Strangers When We Met

ADST-DACOR DIPLOMATS AND DIPLOMACY SERIES

Series Editor: MARGERY BOICHEL THOMPSON

Since 1776, extraordinary men and women have represented the United States abroad under widely varying circumstances. What they did and how and why they did it remain little known to their compatriots. In 1995, the Association for Diplomatic Studies and Training (ADST) and DACOR, an organization of foreign affairs professionals, created the Diplomats and Diplomacy book series to increase public knowledge and appreciation of the professionalism of American diplomats and their involvement in world history. *Strangers When We Met* is a unique addition to the literature about Kuwait and the opening of the Gulf region to Western, and especially American, relationships and influence. It is the 59th volume in the series.

RELATED TITLES IN ADST SERIES

Herman J. Cohen, *Intervening in Africa: Superpower Peacemaking in a Troubled Continent*
Charles T. Cross, *Born a Foreigner: A Memoir of the American Presence in Asia*
Hermann F. Eilts, *Early American Diplomacy in the Near and Far East*
Brandon Grove, *Behind Embassy Walls: The Life and Times of an American Diplomat*
Parker T. Hart, *Saudi Arabia and the United States: Birth of a Security Partnership*
Edmund J. Hull, *High-Value Target: Countering al Qaeda in Yemen*
Cameron Hume, *Mission to Algiers: Diplomacy by Engagement*
Dennis C. Jett, *American Ambassadors: The Past, Present, and Future of America's Diplomats*
Dennis Kux, *The United States and Pakistan, 1947–2000: Disenchanted Allies*
Jane C. Loeffler, *The Architecture of Diplomacy: Building America's Embasises*
Meyer, Armin, *Quiet Diplomacy: From Cairo to Tokyo in the Twilight of Imperialism*
David D. Newsom, *Witness to a Changing World*
Richard B. Parker, *Uncle Sam in Barbary: A Diplomatic History*
———, *Memoirs of a Foreign Service Arabist*
Howard B. Schaffer, *Ellsworth Bunker: Global Troubleshooter, Vietnam Hawk*
James W. Spain, *In Those Days: A Diplomat Remembers*
James Stephenson, *Losing the Golden Hour: An Insider's View of Iraq's Reconstruction*
Wyatt, Susan, *Arabian Nights and Daze: Living in Yemen with the Foreign Service*

For a complete list of series titles, visit <adst.org/publications>

Strangers When We Met
A Century of American Community in Kuwait

W. NATHANIEL HOWELL

Foreword by Shaikha Hussah Sabah al-Salem al-Sabah,
With Contributions by Claudia Farkas Al-Rashoud

An ADST-DACOR Diplomats and Diplomacy Book

Washington, DC

Copyright © 2015 by W. Nathaniel Howell

New Academia Publishing 2016

The views and opinions in this book are solely those of the author and do not necessarily reflect those of the Association for Diplomatic Studies and Training, DACOR, Inc., or the Government of the United States.

All rights reserved. No part of this book may be reproduced or transmitted in any form or by any means, electronic or mechanical, including photocopying, recording, or by any information storage and retrieval system.

Printed in the United States of America

Library of Congress Control Number: 2015953640
ISBN 978-0-9966484-0-0 paperback (alk. paper)
ISBN 978-0-9966484-1-7 hardcover (alk. paper)

New Academia Publishing
PO Box 27420, Washington, DC 20038-7420
info@newacademia.com - www.newacademia.com

Contents

Foreword	vii
Preface	ix
Acknowledgments	xvi
1: An Incidental Encounter	1
2: From Fishing Village to Commercial Port	5
Photo Gallery A	21
3: The Coming of the American Mission	31
4: Decade of Austerity and Promise	59
5: World War II Comes to Kuwait	81
6: From Boom Port to Boom Town	105
Photo Gallery B	123
7: Developers, Dissidents, and Diplomats	133
8: Road to Independence	155
9: Independence	179
10: Growing Pains and Engagement	201
Photo Gallery C	221
11: A Bad Neighborhood	233
12: Sea of Troubles	253
13: Tentative Alliance	275
14: Prelude to Disaster	293
15: Besieged but Not Beaten	321

Photo Gallery D	347
16: The Valley of the Shadow	357
17: Troubled Dawn	395
18: Legacy of Pride and Suffering	413
19: Friends and Allies	439
20: Snapshots at Age One Hundred	463
Appendices	483
Bibliography	501
Notes	524
Index	689

Foreword

In *Strangers When We Met: A Century of American Community In Kuwait*, former US Ambassador to Kuwait W. Nathaniel Howell presents the history of a relationship: the relationship between the people of Kuwait and the people of the United States of America. It becomes evident while reading Howell's book that this is a history driven by people, not governments, although we count the United States as a good and true friend, and not business, although many US companies are represented in Kuwait. This is the story of Kuwaitis and Americans—strangers when they met, friends today.

It strikes me how wonderfully Ambassador Howell delivers the entire ethos of his book in the title "Strangers When We Met." You know immediately that it is a human story of progress, of people who are no longer strangers. Without reading any further you know that these two groups have forged a relationship and even a community. But read on you should, for Ambassador Howell tells a story that is well worth reading.

Ambassador Howell came to Kuwait a stranger. Here during one of the most harrowing times in our history, the Iraqi invasion in 1990, he demonstrated true friendship—standing with the people of Kuwait at great personal peril. In doing so, Ambassador Howell exemplifies the very story told in *Strangers When We Met: A Century of American Community in Kuwait*.

Hussah Sabah al-Salem al-Sabah
Director General
Dar al-Athar al-Islamiyyah

Preface

In 2011 Kuwait marked many pivotal anniversaries. Within that twelve-month period, the nation celebrated fifty years of independence (1961) as well as the twentieth anniversary of its liberation from Iraqi occupation (1991). Parallel with these national events, two benchmarks in the evolution of the relationship between the Kuwaiti and American peoples were also observed: the centenary of the founding of the American Mission and hospital in 1911, and the 60th year since the establishment of the first American diplomatic post in Kuwait, a Consulate, in 1951.

This account of the history of the American community in Kuwait has been more than two decades in the making. It has long been my habit to learn about the history of any place where I live, and so, as soon as I arrived in Kuwait as ambassador in 1987, I began to delve into the historical experience of the host society. As I read and spoke with Kuwaitis and other residents whose personal recollections extended back to the pre-oil era, the small state's extraordinary achievement in surviving and flourishing in an often hostile environment made a strong impression on me. I did not foresee that, before I left, Kuwait would face its most recent and, perhaps, most dire threat in the form of the brutal Iraqi occupation that began August 2, 1990.

A second striking result of these inquiries was a deeper appreciation of the Americans who had lived and worked among the Kuwaitis in times of peril as well as prosperity. I had, of course, a passing awareness of the lengthy contributions of the Arabian Mission (more commonly called the "American Mission") Hospital to the Shaikhdom. As a student, however, I had learned that Kuwait was, until 1961, a British "protectorate." Now, I learned about the longevity of the early American community, which, until the discovery and production of petroleum, outnumbered British expatriates. Indeed, the experience of the Americans, especially in the early decades of the twentieth century, was so inextricably intertwined with the unfolding history of Kuwait that it is impossible to tell their story without reference to the development of the society and polity in which they dwelled. This narrative, then, is also a story of Kuwait's modern history, woven around the ordinary and signal events in the lives of an increasingly numerous and diverse American community. Who could have imagined when my ideas began to take shape in the late 1980s that, within five years, the United States would deploy a half million of its young men and women to spearhead an international coalition in freeing the Kuwaitis from the vicious grip of Saddam Hussein's regime?

Initially, I had the benefit of the oral recollections of resident Americans, British expatriates, and Kuwaitis whose personal experiences and memories reached back to the 1930s, in a few cases to the late 1920s. I am deeply grateful both for their friendship and generosity in sharing treasured memories and materials, including historic photographs. They shared with me as well an enthusiasm for preserving aspects of Kuwait's history that otherwise would probably have gone unrecorded; the text that follows is infinitely enriched by the inclusion of their unique contributions. They help portray a Kuwait that is scarcely imaginable to the modern visitor or resident. Sadly, many of these pioneers are no longer with us, making their recollections and embellishments all the more priceless.

The fruits of my research in Kuwait were at risk following the Iraqi invasion and occupation of that country in 1990–91. In anticipation of my scheduled transfer to another post, our personal effects, including research materials, had been packed and stored in the Residence shortly before the invasion. When the Iraqi regime decided in December 1990 that all Americans were free to leave Kuwait, the Department of State instructed that the embassy run two more evacuation flights for private American citizens who wished to depart and then leave the Embassy open but unstaffed. All the private citizens on the compound and three of the eight Foreign

Service personnel were evacuated on the first of two flights; five of us remained for several days to assure that our citizens in hiding had every opportunity to leave. During this period, we prevailed upon the local Iraqi officials to allow a truck to enter the Embassy compound to pick up "the ambassador's personal effects." We construed that description very broadly to include the personal belongings of the Marine Security Guards (MSGs), silverware, and selected antiques and artworks in the ambassador's Residence, as well as plaques, awards, flags, and other miscellaneous valuables of the Embassy. With a mixture of relief and apprehension, we watched the truck leave the compound for the overland trip to Baghdad, and onward to Turkey. There were no grounds for confidence in the word of the Iraqis, but concern was greater that the compound would be looted once it was unoccupied.

When we met with State Department representatives at a Washington-area warehouse a few weeks later to view the shipment and separate out US government property, we found that it had been unsealed and rifled at some point in the journey. Happily, the looters had taken my personal weapon and some electronics but showed little interest in books, papers, paintings, or other irreplaceable items. The notes and materials laboriously assembled for this book were in disarray but stuffed back in their boxes. *Allah kareem* (God is kind).

Although other activities, especially my transition from the Foreign Service to the faculty of the University of Virginia, were not conducive to the extended task of writing the book, it was possible to continue collecting relevant materials. A review of published works, as well as solicitation of individual memoirs and other unpublished references, continued during succeeding years. Despite concern that it might not prove possible to construct a continuous, coherent narrative of American interaction with their Kuwaiti hosts over the last hundred years, my research produced a surprisingly rich mass of information. For some periods, more material than could be incorporated in the text exists; others are less well documented than I might have wished. For instance, the members of the American Mission Hospital, especially Dr. Stanley Mylrea, were highly literate persons and left an extensive account of the very early decades of the American presence. Personal impressions and recollections of Americans engaged in oil exploration and operations are less likely to have been committed to writing. Nevertheless, I am gratified that it has been possible to piece together a seamless account of the experience of the American community, private and official, for the entire period.

With the approach of the 2011 anniversary, I resolved to make the time to set down this exciting story. If the book was ever to be more than several shelves of books and two milk crates of letters, notes, papers, and photos, it was time to write. And so, I began.

Writing such a book that includes events in which the author has been involved presents special challenges. The Iraqi invasion and occupation of 1990 was a life-changing episode not only for Kuwaitis but for the expatriates caught up in it. This is true also for the author and other Foreign Service colleagues under siege in the American Embassy for more than four months. It cannot but affect the lens through which I have viewed not just that existential experience but the struggle of the Kuwaiti people to maintain their independent existence over the last century. When I returned to Kuwait in 1992 to accept a generous decoration from the Amir, Shaikh Jabir al-Ahmad, I also visited a number of government ministers who were old friends. As I left one ministry, a member of the office staff handed me a note in Arabic. It expressed appreciation for our embassy's refusal to heed Iraqi demands to close after Iraq announced that it was annexing Kuwait. The note was signed, "Your brothers who stayed in Kuwait." We had not realized at the time how important it was to many Kuwaitis to see the American flag flying and to know that they were not alone in their darkest hours.

Persons who share a traumatic experience often develop a psychological bond that is difficult for outsiders to fully comprehend. Those who were present in Kuwait during the Iraqi reign of terror—Kuwaitis, Americans and others—were all affected emotionally and physically by those events. The Foreign Service personnel and private citizens who sheltered on the Embassy compound were no exception; we held three reunions through 1995, two in Virginia and one in St. Louis. Families and loved ones outside Kuwait likewise suffered from fears and uncertainty with the added burden of not knowing for long periods what was happening in Kuwait. Most were traumatized but did not fit within the group bond that developed among those on the Embassy compound. Ideally, hyper-vigilance and persistent anxiety that are functional responses to traumatic situations fade with time; the Kamp Kuwait group, as we called ourselves, outlived its need to get together physically to retell their story. This is a sign of healing. Writing this book while those needs and feelings were fresh and insistent would not have been responsible or appropriate. With the benefit of twenty years, I have been able to review the events of 1990–91 with the balance and objectivity I have sought to apply to the entire book.

Another aspect of the book that sets it apart from many standard diplomatic histories was the decision to rely as heavily as possible on the voices and memories of those Americans and Kuwaitis who lived the history it recounts. While official documents are incorporated, this is not the mechanical, strictly linear account such sources support. I set out to write, insofar as possible, an essentially oral history, as recalled by the ordinary and not-so-ordinary Americans that experienced it. Purists sometimes dismiss oral history as anecdotal, as if that were a disability. I have found, however, these sources to be not only more detailed and relevant to the narrative but, considerably more honest than the formal record. If you seek texture and truth in your history, you must look behind the official records. Failure to do so practically ensures that some of the important aspects of history remain unexplored.

At the same time, I make no apology for my respect and affection for the Kuwaiti people. I found them to be intelligent, persistent, and extraordinarily resilient; otherwise, their small state would have been engulfed by larger, predatory neighbors decades ago. Above all, they are open and plainspoken, seldom concealing their views while defending them with vigor. For some in the United States and elsewhere, this independence is confused with arrogance, as if only the arrogant would not trim their sails to conform to the opinions of others. Kuwaitis are no more perfect than any other people and state and, where I have found actions less than wise or admirable, I have not hesitated to state my view. But, if the reader is expecting another of those Western accounts that are more critique than analysis, he or she will not find it in these pages.

When I consider how far the Kuwaitis have come since the first decade of the twentieth century—when many ills were treated with heated irons or pearl divers died an early death to create relative prosperity—the wonder is not that there have been missteps but that Kuwaiti identity and society have not been crushed by the pace and range of the changes they have absorbed to adjust to modernity. It is no accident, for example, that Kuwait has persisted in its parliamentary experiment for more than fifty years. The impulse of Kuwaitis to participate in their governance is deeply ingrained in the national psyche, a natural outgrowth of the most robust network of *diwanniyas* in the Middle East. The experience has not been easy or trouble-free, and the National Assembly has been dissolved a number of times. But it always comes back, and I find it difficult to conceive of a Kuwait without an elected parliament. Participatory government is the most difficult system, as our own recent experience attests. If it has not been fully mastered in Kuwait either, it will not be for a lack of persistence. As a people, they deserve respect for their achievements and continuing efforts to broaden the role of the citizenry in government.

I hope that the full sweep of this tale will provide crucial context to the story of Kuwait and its American residents. When the American missionary doctors first came to Kuwait at the invitation of the ruler, Mubarak the Great, Americans were as little known to the Kuwaitis as the Kuwaitis were to most Americans—we were literally strangers when we met. Over time and by their good works, the missionaries won the trust and acceptance of the Kuwaitis. Long before American oil workers, businessmen, diplomats, and officials set up shop in Kuwait, these missionaries were paving the way for future friendship and cooperation. Those of us who followed in their wake owe a huge debt to these pioneers for establishing a solid foundation for enduring, mutually beneficial relationships.

The use of source materials and names in Arabic presents a dilemma for which there is no elegant and totally satisfactory solution. Since this book is intended for a general audience as well as Middle East specialists, I have chosen to forgo tortured renderings that seek to approximate the pronunciation of a language written in a totally different alphabet and which includes letters and sounds that have no English equivalents. While striving for consistency, communication and comprehension have been more important to me than linguistic purity. Arabic names are generally written in the form in which readers will be most familiar.

Nat Howell
"Crofton Hill"
Albemarle County, Virginia

Acknowledgments

This story of vast historic scope and human depth could not have been written without the recollections, photographs, and other unpublished materials provided by Americans and Kuwaitis far too numerous to recognize here. While the narrative and interpretations are my responsibility alone, the story is theirs; I hope I have done them and their experiences justice. Many of their contributions are acknowledged in the text and endnotes.

The critical assistance of several individuals deserves special highlighting, however. Claudia Farkas Al-Rashoud, author, photographer and friend, was of vital importance in fleshing out the final chapters, including conditions in connection with the coalition invasion of Iraq in 2003 and the process of blending the American community within Kuwaiti society. As a seasoned newswoman and resident of Kuwait for the last thirty-five years, Claudia is uniquely qualified to describe and interpret a process that now involves a new generation of residents with binational roots.

My Foreign Service career taught me many skills, from proper placement of latrines to improvising a sensor for overhead satellites. It did not, however, prepare me for the complex tasks of editing and configuring this manuscript for publication. I have been extremely fortunate to have the expert assistance of the Association for Diplomatic Studies and Training (ADST) and, in particular, Margery Thompson, the Association's Publishing Director and Series Editor, to guide me through this unfamiliar territory. Special thanks are extended to ADST interns – Gina Larson, Gabrielle Barbour, Nooralhuda Al-azzawi, and Jake Silverman – who stepped up to revise and shape the manuscript and illustrations when the requirements exceeded my expertise. Margery's constant care and supervision have been crucial to bringing this narrative to the printed page.

Finally, I must recognize my proofreader and critic of first resort, my wife Margie Saunders Howell. From first conception through years of research and writing she has been a consistent source of encouragement. Not only has she reviewed the text with an eagle eye and sound judgment; she has not been shy in telling me when she thinks I am wrong. This capacity is just one of the reasons I have been living and working with her for more than fifty years.

1

An Incidental Encounter

It was an incidental encounter, this first American visit to the Shaikhdom of Kuwait, at the head of the Persian Gulf. In the 1880s, an American traveler, accompanying a caravan from Bombay to Constantinople arrived in Kuwait from Busheir in Persia aboard the first mail steamer to call at that port.[1] The traveler, a Mr. Locher, stayed only one day and night; but his account of the episode provides our first glimpse of Kuwait as it was, before it became a British protectorate, before the discovery of oil, and before it became the destination for generations of American missionaries, oil men, diplomats, and soldiers.[2]

Kuwait, a town of an estimated twenty thousand inhabitants, was walled to landward against the episodic threat of bedouin raids, although this fact is not mentioned in Locher's account. Possessing the only natural anchorage on the western coast of the Gulf, Kuwait was already important regional entrepôt for trade with the interior. Locher notes:

> *The male inhabitants of Kuweit (sic) are nearly all either merchants or sailors, trading with Bassorah (Basra), and the Persian coast, or with the wild Bedouin tribes of the desert, in the pearls, frankincense, firearms, ammunition, cloth, saddles, carpets, etc. for skins, sheep's wool, camel hair, gum arabic, coffee, dates, etc.*[3]

Yet, the circumstances of the visit illustrate the lack of familiarity between the indigenous population and Westerners in the last half of the nineteenth century. The steamer anchored a mile and a half from the town because of the captain's lack of knowledge of the coastal waters. The ship's arrival, nonetheless, attracted large crowds of curious and friendly Kuwaitis. Some reportedly had previously seen "fire ships," as the steamers were called, but they were most likely British warships that patrolled the Gulf combating piracy and enforcing a truce among the emirates of the lower Gulf (now the United Arab Emirates).

Shortly after the vessel's arrival and an exchange of cannon salutes, the ruling Shaikh Abdallah II (Kuwait's fifth emir, who ruled between 1866 and 1892),[4] was rowed out to the steamer, where he was entertained and given a tour of the ship. Shaikh Abdallah, in turn, invited the master and passengers to disembark and spend the night in Kuwait, providing them an opportunity to gain a better appreciation of the town. We are the beneficiaries of the fleeting, if sometimes imperfect, impressions of this pioneering American traveler.

Although, the next Americans were not to arrive in Kuwait for two decades, so far as we know, they would recognize many of the features and characteristics Locher described. Established on the edge of inhospitable deserts, the walled town was open to the Gulf, with its commercial fleet of dhows[5] drawn up "high and dry upon the shore" in front of seaside residences.[6] These shores were the shipyards, where vessels were built and repaired, as well as the site where they were stored between voyages to destinations as distant as India and East Africa. Smaller ships were employed in pearling, a grueling enterprise in an era when breathing apparatus was unknown among the divers. In pre-petroleum Kuwait, however, natural pearls were Kuwait's sole export commodity.[7]

Possessing almost no resources besides ingenuity and industriousness, merchants, seamen, and their ships were Kuwait's real wealth. Trade with surrounding territories was the lifeblood of the town, providing necessities such as wood for buildings and ships, and goods for consumption and trade with inland tribes. It was no accident that Mr. Locher's steamer stopped there. One of his fellow passengers on the voyage from Bombay was a Kuwaiti merchant (described only as "a near-relation of the Sheikh of Kuweit") who had purchased "several hundred bales of piece goods" now aboard the steamer.[8] On the night of their arrival the visitors were treated in Shaikh Abdallah's palace to a lavish dinner in their honor, served on Persian carpets set with "silver cutlery of European manufacture."[9]

This touch bespeaks not only the far-reaching regional trade in which Kuwait engaged, but also several characteristics of the Kuwaiti people in the modern era. The first is curiosity and a willingness to innovate. While preserving their essential ethos in the face of other cultures,[10] Kuwaitis demonstrate an extraordinary capacity for incorporating compatible aspects of other cultures into their lifestyle.

Hospitality, another Kuwaiti trait, is an esteemed value throughout the Arab world. In common with other coastal trading societies like Bahrain or Oman, Kuwaitis have centuries of experience in dealing with other peoples and cultures. This corporate history sets them apart from isolated and homogenous societies such as that of the bedu of the interior. With confidence in their distinct identity and the habit of interacting with Persians,[11] Indians, Africans, and, more recently, Westerners, they are open to and tolerant of differences. Shaikh Abdallah and his inquisitive people clearly welcomed these unannounced guests and prevailed upon the steamer captain to make Kuwait a regular port of call.[12]

Locher's memoirs highlight the harsh and unremitting climate that tests not only Kuwait's population but the Americans and other expatriates who have chosen to live there. Situated between sea and desert, Kuwait places substantial demands on the hardiness and resilience of its inhabitants, especially in the era before air-conditioning. Traditional houses were built with flat roofs which served as sleeping platforms in periods of extreme temperature and humidity. At the invitation of Shaikh Abdallah, Mr. Locher and his companions retired to the roof following their dinner. He continues:

> *The whole population of Kuweit seemed to have assembled on roofs to enjoy the refreshing breeze, which came wafted gently across the bay.... An American sleeping for the first time on the roof of an Arabian house feels himself in an extremely awkward position, the privacy of the bedroom is entirely gone, and he feels the unpleasant sensation of being an object of intense curiosity to the occupants of adjoining houses, with all his movements closely watched. The unconcerned manner of the natives however, and their indifference to the scrutiny of their neighbors, soon has a*

reassuring effect upon him, and he retires with the most stoical 'nonchalance.'[13]

To the dying hum of conversation and the howls of jackals and a hyena prowling outside the town walls, he slept al fresco, as succeeding American residents would until the 1940s and '50s.[14]

The following morning, the party from the steamer reembarked to continue their journey, first to Basra and eventually to the Ottoman capital. So ended America's initial encounter with the Kuwaitis, but not before touching a nearby town that would play a key part in the return of Americans to Kuwait, this time for extended residence. As the vessel made its way up the Shatt Al-Arab between Ottoman Mesopotamia and Persia, it passed the Arab sheikhdom of "Mohammera" in what is now the Khuzistan Province of Iran. Locher describes Mohammera as "a fearfully dirty place, inhabited by about five thousand persons, chiefly Persian, who live in wretched little flat-roofed houses built of mud blocks dried in the sun,"[15] Yet, this modest principality and its shaikh would be the catalyst in the decision of the Kuwaiti ruler to invite American medical missionaries to come to Kuwait early in the twentieth century.

We are indebted to Locher for momentarily drawing aside the curtain. His descriptions are quaint and provincial in the tradition of nineteenth century travelers. In some details, he is in error. He asserts that the desert around Kuwait was completely devoid of vegetation, although we know that vast quantities of camel thorn, or *arfaj*, were harvested well into the next century as a source of fuel. Locher's brief stay led to no lasting American-Kuwaiti relationship and his account was only rediscovered after such a relationship had been established. Still, his incidental experience provides a benchmark against which to measure a rich and robust interaction.

The following pages will trace the development of the American community in Kuwait and the growing intercourse and cooperation between the two geographically separated peoples. It is a story that was not inevitable and certainly not predictable from that original meeting. It is a rich tale that younger generations of Americans and Kuwaitis do not know. Above all, it is an account of strangers becoming increasingly familiar with one another and ultimately friends with one another.

2

From Fishing Village to Commercial Port

In the second half of the eighteenth century, two nations widely separated geographically and culturally began to take shape. As the English colonies in North America entered the period of ferment that culminated in independence and the creation of the United States, equally seminal events were occurring on the margins of the Arabian Peninsula on a natural harbor known variously as "Grane" or "Kuwait."[1] The inhabitants of both were recent immigrants; aside from that, there was little at the time to suggest that they would ever interact in any significant way.

The town of Kuwait that Locher described in the 1880s was the outgrowth of seminal events in the first decade of the eighteenth century. Apparently driven by drought in Central Arabia (now Saudi Arabia) in the second half of the seventeenth century, a group of desert dwellers from the Amarat, a subtribe of the Anaza,[2] set out in search of a more hospitable area. Their wanderings through the region between the Qatar Peninsula and Basra finally took them to the shores of Kuwait Bay. Although the area offered some grazing for their flocks, it was probably not as fertile as they had hoped.[3] Nevertheless, perhaps as early as 1710, they settled and began adapting to demands and opportunities, quite different from those of their original homeland. The tribesmen who found a home at the head of the Gulf discovered that sustainability demanded that they develop the skills and specialization required to profit from opportunities in trade, seafaring, fishing, and pearling.[4]

In approximately 1670, Eastern Arabia came under the effective rule of the Beni Khalid confederacy, which had never accepted Ottoman suzerainty over the al-Hasa. In that year, under their leader Barrak, the Beni Khalid successfully expelled the Ottoman governor. It was with their tolerance that the founders of the modern state of Kuwait settled by the waters of the Gulf. A tiny fishing village may have predated their arrival but, if so, it was of little regional significance.[5] The major ports on the western coast of the Gulf were 'Uqair and Qatif and through them passed goods from British India and other states and, thence, by caravan to Central Arabia and onward to the Ottoman wilayets of Iraq and Syria.[6]

A major achievement of Beni Khalid rule was the imposition and maintenance of peace and relative security throughout Eastern Arabia. This policy, entailing control of the bedouin on the margins of the settled coast, was essential to facilitate trade, and the Beni Khalid, based in al-Hofhuf and al-Mubarraz in what is now the Eastern Province of Saudi Arabia, not only provided protection for caravans but dispatched punitive expeditions to the west and as far north as the outskirts of Basra. Taking advantage of this security regime, the founders of the city of Kuwait settled near a small fortification, or *kut*, constructed by the Beni Khalid in the late seventeenth century.

Arab and other histories are vague regarding the date when the proto-Kuwaitis moved to the region, but there is wide agreement in designating them the Beni 'Utba, or 'Utub.[7] Tribally, this grouping of clans and families formed part of the Anazi, whose homeland comprised Najd and Northern Arabia. It seems likely that the 'Utub spent at least half century near the coasts of southeastern Arabia before finally migrating to Kuwait. In the process, this people from the interior acquired an acquaintance with the coastal regions and seafaring that provided the skills needed for the new settlement to flourish.[8]

Regardless of when the first elements of the 'Utub federation arrived in the area that became Kuwait, the development of their entity becomes easier to trace through records and local traditions only after 1750. When the Emir of the Beni Khalid, Sa'dun bin Mohammed bin Ghurair al-Hamid, died in 1752, a succession struggle within his family ensued. The resulting strife and the growing influence of the Wahhabis in the interior of the Arabian Peninsula are thought to have created space for dependent tribes, such as the 'Utub, to acquire a large measure of autonomy, or even independence. The population on the Bay of Kuwait was well positioned to take advantage of this opportunity.

Kuwaiti traditions give no precise date for the 'Utub's transition from dependency to self-rule, although they mark the election of one of their number, Sabah, as shaikh of the town in the mid-eighteenth century as the beginning of a distinct and independent statelet. His election in the tribal tradition "to administer justice and the affairs of the town"[9] strongly suggests that the tiny fishing village at Kut had already grown into a more complex town that supported differentiated occupations and functions. Sabah, the founder of the Al-Sabah dynasty that still rules in Kuwait, was not well known before his selection; there is no mention of him or his family before he became a shaikh. But he must have possessed personal qualities that recommended him to his fellow townspeople for this important role. According to Alan Rush,

> *Unlike the ruling families of countries like Bahrain and Saudi Arabia, they (the Al-Sabah) did not establish their dynasty by the sword. Nor could they claim descent from the Prophet Muhammad in the manner of the Imams of the Yemen or the Sharifs of Mecca and their descendants—the Kings of the Hijaz, Iraq and Jordan. Instead they are said to have acquired the right to rule through a voluntary division of responsibilities between themselves and the other leaders of the community with whom they first arrived in Kuwait as settlers in the eighteenth century.*[10]

The first recorded Western contact with Kuwait occurred in the 1750s. In March of 1758, a Dr. Ives, who was traveling from India to Europe, reached a Dutch trading settlement at Kharg Island. He was told that the fastest passage to Aleppo would be by desert caravan from Kuwait and entered into negotiations with a shaikh (undoubtedly Sabah). They were unable to agree on the price and Ives sailed on to Basra. Nevertheless, the episode provides important clues to the development of 'Utbi Kuwait. First, the tiny fishing village, with its attractive natural harbor, had already evolved into an important town and port for transit trade. Second, the Kuwaitis were already in friendly contact with the Dutch and other traders in the region. And finally, Kuwait's trading relationships were profitable enough that the shaikh felt comfortable in refusing a deal to take Dr. Ives to Aleppo.[11]

Kuwait had developed quickly; fueled by profits from the entrepôt trade. A Dutch document dated 1756 and recently discovered in the archives of the Dutch East India Company, gives the following account of contemporary Kuwait:

> They (the Utubi) have some 300 vessels, but almost all are small because they employ them only for pearl diving. This and fishing during the winter is their only occupation. They number about 4000 men armed with swords, shields and lances.[12]

In pursuit of pearls, the Kuwaiti mariners ranged Gulf waters as far afield as Bahrain, where the richest oyster beds lay. The eighteenth-century Danish traveler Niebuhr estimated about a decade later that the Kuwaiti fleet consisted of more than eight hundred small boats used for pearling, fishing, and other coastal activities.[13]

The new town grew rapidly in the area at the head of the bay, forming the core that can still be located in the modern city of Kuwait. Because the settlers comprised a number of prominent families in addition to the Al-Sabah, its new-found prosperity was widely shared. It is likely that until the beginning of the petroleum era in the mid–twentieth century, many of the leading pearling, merchant, and shipping families were substantially wealthier than the Al-Sabah. Very early in Kuwait's development, notable families settled in the various quarters of the town that came to be known as Sharq (the East) and Qibla (the West, toward Mecca). The Al-Sabah and the administration occupied the center of the town, known as Wasat.[14] While the town has spread in widening concentric semicircles over the succeeding centuries and the major families have moved out to modern suburbs, these original divisions continue to resonate in Kuwaiti traditions today.[15]

For most of its history and until the 1950s, Kuwait was a walled town. The wall does not appear to have been built until after the collapse of the security regime imposed by the Beni Khalid. According to local tradition, the wall—a mud structure that extended in an arc from the sea on both sides of the town)—may have been built around 1760, in the first decade of Al-Sabah rule. In any event, records of the English East India Company describe the town as being walled by 1770. Although the Kuwaiti walls continued to serve their defensive purposes into the first decades of the twentieth century, by the 1950s they were seen as an impediment to the growth and expansion of the city and torn down. All that remains of this defining feature are a single gate and sections maintained as a monument and a ring road that roughly follows its circumference.

Characteristically, from the outset, Kuwait's defense and prosperity owed as much to diplomacy and commerce as to fortifications and arms. A major achievement of Sabah I and his successors was the brokering of a working relationship between the merchants of the town and the bedouin tribes around it. This cooperation was soon sufficient to transform Kuwait into "a staging post on the trade route from Persia, India, and southern Arabia to the Levant and Europe."[16] Offering an alternative harbor secure from the pirates that menaced the Shatt al-Arab and few of the bureaucratic controls of the port at Basra, Kuwait was able to lure some of the traffic from the traditional route. Rush, quoting a contemporary report of the Bombay government, writes:

> *Even the Dutch East India Company began using Kuwait's port; and a certain prosperity was probably achieved as cargoes of 'Bengal Soosies, Coffee, Pepper ... Cotton yarn' and other goods were taken off the ships and transferred to the Safat (open area) behind the town for loading on to camel caravans bound for Aleppo and Baghdad.*[17]

Having successfully managed a potentially delicate relationship with the Beni Khalid regime over the decades of the first half of the eighteenth century, the 'Utub proved equally adept at turning circumstances to their advantage once they attained de facto independence. It was, however, by no means assured that Kuwait and its leadership would be able to keep and consolidate their gains.[18]

An important hurdle was cleared in about 1756, following the death of Sabah I. His youngest son, Abdallah, succeeded his father and thereby confirmed the Al-Sabah dynasty which has ruled Kuwait in an unbroken line to the present day. Abdallah had apparently played a government role under his father, where he is said to have internalized habits of consultation with his kinsmen and other Kuwaiti notables.[19] This practice almost certainly strengthened acceptance of his accession, although Abdallah's selection may not have been universally celebrated. One of the first crises he faced was the decision of the sheikhdom's wealthiest family, the Al-Khalifa, to leave Kuwait in the early 1760s and move to Zubara on the Qatari Peninsula.[20] Whatever the reasons for the migration of this prominent clan, the parting appears to have been amicable as continuing close relationships with Bahrain attest. Nevertheless, this development was a serious blow to the population and prosperity of the fledgling town of Kuwait.

Good fortune again smiled on Kuwait in the middle of the next decade and the Kuwaitis were quick to take advantage of opportunities created by nearby developments. In 1775–76, Persia besieged Basra and broke the tenuous Ottoman hold on that key port city.[21] Although the Ottomans retook and strengthened their grip on Basra several years later, the uncertainties created by the Persian occupation caused a temporary rerouting of trade through Kuwait. England's East India Company diverted its mail and the India trade to Kuwait until 1779. Kuwait then lost much of the economic windfall generated by the Persian-Ottoman conflict, but the commercial powers gained an appreciation of its excellent harbor and, perhaps more important, the reliability of the Kuwaitis as trustworthy trading partners. Kuwait was now firmly on the world's maps.

It was in this period that Kuwait took its first steps as a shipbuilding center and regional maritime power. In the late eighteenth century, the Kuwaitis invested their growing profits in the building of larger and sturdier cargo and naval ships. According to Rush, Kuwait soon possessed "one of the finest fleets in the Arabian Gulf."[22] The record of Kuwait's history contains few instances of warlike activity, and those were of a defensive nature. As early as 1782, however, Kuwait's navy was able to confront and thwart an invasion fleet sent by the Beni Ka'b, a piratical tribe that inhabited the coasts of the Shatt al-Arab.[23]

The development of Kuwait's shipbuilding industry and commercial fleet unquestionably influenced the shape of the growing town. It had always been the practice to use its gently sloping Gulf shore to beach its ships. Buildings were set well back from the water to leave space for these maritime activities.²⁴ With the addition of larger and more numerous vessels, virtually the entire shelf was given over to building ships from the keel up or to careen them for repairs and caulking. Little remains today of the traditional town center; in the 1950s and later most of the older houses were razed, presumably for development. All that remains of this once-thriving area are numerous older mosques that sit forlornly alone and a few original family homes that were fortunately saved for posterity. The shoreline has been filled and altered substantially by the construction of a broad divided roadway, or corniche, and the development of parks and recreation areas. Kuwait's long flirtation with the sea lingers only in memoirs and regrettably few photographs.

Abdallah I became ruler of Kuwait in 1756, a critical time in the young state's history, and ruled until 1814, one of the Al-Sabah dynasty's longest reigns. During his tenure, he was successful not only in advancing Kuwait's commercial activities but in consolidating its independent status—from the Beni Khalid, who were in decline, and vis-à-vis the Ottoman Empire, which was steadily consolidating its control of the neighboring Basra Province.²⁵ Kuwait was coming to enjoy a reputation for good government, reliability, and stability in a region plagued by great power rivalries, growing Wahhabi assertiveness in the desert and endemic piracy at sea. His policies greatly increased the population of the city, both through natural growth and immigration.²⁶ Out of a search for economic opportunity or dissatisfaction with conditions in their homeland, groups from Mesopotamia (Iraq) and Persia (Iran) joined the original 'Utub inhabitants. Their arrival imparted an ethnic and religious diversity that continues to characterize the country to this day. Moderation and tolerance drew the newcomers to Kuwait; their integration into Kuwait's society and economy did much to assure its institutionalization. As Rush observes:

> *Henceforth the original founding families from central Arabia would form an aristocracy whose interests would have to coexist with the often divergent interests of other groups, in particular the ahl al-shimal (people of the north)—a dilemma that continues even today and reflects Kuwait's problematical location on the borderline of Iran, Iraq and Arabia.²⁷*

Small wonder that when Abdallah I died in 1814, an old man who had led Kuwait for more than fifty years, he was a widely respected figure.

The deceased ruler was succeeded the same year by his son, Jabir. According to local tradition, Jabir spent much of his youth in Bahrain and does not seem to have participated in his father's administration. He is said to have had disagreements with Abdallah, the nature of which are obscure.[28] Nevertheless, Jabir's accession was widely acclaimed and he became one of Kuwait's best-loved rulers, earning the title "Al-Aish" (the Rice) because of his commitment to feeding the poor.

During Jabir I's reign, Kuwait suffered two devastating cholera epidemics: in 1821 and in 1831. A contemporary European source puts deaths from the first devastating plague at thirty-five hundred individuals, or probably more than 10 percent of inhabitants.[29]

It was Jabir's adroit handling of relationships with neighbors frequently in conflict with one another, however, that assured his reputation. For example, he continued Kuwait's relationship with the English East India Company and welcomed the brief transfer of its trade post from Basra in 1821 when there were tensions with the Ottoman authorities. He also applauded success of the Bombay Marine, the company's navy, in pacifying the pirate-infested Gulf waters. Although some Kuwaitis had handled pirate loot as well as conventional trade, Jabir reasoned that the elimination of piracy would facilitate Kuwait's growing long-distance trade with India and beyond.

Pursuing a foreign policy that alternated "between opportunism and nonalignment,"[30] he threaded the needle between the competing forces and ambitions of the Ottomans, the Al-Saud Wahhabi insurgency, and the Egyptian forces of Muhammad Ali Pasha who were nominally allied with Ottoman forces in the struggle for control of the Arabian Peninsula. Any of these powers could have threatened Kuwait's independence and prosperity. Under Jabir's leadership, the sheikhdom managed to maintain working, sometimes friendly, relationships with all, occasionally at the same time. As a consequence, Jabir succeeded in maintaining Kuwait's core independence and freedom of action.

Although a detailed exploration of Kuwait's foreign relations in the first half of the nineteenth century is beyond the scope of this narrative, a brief examination of relations with the Ottomans in this period is instructive as a harbinger of Kuwaiti policy into the twentieth century. While Kuwait had provided a haven for opponents of the Ottomans and actually blockaded Basra in the 1830s as part of a regional coalition, these actions do not appear to have permanently damaged the relationship. In 1826–27 the Kuwaiti fleet successfully chased off a combined Bani Ka'b and Omani naval force seeking to besiege the port and was thereby rewarded by the Ottomans. Meanwhile, Jabir I moved to improve relations with the Ottoman rival, the Al-Saud of central Arabia. By 1837, Kuwait was again allied with the Ottomans in reducing the port of Muhammera (present-day Khoramshahr), a trade rival of Basra and Kuwait. For his part in this expedition, Jabir began receiving substantial gifts in the form of dates and ownership of date groves on the Shatt al-Arab.[31] With these and other rewards, Jabir acquired sources of independent wealth that freed the Al-Sabah from sole dependence on duties and the powerful merchant class in Kuwait itself.

Jabir I, who was respected for his modest lifestyle and generosity, presided over a stable and increasingly prosperous state with vigorous pearling, boat-building, and trading industries. As he aged, he devolved some of his authority upon his son, Sabah. A contemporaneous report, not intended for publication, provides a unique glimpse of the Kuwait of 1841, at the height of Jabir I's powers:

> *This Town presents a singular instance of commercial prosperity, although wanting in almost every advantage excepting its magnificent Harbour. Its population is large, as it can produce about six thousand men capable of bearing arms which at a moderate average would make the total number of inhabitants nearly twenty-five thousand individuals... The energy and courage of the people, who are closely united, and free from feuds and factions, render them respected by all the other Maritime tribes... The government of Shaikh Jabir is of a truly mild and paternal character... The small revenue realized by him... (is) ... expended in keeping up a sort of public table [of food] of a plentiful but coarse description to which every one appears to be welcome. This liberality together*

> with the utter absence of all pretension of outward superiority, renders Shaikh Jabir and his son, Soobah (Sabah) ... most popular among his subjects.[32]

When Jabir I died in 1859, after reigning for almost a half century, the succession was seamless. His son Sabah II was already experienced in running Kuwait's affairs, having been, according to some observers, the virtual ruler for the last five years of Shaikh Jabir's life. But because of his father's longevity, Sabah II was already in his mid-to-late seventies. He would rule for only seven years.

While maintaining Kuwait's central practice of nonalignment, Shaikh Sabah moved subtly to bolster relations with the Imam of Najd, Faisal Al-Saud, and his son, Abdallah. An important reason for this policy probably was the pressure being exerted on the Kuwaitis by their nominal suzerain, the Ottoman Empire, which now seemed intent on extending effective control over Kuwait and other areas of the Arabian Peninsula.[33] Kuwait's resistance to increasing Ottoman gestures of intimidation were doubtless buttressed by a conviction that, in extremis, Kuwait could count on support from the Al-Saud, Istanbul's principal rival in the region. At the same time, Sabah II was careful not to provoke the Ottomans gratuitously. When he learned, for example, that they were annoyed that Kuwait had been siphoning off trade from Basra, Sabah II asked the British to suspend port call vessels of the British India Steam Navigation Company.[34]

Diplomacy was the preferred instrument of Sabah II's rule, and he was intent on keeping Kuwait out of the periodic fighting that often swirled close to the gates of the town. Two battles in the vicinity occurred between the tribal forces of the Al-Saud and the Ajman. The Ajman were defeated in both, but Sabah II rejected the request of Abdallah ibn Faisal Al-Saud that Kuwait turn over the Ajman survivors. Instead, Kuwait gave them refuge.

Fundamentally, the business of Kuwait continued to be business. Diplomatic acumen bought, for the town and its surrounding territory, time and space to develop in the areas of trade and pearling. Sabah II took advantage of the growing volume of trade to levy duties on imports. When he proposed a tax on exports, he ran into the powerful merchants lobby and was compelled to yield to their demands. Tension between these dual sources of Kuwait's success and prosperity would continue to be a feature of its society and politics into the modern era.

By the time of the first recorded visit to Kuwait by an American,[35] Kuwait was ruled by Abdallah II, who succeeded Sabah II in 1866.

For Abdallah II, as for many of Kuwait's rulers, the chief preoccupation was to maneuver to preserve the independence of the small shaikhdom, which had a way of exciting the attention and envy of powers around it. In his case, the chief challenge came from a resurgent Ottoman administration in Baghdad. Ottoman policy from the early 1800s had sought to spread influence and control outward and to bind autonomous rulers in the Arabian Peninsula more closely to them. Previous Kuwaiti rulers had managed to parry the Ottoman effort without sacrificing either Kuwait's tradition of self-government or a working relationship with the Ottoman Empire.

Circumstances changed greatly shortly after Abdallah II came to power. Within several years, Midhat Pasha, who would come to epitomize the Ottoman campaign of domination, was named governor in Baghdad, intending to restore Ottoman control in eastern Arabia. The death in 1865 of Imam Faisal ibn Turki, the Saudi emir of Najd, provided the opening Midhat sought. A succession conflict broke out between two of Faisal's sons and, in 1870 one of the contestants, facing defeat, addressed an appeal for help to Baghdad.[36]

When Midhat Pasha bestowed an Ottoman title on the Saudi petitioner and raised a force to subdue Al-Hasa and Al-Qatif, Abdallah was correctly concerned that the Ottoman force could tighten the grip on Kuwait on its way down the Gulf coast. The counterbalances that his predecessors had skilfully employed to fend off an Ottoman embrace were not in play at this juncture:

> *The campaigns of the Al-Saud against the Ottomans had demonstrated the futility of military resistance. Instead Jabir I and Sabah II had relied on diplomacy using the British, Egyptians and Saudis as counterweights to the Ottomans. Now, however, the first two groups were no longer active in the region and the Saudis too*

disunited to do anything but endanger Kuwait's interests. Abdallah II therefore had to cooperate with the Ottomans.[37]

He made a friendly approach to the Ottomans and granted Midhat Pasha the use of Kuwait as a base for his army. In return, Kuwait received a pledge that it would continue to enjoy administrative autonomy, and, of course, profits as a supplier of Ottoman forces.

In a further departure from historical practice, Kuwait provided troops and transport to the mobilizing Ottomans. A cavalry force under Abdallah II's brother, Mubarak, joined other allied tribal forces marching south and Kuwaiti vessels were offered to transport the pasha's troops and heavy equipment. In a gesture that probably exceeded the necessity of Kuwait's unfamiliar role, Abdallah accompanied his fleet to supervise the bombardment that preceded the fall of Al-Qatif and convinced the son of Doha's ruler to accept Ottoman overlordship and fly their flag. As a reward, Abdallah II accepted the position of *Qaimmaqam* of Kuwait.[38] The Kuwaiti ruler was also given title to extensive date gardens in the Basra region by the grateful Ottoman authorities.[39]

Abdallah II ruled Kuwait during turbulent and dangerous times and died in 1892 at the age of seventy-eight. Somewhat surprisingly, Kuwait's friendly relations with the Al-Saud survived his decided tilt toward the Ottomans. As they continued to war among themselves, the Al-Saud found in Kuwait a welcoming haven whenever either side felt compelled to flee the battlefield.

Abdallah II's successor, Muhammad I, came to power in 1892 proclaiming his intention to continue pursuing a pro-Ottoman policy.[40] Instead, he presided over a uniquely divisive and violent interlude in the country's history. The second son of Sabah II, Shaikh Muhammad delegated financial responsibility to one brother, Jarrah, and command of the armed forces to another, Mubarak. A further member of his inner circle was Yusuf Al-Ibrahim, a wealthy in-law who owned estates in Ottoman Iraq and was a leading figure in the pro-Ottoman faction in Kuwait.

Muhammad I enjoyed close working relationships with Jarrah and Yusuf, but relations with the more flamboyant Mubarak rapidly deteriorated. Whether it was because Mubarak appears not to have shared their affection for the Ottomans or they were aware, and fearful, of Mubarak's growing resentment of his limited financial resources and exclusion from real power, he appears to have been largely marginalized.

Under Muhammad I, many of Kuwait's leading families shared a sense of alienation. In part, they were dissatisfied with the shaikh's failure to follow the tradition of consulting with notables on important issues. But there also appears to have been resentment of the prominence of Yusuf Al-Ibrahim and his potential influence on the Al-Sabah figures, whose wealth was largely tied to properties in Ottoman territory. Ultimately, therefore, they were concerned that Kuwait could lose its distinctive identity and become merely an adjunct of the Ottoman Empire.[41]

Within four years of Muhammad I's accession, these currents of concern, nationalism, and resentment merged and Mubarak decided to act. Convinced of the support of tribal elements and a substantial proportion of Kuwaiti townspeople, Mubarak felt powerful enough to seize power. On an early morning in May 1896, he entered the Sief Palace with two sons and a few retainers. Between them, they assassinated the two brothers, Muhammad I and Jarrah. Muhammad I thereby earned the dubious distinction of becoming the only ruler of Kuwait to die violently.

The outline of these events is generally agreed, but there remain aspects that will probably never be completely clear. The Ottoman government in Constantinople immediately surmised that the British were behind Mubarak's coup; unsubstantiated rumors to this effect circulated in the Ottoman capital. For its part, the British government, consistent with its strategic policy of support for, and alliance with, the Ottomans, adopted a conspicuously hands-off posture toward developments in Kuwait. Although none of those involved could know it at the time, the Ottoman Empire was fast approaching its own demise. Within thirty years, this important factor in the evolution of Kuwaiti politics would disappear from world maps. Kuwait would go on to outlive the Ottoman threat.

Shaikh Mubarak (Mubarak the Great) assumed power in Kuwait under precarious conditions. Assassinating his predecessor was an act without precedent in Kuwait's one hundred fifty years of political experience. Additionally, he faced hostility from several directions. Rumors circulated that Yusuf Al-Ibrahim, who had assumed the role of protector of Muhammad I's sons and heirs, was plotting an attack against him.[42] The Ottoman authorities swallowed whatever anger they may have felt and quickly named Mubarak *Qaimmaqam* of Kuwait, but planned to bring the state under direct and unambiguous control. Mubarak I's early efforts to enlist British power as a counterweight foundered on Great Britain's preoccupation with preserving good relations with Constantinople. While they were not willing to formalize the link with Kuwait, the British also were not interested in seeing the Ottomans upset the status quo by incorporating Kuwait. Thus, they were prepared to accede to Mubarak's request for British gunboats to patrol Kuwaiti waters as a strong signal to the Ottomans.

It was not Ottoman policy but the actions of other powers that induced Britain to make an about-face in 1899. The prospect of extending railroad links from Baghdad to the Gulf piqued German and Tsarist Russian interest in Kuwait as a terminus for the projected rail line and a coaling station. The British were not ready to allow these nations to challenge their imperial interests in the Gulf, including the vital connection with India.[43] In January of 1899, Britain agreed to extend its "good offices" (read "protection") to Kuwait. In return, Kuwait undertook not to alienate any of its territory (read "grant concessions"), to exclude other powers, and to place control of its foreign relations in Britain's hands. A political agent was assigned to Kuwait in 1904.

It was more than coincidence that Britain's decision to accede to Kuwaiti requests followed manifestations of the interest of other European powers in the northern Gulf. On the eve of the twentieth century, a German cruiser was dispatched to the Gulf with the clear mission of conducting a survey for the eastern terminus of a railroad to connect Berlin with Baghdad, continuing on to the Gulf at Kuwait. The vessel, variously named as *Ancora* or *Ancona*, visited "...gulf ports, made elaborate soundings, carefully surveyed all likely spots for the establishment of a harbour, and demonstrated to the natives the power of Imperial Germany."[44] Two years later, the Russians also dispatched a warship to Kuwait, the activities of which were the subject of a British memorandum:

> *On the 12th December last (1901), the Russian man-of-war arrived at Koweit from Bushire, half-an-hour before sunset. The next day the weather was stormy, so nobody landed from the ship. The third day, the Russian Consul of Bussorah and two officers of the ship came ashore and visited Sheikh Mubarek. The first question the Russian Consul put to Sheikh Mubarek was whether British men-of-war ever came to Koweit. The Sheikh replied: 'Yes, they are in the habit of visiting Koweit.' The Consul then said the Governments of England and Germany had come to an understanding, and agreed to bring a railway to Kadhima in his (the Sheikh's) territory, and asked if he was aware of that or not. The Sheikh replied he was not aware of it, nor had he heard about it. After some complimentary conversation, the Consul asked Sheikh Mubarek to send Sheikh Jaber (his son) with him to see the man-of-war. Sheikh Jaber was accordingly sent with some men, and at the time of leaving the ship he was given a double-barrel gun and a five-chambered revolver. The man-of-war left Koweit on the 14th December last.*[45]

The arrival of warships of rival powers was a development that Great Britain could not ignore.

The new relationship was not trouble free. Mubarak's impulsiveness and the complexity of British interests and aspirations wove unforeseen tangles in its fabric. The Kuwaitis undertook an unsuccessful campaign against the Al-Rashid shaikhs, who were among the Ottomans' chief allies in the Arabian Peninsula while the British connection emboldened the Kuwaitis to resist Ottoman blandishments and temptations. Kuwait's losses in the conflict with the Al-Rashids were staggering, but had the effect of freeing the Al-Saud to reestablish their position in central Arabia. After the death of Yusuf Al-Ibrahim in 1905, the Ottomans, unquestionably preoccupied by other developments within their Empire, seemed to abandon the drive to incorporate Kuwait, and Mubarak I felt able to relax his guard somewhat.

Kuwait was experiencing growth and commercial prosperity in the first decade of the century, and Mubarak took the opportunity to adopt a more grandiose lifestyle and to absent himself more often from the town. His projects, including the expansion and redecoration of the palace, required increased revenues; soon his taxes and levies for military expeditions began to cause unhappiness among the townspeople. In 1910, several of the leading pearl traders objected by moving to Bahrain. They were eventually lured back but the point had been made.

The greatest threat to Kuwait was yet to come, and from an unexpected quarter. Britain, still anxious to hold the Ottomans within its orbit as World War I approached, signed in July, 1913 a bilateral convention that, among other things, described Kuwait as "an autonomous Caza of the (Ottoman) Empire."[46] Before the convention could be finalized and ratified, however, the First World War erupted and, as feared, the Ottomans allied themselves with Germany. The British-Ottoman relationship evaporated and Britain declared that Kuwait was "an independent Shaikhdom under British protection."

Mubarak received his first word of the 1913 convention while visiting Shaikh Khaz'al, the ruler of the Arab principality of Muhammera (Khoramshahr) on the eastern shore of the Shatt Al-Arab. Travelling on his new yacht, Shaikh Mubarak periodically visited his close friend, Khaz'al, who reciprocated by visiting Kuwait.[47] Mubarak was frequently ill in his last years and died of malaria in November, 1915. His relationship with Khaz'al is of more than passing interest to this narrative, however. From the Shaikh of Muhammera, Mubarak acquired, in part, the taste for pomp and opulence that ran afoul of the sensibilities of many Kuwaitis. More important for our purposes, however, was the influence of Khaz'al in the return of Americans to the Kuwaiti scene.

Gallery A

Gate in the 1921 city wall. The third and final protective wall around the city was built in anticipation of a massive attack by Muslim extremists loyal to the al-Saud family of Central Arabia. The wall was never tested because the attackers were repulsed at the nearby oasis of Jahra. *Kuwait Hilton Hotel Exhibition, February 1988*

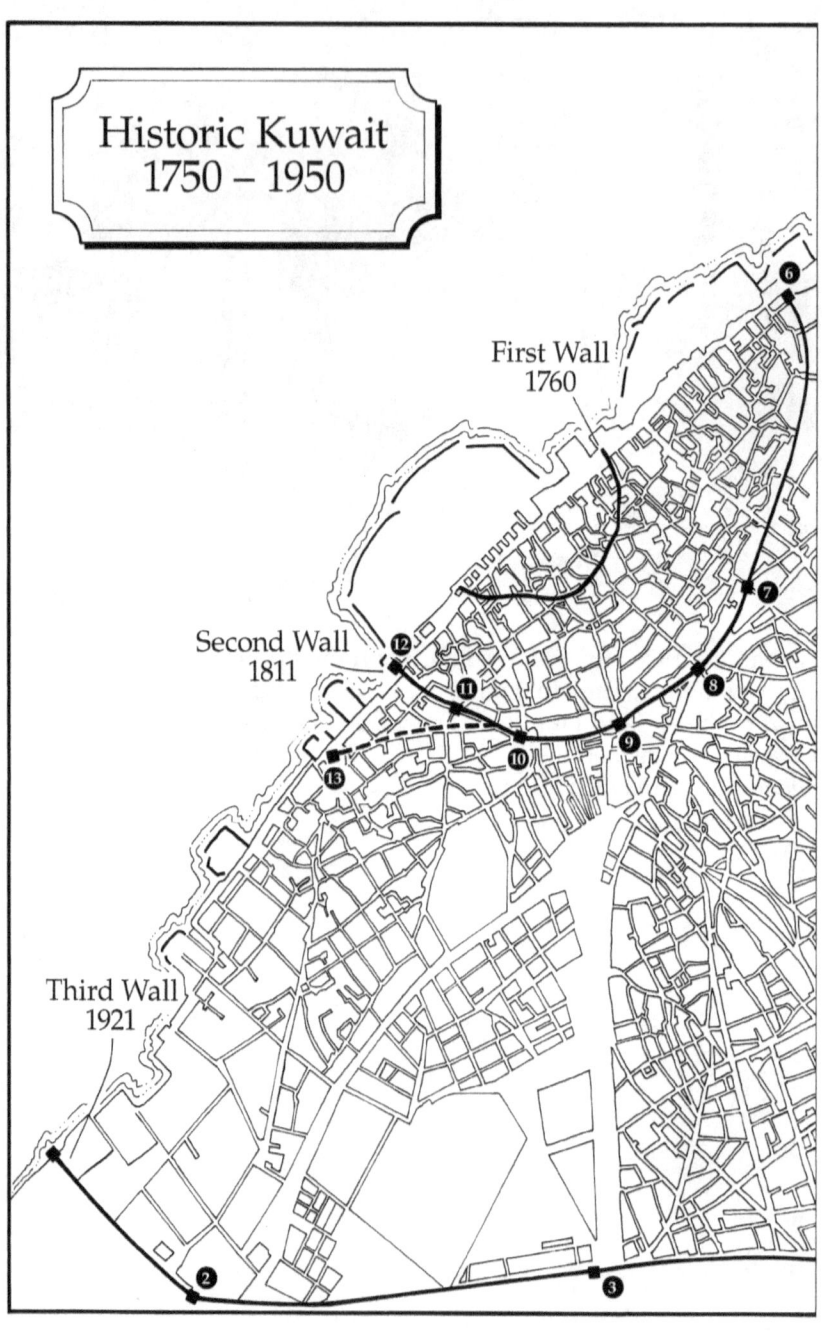

Maps of Historic Kuwait 1750–1950. *Created by Rick Britton (Charlottesville) from various sources and old photographs*

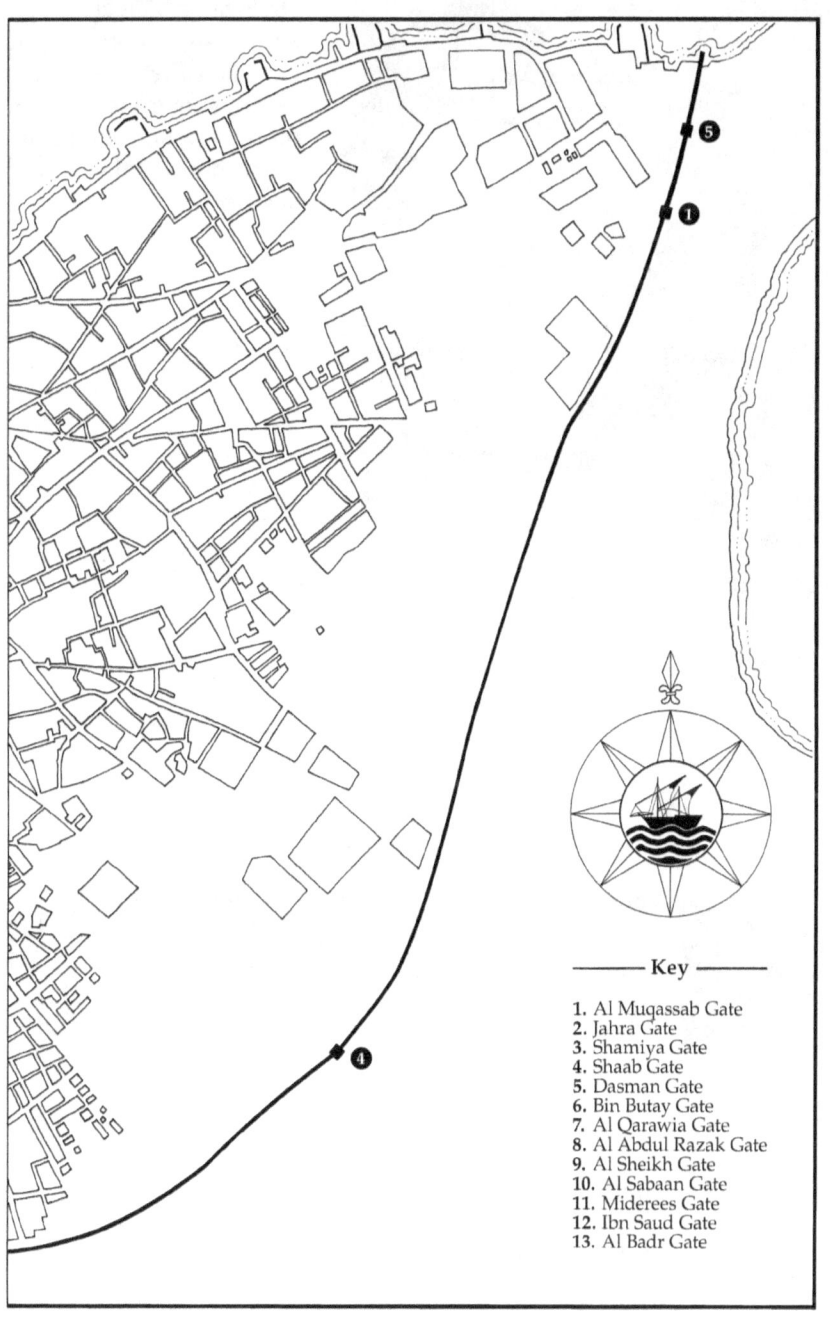

Dr. Eleanor Calverley of the American Mission hospital, Kuwait's first female physician, shown here in 1917 on the donkey she used to make house calls. *Dorothy Scudder papers*

The first American Mission hospital, under construction in 1914. Overlooking the Gulf shore, this and subsequent American Mission buildings introduced modern construction materials and techniques, including the use of concrete and structural steel. *Dorothy Scudder papers*

Dr. Paul Harrison, an early American Mission physician, with patients and visitors at the Hospital Dispensary in 1913. *Dorothy Scudder papers*

In the years before oil production, camels and donkeys bringing huge loads of camel thorn (*arfaj*) into the city were a common sight. The woody vegetation was the major source of fuel for cooking and other needs. *Dorothy Scudder papers*

The Residence of the British political agent was located on the Kuwaiti waterfront near the American Mission compound. Later expanded and modernized, the building still stands as a reminder of the state's history. It was occupied until shortly before the Iraqi invasion in 1990 by Dame Violet Dickson, the widow of Political Agent Col. H. R. P. Dickson. *Dorothy Scudder papers*

First Row: Yousuf al-Fouzan; Abdul Raheem; Eissa bin Abdul Jader; Abdul Aziz al-Humaidhi; Sabah al-Nasser; and Jirjis Eissa.

Second Row: Na'im; Nusrat; Khaled Sulaiman al-Adasani; Hamed Saleh al-Humaidhi; Abu Riziq; and Faqir Mohamed.

Third Row: Sayed Abdul Qader al-Sayed Mohamed al-Rifa'i; Sayed Rajab Sayed Abdullah al-Rifa'i; Sulaiman al-Adasani; Abdullah bin Sarhan; Majed al-Shaheen; Sayed Abdul Aziz Sayed Abdullah al-Rifa'i.

This grainy photograph of the Calverley School, published in a Kuwaiti newspaper, is the only physical reminder of the modern school for boys established at the American Mission in 1911. Under the direction of the Rev. Edwin Calverley, husband of Dr. Eleanor Calverley and first permanent minister of the Mission, the small school offered an English-language curriculum to students from prominent Kuwaiti families. Graduates would later occupy important positions in Kuwaiti administrations. Moved to newly built classrooms in 1916, the Calverley School was forced to close during the Great Depression of the early 1930s. *American Embassy Kuwait archives*

The traditional Kuwait waterfront before the significant development that began in the late 1960s. Many booms and other vessels remained beached, although a new road along the coast reduced the area for careening and building boats. *Kuwait Municipality*

3

The Coming of the American Mission

With the turn of the century, we see the first Americans settle down and call Kuwait their new home. In 1911, the Arabian Mission[1] of the Reformed Church in America purchased, with Shaikh Mubarak's permission, a parcel of land on a small hill outside the walls of the town for its hospital and other facilities. Dr. Paul Harrison was named by the mission to direct the medical work; Edwin Calverley was assigned as evangelist/educator and Dr. Eleanor Calverley, his wife, was sent to handle medical practice among the women of Kuwait.

The arrival of this tiny American community was the culmination of years of effort from the Arabian Mission to gain acceptance of a permanent station in Kuwait. The mission had looked upon Kuwait as a very desirable location for its work almost from its founding in 1892.[2] From its first bases in Basra and, to a lesser extent, in Bahrain, mission personnel visited periodically, beginning in 1895. Early that year, Samuel Zwemer spent three days there, noting the splendid harbor and cleanliness of the place.[3] The following May, two *colporteurs* visited for five days.[4] In an excess of optimism, Zwemer reported "The door is now ajar; one more visit and that by our medical missionary will push it wide open, perhaps off its hinges."[5]

The true situation became clear in 1896, when another *colporteur* passed through Kuwait when Mubarak had just come to power. The new ruler firmly rejected the sale of bibles and other Christian literature. If Zwemer's sense of timing proved inaccurate, the other aspect of his advice was more valid. The mission had initiated the practice of sending its physicians around the Gulf to cultivate contacts and good will.[6] This strategy, however, was not an immediate success. When Dr. Sharon Thoms and two assistants returned to Kuwait in June, 1903, Mubarak had them put on the next vessel departing the harbor that same day.⁷ Despite the rebuff of Dr. Thoms and party, another *colporteur* moved to Kuwait with his large family and operated from a rented house for a year before he had to leave.⁸ A further visit by Zwemer in February, 1904 proved equally unavailing. The prospects in Kuwait appeared so bleak that the mission, at its annual meeting in 1907, considered a motion to divert funds being held to purchase land for a hospital there for uses elsewhere in the Gulf.⁹

Events, however, were about to take an unexpected turn in a dramatic twist worthy of fiction. The mission base in Basra periodically dispatched a physician to tour adjacent towns. In late 1908, Dr. Arthur K. Bennett made a routine visit to Muhammera where he treated an enthusiastic Shaikh Khaz'al for diabetes. Shaikh Mubarak was visiting his friend at the time and Bennett was taken to meet the Kuwaiti ruler aboard his yacht. With Khaz'al's endorsement, Mubarak invited Bennett to come to Kuwait to look at his sister who suffered from eye problems.¹⁰ According to Bennett's subsequent recollection, he successfully performed cataract surgery on the patient, cementing a warm relationship with the ruler.¹¹ The positive impression created by Dr. Bennett's work was further strengthened by the efforts of Sayyid Rajab Al-Naqib, a prominent notable and religious figure in Basra. Highly respected by Shaikh Mubarak, Al-Naqib and his family had also been treated by Bennett and mission personnel. Now, he added his influential voice to those urging that Mubarak invite the mission to establish a presence in his domain. Early in 1909, Mubarak issued the invitation.

Shaikh Mubarak's apparent reversal of position was a fateful one, not only for the Arabian Mission, but for the people of Kuwait and the ruler himself.

One of the leading modern chroniclers of Kuwait's history considers Mubarak's "introduction of modern medicine" to have been the "major achievement in social services."¹² It is not possible, on the basis of available sources, to unravel the reluctance of Mubarak to countenance mission activities prior to 1909. Kuwait was unaccustomed at the time to hosting Western residents who represented a foreign culture and faith; Mubarak may have been uncomfortable with the idea, as were many of the other citizens of the town. But Abu Hakima, in his review of the record, suggests that an entirely different factor may have been in play. He finds no indication in the records of the Arabian Mission that its personnel were aware of the terms of Mubarak's 1899 agreement with the British. Among other things, the agreement stipulated that Kuwait would not sell, rent, or otherwise alienate land to foreigners.[13] Whatever the mix of motives and concerns influencing Mubarak's decision, it seems likely that he obtained British approval before issuing his invitation.

Having secured permission to establish a medical facility in Kuwait, the mission looked forward to building a hospital; for the moment, however, Kuwait was designated an "outstation" of the mission's main lodgement in Basra. Arthur Bennett, John Van Ess,[14] and Gerrit Pennings were tasked with visiting Kuwait to maintain the operation, possibly with the support of a resident Iraqi Christian with first-aid skills. Drs. Stanley Mylrea and Paul Harrison, from the mission's station in Bahrain, shared these itinerant duties. This arrangement did not please Shaikh Mubarak, who was soon pressing for a permanent and independent facility in Kuwait. The first resident staff was in place by December, 1911.[15]

For the first two years, the mission in Kuwait functioned in two rented houses in the center of town. One of them, called Bayt-ar-Rabban, had been the scene of a murder for which the owner was banished and his property seized. Since no Kuwaiti would live there, the mission obtained it for very low rent.[16] The other was in fact an annex of Shaikh Mubarak's palace and served as both a residence and the hospital.[17] The structure had two inner courtyards onto which the rooms opened. The larger section was selected for Dr. Harrison's medical practice and residential quarters. The smaller, more private courtyard was used for Dr. Calverley's practice for women. One room was divided by a calico curtain and functioned as both an office and operating room. The other room was converted into a rudimentary ward. Operations were sometimes performed in the mornings on the roof where light was good and the sun had baked the area. Dr. Harrison, who was replaced in 1914 by Dr. Mylrea, provided a glimpse of the town in his time:

> *The city of thick mud walls and flat roofs spread along the south side of a spacious harbor. Sailing craft of different kinds were built along the shore, and Paul, as he talked with the boatmen, learned that hundreds of them went out each year to the pearl banks and dove for oyster shells. Back of the city the open desert stretched out in unbroken emptiness. There was no drinking water in the city, but water was brought in every day by sailboats that plied back and forth to the mouth of the river (Shatt Al-Arab) fifty miles away.*[18]

The town in which the newcomers settled had not changed fundamentally since the 1880s.[19] Nestled in an arc along the Kuwait Bay, it covered an area of about eight square kilometers and was adapted to both its geopolitical environment and the livelihoods of its inhabitants. The clear, flat shoreline served as a dockyard for vessels of various sizes. (primarily *booms* and *sambuks*) It was employed in enterprises from pearling and fishing to oceangoing trade, while the landward [desert] side had been intermittently fortified against the threat of bedouin tribes, for whom Kuwait was entrepôt and trading post. Harold Dickson described Kuwait's importance for desert tribes in his legendary book, *The Arab of the Desert*:

> *... from time immemorable the Mutair, Harb, Shammar, 'Awazim and northern 'Ajman have done their musabila to that town. This system allows the town authorities to exercise a degree of control over the badawin who market with them, as any misbehaviour may result in the tribe's being forbidden to enter the town—a great hardship.*[20]

There were few monumental buildings in Kuwait in the first decade of the twentieth century with the exception of Seif Palace, the seat of the ruler built in 1904, and a number of minarets. The old city was, in the description provided in the 1960s by a Levantine city planner, "compact, its typical dwelling a courtyard house ..., its scale human." These homes, housing several generations of an extended family, were "strung around main pedestrian traffic arteries ... producing an urban pattern as 'organic' as can be imagined."

Whether approached from the sea or the desert, Kuwait presented the aspect of "a typically Islamic desert Arab city."[21]

One change that had occurred since the first American visit was the dismantling of the mud-brick wall that had been built in the eighteenth century to protect the city from landward attack. As the town underwent normal growth, the wall was removed to facilitate expansion of urban areas. Perhaps, also, the decision to dispense with its protective fortifications reflected an increased confidence and comfort with Kuwait's geopolitical situation. Despite resurgent Ottoman efforts to assert greater control over Kuwait during the empire's twilight years, Shaikh Mubarak astutely gained a measure of security by concluding a formal agreement with Great Britain. Signed on January 23, 1899, the relationship evolved into full-fledged protectorate status for Kuwait by 1903. From London's point of view, the arrangement not only checked Ottoman ambitions but also torpedoed German ambitions to build a Berlin-Baghdad Railroad with Kuwait as its terminus on the Gulf. With the agreement in hand, Shaikh Mubarak felt secure enough to proclaim Kuwait's autonomy from the Ottoman Empire.[22]

With its autonomy confirmed internationally, Kuwait was free to pursue its mercantile vocation. From its seafront on the best natural harbor on the Gulf, Kuwaiti cargo vessels sailed to Basra, Muhammera (in what is now Khuzistan), India, and as far as Mombasa on the African coast. In the Safat, an open desert market at the southeastern edge of town, trade was conducted with the bedouin of the hinterland. Craftsmen practiced their trades in covered *suqs*, or markets, stretching from Safat square toward the center of town, producing goods needed by both townspeople and traders.[23] The new American residents found themselves in the midst of a busy seaport. It was healthier than most because of the absence of mosquito-borne malaria and the cleansing powers of the strong sun, but was apparently not free of vices common to seaports.[24] By 1914, the population was variously estimated at between thirty-eight thousand and fifty thousand souls, there were about thirty mosques, some five hundred shops, and approximately three thousand residences.[25] Dr. Eleanor Calverley, who joined the American Mission in January, 1912, recalled her vivid first impressions of the town on her arrival by steamer from Bahrain:

> *Out of the desert on the horizon appeared a city of low houses the colour of sand. Above the sky was very blue. Beneath, the blue water of the Persian Gulf was dotted with white sails. Beached along the shore a line of brown sailboats awaited the season for pearl diving... In the whole picture was scarcely a tree or a patch of green. And yet Kuwait had a beauty of its own; a beauty of sand and sky and sea....*[26]

The tiny new American community was composed not of adventurers or explorers, although they would experience both adventure and discovery in the course of their work, but rather they were inspired by their faith and the desire to spread Christianity in "that part of the Muslim world which seemed least vulnerable to the Christian message."[27] To that end, the Arabian Mission was establishing "stations" along the Gulf Coast, from Basra to Muscat. As the writings of the early missionaries make clear, however, the ultimate dream of the collective was to penetrate the interior of Arabia.

From its inception, the Kuwait "station" was unique. Whereas other mission stations had a medical component, their activities included a range of activities—including evangelizing and education. Kuwait was from the outset designated as a medical mission.[28] There were probably two reasons for this anomaly. The first was the peculiar combination of circumstances that convinced the ruler to approve its establishment. The second may have been a perception that, aside from its intrinsic importance, Kuwait was a plausible launching pad for the hoped—for jump into Central Arabia. Within a few years, this subsidiary goal was accepted as a forlorn hope as it became apparent that an invitation to establish a permanent presence in Central Arabia would not be forthcoming. Nevertheless, by almost any other measure, the "American Mission" in Kuwait was a spectacular success in transforming health standards, as well as caring for and assisting the emirate with the difficult transition to modernity.

The permission of Shaikh Mubarak to reside in Kuwait and his willingness to sell land to the mission did not assure societal acceptance. This prize remained to be earned even as they set about establishing facilities for their medical practice.

The Kuwaiti townspeople were accustomed to seeing strangers, including Europeans, calling at their port or passing through to other destinations, but they had little experience with European or American-Christian residents. The British Political Agent, with a staff of one or two, had only come in 1904. Most Kuwaitis were initially curious and apprehensive, whereas some were actively hostile. Dr. Paul Harrison, who, a few years earlier, carried out medical work for a period of two months, contrasted the Kuwaiti reaction with the friendliness he had encountered in Oman; "The townsmen showed plainly that they were suspicious of foreigners, and children ran from them in fright when they walked in the streets."[29] Nevertheless, he and his partner, Dr. Gerrit Pennings, made the most of their brief stay. They were warmly welcomed by the nearby bedouin tribesmen who came for treatment and, by the time of their departure, had positively shaped the attiude of the ruler due to their good work. On their parting, Sheikh Mubarak informed them that he had been following their activities closely and added, "I give you permission to return whenever it is convenient for you to do so. May Allah go with you."[30]

It was a start toward breaking down local resistance, but it would take almost a decade for Arabian Mission personnel to achieve full acceptance and integration into Kuwaiti society. Dr. Stanley Mylrea, an Englishman who replaced Harrison in 1913 and went on to achieve legendary status in the country and ultimately choosing to be buried in the city, had left a snapshot of the situation he and his early colleagues encountered:

> ... *While it was true that Shaikh Mubarak wanted us, the great majority of the population including all the leading families were solidly opposed to the policy of allowing Christian missionaries to settle in their city. It was all very well to send for a doctor to come down from Basra to attend an important member of the community who might be ill, but to have a colony of Christian missionaries living in their city? No, they did not want that!*

> *...It used to hurt my pride to realize that in Kuwait I was looked upon as an unbeliever and an infidel. It should be noted that this curiosity and rudeness was a manifestation on the part of the man*

(and the boy) on the street only. The upper classes were aloof and supercilious but they never stooped to the cheap vulgarity of the common people. They kept their good manners and were courteous and civil even when they were probably suppressing inward prejudices. Only a very few were really rude to me.[31]

It should not be concluded from the fear and suspicion of American residents that there did not exist Kuwaitis who, especially those engaged in the international pearl trade with Paris, were aware of events in the United States that could affect their interests. John Van Ess was puzzled to hear the pearl merchants complain about the depressed market in 1909, but noted that they had a single hope for better times:

It was that 'taaf' might happen. I didn't recognize the word and the Arabs themselves did not know either just what 'taaf' was, but anyway if taaf did happen, pearls would jump in value. It did happen. When word came to Paris that Taft had been elected President of the United States, pearls more than doubled in price.[32]

Ready or not, the Kuwaitis were on the brink of being drawn relentlessly into closer contact with the wider world. In 1912, the first automobile arrived in Kuwait, the British-India Steam Navigation Company initiated weekly port calls, and the Hamburg-Amerika Line added Kuwait to its routes.[33] By 1916, Kuwait was connected to Basra and beyond by telegraph. Kuwaiti horizons could never again be confined to the nearby Gulf region.

Equally essential to the mission's acceptance and success in Kuwait was the attitude of the British authorities in the region. At least some of them were initially highly suspicious of these American newcomers who trekked around the Arabian Peninsula interacting, insofar as they were permitted, with local shaikhs, rulers, and tribesmen. With some reluctance, they acceded to Shaikh Mubarak's invitation to set up a medical practice in Kuwait, but not before extracting from the Arabian Mission a written acceptance of Great Britain's "special" status in the Gulf. This agreement, signed at Bahrain on November 18, 1910, also clarified that the mission station in Kuwait would not in any way involve the Ottomans in the affairs of the shaikhdom.[34]

Over time, relationships between the newly established station and the local British authorities developed into mutual respect and even cooperation. While the British establishment was occasionally exasperated by what they regarded as naiveté, brashness and lack of sympathy for colonialism in general,[35] mission personnel were fortunate in the quality of the early political agents, like William Shakespear and Harold Dickson, who came to value the medical and other services they provided. British officials further afield, however, continued to regard mission activities with suspicion and vigilance.[36] By the end of the decade, the British representatives on the ground in Kuwait at least appear to have been won over by the achievements and contributions of mission personnel. In 1919, the political agent there included Dr. Mylrea on his annual honors list. The citation read:

> *Dr. Charles Stanley Garland Mylrea, American Mission, has been of great assistance to my predecessors Colonel Hamilton and Captain Loch as will be seen from this office No. 1465 dated 18.8.18 to your address. He has also been of great assistance to me during the blockade incurring thereby much displeasure among the local population much to the detriment of his own work. His assistance continues and in consideration of his help I recommend him for the honour of O.B.E.*[37]

Undeterred, the mission pioneers went about their medical work while planning facilities, transforming the property, and raising their families.[38] In 1914, Dr. Stanley Mylrea, who had replaced Harrison the previous winter, built his house (the doctor's residence) on a small hillock which he "deemed of great importance."[39] The realization of this project was not without drama and an epic scene worthy of a Hollywood script. Two young American engineers, Charles Shaw and Philip Haynes, were brought in to build the first men's hospital in 1914, where they quickly surveyed the property according to the specifications of the deed of sale. In the process, they found that the property markers were inaccurate and relocated them. An unanticipated consequence of the survey was to exclude two-thirds of the cherished thirty-foot hill! Dr. Mylrea, who had been assigned to Kuwait the previous winter, decided to call on the ruler to ask that the entire hill be included in the mission's property.

Shaikh Mubarak was not amused to learn that the boundaries had been redefined and angrily chastized the mission for delays in the construction of the promised hospital. Mylrea left the audience in a depressed mood.

During the ensuing weeks, the mission sought ways to retrieve the situation, and Mylrea decided to invite the ruler to come to the mission site to measure the property and make a public statement. After some delay, Shaikh Mubarak agreed. The resulting visit is of such supreme importance for the future of the American mission that Dr. Mylrea's recollections merit repetition at length:

The fateful day came and it was raining. Now the Arab hates rain, which indeed converts the cities into quagmires and pools and he usually prefers to stay indoors rather than brave the elements. However, hoping against hope, Mr. Calverley and Dr. Mylrea walked out to the property and sat on the hill and waited. The afternoon wore on and they began to fear the worst. At last, to their relief, a procession came in sight. It was a procession worthy of the "Movies." In front came three carriages, in the first of which was Sheikh Mubarak himself accompanied by his little grandson. In the second carriage was Sheikh Jaber, the heir to the throne. In the third carriage was the resident British Government official who, at the request of Dr. Mylrea, had come to witness the proceedings. Riding alongside of the carriages were all the chief men of the city, out perhaps to see the hated missionaries finally rebuked and dismissed. Accompanying the whole was the usual crowd of small boys hoping to enjoy themselves....

Slowly the cavalcade halted and the Sheikh, accompanied by his son and grandson and by the British Government Official, slowly walked to the top of the hill. The chief men of the city dismounted and also came up the hill. Salutations, barely civil, passed between the Sheikh and the missionaries. Solemnly the official measuring cubit was laid along the Sheikh's arm, to make sure that the official cubit was the right length. At last the measuring was begun. The task took some time but when the figures were given to the Sheikh he could but acknowledge that we had taken only what was our right. His expression underwent a complete transformation and he turned to the missionaries, saying 'Why, this is all right.' He then made a sign to those present that he was about to speak. The gist of his speech was as follows:—'Men of Kuwait. I have summoned you here to-day for a rather unusual purpose. You all know that I am under very special treaty relations with the British Government not to lease or sell any of my territory to foreigners without the sanction of the British Government, and you all know that I have been most scrupulous in observing this agreement. But these people, these Americans, are not politicians or tradesmen. They have come here to teach us and to help us. They have come here to build us a hospital. Now, the doctor here wants something of me. I am not sure just what he does want, but whatever it is I am going to give it to him as a personal expression of my good will.' And then he turned to Dr. Mylrea and said 'Doctor just what is it you want?' to which the doctor replied 'I want you to give us all of the hill'. 'Good' was the answer. 'My men will come out tomorrow and you can tell them where to put the landmarks.'[40]

The first hospital building took shape in 1914 under the direction of engineers Shaw and Haynes. The structure, basically a line of rooms surrounded by a broad veranda, was unique in Kuwait and the Gulf. Because of its use of imported steel beams and concrete, constructing it was more of a challenge than its simple design might suggest. Local builders employed for the project were completely unfamiliar with modern building techniques, and a great deal of on-the-job training was required as the structure was being built. Another feature unfamiliar in Kuwaiti construction was the number and size of windows added for light and ventilation, and the large and airy rooms. Nevertheless, the completed hospital, which was known locally as "the glass house," was so soundly built that its demolition to make room for the Mylrea Memorial Men's Hospital in the 1950s was an unexpectedly difficult task.[41] By 1916, what was called "the padre's house" was added west of the doctor's residence, with an adjacent line of rooms designed originally as the mission school. Finally, in 1919, the mission capped a decade of intensive building with the erection of a women's hospital, similar to the 1913 hospital structure. In the course of this burst of building, the Americans made their mark on the physical face of Kuwait.[42]

Through their writings and other contemporary sources, we know a great deal about these earliest American residents. Dr. Eleanor Calverley, who overlapped with Dr. Harrison and served with absences for leave until 1929, was that rarest of professionals in the region at the time—a female physician. Her gender greatly facilitated interaction with the secluded women of Kuwait and she may have been the first member of the mission to make enduring inroads into Kuwaiti society. As her colleague noted:

> *When it became known that the lady doctor would visit women in their homes, Eleanor Calverley had more work than she could do. Her husband bought a donkey on which she rode to her calls... Her skill began to save lives of child-mothers who so often died giving birth. With her advice babies survived the diseases that usually killed them.*[43]

Dr. Calverley experienced her share of hostility during the first months of her service, however. On one occasion, she was called to the home of a woman experiencing a difficult delivery only to be turned away at the door after hostile midwives had persuaded the family not to let her in.[44] A turning point for her was the case of "Fulana," a Kuwaiti patient suffering from a hernia. Word of the successful operation quickly spread throughout the town; "What do you suppose the doctor lady did? Why, she cut Fulana open, took out her insides, carried them to the sea and washed them and then put them back again."[45]

Edwin Calverley, her husband, a graduate of an Ivy League seminary, was the mission's first permanent minister and educator. Early in his residency, he set up a small modern school with an English curriculum in the line of rooms near the hospital. Elements in the town, who were hostile to the American mission and Shaikh Mubarak's support for it, established a dispensary and competing school which the ruler neutralized by bestowing his patronage on them as well. The dispensary failed in several months but the school, "al-Mubarakiyah" succeeded to become the first modern Arabic school.[46] Some students continued their studies at the Calverley School after completing their early schooling at al-Mubarakiyah.[47]

The iconic face of the mission in its early stages was, however, provided by Dr. Stanley Mylrea. British by birth, he was married to an American, Bessie, who earned the nickname "Khatun Sa'idah" or "happy lady" among the Kuwaitis. Bessie Mylrea was a gifted pianist who imported the town's first piano. Contemporaries recall her pumping and playing the "baby organ" at weekly worship services held by the mission. Mrs. Mylrea attempted to establish a comparable school for girls but was too far ahead of the times. She was compelled to abandon the project by strong religious opposition.[48]

Dr. Mylrea possessed a grave and formal manner, tempered by a dry sense of humor and occasional flashes of exasperation. Lewis Scudder, Jr., who knew him personally in his later years, characterizes him as the epitome of the *hakim*, a "sober man of deep spiritual learning" and wisdom, held in particular esteem in Arab culture: "Even when galloping though the streets of the town on his horse with his dog, Khalaf, pelting along in their train, racing to meet an emergency at some house where illness threatened, he never lost his dignity."[49]

Gradually, the mission began to take shape under the determined leadership of Dr. Mylrea as facilities were built and human relationships were developed.[50] In addition to a growing medical practice among Kuwaitis,[51] mission doctors served as medical examiners for the British political agent. Mission personnel also managed to uphold their evangelical responsibilities. Prior to the construction of a purpose-built chapel twenty years after the arrival of the community, weekly services were conducted in the courtyard of a traditional Kuwaiti house. Although the missionaries would later come to realize the futility of attempts to convert Kuwaiti Muslims, the sounds of their worship and singing often lured passers-by in a town where entertainment was scarce. On occasion, as many as sixty to one hundred Kuwaitis crowded the courtyard to listen to homilies preached in Arabic and to engage in lively discussions of Christianity and Islam.[52] As much as anything else, these early encounters began to undermine the suspicion and hostility within the Kuwaiti population regarding Christians, and laid foundations for the unique level of tolerance among most Kuwaitis today. It was extremely hard to discount these Christian-Americans who had come among them to serve their medical needs.

The Arabian Mission staff, men, and women had the distinction of being the first Westerners to establish a viable community in Kuwait. While small in number, the group was larger than the official British establishment up until the beginnings of the oil industry. With their *colporteurs* and staff from India and other Arab countries, the critical mass for community life existed. Whether single or married, these Americans had come to establish their homes among the Kuwaitis and to interact with their Kuwaiti hosts.[53] To supplement the work of the hospital, a school for boys was established in 1911 with the permission of the ruler and under the direction of Edwin Calverley. In 1916, it moved into newly constructed facilities on the mission compound and continued to operate until forced to close during the worldwide depression. Its curriculum included English, typing, and other modern skills and produced a small cadre of Kuwaiti boys prepared for the demands of modernization that they would confront sooner than they could have anticipated at the time. Among its graduates were the first directors of the Public Works, Health and Customs departments.[54] The Calverley School had an influence on the development of modern education in Kuwait.

Even as the Americans were consolidating their foothold in Kuwait, their sponsor, Shaikh Mubarak, died on November 28, 1915. He was a leader of extraordinary vision and capability. By his adroit conclusion of a protectorate agreement with Great Britain, he secured Kuwait's independence not just against the Ottoman state but also against tribal and dynastic rivalries swirling around him in Central Arabia. Although he occasionally overreached himself domestically[55] and in military adventures abroad in his quest for a greater role in the region, he demonstrated a remarkable capacity for regaining his footing.

In addition to inviting the Arabian Mission to Kuwait to bring modern medical services to his people and presiding over the beginnings of modern education in Kuwait, Mubarak exercised regional influence much greater than Kuwait's size and resources would suggest. Perhaps most significantly he was able to play the part of "king-facilitator," if not "kingmaker," in the Arabian Peninsula. Little-known is the role of Mubarak and Kuwait in the success of Abd al-Aziz al-Saud in consolidating his rule over that vast territory.

The Coming of the American Mission 45

Kuwait's relationship with Abd-al-Aziz and the rise of the Saudi state is a thread that runs through the remainder of this history, a thread in which the members of the nascent American community would sometimes find themselves involved. Here it suffices to set the stage for subsequent developments. Lewis Scudder provides a concise scene setter:

> From 1896 Mubarak was the mentor of the exiled scion of the house of Al-Sa'ud, Abd-ul-Aziz, and protector of his father, Abd-ur-Rahman... He (Mubarak) was pleased to continue giving sanctuary to Abd-ur-Rahman Al-Sa'ud.
>
> Through all these maneuvers, the young Abd-ul-Aziz was Mubarak's observant student, and it was Mubarak who gave his blessing to the undertaking which resulted in Abd-ul-Aziz's dramatic coup against the Al-Rashid in Riyadh in 1902. Mylrea commented:
>
> 'It is to Mubarak that the great king, Ibn Saud, owes his early training, for Ibn Saud spent his boyhood in Kuwait. Mubarak took a great fancy to the young lad and undoubtedly molded his character in the impressionable days of boyhood. It is not too much to say that had it not been for Mubarak, Ibn Saud would never have become the historic commanding figure that everyone acknowledges to be the greatest Arab since the days of the early Caliphs.'[56]

Stanley Mylrea met 'Abd al-'Aziz al Saud in the spring of 1914 when the future Saudi king was encamped in the desert near Jahra for a conference with Mubarak and the British to discuss plans to extend the Baghdad railroad to Kuwait. When fever broke out in the camp among the entourage which had come from malaria-prone Hasa, Mylrea was summoned to treat the victims.[57] Mylrea was quite taken with Ibn Saud and later wrote a lengthy account of their first meeting, including a conversation about faith.[58] They met in Kuwait several times until 1917.

Shaikh Mubarak's death occurred during a period when momentous events that would affect Kuwait and all its inhabitants were unfolding not only in the Arabian Peninsula but also in Europe and the Middle East. These events would shape the future of the country, often in unpredictable ways.

In Europe, even before Shaikh Mubarak passed from the scene, a bloody and protracted conflict involving all of the major powers of the day had broken out. With Britain a leading participant in the Allied coalition on the one hand, and the Ottoman Empire linking its fate to Germany and the Central Powers, it was inevitable that Kuwait's environment would be significantly affected. Since the Ottomans controlled the three wilayets that constitute modern Iraq, hostile forces were a scant seventy miles away and their tribal allies were even closer. Ironically, one of the earliest consequences of the war was to confirm Kuwait as an "independent" state under British protection. Whether the significance of the development was fully appreciated in the town at the time, "November 3rd, 1914 was an historic day for Kuwait since it witnessed the undoing of the [Anglo-Turkish] Convention and the severance of two centuries of diplomatic ties with Turkey."[59] The British political agent in Kuwait had protested his government's ambiguous position on Kuwait's status during the negotiations, but was overruled until changed circumstances made the entire convention a dead letter.[60]

Shaikh Mubarak swore allegiance to the British position in the conflict, but not all of his people were comfortable with his decision. Among these was much of the Islamic establishment in Kuwait who were "embarrassed to be siding with the infidel 'Ingleez' against...the Sultan-Caliph."[61] Interestingly, Mubarak's son, Shaikh Salem, who would himself become ruler in 1917, associated himself, at the time, with the objections of the Islamic party.

At the same time, trade restrictions and shortages associated with the British prosecution of the war added to the difficulties and discontents affecting Kuwaiti society. The British were concerned that the Turks and their tribal allies could not obtain food, arms, and other useful commodities from traditional sources in Kuwait. As a consequence, legitimate commercial activity in the town was seriously depressed. There were some offsetting opportunities for increased trade with British-controlled Basra. Those who were prepared to test the British restrictions could also realize windfall profits by engaging in smuggling—and some did. Ultimately, the British authorities thought it necessary to impose an economic blockade on their own protectorate. To add insult to injury, the worldwide influenza epidemic made its appearance in Central Arabia at the end of 1918. There is little contemporary information on the impact of the pandemic on Kuwait specifically. In Riyadh, the effects were devastating. An estimated ten thousand residents, 10 percent of the city's population, perished.[62] It is difficult to believe that Kuwait completely escaped this highly communicable disease, although mission and other materials of the time are mute on the point. Ironically, the impact may have been mitigated somewhat by the curtailment of normal commercial contacts.

Shaikh Mubarak died, therefore, at a time when Kuwaiti society was experiencing serious strains. Nevertheless, the succession passed smoothly, with his son, Shaikh Jabir, quickly assuming charge. His brother, Shaikh Salem, facilitated his brother's accession when he returned to the capital from a military mission to assist Ibn Saud in a successful campaign against the Ajman, "a powerful tribe that was fighting to maintain its independence of Ibn Saud."[63]

Shaikh Jabir's rule would be extremely brief. By February 5, 1917, a scant sixteen months later, he was dead, having refused treatment by European doctors, including Dr. Mylrea.[64] During his short tenure, Jabir sought to straddle the issue of British trade restrictions, proclaiming loyalty to the British relationship while also sympathizing with merchants disenchanted with constraints on commercial activity. One of the highlights of his rule was a *durbar*, or convocation, called in Kuwait in November, 1916 by Sir Percy Cox, the British Political Resident in the Gulf. The meeting, aimed in large part at heading off a growing rift between Ibn Saud and Kuwait, brought together Ibn Saud, Shaikh Jabir, and Shaikh Kha'zal of Muhammera.[65] After concluding their ultimately unsuccessful political discussions, the three Arab rulers paid Dr. Mylrea and the Arabian Mission the honor of a courtesy call at the recently completed "house on the hill."[66] This was probably Ibn Saud's last contact with the mission in Kuwait.[67] The failure of the conference and other efforts to halt the slide into hostility between Kuwait and the Saudi state had other consequences for the Kuwait station. Originally conceived as a "doorway into the Arabian interior," Kuwait's growing isolation from the Arabian hinterland put an end to that illusion.[68]

On the death of Shaikh Jabir, his brother, Shaikh Salem succeeded him as the ruler. Salem was a complex and religiously conservative man as well as a key figure in Kuwait's bitter feud with Ibn Saud. According to mission personnel, his relationship with his father, Shaikh Mubarak, was troubled; as a strict Muslim, he was known to be highly critical of Mubarak's appetite for luxury as well as his friendship with the more liberal Shaikh Kha'zal. His dislike of "foreigners" carried over to his early attitude toward the Arabian Mission; "For a long time he bore the mission no goodwill."[69] After appointing relatives and loyalists to his new regime, one of Shaikh Salem's first initiatives was a campaign against "immorality" and laxness toward religious observances in the town. Despite his religious orientation, however, he rebuffed a delegation that appealed to him in February, 1917 to take firm measures "against Christian propaganda in Kuwait," allowing the mission to continue its work undisturbed.[70]

Given Salem's alignment with the opposition of the conservative Islamic establishment when Shaikh Mubarak declared support for the war policy of Britain against the Ottomans, it might have been anticipated that his relationship with the British would be troublesome. As ruler, however, he was outwardly friendly toward them, although he may have been less than scrupulous in curbing smuggling. Consequently, in 1918, Britain declared a formal blockade at sea on Kuwait.[71]

Kuwait's relations with the Saudi state would be the central feature of Shaikh Salem's period of rule. He did not come to power with a clean slate on this issue. Despite strains in his relationship with his father, Salem had remained a dutiful son during the former's life. At the moment of Mubarak's death, Shaikh Salem was in the interior where he had been sent to support Ibn Saud.[72] The combined campaign was successful in routing the Ajman forces, but its aftermath laid the groundwork for Saudi-Kuwaiti hostility. Although Salem provided help as ordered to Ibn Saud, there was little love lost between the two men. Perhaps, the origin of this tension lay in childhood; Abd al-Aziz al-Saud knew Shaikh Salem well during his youth in Kuwait. It seems likely that Salem resented his father's high regard for his Saudi guest and protégé. Still other observers suggest that Shaikh Salem and his predecessor, Shaikh

Jabir, may have been concerned by the power and influence that Ibn Saud was accumulating in adjacent Central Arabia. As Rush comments:

> During most of Mubarak I's reign Kuwait had assisted Ibn Saud in extending his authority over Arabia's tribes including the Ajman. By 1915, however, many Kuwaitis—and particularly Shaikh Salim—felt that Ibn Saud's successes had gone far enough and regarded the Ajman as useful agents in curbing his power lest he should ever threaten Kuwait. This was probably the reasoning that led Jabir II to authorize Shaikh Salim to grant some of the Ajman refuge in Kuwait in 1916 even though Shaikh Salim—by order of his dying father Mubarak I—had just helped Ibn Saud defeat them.[73]

The question of whether Ibn Saud would have eventually turned against Kuwait in the normal course of events, as some Kuwaitis feared, will remain moot, although it is not beyond the realm of probability.[74] In the final analysis, the state of Saudi Arabia originated as an empire with tribes and territories from Hasa to the Hejaz incorporated by the sword. The *Ikhwan*, which Ibn Saud harnessed to his purposes until their rebelliousness caused him to curb their power by force, had little love or respect for the townsmen of Kuwait. Whether the motive was the Ajman incident or Kuwaiti refusal to act as tax collector (on behalf of Ibn Saud) with tribesmen from Ibn Saud's territories trading in Kuwait, the Saudi ruler felt highly aggrieved. In 1920, he imposed an embargo on Kuwait's trade with his desert tribes while simultaneously unleashing his *Ikhwan* allies against the city.

Thus began what was arguably the seminal period in the development of modern Kuwait—the Battle of Jahra. In Central Arabia, Ibn Saud's forces finally defeated the Shammar and occupied their chief town of Hail. By May, his *Ikhwan* stepped up raids into Kuwaiti territory, killing some Kuwaiti loyalists and rustling large numbers of camels, sheep, and goats. Kuwaiti forces sent against the raiders that same month, suffered a bad defeat. Ibn Saud's power and prestige were at their zenith and Shaikh Salem had no option but to prepare to receive a major attack.

As noted earlier, the old, second wall encircling the city had been allowed to fall into a state of disrepair as Kuwait had grown beyond its confines. During his rule, Shaikh Mubarak was unconcerned by the lack of effective defenses, describing himself as "Kuwait's wall." Shaikh Salem was not in a position, for personal and geopolitical circumstances, to be so blasé. On May 22, 1920, he issued orders for a new wall to be built immediately, despite intense summer heat.[75]

In a prodigious feat of human will, the inhabitants of Kuwait built the mud and coral wall, three miles in length, over the hottest and most humid four months of the summer. Anchored on the slaughterhouse on the town's west side, it arched around the built-up areas to include Dasman Palace on the eastern shore. The Arabian Mission compound was about one-quarter mile inside the new fortifications.[76] At each end, the wall was extended well out into the waters of the Gulf to prevent attackers from skirting the fortification at low tide. The project required admirable qualities of organization and coordination as well as the corvée labor of every able-bodied man and boy. When completed, it included four fortified gates, firing platforms, and towers and round bastions spaced approximately every two hundred yards along the entire circumference. If there were societal tensions and discontent with Shaikh Salem, the shared threat posed by the *Ikhwan* clearly outweighed them.

It was fortuitous that the construction proceeded so quickly, for the wall was completed just in time. The *Ikhwan* force moved into Kuwaiti territory in early October, less than two weeks after the wall was completed. Before turning its attention to the town, however, the horde camped before the oasis village of Jahra, situated at the head of Kuwait Bay, a key position in any assault on the town itself.

On October 8, the *Ikhwan* force, under the command of their most famous general, Faisal al-Dawish, reached the vicinity of Jahra, barely eighteen miles from Kuwait town.[77] Having anticipated Dawish's opening move, Shaikh Salem had already positioned his main army in the oasis. In the town, efforts to augment the forces were redoubled and an additional few hundred recruits were drafted to man the new wall. Their shouts and war songs to keep up morale during the night were clearly audible at the mission compound.[78]

Two days later, on October 10, the *Ikhwan* launched their attack against the Kuwaiti defenders at Jahra. Dr. Mylrea recounts events in the town as firing from the battle was heard:

> *At once the air became charged with wildly conflicting rumors. Everyone was thoroughly aroused. Young and old, rich and poor, bond and free, streamed past the mission hospital to take their places with those who were holding the gates and the wall. It was quickly realized that should the enemy be victorious at Jahra, Kuwait would be attacked without warning. No one was unarmed and nearly all carried Mauser or Martini rifles with plenty of ammunition, while some had swords and revolvers as well....*[79]

Toward midday, Lt. Col. J. C. More, the British political agent, came to the mission compound with news that he had heard that Shaikh Salem had retreated into the small fort at Jahra and was besieged. More and Mylrea decided to drive around the town and ended up at the main gate where they met Shaikh Ahmad Salem, the heir apparent, who had been left in charge of the town.

Dr. Mylrea recalled the scene of confusion that lay before them:

> *Refugees from Jahra were pouring in at the gate, whole families with their household effects, their camels and donkeys and dogs.*

Each new arrival was immediately beset by questioners, all shouting at the tops of their voices... Little black Badu donkeys struggled manfully in, all of them greatly overloaded and almost invisible from the amount of stuff stowed on top of them. In addition to household goods they carried small children and the blind and the aged.

> *Presently some horsemen galloped in—this looked bad—but it was explained away. It afterwards turned out, as might have been expected, that these horsemen belonged to Shaikh Salim's cavalry....In fact the defeat and dispersal of Salim's cavalry by Faisal Dawish had been the opening move of the Battle of Jahra. There*

was one dominant impression that carried away as we drove home and that was that the town was very nearly in a panic.[80]

In the early afternoon of October 10, the first Kuwaiti wounded arrived at the American hospital. All were cavalrymen who had left the battle early and had limited information about the fighting, which was continuing.[81] Although details were few, in the town it was understood that Shaikh Salem and his forces were surrounded in Jahra fort, with ample food and ammunition but little (extremely brackish) water. During the coming night, the *Ikhwan* would launch three reckless attacks on the fort without success.[82]

Within Kuwait town, the population, including the small American community, knew that the battle was at a desperate stage. Dr. Mylrea captured the atmosphere during that tense and anxious night:

> An hour or so after sunset my wife and I were just sitting down to dinner under the stars when there was a great panic at the eastern end of the town. We could hear the screaming of women and the yelling of boys. All around us rang the cry that the Ikhwan had come in. I called up the Political Agent on the telephone, since the disturbance was at his end of town, and asked for the facts. He replied that it was just a scare. Some fugitives had arrived at one of the gates and the sentries had at first taken them for Ikhwan. The mistake had been explained and the panic had subsided.[83]

There was very little rest in Kuwait town that Sunday evening and none in Jahra.

The following day, October 12, brought a dramatic reversal of Kuwaiti fortunes. Several hundred Kuwaiti reinforcements—Persian coolies and the scrapings of last-minute impressment—were transported across the Bay to Jahra, and six hundred Shammar tribesmen unexpectedly arrived to join the defenders. The latter were traditional foes of Kuwait and allies of the Ottoman state, but the desire for revenge on the *Ikhwan* was uppermost in their minds. The arrival of these fresh forces and Ikhwan's sizeable casualties in the nighttime assaults restored the initiative to Shaikh Salem. The *Ikhwan* forces were quickly routed and asked for a truce. They soon withdrew, taking many hundreds of wounded with them.[84]

The American mission hospital and its small staff were soon overwhelmed with the care of the Kuwaiti wounded. Sixty-three Kuwaitis died in the two-day battle, or one for every twelve of the enemy who died at Jahra. Kuwaiti wounded were about 127 as against the estimated 800 Ikhwani killed.[85] Remarkably for the time, only four of the casualties that reached the mission hospital on October 11 and 12 did not survive. Most of the cases were gunshot wounds, although some had suffered sword and dagger wounds. One of the four who could not be saved with the drugs available in 1920 was a case, rare in Arabia, of gas gangrene, probably contracted because the fighting took place "in the heavily manured date gardens and grain fields of the oasis town."[86]

Dr. Mylrea experienced difficult hours on October 12, but not because of the Battle of Jahra in any direct sense. That morning, he left the hard-pressed hospital to attend to another of his civic duties; as Quarantine Medical Officer for the Port of Kuwait, it was his responsibility to visit and inspect all incoming vessels. As he waited for the launch to take him out to an arriving ship, he probably was not anticipating more crises than he already had on his hands.

He decided to wait in a portside coffee shop, which happened to be occupied by many of the most influential men in the town. Following the exchange of traditional greetings, and as he listened to the talk of the group recently relieved of the stress of the battle, his well-known temper came to the surface, exacerbated no doubt by weariness and lack of sleep.

> There was plenty of pious talk ... but when the twentieth prominent man told me that God would reward me I boiled over and said:
>
> "This is all very fine but talk is the cheapest thing in the world. You people pile all this work on me, but it never occurs to one of you to do anything or help, either financially or in kind. In my country, rulers would be the first to visit the wounded and to do all in their power to ensure that those who had risked everything for the sake of their native land should have the best possible care and attention. Here the Shaikh's slaves dump helpless men on the hospital veranda and depart. That is all there is to it. No thought of how my small staff is to cope with all this extra work."[87]

Years later he recalled saying a good bit more along these lines before he became aware with "horror" that all other conversation had ceased and the entire room, including a senior Shaikh, was listening to his tirade. Without a word, the Shaikh rose, gathered his *bisht* around him and left. All the others followed suit and departed. Mylrea was certain he had made an unforgivable mistake.

He spent a miserable day and it was not until that evening that relief came, in the form of two prominent citizens who had been present in the coffee house that morning. With great courtesy they acknowledged that everything the doctor had said was true, and assured him that the entire city was behind him and ready to help him and the mission hospital. As the spokesman said this, he placed a paper containing the signatures and pledges of many of the leading merchants, as well as a canvas bag containing one thousand rupees, as a down payment.[88] Over succeeding days, additional contributions continued to arrive, and prominent citizens who had been hostile to the Christian mission for most of a decade showed the character to express their new-found friendship for the institution. The American missionaries were no longer an alien community tolerated by the town, but had come to be seen as an important and integral part of the community. Dr. Mylrea concludes his account of this episode which pays tribute to this quality—"Personally I have always felt that the people of Kuwait just did not realize what was being done for them until they were told. When they *were* told they rose to the occasion."[89]

While the *Ikhwan* assault had been repulsed and the American mission was more comfortably settled into its Kuwaiti environment, the threat from Ibn Saud and his *Ikhwan* allies had not ended; it was only in abeyance. The Battle of Jahra had ended with a truce rather than a peace. A scant week later, anxiety was rekindled in the town by the arrival of an *Ikhwan* delegation bearing an ultimatum for Shaikh Salem. A council including many prominent Kuwaiti leaders was convened to consider the *Ikhwani* communication. The proceedings were reportedly heated as some participants pressed Shaikh Salem to invoke the protectorate agreement with Great Britain. Against his own inclinations, the ruler was "more or less forced" to seek British assistance. The request was delivered to them on October 20 and Dawish's ultimatum was officially rejected the same day.[90]

Although the British had earlier warned Ibn Saud that he and his minions must leave Kuwait alone, they were not asked and did not play a role in the Battle of Jahra when the *Ikhwan* ignored their warning.[91] They had, however, initiated contingency measures by sending warships to Kuwait. A second British vessel entered port on October 21 and an aeroplane flew in the same day to conduct reconnaissance.

Dr. Mylrea, who figured so prominently in the events of the crisis, was called upon once more to play an unexpected role at this stage as well. He was having tea with the British political agent when the pilot returned to report that he had not located the *Ikhwan* forces. Mylrea and others familiar with the countryside surmised that Faisal al-Dawish was most likely to have camped at Subahyah, a series of wells about thirty miles to the south. He was amused when the pilot explained that he had been searching for houses and palms and jokingly suggested that the pilot take him along to point out the muddy holes that marked Subahyah. The physician was likely surprised when his offer was accepted.[92]

And so, on the morning of October 22, the head of the American Mission hospital found himself in the open cockpit of the two-seater aircraft, carrying an official British letter ordering the *Ikhwan* out of Kuwaiti territory under threat of being bombed out of it. Numerous enemy tents were soon sighted and the weighted letter, festooned with colorful streamers, was dropped. Almost as soon as a man was observed retrieving the message, the encamped *Ikhwan* poured out of the tents and began firing their rifles at the plane. The pilot prudently gained altitude and returned to Kuwait, his mission accomplished.[93]

Meanwhile, in Kuwait, a third British warship sailed into the harbor bearing Sir Arnold Wilson, the Acting British Civil Commissioner in Baghdad. A council of war (to which Dr. Mylrea was invited) was convened on board to make contingency plans, including, if necessary, the evacuation of British and American nationals in the town.

By October 24, preparations were complete. The wall was fully manned and supplemented by British landing parties with machine guns to secure the town's gates. The next day, a naval signalling party was posted on the roof of Dr. Mylrea's house. The small hill on which it was built made it the best vantage point from which to maintain contact with the supporting British warships in the harbor.[94]

Three days later, having received a defiant reply from Faisal al-Dawish to its formal warning, the British authorities ordered a further air reconnaissance by recently arrived bombers. Dr. Mylrea was once again in the cockpit. The wells at Subahyah were occupied only by several tents, which probably sheltered wounded too ill to ride with the fleeing *Ikhwan* host. A survey far beyond revealed no sign of the enemy. The immediate threat to Kuwait and its inhabitants had passed for the moment.[95]

For several days in October, 1920, the future of Kuwait hung in the balance. It had faced other challenges and threats before in its history, but none more serious and imminent than that posed by "the territorial ambitions of Ibn Saud and his army of zealots."[96] Kuwait would not face a comparable experience again for almost exactly seventy years.

The crisis of 1920 merits serious attention for more reasons than that it greatly impacted the small American community as well as Kuwaiti citizens. As usually occurs when shared trauma affects a group, the events before, during, and after the Battle of Jahra provided the impetus for several important strands of Kuwait's development that would influence the nature of the society until the present day – chiefly, the way Kuwaitis look at themselves, the "others" among them, and their country itself. Among the more important strands are the following:

As already noted, the American Mission emerged from these events with greatly enhanced status. As the redoubtable Dr. Mylrea put it, "For the American Mission, it marked the beginning of a new epoch."[97] Now the mission became not a foreign implant grafted on the body politic, but an institution interwoven into the social fabric. While there may have been a few holdouts in this new embrace, henceforth the mission hospital would benefit from acceptance and material support from Kuwaitis. The ruler, Shaikh Salem, is inexplicably absent from accounts of events after his successful military defence of Jahra and he would die on February 22, 1921, only four months after his victory. Nevertheless, there is strong evidence that he too moderated his attitude toward the American mission as a consequence of its yeoman service during the crisis. He gave the mission additional property to expand its compound and, even more significantly, enrolled his son, Fahad, in Edwin Caverley's school.[98]

In a broader sense, at least two major facets of modern Kuwait may be traced to the traumatic experience in the fall of 1920. It was the date chosen as a benchmark for determining citizenship. As memories of the Battle of Jahra fade elsewhere, outside observers, and possibly even younger Kuwaitis, are frequently puzzled by the emphasis on determining who is a Kuwaiti on the basis of descent from persons who were residents in 1920. Their grandfathers understood that this was an affirmation of the shared anxiety and sacrifice of standing for Kuwait's survival as an independent country in the face of what must have seemed, at the time, an unstoppable *Ikhwani* tide. Nor was this benchmark chosen as an act of exclusion; the shared terror and sacrifice undoubtedly contributed not only to an embrace of the American mission hospital, but to the acceptance of one another as well—Sunni or Shi'a, Christian, Arab or Persian, merchants or Baharna,[99] or tribesman. It may not have ushered in a millennium of tolerance, but it was a way point on the route to the relative tolerance that characterizes most Kuwaitis today.[100]

The second crucial trend originating in this pivotal period was reflected in the dispute noted between the ruler and his prominent counsellors over whether to invoke British support and assistance in the later stages of the *Ikhwan* threat. The delegation of prominent citizens prevailed in this argument and would never again be content not to have a voice in major questions of public policy. Several significant threads combined in the push for a legislative institution, but it is also a familiar outgrowth of crisis situations that demand popular risk and sacrifice. Over coming decades, there would be a series of unsuccessful starts and experiments, but the trajectory which resulted at independence in one of the most vigorous parliamentary experiences in the Gulf region may be plotted from this time.

While these events were playing out, the modern world was relentlessly pressing in on Kuwait. In the 1920s, camel caravans still made their way to Mecca[101] and traditional bedouin raids remained the major threat to Kuwait's security. Change, however, was in the air. Not only was Kuwait connected to the outside world by telegraph, but the grandson of Shaikh Mubarak, Shaikh Ahmad al-Jabir, visited London at the invitation of King George V in October-November 1919.[102] A small water distillation plant installed by the Anglo-Persian Oil Company went into operation the same year,[103] while at the American Mission hospital the first generator was installed in 1921, providing light and a few fans, and making possible the introduction of ice cream.[104] American-made automobiles were also transforming travel and shortening distances. As the mission was taking delivery of its first Model-T Ford in 1921, entrepreneurs in the Levant were pioneering automobile connections with Baghdad and the territories beyond. Employing a succession of American cars and buses, formal service from Damascus to Baghdad began on October 18, 1923 and continued until 1956, when the Iraqis imposed stiff customs requirements.[105] The new influences were not merely in physical objects, as a charming vignette supplied by Bill Brewer illustrates:

> Wanting to encourage Kuwaiti women to remove the veil, Mubarak had the ceiling (of his audience chamber) 'inlaid' with pictures of well-known Western actresses, many of them American. When I took Joe Alsop to call on Abdullah Salim in that room, Joe spent most of his time identifying the various beauties portrayed above us.[106]

4

Decade of Austerity and Promise

By the time of Shaikh Salem's sudden death in February 1921, the American Mission and community were well established within the city's society: "a part of and not just a curiosity within the social fabric of the community."[1] For the mission, 1921 would be a banner year; electric generators for the men's and women's hospitals were installed and the mission received its first motor car, a Model T Ford.[2] But for the new ruler, and all the residents of the city, trying times were still ahead.

The ruler's death came while his successor was out of Kuwait. Ahmad al-Jabir, a nephew of the ruler, was in Central Arabia for meetings with Ibn Saud (soon to be crowned king of Saudi Arabia) when news of Shaikh Salem's passing reached him. He made his way back to Kuwait, arriving by British warship, and was greeted enthusiastically by Kuwaitis on the understanding that he would govern with the participation of a twelve-member Shura (consultative) Council.[3] British concerns that there might be a succession struggle among the Al-Sabah did not materialize and Shaikh Ahmad assumed power without incident on March 24, 1921. His nearly three decades as ruler encompassed troubled times for Kuwait as a result of continuing external threats, stagnant economic conditions, and new intellectual and political currents circulating elsewhere in the Arab world seeped into the society as young people gained education and foreign media became more accessible. Kuwait changed greatly over the course of his rule and the process of modernization brought with it severe challenges and chronic instability.

The threat posed by the *Ikhwan* had not evaporated with Dawish's retreat from Jahra. Although they never again mounted a serious threat to the city, the *Ikhwan* continued to menace outlying Kuwaiti populations and property into the 1930s when King Abd al-Aziz al-Saud decided that this chosen instrument of his empire-building represented a threat to his own authority as well. In November 1927, for example, Dawish and his Mutair tribesmen attacked Busaiya in Iraq and looted at will. Following a raid against bedouin loyal to Kuwait at Umm Rimmam (north of Jahra) that month, the town of Kuwait went on constant alert. The garrison at Jahra was strengthened and the wall was repaired and manned nightly until the end of the year.[4] Problems relating to the bedouin tribes of the region were exacerbated by contemporary efforts to define and enforce new frontiers for Kuwait and two new neighboring states—Iraq and Saudi Arabia.

The British government, involved in each of the three countries, sought to simplify their problems in November 1929 by convening a conference at 'Uqair. Whatever their intentions, theirs was a Solomonic task that could not have satisfied all three and ended by mollifying none. Sir Percy Cox, the British high commissioner, convened a conference of Iraqi, Saudi, and Kuwaiti representatives who proved unable to reach an agreement over several days of discussions.[5] To break the stalemate, Sir Percy took a colored pencil on December 4 and imposed a settlement that deprived Kuwait of between one-half and two-thirds of the tribal territories that had traditionally constituted its hinterlands.[6] His action was not as arbitrary as it might appear. The lines he drew in what was essentially a British agreement with itself, gave to Iraq considerable territory west of the Euphrates that was claimed by Ibn Saud, and compensated Saud for his loss with Kuwaiti land.[7]

Harold Dickson, subsequently, himself the British political agent in Kuwait and an authority on the region and the bedouin, was scathing in his evaluation of the 'Uqair Conference's results:

> By this somewhat strange arrangement, which savoured of surrender pure and simple, to a strong state at the expense of a small and weak one, the obvious end being expediency and desire to mollify the powerful and troublesome Ibn Saud the southern boundary

of the recognized territory of Kuwait was pushed back a hundred and fifty miles, reducing the Kingdom to an area of six hundred square miles.[8]

Although Kuwait paid a very heavy price for the boundary settlement created with Sir Percy's pencil, the agreement failed to bring peace and security for the government and population of Kuwait, including the tiny American community. When word of the proceedings reached Shaikh Ahmad, Kuwait's ruler, he was astonished and angry. There is no hint in the records of the time that he had been alerted that Kuwait stood to lose so much of its traditional hegemony at the 'Uqair Conference. And, of course, he was not consulted or effectively represented there. He apparently managed, with time, to conceal his anger, but Harold Dickson conceded that his trust in Great Britain received a shock from this "betrayal," which he never really got over.[9] The continuing depredations of raiding tribes, including the Saudi *Ikhwan*, and the actions of neighboring countries, must have nourished his resentment; in later crises, implicit references to the 'Uqair formula may be seen in some of his comments at critical moments. But, he was bound by his protectorate agreement with His Majesty's Government, and, more to the point, Kuwait needed a "protector" against these credible threats.

In retrospect, despite British manipulations, it is certain that the commitments of Great Britain to Kuwait and the other shaikhdoms of the Gulf were critical to their survival in the face of Ibn Saud's insatiable expansion:

> *If the British had not guaranteed to defend Kuwait, Qatar and the other shaikhdoms there is little doubt that Bin Saud would have annexed them; as it was he resorted to a policy of harrassment and political pressure. He told the Shaikh of Qatar that he regarded only the towns of the Qatar peninsula as being subject to British protection; the desert, he said, was under his sovereignty.*"[10]

In this context, the destruction of Mohammera by the Shah is instructive.[11] Kuwait was fortunate to have had British political agents —Shakespear, More, Dickson—who were not only sympathetic to the shaikhdom, but effective within the limits of their relatively junior position in the British bureaucracy. They were, however, frequently pitted against colonial bureaucrats who were indifferent to Kuwait's interests at best, and contemptuous at worst. In an unpublished letter to Political Agent Dickson, H. St. J. B. Philby in Riyadh wrote, "Of course the whole trouble about Kuwait is that it is racially and geographically a part of this country (i.e., Saudi Arabia), though it is artificially separated from it by a political barrier which the British, in their folly, prefer to keep up. You might just as well make Hull and its district an independent principality under German protection—it would die, as all traffic would be diverted to Harwich (Jubail) or Dover (Ras Tanura)."[12] Similarly, the British political agent in Bahrain gave private vent to his imperial arrogance in a letter in April 1939: "... we seem reluctant to use the means we possess to deter a crew of feeble and ill-conditioned shaikhs from treating the wishes of His Majesty's Government with quite such persistent disrespect." He conceded, nonetheless, that "We certainly do not wish to administer their disgusting territories and people."[13]

The leaders of the Gulf shaikhdoms could hardly have been unaware of such sentiments and undercurrents within the British bureaucracy charged with their affairs.

The newly drawn desert frontiers on maps appeared definitive, but they could not, in themselves, impede the movement of bedouin tribes, either in search of water, grazing or trade opportunities, or in undertaking raids, smuggling, and looting. Between the successful defense of Jahra in October 1920 and the 'Uqair Conference two years later, four hundred members of the Mutair tribe attacked to within eight miles of the Jahra fort.[14] Over the remainder of the decade, these attacks kept Kuwait in a constant state of alert and apprehension. While these incursions were normally of greater consequence to Kuwaiti bedouin in the interior, they were occasionally of sufficient seriousness to raise anxiety among the townspeople.[15]

Neither did the demarcation of the border between Kuwaiti and Saudi territory, overwhelmingly in the latter's favor, moderate the hostility that Ibn Saud bore toward his smaller neighbor and onetime benefactor. The death of Shaikh Salem in 1921 logically eliminated the personal factor in the Kuwaiti-Saudi relationship.

His successor, Shaikh Ahmad, came to power on reasonably good terms with Ibn Saud. It was not long, however, before Ibn Saud found a new rationale for his hostile attitude.

Bedouin ignored the new political borders not only to raid and attack Kuwait, but also to avoid the controls and taxation that Ibn Saud was implementing in his territory. Some tribes from the Najd sought refuge in Kuwait and continued their traditional trade relations with Kuwaiti merchants. Ibn Saud, upset by the loss of revenue, first sought to send his own tax collectors into Kuwait, and when this was rebuffed, tried to impose on the Kuwaitis the task of collecting taxes on his behalf. The Kuwaitis refused and Ibn Saud imposed a trade embargo on Kuwait in 1923. It remained in effect until 1937.[16]

Against the backdrop of tribal threats, disorder, and commercial stagnation, times were difficult for Kuwait during the interwar period. Economic distress was further exacerbated in the 1920s when Japan began flooding the market with cultured pearls;[17] undercutting another of Kuwait's income-producing industries just before the worldwide Great Depression struck. In fact, the combination of adverse circumstances that Kuwait faced was devastating. The British political agent in Kuwait, writing to the political resident at Bushire in 1936, listed the sources of Kuwaiti income, in order of importance, as follows: "pearling, closely followed by the carrying trade in the Indian Ocean, the Red Sea and along the African Coast, some way behind boat-building and only fourthly ordinary trade."[18] With pearl markets depressed, and the entrepôt in recession and diminished by the Saudi boycott, Kuwait's historic seagoing trade was also undermined by the advent of the steamship which grabbed the lion's share of the carrying trade.[19]

The small American community in the Arabian Mission shared in many of the hardships of the period, but had the consolation from 1921 of enjoying the willing support of both the ruler and the people of the town.[20] In 1920, the mission welcomed its first American-educated nurse, Mary Van Pelt. She remained a primary fixture, known locally as "Khatem Miriam," until 1940, serving as superintendent of both the men's and women's hospitals.[21] Amid the grim economic conditions, there were occasional opportunities to celebrate as when, in 1924, the wife of Dr. Harrison, who had returned for a tour in Kuwait, gave birth to a daughter.[22] The Harrison child was almost certainly the first American born in Kuwait.

Dr. Calverley's school continued to attract eager Kuwaiti pupils through the 1920s, although it remained very small.[23] A contemporary British report puts the enrollment at twenty, including "one Jew, one Negro, and the rest Arabs and Persians." [24] Nevertheless, the school had an impact much larger than its size would suggest; it attracted some of Kuwait's most promising young men, including Shaikh Fahad Al-Salem (Kuwait's first minister of health and public works); Khalid al-Ghunaym (the first speaker of Kuwait's parliament); and several members of the large Behbehani clan.[25] In 1931, economic realities of the depression years caught up with mission's schools in Kuwait and Oman; they never reopened. Despite the unfortunate demise of this seminal school, there can be little question that Edwin Cavlerley and Mu'allim Isra'il, his assistant of many years, made crucial contributions to Kuwait's development.[26] Its operation coincided with a period of initial stirring of modernization in the shaikhdom. In 1928, Abdul Aziz Rasheed, who is considered the father of Kuwait's vibrant press, began publication of a monthly magazine, appropriately named *Al-Kuwait*. He has been described as "a man of great learning and piety with a love of science" who regarded the press as a component of education. The magazine was printed in Cairo and transported overland to Kuwait, where it was read aloud in *diwanniyas* for the benefit of the largely illiterate population.[27] Finally, according to Amb. Faisal al-Mutawa, a few Kuwaitis were sent to Lebanon in the 1920s to study the English language.[28]

The workload on the mission Hospital increased steadily through the two decades following the Battle of Jahra, although the hospital staff and facilities did not grow commensurately.[29] Dr. Mary Allison, the second woman physician on the mission staff, brought some relief when she arrived in October 1934 for a tour that would last until the beginning of World War II. Her introduction to the practice of medicine was abrupt. The initial case—a wife in a prominent family—proved a difficult challenge. The patient was suffering a pelvic abcess and the family was insistent that the surgery be performed in their home rather than at the hospital. Using chloroform and with Dr. Mylrea providing backup, Dr. Allison successfully completed the difficult procedure.[30] Aside from serious cases, the clinical routine was grueling; as many as one hundred women and children gathered on the shore each morning on the women's side alone. Dr. Allison began with innoculations before moving on to widespread roundworm and eye diseases, including tracoma and other less serious ailments. At the men's hospital, the number of patients seeking circumcisions testified to the success of efforts to promote less traumatic procedures for this widespread rite of passage.[31] The personnel worked through the day in primitive conditions[32] until everyone had been seen.

Vaccination against smallpox was a major preoccupation of the mission hospital because periodic epidemics were catastrophic. Their task was as much a matter of education as medical treatment. In 1932, for example, a smallpox epidemic struck Kuwait, killing approximately four thousand in a period of ten days. The ruler, at last, ordered that all residents of Kuwait be vaccinated. Many, frightened of the procedure and convinced that smallpox was an affliction from Allah (God), refused. Finally, after the boys attending Koranic schools were inoculated by force and avoided contagion, others presented themselves for vaccination.[33] Modern medicine was becoming accepted in the town and the American Mission hospital was at the forefront of this societal transformation.

In spite of economic depression, the walled town of Kuwait had grown significantly by the close of the 1920s. In 1927, a British document described it in the following terms: "... about three miles along the shore, having extended considerably in recent years towards the east. Its greatest depth, almost one mile, is near the centre of the town where the long suburb called Murqab has grown out from it towards the southeast."[34]

Contemporary sources make clear that the wall built in the summer of 1920 was maintained, and occasionally manned, during this time of tense relationships with non-Kuwaiti bedouin.[35] It is not absolutely clear whether or not some expansion had occurred outside this defensive perimeter, but it appears unlikely in view of the unsettled conditions in the hinterlands at this period.

With an estimated population of fifty thousand in the town, the community was increasingly diverse. In addition to Persian and Arab immigrants from Arabia and Mesopotamia, there was a Jewish community (mainly of Iraqi origin) of about one hundred, and a few Arab-Christian families.[36] Western residents, of whom the majority were Americans attached to the mission, were a tiny minority; in 1929 the British and Americans together numbered eleven.[37] By mid-decade, there were an estimated thirty-five "Europeans."[38] In appearance, however, the town looked much as it had for decades:

> *The colors were grey and tan and the sun bleached everything toward white. The glare was everywhere while the sun shone, and at night the dark was crisp, so clear the stars shone just beyond the reach of your hand. There were nine trees when we first came. One was just inside the Jahrah Gate and the other eight were on the American Mission compound on the far edge of the Qiblah Quarter. Until the Behbehani Compound was built in the 1950s, all that separated us (the American Mission) from the western end of the city wall was a long stretch of beach. Here some of the ships of Kuwait's great pearling fleet were beached during the season when the trade winds blew.*[39]

The problem of the *Ikhwan*, simmering since the failed assault on Kuwait in 1920, was nearing the boiling point by 1927. The *Ikhwan* mounted raids into Kuwait in 1924 and 1925 on a limited scale, and proceeded to add Iraq to their list of targets. Faisal al-Dawish was back on the warpath and led a more substantial incursion into Iraq at the end of 1927 that alarmed the Kuwaiti ruler. He asked for, and received, temporary British defensive measures in the form of surveillance aircraft and a detachment of armored cars.[40] In January 1928, Kuwaiti forces successfully confronted a separate *Ikhwan* raid in Al-Riqa'i, but the situation was roiled by the growing conflict between Ibn Saud and the uncontrollable *Ikhwan*.[41]

Ibn Saud had found it increasingly difficult since the 'Uqair Conference five years before to manage the *Ikhwan*.[42] By 1927, the Wahhabi tribesmen were openly rebellious against his authority; they had become an embarrassment and potential danger to his designs. For their part, the *Ikhwan* bridled at the restrictions Ibn Saud attempted to impose on their raiding and warfare after they had delivered the Hejaz for him in 1925. When Faisal al-Dawish captured Medina and overthrew Hashemite rule, his forces were forbidden to plunder the rich territory. The *Ikhwan* might have accepted this denial with some grumbling, but they were not ready to accept Ibn Saud's prohibition of further raiding to the north.[43] Among other consequences of their earlier depredation was the arousal of neighboring states and the British themselves. Ibn Saud unquestionably did not want to become caught in the backdraft they were creating. Groups comprised primarily of Mutair, Ajman, and Ataiba attacked bedouin in Kuwait and ranged further afield, raiding into Iraq and Transjordan. The British responded by creating an Iraqi Southern Desert Camel Corps under the leadership of a young former officer named John Bagot Glubb.[44] Working with aircraft of the Royal Air Forces, he also employed Ford trucks with mounted machine guns to patrol Kuwait's frontiers and whittle the *Ikhwan* down to size.[45] By the end of 1929, the *Ikhwan* were back in Kuwait, but this time they were fleeing Ibn Saud and the allied Harb tribe.

Predictably, this turn of events made tensions between Ibn Saud, the beneficiary of previous Wahhabi activities, and Shaikh Ahmad and Kuwait, the victims of their attacks, worse rather than better. The Saudis reportedly believed that the Kuwaiti ruler was aiding the fugitives in the hope of ending the embargo on trade and undoing the territorial arrangement imposed at the 'Uqair Conference. Available sources do not answer the question of what hopes Shaikh Ahmad may have entertained at this juncture. What is fairly well established is that the Kuwaitis and the British were concerned that Ibn Saud might use the circumstances to pursue his designs on Kuwait itself. In any event, the British authorities pushed for (sometimes harshly) and obtained the surrender of the fugitive tribes and deprived Ibn Saud of the pretext they may have provided him.

The injustice that he felt had been done to Kuwait at 'Uqair was manifestly still on Shaikh Ahmad's mind. In June of 1929, he informed the British resident in the Gulf that "though he liked Bin Saud personally, he hated his policy and would like to see him defeated...." and expressed the opinion that the Ajman, Awazim, and Mutair, who had formerly owed allegiance to Kuwait, would return to the fold given an opportunity. The resident's report continues:

> He (Shaikh Ahmad) claims that in addition to aid granted to Bin Saud by the late Shaikh Mubarak, he himself loaned sixty thousand dollars and sent fifteen hundred bags of rice to assist Bin Saud during the siege of Hail. The money has never been repaid and instead of showing gratitude for favours received Bin Saud first rendered Kuwait defenceless by obtaining, with the help apparently of Sir Percy Cox, transfer of allegiance of its tribes, then blockaded the town and ruined its trade for the sake of a difference about customs which could have been adjusted without difficulty. He now calls on the state which he has bereft of its strength and ruined financially to repel from its frontiers its own subjects whom he first seduced from their allegiance and then by treachery goaded to rebellion.[46]

Implicit in the ruler's passionate comments was a corrosive suspicion regarding the British commitment to protect his country. In January 1930, he returned to this theme with Col. Dickson, strongly excoriating what he perceived as coddling of Ibn Saud. In a rare New Year's Day communication to the political resident, he recounted the questions Dr. Mylrea had apparently raised when he called to convey his concerns about the state of Shaikh Ahmad's health.[47]

It seems evident that Col. Dickson was utilizing Dr. Mylrea's concern as a device for conveying his personal doubts, a stratagem familiar to every experienced government official. He continues:

> ... He (Shaikh Ahmad) is obsessed with the feeling common to many other Arabs today, that Bin Saud is the 'big noise' and 'everything' that counts, and that H.M.'s Government fears him and will give him all he asks for.
> The wholehearted support of H.M.'s Government as exemplified by the strong anti-rebel pressure, which has been maintained along the whole southern frontier of 'Iraq and Kuwait by the Royal Air Force, not to mention the sale and manning of aeroplanes, has definitely confirmed this belief ... and where it is obvious to all that our assistance means the definite failure of the rebellion and the practical destruction of the great Ajman and Mutair tribes, Kuwait's protectors since earliest times, and largely the Shaikh's

own kith-and-kin, one can see how deeply their present plight affects the Shaikh. ... this feeling is equally shared by the whole town also, when I say that there exists about 2,000 persons of Awazim, 2,000 of Mutair, and quite 3,000 of Ajman origin in the city at the present day.[48]

That same month the British brought the era of sustained tribal disorder to an end by forcing the surrender of the rebellious tribes—employing starvation as their primary instrument.[49] In the process, they paid a political price in terms of shaken Kuwaiti confidence in their fairness and reliability. The bedouin would never again be in a position to menace the emerging states of the region. The American community was largely unscathed by the instability around them, although there was one death and a second near-miss among American citizens. Charles R. Crane, an American industrialist and close friend of President Woodrow Wilson, was best known as a co-leader of the King-Crane Commission of 1919. Crane arrived in Basra in 1929 to pursue a philanthropic interest in religious causes. He decided to visit Kuwait in the company of the Rev. Henry Bilkert, the field secretary for the Arabian Mission. On January 21, their two-car caravan was ambushed by a small *Ikhwan* party and Bilkert was mortally wounded.[50] He died enroute back to Basra. His death, whether intentional or not, increased apprehension among missionaries and wider expatriate communities far beyond Kuwait.

In the end, the ruler of Kuwait swallowed his anger and revulsion at abandoning the rebellious tribes to their fate, and kept his commitments to Great Britain:

For remaining neutral through the period of the rebellion and keeping his word to Britain Shaikh Ahmad, in 1930, received the KCIE. Though the British government also promised to use its best efforts to bring about the end of Ibn Saud's blockade of Kuwait, this was not achieved for another seven years. It is interesting to recall that after the Uqair settlement, Shaikh Ahmad asked Sir Percy, 'If I become strong like my grandfather will the British government object if I denounce the unjust frontier line and recover my lost territories?' Sir Percy had laughingly given him his blessing. At the time of the Ikhwan rebellion he might have had a chance to do just that. Perhaps it was his Arab sense of honour that kept him loyal to his pledge to Britain.[51]

Although he was fortunate in having a true and honorable friend in Col. Dickson, who served as political agent from 1929 to 1936, and again, for part of 1941, the good will of British officials in the region was not universal. When Kuwaiti interests conflicted with positions of larger neighbors, as in the case of the Saudi embargo, or the dispute regarding taxation of Al-Sabah properties in Iraq, British diplomacy most often proved ineffectual. In connection with the latter issue, several of His Majesty's representatives in the Gulf were explicit to Col. Dickson in their view—"... Kuwait was a small and expendable state which could be sacrificed without too much concern if the power struggles of the period demanded it."[52]

The surrender of the rebellious *Ikhwan* tribes in January 1930 marked the twilight of the volatile bedouin activity that characterized the 1920s.[53] The town of Kuwait would not face the reality of foreign attack again for the next sixty years. That did not mean, however, that the people of Kuwait would experience a new decade of calm and stability. The Saudi embargo continued for seven more years and the Great Depression soon added its weight to the stagnation of the local economy. It will become clear, that with improved communications and other modern developments, the society was being drawn toward the currents and ideas swirling within the larger Arab world. In the 1930s, Imperial Airways (forerunner of BOAC and later British Airways) made a refueling stop in Kuwait on the way to India.[54] As horizons expanded, so did external political influences with significant implications for Kuwaiti society.

Economic conditions compelled the American Mission to make unwanted choices, such as the decision to close the Calverley school. Nevertheless, the small community was able to undertake important improvements to its physical facilities. The original hospital building was completely remodelled in early 1930 and a dedicated operating room was added. The following year, the first chapel was completed by Gerrit DeJong. The chapel, which is still in use,[55] is an innovative structure that combined concrete, steel beams, brickwork, a local mud roof, and heavy stucco. At the end of the decade, in 1939, the original women's hospital was razed and a more modern facility, the Olcott Memorial Hospital for Women, rose in its place. This imposing two-story building, which also survives today, was designed by Dirk Dykstra, constructed by Gerrit Pennings, and incorporates peaked, oriental-style arches suggested by Fred Barny.[56]

With unexpected frequency and despite what must have been a staggering medical and administrative workload, Dr. Mylrea pops up in varying roles and guises in contemporary accounts of the period. He is featured, for example, in a 1937 case of a British-Indian subject accused by Kuwaitis of serving cat meat in his eating establishment. This mundane case is a matter of record because it involved the British Political Agent De Gaury's jurisdiction over non-Kuwaitis. The agent decided that the facts presented were "murky" and dismissed the charges. With evident exasperation, the political resident adds:

> *The American Mission, for some obscure reason, took up the case with considerable élan, Dr. Mylrea playing the part of the local Sherlock Holmes, or rather Dr. Thorndyke, and – analyzing a hair found by the Town Lieutenant on a table in Muttalib's restaurant—certified it to be the same as that of a dead cat in a dustbin in the neighbourhood. De Gaury correctly, to the chagrin of the Mission, decided that this evidence could hold no weight.*[57]

While the desire of the British establishment to dismiss an affair that pitted one of their subjects against Kuwait accusers is understandable, in doing so they appear prepared to ignore the public health implications of consuming questionable foodstuffs, as well as indifferent to the emerging field of forensic science.

As impressive as the buildings were, they were eclipsed by the steady, less dramatic service extended by the American personnel. The mission staff, headed by the redoubtable Dr. Mylrea, not only provided health care over this formative era, but also accustomed their patients to modern medical practices and treatment. Looking back from the vantage point of the late 1940s, Zahra Freeth recorded her reflections:

> *Seeing the crowds of patients who come daily for attention to the state hospitals in Kuwait, it is easy to forget that it has taken many years of exhortation and demonstration to induce these people to submit willingly to orthodox medical treatment.*

The Kuwaitis had largely overcome an ingrained anxiety over unfamiliar Western medicine. Continuing, Freeth credited "the work of a small group of pioneer medical men (sic)" for the enthusiastic acceptance of the expanding Kuwaiti health care facilities in the mid-1940s.[58]

While the motif of the decade of the 1920s was the relationship with Ibn Saud and the resulting warfare and disorder generated by the *Ikhwan* movement, the following decade was marked by the priority of domestic developments.[59] In a sense, Kuwaiti society was losing its innocence under the impact of modernization. The First World War and its political and geographic consequences for the Middle East widened immensely the horizons of Kuwaitis who had not previously been impacted by events and developments beyond their immediate environs: The advent of cable communications and a post office;[60] the presence of British and American communities, however small, in the town; increasing numbers of Arab and European visitors lured by improved transportation links; and the greater availability of newspapers and other printed materials from abroad—all served to bring many Kuwaitis into sustained contact with the political ideologies, intellectual currents and social movements percolating in the wider world during the interwar era. This genie, which interacted with indigenous strains and aspirations, could never be put back in the bottle. Although Kuwaitis would ultimately become more sophisticated and capable of evaluating external ideas, they were henceforth increasingly drawn into the wider world.

As previously noted, Shaikh Ahmad Al-Jabir, had come to power in 1921 with the understanding that he would rule with the advice of a council to represent the views and interests of the merchants and notables.[61] Undoubtedly emboldened by the role and sacrifices of the citizenry in the defense of the town against the *Ikhwan*, the proponents pressed their case with the new ruler, and he agreed. Although a twelve-member council was formed, it soon fell into disuse. The decision of some of the proponents to attempt to play elements of the ruling family off against one another killed whatever chance the experiment may have enjoyed, according to some authorities.[62] Ibn Saud's enforcement of the embargo on trade with Kuwait, as well as the chronic *Ikhwan* threat to the state, probably made it easier for the ruler to relegate the issue to secondary importance.

The idea of shared power, however, did not go away. Developments in the shape of the Kuwaiti body politic, as well as historic experiences, assured that demands for greater participation in governing would persist. Uniquely in the Gulf region, Kuwait had begun to develop a middle class even before the advent of oil income.[63] Great disparities between wealth and poverty persisted but within the context of the social compact that was struck at the beginning of the shaikhdom's recorded history. Essentially, the al-Sabah assumed responsibility for governance so that the merchant class could pursue their economic activities. Until oil income swelled the coffers and called into question this fundamental bargain, merchants "of all classes" were wealthier than the rulers and were expected to pay taxes on their commerce and, periodically, to lend money to the Shaikh. In return, the more important merchant families expected to be consulted on important political matters.[64]

In the 1930s, the parliamentary issue arose with renewed vigor, often stimulated by political turmoil affecting the entire Arab world. In this new manifestation, "ideas of progress and reform coalesced in a constitutional movement in which some of the early pupils of the Mubarakiyya School, mature men by that time, played a significant part."[65] Undoubtedly fed by parliamentary forms in other Arab states, including the new Iraqi kingdom, the movement vigorously demanded a consultative council to advise the ruler on issues of public policy. In the final analysis, the effort was corrupted and undone, fairly or not, by the association of the movement with self-serving Iraqi activities aimed at undermining the position of the ruler and the independence of Kuwait.[66]

When it became feasible to identify the advocates of greater popular participation in governance with Iraqi manipulation, the revived movement was doomed. Nevertheless, and despite the fissures which were exposed by the confrontation, unanticipated dynamics were set in motion that would have important implications for the durability of a Kuwaiti identity: "... the political action of the 1930s reinforced a sense of community among the merchants... Where opponents once migrated to other Gulf ports, the interwar merchants chose to stay and confront the ruler. This choice helped entrench new ideas of state and loyalty to it."[67]

As ferment continued near the surface of public life in the 1930s, propaganda originating in neighboring Iraq engaged the attention and concern of the British authorities by the middle of the decade.[68] An internal memorandum of September, 1935 assessed the purposes of the Iraqi campaign in the following terms:

> (a) ... undermining the authority of the Shaikh of Kuwait with his people
> (b) Bringing into disrepute the good intentions and policy of His Majesty's Government towards the Arab states of the Gulf.
> (c) Arousing the young people of Kuwait to a sense of their supposed danger from the Machiavellian policy of His Majesty's Government and teaching that their eventual salvation lies in union with Iraq.
> (d) Presenting a glowing picture to young Kuwaiti patriots of a future union of all Arab States into the great and indivisible Arab Nation under the aegis of Iraq—a grand conception for immature minds.[69]

For many Iraqis then, and since, Kuwait, with its unrivalled port and later its oil wealth, was viewed as an entity artificially severed from their new state. This thread, which brushed aside the fact of Kuwait's emergence as a distinct and separate international entity *before* the creation of modern Iraq after World War I, was no less compelling to the monarchists of the 1930s than to later "republicans," like Abdul Kareem Qassem and Saddam Hussein. One difference, however, was the fact that some young Kuwaitis of the interwar period were not immune to the appeal. Inspired by their first real encounter with the chimera of Arab unity, impatient with stagnant economic conditions, the slow pace of change in their own state, and motivated by their personal ambitions, there was at least some fertile ground for Iraqi propaganda.[70] A segment of active Kuwaiti youth had formed a "Nationalist Youth Bloc" clandestinely and forged links with Arab nationalist movements in Iraq, Syria, and Palestine.[71] They appealed to King Ghazi of Iraq for support and to embarrass the British and advance his claim to Kuwait with a barrage of propaganda directed against Shaikh Ahmad and the rule of the Al-Sabah family. Baghdad understood in the 1930s, as Saddam Hussein did sixty years later, that their chances of achieving their goal of absorbing Kuwait would be enhanced by the removal of the Al-Sabah who had been inextricably associated with its separate status and identity over its recorded history. One theme of the propaganda campaign, therefore, sought to associate the economic distress affecting the Kuwaiti population with the rule of the Al-Sabah.[72]

In fact, the Iraqi government's propaganda offensive against Kuwait began as early as 1933 with the encouragement of Germany:

Newspapers, including Al Istiqlal, Al Watan and Al Tahreer published a hundred articles, mostly paid for by Germany, in which they attacked Kuwait, its external policy, the state of its education and health insurance, and especially the policy of Sheikh Ahmed himself. The authors maintained that Kuwait was always part of the Basrah Vilayet and demanded its integration with Iraq.

As part of the campaign, Iraqi youth were encouraged to move to Kuwait in the hope of reshaping the society.[73] To reinforce the propaganda campaign, the German ambassador to Iraq, Fritz Grobba, gave the Iraqi king a radio station. During February 1939, the Iraqi regime invited two former members of the Kuwaiti council to Baghdad where they sought to enlist them in a scheme for a "Greater Iraq" incorporating both Kuwait and Bahrain. The following month, British intelligence reportedly uncovered an Iraqi plot, involving an invasion by Iraqi troops and armored cars, that was allegedly aborted only because King Ghazi died on April 4 1939.[74]

By 1938, the ruler, Shaikh Ahmad, came under sustained pressure from internal dissent, as well as seditious Iraqi attacks through newspapers, radio broadcasts, pamphlets, and agents of influence.[75] Although he first denied the seriousness of the call for change within the country, Shaikh Ahmad agreed, under urging by the British and leading citizens, to create another council. Elections were held on June 29 for a council of fourteen members to be chaired by Shaikh Abdulla al-Salem al-Sabah. Over succeeding months, the council debated economic and administrative reforms and drafted a constitution that reduced the ruler "to a mere figurehead," losing control of even the state arsenal.[76]

The British political agent of the day and others appear to have seriously misjudged the unfolding political situation, even though an anonymous "note" dated October 1, to the British political resident gave a detailed account of the turn of the tide.[77] The Shi'a population, a few of whom were among the major merchants, could be counted on to support the ruler. It should probably have alerted the political agent that, in 1938, 4,647 Kuwaiti Shi'a sought applications for British nationality. When the wholly Sunni Assembly refused to moderate their position, the Shi'a went into the streets to demand the abolition of the Assembly.[78] By mid-December he reported that the town was in a disturbed condition "with few armed supporters of the Sheikh war dancing at his Palace. At the other end Council is ready for any eventualities."[79] Four days later, on December 21, Shaikh Ahmad boldly dissolved the council and announced that new elections for a successor with much reduced powers would be held. A further iteration of the council was duly elected, but when the ruler submitted a new constitution that restored his dominant powers, the membership rejected it. On March 7, the British political agent memorialized his meeting with Shaikh Ahmad earlier in the day: "He told me that he would dissolve Council this evening, owing to pro-Iraqi activities of some of its members who have been suborned, and will ask notables to elect an Advisory Council."[80]

With Iraq continuing to stir the pot, the struggle moved into the streets of Kuwait, and one of the most enigmatic episodes in Kuwait's long history.[81]

On March 9, 1938, Ahmad bin Munais (identified by one source as Muhhamad al-Munayyis), a Kuwaiti who had resided in Basra for an extended period, met with a group of Kuwaiti residents to impart a seditious message. The British political agent identified the audience as some former members of the dissolved council, but the meeting appears to have drawn a crowd. There is no ambiguity regarding the speaker's message—the overthrow of al-Sabah rule.

He may have been distributing leaflets as well. According to the British report on the incident, he urged his audience to continue resisting the authorities "until the Iraqi army arrived."

When the Kuwaiti police sought to arrest Munais the following morning, March 10, his followers and supporters intervened and a scuffle broke out. The British account clearly blames the demonstrators for firing the first shot at the police. In the ensuing clash, Yusuf Marzook was wounded in the foot and another rioter, Muhammad Al Qitami, was killed. The ruler himself, when he arrived on the scene, was slightly hurt attempting to restrain his supporters.[82] A court was quickly convened and Munais was found guilty of treason and shot publicly in the main square. In his commentary on the trial, the British political agent concluded: "In the local circumstances (rendered dangerous by and directly attributable to persistent Iraqi propaganda) and as far as I can tell, the judges were justified in their sentence."[83]

Yusuf Marzook was treated for his wounds at the American Mission hospital until he had recovered sufficiently to be imprisoned with other Kuwaiti demonstrators.[84] The men jailed for the 1939 events were released unconditionally on April 25, 1944, and over time returned to full participation in Kuwaiti affairs. Their colleagues who had fled to Iraq were permitted to return home with three specific exceptions.[85]

The unfortunate events of 1938, sometimes called the "Merchants' Revolt," merit discussion in this narrative not because they were typical of Kuwait's history. In fact, the fracas was unique and unprecedented in the two hundred years of political experience.[86] More fundamentally, however, the confrontation must be seen as illustrative of at least two threads that are woven into Kuwait's experience throughout the last century. The first is the persistent pressure to expand the participation of Kuwaitis in governing decisions, a struggle in which the state was far in advance of other shaikhdoms in the region. The effort, which was ultimately successful, generated many scrapes and bruises—but normally did not draw blood. Outside commentators who write of the "absolute" power of the ruler, display a woefully inadequate understanding of the modalities of consultation and consensus-building in entities of bedouin heritage. The ruler might attempt to impose unpopular decisions in the short term, but as even Mubarak the Great recognized on the taxation issue, they cannot withstand widespread opposition over time. Kuwait, in 1939, did not possess the instruments of repression; secret police, intelligence services, a large, well-organized, and dependable armed force, or even a jail.

The second thread is Iraq's repeated intervention in Kuwait's domestic affairs in an effort to manipulate them for Iraq's own interests. At least some of the Kuwaiti opposition swallowed the tainted bait, perhaps out of idealism and naiveté. It is interesting, but futile, to speculate about whether the proponents of participatory government might have won ground sooner if they had eschewed links with a foreign state and not been typecast as agents of Iraqi intervention. It was this connection that alarmed the British and other elements within Kuwait, and allowed the ruler to quash the movement with relative ease. As is frequently the case, overreaching is the enemy of achievement.

Finally, the trauma of the internecine confrontation was one of a series of painful events the residents were compelled to confront together, from the Battle of Jahra in 1920 through the Iraqi occupation of 1990–91. Each affected both Kuwaitis and expatriates and left long-lasting psychological wounds. Reflecting on the 1939 episode, Dr. Lewis Scudder III offers the following comments:

> *Kuwait was a small community, and the high cost of the suppression left scars in Kuwaiti society that are still detectable. While the missionaries were not involved, many of their friends were. The missionaries were grieved by the division of Kuwaiti society. Kuwait was emerging out of an innocent age, and the first signs of a more complex future were becoming evident.*[87]

In spite of preoccupation with chronic economic depression and the challenges of its neighbors, work and daily life continued for Kuwaiti and expatriate alike as the town made its first accommodations to outside influences and modernity. In 1924, Shaikh Ahmad criminalized by decree the import or export of slaves for sale, effectively ending traffic in domestic slaves.[88] The ruler, in fact, was reasonably open-minded regarding many new ideas and technologies. He redecorated a salon and dining room in the palace in European style, with the advice and help of the Calverleys and Col. Dickson. He embraced the automobile, even adapting them to combat *Ikhwan* raiders, as illustrated earlier.[89] And, he came to terms with the idea of negotiating with international companies who suspected that oil was to be found under the sands of his country.

During the late 1930s, small steps were taken to provide the community with amenities—education was a priority. In 1936, a number of teachers recruited from Palestine arrived to staff several newly-established schools. Funding for these initiatives was obtained from a special tax on Kuwaiti merchants. Within a year, the first schooling for 140 girls was offered; "some six hundred boys were in class."[90] Additional attention was also directed toward health care, where the American Mission hospital was by far the most important community asset. In 1939, a rudimentary health ministry was established and a free clinic was opened.[91] Although a new government hospital was envisioned, plans for it had to be abandoned for lack of funds and materials. Nevertheless, these minor improvements were welcomed by the personnel of the strained mission facilities.

As the difficult decade drew to a close, war clouds that would affect them and most of the world eventually, were gathering far away in Europe. To the south of the town, in a region called Burgan, new groups of British and American drillers were at work in primitive and unforgiving conditions. They had not yet significantly influenced Kuwaiti society, but they had produced the first proof that Kuwait contained reserves of petroleum that would transform the country.[92] Better times and new challenges lay ahead for both Kuwaitis and expatriates, but first they had to endure a further ordeal.

5

World War II Comes to Kuwait

In 1939, the last year before the expanding conflict in Europe began to affect life in Kuwait, an Australian mariner from the age of sail slipped into the harbor aboard the Kuwaiti *boom*, "The Triumph of Righteousness." The ship and his Kuwaiti crewmates returned after a voyage of almost one year. From the deck of the vessel, as the twilight faded, the town was completely invisible in the darkness.

Alan Villiers later wrote a book that is a treasury of information about the ocean trade in which the Kuwaitis had long excelled, as well as his positive impressions of contemporary Kuwait. He was clearly charmed by the natives he encountered, whether the skilled seamen among whom he lived on board or the merchants and shaikhs with whom he mingled freely during a stay of several months in Kuwait. One out of a lengthy line of inquisitive adventurers, Villiers recorded his view of the town as the rising sun revealed it the next morning:

> The walled city of Kuwait does not look its best seen from the anchorage, but it has one of the most interesting waterfronts in the world—more than two miles of it. In 1939 the place was one great shipyard of Arab dhows. All along the waterfront running east and west by the shore of the shallow bay, from the British Residency in the east to the American hospital in the west, almost from wall to wall of the town, the big ships and the little ships jostle one another.[1]

When the Second World War began, more than one hundred oceangoing sailing ships still flew the Kuwaiti flag, the bulk of them engaged in trade with India.² However, the Kuwaiti fleet was past its zenith and steamships were already gnawing at the town's maritime commerce. Many of the ships seen by Villiers, particularly the more numerous pearlers, had not been to sea for some years.³ Kuwait launched about 150 pearling ships annually in the early years of the war, and pearling enjoyed a brief revival as the Great Depression eased. Forty years earlier, at least four times that number would have sailed for the season. Although pearls were both plentiful and of high quality in 1939, the war in Europe destroyed the market for such luxury items. The lifespan of this most arduous of Kuwaiti trades was coming to an end. Today, it survives primarily as a commemoration by the youth of an important part of their nation's heritage.⁴

The voyage in which Villiers participated was representative of the most difficult and demanding route the Kuwaiti seamen undertook. Outside observers who have come to regard Kuwaiti society as one of the world's wealthiest and most self-indulgent are generally ignorant of the extreme hardships associated with ocean and desert trades for the centuries before oil. Villiers provided a brief summary of the voyage:

> *Ten thousand miles and nine months of hard life and hard sailing, from mid-August of one year to mid-June of the next —to Basra first, after the summer's lay-up at Kuwait, to load a cargo of dates for Mukalla for orders; then down the Persian Gulf and the Gulf of Oman, standing out into the Arabian Sea before the last of the southwest monsoon had gone, with a call at Muscat for water on the way.*

From Oman, the boom sailed the long, inhospitable southern coast of the Arabian Peninsula through dangerous waters and the threat of pirates to reach the port of Mukalla in the Hadhramaut. There, they took on cargo for Berbera, where the crew discharged the dates for the markets of Somaliland and Ethiopia. Retracing part of their route, the vessel called at Aden and then ran eastward back to Mukalla to load cargo and passengers for Africa. Travelling westward, they made landfall at Ras Haifun in modern Somalia. Proceeding down the east coast of Africa the boom called at

Mogadishu, Lamu and, ultimately, Mobassa, where their passengers disembarked. The next stop was Zanzibar, the "isle of delight," before ending off the Rufiji, a "terrible swamp where all hands grew thin and half of them caught fever while they worked under conditions almost intolerable." Laden with wood for construction and shipbuilding in Kuwait, the seamen retraced their outward route, returning to Muscat, Bahrain, and their home port.[5]

The deep-sea carrying trade was the only relatively vital pillar of the town's traditional prosperity, and merchants, stymied in other outlets, moved into it. While many smaller dhows employed in pearling were moldering on the beach, two or three cargo vessels a month were being built by Kuwait's renowned shipwrights. When effects of the war—shortages, rationing, and other restrictions—struck, the sailing fleet received a welcome stimulus; opportunities for long-distance vessels grew dramatically as competing steamers were requisitioned to support the war effort.[6] The voyages, especially those to and from India, also provided at least some participants opportunities for surreptitious trade in scarce or rationed goods and gold.[7] Violet Dickson recalled that war-related shortages nearly wrecked even the vital shipbuilding industry:

> ... when World War II came, the men who were making the big wooden boats and the pearling boats were desparately short of nails. They'd been getting them from India and now everything from India was shut off. So the builders went to the Shaikh and said, "If the government doesn't want those old metal barges we could break them up and make nails out of them." The Shaikh said, "Nobody wants them. You can do what you like with them." So after that, day and night, whenever there was a low tide there were about 20 men there hammering and banging and cracking away until they broke those barges all up and made nails for making boats during the war....[8]

Kuwait and its immediate neighbors were not directly impacted by the combat operations of the global conflict.[9] Nonetheless, the residents of the town of Kuwait were soon feeling the secondary effects of the war. By the end of 1940, Japanese forces in South East Asia had seized control of the rice-producing regions that supplied

Arabia with much of its imports of this staple. Closer to home, Japanese submarines had begun operations in the Indian Ocean, where they threatened shipping transporting foodstuffs and other essentials to Gulf ports.[10] Taken with the predictable diversion of productive capacity to the war effort, these developments half a world away soon produced shortages and even starvation in the hinterland.

The members of the American community in the mission recalled the grim life all inhabitants endured during the war years. Even the weather seemed to conspire to heighten their misery:

> *The cost of staple goods skyrocketed. Trade was restricted and controlled by the British for the war effort. As Japan threatened to overrun India, even missionaries in the Gulf were enlisted into militias and given basic weapons training. There were a series of extraordinarily hot summers. People seeking relief from the heat lay down on wet beach sand and fell asleep and died in the rising tides. Malnutrition was endemic and heat prostration was common. The winters were, by contrast, bitterly cold, and people died of carbon monoxide poisoning, huddled over charcoal brassieres (sic), their windows closed. The days held abject misery, and Arabian Mission personnel—both medical and evangelistic—found themselves worked to the bone.*[11]

Although contemporary records provide scant evidence, there were probably elements in the Kuwaiti population, especially those recently involved in the power struggle over participation in governance, who questioned the rationale for their state's involvement on the side of Great Britain.[12] They could not have known that effects of the war were being felt worldwide, among those allied with the belligerents and neutrals alike. But there was no escape from their own hardships. Shortages of food and clothing imports caused serious inflation in the price of necessities; the bedouin were especially affected as the costs of dates and fodder for their flocks soared. Thousands had to contend with malnutrition and hunger. Only merchants engaged in the lucrative smuggling trade were able to weather the period profitably. As a result, "income inequalities" in Kuwait sharpened.[13] The final Kuwaiti hope for relief from two decades of economic depression—recently discovered oil deposits—was dashed when the British company decided to plug the proven wellheads for the duration of the conflict.

Amid the gloom of the war period, occasional episodes of humor and irony broke the mood momentarily. The American Mission in Oman suffered that most dreaded of wartime catastrophes—the failure of the tires on its crucial Land Rover. In response to Muscat's call for assistance, Dr. Lewis Scudder, who had just replaced Dr. Mylrea as director of the mission in Kuwait, was able to locate replacement tires in the thriving black market. He sent them to Oman along with the "hefty bill." His counterpart in Muscat, Dr. Thoms, wrote to explain that there was no way his cash-strapped "station" could pay the asking price. A short time later Dr. Scudder replied that there was no problem. The merchant from whom he had purchased the tires had undergone an expensive hernia operation and the account was settled.[14]

Given the distress being experienced by the inhabitants of Kuwait and other states in the Middle East, the British and American governments set up programs to provide subsidies and allocations of foodstuffs on a country-by-country basis. Kuwait and the other Gulf states, as well as the Eastern Province of Saudi Arabia, were supplied out of the Ministry of Food in Delhi, whereas Jeddah, the Levant, Iraq, and Iran received supplies through the Middle East Supply Center in Cairo. Each recipient received specified quantities of cloth, grain, rice, tea, sugar and other commodities, subsidized by the two allies and sold or given to local governments.[15] While the effectiveness of this assistance depended upon the availability of scarce shipping and control of corruption, it played an essential part in mitigating hardships in many localities. Several years after the end of wartime stringencies, the wife of the British advisor to one Gulf Shaikh discovered that a group of little girls born to poor families during the war had been named "Bitaka," Arabic for "ration card."[16]

The fact that Kuwait was outside active combat zones did not mean that it was unaffected by the total war effort. Thousands of combat forces and support troops, as well as contractors, poured into the Gulf to restore order in nearby Iraq and to support a massive supply program for the Soviet Union, now an ally in the war against the Axis. Shipping to support these activities expanded exponentially, and basic decisions affecting Kuwait and the other Gulf states were now made by the British commander-in-chief, Middle East, and other allied agencies and institutions.[17]

An early problem which the war planners encountered was the inadequacy of ports and infrastructure at the head of the Gulf to handle the massive volume of equipment and supplies arriving by ship. Vessels that could not be immediately unloaded began to build up in the waterway as they awaited their turn at the piers and quays. Even as projects were in train to upgrade port and transportation facilities in Iran, military authorities began to cast about for places where stranded ships could wait and give shore leave to their crews. In January 1943, the senior British naval officer in the Persian Gulf suggested using Kuwait Bay as a holding basin for the accumulating fleet of cargo ships: "In view of the number of ships mostly American laying at bar it is proposed to make use of Kuwait as a temporary detention harbour in order to disperse shipping and enable crews to go ashore."[18] The idea ultimately was abandoned because of the inadvisability of unleashing groups of cooped-up seamen on the small town without facilities to receive and accommodate them. The political agent in Kuwait had quite correctly argued that shore parties be strictly limited and under regulations that he would devise.[19] It took only a month for the military authorities to decide not to send the ships into Kuwait harbor, "in view of the prohibition of shoreleave."[20]

Kuwait's contribution to the war, when it came, was much more suited to its heritage and talents. The small state's preeminence in the local oceangoing dhow trade was due not only to the skill and daring of its sailors; it was also home to "the biggest shipbuilding port of the Gulf."[21] Its shipwrights, of Arab and Persian origin, were widely regarded as the masters of their craft, often producing vessels for owners in neighboring emirates. The story is told of a vessel along classic *boom* lines built by the legendary Haji Ahmad under a commission from the ruler of Qatar. When an established British naval architect saw it, he was so struck that he requested to see the plans. One can only imagine his reaction when he was informed that plans were never used. "The builders merely get down the keel and proceed with the job with no more ado."[22] Now the

Americans proposed to employ the skills of Kuwait's ship builders to help meet the need for hundreds of barges to move supplies in the ports and rivers of Iran.

The U.S. Persian Gulf Command was established in December 1942 for the sole purpose of delivering "American supplies to the Russians as rapidly as possible in the largest possible quantities."[23] In its two years of operation, the PGC delivered through the Gulf and across Iran four and one half million long tons of supplies and 143,000 vehicles of every description. The story of this herculean operation was published in the *New Yorker* magazine, and adapted as a book at the end of the war. Aside from its intrinsic interest, these accounts appear to be the first mass exposure of the American public to Kuwait and its contribution. The somewhat quaint description of the town in Sayre's book bears repeating:

> *South of Iraq, on the western shore of the Gulf, is a tiny sultanate called Kuwait, whose marine Arabs have been famous since Marco Polo's time for building dhows, high-decked sailing vessels that look like the caravels of Columbus. These Arabian Yankees of Kuwait—magnificent, big, clean men—had built from furnished parts about five dozen Higgins barges for the Command, and they were used for unloading the Liberties offshore. This helped some but not nearly enough. Cargo was being moved far too slowly off what few docks there were.*[24]

The official United States Army history of "Al Kuwait Station," as the facility was called, is less fanciful but more complete.[25] In November 1941, the U.S. and British high command drew up a list of priorities, assigning to the Americans the task of assembling knocked-down barges for delivery to the Inland Water Transport unit of the British Tenth Army. Early in the following year, the British called for large numbers of additional barges for use on the rivers in Iran. The Iranian District engineer was tasked to meet this requirement and appropriated an initial $100,000 for local reassembly. By April 1942, the first sixty-two barges had been designed and built in the United States and were ready for shipment to the Gulf. The Army contractor engaged to accomplish the reassembly reported that it would be in place by June 1.

The normally staid Army historian was unable to resist an element of romanticism when he wrote:

> *The site chosen for the barge assembly operation was the picturesque Arab town of Kuwait in the Sheikhdom of Kuwait, a British protectorate sandwiched between Iraq and Saudi Arabia at the northwest corner of the Persian Gulf. Here an ancient hereditary guild of shipwrights, whose oral tradition claims that they once sent a party to the Mediterranean to instruct the Phoenicians, carried on a thriving native boat-building industry. An adequate force of native craftsmen and carpenters was available to work under the supervision of a small number of American civilians responsible to an area engineer delegated by the Iranian District engineer.*

A planning meeting in Kuwait, convened on May 21 by the colonel in charge, brought together representatives of the American civilian contractor, the British Political Agency, the Kuwait Oil Company, and Haji Ahmed bin Salmon, 'the adaptable and cooperative chief of the native boat-builders's guild.' Since the ruler reportedly objected to locating the assembly plant within city walls, a site on a flat beach near the oil company pier at Shuwaikh was selected.[26] Paul Edward Case, author of a National Geographic article about Kuwait in 1952, was in the United States Navy at the time and worked on the reassembly project:

> *We were far out of town and almost the only persons beyond the walls. Some bedouins, in tents clustered at the base of the city walls, were the only other outsiders... Today (1952) our former house and cookhouse are homes for English oilmen. The barren beach has sprouted the town of Shuwaikh....*[27]

The local planners were dealing with inadequate and inconsistent information from the War Department regarding the number, unit weights and sizes, and delivery schedules, and decided that the Kuwaiti shipwrights would assemble a sample barge to produce cost and time records for calculating compensation for large-scale production.

A U.S. Army Lieutenant of Engineers arrived in Kuwait with twenty-two American civilian contractors on June 22. Their task was to establish sufficient facilities to begin the assembly process. With the cooperation of Kuwaiti laborers, they had constructed a barebones plant at Shuwaikh:

> *Camp facilities were prepared by renovating, repairing, and adapting two stone buildings formerly used as a community isolation hospital.*[28] *These provided space for dormitories, offices, recreation, kitchen, and mess hall. Frame wash and latrine buildings were erected along with two Quonset huts for additional sleeping quarters and a first-aid station. A small stone house was put up for the area engineer and the camp manager. Other construction provided 2,000 square feet of floor area in two warehouses, and about 16,000 square feet of other space, of which nearly 11,000 were for two planking sheds, and the rest divided among repair shop, power plant, paint shop, carpenter shop, fuel storage, huts for interpreters and guards, and sun and cutting shelters.*[29]

The first barge, begun on July 7, was rolled out of the sheds two weeks later.

Mass production was initiated on July 22, employing dual assembly lines. One barge was laid down each week and by October more than twenty were in production at the same time. The techniques involved, including working with plans and specifications, were new to the Kuwaiti shipwrights, but, in the words of the Army historian, "they took to it expertly." The adaptability of the skilled local craftsmen was all the more notable because of the magnitude and complexity of the assembly process. The individual barge, sixty feet long and weighing approximately seven tons, arrived from the United States disassembled. The framework for the hull was bolted together and planked and sealed with the vessel upside down. Next, they were turned upright by cranes in an improvised turning rig so that deck planking and hardware could be installed. Finally, the completed craft were launched for towing by sailing ships or motor launches to either Basra or Khorramshahr where they were delivered to the allied Inland Water Transport.

By the time this largest industrial operation in Kuwait's history ended on June 28, 1943, 368 barges had been completed and sent to the head of the Gulf, and ten remaining kits were turned over to the Russians. The first shipment received came from Higgins Industries, Inc. in New Orleans[30] and was accompanied by blueprints and planking schedules. In other cases—from shipbuilders in Palatka, Florida; Duluth, Minnesota; Brownsville, Texas; Whitehall, Michigan; and Toledo, Oregon—they often arrived before, or even without, plans. Procurement from multiple sources sometimes meant slight variances on specifications that American and Kuwaiti workmen had to resolve; the planking on forty barges from one supplier proved to be one-quarter of an inch off.

By almost any measure, nonetheless, the American-Kuwaiti collaboration on the barge assembly project proved to be a signal success. Eventually, the twenty-two Americans were reduced to eighteen and, finally, to none—leaving the district engineer to complete his assignment with some 185 Kuwaiti carpenters and about 85 unskilled laborers.

Amidst all of the strains and activities associated with the war, the ruler, Shaikh Ahmad, suffered a serious, potentially fatal, heart problem. The British political agent reported on April 4, 1942 that he had learned from Dr. Scudder of the American Mission that "His Highness had a very serious heart attack this afternoon and that he is dangerously ill." Scudder added that he hoped the gravity of the ruler's condition could be kept secret so that he could get as much rest as possible.[31] As the ruler responded to treatment and the prospect of a potential succession crisis receded, the political agent reached out to Dr. Mylrea, who had moved to India following his retirement. "I was talking to His Highness this morning and he told me that he had written and suggested that you return to us in Kuwait." He added his own invitation to that of the ruler, explaining that Shaikh Ahmad "has a sincere admiration for you and a genuine fondness and I should welcome your presence knowing as I do that your advice, both medical and otherwise, would be sound."[32]

The ruler not only survived this first heart attack but was soon recovering his health. And, Dr. Mylrea did return to see his old friends and home, as he would continue doing as long as he lived. At the end of the year, on December 21, 1942, the political agent recounted a talk with Dr. Mylrea:

> Dr. Mylrea told us that he had just seen the Shaikh and was pleased with his condition. His Highness had been most pleasant and had pressed him to return to Kuwait and make his home here but Dr. Mylrea had not felt that he could make a definite decision yet and had told His Highness that he much appreciated his kind suggestion but he did not feel that he could give any assurance at the moment, that he proposed to remain here for two months and that as soon as he had made up his mind he would inform His Highness.[33]

These exchanges are a vivid indication of the degree to which the American Mission had been able, through its years of work and service, to incorporate itself not only within Kuwaiti society but in the affections of the Kuwaiti ruler.

The long-established American community at the mission was dealing with important physical and personnel changes, not least of which, the first change of leadership in three decades. Dr. Stanley Mylrea, who had witnessed and participated in more of Kuwait's recent history than any other expatriate, retired to India with his wife, Bess, in 1941.[34] In 1939, Dr. Lewis R. Scudder with his wife, Dorothy, a nurse, joined the mission to succeed him as Director of the Mission and Hospital. Scudder offered the flavor of Kuwait as he first saw it in a 1971 commencement address at the American School of Kuwait:

> Inside (the walls), we found ourselves upon a broad sandy open space between courtyards on either side along the middle of which meandered the sandy road that led to the Safat which at that time was the sheep and camel market. We were not a little surprised to see just in front of us... a pile of camel thorn used as fuel for making coffee and tea, ten or more feet high moving along the road with no apparent means of locomotion. As we passed it we saw under it the bobbing head and ears of a small donkey attached by a rope to the owner....
>
> ... The building complex of the Mission then included two missionary homes, another for the hospital pharmacist, another the mission chapel, and on the shore a two storey stone and cement women's hospital not yet completed and finally a sprawling

one storey eight-room little hospital for me that had served the medical and surgical needs of the entire population of Kuwait for more than thirty years.

The Kuwait of that time was a quaint, quiet, sandy little desert town whose main livelihood was the sea. It was often, therefore, that we heard the characteristic rhythmical sea chants of the sailors as they rowed boats on the bay or labored at raising the sail of a boom as she sailed off on her voyage to India, Zanzibar, or off to the pearl fishing grounds....

We had a small circle of good friends that were much together in simple amusements and recreation such as tennis and bridge. For us of the Mission medical personnel, however, the hospital created more than a full-time job, so we never lacked for entertainment. There was little outside the walls of Kuwait except for a few drillers' houses and workshops at Magwa. The whole of Ahmadi was bare hillside right away to the sea. There were only the tiny oases of Fantas, Abu Halafa, and Fanaitees scattered along the coast.[35]

Dr. Lewis R. Scudder, who would earn the respect and affection of the Kuwaitis in his own right, was the scion of a distinguished family of missionaries. His ancestor, Rev. Dr. John Scudder, went to Ceylon in 1819 and thence to India, "founding a dynasty of forty-two missionaries" extending over four generations. Ethel "Beth" Talcott Scudder, his great granddaughter, married Dr. William Wells Thoms in 1930 and served in Kuwait during the following decade. Dr. Lewis R. Scudder, a grandson, died and was buried in Kuwait.[36] He was accompanied by his wife, Dorothy, a trained nurse who became the administrator of the mission hospitals and died in 1991. It is thanks to her memory and longevity that precious details of life in Kuwait at the time have been preserved.[37]

The Scudders were met in Basra by Khatem Miriam Van Pelt, driving the mission's new Ford automobile. The trip to Kuwait was a gruelling trek of five and one-half hours over a deeply rutted track through a landscape that supported considerably more *arfaj*, or camel thorn, than today. Shortly after their arrival, the Scudders were invited to dinner with the Dicksons at their black bedouin tent near Khaitam. During the dinner, darkness fell, and when they were ready to return to town, no lights were visible from Kuwait to guide them. The Dickson's cook helpfully showed them how to navigate by observing the ripples caused by northerly winds and they made it back to the town gate. The gates were closed and locked at sundown, but the gatekeeper opened it for them.[38]

The main form of entertainment for "Europeans" in Kuwait consisted of dinners and other gatherings in their homes. In an effort to adapt these events to the heat and humidity, the ladies promoted more comfortable attire for these occasions which they dubbed "Gulf Kit." Men wore business or formal trousers and dress shirt (and cumberbund) without coat and tie. This innovation caused confusion at first. On one occasion the Dicksons arrived in golfing clothes and carrying their clubs, having misread the "Gulf" on the invitation for "Golf." Whatever its origins, "Gulf Kit" caught on and was common throughout the Gulf into the 1970s, when widespread air-conditioning reduced the need.

It was traditional for prominent Westerners who had deep roots in Kuwait to call upon Kuwaiti friends at the Eids or holidays. Some remnants of this custom persist, especially in the calls by the British and American Ambassadors. The return calls that Kuwaitis made at Christmas have receded into memory today, although several Kuwaiti friends visited on Christmas Day when I was Ambassador there in the 1980s. These friendly calls were a major event as recently as the 1940s. Dorothy Scudder recalled "One Christmas," when "we had 425 men starting from 7:30 in the morning and going on until about 1:00 o'clock. We would serve bitter coffee, cigarettes and candy. ... I always had some of our boys from the hospital right by the door, one taking down names and one bringing coffee and pouring coffee and cigarettes. It was quite entertaining but it was wonderful when they would all come in and wish us a Merry Christmas."

While Dr. Scudder was preparing to take the reins of the mission from the estimable Dr. Mylrea, Dorothy Scudder was also benefiting from his experience, studying bookkeeping and other skills she would need as she moved into the administrative supervision of the increasingly complex institution.[39] Stanley Mylrea and Lew Scudder were leaders of differing personas—Mylrea projected a "stern and sometimes tempestuous" exterior, whereas Scudder was a man "with gentle strong hands, soft smile, and reassuring bass voice" whose empathy was apparently nearer the surface.

What both of them shared, other than medical and surgical skills, was a strong commitment to their faith and mission, an ability to inspire their harried and hard-pressed staff, and an abiding commitment to Kuwait and its people. In return, they both earned the respect and admiration of their patients and friends, and neither would ever leave them, even in death.

In their almost sixty years of service in Kuwait, Drs. Mylrea and Scudder continued to refine and develop the facilities of the mission hospital even as they ministered to medical needs. In the early years of the new decade, despite a depressed economy and wartime stringencies, the Olcott Memorial Hospital for Women was completed, a building to house the laboratory was added to the complex and Kuwait's first x-ray unit was installed.[40] In the same period, Kuwait also received its first telephones. In the words of Dorothy Scudder:

> ...in 1940 we had our first telephones. Shaikh Ahmed had number one and we had number twelve... One day he called up soon after he got his telephone...and he said, 'Hello, Scudder? This is Ahmed. I am calling you to see if you can hear me. Can you hear me?'[41]

In spite of the completion of the women's hospital and other facilities, the life and work of the mission staff remained challenging and conditions relatively primitive. There was no reliable electricity on the mission compound until 1943 when a generator arrived from a church in the United States.[42] The new generator, however, was not large enough to power air-conditioning and the atmosphere in the operating room was often uncomfortable. There were no screens to cover the open windows, so a man was positioned beside the operating table with a feather duster to chase the flies away. The surgeon, Dr. Scudder, perspired freely and wore a cap and mask made from Turkish towels to catch the sweat. "We were very fortunate," Dorothy Scudder recalled, "we had few infections because we always put sulphur powder inside before we closed the incision."[43]

Fresh water, which had to be brought down from the Shatt

al-Arab, was also in short supply. It was used almost exclusively for drinking. Elaborate procedures were followed to make optimum use of the scarce resource:

> *The wells in town produced brackish water hardly less salty than that in the sea. Even in the late 1940's, when the Mission had arranged to pipe brackish water into our homes, we hoarded it. We would shower in the brackish water (when before we had dipped it by hand), then rinse off with one pitcher of sweet. All the water we caught in a tin tub and used it to water the scrawny salt pine trees.*[44]

Daily clinics continued to draw large crowds, and women began doing their laundry while they waited to be called. The staff also held clinics outside the town. Again, Dorothy Scudder: "In those days, everybody had worms until we'd take our bag with all this medicine and one of the Shaikhs would open his house and we'd have a regular clinic once a week in Jahra."

During the decade of the 1940s, the American Mission was able to place increased emphasis on the training and development of support staff. From its opening at the begining of the century, it reached out to enlist support from the local society, particularly Arab-Christians and "the enterprising Iranian Shi'ahs"[45] Under the tutelage of Dr. Mylrea, a number of nurse's assistants, or "dressers," joined the hospital staff to supplement the work of American caregivers. As the years passed, first bedouin and Shi'a and ultimately the majority of Sunnis in the society took advantage of the medical facilities, and many of them came to have feelings of gratitude to the mission doctors and clergy. One of these, Muhammad 'Abu-Jasim, was a key figure in the blossoming of the hospital:

> *Through the Great Depression and Second world War, when times were hard, the clergy of the mission (foremost among them the matchless Gerrit Pennings) paid close attention to that wiry and hard-working man and his growing family. Perhaps in thanks, all of Muhammad's sons enlisted in the service of the mission in one way or another.*[46]

His eldest son, Jassim, apprenticed as a cook and remained until the era of oil wealth when he left to take a position with the Kuwaiti ports. It was his younger brother, Haidar al-Khalifa, who would become a skilled and indispensable member of the hospital team.

Haidar went to work as a teenager in the early 1940s as a domestic servant in the home of Gerrit DeJong. Recognizing his promise, Mrs. DeJong (Everdine) tutored Haidar in English and sent him to the hospital to be trained as a nurse. He was soon working as an assistant to Dr. Scudder, scrubbing in for surgeries, and even learning to perform simple procedures under supervision. Two of his younger brothers also trained at the hospital. He was at Dr. Mylrea's bedside when the visiting physician died in 1952. In what may have been his final words, Mylrea said, "I took care of your father when he was sick and almost died, and now you're taking care of me. It balances things out, doesn't it, Haidar?" Haidar went on to become the first trained radiologist in the country and was serving as the Administrator of the American Mission Hospital when it shut its doors in the 1960s. Twenty years after that closure, the last American veteran of the Mission Hospital remaining in Kuwait, Dorothy Scudder, gave expression to the affection and respect in which Haidar was held:

> ... he was a wonderful helper to all of us and he's still a big help to me. He has a family of fifteen children, two boys and thirteen girls... and they're wonderful children. They've all grown up through university and one's a doctor and one's a major in the police force, and many teachers and ... I'm always pleased when Haidar tells me how his family is.[47]

As the World War drew to a close, Dr. Scudder introduced a program for training practical nurses of Kuwaiti nationality with the assistance of Mrs. Eleanor Heusinkveld (1945–49) and Jeannette Veldman (1956–59).[48] By degrees, additional Kuwaitis, like Haidar al-Khalifa, augmented the ranks of the professional staff: Suleiman Sim'an Shammas, the first pharmacist and practical nurses Alie Yaqoub Shammas, Farida Yaqoub Shammas, Abbas Radha, Ibrahim Hasan, Abdallah Abbas, Ali Abbas, Ramadan Al-Khalifa, and

Ali Shatti. The contributions of these new colleagues to the work of the mission was crucial to its ability to cope with the increasing demands of the growing shaikhdom.

Without question, the greatest disappointment of the wartime was the suspension of oil exploration and production for the duration of the conflict. Beginning in the 1930s, when the ruler awarded the first concession, oil had become the major hope for relief from the stagnant economy of the small state. By the time the war closed in on the operation, the British and American drillers had proven the presence of petroleum in exportable quantities beneath the sands of Kuwait, and had begun to transform areas outside the town.

The story of the negotiations leading to the first concessions for oil exploration is complex (it has been related in great detail elsewhere).[49] Nevertheless, some understanding of how American firms and citizens came to play a partnership role in what was initially a British preserve, is essential. In fact, the early American interest in Kuwait's oil prospects is of more than passing significance because it was also key to launching the Kuwaiti industry "sooner than might otherwise have been possible."[50]

The British were looking at the petroleum potential of Kuwait and other areas of the Gulf as early as 1913, as they were converting the Royal Navy from coal to oil-fired boilers. That year, Admiral Sir Ernest Slade, RN, visited Kuwait and met with Shaikh Mubarak to assess prospects for oil in the Gulf.[51] It must have seemed to London, however, that there was little cause for urgency. Though, unlike the United States, Britain possessed no domestic oil deposits, its far-flung empire and wide influence gave it access to the increasingly important resource. It was developing substantial proven oil production in Persia and, through its treaties with Kuwait and other Gulf principalities, London was probably comfortable regarding the possibility of rivals for the region's suspected petroleum reserves.

The first test of the wills of British and American oil companies occurred in Iraq rather than Kuwait. With the collapse of the Ottoman Empire following World War I, Britain assumed a League of Nations Mandate over the new Iraqi state. Skillfully absorbing the wilayet of Mosul which France had claimed, Britain was apparently free to monopolize the oil resources of Iraq. With the active support of the U.S. State Department, American companies pressed for a share in the Iraqi reserves over British objections. London argued that since the United States had not joined the League of Nations, America "had no claim to share in the commercial development of territories such as Iraq, which were administered under a League mandate."[52] After protracted diplomatic exchanges, U.S. insistence on an equal share in development of mandated territories won out. In 1927, American oil interests (Socony Vacuum, later Mobil, and Standard Oil of New Jersey, subsequently Exxon) were accorded a 23-and-three-quarters percentage share in the Iraq Petroleum Company (IPC).

The agreement on Iraq did not resolve the issue of American participation in petroleum exploration in Kuwait and other parts of the Gulf littoral. Bahrain was the next arena of rivalry. U.S. oil interests continued to run into treaty provisions, giving Britain a veto over granting concessions to foreign governments and companies. It is unfair to generalize about the reaction of British officials regarding the inroads being made by Americans in these British preserves. Many were legitimately concerned about the precedents being established and others were welcoming to American colleagues. It is nonetheless true that that some British officials deeply resented American "intruders" and reacted with near paranoia.[53]

Even as a resolution of the issue of American participation was being shaped in Iraq, the United States set its sights on Bahrain, which was constrained by treaty provisions similar to Kuwait's. If the politicians who had drafted the "non-alienation" clauses in these agreements thought they had locked foreign interests out of their Gulf client states, they had not reckoned with the labyrinthine world of oil exploration. The American share of the Iraq Petroleum was won by frontal assault; the Bahraini prize was pursued by stealth and maneuvering.

Major Frank Holmes, a British subject and pioneer oil prospector in the region, established a British company—the Eastern and General Syndicate (EGS)—in 1925 as a vehicle for his pursuit of Gulf concessions. Stymied by British obstructions in a direct approach, Eastern Gulf Oil, an American firm, was successful in acquiring two option contracts held by EGS, the first on a concession in Bahrain and the second on an unassigned concession in Kuwait in November 1927. The contract for Bahrain was transferred a year later to Standard Oil of California. In association with the Texas Oil Company, the Bahrain Petroleum Company (BAPCO) was formed and registered as a British corporation under the laws of Canada.[54]

The British were alarmed to find the camel's nose under their tent and raised obstructions that threatened the Bahrain deal. The U.S. Department of State again took up the interests of the American participants; in March 1929, it demanded a clear statement of British policy regarding concessions in the shaikhdoms of the Gulf. The formal British response, when it came, confirmed that the Foreign Office would accept participation of American companies if they satisfied specified conditions governing the use of American capital. Implementing negotiations between the State Department and the British India Office resulted in an acceptable compromise.[55]

As the British had correctly suspected, Eastern Gulf Oil followed up its success in Bahrain by turning to the Kuwaiti portfolio, where the Anglo-Iranian Oil Company had shown little interest or sense of urgency. Britain, determined to stop the erosion of its monopoly position, was adamant in applying the "national clause" in its treaty with Kuwait, meaning that no non-British company could receive a concession. Finally, in November 1931, the Eastern Gulf Oil Corporation took the problem of Britain's position to the State Department once more. The American pressure had another significant effect on the British; the Anglo-Iranian Oil Company, which had heretofore shown little serious interest in Kuwait, now hastened to negotiate with the ruler for a concession there, as did representatives of the American company.

Simultaneously pursuing contacts with British and American oilmen greatly strengthened the position of the Kuwaiti ruler. The American government, furthermore, was, from December 1931, pressing London for equal treatment of American companies in Kuwait. Britain's preferred strategy apparently was to press for Shaikh Ahmad's decision before they had to consider the American demands, but the Kuwaiti ruler refused to be rushed. During this period, Colonel Dickson, the well-informed British political agent in Kuwait, reportedly reached the conclusion that Shaikh Ahmad would take his time and was leaning toward the American syndicate. In his view, the Shaikh doubted that the AIOC, which had virtually ignored his country until the Americans arrived on the scene, was ready to develop Kuwait's oil resources vigorously. Dickson also believed that the ruler was influenced by the ineffective British efforts to resolve two other issues of deep concern to him: the continuing Saudi embargo on trade with his country, and Iraq's taxation of date gardens which he owned.[56] He no doubt recalled the outcome of the 'Uqair conference as well.

The official British response to the American Embassy in London reflected none of the nuance and uncertainty of Col. Dickson's appraisal. After reviewing the many exchanges between the two governments, the Foreign Office concentrated on the embassy's assertion that the Kuwaiti ruler was amenable to the operation of the Eastern Gulf Oil Company in his country.

The British letter, signed by Sir John Simon, commented as follows:

> His Majesty's Government have caused enquiries to be made of the Shaikh, who replied that he was still averse from receiving in his principality a company other that an entirely British one.... It will be observed from a reference to the Shaikh's letter (to Holmes) that its final sentence only expresses a readiness to discuss the matter further with Major Holmes, after agreement has been reached between the syndicate and HM Government.

The actual situation appears, particularly in retrospect, to have been considerably more fluid and ambiguous than the letter purported. Nevertheless, while restating the British position that the British corporation had a preemptive claim to negotiate with Shaikh Ahmad, Sir John conceded that "His Majesty's Government are, however, now prepared, for their part, not to insist in this case that any concession must contain a clause confining it to British interests, if the Shaikh for his part is willing to grant a concession without such a clause."[57]

By the mid-1930s, the competitive bidding between British and American oil firms had raised the projected cost of the concession. The time was ripe for a compromise. On December 23, 1934, the Kuwaiti ruler awarded the country's first oil concession: a seventy-five year grant to the Kuwait Oil Company (KOC), a subsidiary of the Anglo-Iranian Oil Company, and the Gulf Exploration Company, a subsidiary of the Eastern Gulf Oil Company.[58]

Anglo-American drilling operations began in 1936, bringing a small number of expatriates to the small country. The first exploratory well was drilled at Bahra, on the north shore of the Bay of Kuwait, but it proved to be a dry hole. The drillers then moved their rig further afield, to a site near the Burgan Hills, about thirty miles south of the town, and fourteen miles inland from the coast. The second test well struck oil at an exploitable depth on February 22, 1938, with considerable drama. One of the participants in the operation recorded a graphic account of the near-disaster:

> *On the night when the main oil horizon was struck, at the inconvenient hour of 1 a.m., Tom Patrick, the drilling superintendent, and the duty driller took exactly the correct action. They pulled the drilling tools up into the cased hole and continued to circulate mud fluid (bayrite) in order to keep the well under control and prevent the drill pipe from getting stuck. Fresh mud was pumped into the casing but it soon became evident that mud stocks were becoming exhausted. We then decided to plug the hole with a ship's mast. Donald Campell obtained a suitable pole from one of the shipyards which we tapered to a length of about ten feet. Then, the drill pipe was pulled out of the hole and the mast driven by the pipe into the pilot hole, giving us a complete closure of the formation. The main valve was then replaced.*[59]

The oil bearing structure of Kuwait which they had tapped is, in many respects, ideal. The oil is forced to the surface by internal pressure without the need for pumps and, then, flows to the Gulf shore by gravity, again obviating the need for elaborate and expensive pumping mechanisms.

Through 1936 and 1937, as the drillers labored in the barren desert, company geologists carried out gravity, magnetic and seismic surveys to identify promising formations. The team, which included Americans like Paul Boots, had investigated the area of known bitumen deposits in the vicinity of Burgan and pinpointed it as a promising location.[60] Burgan ultimately became a major center of producing wells, with more than one hundred drilled around the initial strike.

The work of these oil pioneers would have momentous implications for the future of Kuwait. But the first workers were relatively few in number and had an extremely limited footprint well away from the town. To support their operations, a primitive camp was set up at Magwa, approximately midway between the Burgan field and the town of Kuwait. Aside from a small clinic, it boasted few amenities. Nevertheless, they had set in motion a process that would alter the country and its society in ways that could hardly be imagined at the beginning of the 1940s:

> *One of the most striking changes brought about by the oil companies was the opening up of the region to the outside world. Until then, the British authorities had granted very few entry visas there, and allowed only minimal reference to the Gulf states to be made internationally. Once the oil concessions had been signed, control of foreigners could no longer be tightly restricted; geologists, refinery workers, managers, etc. all began to arrive in increasing numbers.*[61]

Before the full potential of the petroleum discoveries could be realized, however, the oilmen and the Kuwaitis, would have to wait several additional years. As an active theater in the Second World War, the Gulf region was subject to the decisions of the Commander-in-Chief Middle East. In late 1942, the oil company employees were ordered to mothball their operation and relocate to Abadan. Well heads were concreted shut and the oil men and the few families that had joined them had all left Kuwait by July, 1943. Col. Dickson, who had by then left government service for a position with the Kuwait Oil Company, and one other executive, remained behind to guard the nine disabled wells and several water wells that had been left functional to serve the needs of the bedouin and other specified purposes, such as the U.S. Army barge assembly operation.[62]

Kuwait had reason to hope for better times as World War II ended in Europe and Asia. In addition to the prospect of long-delayed oil revenues, the troubled relationship with Saudi Arabia improved markedly in 1942. On April 20, the British Minister in Jeddah signed, on behalf of Kuwait, several agreements with Shaikh Yusuf Yasin for the Saudi government.[63] The regularization of relations with this key country added an element of stability for Kuwait, eliminating the threat of hostile actions on its western and southern borders for the first time since the era of Mubarak the Great.

Another consequence of the war, and America's worldwide responsibilities in prosecuting allied military operations, was a small, but enhanced U.S. interest and official presence in the region. The barge-assembly project brought the first representatives of the U.S. government to Kuwait (although they remained only until the job was done), and countless American-registry cargo vessels discharged their cargos in the port. The involvement of American oil companies in exploration, and later, the production of petroleum, gave Washington an economic interest in Kuwait.[64] Surprisingly, the U.S. interest was strategic and commercial, rather than tied to a perceived need for oil:

> *The petroleum resources of the Middle East are so much a part of modern life that it is hard for Americans in the 1990s to consider the strategic importance of the Persian gulf in terms other than oil. Nevertheless, a focus on oil interests alone is insufficient to explain the directions taken by American policy in the years immediately following the Second World War. NEA's (Department of State Bureau) memorandum of October 1946 on United States policy toward Iran, for example, never once mentioned oil.*[65]

Nor does it appear that Washington had the intention of replacing the British in the Gulf, although given the power disparity at the war's end, the British may be excused for fearing otherwise. When the Department of State requested permission in 1942 to station a consul in Bahrain, the Government of India advised that "opposition to U.S. proposal should be pressed to utmost," adding that "...we surmise that U.S. government have other objectives in view beyond those they have so far discussed, including possible visions of oil and air hegemony along the entire length of Arab coast."[66] Five years later, the British political agent in Kuwait was equally adamant: "I consider it probable that the Shaikh would endeavour to 'play off' the British and United States representatives against each other and that this might weaken our influence with him." [67] British representatives in the Gulf were intent on establishing the *status quo ante* following the end of hostilities, but it was not to be. More than the heightened American visibility, Britain's economic exhaustion and the evolving attitudes of the Kuwaiti people would see to that.

On September 28, 1945, one month after the surrender of Japan, President Harry S. Truman approved completion of the U.S. airbase at Dhahran, an "airfield that would play a key role in Operation Desert Shield/Storm forty-five years later."[68] The next two decades would witness great changes that few politicians could then imagine. As the decade drew to a close, the U.S. military, especially the navy, deployed worldwide since the begining of the world war, was becoming heavily dependant upon petroleum supplies from the Middle East.[69] Without a conscious policy decision in Washington, Kuwait's strategic location and oil resources acquired a new salience for the United States.

6

From Boom Port to Boom Town

As the Second World War drew to a close, first in the European Theater and within months in the Far Eastern, Kuwait was poised to enter a new and unimaginable phase in its development. Even as much of the world began the process of recovery from the human losses, physical devastation and economic distress of six years of war, the town, with an estimated population of about one hundred thousand, was about to undergo changes—physical, economic, and societal —that were genuinely transformative.

A reliable supply of potable water was a limiting factor in sustaining a growing population that was about to explode with postwar development. When Kuwait was established, nearby wells, although located outside the walls, were sufficient for its modest needs. As the town grew, however, demand began to outstrip available fresh or brackish water resources; early in the last century finding a new source was imperative. The solution found capitalized on Kuwait's shipping assets:

> *In 1925, with typically Kuwaiti ingenuity and business acumen, a local mariner thought of the idea of transporting empty barrels in the hold of his vessel and sailing up the Shatt al Arab, near Basra, filling up his barrels with fresh river water and returning with his precious cargo to berth at Shuwaikh jetty....*[1]

The experiment was so successful that soon additional sailing vessels, some reconfigured as tankers, were plying the one hundred miles to the Shatt and transporting large quantities of water that served the needs of residents as late as the 1940s.

A complementary infrastructure was created in the town. Large collecting tanks, into which the ships could unload, were constructed, and a distribution network, based largely on donkeys that could negotiate the narrow streets and lanes, grew up to deliver water to individual Kuwaiti households. In 1946, Zahra Freeth found fresh water on sale at one and a half annas per four gallons. Poor families who could not pay the additional charge for home delivery collected their water from the discharge basin:

> *I watched the poorer women .... Each brought with her a four-gallon petrol can, and after filling it within the courtyard, handed a coin to the attendant at the gate, and went on her way with the full tin on her head, carrying the four gallons with an easy grace.*[2]

The volume of fresh water brought in by dhow eventually reached around 96,000 gallons a day. Ships anchored offshore to allow sediment to settle before discharging their cargos at the jetty, where *candaris*, or water carriers, peddled the precious cargo from goatskin bags.[3] The reliability of the water supply was dependent, however, upon favorable winds, and the system would soon be overwhelmed by a burgeoning population and the requirements of development. Plans were laid down in the second half of the decade for a massive investment in technology to distill seawater on a hitherto unknown scale.

A Kuwaiti miraculously transported from the eighteenth century to the early 1940s could have felt at home in prewar Kuwait. It was larger and more complex than he or she would have remembered, and a number of unfamiliar innovations—automobiles, steamships, the telegraph, and advanced medical care—had made their appearance. By the end of the decade, however, the town was not only experiencing rapid development, but struggling to catch up with expanding needs. In 1948, for example, work on a municipal power station began but was delayed when British electricians failed to arrive on schedule. In June, a serious fire broke out in a flammable shipyard beside the ruler's palace. Lacking a municipal fire department, the blaze was only contained by the arrival of the fire brigade from the Kuwait Oil Company.[4] Nevertheless, the time traveller would have readily recognized the architecture, the physical layout of the town and many other features of everyday life. Within a few short years, this would no longer be the case. As a longtime Western resident observed, the year 1946 "was perhaps the last in which the stranger might have seen Kuwait in anything like her old traditional form."[5]

The catalyst for the revolutionary transformation was, of course, the exploitation of the country's petroleum resources, discovered in the late 1930s and placed on hold for the duration of the War. For if the icon of the traditional Kuwait and its well-being was the *boom* (the signature vessel of its skilled shipwrights and sailors), the symbol of the new age would be the oil rig which fuelled an unprecedented economic "boom."

Hardly had the guns fallen silent in the Pacific when the first wave of oilmen returned to Kuwait. These early arrivals were mainly veterans of the exploration of the country between 1935 and 1942, when they were ordered to leave by military authorities. At least some of them had withdrawn no further than Abadan where they spent the war years, "... but they were soon joined by a host of American and British drillers."[6] Over the next few years, Kuwait was flooded with drillers and others who literally rearranged the landscape south of the city.

Unlike the Americans of the Arabian Mission who left extensive memoirs and other writings, the British and American oil workers seldom recorded the details of their daily experience in Kuwait. The vast majority of them seem destined to remain anonymous, unfortunately. Nevertheless, there are occasional glimpses of some of the American oilmen who contributed to the development and exploitation of Kuwait's oil wealth and swelled the tiny American community established over three decades earlier. The top company executive who set up in Kuwait City after the war, was Tom Patrick, the American deputy manager, who took up residence near the western gate of the city walls. The Kuwait Oil Company (KOC) guesthouse, located just inside the Jahra gate in the city wall and on the site of the present Sheraton Hotel, was the only place that expatriates could entertain or be entertained.[7] The expatriates named their headquarters in the nearby Behbehani Compound "Marble Arch"[8]

Another American on the scene periodically was General Walter B. Pyron, a veteran oil man and Gulf Oil vice president. During the war, he had served with the Texan 4th Cavalry Division and, as soon as he had donned mufti, he began periodic visits to monitor progress. If the characterization of his manner is accurate, he had not made a complete transition from his military persona. According to a well-informed observer, "His approach was never less than brisk. He wanted to see oil in the pipeline without delay—by what means or method he was not greatly concerned, so long as it did not cost too much."[9]

The first task of the returning oilmen was to tie the producing wells that had been capped and abandoned three years earlier to the gathering facility.[10] By the end of 1945, a pipeline was built from the field to a group of storage tanks atop the Dhahar ridge, a topographical feature running parallel to the Gulf Coast. From there, the oil would depend upon gravity to flow to the shore at Fahahil, the site selected for the marine terminal.[11]

The building tempo associated with development of an oil industry inexorably altered what had been a pristine desert landscape, unchanged and hardly touched for millennia. The primitive and minimal support camp set up by the original explorers at Magwa—between the Burgan field and Kuwait City—quickly assumed the aspect of an industrial park. More substantial operational structures had been constructed, and vehicles and equipment from Abadan and elsewhere filled the horizon.[12] Where small coastal villages and bedouin encampments had previously been the only intrusions on nature, hundreds of workmen—Britons, Americans, Arabs, Indians, and Pakistanis—were transforming the face of Kuwait permanently.

The Americans who arrived in Kuwait in this new wave of expatriates were distinctive in several respects. The majority of drillers, roughnecks, and mudmen tended to be from the Southwest—Texas, Louisiana, or Oklahoma—having gained their experience and honed their skills in the oil-producing regions of the United States. They were, in the main, hardworking, hard-partying men who spoke with a broad accent that was unfamiliar to English-speaking Kuwaitis and even their British colleagues. But they left their mark on the American community there and, in some respects, on the culture itself.¹³ Moreover, like the the personnel of the American Mission, the newcomers were committed, when possible, to having their families with them even in an environment as harsh and unfamiliar as Kuwait in the 1940s. Among the early arrivals on the oil scene was a group of wives from Texas.¹⁴

As a rule, though lacking in sophistication and experience abroad, the American oilmen worked well with local peoples, possessing little of the aloofness or class consciousness of more refined expatriates. The evidence of this working relationship may still be encountered in the Arabic of eastern Saudi Arabia and other areas of the Gulf where they labored. The late Joe Twinam, an American Foreign Service officer and ambassador to Bahrain, spent much of his career in the Gulf, including a tour in Kuwait in the 1960s. He correctly attributes to private Americans—missionaries, educators, oilmen, and businessmen—the laying of the foundations for the cooperative relationships between Americans and Gulf societies. Shortly before his untimely death, he wrote:

> *To a remarkable degree, private Americans pioneered the American connection with these countries, providing some solid base of goodwill on which the U.S. Government could in time move to build official relations.*¹⁵

Among the lasting effects of their interaction with the local society, Twinam notes the fact that "...for many years the Gulf Arab word for tractors and the like was 'caterpillar'."¹⁶

While the large American firm, Bechtel, was gearing up to construct the Kuwait Oil Company's gathering, storage, refining, and delivery systems,¹⁷ a more permanent facility, destined to become Kuwait's second major town, was being laid out at a site on the empty Dhahar ridge just north of the newly built tank farm. Here, a complete modern town was developed over succeeding years. The emerging town and port was aptly named Ahmadi in honor of the ruler who had presided over the beginnings of Kuwait's lucrative oil industry and the physical, economic, and social transformation that flowed from it.¹⁸

In June 1946, the eight proven prewar oil wells were connected to the new gathering center and the country was producing thirty thousand barrels per day, primarily for domestic consumption. At the end of that month, Shaikh Ahmad ceremonially inaugurated Kuwait's oil era by opening a special silver valve and sending crude oil from the storage tanks to a tanker, *British Fusilier*, at pierside.[19] The occasion was marked as well by probably the first massive fireworks display in Kuwait's history. KOC officials had procured an impressive display of 'victory' fireworks from the Anglo-Iranian Petroleum Company and "the night sky exploded with rockets, comet trails, shooting stars, and the thunder and lightning of a 'set piece'."[20]

The symbolism of Kuwait's first oil export, while important, was only one milestone on the path of industry development that was to come. Members of the American community, although less numerous than the workforce from Britain and other countries, nevertheless played vital roles at all levels—from skilled drillers and engineers in the fields to KOC executives. On the departure of L. D. Scott in 1946, operational responsibility fell to Tom Patrick, recalled as a professional who demanded the best from his subordinates. He unfortunately fell ill in 1948 and returned to the United States where he succumbed to a brain disorder. That same year, L. T. Jordan arrived from Texas to become general manager of the company. Jordan earned a reputation as "unquestionably the man for the occasion," and the executive credited with encouraging "a unique community spirit among the oil people of Kuwait."[21]

The development of the oil port, Mina Ahmadi, proceeded at a rapid pace.

By 1947 a water distillation plant, power station, and the first small refinery were operational. The refinery produced gasoline and paraffin needed by the company, as well as supplying the local market. It also provided fuel oil to tankers, dry cargo ships, and vessels of the British and American navies.[22] Two years later, in 1949, the massive oil loading pier (the largest in the world at the time) was completed. It extended 4,100 feet out into the Gulf waters and its T-shaped head provided spaces for eight tankers to berth. Six additional submarine pipelines were extended out to single point mooring buoys, permitting additional tankers, including the larger vessels, to load offshore.[23]

Even as the operational facilities needed by the KOC were being rushed to completion, the provision of permanent accommodations for expatriate employees, housed in temporary buildings at Magwa and Wara, was a simultaneous priority. Nothing less than a wholly new town was envisaged.

The temporary housing, in which KOC personnel and contractors lived, left much to be desired. The company bought and erected thirty aluminum prefabs from Reynolds Aluminum Company for American drillers, including those who had brought their wives and children. Accommodations were barracks-style with meals taken in a common mess hall. The one advantage of the temporary housing was that air-conditioning was more effective than the systems in the newly built permanent houses. Some of the residences in Ahmadi were ready for occupation before the Geerhart family arrived and they moved in directly:

> We moved to one of them and the social life of these Texas and Oklahoma oil company people seemed in a way a strange culture to me, even though I was from California. We were all so well received and taken in, anything that oil company had or did, we were part of.[24]

In contrast to the "speadeagled dwellings" from which they moved, the British, American, and other employees discovered at Ahmadi a "pleasantly ordered suburban" community that would not have been out of place in the desert southwest of the United States. With precisely aligned and numbered streets, avenues, and a central thoroughfare, Seventh Avenue, bisecting the town, gave it an aspect totally at odds with the narrow, twisting lanes of old Kuwait. The houses incorporated Scandinavian and American flourishes and were set on lots that must have seemed forlorn patches of desert to the first arrivals. The first tree was imported and planted in March 1948, a harbinger of things to come, as the company and residents worked in tandem to establish tree-lined streets, evergreen hedges, and colorful flowerbeds. By 1952, some 350 staff houses and seven hundred residences for payroll employees had been erected.[25]

Ahmadi, however, was more than a bedroom community and took years to unfold fully; It was the hub of the oil community, providing for health and welfare and all the social, cultural, and sporting amenities of an advanced and well-off, multinational work force. KOC now assumed the responsibilities of a municipality—road building, health care, education, and long-term planning. In 1947 an Anglo-American school was established for six pupils.[26] By the middle of the 1950s, the town boasted a swimming pool, an ice-making plant, a public security headquarters, a post office, a laundry, a bakery, bus service, and a church and mosque.[27]

Driving along the well-established streets of Ahmadi town today, or looking at the expanded oil and port facilities of Mina al-Ahmadi, it is hard to imagine the hardships and difficulties faced by the first generations of oil workers, laboring in what was then little more than raw desert. Zahra Freeth had a unique appreciation of this achievement:

> *The obstacles which the Kuwait Oil Company has had to overcome in the development of Kuwait's oil resources make its achievement in the years since the war all the more remarkable. It began work in a country where industry, and therefore men trained in industry, were nonexistent, a country which lacked even the most elementary port and transport facilities for unloading heavy equipment and shifting it to the site of operations. And over and above the great technical difficulties with which the company was faced, it had to contend with a climate in which the intense heat of summer raised fresh problems in the fields of both mechanical and human activity—making life almost unbearable for the men who had to work through the heat without the benefit of the amenities which today make the summer tolerable.*[28]

American oil workers and interests began to appear elsewhere in Kuwait over the post–World War II decade. In 1948, the ruler granted a concession to the American Independent Oil Company (AMINOIL),[29] a consortium put together by Ralph K. Davies, a former vice president of Standard Oil of California, in Kuwait's half of the Neutral Zone shared with Saudi Arabia. The Saudis had earlier given a similar concession in their part of the zone to the Pacific Western Oil Corporation, and the two companies agreed between them that AMINOIL would be the operating company, working on a joint account basis.[30]

After drilling five dry holes in the Neutral Zone, AMINOIL struck oil near Wafra in March of 1953, and within about a year had proved fourteen producing wells. The crude produced in the zone was transported by a pipeline of over thirty miles to Mina Abdullah within Kuwaiti territory. Initially, both AMINOIL and Pacific Western loaded crude at this facility, which would eventually include a refinery. The first export from Mina Abdullah occurred at the beginning of 1954 and over the next few years one fifteen-thousand-ton tanker a week was loading there, primarily for the Japanese market.[31] AMINOIL also acquired in 1949 exclusive rights to explore for and develop petroleum on the islands of Kubba, Qaru, and Umm al Maradim in the Gulf off Kuwait and the Neutral Zone.

The Americans, some with families, arriving to participate in Kuwait's oil industry and to help build the infrastructure and amenities made possible by the country's new-found wealth, swelled the tiny community represented by the American Mission. The numbers of the mission staff, now in its fourth decade of operation, had been remarkably stable over those years. And, unlike the newcomers, mission personnel generally regarded service in Kuwait as a long-term commitment, despite the difficult challenges of climate, isolation, and relatively primitive conditions. With some exceptions, the new American expatriates possessed less interest in the culture and society around them and planned to leave once their project or assignment was completed.[32] The numbers of British and Americans in the women's group at Ahmadi, for example, remained roughly stable through the 1950s but in the next decade, as drilling tapered off, American families began to depart.[33] In contrast, the mission staff had embedded themselves in Kuwaiti society and affected Kuwaiti perceptions of the American people in ways that their later compatriots could not.[34]

The influx of American and other expatriates added to the strain on the small mission staff, particularly before the KOC had completed its own medical facilities and other amenities. The mission, however, had a good relationship with the companies and received generous support from them and their personnel in return for its services.[35] One noteworthy case was that of John Buckley, the chief engineer of the port of Mina al-Ahmadi. Lewis Scudder provides the following sketch of Buckley, who married Joan Oltoff, a nurse at the American Mission hospital, in 1949.

> *Joan, John, and their children were included in all mission family celebrations, and if Dorothy Scudder ever ran up against a sticky engineering or construction problem, the first person she called was John Buckley. His ebullient sense of humor and his resourcefulness made him a much appreciated individual. The Buckleys retired from KOC in 1968 and lived in Cornwall, England, where Joan continues to live. John died in 1984.*[36]

Additional Americans and their families, as well as Arab-Christians, swelled attendance at the mission chapel. An Anglican church was established at Ahmadi in 1947 and enlarged in the 1950s; a small informal fellowship grew up at the AMINOIL camp at Mina al-Abdullah.

For the first several years following the Second World War, the Mission Hospital remained the sole modern medical-surgical facility serving the burgeoning population of the country. Drawing on the newly created wealth from the oil industry, the Kuwaiti government began to build a medical infrastructure of its own.[37] Nevertheless, the mission, under the direction of Dr. Lewis Scudder, Sr., continued to plan for the construction of a new and more modern hospital on its compound. In January 1947, Gerald Nykerk wrote to British Political Agent Major Tandy, that the mission had accumulated "three and one quarter lacs of rupees" and envisaged the beginning of construction as soon as materials became available.[38] As it happened, his prognosis was overly optimistic; almost seven years passed before ground was broken for the new sixty-bed facility.

It was during this postwar decade, too, that the United States government began to play an active role vis-à-vis Kuwait and its people. With the possible exception of the U.S. Army barge assembly project during the War, private Americans and corporations had been the face of the United States for Kuwaitis and their government. In conformity with the Kuwaiti agreement with Great Britain, Washington had dealt exclusively through the British government.

While this paradigm continued to govern official U.S. policy in the country, increasingly, Kuwaitis would encounter U.S. civilian officials and military among them, reflecting America's newly recognized influence, interests, and responsibilities following the War.

As we have seen earlier, wartime exigencies brought massive American shipping into the Gulf as part of the allied effort to supply the Soviet Union through Iran, and to help meet the pressing needs of the Gulf state populations, including Kuwait. The subsequent development of the oil industry kept them coming after the war, both to deliver the materials needed for extensive construction projects and to transport oil exports to foreign markets. The U.S. Navy naturally followed the merchant marine traffic, purchasing needed bunkering from Mina al-Ahmadi after production was established.

To fulfil and support its new responsibilities for patrolling the Gulf and adjacent waters, the U.S. Navy created in 1949 Commander Middle East Force (COMMIDEASTFOR)[39], a very small command to cover not only the Gulf but also the Red Sea, the Gulf of Aden, the Arabian Sea, and the Bay of Bengal. Based at a small shore facility, co-located until the early 1970s with the Royal Navy at Jufair in Bahrain, the ships "chopped" to the Commander often were resupplied from merchant ships at sea. The Commander, for most of the Command's history, had control of only one vessel, generally a seaplane tender reconfigured as a command ship.[40] Pairs of destroyers were periodically dispatched from the Sixth Fleet in the Mediterranean, and later from USPACCOM in the Pacific to augment the command ship and to undertake port calls on goodwill missions.[41] Visits by ships of the U.S. Navy became a routine occurence in the 1950s. William D. Brewer, who was U.S. Consul in the period recalled:

> The Kuwaitis liked them, for it gave them a chance to appear somewhat more independent, even though all top contacts were always through the political agent. Looking back, I think we had many more than the Royal Navy. I was there, however, when the Vice Admiral Commanding the Indian Ocean paid, what proved to be, the final British visit at that level. In a way, it marks the beginning of the end of the special British position in the Persian Gulf.[42]

Visiting naval vessels provided U.S. diplomats with an opportunity to replenish their larders from ship's store, and occasionally livened up the social scene. Rear Admiral "Skip" Beecher, the second COMIDEASTFOR, had a widespread reputation as a vocalist, composer, and ukelele player. By the time his flagship made an official visit to Kuwait, he and his staff had created an operetta, matching new lyrics to familiar tunes. At dinner on the ship for a group of Westerners, including the political agent, the guests were convulsed by tunes such as "Bah, Bah, Rein" (the Yale tune) and "Kwait till the Sun Shines, Nelly."[43]

As oil production and other developments expanded and the resident American community grew accordingly, it was logical for the U.S. government to begin thinking about consular services, including the protection of American citizens. The process leading to the establishment there of a U.S. Consulate proved to be a lengthy one, but evidence of interest in the welfare of American expatriates can be traced back to the late 1930s. In 1938, the American Consul in Baghdad made inquiries through his British counterparts regarding applicable Kuwaiti laws.[44] There is no evidence of a serious followup at that time, and the intervening wartime crisis undoubtedly delayed active pursuit of this issue.

By agreement between the British and Kuwaitis, the political agent exercised responsibility for expatriates even after the creation of a court system for Kuwaitis. Encompassing not just Western expatriates but South Asians and others as well, the arrangement worked reasonably well, with the political agent occasionally rendering judgements, so long as the numbers involved were relatively small. However, once workers poured into the country following the war, the limited resources of the agency were soon strained.

At least some British officials, available records show, held highly stereotypical views of working class Americans which colored their attitudes. Miriam Joyce, who reviewed archives and diplomatic correspondence extensively, summarized the viewpoint of these elements:

> ... the British expressed uneasiness about Americans employed in the oil fields. These Americans were depicted as unpolished roughnecks, tough men who carried weapons. 'We do not want to run

> the risk of American gunmen and others shooting up each other in the camps, or Arabs outside the camp, especially as there is at present no police force capable of dealing with such a situation if it were to arise.'[45]

It is not possible to determine how widely this "cowboy" mythology was shared, but no documented instances of extraordinary difficulties attributable to the American workforce have come to light. Since the local British officials had no similar problem working closely with American oil executives, it is likely that British "concern" flowed more from class consciousness than national animosity. Another instance of British angst at about the same time reinforces this judgement. In the spring of 1949, the political agent in Kuwait raised the question of the ruler's new yacht, a gift of the AMINOIL company. Apparently, the ruler was not "entitled" to exhibit the gold "coronet" emblazoned on the vessel's smoke funnel. He thought, however, that he had resolved the protocol gaff: "I think it was more likely put there by the American donors."[46] He was probably correct. This was something the average American would not have given a second thought. But it does illustrate the cultural gulf that still divided the British and American allies.

Across this gulf, exacerbated by Britain's efforts to maintain its privileged position in Kuwait in the face of domestic opposition, Great Britain's postwar economic distress, and the emerging power of the United States, the two governments engaged on the issue of American consular representation from differing perspectives. For London, the American workers in Kuwait constituted a potential source of disturbance, while Washington saw them as a vulnerable population in need of consular protection. The British were also concerned, with some legitimacy, that accreditation of an American Consulate would establish a precedent that Arab states with nationalist regimes would try to exploit. The United States accepted the argument initially, agreeing instead that it would establish a consulate in Basra with a mandate to make frequent visits to Kuwait. This would ultimately prove unsatisfactory due to the rigors of travel over the largely unimproved track between the two cities. Within several years, the United States was back, renewing its request for a consular presence in Kuwait itself.[47]

In 1949, the Department of State resumed its negotiations through the American Embassy in London. Anticipating the British government would again raise the argument that a U.S. Consulate in Kuwait would open the field to other, more troublesome, countries, the embassy made the case that its needs for consular representation were more pressing than those of other foreign states. Despite monthly visits to Kuwait, the American Consulate in Basra had been unable to keep up with the workload being generated by the enlarged American community. Citing the requests for consular services being pressed by Gulf Oil Company and the American Independent Oil Company operating in the Neutral Zone, first secretary of the Embassy in London G. Lewis Jones detailed the growing demands for passport services—"Passports had to be renewed or replaced, family members included or excluded. Consuls were needed to witness marriage ceremonies, and to record births."[48] Perhaps sensing that British reservations were weakening under the weight of the U.S. case, Jones closed his presentation by asserting that an American consular presence in Kuwait would be a positive development, benefiting Anglo-American relations and contributing to "the harmonious development of our commercial relations in Kuwait."

The British remained reluctant to approve an American consular mission in Kuwait, but were realistic enough to recognize that the U.S. case rested on "extremely strong practical grounds." They were also concerned that if they rebuffed Washington's request outright again, the United States could begin to question Great Britain's special position in Kuwait and the rest of the Gulf. They, therefore, turned to devising an arrangement that would fulfil American requirements without compromising their unique status in Kuwait.

When Sir Bernard Burrows next met with Jones, he explained that the British government was prepared to offer a solution permitting an American consul to fulfil the practical requirements outlined, so long as the incumbent would have no direct access to the ruler of Kuwait. Reverting to continuing concern that the arrival of an American Consul not open the floodgate to demands from other countries, Sir Bernard emphasized that Britain was prepared to accede to the American request only on condition that the consul be accredited to (i.e., receive his credentials or exequatur from) Britain rather than Kuwait. Further, the arrangement would "in no way alter British jurisdiction over foreigners or relations between Britain and the oil companies."

Although Great Britain accepted that it could not simply continue to stonewall in the face of American pressure and had devised what would prove to be a workable solution, it still entertained some hope of being able to convince Washington to back off its strong position. When Sir Bernard committed the terms he had conveyed orally to First Secretary Jones to paper in August 1949, he also made one last attempt to dissuade the State Department. Elaborating on the implications of a resident American consul, he outlined feared consequences:

> He ... pointed out that Baghdad too had requested a consul in Kuwait and that if the answer was yes, Egypt would expect representation. At this juncture, the United States was the only country with which Britain had a consular convention, but London was in the process of negotiating such a convention with Egypt, a convention stating that a consulate may be opened in any location where a consulate of a third country was established. Thus, if an American consulate opened in Kuwait, after concluding a consular convention with Egypt it would be impossible to prevent an Egyptian Consulate in Kuwait. Of course, after admitting Egypt it would be difficult to refuse Iraq. Kuwait would then become involved in Arab League affairs and 'in all the rivalries and intrigues' that divide the Arab states.[49]

The U.S. demand, he concluded, presented the British with a dilemma that they continued to hope Washington might resolve without establishing a consulate in Kuwait.

Washington undoubtedly shared some of London's concerns. The United States had no interest in introducing virulent strains of inter-Arab rivalry and politics into the relatively isolated Kuwaiti body politic; memories of Iraqi exploitation of the country's domestic troubles a decade earlier were still relatively fresh. Nevertheless, the needs and pressures on the Department of State were real and likely to grow. The "circuit rider" concept had been tried and proven ineffective. Short of a floating consulate on a U.S. vessel—which was evidently never seriously considered—there was no viable alternative to an American consulate on Kuwaiti soil. Washington, therefore, accepted the British proposal.[50]

Typically, the Department of State, having won British acquiescence in a consulate, was not ready to implement the arrangement expeditiously. Whether some department officials now entertained second thoughts or had not anticipated the practical problems of finding premises in the relatively undeveloped boomtown, many months were to pass before the first American consul was in place. In her excellent account of this episode, Joyce asserts that questions were raised of whether "the cost of establishing and maintaining a consulate would be out of proportion to the results...." This explanation of State Department behavior has the ring of authenticity.[51]

In any event, the ruler, Shaikh Ahmad, who had approved Anglo-American arrangements for the U.S. Consulate, passed away before it was staffed. The British political agent expressed concern on January 18, 1950 about the ruler's heart and the potential instability that could result from his death:

> *I am not at all happy about the question of succession here. I have no news of Abdulla Salim but presumably he cannot, even if he wanted to, come back quickly. Abdulla Mubarak is receiving at the Palace in ruler's stead and if the ruler were to die Abdulla Mubarak must be expected to try to succeed him.*[52]

Shaikh Ahmad ruled Kuwait for three of the most turbulent and momentous decades of its history—bracketed by the almost medieval battle of Jahra and the explosive development fueled by new oil wealth. He passed away January 29, 1950 with Dr. Lewis Scudder of the American Mission hospital as attending physician.[53] He had survived serious coronary thrombosis for eight years before suffering a second, fatal heart attack. Shaikh Ahmad was approximately sixty five years old.[54]

The ruler's sons, Jabir al-Ahmad and Sabah al-Ahmad, both of whom would succeed him after an interval, were also at his bedside. They were reportedly so affected by his death that they collapsed and were unable to appear in public until they had regained their composure several days later. Dr. Lewis Scudder and Mrs.

Dorothy Scudder took the young men into their home "on the hill" in the mission compound to give them the time and support they needed for recovery.[55]

During his long rule, their father had sometimes been opposed and reviled by elements of his own population, but more often was respected by the Kuwaitis for the steady hand with which he navigated the physical, political, and economic challenges of his time.[56] His political judgement and survival instincts had proven, at several junctures, more sound than those of many observers, including some of his British advisors. Now, he once again had the last laugh.

Expecting serious tension among the members of the Al-Sabah family, the British political resident predicted a power struggle "between the heir apparent Abdalla Salim..., Abdalla Mubarak (who controlled the Kuwaiti police and relations with the Bedouin), and the sons of Ahmad..."[57] The British moved military forces forward toward Kuwait and considered flying in troops. In London, the Foreign Office proposed withholding recognition of the new ruler until British advisors had approved the choice. Fortunately, such intervention proved unnecessary because it is far from clear what the popular reaction might have been in a country already beginning to chafe against foreign influence. Instead, the underlying stability of the Kuwaiti society again saw the state through this transition; the accession of Shaikh Abdallah Salem occurred peacefully, vindicating, perhaps, Shaikh Ahmad's farsightedness.

As soon as he received word of the death of the ruler, Clifton P. English, the American Consul in Basra, decided to travel to Kuwait immediately to offer condolences. His only option was to drive the hazardous one hundred mile track linking Kuwait. He decided not to try the trip at night and arrived in Kuwait on January 31, 1950. Although he was too late to attend the actual funeral, Mr. English became the first official American to be present at a state occasion in Kuwait.[58]

Changes in Kuwait over this tranformative period were not merely physical. Under the influence of oil wealth, the experience with representative institutions during the interwar decades, and the growing numbers of Kuwaitis, exposed to life abroad for educational and other activities, the traditional paradigm—ruling family, prominent merchant families, and tribal elements/minorities—was losing its sharp definition. An increasingly numerous and influential middle class mitigated traditional class and communal rivalries and bolstered the "fundamental national consensus."[59] Crystal argues, not entirely convincingly, that in the postwar years the merchant class withdrew from "formal political life":

> *Where economic elites once entered politics to protect their economic interests, after oil, merchants left the realm of formal politics to preserve those interests.*[60]

It was not so much that they withdrew from politics, as their future participation in parliamentary affairs would show.[61] What was occurring was that the stark juxtaposition of the merchants as the single pole challenging the ruling family was diluted by the emergence of the middle class, the increasing urbanization and educational levels of tribal elements, the mass influx of expatriates to support the petroleum industry, and other facets of rapid development. Masses of new workers poured into the country to meet the demand for manpower, from: Iran;[62] Iraq; Egypt; Syria; Lebanon; and Palestine. Further economic immigrants from India and Pakistan came somewhat later, giving the society a new and decidely more diverse complexion.

The task of dealing with this new society and the external ideas and influences the new expatriates brought with them, would fall to Shaikh Ahmad's successor.

Gallery B

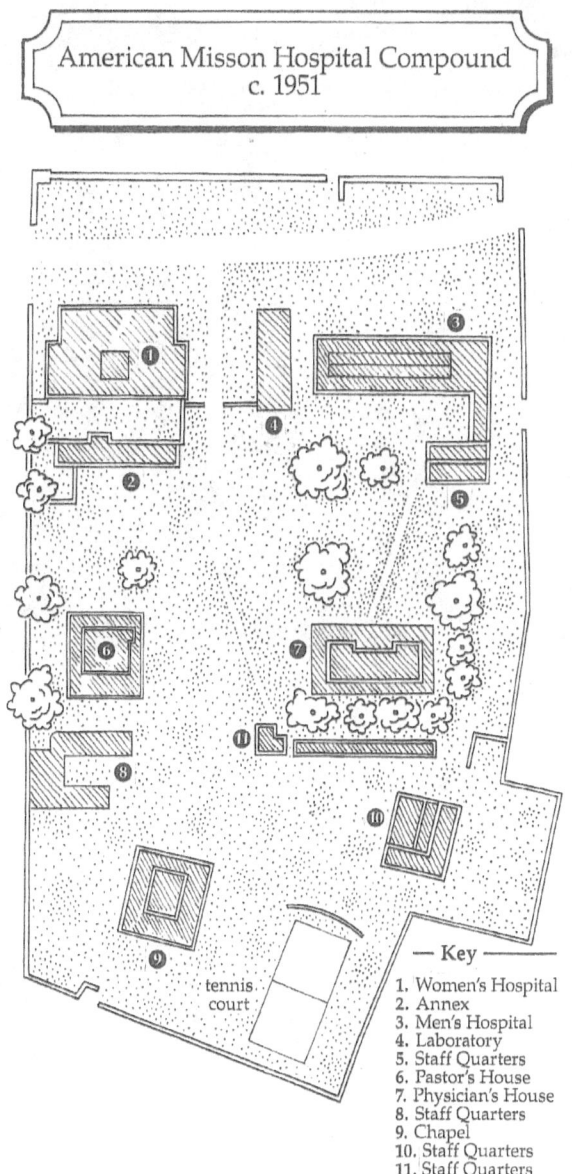

Diagram of the American Mission compound at the height of its influence in 1951. An expanded Men's Hospital was added in 1954 on the site of the first hospital. *Executed by Rick Britton from photographs and other sources.*

Unidentified U.S. Navy officers with prominent Kuwaitis during a port visit in the early 1950s. The central figure (to right of ship's captain) is Shaikh Fahad Salem al-Sabah, an early supporter of the American relationship. U.S. Consul Enoch Duncan stands at extreme left. The ship was probably the U.S.S. *Duxbury Bay*. *Dorothy Scudder papers*

Friends and colleagues gather in 1952 to bid farewell to C. A. P. Southwell, the American managing director of the Kuwait Oil Company (KOC). Americans, from executives to drillers and "roughnecks," participated in significant ways in developing Kuwait's oil industry. *Kuwait Oil Company*

Americans celebrate Independence Day at the oil company guesthouse in Ahmadi on July 4, 1953. Dr. Lewis Scudder, director of the American Mission Hospital, is seated at the table of four, to the left of the server. *American Embassy Kuwait archives*

The dedication of the Men's Hospital at the American Mission in 1954 was a major civic and social event that drew large numbers of Kuwaitis and expatriates. *Dorothy Scudder papers*

Dr. Lewis Scudder (second from left), director of the American Mission, presides over the head table at the dedication of the Mylrea Men's Hospital in 1954. Named for the iconic former director, Dr. Stanley Mylrea, who had recently died, the modern facility was completed at the zenith of the Mission's influence among Kuwaitis and expatriates alike. *Dorothy Scudder papers.*

For the 1954 dedication of the Mylrea Men's Hospital, the facade was festooned with flags. Shown here is the historic flag of Kuwait (red emblazoned in white with "Kuwait" in Arabic), flanked by the Union Jack (in recognition of Kuwait's status as a protectorate of Great Britain) and the Stars and Stripes, denoting the sponsorship of the American Mission medical facilities. *Dorothy Scudder papers*

Workers demolish the 1921 wall girding historic Kuwait to facilitate the expansion of the city in the 1950s. Spurred by development and the availability of oil wealth, the city quickly spread to take in open desert and outlying villages. *Kuwait Hilton Hotel Exhibition, February 1988*

[front row, from left:] Dr. Lewis Scudder, unidentified U.S. representative of the Foreign Mission board, and Shaikh Abdallah Al-Salem Al-Sabah, ruler of Kuwait, officiate at the dedication of Mylrea Men's Hospital in 1954. *Dorothy Scudder papers*.

After the advent of oil wealth, Safat Square continued to be a focus of commerce in the 1950s. Gone, however, are the bedu and their camels and donkeys. In their place new roads and parking lots have transformed the shopping center. *Kuwait Municipality*

The unprecedented development of the late 1940s and early 1950s included vast tracts of new housing in areas surrounding the historic city. Shown here are entire new neighborhoods to house the expanding Kuwaiti and expatriate populations. *Kuwait Municipality*

Consul Dayton Mak presenting his credentials as the chargé d'affaires of the U.S. Embassy in Kuwait, to the ruler, Sheikh Abdallah Salem al-Sabah, in September 1961. When Kuwait achieved independence, the American consulate was elevated to embassy status. Ambassador Parker Hart, resident in Jidda, was named the first ambassador to Kuwait and presented his credentials on a visit in January 1962. *American Embassy Kuwait archives*

Kuwait's first ambassador to the United States, Abdul Rahman al-Atiqi, with President John F. Kennedy in 1962. *American Embassy Kuwait archives*

7
Developers, Dissidents, and Diplomats

In accordance with local custom, Shaikh Ahmad al-Jabir was laid to rest on January 30, 1950, one day after his death. Shaikh Abdallah al-Salem Al-Sabah, the Heir Apparent, was not among the mourners arriving by boat from Oman on January 31.[1] The Reverend De Jong of the American Mission was among the "packed crowds" that gathered to honor the long-serving Shaikh Ahmad.[2] Shaikh Abdallah was confirmed as the ruler of Kuwait on February 25.[3] Representing the United States at his confirmation was Captain Anderson, commander of the U. S. Navy vessel *Maury*.[4] *Maury* and the British naval ship *Wren* fired salutes at noon to mark the occasion.

The new ruler would not serve as long as his predecessor, but Shaikh Abdallah would face challenges no less daunting. Spurred by the oil industry and the wealth it produced, the country was experiencing remarkable economic and population growth that would continue over the remainder of the decade. The city and environs resembled nothing so much as a gigantic workshop. A British anthropologist who conducted field work in Kuwait in the early 1950s, offered a vivid vignette of the area around Shuwaikh at the time:

> Half an hour after Jahra, we reached the outskirts of the city, and modern confusion began. We drove through a suburban shanty town, consisting mostly of reed hutments (barasti), with some cement buildings and corrugated iron roofs. In Col. Dickson's The Arab of the Desert, the suburb had been described as the home of Kuwait's semi-settled bedouin.[5]

Some recently settled bedouin may have remained in the area where the U.S. Army had recently overseen the assembly of barges, but the bulk of the inhabitants were immigrant laborers. They lived among "stacks of girders, planks, sewage pipes and cement bags, the noisy power generators, the smelly tar burners, and the gangs of labourerscarrying baskets of bricks and pans of mortar on their heads." Aside from the disruption and inconvenience of a development phase that was without precedent, the governmental mechanisms more suited to Kuwait's simpler past were strained and stressed beyond capacity by the requirements of planning and overseeing multiple major projects consuming millions of Pounds Sterling.

The British government sought to meet this new challenge, and insitutionalize their influence, by pressing the new ruler throughout his first years in power to accept larger numbers of British experts and advisors with limited success. In fact, the almost one-month delay in their formal recognition of Shaikh Abdullah was an effort to secure his agreement to these appointments. But, they had other concerns as well. As Kuwaitis were drawn ever closer to the nationalist currents coursing through the Arab world—from students studying in Arab capitals, the influx of Egyptians, Palestinians, and other Arabs who swelled the workforce, or vastly improved awareness of developments in the outside world[6]—the British began to sense that their special position in the country was eroding, as indeed it was. Placing additional British advisors in key administrative positions was viewed naively as an antidote to this erosion.

The heightened volatility of Kuwaiti society, including recurring demands for greater participation in decision-making, presented a challenge for Shaikh Abdallah who was simultaneously dealing with British pressure. While there is little indication that the United States sought to displace Britain's preeminence in the country, Washington did aspire to establish a consular presence there and to share in the projects on Kuwaiti drawing boards. For some British officials, however, American entry on the scene was viewed as less than benign. The documentary evidence of the period often makes this point explicitly, and it seems more than accidental that the local personalities of whom they complained to one another had at least one thing in common—an openness to American influence.

***

The U.S. government did not press ahead expeditiously with the opening of the consulate accepted in 1949. However, Consul English from Basra took advantage of his visit on the occasion of Shaikh Ahmad's death to meet with Shaikh Abdallah Salem on February 1, 1950.[7] In his subsequent dispatch to the Department of State, English reported that "Shaikh Salim [sic] was almost embarrassingly cordial." Judging that Shaikh Abdallah was pleased and "relieved" to receive an American official, English added that American representatives were encouraged to visit Kuwait more often. During the audience, James MacPherson, the AMINOIL chairman, arrived to assure Shaikh Abdallah that the resources of the company were at his disposal. In his comment on the events, English opined, astutely, that while the British position remained strong, Shaikh Abdallah Salem was maneuvering to avoid being viewed as controlled from London.[8]

Consul English's eventful visit to Kuwait in early 1950 may well have been instrumental in reinvigorating State Department efforts to locate a resident consul there. The rigors of road travel from Basra and the apparent warmth of Shaikh Abdallah Salem's welcome were powerful incentives to move forward. In any event, exploration of suitable locations for residences and offices was soon initiated. The challenge to find accommodations was by no means minor in a city undergoing a major transformation and simultaneously attempting to house the massive influx of needed workers. Initially, the Department of State informed the Foreign Office that a consul would be appointed by June 30, 1951. Although the projected date was later revised to August 1, Enoch S. Duncan actually arrived to take up his duties as the first American Consul on June 28.[9] He was undoubtedly under instructions not to exacerbate British sensitivities and reportedly informed the political agent that he did not intend to adopt anti-British positions.[10]

It is not possible today to locate precisely the site of the first U.S. Consulate because of subsequent redevelopment of the waterfront and the creation of a sweeping Corniche along the coast in the 1970s. We know that it was in the vicinity of and to the west of the American Mission.[11] The building occupied by the first consulate seems to have survived until the mid-1950s. A photograph of the dedication of the Mylrea Hospital in 1954, shown by Dorothy Scudder, apparently showed the corner of the structure in which the consulate was housed. The transcription of her slide talk reads:

> *This is the women's hospital... and behind that is where our first American Consulate was, you can see the house that they used.*[12]

The Olcott Women's Hospital, completed in 1939, still exists, so it is possible to approximate the site of America's first diplomatic mission.

The problem of appropriate facilities was solved by Shaikh Fahad, a prominent member of the Al-Sabah family who had visited the United States.[13] Shaikh Fahad al-Salem made available to Duncan, a traditional Kuwaiti house that reportedly belonged to one of his wives.[14] Duncan engaged a close friend of Shaikh Fahad, Salim Garabet—known as Abu Alwan—to be his interpreter. Garabet was an Iraqi national who had worked for the U.S. Army during World War II and maintained close relationships with American Mission hospital personnel.[15] He would appear, therefore, to have been a logical addition to the staff of the newly operational consulate.

Despite Consul Duncan's determination to avoid challenging Britain's special status, his very presence introduced a new dimension to the Kuwaiti scene, and the British attitude toward this development was decidedly mixed. Taking note of the friendly relationship between Duncan and Shaikh Fahad (whom the British had long found to be troublesome), the political agency shrugged off the association as giving the Shaikh something to preoccupy him.[16] Nevertheless, regional British officials speculated that Duncan was naive and probably did not recognize the "risks he may run" by becoming closely identified with the Shaikh whom they described as "both unruly and unpopular."[17]

The opening of the first American Consulate in 1951 coincided with heightened British angst and frustration. Kuwaiti society was greatly changed by increasing currents of Arab nationalism and vastly improved access to news about developments in the Arab world and beyond.[18]

Kuwaitis were travelling and studying abroad with greater

frequency and bringing back with them experiences and ideas that were previously unknown in the state. Nationalism and identification with broader Arab issues easily translated into open opposition to continued foreign tutelage. These elements confronted the ruler with difficulties almost from the beginning of his term, but for the British they represented a direct challenge; in the early 1950s, the staff of the British Political Residency was enlarged substantially.

Alongside the rising sentiment in opposition to the British protectorate, Britain was also concerned with the chaos that attended the early phases of Kuwait's development. The traditional mechanisms of Kuwaiti administration were clearly overtaxed by the multiple projects and huge expenditures that oil wealth made possible. Real or exaggerated problems of corruption, waste, and incompetence filled British memoranda and reports of the period, as well as a growing determination to overcome them, and to shore up its domestic position by pressing for the assignment of British "experts" to key financial, planning, and oversight positions. There is little evidence in the early 1950s that they considered the contradiction between defusing criticism of their influence and increasing the role and visibility of British decision makers.

The American Consulate's arrival did not create the problems faced by the British, but it easily became another indicator of threat to their fortunes and a convenient scapegoat for frustrations. Duncan's presence was clearly associated in some minds with the other adverse trends with which the British were contending. While exonerating Consul Duncan from responsibility, a British contemporary expressed the view that:

> ... *certain elements in Kuwait Town, led by Shaikh Fahad al Salim, tried to adopt him as the focus of an 'American' party of Kuwaitis in opposition to, or, at least, divided from, the British. Nothing much, except a good deal of talk, resulted but it might cause trouble, without necessarily benefiting the Americans. The numerical justification for the post in the numbers of American citizens is as exiguous as ever.*[19]

The final comment suggests that some British officials continued to believe that the American Consulate had been pushed by the Department of State for spurious reasons that were related, perhaps, to the broad American position in opposition to remnants of colonialism. While Kuwaiti nationalists probably welcomed other friendly powers within the country, the implicit suggestion that they were interested in trading Britain's strong influence for America's speaks eloquently of the British mindset at that time. For whatever reasons, the British who were engaged at the time of Consul Duncan's arrival in planning for the security of Kuwait's oil infrastructure against internal attack, decided against involving the American Consulate.[20]

The British dilemma, as well as its associated sensitivities, was intensified by the fact that the underlying equation of the relationship with Kuwait had changed fundamentally. Kuwait was still dependent upon British protection as its ultimate defense against the designs of neighboring states, but, since the beginning of the oil age, Great Britain had seen its interest there change from a strategic convenience to a vital economic asset. In fact, the dependence was now mutual, and it is therefore understandable that the British were intent upon checkmating potential rivals and identifying those who might undermine their position.

For some years, they had identified Shaikh Fahad al Salem as a thorn in their sides. Now, in addition to other charges against this influential figure, he began to be associated in their minds with a potential American challenge.

They were, in fact, correct that Shaikh Fahad had shown himself to be favorably disposed toward the Americans in Kuwait. He had been on friendly terms with the personnel of the American Mission since childhood and, through them, arranged for the education of his children. When the first American oilmen arrived in Kuwait in the 1930s, he welcomed them warmly. It was no surprise, therefore, when he embraced the American Consulate in 1951. Whether or not his primary goal was "to supplement or replace British skills and services with American expertise,"[21] there can be little doubt that his feelings for the American people were genuine. In the 1980s, I was reminded by Kuwaitis that Shaikh Fahad expressed the view that "the Americans came here to help us when we had nothing."[22]

Shaikh Fahad was the first senior member of the Al-Sabah family to visit the United States as well.[23] He was welcomed and feted by the Department of State as well as the Gulf Oil Company. Every indication is that the experience deepened his friendly feelings for America; as he departed to return to Kuwait, he took the time to write from the Savoy Plaza Hotel in New York City to Under Secretary of State George C. McGhee. He closed with the wish that God would bless "America and her people."[24] Shaikh Fahad's tour of the United States was considered significant enough to rate inclusion in the political agency's "Administrative Report for 1951":

> *Fahad al Salim returned in the beginning of the year from his protracted trip to Europe and the United States where he was given civic receptions and presented with the keys of no less than eight towns. Though darker and more 'negroid' than most American negroes, he was also photographed drinking beer at a fashionable beach resort in Virginia.*[25]

It is informative to note that the British establishment, frustrated in their attempt to fortify their own position in Kuwait, was not only keen to identify individuals under the influence of American interests,[26] but believed they could find lessons from the success of Shaikh Fahad's American visit. Later, when Shaikh Abdallah, whom the British also considered a spoiler, expressed a wish to visit Great Britain, a British document worried that he might also decide to include the United States on his itinerary. This would be "unfortunate," it commented, "because the experience of Shaikh Fahad has shown that Kuwaitis do not take kindly to the United Kingdom if they go there after visiting the United States."[27]

The most serious and self-defeating flaw in British policy in the early 1950s, however, was the underestimation and misunderstanding of the new ruler. That this should have been the case is all the more startling because Shaikh Abdallah had been a player on the Kuwaiti political scene for over three decades. On the death of his father, the ruler, in 1921, Abdallah had stepped in as temporary ruler until Shaikh Ahmad al-Jabir returned from abroad where he then stepped aside in his cousin's favor.[28] During the agitation in the late 1930s for popular participation in governmental decisions,

Shaikh Abdallah was more sympathetic to the "reformers" than Shaikh Ahmad and many family members of his generation:

> As criticism of the government increased, Abdallah became the patron of a movement aimed at introducing wide-ranging reforms and a system of government that would restrict the powers of the ruler. Awkwardly placed between the reformists and his relatives, Abdallah behaved with great tact, particularly in 1938 when he presided over a Legislative Assembly that the ruler had authorized with extreme reluctance. ...Abdallah headed another abortive council and played an ambiguous role in the events preceding March, 1939 when Ahmad I reasserted his full authority.[29]

And finally, before and during World War II, Shaikh Abdallah had been accused of "pro-Axis leanings" which may have given the British pause that he might not be amenable to their goal of "controlling" Kuwait's development into a full-fledged oil state."[30] They were correct to be concerned, for Shaikh Abdallah was clearly a Kuwaiti—and at least, by inclination, an Arab—nationalist with reformist tendencies and a determination to maximize Kuwaiti control of its affairs within the framework of the British protectorate.[31] In the final analysis, the British could not identify a more malleable alternative and accepted Abdallah al-Salem despite clear misgivings.

In this atmosphere, Duncan and his successors attacked the substantial, practical, and logistical challenges of establishing the consulate. The U.S. Consulate in Basra played an important supporting role in the process. On December 19, 1950, the Department of State asked that Vice Consul Robert E. Moberly make inquiries about available residential and office space in Kuwait on his next monthly visit there. In carrying out its instructions, the diplomat from Basra indicated that he would enlist the advice and assistance of the American Independent Oil Company already on the ground there. Department of State records do not report the details of these consultations, but on June 27, 1951 Basra informed Washington that Consul-designate Enoch S. Duncan had proceeded to Kuwait following several days of consultations in Basra.[32]

It was not until October of 1951 that the first shipment of essential office equipment and supplies arrived in Kuwait. By that time, a building had been prepared for the initial consulate. Two rooms were fitted out as office space and the rest of the house served as living quarters for an unidentified foreign service clerk detached temporarily from Basra.[33] Sources agree that Consul Duncan and his wife lived in the vicinity of the present-day Sheraton Hotel. His house was outside the Jahra Gate and near the KOC Guesthouse.[34]

Within a short time, the consulate rented a larger building outside the town and on the shore from Shaikh Abdallah Jabir, who later became the minister of commerce and industry.[35] These premises were used for offices and quarters for the principal officer until 1961, when all operations were moved to a new compound near Bneid al-Gar. Harry Symmes, who suceeded Duncan, moved into the "villa" immediately and provided details about its amenities. Four rooms used as offices were connected by a corridor to the "residence," consisting of two bedrooms with baths, a living room, and a dining room. Cooking facilities were located under a tin shed on the roof. A water tank on the roof connected to the bathrooms and sinks; "It was our practice to draw water for baths early in the morning so that it would be cool enough for a bath in the late afternoon," Symmes remembered. Located one-half mile outside the town wall, the consulate was protected by several Kuwaiti policemen seeking whatever shade they could find. The consulate was connected to the town electrical grid in 1952–53.[36]

A major priority for the new consul was the acquisition of adequate apartments for the vice consul and the American clerk. Unfortunately, the Department of State appeared less than eager to assist. It took Symmes months of effort to induce a representative from the State Department's Foreign Buildings Office (FBO) to travel to Kuwait to survey the haphazard collections of furnishings and to approve construction of rental apartments for the staff. The obstacles he faced included the necessity of disabusing FBO of the idea of adopting a "Hawaiian design."[37] Finally, however, the new staff residence was leased at a location inside the wall near Dasman Palace in 1954, and the Consulate building was refurbished at the same time.[38] In 1956 and again in 1957, the consulate rented employee residences in the vicinity of the Dasman Palace to accomodate additional personnel.[39]

***

Kuwait Town had not yet shed its historic personna when Harry Symmes arrived in 1953, although it was on the verge of transformation. As he saw it then, the town was "an assemblage of mud buildings encircled by a mud wall alongside a large bay—treeless except for a few spots of green around what I was to learn were Dasman Palace and the British Political Agency—an unpaved airport with a small mud building—a web of vehicle tracks going from the town and from the airport aimlessly, it seemed into the desert surroundings."[40] He was met at the airport by the consulate official car, a rusting Chevrolet sedan scarred by blowing sand and sporting two overlarge flags on the front fenders.[41]

Although the American community had grown by several orders of magnitude with the influx of oil executives and workers, the number living in Kuwait Town was still limited.[42] The consulate enjoyed cordial and supportive relationships with the Scudders at the American Mission, as well as L. T. Jordan, the American head of KOC and "Mac" MacPherson of AMINOIL.[43] In contrast, despite his success in eventually generating action by the Foreign Buildings Office, Consul Symmes remained bitter at the reluctant and delayed support the new post received from the Department of State. In the midst of the post's struggle to establish itself on a sound and sustainable basis, for example, the department imposed a 30 percent cut in all Foreign Service posts:

> *Looking back on the administrative support we received, I am still resentful at the grudging way in which it was supplied, as well as by the general failure of NEA to appreciate how important it was to our national interest to have a properly functioning post in the rapidly changing political situation.*[44]

Consulate communications were an additional irritant. Kuwait was primarily dependent on weekly diplomatic pouches to and from Washington. This link was frequently routed through the Consulate-General in Dhahran, Saudi Arabia, several hours away by desert track.[45] Pouch schedules were neither reliable nor timely because of limited plane schedules and the vagaries of the local weather, but Washington frowned on the use of telegraphic communications which were sent through cable and wireless "at great expense."[46] The Consulate did not have a telephone until at least 1955.[47]

The consulate's relations with Kuwaitis were good. Harry Symmes attributed the warm reception accorded the first American diplomats, in large part, to the atmosphere established by the American Mission over the previous forty years:

The American Mission Hospital was highly respected and loved by the ruling family and the townspeople. In a concrete way it exemplified American virtues and ways of doing things....

He felt this factor was important in blunting negative reactions to the creation of the State of Israel and the perceived injustice done to the Palestinian refugees or rare incidents involving American seamen or oil workers. Concern with the Arab-Israeli problem, however, was kept alive by the influx of large numbers of Palestinians into Kuwait in search of employment: By 1953, Kuwait had become, in some respects, analogous to Beirut: a haven for exiles, malcontents, entrepreneurs, and political operators."[48] To this potentially volatile mixture was added Muslim Brothers (*Ikhwan al-Muslimeen*) from Egypt as a result of Gamal Abdel Nasser's crackdown on the organization.

Unlike the Europeans and Americans at Ahmadi who had little contact with Kuwaitis and other Arabs, consulate personnel developed personal and professional relationships with Kuwaiti society. Vice Consul William A. Stoltzfus, Jr., (1954 to 1956) and ambassador in the 1970s, later reminisced fondly about members of the ruling family who were especially hospitable to the consulate personnel.[49] Among those he singled out were Shaikh Abdullah al-Jabir,[50] Shaikh Fahad al-Salim, head of the Public Works Department,[51] and Jabir al-Ali.[52] Kuwaiti society, with its long tradition of *diwanniyas*, was then, as now, unique in the Arab world for the accessibility of a wide range of Kuwaiti personalities. In the early 1950s, it was even more informal than it later became and, on feast days, British and American representatives made a lengthy series of calls on the ruler, shaikhs, and "heads of old town families and notables." On July 4, Christmas, and New Year's day, Kuwaiti officials and important town residents reciprocated with calls on the U.S. consul.[53]

William D. Brewer, son-in-law of John Van Ess of the Arabian Mission, replaced Harry Symmes as the U. S. Consul in 1955. The consulate was firmly established and growing when he arrived but there were still important refinements that claimed his attention. Building on the efforts of his predecessor to engage the Department of State with deficiencies in Kuwait, Brewer oversaw improvements to the consulate premises; enhancing functionality and representational posibilities. Among his projects were the addition of a proper kitchen next to the dining room, a third bedroom, and convincing the Department of State to install modern window airconditioners to replace "huge Remington consoles that provided more psychological than physical relief."[54]

Several houses were built near the consulate during the late 1950s but the complex remained remote from the town. There was no paved road until the main route to Salmiyyah, and "depending on the season, sand or mud was sometimes a real hazard."[55]

Bill Brewer continued the close cooperative relationship with KOC, whose manager and all members of the Oil Operations Group (responsible for extracting the oil) were Americans. He had more difficulty with senior British officials who visited from London. Their inclination was to deal only with the British political agent on essential business and ignore the American Consulate. Over time, his efforts enjoyed some success in breaking down the reserve of London-based company officials. He also visited AMINOIL and Getty operations in the Kuwait/Saudi Neutral Zone (which were within his consular district) several times, and invited Americans there to consulate functions, but had only sporadic contact with the two American operating oil companies—AMINOIL and Getty.[56]

The American community in Kuwait, while not large in absolute numbers, had grown significantly since the mid-1940s and would continue to be augmented over the next ten years. It was by no means as tight-knit or as plugged into Kuwaiti society as it had been when the personnel of the American Mission Hospital defined it. But, with an American Consulate in place, the community's profile was higher than it had been.

Long-established missionaries and medical personnel still provided an element of continuity and credibility to the American community as individuals associated with petroleum, construction firms, and the Department of State swelled in numbers. Despite the new Kuwaiti medical facilities that were opening in the town, the influx of workers (both American and non-American) stressed the personnel and facilities of the mission hospital immensely.

> *The 1950s ... saw a massive influx of migrant workers, a mechanization of trans-desert travel, and a mental breakthrough as well. People who only a decade earlier would never have considered abandoning village or tribal medical practices and who considered foreigners and Christians to be unclean, now began to attend the mission's clinics in droves. The number of cases treated jumped fantastically, and people who once were merely overworked were now inundated by the demands placed upon them. There was the old Christian physician's habit of not being able to say no to a person in need, and there seemed to be no way to slow the voracious demand that had suddenly developed. Physical facilities were taxed to the breaking point, and medical professionals were strained beyond levels of normal endurance.*[57]

The passage of the years as well as operational strain were taking their toll of long-serving mission personnel. Some retired and were replaced and others were periodically absent on leave, but a major blow occurred in January, 1952. The redoubtable Dr. Stanley Mylrea passed away while on one of his regular visits to Kuwait. He was staying at the "house on a hill" on the mission compound that had been his residence for so many years. Having served the American Mission from its inception and Kuwait through critical decades of its history, he was fittingly buried in a small Christian cemetery just outside the old wall. His simple headstone reads "The Son of Man came not to be ministered unto, but to minister...."[58]

The American Mission, which remained an integral part of Kuwaiti society,[59] was more focused on the future than its history. In 1952, it was busily planning for the construction of a new men's hospital. The same year, the mission purchased a small shop on the edge of the covered *suq*, a mile and a half from the compound.

These premises had been leased for years as a religious bookstore and reading room where the *colporteurs* could receive and interact with their contacts.⁶⁰

Since the mid-1940s (See Chapter 6), the American mission had been collecting funds and laying plans for the new hospital building. Buoyed by the outpouring of Kuwaiti support, both financial and moral, the Kuwait station envisaged a truly modern facility—fully enclosed and centrally air-conditioned. The opposition they encountered came from church officials in the United States and presaged a continuing troublesome relationship for the future. The governing Board of Missions appears not to have fully appreciated the affection and esteem in which Kuwaitis held the American Mission.⁶¹ Even though the finances for the new hospital would come from local sources, Henry Bovenkerk, who was in charge of financial affairs for the board, insisted that central air conditioning was a conceit and demanded that the plans be revised; "The main wards were not to be air conditioned. Central air conditioning was applied only to the central block—doctors' offices, waiting rooms, operating theaters, laboratories, xray, and two private care patient rooms." As a consequence of his insistence on this point, almost as soon as the new hospital was opened, it had to be retrofitted with air conditioning units that gave it a patched appearance. The new building became, in the words of the chronicler of the American Mission, a monument to "how micromanagement from a remote position could not only be short-sighted, but prejudicial to the mission's best interests."⁶²

The funding for the new hospital, which would be named the Mylrea Memorial Hospital, came largely from the people of Kuwait. The ruler, Shaikh Abdullah Al-Salim made the largest single contribution, but other prominent Kuwaitis, including Abdullah al-Uthman, a leading Muslim spiritual figure, either made donations to the fund or endowed expensive diagnostic machines, or wards, such as that for indigent patients.⁶³ By any measure, the campaign to fund and build the new hospital was remarkable, all the more because it took place at a time when the American Mission was no longer the only modern medical facility in Kuwait. In the words of one who was present in that exciting time, the effort "brought together in one intent the aspirations of the mission and the hope and good will of the Kuwaiti Muslim community. A genuine sense of shared values was involved, and the Kuwaitis again adopted the mission as their own."⁶⁴

The Mylrea Memorial Hospital was located on the site of the old hospital at the northern edge of the compound, facing the Gulf. It opened officially on October 8, 1955 in the presence of the ruler and a host of prominent Kuwaitis and Americans.⁶⁵ The American Mission, headed by Dr. Lewis R. Scudder, made extensive preparations for the festivities, spreading oriental carpets over the tennis courts for the guests, with flags (Kuwaiti, American, and British) and a celebratory meal:

> *The Mylrea Memorial Hospital was dedicated at the time of the mission's full annual meeting. I remember the event as a whirlwind of activity. The full assembly of the mission (children included), along with all of Kuwait's notables, high brass from the local expatriate community, and Henry Bovenkerk... made for a massive affair. In spite of its design drawbacks (upon which Bovenkerk had insisted), opening the new hospital was deemed a worthy achievement.*⁶⁶

It is difficult to overstate the symbolic significance of this moment at a difficult and sometimes troubled era in Kuwait's development. Through decades of dedicated service and good works, the members of the American Mission had shared Kuwaiti travails and joys and had woven bonds between the two peoples of a quality and intimacy rarely achieved. How sad that the mission board in the United States had not grasped the fact that what its station in Kuwait had accomplished was more transformational and enduring than a small number of conversions. The Kuwaitis and Americans were strangers no more!

The opening of the new hospital was followed in the 1950s by other less dramatic changes to the mission compound. Lighting was added to the tennis courts, and a rented building on the eastern boundary, used for housing missionaries, was demolished to make way for a new roadway running along the entire shoreline; it was replaced in 1957 by a new building at the northeast corner of the 1931 chapel. The following year, the capacity of the chapel itself, which was serving increasing numbers of European, Arab, and South Asian Christians, was doubled by the addition to the east of an activities hall. The sanctuary was refurbished at that time with rosewood pews and chancel furniture produced by the industrial school of the Arcot Mission at Kadpadi in South India.[67] These were important improvements, but not on the scale of the new hospital which would be recalled as "among the last major celebrative events of the mission."[68]

Kuwait's oil resources generated both great wealth and unprecedented change in a very short period, but it could not, in itself, assure happiness and stability. Though his people were already benefiting from amenities—abundant water, reliable electric power, growing opportunities for education—that were unimaginable a scant few years earlier, the first years of Shaikh Abdallah Al-Salem's rule were difficult and troubled. Furthermore, its oil wealth "made Kuwait politically insecure and dramatically aggravated the ambitions of its powerful neighbors."[69] At the same time, the country's oil wealth made maintenance of Britain's control more crucial to London at the very time that its grip was slipping.[70]

The British experience in attempting to impose greater influence over Kuwait's internal affairs—an area that had not been contemplated under the "protectorate" arrangement—was not a happy one. Having failed in a ploy to exchange their recognition of Shaikh Abdallah as ruler for acceptance of multiple British advisors in 1951, the British government persisted in these efforts over the next few years. The ruler parried their pressures and entreaties with a skill that preserved the British relationship and protection while earning him a reputation as indecisive by some British officials. He agreed to accept financial (Col. G. C. L. Crichton) and customs (H. L. Roper) experts in 1951[71] and a retired Indian Army officer (Major General Hasted) to advise on the massive development program. But he temporized, delayed and ignored the British when they pressed him to appoint senior British advisors to decision-making positions. In 1953, when these and other pressures on the ruler reached a crescendo, rumors circulated that Shaikh Abdallah Al Salem was thinking of abdication.[72]

In reviewing the documentary record of the period, it is difficult not to conclude that H.M.'s Government was either tone deaf to the advice of its Middle East specialists, or was not well served by officials on the ground. Dickson, Shakespear and other early political residents and agents, would doubtless have quickly recognized the Kuwaiti "No" and the basis for it. Instead, however, a "Kuwait Working Party" was assembled in London and even the prime minister, Sir Winston Churchill, was enlisted in the unsuccessful effort to convince the ruler to acquiesce in an expansion of British control over Kuwaiti decisions during his visit to London for the coronation of Queen Elizabeth II.[73]

Whatever the contributions of British missteps, the massive development program was in genuine need of institutional and administrative reform. The scope and value of construction was unprecedented not merely in Kuwait's experience but Great Britain's as well. The rudimentary government that evolved when Kuwait was a simple town was not capable of coping with the requirements of planning, coordination, financial oversight, and the control of corruption on a massive scale.[74] Roads, schools, housing, and other infrastructure were being completed at a rapid pace; the first government plant for water distillation began operation at Shuwaikh in 1953 and a power station was completed a year later.[75] But there were more than the usual teething problems. The power plant had to be reworked in 1958, and at least one imposing school building was completed without electrical wiring or pipes for water.[76] More serious, however, was the state of the Kuwaiti treasury and the frustration, anger, and mutual recrimination gripping the country:

> *By 1953, anger and concern were mounting over Kuwait's deteriorating situation. For the astonishing truth was that, despite all the new wealth, Kuwait was approaching the brink of bankruptcy. Many leading shaikhs, with the exception of the abstemious ruler, were charged with plundering public assets and ignoring the people's rights. Others, including the shaikhs' partners in the merchant community, were denounced for dealing with the notorious 'Big Five' companies that were dominating the development programme and making unseemly profits through contracts based on the questionable 'cost plus' principle.[77]*

The sheer volume of spending injected into the economy created huge inflationary pressures that undermined the public's sense of well-being.[78]

The details of the British struggle to overcome resistance to their effort to seize greater control over the organization and implementation of Kuwaiti development are beyond the scope of this narrative. It is noteworthy, however, that their hopes foundered not just on the resistance of the ruler and others in the hierarchy, but also their own mistakes, including the suitability of the "advisors" they succeeded in placing within the Kuwaiti administration. As early as 1952, the British Political Agent drew attention to difficulties with Crichton and Hasted.[79] Hasted, however, was much the greater problem. His brusque, martinet manner and lack of cultural sensitivity alienated the Kuwaitis and, eventually, the British establishment itself. By the following year, the more admirable Crichton was moved to send him an extremely frank and critical letter regarding his performance.[80] Hasted was not above feeding British suspicions of American influence to account for his difficulties. Eventually, his British contacts learned to discount his claims and explanations:

> *Hasted reports a move on the part of Fahad, Izzat Jaafar, and group of supporters, which he alleges is designed to wrest control of the placing of contracts from the hands of his department. They would then, it is reported, be put out to world tenders to bring in Americans and others 'who would live in tents'... Fahad and his group are said to be in the pay of American interests... There is no evidence for any of this....*[81]

The drama of the British campaign to implant powerful advisors into the Kuwaiti decision-making process was poisoned further when the behavior and huge profits of the British companies that had dominated early construction became a public issue. The British decision to mobilize five of their large concerns, each associated with a Kuwaiti partner, at the outset of development probably made sense given the pressures to begin construction quickly and the virtually unlimited need for infrastructure. To encourage the companies to deploy the men and equipment required for these large undertakings, they were accorded extremely generous terms—cost plus 15 percent—and guarantees of further work. By the mid-1950s, they were firmly ensconced, fully employed, and continuing to benefit from exceptionally remunerative terms. At least some of the companies had come to view their advantageous position as an entitlement. Against the backdrop of growing nationalist sentiment within the country, the issue came to a head. To the other sources of dissatisfaction with MG Hasted was added the charge that he was "directing lucrative contracts and special privileges to his fellow countrymen."[82] The American consul reported that priority in construction appears to have been accorded to housing and other amenities for expatriate workers.[83] To their credit, some British officials seem to concede that "Big Five" firms had brought this negative attention on themselves by their avaricious behavior.[84]

The controversy over the "Big Five" companies resonated in Kuwait on several levels. For nationalists, beginning a flirtation with Arab nationalism and, especially, Gamal Abdel Nasser's influence in Egypt, the situation was symbolic of foreign domination and what they believed was their ruler's acquiescence in British control. For those concerned with the success and cost of the development program, including some British officials, it was seen as an example of greed, extravagance, and a sense of entitlement by the companies involved. For Kuwaiti merchants and notables not associated with the "Big Five," it was regarded as a case of an unfair distribution of opportunities and profits from development. For many others it was further evidence of the hidden agenda of General Hasted and the British advisors.[85]

Some action to assuage these converging criticisms was inescapable; the "Big Five" companies were allowed to carry on with their existing contracts but excluded from the next round of projects, including the lucrative port project. Expanding and modernizing the port and cutting a deeper channel through the rocky harbor bottom were major priorities since congested piers and overfull warehouses were limiting the pace of overall development.[86] The affected British firms did not accept the Kuwaiti decision easily. They enlisted the support of their government to press the ruler to reverse the decision to move to open competition. Shaikh Abdallah Al-Salem not only did not budge but, according to the political agent's report of the conversation:

> *The ruler replied that my remark forced him to reveal some of his secrets which he has kept to himself for fear of being thought boastful. It was he (mistakenly) who had got 15 percent for British firms when the Education Committee wanted to give them only 10 percent. The members of the Committee thereupon resigned. He had also resisted the effort of Westinghouse to get the contract for the supply of the second distillation plant, and had seen that it went to Weirs of Glasgow.[87]*

By the mid-1950s, Britain's effort to strengthen its participation in Kuwait's internal affairs through the appointment of powerful advisors had foundered. In part, the exercise was undermined by a certain arrogance,[88] and the personal behavior of the British incumbents which Kuwait had accepted. In the main, however, it failed because of the skilful evasion of the ruler and the outright opposition of other figures in the Kuwaiti establishment. Shaikh Abdallah Al-Salem's achievement in evading pressure while maintaining cordial relations with British representatives was notable. As he exerted his authority not only vis-à-vis Great Britain but also over other members of the Al-Sabah, intentionally or not, the British underestimated this ruler,[89] who presided over "the emergence of a new state structure"[90] more suited to managing a modern state.

In mid-decade, some knowledgeable British experts showed an awareness that their special status was likely unsustainable.[91], British Political Agent Sir Gawain Bell, who served from 1955 to 1957, advocated the institution of a representative government and some governmental functions, such as control over stamps and post offices were transferred to the Kuwaiti government. A Kuwaiti bank, formed by ten Kuwaitis, was chartered by the ruler in 1952[92] and within a few years Kuwait adopted its own currency, replacing the Indian Rupee in use since the days of the Raj.

Faced with the evolving situation, Britain fell back on the political agency as its primary instrument and line of communication in the country. The agency was upgraded and additional staff were assigned, and it was given a direct organizational line to the London Foreign Office, bypassing the political resident in Manama, Bahrain. Despite this enhancement, there are circumstantial indications that the political agent's historically intimate relationship with the ruler and other Kuwaiti notables had deteriorated, perhaps under the strains of the campaign to install advisors. In a report dated September 16, 1954, the political agent wrote:

> *I have the honour to report the formation of a union amongst employees of the Kuwait Government. I had not heard of its existence until a few days ago I was given a copy of the constitution by Mr. Symmes, the U.S. Consul. At the same time reference to it was made in Sada al-Iman, the newspaper which was published by the National Cultural Club at the beginning of this month but which has since been suspended....*
>
> *Mr. Symmes tells me that he obtained his copy of the union's constitution from a former employee at the U.S. Consulate who had previously been dismissed by the Kuwait Oil Company for trying to form a union amongst their employees. This man has told Mr. Symmes that the long term aim of the union is to replace all foreigners including non-Kuwaiti Arabs who are holding important positions in departments of the Kuwait Government. He claims that they have already forced several dismissals including in one department that of a British section director....*[93]

Times were clearly changing, and with them, the relationship between a more assertive Kuwait and their British protector. This was not, however, the only change challenging Kuwait and its inhabitants during this critical phase of its transition.

8

Road to Independence

The decade of the 1950s brought changes for residents of Kuwait that were without precedence in their scope and rapidity. The town underwent physical transformation through development that irreversibly altered its shape. Scarcely less wrenching were the pressures on traditional society generated by substantial population growth as non-Kuwaitis—Arab, Western, and South Asian—flooded the country in response to needs and opportunities. Life for many residents improved as new infrastructure and conveniences came on line, but Kuwaitis were challenged to both adjust and forced to contemplate which facets of their culture they would refuse to surrender to preserve their sense of identity, integrity, and cohesion. In retrospect, Kuwait was moving toward independence and membership in the Arab world less quickly than many nationalists of the period desired, but more rapidly than most realized at the time. Such transitional eras are inherently unstable and Kuwait was no exception to this rule.[1]

The town had, by this time, spilled out well beyond the third city wall built in response to the Ikhwani threat in the 1920s. Although it still girded the city's core, it no longer shut the world out nightly, as it had done as late as 1939.[2] The oil company town at Ahmadi created, for the first time in Kuwait's history, a second important population center. But it was the development of suburbs around the walled city that opened up the society geographically, economically, and psychologically. In fact, the pace of expansion was outstripping even the imagination of planners and dreamers.

The initial designs for the redevelopment of the city concentrated first on the area within the walls. Drawn up by British firms in April, 1951, the plan envisaged cutting new, modern avenues and widening and improving some of the narrow alleyways that criss-crossed the historic town. Naif Avenue was to become that "Whitehall" of Kuwait, providing spaces for government offices. By early the following year, however, the consultants had concluded that plan was somewhat out of date because it did not encompass a wide enough area:

> *The city is already tending to spread outside the walls, and will, in a comparatively short time, spread from Kuwait to Dimna, including Shuwaikh. It is therefore of the utmost importance to control, plan, and develop those areas before it is too late and they grow into areas of congestion such as now exist within the walled city. However, if this is done immediately and housing estates erected, it will provide alternative accommodations for those whose houses have to be demolished within the walled city to make roads, etc., thus causing the least dislocation and distress to the people.*[3]

Outside the perimeter, more than twenty areas were sketched out, each identified by a letter from "A" to "W" and a notional indication of its primary use—"port," "residential," "hospital," and so forth.[4]

More than two thousand houses within the wall were scheduled for demolition in order to create space for roads and other infrastructure. The displacement of a significant percentage of inhabitants made construction of replacement housing in the designated growth areas an urgent priority. Developers estimated that a minimum of five thousand housing units were required in the shortest possible time, with a total of ten thousand units in the coming five years, to make a dent in the existing housing shortage. Thereafter, an additional five hundred to one thousand residences a year would be needed "to meet expanding population, and raised standards of living."[5]

To many Kuwaitis and long-term American and other expatriates, it must have seemed that the world they had known was being turned upside down. To be sure, oil wealth, and the amenities it could purchase, made life more pleasant, but these advantages were not immediately accessible. In the meantime, it was necessary to endure the dislocation, inconvenience, and psychological trauma of the construction phase. Familiar neighborhoods and homes were torn down in wholesale lots to make it possible to drive wide avenues through the town. "New Street," (*al-Sharia al-Jadid*) capable of carrying automotive traffic from the old dhow harbor near the American Mission compound to the *Safat*, was one of the first fruits of the disruption.[6] "Progress" almost always comes at a price, however. Many old houses and the sense of neighborhood were lost in the process – and even worse was to come. In 1957, it was decided to tear down the city walls, which had been so intimately associated with Kuwait's identity, dangers, and triumphs.[7] Vestiges of the Jahra and other gates, as well as several historic homes, were saved as reminders of a shared heritage.

The crucial issues of identity and adjustment to sweeping cultural change were, in essence, psychological, hence, largely invisible to outside observers. A hint of what was surely occurring beneath the surface is provided, however, by the national choice of clothing. After the Second World War and into the following decade, many Kuwaiti men shed their traditional *dishdashas* in favor of denim overalls and were hardly distinguishable from Palestinians and Persians wearing shirts and trousers.[8]

Over the next several years, as if by common accord, the trend reversed:

> *Students put their suits away and changed back into local dress. Kuwaiti dress had now become a mark of identity, a signal announcing that the wearer was Kuwaiti, one of the people who belonged there in Kuwait (ahl al-bilad) and, even more important, that the wearer was not an immigrant.*[9]

Preserving their sartorial heritage was an important assertion of identity and continuity in a sea of change.

While the city changed around it, the American Mission hospital and compound remained rooted where they were first laid out in 1911. The only significant project was the addition in October, 1958 of a "parish hall" that effectively doubled the capacity of the chapel.[10] As a consequence of the influx of foreign workers, the mission was ministering to growing numbers of newly resident Christians, including a significant congregation of Arabs from Lebanon, Palestine, and elsewhere.[11] The American Consulate, however, did not have similar deep roots and was eventually moved to newly built facilities in the suburb of Bneid al-Gar, outside the old wall.

The early years of Shaikh Abdallah's tenure as ruler posed serious challenges quite aside from the thrust and parry of the relationship with Great Britain. Traditional society had been relatively simple and straightforward and composed essentially of three classes—the ruling family, the merchants or "notables," and a working class primarily comprised of sailors and pearl divers, according to a prominent Kuwaiti political scientist. In this mix, he attributes "vast power and authority" to the merchants who controlled the economy.[12] Once oil earnings began to flow, the equation was turned on its head as huge sums accumulated in state coffers under the control of the ruler and the Al-Sabah. In a sense, the history of Kuwaiti politics now became a struggle for control of these profits and the power they conveyed. Meantime, as young Kuwaitis went abroad for study in hotbeds of Arab nationalism (such as Egypt or Iraq), new and unfamiliar influences and ideas were introduced into the society. Foreign workers (including displaced Palestinians) entering Kuwait to work in the oil industry and development projects often brought with them their own preoccupations, ideologies, and agendas—further roiling the waters. Instability was in the air.

Almost from the beginning of his rule, Shaikh Abdallah was confronted by an organized and sustained opposition, which challenged the very underpinnings of Kuwait's long-standing political system. The country had largely been free of the kind of disruption represented by the Majlis movement of the late 1930s. The relative calm of the 1940s ended with a vengeance and a growing stream of oil wealth at the end of the decade. Longtime American residents observed these changes with concern:

> *On the heels of extreme hardship and suffering, oil wealth came as something of a 'rear-end collision' and had what can only be described as a 'whiplash' effect upon the moral, spiritual, and cultural dimensions of society not only in Kuwait but in the Gulf as a whole.*[13]

Discontent was fed by, and focused initially on, perceived rivalries between leading members of the al-Sabah and new opportunities for extravagance. But the brew was much more complex; some elements were genuinely inspired by ideas of enhanced democracy, while others probably used the concept to advance other agendas. The reform efforts of the 1950s, however, differed importantly from earlier movements. Participants included not only young Kuwaitis who had been abroad for education, but "politically sophisticated Egyptians, Lebanese, Iraqis, and Palestinians who were working in Kuwait."[14]

The Department of State in Washington, D.C., was not indifferent to the instability in Kuwait. In the vernacular of the period, it viewed those challenging the *status quo* as "communists." The U.S. Consulate, however, took a more nuanced view, reporting that there were only a few Kuwaitis affiliated with the party and that the majority of activists were Palestinians, with a sprinkling of Egyptians, Lebanese, Iraqis, and Syrians who worked through cultural clubs and among expatriate teachers.[15] With more enthusiasm than prudence, the United States sought to involve itself in the volatile local situation at this critical moment. In 1952, the Americans raised the possibility of locating a Voice of America station in Kuwait to broadcast in Arabic and in Russian to the Soviet Union. For a variety of reasons, including the preservation of their special position, the British rebuffed the proposal.[16] Three years later, an American official put out feelers regarding even greater involvement in Kuwaiti affairs. An annex to the "Kuwait Diary No. 7 of 1955" contains the following note:

> Mr. Herbert Hoover suggested to H(er). M(ajesty's). Ambassador in Washington that the U.S. Government ought to share the responsibility for affairs in Kuwait as the United States had an important investment there. H.M. Ambassador gave him no encouragement. This conversation seems to follow a discussion of the political situation in Kuwait which Mr. Hamilton of Gulf Oil Corporation had with the U.S. Consul in April. Mr. Hamilton later saw Mr. Hoover.[17]

Once again, the United States was saved from itself and the

building Kuwaiti opposition to the British protectorate by London's sense of exclusivity.

The vehicle favored by the opposition for their agitation in this phase was the series of professional and "cultural" clubs that emerged as the society became more diverse and contentious. These associations were by-products of the expansion of civic spaces and took their place alongside traditional fora like *diwanniyas*. They offered discontented elements settings in which to congregate, debate, and prepare their campaigns for reform. The focus at the outset was on domestic issues such as corruption, governance, and accountability. Beneath the public face of these movements was a more ambitious goal held by at least some of the activists. By 1954, a group calling itself the Kuwait Democratic League began issuing pamphlets and other propaganda critical of the ruler. as well as other members of the Al-Sabah.[18]

Arab nationalism, especially the building phenomenon of "Nasserism" promoted by Egypt, lay just below the surface of events in Kuwait. The participation of non-Kuwaiti Arabs in the movement almost certainly assured that larger Arab causes, such as the Palestinian question, were featured in internal discussions and decisions. It was the increasing regional influence of Gamal Abdel Nasser of Egypt and the Suez Crisis of 1956, that interjected wider currents openly into the confrontation in Kuwait:

> *In August 1956, in response to Nasser's call for a strike, four thousand demonstrators met at the National Culture Club, the new center of radical opposition, to hear pro-Nasser speeches. In September more disturbances followed. In October a strike protesting the French arrest of Algerian leaders closed government offices and shops. After 1956 anti-British and anti-French sentiments were grafted onto the anti-government statements.*[19]

The two threads of internal protests—agitation for regime reform, and a sense that Kuwait should be more deeply involved in pan-Arab causes—came together to create massive instability in response to Egypt's nationalization of the Suez Canal in 1956 and the British, French, and Israeli military reactions. The "Committee of Clubs" stepped forward to organize and coordinate widespread protests in support of Egypt.

President Nasser enjoyed widespread popularity throughout the Arab world as a strong leader who tweaked the "imperialist" powers and promised to reverse the humiliations most Arabs felt they had suffered from the West. An evaluation by the British Agency in Bahrain made the point forcefully in August 1956:

> Nasser is still a hero to almost all Arabs. His defeat by us would be regarded as a humiliation to the Arabs, generally, and would cause resentment rather than respect. In a year or two, many Arabs will probably have seen through Nasser, or come to understand the threat he poses for the rest of the Arab world. At present this is nowhere understood and our propaganda cannot succeed in getting it across in the course of a few weeks.[20]

Kuwait was no exception.

The building tension in Kuwait bubbled over in 1956. The flames of support for Nasser in his confrontation with Britain and the West were fanned by Egyptian and Palestinian teachers in the country's new schools, but a significant number of Kuwaitis responded to their agitation.[21] Following a series of low-grade demonstrations over preceding weeks, the Anglo-French air strikes on Egyptian airfields on October 31 sparked calls for mass action and, ultimately, violence against British interests and those of its allies. A massive meeting was called to press for the expulsion of all British subjects in Kuwait. The ruler, recognizing the potential threat to the government inherent in such demonstrations, banned all demonstrations, strikes, and other public meetings—the meeting did not take place. Tensions continued to rise, however, and Britain took the precaution of moving troops to nearby Bahrain.[22]

Pamphlets prepared by the "Committee of the Clubs" appeared in the street on November 2 to denounce Britain's attack on Egypt and to call for a major show of force and a strike.[23] The Police Department responded with a public notice banning all such public manifestations and prepared for a confrontation the following day with the "reformist movement" near the main bazaar mosque. The test of strength was a stalemate as shops that opened normally were quickly shuttered at the approach of the crowd of several hundred demonstrators. Businesses in other parts of town followed suit, while the police and other security forces dispersed the crowds with only minimal injuries in two hours. In classic style, small bands (mainly youths) broke off from the main confrontation to rove the town—throwing stones and yelling. One of these splinter groups moved in the direction of the British Political Agency. Shaikh Mubarak Abdullah personally led the security forces, wielding a cane, to drive off the group. Although the commercial sector was shut down, government departments and development work were unaffected.

Expatriate communities in Kuwait were, for the first time, more than interested observers of popular demonstrations and opposition activity. With increasing anger directed particularly against the British presence, ordinary British citizens were potential targets of mob violence. The Kuwait Oil Company management warned all Europeans living in Ahmadi to remain in their homes and to avoid travel to Kuwait City. For its part, the American consulate advised its citizens to be cautious as well, citing the possibility that they could be mistaken for "Englishmen." The fact that these cautionary advisories (which have become routine throughout the Middle East since) merited comment in the records of the time is a measure of the relative innocence of that period. Nevertheless, the advice was prudent. Dr. Mary Allison, who had served for many years with the American Mission Hospital, was pelted with onions by boys as she drove through the *suq* area.[24] Gone was the intimacy of old Kuwait where expatriates were few in number and known, at least by sight, to practically the entire population.[25]

The Committee of the Clubs sought to extend the disorder by issuing a call on the afternoon of November 3 for a continuation of the strike the following day. Nearly all shops chose to comply and several schools, under the strong influence of Egyptian and pro-reform elements in the Education Department, did not open. The response in the streets, however, was spotty. Several small groups in Kuwait Town and a single group in the Arab quarter of Ahmadi, were dispersed without difficulty by security forces. Perhaps as a result of the weak turnout, the Committee of the Clubs announced that henceforth it would continue its campaign with other tactics. They revealed in a circular that new tactics would consist of "committees to organise (a) future strikes; (b) a boycott of British and

French goods, vessels, and aircraft; (c) the recruitment of volunteers to fight in Egypt, and (d) the raising of funds for Egypt."[26] Representatives of the clubs and the Education Department reinforced their demands over the next two days in contacts with the ruler and other members of the al-Sabah, elaborating a program that included approval to collect public funds to support Egypt; opening offices to recruit volunteers to serve with the Egyptian armed forces; recognition of the cancellation of contracts with British companies; a boycott of British and French products and refusal to serve customers from those countries; and dismissal of state employees of British nationality. The ruler accepted the first two demands, but rejected the fourth which would affect government interests. He, likewise, refused to cancel contracts with the British which also could adversely affect the operations and development program of the Kuwaiti government. Private merchants and shopkeepers were free, he observed, to do as they wished regarding British goods and customers.

The situation remained quiet but tense over the next several days and schools were officially closed until November 10. Many shops in the *suq* sprouted placards announcing that British customers would not be served—banners, which were soon blown down by strong winds, appeared in the streets bearing pro-Egyptian and anti-British slogans. Those in the vicinity of the British Political Agency proclaimed "Death for Enemies." Despite the obvious anger in the city, no serious incidents took place beyond catcalls and angry glares whenever a Briton, or others mistaken for them, ventured outside.

The Committee of the Clubs, bolstered by the support of the Director of the Education Department as well as Colonel Jassim Qatami, former Director of the police (who defected to the opposition), concentrated on attempting to press the powerful merchants to implement the boycott. On November 8, approximately fifty commercial notables convened to discuss further measures. The instigators had met the previous day with commission agents to discuss proposals, including the blacklisting of British goods already imported, and creation of a register of surrendered agencies so that they might be reclaimed in the future. The discussions were heated and contentious. Ultimately a ways-and-means committee of sixteen was created with the merchants, making certain they were well represented. The apparent consensus of the commercial class was that they would be financially incapable of dealing with a complete break with Britain. They were also convinced that any agency agreements given up would be snapped up by competitors. The boycott movement was running up against the commercial heritage of the country; the merchant class was not eager to commit economic suicide to satisfy the agitators.

The boycott, aside from inconvenience or unpleasantness for individual shoppers, proved less than effective. Government departments (with the notable exception of the Education Department[27]) do not appear to have canceled British contracts; British-associated banks continued to receive business and deposits, and lines of credit never ceased to be opened in the United Kingdom. Even in the retail sphere, many shopkeepers were reportedly embarrassed by the pressure to deny service to old customers and found ways around the intent of the boycott; some sent goods out, while others exhibited no hesitancy in dealing with the servants of Europeans.[28]

With the Anglo-British withdrawal from Port Said in Egypt and the passing of time without serious incident, the expatriate community began to hope that the worst was behind them and to look forward to a more normal Christmas season.[29] The British Political Agency expressed the opinion that the boycott was losing steam not only due to the improving politico-military situation, but also to the concern of Kuwaiti merchants that they would lose the lucrative holiday trade.[30] The charged atmosphere of the period was broken by an event of great significance to the European community, when the St. Paul's Church at Ahmadi was consecrated in late November. The main address at the ceremony was delivered by the Anglican Bishop of Jerusalem, assisted by the Bishops of Iran and of South India, and the Reverend de Jong from the American Mission in Kuwait. The political agent and Mrs. G. W. Bell, as well as the U.S. Consul and Mrs. William Brewer, attended the impressive ceremony along with senior staff from the Kuwait Oil Company.[31]

During a mid-December rainstorm, the confrontation took a violent turn. Without warning, on December 10–11, ten explosions occurred in the oil-related areas of Mina al-Ahmadi, Ahmadi, and Magwa. Political and company officials reconstructed these acts of sabotage:

> ... a small party of saboteurs... left Kuwait probably in a single vehicle and drove to Ahmadi by the coast road. Three charges were laid on the underwater pipelines at Mina-al-Ahmadi and two portions of the boundary fence of the new refinery area were blown in. The saboteurs then continued to Ahmadi itself and laid charges on three oil wells. They returned towards Kuwait Town via the main Ahmadi/Kuwait road laying three separate charges on gas scrubbers on the gasline which supplies the power station and distillation plant for Kuwait Town.[32]

Fortunately, several of the charges failed to detonate and most of the damage was minor and easily repaired. One producing well, however, was set afire and burned off initially at a rate of three thousand barrels a day. Technicians from the oil company, with the assistance of the Kuwait Fire Service, were able to reduce the burn. The legendary Red Adair was summoned from Texas and succeeded in suppressing the blaze on December 14.[33] Although the effects of the attacks were minor (mainly because of the incompetence of the saboteurs), and the government and people of Kuwait were spared an interruption of the gas supply, immediate measures were taken to prevent a repetition. Security measures were tightened at oil installations and pipelines, checkpoints were established on the roads leading to Admadi, and a nightly curfew was imposed in the vicinity. Psychologically, the results were serious:

> After the 1956 acts of sabotage, the situation in Kuwait grew tense again and security measures were increased—and the prospects of Christmas shopping in the town, which the withdrawal from Port Said had made more than probable, were now dismally extinguished.[34]

The local atmosphere was so toxic that rumors were spread, with the aid of Kuwaiti newspapers, that the British had planted the explosives in order to provide a justification for landing troops in Kuwait.[35]

The disorder surrounding the Suez Crisis was a defining event for several factions, at least for the foreseeable future. The instigators,

Kuwaitis and foreign Arabs alike, had harnessed genuine popular anger to produce large demonstrations and even a violently anti-British campaign.[36] Buoyed by this experience, they were now prepared to continue their agitation. While this alienated element seemed to embrace a spectrum of aspirations, from young Kuwaitis fired by the idea of broader participation in running the country to hard-core "revolutionaries" seeking to overturn the existing order entirely, all were increasingly under the influence of Arab nationalists from Egypt, Iraq, and Palestine.

The ruler, Shaikh Abdallah, was wily beyond the appreciation of most of his contemporaries. He recognized that the wind blowing across his country, particularly from Nasser's Egypt, had freshened and shifted. Like the expert mariners of his society, he recognized that he must tack with it or risk foundering, for beneath the anti-British motif of the "reform" movement lay at least some who posed a challenge to his rule and the Kuwaiti system—as subsequent events would make clear. Efforts to obstruct an alliance between the expatriate Arab radicals and their Kuwaiti disciples through improvements in the quality of life and gradual change, had proven unsuccessful. Out of personal conviction or expediency, Shaikh Abdallah assumed a posture that supported Nasser "at least with regard to his stand against colonialism," without outwardly challenging the continuing British position in Kuwaiti affairs.[37] Over the early years of his rule, Shaikh Abdallah also had to contend with rivalries among senior Shaikhs within his own family. Shaikh Fahad al-Salem, the head of the Public Works Department, looked toward a larger role for the Americans[38] while Shaikh Abdallah Mubarak, who had charge of the armed and public security forces, "tended to support, and be supported by, the British."[39] Nevertheless, the appearance on the scene of a virulent opposition movement temporarily overshadowed jockeying for position within the al-Sabah (over the longer term, the towering figures of the older generation would shortly pass into history.)

The ruler certainly did not welcome the more robust challenge to the status quo and, ultimately, his own position. He had been quietly improving the lives of the Kuwaitis through development of reliable water and electric supplies, housing, schools, hospitals, and other amenities, as well as creating the elements of a welfare state. As we have seen, Shaikh Abdallah had also parried British efforts to tighten its control over events in Kuwait without pushing his relations with them to the point of rancor. The intensification of popular anti-British sentiment and the growth of independence movements in many parts of the British Empire, strengthened his hand on this issue:

> Abdallah III became all the more assertive of Kuwait's freedom in internal affairs. Backed by the notables and assisted by his strong-minded nephew, Shaikh Jabir al-Ahmad... he applied every form of discreet leverage in his outwardly cordial relations with the British...[40]

Methodically, he expanded spheres of autonomous action ranging from banking and currency, to the post office. Internationally, he took the first tentative steps toward creating an identity distinct from that previously permitted under the protectorate agreement with the United Kingdom when Kuwait had joined UNESCO and the Organization of Petroleum Exporting Countries (OPEC) in its own right. Nevertheless, Shaikh Abdallah exercised care not to call into question the fundamental British guarantee of Kuwait's security, on which the country still depended. The Suez Crisis and its local repercussions emboldened many Kuwaitis to question the wisdom of the British protectorate, and some to continue active steps to undermine this and other facets of the existing order, but this view did not resonate with the ruling family.[41]

British policymakers appear to have been thrown into some disarray by the strength of the popular reaction to the Suez Crisis in Kuwait, and Bahrain in particular. Several years before 1956, more perceptive members of the British establishment had come to recognize that efforts to tighten their influence in Kuwait were unlikely to succeed. Other elements, however, forged ahead as if the small American presence in the country was the principal impediment to their ambitions. Ironically, the popular reaction to the Suez Crisis brought the American Consulate out of the British shadow. Bill Brewer looked back over his tour there:

> *The only time when I took a lead was during the Suez Crisis. The British were in the doghouse, their local officials were not embarassing Kuwaitis by contacting them, and I was therefore the contact point with the GOK on matters affecting the Western community.*[42]

Increasingly, British unhappiness with the United States focussed on threats to the United Kingdom's economic and commercial dominance. In February 1956, the Foreign Office was concerned by rumors that senior Kuwaitis, in particular Shaikh Fahad, were moving sizeable funds to the United States, "possibly as a hedge against future trouble."[43] Although American consul Talcott Seelye complained in 1959 that the one-man commercial office within the consulate "could not compete,"[44] U.S. firms were in fact making inroads that disturbed British competitors.[45] A case in point was the award of a contract to Westinghouse in early 1956 to supply an additional set of evaporators for the expanded distillation plant. In sharp contrast to the views they had defended regarding the work awarded without open tender to the "big five" British corporations, British officialdom now complained that "It might be said that ordering this additional plant from Westinghouse without going out to tender discriminates against other manufacturers."[46] Even more devastating to their hope to maintain Kuwait as a British preserve was the choice the following year of the American firms, Pomeroy and Hawaiian Dredging, in a hotly contested competition to perform extensive dredging and construction work for the new Kuwait Port.[47]

Strains and tensions also arose between the British and American views on issues such as the appropriate relationship with the local society and non-European expatriates. Largely out of the need to develop facilities at Ahmadi to support the oil industry, KOC constructed surprisingly pleasant housing for the British, American, and other expatriates surging into the country, with a separate area for Arabs. This arrangement was evidently seen as "natural" by the planners. The result, however, was what an expert observer described as "a little, inward-looking, colonial-type community ... at Al-Ahmadi."[48] The development pattern, chosen by AMINOIL for its operations, contrasted sharply with that of KOC and elicited the following comment from the British Political Agency:

> ... their colourful, popular and forceful General Manager, Mr. MacPherson contributed and, in a small way, enforced an idea which may have an effect on the vexed question of the relationship between oil company personnel and local population. He would have none of the oil 'camps' for European and American employees which are such a feature of other companies operating overseas. In the fields, only those actually engaged in production would work and live. All the personnel of ancillary services would have their offices and living quarters in the local towns in the midst of the local population. The idea is to avoid the segregating effect of the camps. It has its origin in another, typically American, one: to the effect that the more you mix colour, caste and creed in the nearest approximation possible to the American way of life, the more likely they are to get on well together.[49]

The British, concerned by the part Arab expatriates played in the disorder in Kuwait during the Suez crisis and later, made attempts to discourage American firms such as Getty, AMINOIL, and Pomeroy from hiring Palestinians welcomed by the Kuwaitis. In the summer of 1957, the Foreign Office cautioned that this goal be pursued "in a manner that will not lay us open to any charges of wishing to obstruct the employment of refugees."[50] The instruction did not offer guidance on how these contradictory goals were to be pursued simultaneosly.

Such skirmishes and disputes were, in the final analysis, little more than a rearguard action against new forces and influences gaining a foothold in Kuwait. Britain's hope was to keep Kuwait and the other Gulf protectorates free of the strains of Arab nationalism which were destabilizing the Arab East. The Suez Crisis, and the popular movements it fed, were a vivid warning for Britain and the West that a policy of dealing with the small Arab states of the Gulf in isolation was no longer feasible. "The protectorates had begun to lose their immunity; political developments and events in the rest of the Arab world were beginning to impinge on the isolated Gulf region."[51]

Gamal Abdel Nasser, who struck an enduring chord in Arab countries that resonated to the idea of the Arab "strong man," continued to play a role in the domestic affairs of Kuwait, as in many other countries, throughout the 1950s and well into the next decade. Through the propaganda of the "Voice of the Arabs" radio in Cairo, as well as young Kuwaitis who had studied in Egypt, Egyptian teachers and other Egyptians sent abroad to work, Nasser's influence was massive.[52] He could be charming, but, at heart, he was no friend of monarchical regimes like Kuwait, as Shaikh Abdallah no doubt recognized in his careful response to Egypt's offensive.

The first anniversary, in 1959, of the founding of the United Arab Republic (UAR), uniting Egypt and the Syrian Arab Republic, provided an occasion in Kuwait for the revelation of the real objective of some of his supporters there. For the celebratory rally, Ahmad Said, the director of the "Voice of the Arabs" radio, was invited to Kuwait by the opposition weekly, *ash-Sha'ab*. The Committee of Clubs planned another event at a Kuwaiti secondary school. After months of agitation, the "reformists" abandoned caution in putting forward two demands: immediate change in the system of government involving popular participation; and Kuwait's embrace of Pan-Arabism, a code word for Nasserism. With a crowd of some twenty thousand persons in attendance, the leader of the opposition, Ahmad al-Khatib, opened the meeting and turned the podium over to Jasim al-Qatami, who had resigned from the police in opposition to the banning of public demonstrations at the time of the Suez Crisis. For unknown reasons, al-Qatami abandoned his prepared speech and declared:

> *The Sabah became the rulers of Kuwait three hundred years ago. They ruled autocratically and arbitrarily then. They cannot expect to do the same in the latter part of the twentieth century. Either they grant the people the necessary reforms at once, or the people will take power for themselves.*[53]

The gauntlet had been thrown down; the ruler could not pretend he was unaware of the nature of the challenge he was facing.

It would become fully apparent, only in retrospect, how much Shaikh Abdallah had achieved by his quiet incremental steps to promote modernization in Kuwait and lay the groundwork for the country's independence. Certainly, the "reformists," caught up in the appeal of Nasserism and Pan-Arabism, did not consider the ruler's accomplishments significant or sufficient. Nevertheless, he accelerated reforms by encouraging the development of comprehensive legal and legislative systems.[54] To undertake the codification of these laws, Kuwait called upon an Egyptian expert, Abdul Sanhouri, who had apparently developed a positive relationship with the American Consul. Sanhouri told Consul Seelye that he was encountering trouble conforming the new laws to the "traditions and habits of the country."[55] Despite these difficulties, he was able to complete the law on organization of the judiciary by 1960; implementation was delayed while the expert drafted additional laws, including a penal code. In reporting positively on Sanhouri's work, Seelye commented:

> *Considering the determination with which the Subah shaykhs usually protect their own vested interests, the relative speed with which Sanhouri's new laws have been passed by the all-Subah Supreme Council is noteworthy. For these laws, if properly implemented, will seriously undermine special shaykhly prerogatives.*[56]

Egypt, and the internal tensions flowing from its policies, was not the only major Arab state on the radars of Britain and Kuwait. Neighboring Iraq was always a factor in Kuwaiti calculations, in good times and bad. Baghdad, which had several times claimed Kuwait and, just as often, acknowledged Kuwaiti separateness, had always been an unpredictable neighbor. The frontier between the two countries had never been agreed and demarcated.

The border between Kuwait and the Ottoman provinces later incorporated into the modern state of Iraq, had been spelled out in the Anglo-Ottoman Convention of 1913. The Convention was never ratified and the Ottoman state disintegrated following World War I. In 1923, the British High Commissioner to the Iraqi government installed by Great Britain redefined the frontier in an official letter. In neither instance was the border demarcated between them.

Following the First World War, the Kuwaitis and Iraqis reportedly accepted the placement of a signboard south of Safwan[57] as the frontier at that point. The signpost was removed by the Iraqis in 1939 at a time when they were stimulating unrest in Kuwait with claims to its territory (See Chapter 4). The British decided to replace the marker despite Kuwaiti concerns not to exacerbate relations with Baghdad. Col. Galloway, the British political agent in Kuwait, drove to the vicinity of Safwan in June. 1940. He was accompanied by Ali Khalifa, the ruler's representative, who knew the area intimately. Together, they planted the new post in the location of the previous one and were observed by an Iraqi official from the Safwan post. The Iraqi posed no objection to the new marker but suggested that the wind might disturb the new sign. It was again removed shortly thereafter.[58] By the time the British got around to demarcating the reference point in 1951, this time with the added factor of delimiting oil fields in the equation, too much time had passed for Col. Dickson to be certain of the location of previous signposts.

Iraq showed little inclination to settle the location of the frontier, but made efforts to enlist Kuwaiti cooperation in Baghdad's regional policies. Disturbed by the growing assertiveness of their regional rival, Egypt, the Iraqi monarchy was soon seeking to draw Kuwait into its orbit. In 1954, Nuri al Said, the pro-British Iraqi prime minister, proposed that Kuwait join the projected Baghdad Pact.[59] Shaikh Abdallah predictably rejected Kuwait's entanglement in the alliance. Kuwait did, however, show initial interest in a proposed scheme to bring fresh water to Kuwait by pipeline. By the early 1950s, burgeoning Kuwait was desperate to find a permanent solution to the perennial problem of a reliable fresh water supply. Since the dhows that had plied the Gulf between the Shatt al-Arab and the city of Kuwait were no longer a viable solution, the idea of replacing them with a new pipeline was suggested. The concept aroused skepticism from the outset on political and engineering grounds; the British political resident in Manama took a nuanced position on March 19, 1953:

> *I am of the opinion that in view of the political dangers inherent in it we should not go out of our way to encourage it. On the other hand, if the Kuwaitis want it we should not oppose it, though we should make sure they fully realise the dangers to which I have referred.*[60]

The pipeline project, nonetheless, continued to be considered for three more years, promoted in some degree by the substantial commercial opportunities it promised. Sir Alexander Gibb and Partners, a British company, was appointed consultant for the pipeline. The British Political Agency in Kuwait reported in January 1954 that the firm was moving quickly to undertake to complete the field work for the feasibility survey, opining that "British prestige here is linked closely to it."[61] It is not clear from the available records how much preparatory work was undertaken before the ruler scratched the project in favor of constructing additional distillation capacity.[62]

There can be little doubt that Shaikh Abdallah's decision was based primarily on his reluctance to place control of the water supply in the hands of the unreliable Iraqi regime. It is also likely that he allowed discussion of, and speculation about, the project to continue in order to mollify commercial and political interests of Britain and the United States.[63] According to Bill Brewer. the U.S. consul at the time:

> Not surprisingly, the Kuwaitis weren't interested. 'What will Iraq do' one asked me rehetorically, 'once we get our fields all prepared and crops planted'.[64]

Aside from Baghdad's quixotic attitude over the decades to Kuwait's independent status, the ruler was following the internal situation in the neighboring state with concern, despite the instability in his own country. The British political agent reported on a conversation with Shaikh Abdallah on July 9, 1958, quoting the ruler as noting that the position of the king of Iraq was very insecure; "it enjoyed no support among the people." Such popular support was the final and enduring foundation for a ruler. If the Iraqi régime were overthrown, it might well be his own turn next.[65] Within days, his worst fears were confirmed when the monarchy in Baghdad was swept away in an army coup led by Abdel Kareem al-Qassem.

The new leadership in Baghdad was a largely unknown quantity when it assumed power in July 1958. Kuwait's relationship with Iraq under the deposed monarch had been far from exemplary, but the Kuwaiti leadership could have hardly been reassured by the fall of another Arab monarch. Kuwait, predictably, pursued a policy of accommodation with the new Iraqi leadership. An early Kuwaiti visit to Baghdad in 1958 for official talks produced no unpleasant surprises, including any reference to an Iraqi claim against the country.[66] Nevertheless, the Kuwaiti authorities took prudent precautions domestically. The Kuwaiti Army was placed on alert; units deployed from Jewan Camp and all military personnel in the town carried arms. Areas near the British Political Agency and the American Consulate were placed off limits to the general public and checkpoints were established to clear those on business.[67] Yet there were soon indicators that the relationship would continue to be troubled. In May 1959, the Kuwaitis discovered a plot to infiltrate the country; two hundred Iraqis were located encamped in the desert and escorted away.[68]

At least initially, President Nasser, and his supporters in Kuwait and elsewhere, regarded the violent overthrow of the Iraqi monarchy with enthusiasm. The fall of another Arab king must have appeared a step on the march of Pan-Arab republicanism. Surely Iraq would soon cast its lot in with the United Arab Republic. Such emotions may have emboldened elements of the Kuwaiti opposition to challenge the ruler and traditional system openly. In this, they were quickly disabused of their illusions. They had badly underestimated the historical rivalry between the Nile Valley and the civilization of the Tigris-Euphrates, the "Fertile Crescent," which proved much more potent even than Nasserism.

The decade of the 1950s was arguably the most tumultuous and transformative in Kuwait's more than two hundred years as a principality. By 1961, the population was an estimated 320,000[69] compared to about 160,000 in 1950.[70] Perhaps more important was the substantial diversification of inhabitants. The British Political Agency recorded some 6000 British subjects (including South Asians) and 850 "foreigners" (including Americans) registered at the beginning of the decade,[71] whereas ten years later the total included 3000 British, 400 Americans, 26,000 Iraqis, 20,000 Iranians, 15.000 Jordanians (primarily Palestinians), and smaller numbers of Saudis, Indians, Pakistanis, and Lebanese.[72] The number of Shia Muslims rose significantly following World War II, although they were not a homogeneous community. The largest cohesive group were Shiites of Persian origin, whose families had lived in Kuwait for several generations and were considered Kuwaiti subjects. Shiite laborers from Iran (many displaced by the nationalization of the British petroleum facilities at Abadan) and Iraq flowed into Kuwait in large numbers in search of work. The tiny Jewish community of Iraqi origin had decided to immigrate to the new state of Israel. They had been prominent in the cloth trade and older Kuwaitis recalled that they were able to sell their property and depart freely.[73] In ten short years, Kuwaiti society had doubled in size, its historic cohesion and shared experience diluted by greater diversity.

No development of the era was more important in terms of Kuwait's future than the explosive growth in educational activity. In addition to the large investment in school buildings within the country, young Kuwaitis were provided with new opportunities to study in other societies, with all the benefits and drawbacks of exposure to foreign social and political cultures, including that in the United States. Farsighted officials acknowledged early on that not only was this trend essential, but that it would have significant repercussions. The British political resident wrote in 1953:

> *As educated Kuwaitis become available we must ensure that they are absorbed, not only by the Kuwait Oil Company, but by British firms in Kuwait generally, and we must also recognize the fact that the British employees of the Kuwait Government must be gradually replaced by them. In the pursuance of the policy which has been agreed upon we shall have, in due course, to hand over to them all internal activities with which we are concerned, such as Posts and Telegraphs and Civil Aviation.*[74]

The giant steps that Kuwait had taken are nowhere more evident than in the education of girls. By 1952, more than 2,500 girls were enrolled in ten schools, including two in villages, and two more the following year. Starting from a base of zero, girls' classes were progressing toward secondary education.[75]

Not surprisingly, given the other stresses that Kuwaiti society was under at the time, education contributed to the instability of the 1950s. Initially, the government looked to other Arab countries, particularly Egypt, for assistance in this important area. Lacking sufficient Kuwaiti teachers to staff the new schools, Egyptians and some Palestinians were employed in the Education Department. As employees of the Egyptian government, many brought with them outlooks and agendas that were not oriented toward Kuwait's needs or interests. The British Council Centre in Basra, Iraq noted following a survey that "... the Kuwait schools are now using a syllabus nearly identical throughout with the Egyptian Schools."[76]

Egypt also figured prominently in the new Kuwaiti program of financing study abroad at the outset. In 1954, for instance, there were about 183 young Kuwaitis in schools at all levels overseas. Fifty-three were enrolled in an Egyptian elementary school, and smaller numbers were pursuing studies in "industrial studies," law, commerce, and medicine. Thirty-eight Kuwaitis were in British schools, with a few in Iraq, Lebanon (the American University of Beirut), the United States, and one in France.[77] This distribution would have significance for the "reformist" agitation within Kuwait, in which Egyptian teachers and their Kuwaiti students played a leading role as Gamal Abdel Nasser reached for regional dominance through promotion of his vision of Pan-Arabism.

The exposure of young minds to new ideas and cultures can have less predictable effects on society as well. Newly educated young ladies in the country were also becoming a catalyst for change. Episodes in the spring of 1956 offer an illuminating case study. A group of fifty Kuwaiti girls were planning to visit Egypt with their instructors during a break in classes. They rejected the demand of the Education Department that the girls wear veils on their trip and the travel was cancelled. Protests against veiling persisted, and the same year four young ladies from notable merchant families took off their *abayas* and burned them in their schoolyard. Shaikh Abdallah Jabir, the head of the Education Department, expressed understanding of their actions in a meeting with the protesters, but suggested that they take account of the views of their fathers while they completed secondary studies. When they went abroad to continue their studies, he counselled, they would not have to wear the veil. When they returned to Kuwait, they would no longer have to cover their faces.[78] In fact, in the turbulent 1950s, many Kuwaiti women shed their veils. According to a widespread account, Kuwait's first feminist demonstration occurred in the mid-1950s, probably in *Safat*. Fatima Hussain, who had been educated in India, joined other Kuwaiti women as they marched to the public square and burned their abayas (long black cloaks).[79]

The fact that this revolutionary moment is largely unremarked in the documentation of the period suggests that it stirred little controversy.

Kuwait was not the same place at the end of the decade. Irrespective of domestic strife and external threats, Shaikh Abdallah had steered the country through dangerous shoals and fast-running currents. Kuwait was now a major oil producer enjoying the huge proceeds of its exports,[80] and well on the way to creating a network of subsidies and other benefits to the Kuwaiti people. Sooner than the ruler and others involved might have anticipated, Kuwait would achieve full independence, shedding its protectorate status while retaining a vital defense commitment from the United Kingdom.

9

Independence

Without fanfare, Kuwait was moving rapidly toward independence in mid-1961. On June 19, 1961, documents were exchanged between the ruler and the British political resident in the Gulf, Sir William Luce, by which Her Britannic Majesty's Government formally recognized the state's full independence and sovereignty.[1] The same day in London, Lord Privy Seal Edward Heath was announcing in the House of Commons that the "obsolete and inappropriate" treaty of 1899 had been replaced with an agreement of "close friendship."[2]

While the protectorate that had governed Great Britain's relationship with Kuwait for sixty years was terminated, the new treaty, and the unpublicized negotiations leading to it, envisaged continued close relations in the field of regional security. The ruler, Abdallah al-Salem, and the Kuwaiti government were confident of their ability to maintain internal security, particularly with the enhancement of capabilities undertaken in the years prior to 1961. With good reason, however, they were less sure of the newly created Kuwaiti army's capacity to protect against serious external threats.[3] During discussions preceding the new treaty, the ruler secured a "firm British commitment" to assist Kuwait against any challenge to its independence.[4] The menace of *Ikhwan* attacks and the Saudi appetite for Kuwaiti territory that loomed so large in the 1920s and 30s had faded into insignificance as relations with Saudi Arabia warmed greatly—but Kuwait's neighborhood could still be a rough one.[5] Ironically, Kuwait felt compelled to invoke the British commitment almost immediately.

For the American and other expatriate communities, Kuwait's transition to full independence was more than an event of historic significance; among other effects it had practical implications for their status and communal experience. J.C. Richmond, the last of the British political agents in Kuwait, was appointed Britain's first ambassador, and the agency was transformed into the British Embassy. The new "State of Kuwait" adopted an official seal, based on one the ruler had adopted in 1956 to symbolize the country's maritime and desert heritage. A new national flag incorporating green, white, and red stripes and a black trapezoid replaced the traditional red banner with "Kuwait" in white. And, finally, the ruler adopted the title of "Amir" to emphasize his new status in the international community.[6]

Among the many changes and adjustments necessitated by independence was the legal basis for the American diplomatic mission and the American community. The British government formally ceded control over Kuwait's foreign relations.[7] Even earlier, Britain announced that it would be abolishing the separate law court under which the political agent sat in judgement over cases involving Americans and other foreign nationals.[8] It soon became evident that once London relinquished jurisdiction over non-Kuwaitis, "it would no longer be able to protect American citizens or even guarantee the continued functioning of the American consulate."[9] Britain's solution to this conundrum was a recommendation that the Foreign Office issue an "agreement to function," and that the ruler specify, in writing, to the political agency those rights, privileges, and immunities that Kuwait would assure to the consulate and its personnel. Both U.S. and Kuwaiti interests were served by assuring the uninterrupted operation of the American Mission.

The United States administration was unambiguous in its support for the new Kuwaiti state. Quickly, on June 27, a Department of State spokesman confirmed American recognition of Kuwait as a "sovereign state."[10] The American Consulate, now located on a new five-acre site in a sparsely populated area outside the city walls, was redesignated an American Embassy. Consul Dayton Mak was appointed chargé d'affaires on September 22, 1961, a position he held until January 7 the following year (see Appendix D for a listing of U.S. Chiefs of Mission).

Kuwait moved with even more dispatch in normalizing diplomatic relations with Washington. Despite other preoccupations of the moment, Amir Abdallah wrote to President John F. Kennedy to introduce Kuwait's first ambassador to the United States, Abdul Rahman al-Atiqi. When the president met with Ambassador al-Atiqi to accept his letters of credence, he spoke warmly of the role American business played in Kuwait's rapid development.[11] One month later, the United States reciprocated when the president announced the appointment of Parker T. "Pete" Hart as nonresident ambassador to the State of Kuwait. Pete Hart, a seasoned American diplomat, was already ambassador to Saudi Arabia and minister to Yemen and continued to hold those posts. Ambassador Hart later recalled: *"On January 5, 1962, I presented, according to traditional diplomatic custom, a copy of my credentials to Foreign Minister Sabah al-Salim Al Sabah, brother of the emir."*[12]

With the establishment of the U.S. Embassy and the normal relationship between independent states it betokened, leadership of the American community shifted naturally to the ambassador. In Kuwait, as in many other parts of the Middle East, the flag followed private Americans rather than the other way around. Missionaries, archaeologists, educators, explorers and, later, oil men and merchants, were the pioneers—establishing beachheads in the Levant, in Turkey, and along the Gulf coast. In Kuwait, the American Mission occupied a unique and pre-eminent position in the community and the surrounding society. Although it would continue to occupy an important and respected position following Independence, the director of the mission no longer bore the predominant responsibility for community health and safety that Doctors Mylrea and Scudder shouldered over many decades.[13]

A British anthropologist, who conducted field work in Kuwait in the late 1950s, viewed the British and American communities as constituting "a little, inward-looking, colonial-type community... at Al-Ahmadi."[14] While the oil town at Ahmadi was the largest concentration of Western expatriates in Kuwait at the time, it was by no means the whole story. The American Mission and its personnel had operated and lived in close association with Kuwaitis for forty years by the time Lienhardt conducted his research. Other

American residents, not subject to the contemporary practices of the Kuwait Oil Company (KOC), were not completely comfortable with the company's strict segregation of European workers from Kuwaiti and other Arab colleagues. In fact, even in the case of KOC, it was American personnel who led the way in bringing wives and families with them. The long-established members of the American community could have enriched Lienhardt's understanding of Kuwaitis and their society.

With the expanded facilities of the men's hospital completed in 1954, the American Mission constituted a prominent presence in the country into the 1960s and 70s. From modest beginnings in the late 1940s, the Kuwaiti government had built an impressive modern medical infrastructure. Nevertheless, the mission continued to occupy a unique niche in society and in the affections of most Kuwaitis.[15] Among its other achievements, the American Mission had waged a long and often frustrating war against the scourge of smallpox. There was a small-scale outbreak during 1956 that was quickly contained because widespread innoculation was accepted.[16] Ambassador Joseph Twinam, a distinguished Gulf specialist who served in the Embassy in Kuwait shortly after independence, reflected on the situation in the mid-1960s:

The government had, by then, provided large and well-staffed public hospitals with the most modern of equipment, but many Kuwaitis still preferred to be cared for in the modest, relatively primitive, American Mission Hospital.[17]

The continuing demands on the medical staff exacted a heavy toll in 1964.

Gerald Nykerk, who had come back to Kuwait in order to provide relief for the overstressed Dr. Lewis Scudder, died on March 20 from a heart attack. The following August, Lew Scudder also collapsed and was quickly flown to the United States to undergo emergency surgery to remove a critical subdural hematoma. With its two senior surgeons gone, the hospital was in crisis. Much of the burden fell on Dr. Alfred Pennings—an internist by training and a scion of a long-serving missionary family—and a small group of Indian associates.[18] Dr. Egbert Fell, a friend of the Scudders from their student days at Rush Medical School, had just retired from the University of Chicago Medical School and volunteered to come to Kuwait in the winter of 1964 to assist during the crisis.

Dr. Scudder's major surgery in Chicago was successful and he recovered quickly, but convalescence required more than a year. During this time, the secretary for the Middle East for the Board of World Missions pressed Lew and Dorothy Scudder to take early retirement. By early 1966, however, the dedicated couple decided, given his satisfactory recovery, they would return to Kuwait to continue their more than twenty years of work. Needs at the hospital were urgent and they felt capable of resuming their duties.[19]

All too often, Western analysis of non-European societies focuses on one side of the relationship, treating indigenous peoples as receptors or objects rather than actors. Lienhardt's field work in Kuwait tends to emphasize non-Kuwaiti attitudes and behavior, perhaps because of his limited access to Kuwaitis. He concluded that "the Arab immigrants (sic) displayed no more interest in Kuwait than did the oil camp community..."[20] Lienhardt's analysis reveals little about Kuwaiti attitudes toward Arab expatriates and argues that the indifference of the latter was based on an unfavorable comparison of Kuwait with their countries of origin:

At that time, there were many ways in which Kuwait could not compare with the major cities of their own countries, and from the immigrants' point of view it was no more than a smallish place which had had the luck suddenly to become rich, but which did not, so far, understand much about the metropolitan idea of 'progress'."[21]

A close reading of the limited historical record suggests a major factor in Kuwaiti responses to Americans (and other expatriates) was the interest and respect they showed for Kuwaitis and their culture.

Unsurprisingly, American Mission personnel were not greeted with immediate acceptance. The Americans had more than a decade of experience in the Gulf and Arabian Peninsula when they established their hospital in 1911, but still had much to learn about Kuwaiti society. They were, however, pleased to be there and fired by enthusiasm for their missionary, medical, and educational work. Kuwaitis possessed even less familiarity with Americans and their culture. The road from strangers to friendship led through lengthy exposure to one another and shared experiences. Within a decade, the mission had proved itself not simply durable but beneficial to Kuwait. Acceptance, and even affection, followed despite cultural differences.

Nor was the American Mission unique in gaining trust and entrée into the Kuwaiti community. The adventures of the Australian seaman, Alan Villiers, with Kuwaiti sailors on a harrowing trip to the African coast in 1939 (see Chapter 5) earned him a welcome into the society on his return to Kuwait. As he recalled:

> *The Kuwaitis, with their background of desert hardship and of troubles elsewhere, appreciated the comparative quietness of Kuwait, and I found in them all a great love for the city-state. Sometimes the intelligentsia, dropping in at these evening talks, were more apologetic than they needed to be, and spoke of the democracy of Iraq as an ideal to strive for. Youths coming back in silk trousers from Iraq affected a great discontent with their own Arabian Kuwait: but it seemed to me an honest, straightforward, and satisfying place, despite the backwardness which they alleged. The silk-clad youths could leave again, if they did not like it.*[22]

The people of Kuwait were inevitably changed by exposure to other cultures, lifestyles, and technologies. Indeed, it is remarkable that they were not swamped by the pace of breakneck growth and development. The country's population is estimated to have increased by over 500 percent over the period 1957–1975, primarily as a result of the influx of foreign workers. By the mid-1960s Kuwaitis were a minority in their own country.[23] Such a massive demographic shift poses profound challenges to the stability, sense of identity, and integrity of large groups. Responses can range from a descent into isolation and insulation from external influences, to a reinforcement of a sense of distinctiveness that makes openness to the "other" less threatening. On the whole, Kuwaitis chose the latter course.

One indicator of the consolidation of a distinctive identity was reflected in the issue of dress. As Villiers noted above on the eve of World War II, some elements of the society—"the silk-clad youths"—initially responded to contact with more developed Arab societies by romanticizing their ideas and trappings as if the Kuwaiti heritage was flawed and inferior. This attitude also influenced internal politics by attributing, for example, a credibility to "Iraqi democracy" which later proved to be an illusion. Recognition of this illusion and acceptance of the positive aspects of Kuwaiti values and traditions would take some years to occur. The widespread reversion to traditional dress—*the dishdasha*—was much more than a fashion statement; it was the outward manifestation of an internal struggle to assert Kuwait's separate and unique national identity.

An important catalyst of change was the substantial number of young Kuwaitis sent abroad for higher education and training beginning in the 1950s. Initially enrolled in the institutions of other Arab countries, a significant number were sent to Britain and the United States as the demand for petroleum and general engineering and other sciences grew in importance. Some matriculating to the United States were first enrolled in high schools where they were hosted by carefully selected American families.[24] The first cohorts of overseas students were reportedly discouraged from marrying European women. Those who ignored this admonition could be shunned by their families, a daunting sanction in traditional Kuwaiti society. They reportedly also faced the possibility of losing government financial support.[25] It is not possible to determine from the historical record how widespread this negative attitude was or when it changed. But the significant number of successful marriages between Kuwaiti men and American women, and the sizeable number of dual-national children registered with the American Embassy, suggest that it was neither effective nor long-lasting.

Educational exchanges with the United States were such an important and integral element of relations between the two peoples that it is easy to forget how modest the first tentative steps were. In 1956, the Kuwaiti Department of Education asked AMINOIL to help place a small number of Kuwaitis in American institutions of higher learning. With no Kuwaiti representation in the United States at the time, the department needed a point of contact there. AMINOIL, with headquarters in San Francisco, naturally concentrated its search in the western United States. The first cadre of Kuwaitis to continue studies in the United States. included: Hisham Hussein; Mahmoud Khalid Al-Sane (later Under Secretary of Education); Mohammed Sayed Abd al-Muhsin al-Rifai; Abdallah Shirhan; and Ahmad Nouri. A second tranche was comprised of: Dr. Abd al-Aziz al-Sultan; Fawzi Musaed al-Salah; Faisal Sultan Al-Eassa; Abdallah Al-Dakhil; and Abd al-Rahman al-Houti (subsequently Minister of Public Works).[26]

Under Secretary of Education Faisal al-Mutawa traveled extensively in the United States in 1958 to consolidate the program, and the Kuwait government soon established an office in New York City to oversee the young people enrolled in American colleges and universities. The office was initially headed by Clyde Lee Masters, who was subsequently an advisor to the Saudi Ministry of Education.[27] The ground that they prepared was so fertile that by the end of the twentieth century Kuwaiti graduates of U.S. institutions numbered in the thousands. During the fall of 1988, my wife and I hosted a large reception attended by many Kuwaiti alumni of American schools. In its coverage of the event, a Kuwaiti daily reporter quoted Jassim Mohamad al-Wazzan:

> *I am a father of five sons who all graduated from American universities. I also have eighteen grandchildren of whom two hold American citizenship by birth while their parents were studying.*[28]

While anecdotal, al-Wazzan's situation is not unique and illustrates the extent to which educational cooperation has woven a durable fabric of relationships between the Kuwaiti and American peoples.

As Kuwait began its history as an independent state, the small American community there included many who had developed friendly and comfortable relations with Kuwaitis. For the first time, their fellow countrymen back in the United States were beginning to see news and information about Kuwait in their newspapers and other media. During the turbulent period of the Anglo-French invasion of the Suez Canal, at least three American journalists reported from Kuwait. In the mid-1950s, General Electric Airconditioning ran an advertisement with photos of contemporary Kuwait in *Life* magazine, touting its products in the offices of a prominent Kuwaiti company. It was a tiny beginning that would pale in comparison with media coverage over later years, but Kuwait was now on the radar of the larger American public.

The people of Kuwait scarcely had an opportunity to savor the moment of independence before they were menaced from a familiar direction. As the celebration of the first National Day drew to a close, President Qassem of Iraq laid a dramatic Iraqi claim to Kuwait on June 25, 1961.[29] At a press conference, the Iraqi leader declared that Kuwait was an inseparable part of his country and he would "demand every inch of its territory."[30] The message was not unprecedented in the history of Iraq-Kuwait relations but from Qassem it came as a surprise. Since he seized power in a 1958 coup against the monarchy, Qassem had carefully avoided explicit claims against Kuwait. Nevertheless, in retrospect, there had been several straws in the wind over preceding months.

The previous summer, in 1960, Iraqi police arrested a party of engineers paving the road from Jahra to the frontier with Iraq. Baghdad initially asked Kuwait to stop paving but later agreed that the Kuwaitis could complete the road as far as the Iraqi border post at Safwan. At the same time, the Iraqis were preparing to construct a new port at Umm Qasr. Maritime access to Umm Qasr is possible only through Kuwaiti territorial waters in the area of Bubiyan Island, but Baghdad neither officially informed Kuwaiti authorities of their plans nor sought an agreement for access.[31] It is tempting to see in Iraq's behavior, including the reversal of position on the paved road, an anticipation that it would soon control both the improved road and the nearby Kuwaiti waters. In April 1961, amid unfounded rumors that Kuwait would seek Commonwealth status, Qassem delivered a speech in which he casually asserted that there was no frontier between Iraq and Kuwait.[32] Finally, on June 20, Qassem sent a telegram to the Kuwaiti ruler in which he argued that British protection on the basis of the Anglo-Kuwaiti agreement of 1899 was invalid because "it was ... 'unlawfully' concluded...."[33] Qassem's blunt assault on Kuwait's independence and integrity on June 25 may thus be viewed as the culmination of a series of subtle signals. In the judgement of Miriam Joyce, "... as soon as Kuwait declared independence it was clear that General Qasim's intention was domination rather than cooperation."[34]

With one notable exception, the reaction of the international community to Iraq's assertion of entitlement to Kuwait ranged from stunned surprise to expressions of support for the new state. Probably hoping to curry favor with Baghdad, broadcasts from Moscow took the line that nothing had changed as a result of the Anglo-Kuwaiti agreement and that "British influence and exploitation continued."[35] At the United Nations headquarters in New York, the Soviet Union vetoed Kuwait's application for membership. Effectively frozen out of the Gulf region,[36] Moscow changed its position only when Kuwait agreed to establish diplomatic relations with the Soviet Union.

Recognizing its vulnerability to a determined Iraqi effort to enforce its claim militarily, the Kuwaiti government sought support from Britain and Saudi Arabia and dispatched a number of diplomatic missions to Arab and other countries to explain its position.[37] With the exception of Saudi Arabia, which strongly supported Kuwait from the beginning of the Iraqi-generated crisis, the initial stance of the Arab governments gave the Kuwaitis little comfort. But, as Saddam Hussein would also do almost thirty years later, Qassem misjudged the moment. His initiative was launched in an atmosphere of intensive competition with Nasser's United Arab Republic for leadership and influence in the Arab arena. Nasser was undoubtedly aware that, should Iraq gain control of Kuwait and its wealth, it would be to his disadvantage. Therefore, after initially waffling, the UAR came down in support of Kuwait and its independence.[38] As the Arab League met in Cairo to consider Kuwait's application for full membership, other Arab capitals supported Kuwait's position in the dispute.

Kuwait had taken steps to enhance its military capabilities, but it still was not a match for the much larger Iraqi armed forces. As early as the late 1930s, Kuwait had initiated reforms to build an army for external defense, as well as transform the traditional guards and tribal levies into more organized internal police and security forces.[39] The process continued through the 1950s[40] and, by decade's end, they had created a small professional military, including sixteen advanced Centurion tanks (eight of which were to be prepositioned for use by British forces in the event that they were required to come to Kuwait's defense). Twelve Saladin armored cars were ordered for delivery in late 1959 and military cooperation with Britain, including armor training, took place behind the scenes. It was a measure of the sensitivity of the Anglo-Kuwait relationship in the contemporary Arab milieu that Shaikh Abdallah Mubarak asked that "visits from British officers be kept quiet to avoid 'provoking' Iraq or providing Cairo Radio with an opportunity to point to such visits as evidence that Kuwait was becoming a British military base."[41]

Although they had prudently included provision for British assistance and support against external threats in their agreement, neither Kuwait nor London looked with enthusiasm at invoking it in 1961. The ruler and the Kuwait government were concerned with domestic opposition elements and, particularly, Arab world opinion—which was all too ready to criticize the new relationship. For its part, London had regarded Kuwait as its most important protectorate in the Gulf once oil production began. While it had relied upon naval guns, small detachments of naval infantry, and a few aircraft during earlier threats to the shaikhdom, Britain had given thought to possible contingencies that would require larger ground forces. By the time the monarchy in Iraq was overthrown by Qassem in July 1958, the British had plans in hand for a military intervention.[42] Nevertheless, chastened by the traumatic experience of the Suez intervention, which the United States opposed, senior British officials were reluctant to contemplate a deployment in the region without "clear and public support" from the United States government.[43]

A month before Qassem's inflammatory statements of June 25, the British were concerned by the perceived American posture. The Permanent Under Secretary at the Foreign Ministry decried the lack of Anglo-American joint planning for security in the Gulf. Warning that a sudden emergency in the area could have serious consequences, he continued that it is "really rather ludicrous that there should be an American Admiral stationed in Bahrain alongside a British Admiral... both of them apparently working in watertight compartments and not having much idea of what the other is doing." Immediately following Qassem's press conference, the Foreign Office complained:

> *The United States authorities have shown increasing reluctance to discuss military plans for the area. The State Department has been most careful to avoid any commitment that the United States Government would support the United Kingdom Government if the latter took action in Kuwait.*[44]

The initial American response to Qassem's public claim to Kuwait was tepid and almost nonresponsive to the implied threat. The State Department characterized the crisis prompted by Iraq as "basically (an) inter-Arab controversy" and added that were the United States to interject itself into the crisis it might "goad Qasim to new intemperance." These early comments entirely ignored Iraq's challenging Kuwait's independent existence, hardly a simple inter-Arab disagreement.

The British government, nonetheless, sent a message to Secretary of State Dean Rusk that expressed the hope that the British and American governments would "act with the closest cooperation" in confronting the Iraqi challenge. The British demarche stressed that "The importance of Kuwait to the Western world is such... that we cannot take the risk of allowing Qasim to seize it unopposed." Secretary Rusk's reply was much more satisfactory to London. Rusk wrote, "We understand the depth of your obligation, we agree that the independence of Kuwait must not be destroyed by force, and we are prepared to render the full political support you request."

Secretary Rusk also offered to urge Saudi Arabia, with which the British did not have diplomatic relations at the time, to attempt to defuse the situation. While certainly not the only factor in hardening the American position, the Gulf Oil Company, a partner in KOC, employed its influence to stiffen the U.S. position. Senior officials from Gulf and the State Department conferred in Washington on June 30, 1961. A major concern of the oil executives was that the United Kingdom might not have the military weight to deal with the Iraqi threat. They sought, and received, assurances that the United States would assist militarily if Britain requested such support. The Kennedy Administration representatives stressed that, while protection of Kuwait was still a British responsibility, they would reply favorably to a British request.[45]

Meanwhile, British planning continued for a possible intervention at Kuwaiti request. The British plan, "Vantage," for the defense of Kuwait was on the shelf. It had been drafted some years earlier and before Kuwaiti independence.[46] Although a new plan, called "Bellringer," was being finalized as a replacement, the decision was made to use the existing plan with some modifications.[47] Even so, the British force would be far from self-sustaining. The planning depended not just on Kuwaiti support and cooperation, but use of 680 civilian vehicles from the Kuwait Oil Company as well as gas and lubricants, housing for administrative functions, and drinking water and some foodstuffs.[48]

By the end of June, the British government had concluded that Qassem would be deterred only by large British forces on the ground. Despite concerns regarding hostile reactions to its military intervention, the decision was made in London to proceed. On the night of June 31, a British diplomat in Washington went to the residence of a senior State Department official to inform the United States that the first wave of British troops would arrive in Kuwait on July 1.[49] Marine commandos landed from HMS *Bulwark* without incident.

A delicate diplomatic and propaganda minuet surrounded the insertion of British forces in defense of Kuwait. The British had obtained American promises of support, but London and Kuwait knew there would be reflexive hostility to the British continuing role in the region. Kuwait had invoked the new protection provisions[50] and succeeded in lining up UAR and Arab League support against the Iraqi threat, but was sensitive to appearances that it remained a dependency of Great Britain. Saudi Arabia, for instance, was strongly committed to Kuwait's independence but its relations with Britain were in abeyance. Nasser's UAR supported Kuwait largely out of a concern that archrival Iraq not derive an advantage, but was loathe to tarnish its revolutionary and anti-imperialist credentials. Irrespective of what was happening on the ground, managing the risks and disconnects among Kuwait's supporters was a daunting task.

Even as the first contingents were establishing their beachhead, planning for the evacuation of Western expatriates was under way. As the British Embassy finalized arrangements for the safety of British subjects, the American Consulate, for the first time, was totally on its own in discharging this fundamental protection responsibility. Planning likely called for American civilians to be evacuated aboard U.S. destroyers staging out of Bahrain.[51]

Landings of Marine commandos and elements of the Dragoon Guards from assault craft took place in scorching summertime heat and dust. Among the estimated three thousand troops that had been deployed ashore by the night of July 2, the only casualties were a number of cases of heat exhaustion.[52] Between five thousand and six thousand British personnel had taken up positions in Kuwait by the time the flow ended. Later components arrived by air.

The troops of the British expeditionary force had begun to lay minefields in the northern Kuwaiti desert when Kuwait delivered its defining statement on July 5:

> *Kuwait has always guarded her independence and sovereignty and will continue to do so. Besides, this attitude becomes even clearer if one remembers that during the long period when Kuwait had treaty relations with Britain, no British forces ever landed in Kuwait. The Arab people in general, and Iraqi people in particular, and especially the leaders of the Iraqi Revolution before others, know that throughout the crises the Middle East has experienced in its distant and more recent past—the Suez War and the July Revolution (in Iraq)—Kuwait has never been used as a military base, and no foreign troops ever landed on her pure soil.*[53]

Feeling the need for British assistance in view of Iraq's threat, yet aware of the negative reaction among Arab countries (such as Egypt) that had come down on Kuwait's side of the dispute, the Kuwaiti government sought to isolate itself from their criticism. Although the wording was artful, it was not entirely effective in resolving the contradictions.[54]

Accurate intelligence regarding Iraqi capabilities and intentions was extremely scarce. The British and Kuwaitis alike were dependent upon the British Agency/Embassy to provide the information needed for their analysis. Mustafa Alani, in his study of Operation Vantage, concluded that "Apart from a small U.S. consulate, the agency was the only foreign diplomatic establishment in Kuwait capable of helping them to obtain firsthand information on the situation vis-à-vis Iraq."[55] As is frequently the case in building crises, information regarding Iraq's real intentions was missing or inconclusive; a vigorous debate seems to have developed within the British establishment over the need for, or wisdom of, military intervention. One of the officials who argued strongly against landing a British force was Politcal Agent Sir John Richmond, later, ambassador to Kuwait. He reportedly argued that "Arabs do not attack other Arabs except by radio propaganda..." believing that Qassem might threaten Kuwait verbally but would not invade.[56] Whatever the basis of his conviction, it did not prevail and seems a quaint conceit in light of subsequent events, including the Iraqi aggression against Kuwait in 1990. When intentions are unclear, decision-makers have no choice but to fall back on perceived capabilities, which is the factor that appears to have moved the British government. The power disparity between Iraq and Kuwait, and the close proximity of the two states, likely tipped the balance.[57]

In the same time frame, Kuwait agreed that the Arab League force that would replace the British troops as they withdrew. The British did not object to the plan, although the Foreign Office was concerned that the projected League force included neither armor nor air support. In Bahrain, the British Political Resident for the Gulf was positive about the plan but less than confident that the multilateral force would really come into being.[58]

Nevertheless, Britain began to draw down its forces almost as soon as the deployment was complete; by the end of July, and despite the snail-like pace of Arab League efforts, only two thousand British troops remained in northern Kuwait.[59] A League military delegation arrived in Kuwait a week later to discuss preparations, and four days later Secretary General Hassouna and the ruler signed a formal agreement for a force of up to 3,500 Arab troops. As part of the agreement, Kuwait expressed readiness to join the Arab League Mutual Defense Pact and bear all costs of the operation, except salaries. The organizers, meanwhile, were encountering varying degrees of enthusiasm and cooperation from member states.[60] A force of 3,300 soldiers made up of units from Saudi Arabia, the United Arab Republic (UAR), Jordan, Sudan, and Tunisia which finally appeared during September. This force was commanded by Col. Dabbagh, a Saudi who was under orders to avoid contact with the British military. Despite the resulting chaos and lack of coordination, the last of the British troops withdrew in October.[61]

It will probably never be known what Qassem's real intentions were when he precipitated the crisis by his stark claim to Kuwait. Was his premeditated declaration a trial balloon designed to see whether anyone was prepared to stand up for the newly independent state of Kuwait? Would Iraq have moved militarily in the absence of firm international support for Kuwait's survival and integrity? In any event, the prompt British military riposte, as well as eventual Arab League mobilization and the rejection of Iraq's threat by the wider international community, rendered any Iraqi adventure foolhardy.[62]

Kuwait had survived its first test as an independent state and two years later, in October 1963, Iraqi and Kuwaiti officials signed a minute recording Iraq's recognition of the "independence and complete sovereignty of the State of Kuwait within its frontiers as specified in the letter of the Prime Minister of Iraq dated July 21, 1932."[63] Despite the reiteration of this Iraqi recognition, Kuwait would again face Iraqi aggression in the future. For the moment, however, the residents of Kuwait confronted the task of recovering from the stress and pain of the country's birth.

The international response to Iraq's threat succeeded in sparing Kuwait from attack, but it can hardly have been a satisfactory experience for any of the players. As veteran Middle East correspondent, David Holden, later pointed out, the Iraqi dictator was "scared off" and barely managed to deploy about six thousand troops for a brief period. Most disturbing, however, was the feckless Arab League performance. The member states initially refused to support Kuwait, which turned to them first. When shamed into action, "the League took several weeks to produce a force of its own to replace the British troops." Within months, forces had disintegrated.[64]

Despite continuing pressure domestically and within the Arab world for him to renounce the defense agreement with Britain, the amir refused and eventually sought external support further afield. Two years later, Kuwait's long-serving foreign minister and subsequently amir Shaikh Sabah al-Ahmad asked American chargé William Stoltzfus[65] if the United States would protect small states under threat of aggression. Stoltzfus replied to the hypothetical query that the United States would determine its response based on the facts of individual cases. He was later instructed by the Department of State to add that Washington considered Britain to have primary responsibility for Kuwait's defense but that in any such contingency the United States would support the British in any way possible.[66] In fact, both the American and Kuwaiti governments were groping their way toward an appropriate security relationship. In 1962, the American admiral in Bahrain requested approval of visits to Kuwaiti ports by naval vessels as a demonstration of support for Kuwait's independence. When the Gulf flagship, USS *Valcour*, requested agreement for a visit from June19 to June 22 to Mina al-Ahmadi, the Kuwaiti authorities denied the request. They explained that, while Kuwait welcomed the vessel, its presence at the time of national day celebrations might cause embarrassment.[67]

The American Consulate, redesignated an embassy in the midst of the Qassem crisis, was an interested observer of these and other significant events of the time. The consulate had been established against the better judgement of the British government. Although its personnel developed good working relations with many British counterparts, American diplomats were conscious of the fact that they were under constant scrutiny by the political agency.[68] Despite persistent suspicions, there is no evidence that the British ever had grounds to accuse the consulate of seeking to undermine Britain's unique position in Kuwait. As the instances cited above attest, American representatives continued to show deference to the British in defense matters as long as the United Kingdom maintained a military capability "east of Suez."[69]

By the time of Kuwait's independence, the consulate had moved to a five-acre site leased from the ruling family of Bahrain near the villa of Shaikh Abdallah Jabir. On the site fronting the Gulf, three buildings had been constructed by Shaikh Abdallah Ali Reza: a two-story house as a residence for the principal officer; a three-story building with apartments for other American staff; and a long one-story structure as a Chancery or office. Except on the Gulf side, a waist-high cinderblock wall surrounded the compound. Prior to the construction of the Gulf Road along the coast, the rear of the Residence offered direct access to the beach. According to a number of longtime residents, both Kuwaiti and expatriate, the "Embassy Beach" provided a family-friendly place to gather for many in the community.[70]

The American Consulate had the new compound constructed in the late 1950s. James E. Akins[71] had primary responsibility for overseeing construction on the site for which Talcott Seelye had negotiated a long-term lease. Seelye pushed hard to have the premises designed for an embassy because he foresaw Kuwait's independence. The Foreign Buildings Office in the Department of State balked and demanded a guarantee that the post would become an embassy in the immediate future. It then proceeded to build facilities for a consulate. Even so, the FBO designs left much to be desired. Through persistence, the consulate obtained minor modifications but was unsuccesful in getting the Washington bureaucracy to put balconies in the staff apartments on the Gulf side rather than overlooking *barasti* huts on the desert side. The resulting structures were modest and, in some respects, totally inadequate. The original plans called for the dining room in the principal officer's residence, for example, to be only as long as the width of the living room. It was lengthened through tough negotiations until it was large enough for a small sitdown dinner. The slit of tiny windows at eye level had to be enlarged to accomodate proper windows overlooking the seashore.[72]

The compound, intended to house a consulate but served as the American Embassy until 1996, was augmented with additions and temporary structures for additional staff and functions.[73] Despite its shortcomings, it had evolved into a pleasant site with trees, lawns, gardens, and a large swimming pool. Department of State Inspectors who visited shortly before the Iraqi invasion in August 1990 characterized it as having the appearance of a well-maintained "boys' camp." Whatever the limitations of the facilities, the Embassy compound was comfortable, functional, and well situated as the city grew around it. Around 1970, a high-rise Hilton Hotel overlooking the Embassy grounds was built across the street.[74]

The establishment of formal diplomatic relations between Kuwait and Washington did not sit well with the Qassem regime in Baghdad. When the United States appointed its first ambassador to Kuwait in January 1962 the Iraqi Foreign Minister convoked the

American Ambassador to Iraq to warn him that Baghdad valued relations with the United States but was reassessing them and might withdraw the Iraqi chief of mission in Washington. After the new Kuwaiti Ambassador to Washington presented his credentials, the Iraqi government demanded that the American Ambassador depart Baghdad.[75]

As bilateral relationships grew, American diplomats in Kuwait had much to ponder in addition to the Iraqi threat during Kuwait's first months of independence. In September 1961, as the Arab League force was at last taking up positions in the country, the Kuwaiti government made its first request for American military equipment.[76] On 18 September they asked for the sale of jeep-mounted recoilless rifles with ammunition and a four-year stock of spare parts. Far from being eager to displace the British, however, Washington was reluctant to become a significant source of military equipment in the Middle East. Chargé Mak explained U.S. hesitancy and suggested that the contemporaneous Berlin crisis could make it difficult for the United States to spare the weapons. The Kuwaiti authorities persisted, believing that the recoilless rifles were most suitable for their needs. Mak broached the issue with British counterparts who agreed that the Kuwaiti requirement was logical and suggested an arrangement to enable the British to provide American military equipment to Kuwait.[77] The first, tiny steps toward bilateral defense and security cooperation were thus taken during this formative period. When the Cuban missile standoff between the United States and the Soviet Union occurred, the amir wrote a letter of support to President Kennedy and ordered his air force and police to be on alert for potential attacks on American interests.[78]

Kuwaiti efforts to strengthen credible military and civil services staffed by Kuwaitis resulted in the resignation or retirement of high-ranking officials of Palestinian origin during the years following independence. A significant number of this intelligentsia who had come to serve in Kuwait prior to the advent of oil wealth were granted Kuwaiti citizenship for their services.[79] In education, the police, and the armed forces, expatriates from Palestine played an important role in shaping institutions.

Behind the headlines and military and diplomatic activities, important domestic reforms that would shape Kuwait's future were in progress. The ruler had announced plans to oversee the drafting of a constitution for the country. Six months after independence, on December 30, 1961, Kuwaiti voters went to the polls to elect a twenty-member constituent assembly charged with drafting the new constitution. The assembly completed the task in less than a year, and by November 11, 1962, it was ready for the amir's signature. By signing the document, Amir Abdallah made history in becoming the first and only constitutional monarch in the Gulf, a momentous development in a process that had periodically divided Kuwaitis since the 1920s and 30s.

The 1962 constitution was a hybrid document, embodying, in the judgement of a prominent Kuwaiti political scientist, "a compromise between two aspects of Kuwaiti political culture: traditional hereditary rule and modern representative forms."[80] It did not resolve all future differences; crises involving the National Assembly would continue. It did, however, provide the first written guarantee of fundamental rights and freedoms. And drawing upon Kuwait's long tradition of consultation and consensus-building, it committed the nation irrevocably to representative government. These pioneering achievements have not often received the credit they merit in both "opposition" politics or Western commentaries. The situation, Ghabra elaborates, "can be characterized as a transition from semiauthoritarian rule to semidemocratic rule whereby elections and a democratic process empower a parliament to balance and check the executive branch...."[81]

Political struggles with "opposition" members of the new National Assembly soon arose. In 1963, twelve deputies from the Arab nationalist bloc proposed that the defense agreement with the United Kingdom be abrogated. Apparently undeterred by the ineffectual Arab League response to Kuwait's defense in 1961, they envisaged the abrogation as a prelude to Kuwait's adherence to President Nasser's United Arab Republic (UAR). The failure of this initiative on the part of the national bloc illustrates an important lesson regarding elements that identified with pan-Arab currents and non-Kuwaiti Arab expatriates:

> Electoral success required Kuwaiti support. Arabs, from outside Kuwait, no matter how enthusiastic, could not vote. Because of the large number and placement of nonnationals, foreigners, even Arabs, were seen by many Kuwaitis as potential enemies, not allies. It was easier to galvanize a crowd with xenophobia, offering the expatriates as scapegoats, than as Arab allies.[82]

Dr. Ahmad al-Khatib, a perennial figure in the Kuwaiti "opposition"[83] who was a leader of the bloc, delivered a speech in the National Assembly in 1963 advocating that the rights and privileges of Kuwaiti citizens be extended to Egyptians, Palestinians, and other Arab workers in the country. This obvious effort to expand his constituency fell flat, and in the process narrowed the future focus of the assembly to Kuwait's (rather than Pan-Arab) issues and interests. The public reaction to al-Khatib's proposal was so strong and negative that he was compelled to back off. Nevertheless, any who had suspected that the parliament would be little more than a rubber stamp for the cabinet had been proven wrong. "Kuwait," according to a knowledgeable observer, "has somehow managed to combine American and British procedural features."[84]

The era of Shaikh Abdallah Al-Salem Al-Sabah's rule (1950–65) was arguably the most important of the country's modern history. Neither Kuwaitis nor American and other expatriates could have possibly conceived of the changes that would occur under his wise and understated leadership. Indeed, during frequent periods when he was challenged by internal critics and occasional violence, the casual observer might have doubted the course he had set, or his popularity among his people. His rule was not serene and trouble-free, but, at the end of the day, his achievements overshadowed the turbulence. "Despite their varying opinions on most subjects, Kuwaitis are unanimous in ranking Abdallah III the greatest of their modern rulers." [85]

No less an authority than Alan Rush clearly concurs in this judgment. With consummate skill, Shaikh Abdallah fended off persistent British efforts to tighten their control over Kuwaiti domestic affairs. In the process, he brought Kuwait rapidly to independence without sacrificing a cordial relationship with London, including an extended commitment to Kuwait's security. In a similar manner, he fended off the influence of powerful Arab states (particularly Egypt and Iraq, and Kuwaitis inspired by them) and successfully brought Kuwait into the Arab League and United Nations. At the same time, the country was undergoing unprecedented development of infrastructure and other facilities, including education, while the rudimentary traditional administration was being upgraded to meet the demands of a modern economy. In Rush's words, "...[Shaikh Abdallah] achieved Kuwait's transition from an obscure old-world shaikhdom into an internationally known, oil-rich state and willed into existence the standards of tolerance and fair play by which his successors have been, and always will be, judged."[86]

The amir was not, despite his achievements, a highly vocal or charismatic leader—which may explain why rivals and detractors appeared to dominate the scene in the early years. He exhibited calm and an aversion to recklessness during crises; whether the fallout from the Suez Crisis or Iraq's invasion threat at independence. Undoubtedly, his quiet, resolute demeanor in periods of danger and instability contributed to the enhancement of his reputation among his people and permitted him to change the paradigm of national political culture.

> *Faced with danger from outside the country, the eyes of the Kuwaitis had been opened. Suddenly they could see that, whatever its faults, the Al-Sabah dynasty is the irreplaceable symbol of Kuwait's independence and traditions, its only acceptable stabilizing force, and this in turn increased Abdallah III's resolve to trust the people and encourage the establishment in Kuwait of a political system offering more civil and political rights than were available to his Iraqi critics in their own country."*[87]

10

Growing Pains and Engagement

The Kuwaiti ruler, Amir Abdallah Salem, fell ill in October 1965, and following a massive heart attack, passed away on November 24. He was survived by three sons, including Shaikh Sa'd al-Abdallah who was destined to become a long-serving crown prince/prime minister.

Shaikh Sabah Salem,[1] the prime minister and half brother of Amir Abdallah, was selected as the new amir. Shaikh Sabah's accession was met with widespread enthusiasm because he represented continuity; his rule was regarded as a continuation of Shaikh Abdallah's and he was viewed as personally sympathetic to liberalizing trends. The new amir named Prime Minister Shaikh Jabir al-Ahmad as the Heir Apparent in May 1966.[2] With this decision, the collateral Jabir branch of the ruling family was brought back into the line of succession, setting up a return to the earlier practice of alternating with the Salem line.[3]

If either the government leadership or the inhabitants of Kuwait had hoped for a period of stability and calm following a decade of unprecedented change and a renewed Iraqi threat, they were soon disappointed. There would be no time to digest or adapt to the vast physical, societal, or individual changes, including the adoption of the first and most revolutionary experiment in parliamentary government in the Gulf region. Instead, in January 1963 the people of Kuwait experienced a shock and challenge almost from the moment Shaikh Sabah al-Salem became prime minister.

Although knowledgeable observers were aware of the internal turmoil that fed on events like the Suez Crisis and the campaign of the United Arab Republic and others to spread the ideas of

Pan-Arabism in the late 1950s, it was hoped that improved living standards, domestic reforms, and the experience of an open attack by a neighboring Arab country would usher in a period of relative domestic unity and peaceful evolution. The idea of association with the larger Arab world was an attractive and understandable one for the people of a small Gulf state. Only over time would most Kuwaitis come to appreciate that, as often as not, the prophets of Pan-Arabism were concerned not with what was good for Kuwait but with their own power and influence. The dichotomy is reflected in the contrasting views of Kuwait's immense oil wealth:

> *To Kuwaitis or Saudis, who generally take their Arab nationalism seriously, the oil wealth is theirs to be spent as their leaders determine. To share a portion of it with fellow Arabs is an act of generosity, or geopolitics. To the peoples of the have-not Arab countries, this is apparently Arab oil wealth; they are not grateful for, but dissatisfied with, the share they have gotten.*[4]

The election of 1963 for the first National Assembly produced an unexpectedly "cantankerous opposition group" that was anti-Western, Arab nationalist, and radical socialist in orientation.[5] Hardly had the new assembly been seated when this "opposition" adopted extreme positions on a range of issues.[6] They belittled the reforms engineered by Amir Abdallah as half-measures, attacked the government for working with the most powerful merchants, and called for a reduction in the al-Sabah privy purse. Predictably, and without regard for the recent experience with Iraq, the opposition spokesmen demanded the abrogation of the 1961 defense agreement with Britain. With regard to the latter issue, the "opposition" position was indistinguishable from that of the Soviet Union, the UAR, and their regional allies. For example, in May 1964, Soviet Premier Nikita Khrushchev told an audience in Cairo that

> *... imperialists were still in Kuwayt where there was a Muslim Arab amir ... who is paid a bribe ... who lives to be very rich trading with the wealth of his people, and his conscience does not disturb him in this respect.*[7]

It became increasingly evident that the "opposition" deputies were acting in conjunction with, if not at the behest of, foreign elements whose agenda was inimical to Kuwaiti interests.

The untenable political situation came to a head in December of that year when the radical deputies, no more than one quarter of the National Assembly, succeeded in forcing the cabinet to resign, and a new government (omitting ministers unacceptable to the "opposition") to be formed.[8] The success and intemperance of the assembly hard-liners in making the pursuit of normal political and social life impossible within Kuwait also unmasked their real ideological loyalties and goals. As Rush concluded, the extremism revealed "first alienated, then alarmed, the conservative majority of Kuwaitis, and even split the ranks of the unofficial opposition" within the assembly.[9]

With the support of Amir Sabah, the government counterattacked with increased candor and firmer security measures in 1965.[10] The campaign was spearheaded by two capable and popular figures Crown Prince Shaikh Jabir al-Ahmad and Shaikh Sa'd Abdallah, who was in charge of Defense and Interior. Illustrative of the new strategy were their frank statements of the time. In a speech before the National Assembly in May 1966, Shaikh Jabir "reminded Arab nationalist deputies that their chief duty was to serve Kuwaiti, and not Egyptian or pan-Arab, interests. He also accused them of 'spreading a spirit of disregard ... for the traditions with which we have been brought up'." For his part, Shaikh Sa'd warned that "The government was very lenient in the past... [but] now ... finds itself compelled to strike with iron for maintaining peace and order so that our people can live in happiness."[11] To underline the new determination, the authorities questioned hundreds of Egyptian, Palestinian, and other Arab expatriates and deported many who were believed to be colluding with and supporting the Kuwaiti minority represented by dissident members of the assembly. Clubs that had long provided a base for political agitation among teachers and journalists were closed, and stricter controls were imposed on the press.[12]

The "opposition" responded emotionally to these measures; eight deputies resigned from their seats in the assembly. Their departure made governing easier and paved the way for an orderly election of deputies to the 1967–1971 National Assembly. Buoyed by their success, the government dismissed the municipal council which chronically criticizied land acquisition policies and leading land speculators. Pan-Arab candidates suffered unanticipated setbacks in the next assembly election.[13] While rocky, Kuwait survived its initial experience with parliamentary government with its commitment intact. There would be continuing tussles over coming years, but the National Assembly was firmly ingrained in Kuwaiti political consciousness.

The fledgling American Embassy was an active observer of these internal developments. There was not yet the matrix of bilateral relationships between Kuwait and the United States that would evolve over the remainder of the twentieth century, but the old constraints on direct contacts with the amir and senior Kuwaiti officials had been lifted with the end of the British protectorate agreement. Dayton S. Mak, who was assigned to the country to serve as chargé d'affaires during and after the transition to independence, provided insights into the activities of American diplomats during this crucial period.[14]

Parker T. "Pete" Hart, the first U. S. ambassador to Kuwait, was resident in Jidda.[15] Ambassador Hart undertook only two visits to Kuwait during his tenure, although he had visited there as early as 1950 and continued to visit after he joined Bechtel following retirement from the Foreign Service. He died, regrettably, before he was able to record his rich experiences for the Foreign Affairs Oral History Collection. Fortunately, he was an old friend of mine and kindly shared some of his insights by letter.

Ambassador and Mrs. Hart traveled to Kuwait in January 1962 to present his credentials to Amir Abdallah al-Salem:

> The credentials presentation was managed with almost British style by the Kuwaitis, red jacketed bagpipers, spit and polish, precision honor guard marching, fife, and drums. The Amir answered my speech given in Arabic (prepared with the indispensable help of Isa al-Sabbagh, my Cultural & Public Affairs Counselor) by a warm welcome, and I had later a follow-up visit to him in his modest office on the sea near where dhows were repaired or built.[16]

Ambassador Hart raised the deteriorating situation in Yemen and asked if Kuwait might join countries providing the Mutawakkilite Kingdom with economic assistance. The Amir responded with a proverb —"'One makes one's bed by the length of the blanket" and explained that "aid to Yemen was wasted as long as Imam Ahmad ruled." Hart observed that he found out that Amir Abdallah was "dead right." This typified Pete Hart's appreciation of interactions with Kuwaiti officials and businessmen. He summed up his experience concisely: "I always found Kuwait and Kuwaitis, in my follow-up visits on Bechtel business, to be anchors of common sense in a swirling political environment. I regretted that my time in stable, practical Kuwait was so short, for I felt so relaxed there...."

Mak recalled the amir of his time, Shaikh Abdallah, as a warm man who was "quite approachable" but seldom inclined to substantive discussions. Amir Abdallah periodically invited diplomats and their wives to dinner at his palace. His habit was to devote time talking with his guests and to take the ladies away for more conversation before the guests departed about 7:00 pm.[17] As the primary U.S. representative, Chargé Mak recalls easy access and cordial exchanges with a number of ministers and other senior officials. Crown Prince Shaikh Sabah al-Salem was handling the foreign affairs portfolio during that period. Mak remembers that he was very welcoming:

> "... I would go and visit him fairly often, at least once a month. He had an office in the Foreign Office at that time and he also had an office elsewhere, but I'd visit him and discuss general problems with him either at the Foreign Office or at his home. We had very few immediate problems to discuss, although there would be general area problems on which I sought his views."

Among the frequent subjects on which views were exchanged were President Nasser of the United Arab Republic (UAR), his influence and activities, and Iraq, which was still claiming Kuwaiti territory. "I would discuss," Mak relates, "with the foreign minister, the deputy emir, and the defense minister general ideas of Kuwait and its requirements for outside protection."

The embassy maintained close contact with the officials of the

Kuwaiti foreign affairs department (later the Ministry of Foreign Affairs) which Mak visited at least weekly for far-ranging discussions. The minister and "all of his staff ... were people I could pop in on like I did in London. They were that kind of people."[18] Mak summarized his experience as the senior American on the scene as "a very friendly arrangement."

In addition to its function in conducting contacts and exchanges with the host government, the new embassy assumed responsibility for the American community in Kuwait. It was still a relatively small community —not more than three hundred—and widely dispersed in oil and company compounds throughout the country and in the Neutral Zone shared with Saudi Arabia. In addition to the Americans working with the Kuwait Oil Company (KOC),[19] Bechtel, Schlumberger, Getty, AMINOIL, and several large construction firms were among the major American employers. Only a few of the senior personnel resided in Kuwait city, which meant that opportunities for interaction between the subgroups were few. The embassy was staffed by five Foreign Service Officers, three clerks/secretaries[20], and four or five local hires and provided whatever nexus existed for the American community.[21] Unofficial Americans and their families were welcomed to the compound for swimming, volleyball, and tennis. The entire community gathered at the embassy annually for Independence Day celebrations.[22]

Despite the looming storm clouds caused by the Iraqi threat to Kuwait's independence, the embassy commemoration of American Independence Day in July 1961 was a memorable event. Not only the American community but "droves" of Kuwaiti shaikhs, merchants, and others came to see the the new Embassy facility which, despite its austerity, was different from other buildings in the Kuwait of the day.[23] Kuwaitis, including members of the ruling family, regularly attended embassy functions in those simpler less formal days.

The new Embassy grounds were doubly important to the far-flung Americans who had few institutions to sustain a sense of community.[24] There was no American school at independence and parents could either enroll their small children in the British school or take on home schooling under the so-called Calvert system.[25] In about 1962, a small school with some half-dozen American and Palestinian students was set up in part of the Chancery building under the guidance of a talented Palestinian female teacher.[26] This was the first American school in the country since the pioneering school of Dr. Edwin Calverley was compelled to close in the 1930s.[27] Although several children of private Americans attended the embassy school, it was not large enough to meet community needs.

Given the priority Americans attach to educational opportunities for their children, it was only a matter of time before the community turned its attention to the establishment of an appropriate school.[28] The embassy, in cooperation with the American Mission, took the initiative to create the International School of Kuwait (ISK); the new school admitted its first pupils in September 1964.[29] In preparation for this momentous opening, Dorothy Scudder wrote to her sister, a superintendant of schools in the United States: *"I said there are no books here... so when she was changing her books..., she would send them to me... the American school here started off with those books and a couple of the women who were school teachers."*[30]

The new school became the catalyst for a revolution in expatriate education in Kuwait. By the 1980s, there were three schools, including ISK, teaching an American curriculum through high school and accredited in the United States. Young Kuwaitis planning to pursue higher education in the United States, Britain, or elsewhere also take advantage of these institutions.

The American Mission hospital continued to operate through the 1960s within the new system of state hospitals and clinics. It was, however, in the twilight of its fifty years of dedicated service to the health and well-being of the society. In 1966, the National Evangelical Church in Kuwait was registered with the authorities and, under the direction of American pastors, held Protestant services in English, Arabic and, eventually, South Asian languages and Tagalog at the expanded chapel on the American Mission compound. The Evangelical Church, along with a later Catholic cathedral and the Anglican Church at Ahmadi, continue to minister to spiritual needs of expatriate communities today.

For the last several decades of its operation, the American Mission and its hospitals had been largely financed by local patronage and subscriptions. Capital building projects benefited from the support of grateful Kuwaitis, including the Amir. Nevertheless, the venerable institution came under increasing pressure from Church authorities in the United States who argued that "what had begun as a charitable undertaking could no longer be justified in what had become the world's most lavish welfare state." Reportedly, the amir offered to pay the costs of its continued operation, but the Church officials could not be swayed from their determination to shut it down.[31] Some observers suspected that the real motivation was the fact that the American Mission, despite its good works, had never achieved the number of conversions to Christianity that the Mission Board felt necessary to justify its continuation. In 1973, the "Arabian Mission was dissolved as an entity."[32] The coup d'grâce was administered, not by the Kuwaitis who had embraced it, but by the staff's fellow countrymen who had launched it.

Dr. Lewis Scudder, Sr. and Dorothy Scudder remained in Kuwait, embraced by the Kuwaiti government and population. They continued to reside in the "house on the hill" built in 1914 for the hospital director with momentos and photos of their decades of residence. Both Lewis and Dorothy were given employment within the Kuwaiti medical establishment and their son, Dr. Lewis Scudder, Jr. recalls that his father was offered Kuwaiti citizenship several times:

His Kuwaiti friends were rather surprised when he politely refused it. His answer, invariably, was that to have accepted it would have made it appear that he was trading upon his years of ministry as a missionary. He would not throw away the gold for silver.[33]

It is appropriate that the epitaph for the intrepid medical missionaries of the Arabian Mission, and their invaluable contribution to the development of relations between the American and Kuwaiti peoples, was written by Ambassador Joe Twinam before his own untimely death in 2001:

Suffice it here to say that the missions came to convert, ran into the strength of Islam and stayed to heal. In the long and arduous process they created a firm impression that Americans are basically decent folk who want to help if they can. That perception, which many other Americans of more worldly interests also subsequently nurtured, has done much to develop and sustain the American position in the Gulf over the years.[34]

Initially, the staff of the American Embassy did not face an overwhelming workload but with the passage of time and the measured withdrawal of British assets, its agenda of issues with the Kuwaiti government grew.[35] At the outset, it was dependent upon the commercial cable system to communicate with the Department of State and other diplomatic posts in the region:

Our telegrams we would type on a local form, take it down to the local (Cable & Wireless) telegraph office and send it off. Now this, of course, was quite adequate until we had real problems; in other words when the threat of Iraq happened this was no longer possible. So we had a terrible time. Very quickly the Department put us 'on line' ....[36]

Security issues and concerns, such as those posed by Iraq, were a continuing preoccupation of the Kuwaiti authorities and the embassy, and soon became the subject of exchanges and cooperation between the two. The Iraqi threat to Kuwait's independence, issued by Qassem, gradually lost its immediacy—in part because of the demonstrated willingness of the British and international community to confront a military adventure, and in part because Qassem was facing serious internal opposition. To bolster his position, Qassem became increasingly dependent upon an alliance with the Iraq Communist Party. On February 8, 1963, a coalition of Ba'athist and Pan-Arab officers more closely aligned with President Nasser overthrew and executed Qassem, providing some breathing space for Kuwait. On February 18, the border between Kuwait and Iraq was reopened and within days trade, currency, and diplomatic relations were restored.[37] The National Assembly, still dominated by the radical "Pan-Arab" minority, did not seem to have drawn any useful lessons from the recent crisis,[38] but the government remained wary. When an Iraqi delegation headed by Iraqi Prime Minister Bakr and including the Minister of Defense visited Kuwait October 10–14, the Kuwaiti hosts took advantage of the opportunity to make a point:

> In response to the heavy demonstration of Iraq's military might at the earlier Kuwaiti delegation, the Kuwaiti Government now laid aside its usual high-level visitors' sightseeing program of central kitchens, kindergartens, and institutes for the blind and gave the Iraqi delegation a dose of new Kuwaiti military installations and equipment. In this way they hoped to show that Kuwait would not be a pushover.[39]

Irrespective of those inside the country calling for an end to Kuwait's dependence upon British assistance as a last resort, events elsewhere were laying the groundwork for the agreement's termination. London was finding its commitments in the Gulf too costly to sustain and its withdrawal accelerated as the decade came to an end. On December 24, 1965, the British Defense and Overseas Policy Committee took the initiative to amend the Kuwait agreement to limit its commitment to air forces unless "the ruler gives us adequate time to move inland forces from the United Kingdom or Far East to Kuwait'"[40] The British prime minister took the final step when he announced publicly (in January 1968) that all British forces, including the naval facility at Jufair in Bahrain and the base at Aden, would be withdrawn by the end of 1971. This decision also presaged an end to Britain's special treaty relationship with Bahrain, Qatar, and the Trucial States.[41] Britain, for so long Kuwait's defender *in extremis*, was no longer an option:

> It was against this background that Shaikh Jabir announced the abrogation of the exchange of letters and the effective ending of Britain's special position in Kuwait. When the al-Sabah again looked for external support following the Iraqi invasion of 1990, it was the United States, rather than Britain, which acted as guarantor of Kuwaiti independence.[42]

Washington quite naturally followed developments in the region closely because of its interest in maintaining stability and global access to the immense petroleum resources there. Its primary focus at the time, however, was to prevent the Soviet Union and other hostile forces, including radical Pan-Arabism, from establishing positions of strength and influence in the region.[43] As a result, it took no measures to rush in to replace the departing British, and the U.S.-Kuwaiti security relationship was slow in unfolding. Dangers inherent in the Arab-Israeli dispute claimed a far greater portion of American diplomatic attention and effort. In this respect, U.S. foreign policy failed when it was unsuccessful in preventing the June War of 1967.

By the time that conflict occurred, a denouement in the earlier struggle between the Arab "republics" (of which President Nasser was the primary protagonist) and Arab monarchies, (epitomized by Jordan and Saudi Arabia) had taken place. The accompanying reduction in area-wide tensions helped facilitate the Kuwaiti "establishment" in wresting the domestic initiative from "opposition" elements in the parliament and other institutions.[44] The improved inter-Arab atmosphere made it easier for King Hussein of Jordan to reconcile with Nasser and commit Jordanian armed forces to the battle in which Jordan was forced out of the West Bank. It also encouraged countries like Kuwait to throw their diplomatic and financial assets into the Arab effort and even provide Kuwaitis to fight with Arab armies.[45] When the guns fell silent, Kuwait absorbed a further wave of Palestinian refugees and contributed heavily to the damaged economies of the "confrontation states" bordering Israel.

The 1967 Arab-Israeli war inevitably affected the evolving relationship between Kuwait and the United States. Chuck Cecil, who began his Foreign Service career as a JO (Junior Officer) in Kuwait from 1966 to 1968, recalled that there was "a day or two of uncertainty" about whether diplomatic relations would be broken.[46] The amir, however, received Ambassador Cottam a day or so later and assured him that relations would be maintained. The Kuwaiti police and Army set up checkpoints just beyond Dasman Palace and the circle on First Ring Road, and halted crowds that attempted to move toward the Embassy compound.[47] The ambassador had planned a lunch shortly after June 5 and most of the guests called to regret. Only one, Mohamed al-Sharekh, Deputy Director of the Kuwait Fund, managed to talk his way through the police cordon.

The embassy in Kuwait[48] was awarded a group Meritorious Honor Award in October 1967 which read in part "... by exceptional devotion to duty under adverse circumstances, provided effective protection of American interests in Kuwait, (the embassy) provided advice, comfort and assurance to the American community in Kuwait and kept official and unofficial channels to Kuwaitis open, paving the way for an early return to the normal, beneficial relationships between Kuwait and the United States."[49] But it turned out to be more of a hiccup than a convulsion.[50] Probably out of genuine support for Arab positions on the Palestine Question, but also to protect its position within that community of states, Kuwait observed the embargo of oil exports to the United States and others considered to be allies of Israel,[51] but maintained the embargo for only three months. On September 3, loading of oil to all destinations was resumed.[52] Even more significantly, Kuwait bucked the Arab trend by refusing to break diplomatic relations with Washington and London, fending off pressures from Arab governments in doing so. The following year, 1968, Amir Sabah accepted an invitation to make a state visit to Washington, the first Arab head of state to visit the United States since the 1967 war.[53]

At the time of the June War and for several years thereafter, United States Navy assets in the Persian Gulf operated out of a facility at Jufair in Bahrain. The token force included the command ship U.S.S. *Valcour*, a converted World War II seaplane tender that was painted white. The "Great White Ghost of the Arabian Coast" (as *Valcour* was known at the time) was a familiar sight in the Gulf and Indian Ocean as it made port calls throughout the area. This permanent flagship was supplemented by one or two pairs of destroyers, detailed alternately from the Atlantic and Pacific fleets, for limited periods of duty. Among the memorabilia Dorothy Scudder had collected were photographs showing unidentified U.S. Naval Officers in uniform during friendly visits to Kuwait. Unfortunately, her possessions were trashed and destroyed by Iraqi troops during the 1990–91 occupation of the country. Arab and South Asian members of the National Evangelical Church adjacent to her home partially documented the gratuitous destruction. Several historic photographs that had been given to me by Mrs. Scudder survived.[54]

In the early 1970s, the future of the U.S. Navy facility in Bahrain was in jeopardy for several years, particularly following the 1973 Arab-Israel War and the imposition of the Arab oil embargo. The U.S. government conducted an in-depth review of its policy in the Persian Gulf as the British withdrew from the area. Still involved with the conflict in Vietnam, Washington "decided that the United States would not try to replace Britain in the Gulf, but it would maintain its small Middle East naval presence there which was known as MIDEASTFOR."[55] As part of this same decision, Ambassador Bill Stoltzfus was accredited to Bahrain, Qatar, the United Arab Emirates, and Oman in addition to his responsibilities in Kuwait. Modest embassies were established in Manama, Abu Dhabi, and Muscat under chargés d'affaires. In 1974, however, the short-lived Bahraini parliament adopted a resolution calling for the Navy to leave its tiny facility. Although the Bahraini government was taken by surprise, it did not feel it could simply overrule the parliament (within a year, it dissolved the parliament itself). Admiral William J. Crowe, Jr., who would go on to occupy increasingly senior Navy posts and, ultimately, was Chairman of the Joint Chiefs of Staff (CJCS), assumed command in Manama, and it fell to him and the U.S. Ambassador (Joseph Twinam and, later, Wat Cluverius) to work out a mutually-acceptable solution.

Admiral Crowe's tenure as COMMIDEASTFOR was not a pleasant one, and may well have colored his subsequent view of the region negatively. Nevertheless, he was instrumental in crafting a workable compromise. Despite high tension and uncertainty, the purpose-built command ship U.S.S. *La Salle* (AGF-3) replaced the aged *Valcour* as flagship in the Persian Gulf/Indian Ocean.[56] The U.S. Navy facility at the Jufair location vacated by the Royal Navy in 1971 survived, although it looked for a time as if naval vessels would have to function without land support. In his memoirs, Crowe summarized the way in which the impasse between the United States and Bahrain was resolved:

> *The guts of the concept was that most of the [Navy] dependants would move out of Bahrain. The flagship was a 31,000-ton amphibious landing ship ... which accommodated a crew of about twelve hundred people. Of the twelve hundred, three or four hundred had families that would normally be living in Bahrain. But in fact all but about a hundred and fifty families had already left since the Bahraini announcement about closing the base. Now we were preparing to move all the remaining families except those of people manning the base facilities. Over half of the base personnel*

were young and single, and when we were finished there would be only about thirty or forty families left.[57]

Since both the American and Bahraini governments were looking for a way out, this strategy made it possible for the U.S. Navy to retain its vital support facilities on shore while the Bahrainis could continue to argue in 1977 that the Navy was withdrawing. The strategic importance of this accommodation is difficult to overestimate. As Adm. Crowe concludes:

> If we had lost our access to facilities in Bahrain in 1977, we would not have been able to accomplish what we did in the Earnest Will convoying operation during the Iran-Iraq war. Desert Storm (the liberation of Kuwait) would have been more difficult.[58]

The retention of modest U.S. Navy facilities provided an essential fulcrum when the United States was called upon to mount security operations in the Gulf region. Their loss would have had costly consequences for Kuwait when its more powerful neighbors attacked it and its vital interests.

The investment in naval support facilities reflected heightened American interest in security and stability in the Persian Gulf, including Kuwait. Enhancement of naval facilities went hand in hand with the adoption of a more forthcoming position on the sale of U.S. military equipment to smaller Gulf states. Ambassador Twinam, who was actively involved with the implementation of U.S. policy toward the region, deemed it "remarkable" that until the 1970s Washington "adopted a policy of relative restraint toward selling military equipment in a region in which the future character of newly independent governments and of their relations with one another was not yet certain."[59] At Kuwait's initiative,[60] U.S. regional policy took a definite turn in 1973 when the U.S. Administration agreed to a Kuwaiti request for vital air defense systems, including I-Hawk ground-to air missiles and modern fighter/interceptor aircraft. This development added a new and increasingly robust dimension to bilateral relations.[61] First, however, the two governments had to exercise ingenuity to make this program work since Kuwait does not allow military attachés. The solution was the creation within the American Embassy of a cadre of military administrators and logistics, and maintenance specialists called the U.S. Liaison Office Kuwait or USLOK.[62]

Kuwait had proclaimed itself "non-aligned" in international relations—consistent with its historic effort to maintain the best possible relations with states that might threaten its security and interests.[63] When the British Conservative party came to power and launched a re-evaluation of the decision to withdraw from "East of Suez," for example, Shaikh Jabir al-Ahmad, was blunt: "We do not accept any foreign presence in the area, be it British or anything else."[64] This position could be interpreted as a criticism of the U.S. Navy presence in Bahrain at a moment when its future was in doubt. It was certainly not helpful to the amir of Bahrain who was also looking for a way to resolve the impasse on the issue to the satisfaction of both parties.

To give substance to its position on nonalignment, Kuwait moved deliberately to establish diplomatic relations with Moscow and other communist states. The Soviet Union had blocked Kuwait's application to join the United Nations until Kuwait agreed to exchange ambassadors.[65] Diplomatic relations with other Eastern European states followed. The United States regarded this facilitation of a hostile presence with surprise and concern. American Chargé Dayton Mak, recalled discussing these concerns with Shaikh Sa'd Abdallah, the minister of defense at the time:

> I ... remember ... speaking to him one day about the Kuwaiti decision to allow the Russians to establish an embassy in Kuwait. I told Sheikh Saad [sic], 'You know they aren't coming in because they love you, they will be coming in here trying to undermine you and who is going to keep an eye on all these people?" He ... looked at me and laughed with a twinkle in his eye and said,"'Well I expect you Americans to do that."[66]

Adherence to a nonaligned posture offered advantages in the Kuwait government's estimation; it provided a degree of immunity from radical elements of the domestic opposition as well as more extreme republican regimes in the Arab world. Additionally, it gave the Soviets and others who were not natural allies of a monarchical government an incentive to eschew mischief-making. On the other hand, it unquestionably gained the attention of the West. In the process, some officials in the West, who did not see the nuance behind the words, concluded that Kuwait might not be a reliable partner despite many shared interests and goals.[67]

Beneath the occasionally intemperate rhetoric, the U.S.-Kuwaiti relationship was sound and continued to mature as both nations learned to deal constructively with an increasing range of issues and interests. Strong words were sometimes delivered more for effect than to give offense. William Stoltzfus, who was ambassador to Kuwait from 1972-76, offered an illustrative case from his experience there.[68] He was meeting with a senior Kuwaiti at the time Kuwait was purchasing U.S. armaments. The discussion turned to the costs of the package. The Kuwaiti opened with a "blast": "You [the United States] obviously don't consider us friends... you have no respect... we are just little inferiors to be treated like dirt and taken advantage of...." The Kuwaiti official then dismissed his deputy and proposed tea, during which the conversation was pleasant and non-contentious. Ambassador Stoltzfus reported to the State Department that he and the official had discussed the cost of military sales and expressed hope that the prices could be kept as low as possible. Just as the veteran shopper in the area learns the point at which bargaining with the shopkeeper has achieved its purpose, experienced diplomats in the field learn to differentiate between interpersonal anger and situational requirements. This facility allows genuine feelings to be conveyed without destroying interpersonal and bilateral relationships.[69]

Diplomatic relations between Kuwait and the United States survived the fallout from the 1967 and 1973 Arab-Israeli wars—particularly the former, when many Arab states broke diplomatic ties.[70] Aside from working contacts at the embassy level in Kuwait and Washington, there was a surprisingly robust exchange of high level visits and consultations. The decision of Shaikh Sabah al-Salem to make a state visit to the United States in 1968[71] was not only an act of courage and leadership in the regional atmosphere, but testimony to the importance his government attached to the relationship. The travel of senior U.S. officials to Kuwait over the period was a demonstration that Washington reciprocated this view.[72]

The bilateral agenda was broad and diverse and, as Chargé Mak's anecdote about the decision to open relations with Moscow implies, more relaxed and friendly than the public posture suggested. Kuwait's security, and that of the region, was a continuing subject of consultation as the two states moved toward Kuwaiti acquisition of major U.S. weapon systems. Such cooperation implies much more than a simple transfer of military hardware. Following the announcement regarding the sale of fighter aircraft in 1973, as an example, Minister of Defense and Interior Shaikh Sa'd al-Abdallah announced that twenty-four Kuwaiti pilots would go to the United States for long-term training. These sorts of continuing interactions foster mutual familiarity and, often, strong personal and professional relationships.[73]

Petroleum and financial affairs were also staple items on the bilateral agenda. The Kuwaiti government had sought to improve its stake and income from oil since 1950, shortly after exports began. As it grew in technical competency and economic sophistication, Kuwait was interested in maximizing its income to finance development and underwrite the rising standard of living of its people. There were limits on the volume produced and market constraints on pricing, but the oil embargoes in which Kuwait participated following the Arab-Israeli wars of 1967 and 1973 made it possible for OPEC to raise base prices and end the era of cheap petroleum.[74] The experience also strained relations with some of the foreign oil companies.

A complicating factor for Kuwait's petroleum policy was the intervention of the unruly National Assembly into the state's relationship with foreign concessionaires. The Kuwait government had gradually increased its stake in the Kuwaiti Petroleum Company (British Petroleum and Gulf Oil Company) to 60 percent. In December 1975, pushed by largely radical deputies, Kuwait took full control of the company.[75] Two years later, in 1977, Kuwait likewise nationalized AMINOIL. These measures were in no way welcomed by the U.S. government or the American oil companies, but they passed by without apparent rancor. The United States recorded its reservations in accordance with its long-standing position on "fair compensation" in cases of nationalization of American assets abroad, but the U.S. corporations involved seemed resigned to the final terms which included assurances of access to Kuwaiti crude in the future.[76] *"The history of these takeovers, a remarkable episode of generally amicable host-government acquisition of foreign investment, say something about the quality of relationships which American oil men and Gulf Arabs had built over the years."*[77]

Despite the continuing expenditures for development, including policies to subsidize and support a rising standard of living for Kuwaiti citizens, Kuwait began to realize budgetary surpluses in the decade following independence. The increase in oil revenues confronted the government with the question of how to invest the profits. The solution adopted would prove very prudent and prescient in the future, especially in the recovery from the ravages of the Iraqi occupation in the 1990s. Shaikh Jabir al-Ahmad played a leading role in the establishment of a "Fund for Future Generations"[78] to absorb excess funds. Kuwait was estimated to have proven petroleum reserves sufficient to last for two hundred years at current levels of production. Nevertheless, the new fund took account of potential needs in the distant future when the oil reserves might be exhausted. Details regarding the fund were not officially disclosed, but Kuwaiti and other knowledgeable experts estimated that the fund value was at least one hundred billion dollars in the late 1980s when I arrived in Kuwait as American Ambassador.

Management of the Fund for Future Generations was not a topic for diplomatic discussion because the investments were made in private funds and corporations, but American bankers and financial specialists were consulted.[79] According to reports, the fund invested in countries around the world based on a formula keyed to the relative weight and risk of the various national economies. The largest proportion were invested in the United States. In short, the fund was an extremely sophisticated solution for Kuwait's surplus income.

Another area of interest to the United States—trade—thrived in the 1960s and 70s. In addition to large projects, which were less numerous than earlier, Kuwait was an important market for American machinery and vehicles. Familiar with U.S.-manufactured automobiles since Dr. Mylrea and the American Mission began importing them for their own use, Kuwaitis bucked the trends elsewhere in the region and supported the largest General Motors (GM) dealership outside the United States:

> In all the states of the lower Gulf in the 1970s, the Japanese took the market by storm, pushing their sales from a nominal few percent to between half and three-quarters of the total. Rather to everyone's surprise, Kuwait stood out against the onslaught. Much of the explanation for the resilience of American cars in Kuwait has been put down to the fact that Kuwaitis are richer than the lower Gulf Arabs. The highly competitive price of Japanese cars has less appeal to them. Whereas the taxi drivers in Saudi Arabia and the lower Gulf have Datsuns, Toyotas, or Mazdas, in Kuwait most of them seem to run to Chevrolets.[80]

The price explanation seems too facile since there are many wealthy persons in the Lower Gulf and a good proportion of the Japanese cars they bought were higher-end models. A substantial part of the answer would appear to lie in Kuwait's earlier familiarity and comfort with U.S. vehicles. Bedouin, and those with recent bedouin roots, seemed to favor Chevrolet or Ford pick-up trucks and SUVs. These vehicles, often with a young camel or other livestock in the truck bed, are still a common sight in Kuwait's Friday market. Access to Ford vehicles was curtailed when Ford was placed on the Arab Boycott list in the 1960s. When Ford returned to the market at the end of the 1980s, the Kuwaiti police quickly acquired powerful Ford patrol cars.[81]

Substantive relationships between the United States and Kuwait deepened in the 1960s and 1970s, despite what a U.S. diplomat described as a certain "prickliness" in other aspects of the dialogue.[82] Joe Twinam, who was Ambassador to Bahrain in the early stages of the effort to preserve U.S. Navy access there and continued to be involved in Gulf affairs over the remainder of his Foreign Service career, characterized the era as follows:

> In its first quarter century on the world scene, Kuwait may have appreciated the global U.S. role in maintaining a strategic balance, but it felt no specific political debt in return. Having been pressured into relations with the Soviet Union as the price of admission to the United Nations, Kuwait made the best of the situation

> by publicly espousing many 'nonaligned' positions and, in time, turning to the Soviets to purchase weapons systems, particularly when the United States seemed reluctant to provide similar arms. Moreover, except of course for Iraq, Kuwait was the sharpest critic in the Gulf of great power military presence there. Kuwait was generally unwelcoming of the U.S. Navy presence in Bahrain or, subsequently, the U.S. agreement with Oman to use air and port facilities in that country.[83]

Paradoxically, Kuwait sold critical specialty fuels to the U.S. Navy that were unavailable from other sources in the area.

Beneath the discordant mood music, strong personal and institutional relationships were forming in areas where cooperation was in the interests of both countries. Time would prove their durability. The private American community in Kuwait was scarcely touched by differences between the two governments. While Kuwait counted on support from the United States and others against threats by their more powerful and unpredictable neighbors, it was far from clear that they fully comprehended the logistical requirements and demands inherent in projecting power at the head of the Persian Gulf. In time, no doubt, Kuwaitis came to be grateful that their position on the U.S. Navy presence in Bahrain, for example, did not prevail. The chronically-troubled relationship with Iraq eased after the Ba'athist overthrow of Qassem in February 1963. The honeymoon, however, was brief. By the late 1960s and into the 1970s, Kuwait was once more facing a hostile and threatening Iraqi regime.

Gallery C

The Kuwaiti Crown Prince/Prime Minister Sa'd Abdullah and his delegation in policy discussions with President Ronald Reagan and his senior advisors during an official visit in 1988. *Department of State photo*

Crown Prince and Prime Minister Sheikh Sa'd Al-Abdallah Al-Sabah, with President Reagan, during his official visit to the United States in 1988. *Department of State photo*

Newly constructed compound in 1962, showing the Chancery (one-story building at upper left), staff apartments (at upper right), and ambassador's Residence at center. The staff apartments were later converted to administrative functions. The building was heavily damaged by a truck bomb in 1983 and rebuilt. The beach in the foreground originally extended to the Gulf shore. *American Embassy Kuwait archives*

The American Embassy compound, photographed from a nearby hotel, as it appeared in 1990. This photo was confiscated, for security reasons, from a hotel guest who had innocently violated hotel policy against taking pictures of the Embassy. Beginning in August 1990, U.S. officials and private citizens on the compound were under siege by invading Iraqi forces for nearly five months. The Kuwait Towers and Gulf shoreline are visible at upper right. *American Embassy Kuwait archives*

The American Women's League (AWL) booth at one of the periodic international charity events, fairs, and social occasions sponsored by the League. The AWL is open to all American women, including many who are spouses of Kuwaitis. *American Embassy Kuwait archives*

Margie Saunders Howell leads off an AWL fashion show at a Kuwaiti hotel on May 15, 1990. By tradition, the wife of the U.S. ambassador is the honorary chair of the AWL. *American Embassy Kuwait archives*

Commencement exercises at one of three high schools in Kuwait accredited in the United States. This ceremony took place in the ballroom of the Kuwait Regency Palace Hotel in the spring of 1988. *American Embassy Kuwait archives*

The American Embassy "Ambassadors" competed in the Kuwait Little League in the late 1980s. With American, Kuwaiti, and other children, Kuwait was a leader of Little League and T-ball in the Middle East. It also started the first teams for handicapped players in the region. *American Embassy Kuwait archives*

Dorothy Scudder, the last member of the American Mission resident in Kuwait, was honored by the American embassy in conjunction with the July 4th celebration in 1989. A restored traditional Kuwaiti doorway was installed as the public entry to the Residence garden. Named the Scudder Gate, the portal was dedicated to the members of the Mission who opened the door for the American community in Kuwait. Here Mrs. Scudder, who was marking her 50th year of residence, examines the plaque. The widow of Dr. Lewis Scudder, the last director of the American Mission Hospital, she was on home leave at the time of the Iraqi invasion and passed away in the United States in 1991. *Howell photo*

Members of the embassy's "Eagles" softball team, posing after a game with the "Falcons" in 1989. The Kuwait Industrial League, comprising Americans, Kuwaitis, and other nationalities, played Friday mornings on fields on the Sixth Ring Road. *American Embassy Kuwait archives*

The crew of the American Embassy entry awaits the next heat in the Messilah raft races. The pontoons made from oil drums welded end-to-end were later adapted to line the well dug on the Embassy compound during the Iraqi siege in late 1990. *Howell photo*

Mrs. Howell welcoming the "Hungry Bunny" mascot, circa 1988. "Hungry Bunny" is the Kuwait franchise of a well-known American fast food chain, which was a regular supporter of embassy and other American social functions. *Howell Photo*

Santa Claus brings holiday cheer to the traditional Embassy Christmas celebration for all employees and their families. For the first decades of the resident American community, prominent Kuwaitis were welcomed into homes on Christmas day, and Americans made reciprocal visits on Islamic Eids. *American Embassy Kuwait archives*

11

A Bad Neighborhood

Throughout its recorded history Kuwait's relationship with its northern neighbor has been troubled and problematic. Whether under Ottoman governors, the Iraqi monarchy, or the "republican" regimes that succeeded them, Baghdad and Basra have cast covetous eyes on the small shaikhdom. At times, their tactics have been subtle, but periodically they resorted to strong-arm methods and even military incursions, as was the case with Qassem's open challenge to Kuwait's independence and integrity in June 1961.

Following replacement of British troops by a shaky Arab League force, the possibility of an Iraqi military incursion eased, but Qassem continued to try to stoke tension. In late December 1961, he announced that Iraq would remobilize its forces to "liberate" Kuwait, prompting the British to place a small contingent on a twelve-hour alert.[1] Iraq then complained at the UN Security Council of "provocative measures" taken by Britain. Kuwait countered in the same forum with a protest over Iraq's "continued pressure and concentration of its military forces."[2]

By March of 1962, the Qassem regime appears to have concluded that there was no benefit in prolonging the tense situation. Whether because of internal challenges it was facing or the response of the international community, the Iraqi Permanent Representative at the UN delivered a letter to the Security Council pledging that Iraq would depend upon peaceful methods "to restore its legitimate rights to Kuwait."[3] The American chargé on the scene summed up his recollections of the episode:

> It was a very tense time, but perhaps the whole thing sounded a bit more tense outside than it really was inside. Very few people that I talked to in Kuwait, either among the Kuwaitis or among the British, really thought that Qasim intended to come in and take over Kuwait. Particularly after the British moved in with their ships and landed their forces, it seemed unrealistic that Qasim would try to move in. Anyway, he didn't and things died down after a while.[4]

The violent coup that ousted Qassem in February 1963 appeared to further ease the relationship with Kuwait. In the ensuing power struggle, the ruling coalition, led by Abd al-Salam 'Arif (which included Baathist elements), succeeded in defeating a challenge from the Communist Party of Iraq, but was soon engulfed in a power struggle with radical leftists within the Baath Party of Iraq.[5] With Iraq preoccupied by internal infighting, the intensity of the threat to Kuwait passed and relations fell into a now-familiar, post-crisis pattern.

In June 1963, the leading Cairo paper, al-Ahram, cited "informed" Kuwaiti sources saying that agreements had been reached between Baghdad and Kuwait resolving the question of Kuwait's independence. As part of the settlement, the daily reported that the Kuwait Fund for Arab Economic Development had agreed to lend the equivalent of ten million Iraqi Dinars (ID), as well as an additional ID20 million to be repaid over twenty years. In return, Baghdad was to recognize Kuwait's independence.[6] Oil wealth was an important aspect of Kuwait's diplomatic toolbag. Kuwaitis were genuinely committed to mainstream Arab causes and saw the development of other Arab states to also be in their interest. At the same time, however, it was hoped that their generosity would dissuade their potential enemies and build goodwill in friendly Arab capitals.[7]

The National Assembly voted unanimously in September 1963 to establish diplomatic relations with Iraq.[8] The following month, Prime Minister Shaikh Sabah al-Salim made the gesture of visiting Baghdad for discussions with the new Baathist regime on relations between the two states.[9] In return he elicited another Iraqi announcement recognizing Kuwait's independence and sovereignty.[10] The normalization process was proceeding so rapidly that Kuwait signed an agreement with Iraq to revive the old project to pipe potable water to Kuwait from the Shatt al-'Arab.[11] A Water Authority to oversee the sweetwater project was created under the leadership of Jasim al-Saqr.[12] The proposed project, similar to a scheme considered in the 1950s, did not come to fruition, and the prospect was soon eclipsed by renewed tensions with Baghdad.[13] The deterioration in the relationship with the new Iraqi regime was neither as sudden nor as dramatic as it had been with Qassem. The Kuwaiti government gave every indication of a concerted diplomatic effort to nourish and sustain the promising era ushered in by Qassem's demise. Minister of Foreign Affairs Shaikh Sabah al-Ahmad undertook a two-day visit to Baghdad shortly after the Baathist coup (March 1963) to congratulate the new leadership there.[14] A four-day state-visit by Amir Shaikh Sabah al-Salem in June 1966 resulted in agreement to create a "border committee" to demarcate the frontier between Kuwait and Iraq.[15] The Iraqi regime reciprocated with high-level visits to Kuwait. Iraqi Vice President Hardan al-Tikriti arrived in Kuwait in May 1970 for a three-day visit that reportedly featured discussions of the situation in the Gulf as well as the Palestinian issue. This was closely followed by a four-day stay by the Iraqi Minister of Economy, Fakhri Qadduri.[16]

The appearance of normal, cooperative relations was deceptive; for there were periodic discordant notes. In August 1970, for example, the government-controlled press in Iraq charged Kuwait with collecting duties on Iraqi exports in violation of a 1964 economic agreement.[17] Baghdad's policy of harassment reached a crescendo by early 1973 when Iraqi troops occupied one border post at al-Samitar and shelled another Kuwaiti installation. Kuwait responded by reinforcing its forces, declaring a state of emergency, and closing the frontier. The situation was considered grave enough for Mahmoud Riyad, the Arab League Secretary General, to fly immediately to Kuwait to mediate the emerging conflict. Egyptian Foreign Minister Muhammad al-Zayyat arrived in Kuwait several days later following his visit to Baghdad. Finally, on April 5, Iraq announced that its troops had withdrawn from the positions occupied on March 20.[18]

William A. Stoltzfus, who was the American Ambassador at the time of the crisis, characterized Iraqi behavior as follows:

> In March of 1973 Iraqis made some threatening moves on the Kuwaiti border.... the Iraqis backed off and just harassed the Kuwaitis. They are very good at that. They would take any occasion to harass the Kuwaitis, trying to keep them off balance.[19]

Baghdad's policy was undoubtedly calculated to sustain a high level of tension and uncertainty about their military goals, and it apparently had the desired effect. Walter McClelland, deputy chief mission in Kuwait in 1970–74, recalled that the menacing rhetoric from Baghdad "kept the Kuwaitis—and us—a bit nervous" because there was little doubt that the Iraqi regime was capable of using force in pursuit of its objectives. "When Iraq finally did launch a massive attack on Kuwait in 1990, the possibility had been entertained for a long time."[20]

Hardly noticed among other more dramatic events of the period, the Iraqi menace of 1973 moved the Kuwaiti authorities to request that the United States government send a military team to Kuwait to survey the country's defense needs.[21] The survey team's conclusions highlighted the need for air defense capability, tanks, and acquisition of aircraft capable of providing air cover on an expedited basis. The United States arranged a demonstration of the Navy F-4 Crusader, which was being replaced in the U.S. Navy and was available immediately.[22] The Kuwaiti military also bought the U.S. Hawk ground-to-air missiles and supplemented their Mirages in 1976 with American A-4 aircraft.[23] These initial sales proved to be the seeds of an increasingly robust security relationship between the two countries, culminating, after the liberation of Kuwait from Iraqi occupation in 1991, in a security partnership.

But, first, the parties would face yet another obstacle in the form of the 1973 Arab-Israeli conflict. In the resulting hostile atmosphere in the Arab world, American communities faced palpable risks. "The Kuwaitis, however, were very anxious to keep everything calm, and they did remarkably well on that."[24] No demonstrations developed and Americans were not placed in serious jeopardy. As in 1967, Kuwait did not interrupt diplomatic relations with Washington, but it did join other Gulf oil producers in imposing an embargo on oil shipments to the United States and other select Western countries:

A Bad Neighborhood 237

> ... *on October 22 [1973] the New York Times reported that 'four Persian Gulf oil producers—Kuwait, Qatar, Bahrain and Dubai—announced a total embargo of oil to the United States.' The embargo lingered on in one form or another until March 18, 1975, when at a meeting in Vienna most of the Arab oil countries announced officially they would lift the embargo of oil shipments.*[25]

The Gulf states learned important lessons in 1973; as they became more heavily invested in Western economies, embargoes became a less attractive and cost-free strategy. The truth of the increased interdependence between the Gulf shaikhdoms and the West was acknowledged by the often ascerbic 'Abd al-Rahman al-Atiqi who was Oil Minister in the early 1970s. Kuwait, he announced in December 1974 would not reduce its production enough to harm Britain and the United States because of its investments there.[26]

A decade following the embassy's establishment, it was now a modest mission of about a dozen Foreign Service personnel. The American staff was assisted and augmented by Foreign Service Nationals or FSNs (personnel recruited locally) of Arab or South Asian origin. A number of these FSNs served the embassy loyally for decades and provided an important element of institutional continuity and stability. Among this select group was Abdul Mu'ti Haroun, the driver for the chief of mission[27]; Gulzaman, the Residence butler who died in service at the Ambassador's Residence in the 1970s[28]; and Fawzi Dalloul, probably the longest serving employee, who worked for the United States Information Service (USIS) with the American Public Affairs Officer (PAO). Fawzi was a key member of the embassy staff when I arrived in Kuwait in 1987. He retired in the 1990s and emigrated with his family to the Atlanta area under a program that facilitated the acquisition of American citizenship for FSNs who have provided extraordinary service abroad. Unfortunately, Fawzi passed away several years ago. While not American citizens, they and their families were in every other sense part of the embassy community and were included in embassywide gatherings such as holiday parties at the Residence.

A succession of American Ambassadors left their marks on the embassy over the years of the 1960s and 70s. Howard Rex Cottam replaced Pete Hart in late 1963 and became the first ambassador resident in Kuwait. When he departed in July 1969, he had witnessed a key formative period in Kuwait's development as a modern state. Regrettably, he appears not to have recorded his experiences and impressions. George Quincey Lumsden, who was assigned to Kuwait as economic officer from 1969 to 1972, provided a glimpse of Cottam:

> *Howard Cottam was there when I made my first trip to Kuwait. He left just as I arrived in the summer of 1969. I didn't get much chance to serve under him, but he was a wonderful, avuncular gentleman who was very popular with the Kuwaitis, who was the right type of person for Kuwait at the time of its affluence and did not put huge political pressure on anything, very, very well liked, distinguished, and I think did an excellent job there. I believe he retired after Kuwait.*[29]

William D. Wolle, who was deputy chief of mission in 1968–70, holds a similarly positive view of Ambassador Cottam's effectiveness in Kuwait. He recalled that Cottam was highly interested in Kuwait and its people and enthusiastic about the assignment, his first as principal officer. In particular he worked to immerse himself in Kuwaiti society: "how they were interrelated... who did what, and who relied on whom."[30] According to Wolle:

> *He was close to the American companies that were represented there. His door was always open. He was a hard worker. I felt that he really did a marvelous job in Kuwait. He also would go on the speaking circuit back in this country whenever he was back on leave, etc. and try to portray this image of a very small, but in its own way, a very dynamic country. He was a superb ambassador for Kuwait's interests as well as our own, I thought.*

Ambassador Cottam retired from the U.S. Foreign Service when he departed Kuwai. He died in 1984.

John Patrick Walsh became ambassador in November 1969, although his tenure was cut short, leaving the post in December 1971. It is beyond the scope of this narrative to analyze or judge individuals, but the testimony of other senior diplomats in the embassy leaves little doubt that post morale suffered under his leadership.[31] Walsh was the Executive Secretary of the State Department prior to his assignment but had no previous experience in the Middle East or as an ambassador. He had recently lost his wife and his son was apparently seriously wounded in Viet Nam.[32] Another possible factor in his controversial tenure and eventual recall lay in the reported close relationship he had with the Democratic Party, and especially the Daley machine in his hometown, Chicago. In any event, he seems to have been incapable, or unwilling, to take advantage of the talents of his deputy, Wolle, or other members of the staff.[33]

Unhappiness and discontent within an embassy does not remain an internal matter, and State Department officials, including inspectors who periodically evaluate embassies and consulates, were soon aware of a morale problem in Kuwait.[34] The denouement of the situation apparently came as a result of an official visit by then Vice President of the United States Spiro Agnew. In connection with that visit, a Kuwaiti English-language newspaper, the *Daily News*, published an article attributed to Ambassador Walsh, stating that the United States was not serious about resolving the Arab-Israeli conflict and that Agnew's visit was merely an element of the Republican strategy for the 1972 election in America.[35] In any event, Walsh left Kuwait in late 1971, although one source attributes his departure to "a political dispute with local dignitaries."[36]

Vice President Agnew's visit to Kuwait and neighboring states was not just the catalyst for the early departure of Ambassador Walsh but also apparently decisive in the choice of Walsh's successor. After Kuwait, the Vice President continued on to Jeddah where the U.S. Embassy to the Kingdom of Saudi Arabia was located at the time. During his stay in Jeddah, Agnew met William Stoltzfus, who was the Deputy Chief of Mission. When the Vice President returned to Washington, he appears to have recommended that Bill Stoltzfus replace Walsh in Kuwait.[37]

The embassy that Ambassador Stoltzfus inherited in early 1972 was a small, Class Three Foreign Service post constructed in a prime location to house a consulate, and staffed to deal with a limited but growing agenda of bilateral issues. The new ambassador found that the official Residence was not adequate to accommodate his family and the increasing number of official visitors arriving in Kuwait:

> *The Chancery itself was just one of those, what do you call them? Pre-fabs... The Ambassador's Residence was nice but small. There wasn't enough space for our children still at home and our many guests. So we had it redone. My wife, our three girls and I moved out to Salmiya, which is a suburb of Kuwait City, and rented out there for at least four or five months while the residence was being worked on. We had a guest wing put on and the whole interior upgraded. In fact the first person who came to visit and stayed in our guest suite was Senator Fulbright. So it was known thereafter as the "Fulbright Suite." It was an attractive set up we had.*[38]

The basic structure of the ambassador's Residence was largely unchanged from the 1970s until after the Iraqi occupation of 1990-91. In the mid-1990s, the embassy moved from its historic location on the Gulf to new premises inland at Mishrif.

The other buildings on the compound also underwent changes to accommodate increasing staff and expanded functions. The largest structure that had been built as staff housing was converted to administrative and other offices by the end of the 1970s,[39] and a new wing was added to the long low building that served as the Chancery. In the same period, a sub-basement was dug under the original Chancery which required strengthening the existing slab floor. "Lovey" Edwards, a locally hired employee who served on the embassy staff from 1966-88, remembered that the unusual project attracted close attention from the Kuwaiti press:

> *... the newspaper said that the embassy was constructing an underground passage as an escape to the sea in case of political upheavals in Kuwait because at the time there was a question of Kuwait's borders.*[40]

The grounds of the compound had been transformed from arid desert to a virtual oasis with trees, shrubbery, and lawns sufficient for the several sheep that Ambassador Stoltzfus kept while he was in residence. During his tenure as ambassador, security concerns also became another catalyst for alterations to the site. While remodeling to provide enhanced protection for the compound would become a continuing project over the next two decades, the initial "hardening" of the site seemed minor in retrospect. The first precautions were occasioned by the murders of two American ambassadors in the region. Ambassador Stoltzfus recalled the physical and psychological ramifications of those two crimes:

> *Then came the assassination of Roger Davies in Cyprus and of Cleo Noel in Khartoum.... Those were depressing times. I lost a lot of enthusiasm for what I was doing when that sort of thing happened. It is not only that you are concerned about your own safety and that of your wife and children. All Americans were at risk. The children were going to school in town. We would get CIA reports on hit squads in town. So you had a car follow you everywhere.*
>
> *The embassy did a complete job of installing iron grilling and sub-machine guns and surveillance equipment in the Chancery and the Residence.*[41]

Security was not the sole determinant of important changes at the embassy. The Gulf region was in an historic transition and, at the beginning of the 1970s, Great Britain was in the process of withdrawing from the Gulf and the small shaikhdoms of the Trucial Coast and Oman. The independence of these new states presented the Department of State with a challenge—how to assure continued U.S. representation—for which it was ill-prepared, both conceptually and financially.[42] The situation was further exacerbated by lingering uncertainty about the number and shape of the successor state or states.[43]

The Near East Bureau (NEA) ultimately decided to establish three small embassies in Manama (Bahrain), Abu Dhabi (UAE), and Muscat (Oman), although in reality it could not commit funds sufficient to open even one mission properly. Each new embassy was under a chargé d'affaires with a minimal staff of American officers to discharge consular and commercial functions assisted by a limited number of locally-hired employees. Despite the hardships of carrying out the assigned mission, this was a welcome opportunity for middle-level officers who responded enthusiastically.[44]

The ambassador in Kuwait was assigned the additional duties of nonresident ambassador to the three new posts and Qatar.[45] Embassy Kuwait, already under strain from the growth in workload and personnel, was now asked to provide administrative support to the posts in the Lower Gulf.[46]

Richard W. Bogosian, the economic officer in 1972–76, later described the situation

> *I think the Bureau has, over the years, had a succession of fairly good executive directors, who have, for one thing, managed money very carefully and, as a result, probably have a little more financial flexibility than otherwise. The notion that these are tough posts and you need to be sympathetic to them has become almost a philosophical fundamental. Those notions were present then. I don't know that they were quite as deeply embedded. ... there is kind of a perverse sense that you know where you're going, you've got to expect to suffer. ... I was in Kuwait at a time when that post grew rapidly as well, and there were some real strains, and our administrative officer reported that, and the people in Washington said he's lying; "we were there two years ago, and we know it isn't that way." What Washington had difficulty understanding was what it's like at a post that's rapidly expanding. It's difficult to keep up with it. Even if they understand it, by the time you get the budget, by the time the money comes, by the time whatever it is you've ordered gets there, it can be months and months and months. I had to entertain the dean of the diplomatic corps, the Nigerian Ambassador, who was leaving, at a time when the roof was leaking and we had pails all over the ambassador's office.[47]*

Already coping with its own difficulties, Embassy Kuwait became another layer in the cumbersome budgeting/procurement process for the new embassies. Small wonder, then, that the jerry-rigged system of support proved a logistical nightmare for the newly minted embassies further down the supply line. Starting at ground zero with whatever supplies could be spared by the Consulate-General at Dhahran, they were frequently without office supplies as basic as legal pads, telegram forms, and pens and pencils.[48]

Within two years, resident ambassadors were named to the new embassies and the staff was augmented. In the meantime, Ambassador Stoltzfus made periodic visits to Bahrain, the UAE, and Oman for meetings with host-country officials. In general, his visits had little impact on the operation of the embassies and, so far as the resident staff in Abu Dhabi were aware, he never visited the embassy premises or met with the staff while in the UAE.[49] As part of the arrangement, a few "regional" officers, such as a budget and fiscal specialist, were posted to Kuwait partially to support the subsidiary embassies. The resulting diffusion of responsibility and crossed lines of command created more problems than they solved.[50] There was widespread relief when the arrangement came to an end.

In the two decades following independence, the inconveniences of the early period of development receded from public consciousness for Kuwaitis and expatriates alike. The quality of life improved and prosperity and benefits of oil wealth spread to all levels of Kuwaiti society. These changes had repercussions in the political and social spheres, including the consolidation of the influence of the amir and the al-Sabah family:

> *In particular there was a growing recognition of the government's success in providing better state housing, hospitals, schools, and other social services that are available in some socialist republics. Critics of the government, on the other hand, took these achievements for granted, preferring to accuse ministers of mismanaging state enterprises and failing to curb speculation.*[51]

The government continued to contend with opposition and, in some instances, simple obstructionism in the National Assembly where succeeding elections produced some deputies opposed to the prevailing paradigm. Nevertheless, Kuwait demonstrated dogged determination to continue its groundbreaking parliamentary experience, long after other states in the region had either decided not to follow suit or, like Bahrain, had abandoned legislative experiments after a brief trial.[52] Joe Twinam years later attempted to illuminate the difficulties that the reality in Kuwait and other small

Gulf states posed for Western social scientists seeking to analyze their political systems:

> ...there are common characteristics of these polities that tend to make standard Western analytical approaches to the issues of political harmony sometimes irrelevant, if not misleading. If one worries for instance about the absence, even at the moment in Kuwait, of the classic Western vehicle for expressing the public will—the elected legislative branch- it is important to keep in mind that the states involved are only recently into establishing what the West would recognize as an executive branch in order to meet public aspirations.
>
> These are basically tribal societies in which the ruler has a legitimacy hard to evaluate by modern Western standards. He is more accessible to his people, and much less august in their eye, than most of his Western counterparts. Indeed one of the complaints of some Gulf citizens, as sophisticated modern public administration has replaced the simpler patterns of a day well within the memory of many, is that they can still get justice from the sheikh but have a tough time getting a fair shake from those bureaucrats administering his government.[53]

The increasing satisfaction of Kuwaiti citizens with their government deprived opposition deputies of much of the receptive audience on which they counted. State Security Courts were established to handle cases of alleged subversion and threats to public security.[54] The situation was especially delicate because Kuwaiti citizens had become a minority in their own country, and earlier disruptions were often instigated by expatriates of Arab origin. Palestinian refugees who had been welcomed to work in Kuwait were a particular concern because they constituted an estimated 25 percent of the total population:

> There was a very close control over the Palestinians. The head of the Palestinian Community was closely supervised by the Interior Minister, and if anything got out of control, he was held responsible for rectifying the matter. Kuwaiti security knew all about the Palestinian community and it took swift and drastic action in case

of any political movement or strike or other perceived threat to the Kuwaiti monopoly of power.[55]

Labor unrest and other ordinary forms of societal protest do not appear to have been a problem as income and quality of life improved for Kuwaitis, as well as for many in the expatriate population who occupied professional and skilled positions.[56] On the other hand, the potential for subversion was high in a region where Iraq was actively seeking to extend its influence. Iraq was playing out rivalries with Iran and other Arab regimes, as well as radical Palestinian organizations, such as Black September, which were involved in acts of terrorism. The Kuwaiti authorities prudently kept a watchful eye on evidence of foreign, covert activities and contacts with residents.[57] Aside from its strategy of keeping Kuwait on edge and off balance, the Iraqi regime of the time was aggressively conducting covert activities throughout the Gulf region.[58] The Iraqis were reportedly not beyond undertaking clandestine operations inside Kuwait for their intimidation effect. On one occasion, the Iraqi regime allegedly sent a member of the Tikriti clan, who had run afoul of the ruling cabal to Kuwait, to meet with the amir. He was assassinated on his way to the meeting, apparently to demonstrate their reach and ruthlessness to the Kuwaitis.[59] In the atmosphere fostered by the murders of the U.S. Ambassador and others in Khartoum, these activities created high levels of stress among both the indigenous population and American community.

The Iraqi regime played periodically on Kuwaiti nerves in a series of feints and parries. In late 1974, Iraqi troops infiltrated more than one mile into Kuwait before setting up military posts, provoking 'Abd al-'Aziz Musayd, the chairman of the Assembly foreign affairs committee, to declare that Baghdad was intent on seizing the two Kuwaiti islands (Bubiyan and Warba) that Iraq had long conveted.[60] Two years later, in September 1976, elements of the Iraqi army were back in Kuwaiti territory pitching tents a kilometer beyond the frontier.[61] In a post-crisis dance that had become routine, Iraqi-instigated incidents were followed by a flurry of diplomatic activity to "resolve" the crisis. The Iraqi interior minister, 'Izzat Ibrahim al-Duri, met his Kuwaiti counterpart, Shaikh Sa'd Abdallah, in November. Later that same month, Iraqi Foreign

Minister Sa'dun Hammadi flew to Kuwait for further discussions.[62] The content of these consultations was not made public, but their import can be inferred from the fact that the Acting Prime Minister of Kuwait, Shaikh Jabir al-'Ali, felt it necessary to issue a public statement disputing the contention that the two islands in the Khor Abdallah belonged by right to Iraq.[63] Nevertheless, Kuwait continued to place its confidence in its diplomatic skills and announced in July 1977 that it was reopening its border with Iraq for the first time since 1972.[64] Tensions with Iraq would indeed ease in time, but the outbreak of the Iraq-Iran war was the principal catalyst for an interlude of "friendly" relations between Iraq and Kuwait.

In July 1977, even as tensions with Iraq were abating, Kuwait faced its first major confrontation with the forces of international terrorism. It was the era of aircraft hijackings which had begun to afflict the Gulf region earlier in the decade. Twelve Arab radicals seized a Kuwait Airways jet in flight and compelled it to land in Kuwait for refuelling. At least some passengers were released during the stop, reportedly in exchange for the hijackers' safe conduct to the Peoples Democratic Republic of Yemen (PDRY). The PLO condemned the hijacking (according to the *New York Times*) and identified the leader of the operation as a member of the renegade PFLP-General Command. The plane made it only as far as Damascus, where the perpetrators surrendered to the Syrian authorities.[65]

The Kuwaiti government, facing a full plate of security and other challenges, found it increasingly difficult to govern with what it regarded as obstructionism on the part of the National Assembly. Among other problems, some deputies appeared ignorant of, or indifferent to, the effects of their statements and actions on relations with foreign countries. In the 1973-75 period, for example, Kuwait relied upon the support of other Arab heads of state and the Shah in Iran to forestall Iraqi aggression.[66] When Iran occupied three islands in the Gulf claimed by Sharjah and Ras al-Khaimah, the Kuwaiti government stated its official opposition, but the National Assembly went several steps further and called for severing diplomatic and economic relations with Iran and, for good measure, with Britain as well.[67] On August 29, 1976, Prime Minister Shaikh Jabir al-Ahmad stunned the assembly by abruptly resigning and declaring that the assembly's refusal to cooperate was harming national interest.⁶⁸ The amir dissolved the National Assembly, reappointed Shaikh Jabir as prime minister and announced his intention to seek revisions to the constitution. He stressed that the dissolution of the assembly was a temporary measure.

Over the preceding years, there were numerous episodes and incidents that led the Kuwaiti authorities to take this drastic step. The case for the measure was sufficiently convincing to win widespread understanding among the Kuwaiti populace. An American scholar concluded that there were "four factors" at play in the Amir's decision: the cumulative effect of assembly obstructionism on a range of issues; the growing dissatisfaction of domestic constituencies; opposition identification with outside groups and states; and the suspicion and hostility of Saudi Arabia and other more autocratic Gulf states toward parliaments.⁶⁹ The obstreperous members of the National Assembly had badly overplayed their hand and for the remainder of the 1980s Kuwait functioned with the legislative branch on the sidelines.

American interactions with Kuwait and its people expanded and diversified greatly in the first two decades following independence. Historic changes in the resident American community accompanied the growth of personal and institutional relationships. As noted previously, the American Mission and its hospital were terminated in this timeframe, its functions absorbed by the new system of state-sponsored healthcare and most members of the staff departed. Dr. Lewis and Dorothy Scudder elected to remain with the blessing of the Kuwaiti government and people until their deaths; they continued to live in the "house on the hill" built in 1914 for the Mission's senior physician.⁷⁰ The National Evangelical Church in Kuwait registered in 1966 and its ministry continues to be housed in the chapel and several other buildings on the compound. The two hospital buildings were reportedly integrated initially into the state health system but then, abandoned for many years, becoming mute testimony to the time when this element of the American community was deeply embedded in the daily lives of Kuwaitis.

The era was also one in which veteran American oilmen from Gulf Oil Company and, subsequently, AMINOIL⁷¹ began to withdraw from Kuwait as educated Kuwaitis replaced expatriate professionals and the companies were nationalized. The question of ownership came to a head in February 1972 when the partners in ARAMCO rejected a Saudi request for an initial 25 percent of ARAMCO's shares.[72] With the Saudis in the lead, existing ownership arrangements throughout the Peninsula quickly began to unravel, leading to nationalization.[73] While this was probably a natural evolution, many Americans from this segment of the community were taken by surprise. These were unpretentious and down-to-earth men who felt they had developed a sound partnership with their Kuwaiti colleagues. Quincey Lumsden, who was assigned to the embassy as the takeover was building, described these Americans as "good ole' boys who like hunting and guns and things and go on a first-name basis right away."

It was this rapport that misled Gulf Oil into thinking that they had it made in Kuwait, that they'd never be thrown out, because they weren't the British colonialists.[74]

In the end, the American oil companies accepted Kuwait's nationalization with relatively good grace, accompanied as it was with an assurance of continued access to Kuwaiti oil. Nor did the evacuation of the company oil camps signal a total end of American drillers, "mudmen" and "roughnecks" in the country. In subsequent years, American oil service companies would continue to undertake exploration and well development as subcontractors to the Kuwait Oil Company and the Kuwait Drilling Company.[75]

The makeup of the American community was altered as missionaries and workers in the oil industry departed and were replaced by a new generation of expatriates working in business, education, and diplomacy. Personnel from Raytheon and Lockheed, for example, joined the community to support the U.S. weapons systems purchased by Kuwait in the 1970s and, as previously discussed, American military and civilian personnel were assigned to the embassy staff to provide assistance to the Kuwaiti military in training, maintenance, and logistical support for complex aircraft and missile systems.[76] In the same period, burgeoning trade between the United States and Kuwait attracted company representatives and technicians to join Americans employed by U.S. contractors—

selected by Kuwait—to implement major projects. Dick Bogosian, the Embassy Economic Officer from 1972-76, estimated that American exports to Kuwait increased by 400 percent during his tour. He was hosting eight U.S. trade missions annually when he was transferred.[77]

Education was another area of cooperation that brought American teachers, professors and administrators to Kuwait while hundreds of Kuwaitis went to live and study in the United States. The Kuwaiti government spent lavishly to educate its young people and by the 1960s a sizeable cohort of students had worked their way through secondary school and were prepared for a university education. In 1968, more than 150 Kuwaitis graduated from British, American, and regional universities. In succeeding years that number would grow significantly and those studying abroad increasingly attended American institutions of higher education.[78] Kuwait University was established in the mid-1960s with an initial student body comprising four hundred undergraduates.[79] In 1975, the Egyptian education system, on which its curriculum was originally based, was abandoned in favor of the American system of credit hours.[80]

The harmonization of American and Kuwaiti education greatly facilitated the transition for young Kuwaitis enrolling in colleges and universities in the United States. It is difficult to overstress the impact of the thousands of Kuwaitis who studied in America in bridging the two cultures. Aside from the value of their academic studies, the students lived among Americans for the years of their enrolment, coming to know the country and its people. For Americans, it was a rare opportunity to become acquainted with individual Kuwaitis and to develop an interest in and curiosity about the small state half a world away.[81] Both sides profited from the interaction. By the time I served in Kuwait in the late 1980s, the American Embassy estimated that as many as fifteen thousand Kuwaitis had completed studies at American universities and colleges. This substantial number of students is even more significant when one considers the size of the Kuwaiti population base, estimated at about six hundred thousand at that time.

Sending so large a number of vigorous, inquisitive young people to live and study in a free and unfamiliar society was not, of course, without its problems. As with all college-age people, much depends on the maturity and experiences of the individual. A small number of Kuwaiti students, who tended to be in engineering and the hard sciences, were offended by the material aspects of American popular culture and returned home more committed to conservative Islam. A larger number returned with more liberal ideas that made their elders uncomfortable.[82] On balance, however, the experience must be counted a considerable success, imparting the knowledge and skills Kuwaitis needed to assume positions of authority in government, industry, and education. The incidental benefits were no less salutary in breaking down barriers between the two societies—American wives, dual-national children (born in the United States), and even Little League baseball became more common in Kuwaiti society..

Kuwait was very much on the radar in Washington and, during the 1970s, another variety of American—the high-level official visitor—came to Kuwait in appreciable numbers. In addition to Vice President Spiro Agnew,[83] Secretary of State William Rogers added both Kuwait and Bahrain to his itinerary in 1972 on a trip devoted to advancing the "Rogers Plan" for a resolution of the Palestine issue.[84] Members of the U.S. Congress joining the parade included Carl Albert, Speaker of the House of Representatives;[85] Congressman Poage, Chairman of the House Agriculture Committee; Senator Mark Hatfield; Senator Charles Percy; Congressman Steve Solarz; and representatives from North Carolina, South Dakota, and California. Some were seriously seeking to enhance their understanding of Kuwait but others were merely along for the ride. A notable exception to the latter group was Senator William Fulbright. He visited in December 1972 while he was still Chairman of the Senate Committee on Foreign Relations[86] and, subsequently returned as a private citizen after he left the Senate. Fulbright had been in Tehran and continued on to Abu Dhabi and other Gulf embassies.[87] Aside from the succession of "official" visitors, the embassy received or hosted a number of senior private businessmen, including a "blue ribbon" mission of top U.S. corporate executives. Among them were Lee Iacocca of Ford Motor Company and a senior official of the Coca Cola Company, both of whose companies were on the Israel Boycott list. This fact did not prevent them from undertaking constructive contacts with Kuwaiti businessmen who were eager to obtain the agencies for these premier corporations. Ultimately, they were removed from the list and returned to the Kuwaiti market.

Considerable progress was achieved by Americans and Kuwaitis in the two decades of Kuwait's independence in learning to deal effectively with one another. Both are proud nations which do not believe in concealing their thoughts and feelings. Often positions taken publicly by Kuwaiti spokesmen belied the substantial areas of agreement and cooperation achieved together, for example, in security policy, in the economic and commercial fields and elsewhere. Kuwaiti criticism may have been irritating to those who were thin-skinned, but the frank relationship was appreciated by others who understood the imperatives acting upon Kuwait. Joe Twinam summed up the context succinctly:

> ... *Kuwait was for long the most outspoken of the friendly Gulf states in public criticism of U.S. or other great power military presence in the region.... On the other side there is substantial, if quiet, Kuwaiti appreciation of the U.S. role in maintaining a peaceful global order, and Kuwaitis admire not just American technology but also certain of the basic ideals which motivate the American national purpose.*[88]

The Kuwaiti leadership was very capable and certainly hoped that they could preserve their country and its independence by clever diplomacy, but they were not ignorant of the potential perils in their neighborhood and, at some level, probably understood that they would need external support and protection against vastly larger and more ruthless neighbors such as Iraq and, later, "revolutionary" Iran. Hence, although Kuwait's strategy was to join the consensus in the Arab world whenever it could find one, it was careful to preserve its relations with Washington after the Arab-Israeli wars of 1967 and 1973 when many other Arab capitals were indulging their emotions by breaking diplomatic relations.

The American diplomats who left their impressions of serving in Kuwait at the time have recorded more than the events and visitors; they have also provided a reading of the atmospherics of working there. They are unanimous in agreeing that relations were good and productive and that there was no personal animosity from their Kuwaiti contacts, no matter how critical they might have been on this or that aspect of U.S. policy. Some found the Kuwaitis to be opinionated, "sanctimonious," or always ready to criticize—as indeed they could sometimes be. These are attributes that observers have occasionally detected in U.S. policy as well.[89] The recollections of Dick Bogosian are particularly insightful. He was enthusiastic about his assignment to Kuwait:

> ... Kuwait was one of the most exciting places to be in the Arab World, partly because in Arab terms it was relatively free. There was a vibrant press; there were people from all over the Arab world; there were organizations like the Kuwait Fund and the Arab Fund and the Organization of Arab Petroleum Exporting Companies that were based in Kuwait, as well as some major new initiatives underway. So that there was an interesting mix of people. It was very cosmopolitan.[90]

Bogosian was an officer who was able to take his Kuwaiti colleagues as they were and work with them to attain shared objectives; "We liked the Kuwaitis because they were very frank...." Like many of the professionals working in the region, he probably knew the Kuwaitis were saying out loud what other Arabs were only whispering to one another, and it made officials in Washington uncomfortable. The Kuwaitis were not always right or prescient, as the existential threat from Iraq in 1990 would ultimately prove, but neither did they conceal what they were thinking.

On the last day of 1977, Amir Shaikh Sabah al-Salem passed away at the early age of 52. His death from cancer was widely mourned by those who saw him as a vital connection with the previous amir and his half brother, Shaikh Abdallah al-Salem.[91] He was survived by five sons and seven daughters.

12

Sea of Troubles

Shaikh Jabir al-Ahmad, prime minister and heir apparent since May 1966, became amir in 1977. Educated at the Mubarakiya School and by private tutors, he had been identified at an early age as a promising member of the younger generation of shaikhs. Beginning in the late 1940s, he occupied a series of important positions in public security, petroleum affairs, and housing. His primary focus, however, was in finance and budgetary policy, serving as Kuwait's first Minister of Finance and Economy beginning in 1962. The following year, he added deputy prime minister to his responsibilities. He was the first ruler in Kuwait since Mubarak the Great to assume power without the American Mission Hospital in operation.

Shaikh Sa'd Abdallah al-Salem was named crown prince in January 1978 and prime minister one month later.[1] A popular and gregarious figure, Shaikh Sa'd joined the Metropolitain Police in 1945 and held increasingly senior ministerial positions in police and defense affairs until his elevation.[2]

Between them, the new amir and crown prince brought decades of sustained and varied experience to their new responsibilities. The next fifteen years—another time of national peril—would demand all of the skills and experience they had acquired over the years.

The final years of the 1970s witnessed instability and change in neighboring countries—notably Iran and Iraq—as Kuwait enjoyed an orderly transition in leadership. The opposition to the Shah of Iran, comprised of imams of the Shiite establishment as well as secular liberals and leftist elements, was gathering steam. While the unrest and demonstrations may have initially appeared manageable, they eventually compelled the Shah to flee into exile. In 1978 another exile, the Ayatollah Rouhollah Khomeini, was also on the move. His agitation against the Shah's regime had earned him a period of exile in Iraq, where he continued his outspoken attacks from the Shiite center at Najaf. Finally, the Iranian government convinced Iraq to give Khomeini no choice but to leave Iraq. In October of the same year that Shaikh Jabir al-Ahmad assumed the rule in Kuwait, Khomeini presented himself at the Iraq-Kuwait border post, but was refused entry. Instead, the Ayatollah went to a quiet suburb of Paris, from which he continued to preach against the Shah's government and inspire revolutionaries in Iran. In less than a year, he returned to Iran in triumph and set about carrying out an Islamic revolution there.

In Iraq, meanwhile, another leadership transition, less publicized but equally ominous, was underway. Saddam Hussein, nominally the Vice President of the Baathist regime, moved decisively to claim undisputed rule of the country.[3] Saddam was recognized as a ruthless Baathist thug within the Department of State, but was virtually unknown in the United States at large. In retrospect, his shedding of the mantle of anonymity was presaged by a telephone call I received at the Department of State one Saturday morning in 1979. The head of the Iraqi Interests Section announced that "Mrs. Saddam Hussein" would be arriving in New York for medical treatment and required security protection. He was so insistent with complaints over succeeding days that he conveyed a strong impression that more than his career was at stake.[4]

From Kuwait, instability in neighboring Iran was followed with concern, if not yet alarm, as Kuwaitis and expatriates alike went about their normal affairs. If the emergence of Saddam Hussein from the shadow of the ailing Baathist figurehead, General Ahmed Hassan al-Bakr, generated undue excitement, the fact is not reflected in the historical record; knowledgable Kuwaitis had long been aware of Saddam's influence behind the scenes. Few in the region, or in world capitals, foresaw that soon Iraq and Iran would be engaged in a massive war that would neither affect the flow of petroleum significantly nor draw in other countries.[5] The Kuwaitis were much more absorbed by internal issues, including the most recent glitch in the country's experiment with representative government.

Ambassador François "Fran" M. Dickman arrived in Kuwait on October 20, 1979, to replace Ambassador Maestrone who departed post earlier in the year. He was met by Chargé Affaires Peter Sutherland as well as other senior members of the embassy staff. Fran Dickman was an experienced "Gulf hand," having served as ambassador to the United Arab Emirates and, prior to that, as country director for the Arabian Peninsula (NEA/ARP) in the Department of State. Within four days, he presented his credentials to Amir Shaikh Jabir al-Ahmad.

The American Embassy over which he took charge was considerably larger than his previous embassy in Abu Dhabi. Approximately eighty Americans and more than one hundred local employees (FSNs) made up the staff which reflected the expanding range of U.S-Kuwaiti interactions. In addition to diplomatic, consular, and administratice officers of the State Department, the total included a seventeen-person military liaison group commanded by a colonel (USLOK) as well as teams representing the Federal Highways Administration, the Federal Aviation Administration (FAA), and the Civil Service Commission that were providing reimbursable technical assistance to the Kuwaiti government. Unlike most other Gulf posts at the time, Kuwait also had a Marine Security Guard (MSG) detachment, normally a noncomissioned officer-in charge (NCOIC) and five or six watchstanders.[6] The Chancery, Administration building, and Residence were surrounded by a high wall and access was provided by a single steel gate. As a result of development of the surrounding neighborhood, a multistory Hilton Hotel stood next to and overlooked, the compound.[7]

If Fran Dickman had expected a routine tour of duty dealing with bilateral relations, he was quickly disabused of the notion. The Islamic revolution in Iran soon cast its shadow over neighboring Kuwait. Dickman received an urgent call from the State Department Operations Center in late November with an unusual request; could Embassy Kuwait contact the U.S. Embassy in Tehran? That embassy had apparently been taken over for a second time by Iranian students and Washington was unable to establish a link. Although connectivity between Kuwait and Tehran was normally relatively good, Dickman and his staff drew a blank. Dickman recalls that the only news he could pass to Washington was the fact that the U.S. Agricultural Attaché in Iran had been able to reach the relative security of the Canadian Embassy there. The unfolding revolution in Iran affected Kuwait and its inhabitants for the remainder of the decade; the violence it spawned soon touched Kuwaitis and the American community living in Kuwait.

At the end of November 1979, an anti-American mob of several thousand gathered outside the Embassy compound in support of the capture of the U.S. diplomatic hostages in Iran, and moved to enter the embassy. According to the *New York Times* account, the demonstrators, made up of resident Iranians and Kuwaitis who were largely Shiites sympathetic to Iran, were efficiently dispersed by Kuwaiti security forces using tear gas and truncheons.[8] Still, at this early stage, there was ambivalence on the part of at least some senior Kuwaiti officials despite the seizure of the American Embassy and its diplomatic personnel in nearby Tehran. Several days prior to the attempted demonstration, U.S. Treasury Secretary William Miller visited Kuwait for important conversations about oil pricing and the measures the United States was undertaking to maintain the strength of the dollar. He was received by the ruler on November 27.[9] In preparation for the visit, Dickman had met with Minister of Finance Abdul Rahman al Atiqi who had a reputation among diplomats as a "difficult" person. The Americans found al Atiqi angry that the United States had frozen Iranian assets worth approximately $10 billion and asked what assurances Kuwait had that the same thing would not happen to Kuwait's investments in America.[10] Al Atiqi later went public on the issue in an interview reported by the Middle East Economic Survey. The U.S. decision, he is quoted as asserting, has "implications of a most dangerous and serious kind."[11]

The seizure of Embassy Tehran and the aborted demonstration in Kuwait generated a major internal review of security procedures at the embassy. The wisdom of this review was later confirmed by the publication of classified materials that had been captured in Tehran, including shredded material laboriously pieced together by the Iranian revolutionaries. Under the direction of Kuwait Security Officer Mark Sanna, Marine Security Guards destroyed all but the most essential working files; others of historical interest were sent to Washington by courier.[12] Stringent procedures were established for securing working papers of embassy sections at night and a log of cables was created to replace the actual documents.[13]

The physical security at the Embassy compound had already been upgraded during the tenure of Ambassador Stoltzfus (see Chapter 12). Long gone were the early days when the property was surrounded on three sides by a waist-high cinder block wall with open access from the beach side. The unguarded gate by the Chancery building across from the Hilton Hotel had been blocked by a tall wall surrounding the entire compound.[14] The single point of access on a side street was defended by a reinforced steel gate.

Four years later, these precautions proved only partially effective against a determined terrorist assault. On December 12, 1983, a truck packed with explosives rammed the gate and exploded, doing structural damage to the embassy's administration building. A particularly graphic account at the time reported that "... two men in an open truck loaded with explosives drove through the gates in a suicide mission reminiscent of the attack on the U.S. and French military compounds in Beirut in October."[15] The Chancery nearby also suffered damage in an explosion so powerful that a vehicle tire was still lodged in the top of a tree across the street in the 1990s.[16] Five persons were killed in the attack, including three Foreign Service Nationals (FSNs) working there.[17] The suicide bomber(s) and a Kuwaiti visa applicant also died of their injuries, and twenty additional FSNs and seventeen visitors were wounded.[18]

Across Kuwait, five additional truck bomb attacks occurred almost simultaneously at the French Embassy, the airport, two residential areas for private American expatriates, a power station, and an oil facility in Shuwayba in a carefully-prepared campaign against not only the American community but Kuwaitis and other expatriates as well. There could now be no doubt that modern terrorism had come to a country with limited experience with such violence.[19]

For its performance in coping with the truck bombing and its aftermath, the embassy in Kuwait was awarded the Department of State's Superior Honor Award in April 1984. The accompanying citation read:

> *In recognition of the courage, resilience, and resourcefulness by the American, Foreign Service National, and contract employees of the American Embassy Kuwait following the tragic terrorist bombing there on December 12, 1983 which took the lives of three of their colleagues, Mufeed al-Hakim, Ali Jumal, and Ahmed Mahmoud. Despite the devastation wrought at the Chancery compound, Mission employees demonstrated uncommon loyalty, hard work, and courage in undertaking the difficult tasks associated with continuing reporting and functional responsibilities, restoring basic embassy services and facilities, and reassuring the large American community resident in Kuwait. The embassy's superlative performance in all of these areas has been commented on by official visitors and by U.S. Government agencies directly concerned with U.S. interests in the region and reflects the finest traditions of the Foreign Service.*

The decade of the 1980s was a time of high tension for Kuwait and its residents, as the country found itself a focus of the blowback from developments occuring all around it. The American community shared in the apprehension. As early as late 1979, in the wake of the turmoil in Iran, the U.S. Embassy began to receive credible reports of possible attacks. Near Thanksgiving Day, Ambassador Dickman was asked to call on the chief of Kuwait's Criminal Investigation Department (CID) who informed him of reports of talk in some Shia Hussainiyas of imminent anti-American demonstrations that could develop into an assault on the Embassy compound.[20] These unfolding events greatly concerned the Department of State which instructed Dickman to encourage embassy dependents to depart voluntarily.[21] As the evacuation of official dependents proceeded, the embassy received additional warnings from the Kuwaiti authorities. The final warning on November 30, the day of the large demonstration at the embassy, was more specific and included reports that police had arrested persons filling water bottles with gasoline not far from the compound. The day also happened to be *Ashura*, the holiest day in the Shia Muslim calendar, meaning that large numbers of emotional believers would be congregating. Fortunately, the Embassy premises were nearly deserted.

As the mosques let out following Friday prayers, a large and raucous crowd gathered outside the Embassy perimeter and attempted to enter the compound.[22] The crowd was composed of Kuwaiti Shias and expatriate Iranian workers. The duty officer at the Foreign Ministry was contacted and within an hour the rumble of tanks was audible from the compound as Kuwaiti security forces swept in to disperse the rioters with tear gas and truncheons.[23] Thousands of discarded sandals littered the area around the Embassy as the demonstrators fled.[24] Although the demonstration was aborted by the timely arrival of Kuwaiti forces, the accumulating evidence of the volatility of the situation in the region convinced the State Department that a mandatory evacuation of dependents was the prudent course.[25]

An ordered evacuation of official dependents or employees inevitably raised the dilemma that Embassy Kuwait faced in providing advice and guidance to private American citizens. While the embassy has responsibility for the welfare of all members of the community, it has no authority to compel them to act. The uncertain situation in Kuwait had unique implications for a growing segment of the American community living in the country. A "large number" of women had married their Kuwaiti husbands while they were pursuing university studies in the United States.[26] Many of the children were either American citizens or dual U.S.-Kuwaiti nationals registered with the embassy. These citizens were unlikely to evacuate in the absence of an unambiguous threat. Rather than encourage the private community to depart along with official dependents, the embassy fell back on the most effective tool it possessed—enhanced communication. Monthly meetings at the Embassy Residence were instituted for the community, where the ambassador and other officials could provide information on the evolving security climate and interact with members of the community on issues of concern to them. The Embassy Warden network was likewise reviewed and tightened to insure that the ambassador could reach American residents with critical information and advice between meetings and in times of dire threat.[27]

The American community shared with Kuwaitis and other expatriates an awareness of their vulnerability to events occuring beyond the borders and control. Tensions were perhaps as high as at any time since the Battle of Jahra in 1921 when a hostile *Ikhwan* force was literally at the gates of the city (see Chapter 3 supra). Tensions and violence would get worse and persist throughout the decade.

The National Assembly, suspended in 1976, was restored in time for a new round of elections in 1981. Islamic conservatives, especially Sunnis, increased their representation in the supercharged atmosphere.[28] The new assembly would prove no less contentious than its predecessor, and a great deal more divisive at a moment when internal cohesion in the entire region was under increasing strain. Without effective restraint from moderates and secular deputies, representatives of the Islamic movement and the Social Reform Society had the capacity to dominate the proceedings.[29] The agenda they enacted included not only opposition to voting rights for Kuwaiti women,[30] but measures inconsistent with Kuwait's long tradition of moderation and tolerance. Legislation was proposed confining naturalization to Muslims,[31] banning the importation of alcohol by foreign embassies, and prohibiting public decorations and celebrations at Christmas.[32] Such measures did little to promote societal cohesion at a time when it was most needed, but it was the challenge of protecting the country from the effects of the rivalry of Kuwait's more powerful neighbors that most preoccupied the amir and crown prince; public criticism by deputies of other Arab states was an embarrassment to the government.[33] In time, as Kuwait experienced unprecedented internal violence, it became evident that its population included not just Arab expatriates, but some Kuwaitis who sought to overturn the system.[34]

Violence and acts of sabotage and terrorism came to the streets of Kuwait slowly at first, but soon established a cadence and momentum. It became clear that these activities were directed not simply against expatriates but targetted ordinary Kuwaitis, the regime, and the amir personally. By 1980, the first attacks lashed out at vulnerable Kuwaiti targets and interests. In April, gunmen fired on the motorcade of Iranian Foreign Minister Sadiq Qutabzadeh as he drove to meet with the amir.[35] Any illusion that this attack was an aberration reflective of conflicts abroad was quickly dispelled after a succession of attacks: a bomb exploded at the London office of the Kuwait Oil Company; two explosions took place at the offices of the local newspaper, Al-Ray al-Amm; and two Jordanians hijacked a Kuwaiti airliner and forced it to fly around the Gulf before surrendering.[36]

By 1982, even more violent attacks resumed in earnest with the wounding of the United Arab Emirates chargé d'affaires in Kuwait. In Madrid, Kuwaiti First Secretary Najib Sayyid Hashim Rifa'i was killed around the same time that the acting Kuwaiti consul general in Karachi was wounded.[37] In spite of the fact that these criminal acts occurred outside Kuwait, the government had evidently concluded that there were elements living within the country that posed an even more immediate security threat. In October 1982, the issuance of entry visas was suspended temporarily, probably as part of a broad review of procedures and enforcement. The decision of the Minister of Interior the following month to deport more than twenty-five thousand illegal aliens seemed to be one result of the review.[38] The evolving situation had focussed the government on potential subversives already within the country.

The intense Iraq-Iran War, which began in 1980, posed significant challenges for Kuwaiti foreign policy-makers (which will be discussed elsewhere). Equally critical was its impact on Kuwaiti society and internal security. Kuwait, like Bahrain, the United Arab Emirates, and the Eastern Province of Saudi Arabia, has a sizeable minority of Shi'a Muslims, the backbone of which are old established merchant families of Iranian origin. While the latter constitute a stable and loyal element of Kuwaiti citizens, the revolutionary Islamic regime in Tehran was hostile to the Arab emirates of the Arabian Peninsula and bent upon exporting its ideology. Among some younger Shi'a in Kuwait, and especially among later Persian immigrants and resident aliens, the appeal and struggle of co-religionists in Iran not surprisingly exerted a strong attraction in the early phase. For a small portion of the Shi'a population of Iranian origin, the pull was compelling.[39]

In the tense atmosphere in 1982, Kuwaiti police dispersed a procession of Kuwaiti Shi'a mourning the death of Hussein, the venerated founder of Shi'ism nearly fourteen centuries earlier. The Iranian Ambassador to Kuwait immediately protested the police action, leading a Kuwaiti official to state that Iran would not be allowed to "exploit religious occasions." The Iranian regime later formally protested this treatment of Iranian "nationals" and warned of consequences.[40] Thereafter, the Iranian hand behind the security threat confronting Kuwait became increasingly evident. The perpetrators were often Iraqis, Lebanese, Palestinians, or even Kuwaiti Shi'as, but their direction and inspiration was traceable to Tehran.[41]

Kuwait's stuggle to deter and contain elements attempting to undermine the nation's security and stability reached a critical stage in 1984. Police and security forces demonstrated growing effectiveness against the agents of disorder as their identity and the expansiveness of their objectives became clearer.[42] These successes did not end the threat and, indeed, the sentencing of the accused became the rationale for further terroristic acts—but the tide nonetheless had turned somewhat.[43] The Kuwaiti government and public, with a new appreciation for the stakes involved in the struggle, were no longer playing defense in the dark.

On May 25, 1985, the motorcade of the amir was attacked by a suicide bomber as it drove through the streets of Kuwait. Four people died in the suicide bombing, but the amir escaped serious injury thanks to the instinctive reaction of his security detail which interposed their follow car between the approaching bomber and the amir's sedan.[44] "Islamic Jihad" claimed responsibility for the attempt to assassinate the Kuwaiti ruler and demanded release of the group's members imprisoned in Kuwait for earlier bombings. Kuwaiti police quickly identified the bomber as an Iraqi, holding a Pakistani passport, who belonged to al-Dawa (the Call), an Iraqi organization that supported Iran. By the end of May, twenty suspects had been rounded up on charges of involvement in the attack.[45]

The audacity of the plot to eliminate the amir, the head of the Kuwaiti state and symbol of Kuwait's independence and identity, served as a catalyst for a fundamental change in the attitudes and perceptions of the Kuwaiti government and people. Kuwait's enemies were not simply a repulsive nuisance that kept the residents on edge, but a threat to the very survival of their society. Terrorist attacks at home and abroad continued but would never again attain existential immediacy. Almost imperceptively, Kuwait's foreign policy posture shifted, easing the sometimes testy relationship with the United States and other Western and moderate Arab friends, and acknowledging the futility of trying to placate states and forces dedicated to Kuwait's destruction.[46]

Several months before the foiled assassination plot, terrorists intent on freeing colleagues imprisoned in Kuwait directed their efforts against a Kuwait Airways jet on a routine flight from Kuwait to Karachi. On December 4, 1984, four gunmen who had embarked in Kuwait hijacked the aircraft and forced it to divert to Tehran. Among the approximately 162 persons aboard were six American citizens, including three auditors for the American foreign assistance organization (USAID).[47] While one American official was murdered, more than forty women and children were released by the hijackers who announced that they would destroy the aircraft unless Kuwait freed those convicted of the December 1983 bombings. When the Kuwaiti government refused, a second American was murdered and other American and Kuwaiti passengers were savagely beaten. On December 9, Iranian security stormed the plane, captured the hijackers, and freed the remaining hostages. Iran rejected requests to extradite the hijackers who were Lebanese and/or Iraqi Shi'as. Instead, Iran announced on December 18 that the perpetrators would be tried in accordance with Islamic law.[48]

Even prior to the attempt to kill the amir, Kuwait had begun to stiffen its response to the persistent attacks against it. Now, as the terrorists turned their bombs on innocent Kuwaiti civilians,[49] Kuwaiti concern became obsession.[50] The Kuwaiti authorities attacked the problem on several levels, including developing a robust system of anti-terrorism laws and prosecutions. In June 1985, the cabinet endorsed a stringent law imposing the death penalty for acts of terrorism that involved the loss of life.[51] In the aftermath of a further hijacking of a Kuwaiti airliner in April 1988, the minister of state for services announced that capital punishment would be introduced for damage to aircraft or airports as well.[52] Finally, the office of the attorney general made clear that persons, including Kuwaiti citizens, advocating the overthrow of the regime would be prosecuted to the maximum extent of the law.[53]

On another front, Kuwait intensified efforts to identify and deport expatriates considered a threat to public order and security. While Iranian nationals received special attention, others, especially Palestinians, Lebanese, and Iraqi Shi'as, were also carefully scrutinized.[54] Major sweeps were conducted in 1985 to locate potential subversives following the attack on the amir. Minister of the Interior Shaikh Nawwaf al-Ahmad al-Sabah claimed in August that 90 percent of the individuals posing a threat to domestic security had been deported.[55] While accurate figures for the number of persons affected by these deportations are difficult to compile, an announcement from an Interior Ministry official in November 1986 provides a rough order of magnitude. He reported that 26,898 persons had been expelled over the preceding year.[56] These numbers probably understate the effect of Kuwaiti security measures. Sources in the region, for instance, alleged that Kuwait had quietly removed a number of non-Kuwaiti Arabs from sensitive positions in the government. Such individuals do not appear to have been subjected to deportation.[57] Deportations seem to have peaked in 1985, but there is evidence that the operation continued routinely after that. The Interior Ministry reported in the late 1980s that it continued to expel fifteen to twenty illegal immigrants a week.[58]

Finally, police and security forces stepped up investigations and arrests in connection with bombings, arson, and other breaches of internal security and tried suspects on a regular basis. In the main, serious cases were heard in the Special Security Court established in 1984 to prosecute those charged with bombing the American Embassy and other targets.[59] Although the trials were held out of the public view, the public record of convictions and acquittals suggests that relatively rigorous procedural and evidentiary practices were followed. For example, in July 1987, the court tried eight suspects accused of distributing leaflets calling for the overthrow of the government and assassination of the amir. Six of the defendants in this highly-charged case were convicted and two were acquitted.[60] Incidents continued to occur periodically until the truce in the Iraq-Iran war in 1988, but the adversaries of the Kuwaiti government were unable to mount further spectacular attacks. Much more delicate and disturbing than the ongoing incidents were two aspects of the sabotage campaign: The first was that some Kuwaiti nationals, particularly young Shi'as, were involved,[61] and the second revelation was that the objective of some of these elements was not policy change but the overthrow of their own government.[62]

Faced with the difficult internal security situation on the one hand, and dangerous foreign policy challenges posed by the vicious conflict between Kuwait's more powerful neighbors, Shaikh Jabir al-Ahmad dissolved the National Assembly for a second time in July 1986, and suspended several articles of the constitution. Crown Prince and Prime Minister Shaikh Sa'd al-Abdallah was asked to form a new government.[63] The decision to suspend the Assembly was accepted with equanimity among the Kuwaiti people; numbed by the insecurity around them and worried by Iranian efforts to export its "Islamic" revolution.[64] The government's explantion that the measure was prompted by security concerns, the exacerbation of divisions within society, and the challenges of the Iraq-Iran war resonated with a population normally predisposed to support legislative government.[65] Commercial interests welcomed the stability created and the wider public appeared to welcome relief from the carping of the assembly members.[66]

The well-established American community shared with their Kuwaiti neighbors the anxieties resulting from uncertain internal security conditions, particularly as the bombings and other violent attacks moved into restaurants, workplaces, and other locations frequented by civilians. Meanwhile, the largest conventional conflict since World War II, often audible in Kuwait City, unfolded just north of the border in Iraq. No known American casualties occurred within the country, but the community was well aware that Iran, their Lebanese and Iraqi allies, and radical Palestinian organizations were not reluctant to attack American civilians. Indeed, they were intentionally chosen for murder and mistreatment during contemporaneous aircraft hijackings.[67] American expatriates in Kuwait were not directly impacted by the regime's counterterrorism measures, although an unidentified Kuwaiti politician unintentionally injected a note of absurdity into the somber atmosphere when he called for the deportation of twenty-three alleged American Jews working on the Mina 'Abdallah refinery because he believed they constituted "a threat to the country."[68] He was totally ignored.

In the unsettled situation and with the staff of Embassy Tehran held hostage by the regime in Iran, security of the embassy and protection of private American citizens were top priorities. The embassy institutionalized monthly meetings with the community at the ambassador's Residence.[69] These sessions facilitated regular interaction between the ambassador and the staff about regional and internal security conditions and other developments of interest, such as the controversial U.S. extradition of an accused Palestinian bomber to Israel, a well-publicized child custody case involving the Embassy Consular Section, and current issues in the U.S.-Kuwaiti relationship.[70] Open communication of this kind was essential to maintaining confidence among American expatriates that their embassy had a grip on the things that worried them. Meanwhile, spurred on by the Iranian capture of the embassy there and the subsequent publication of reconstructed classified documents, the embassy staff in Kuwait continued to refine and exercise procedures to improve physical security.

Iraq's surprise attack on Iran in September 1980 faced both Kuwait and the United States with an unfamiliar and unpredictable situation. The two countries had engaged in a war of words and subversion for some months,[71] but the thrust by nine Iraqi divisions on September 22, 1980 into the oil-rich province of Khuzestan had not been foreseen in Washington.[72] The United States now confronted a war with dire potential implications, including the welfare of the hostages, without normal diplomatic relations with either belligerent; the diplomatic staff in Tehran was held captive and American diplomats in Baghdad were operating as an Interests Section under an allied embassy. Neither country was friendly. Questions were numerous but answers were few as the United States pondered its options.

The embassy in Kuwait had scant opportunity for reflection because it was immediately drawn into the crisis. Radio broadcasts on September 22 carried reports of Iranian air attacks on the petrochemical facility being built at Zubair in Iraq; the news was delivered to the embassy at mid-morning by two American engineers. An Iranian bomb had fallen on a construction office killing or injuring several company employees, including Americans. The company was evacuating personnel and dependents at Zubair but were facing difficulties at the Kuwait border because few had visas and most passports had been kept in a safe in the destroyed offices. The engineers requested assistance in facilitating entry into Kuwait and in arranging onward transport to the United States and Europe.

Brooks Wrampelmeier, charge d'affaires in the absence of

Ambassador Dickman, dispatched Regional Security Officer Mark Sanna and Vice Consul Keith Loken to the Abdali border post to assess the situation while Consul Karla Reed contacted the Foreign Ministry to request permission for the evacuees to transit Kuwait on their way to safehavens. The Kuwaitis agreed that they could enter on condition that they departed the country within forty-eight hours. At the border, meanwhile, the extent of persons without any travel document was becoming clear. Consul Reed was able to elicit Kuwaiti agreement that the embassy could issue a "laissez passer" to individual Americans in this category. This solved a major problem but created another since the United States did not have an official "laissez passer." Karla Reed cleared this hurdle by creating one festooned with an impressive array of seals and ribbons.

In this manner, several hundred American citizens and nationals were able to enter Kuwait, the last of whom did not reach Kuwait City by leased busses until midnight. Most of the evacuees went to hotels and a few with injuries were hospitalized. In addition to leasing busses, the Administrative Section, headed by Bill Hoffman, was working with company officials in home offices to arrange charter aircraft. Wrampelmeier also sent the embassy nurse, Edna Farrington, to the border with first-aid supplies and tranquilizers for those in need, including the wife of an American citizen killed in the air raid. An embassy officer's wife, who was a registered nurse, took over the embassy health unit to provide support for arriving evacuees in need. Consul Reed spent considerable time visiting those in hospitals to check their welfare and to collect sufficient eye-witness testimony to make out death certificates for the deceased.

With the onset of the war, journalists had descended in force on Kuwait. As Charge Wrampelmeier recalls:

> We were also having to deal with the American and other media who pressed us for interviews and information, especially about American casualties in the Zubair bombing. PAO (Public Affairs Officer) Ray Peppers rescued me from two persistent journalists, irate over my refusal to allow them on the compound after official office hours or to grant them an interview at a time when I was frantically drafting a reporting cable to the Department. Ray even

received a telephone call from a radio station in some Canadian prairie town. The caller announced to a still groggy Ray that he was 'on the air' and would he say a few words about the situation to the radio audience![73]

The Department of State appropriately awarded individual honor awards to Sanna, Loken, and Reed for their innovative and effective handling of the emergency. A Group Superior Honor Award was given to Embassy Kuwait for its exemplary performance.[74]

While the Kuwaiti authorities were probably caught off guard by the timing of the conflict, they may not have been taken totally unawares. The new Iraqi President, Saddam Hussein, clearly was banking on the post-revolutionary disarray of Iran's professional military to facilitate Iraq's domination of the battlefield,[75] but he also reportedly told the Kuwaitis that he had counted on the largely ethnic Arab population of Khuzistan to rise up and welcome the Iraqi army.[76] Kuwait, already concerned with the extremism of the Iranian regime, undoubtedly sympathized with Iraq as a bulwark against Iranian influence and subversion, but it was also intent on maintaining working links with Tehran. With fighting along the Shatt al-Arab making the Iraqi port of Basra unseviceable, Kuwait granted Iraq effective control over several berths in its own port for the duration of the conflict.[77] At the same time, given the troubled record of its relations with Iraq, it is likely that Kuwait was ambivalent regarding a potential increase in Baghdad's strength and influence as a consequence of an outcome favorable to Iraq. In the judgement of Ambassador Dickman, "The [Kuwaiti] leadership had traditionally sought to compensate for the country's weakness by avoiding entangling alliances, by trying to play one strong neighbor against the other, and by avoiding public stances that would antagonize any of its near neighbors."[78] The all-out war now unfolding made pursuing these goals immeasureably more difficult.

In strategic terms, U.S. and Kuwaiti views of the conflict were congruent.[79] American concerns were further heightened by the fact that the USSR had invaded Afghanistan in December 1979, bringing Soviet tactical aircraft at Kandahar to within four hundred miles of the Gulf—potentially positioning Moscow to exploit the fallout from the Iraq-Iran war.[80] Kuwait condemned the Soviet occupation of another Muslim country but seemed no more concerned with Moscow's action than with U.S. efforts to strengthen its military posture in the Gulf in response to moves by its Cold War adversary.[81] What should have been a reasonably harmonious period in bilateral relations became a time of prickly exchanges.

Kuwait's posture in the early years of the decade was one of strict pan-Arab orthodoxy, partially out of conviction but also almost certainly as a defensive gambit in dangerous times. As the American Embassy saw it, Kuwaiti policy makers sought to deal with the shocks and threats they saw all around them "by trying as much as possible to burnish their nonalignment image" and portraying themselves "as more Arab than the Arabs." This brought the two states into collision over a series of out-of-area issues: the U.S. extradition of a young Palestinian charged with a bombing;[82] the Egyptian-Israeli peace treaty and the Camp David Agreement; US freezing of Iranian assets after the seizure of the American Embassy; and the egregious Israeli invasion of Lebanon in 1982, to cite only the most noteworthy.

The Kuwaiti press echoed the regime's criticism of U.S. policy decisions adding to the sour atmosphere. In a poignantly ironic twist, the Kuwaiti media strongly objected to President Carter's declaration in his January 1980 State of the Union address that the United States would use force, if necessary, to prevent domination of the Gulf by a hostile power (the "Carter Doctrine") just as they opposed U.S. military access and facilities in Bahrain and Oman. A scant ten years later the doctrine would become the basis for a massive effort to liberate Kuwait, and the facilities made available by more farsighted neighbors would expedite the required military buildup.

In the first months of the Iraq-Iran conflict, even as Iraq's initial armored thrust began to grind to a halt, an important goal in Washington was to prevent the war from expanding to friendly states in the Gulf and the wider Middle East. Alarmed by Iranian efforts to export its extremist brand of Islam, many observers were inclined to view Iraq as an essential bulwark against this virus. Iraqi bombers were soon detected on deployments to Yemeni and Omani bases with the potential of drawing those states into the conflict.

In the latter case, a word to the media was enough to effect their withdrawal. In the spring of 1982, a substantial tent encampment in the desert outside Kuwait City raised concerns by analysts that Kuwait was mobilizing its armed forces. Wiser heads soon pointed out that the occupants were Kuwaiti civilians who annually made a pilgimage back to their bedouin roots for several months in the spring.[83]

Whatever hopes the Kuwaitis may have entertained at the outset of the war turned to anxiety about internal security as the war settled into a stalemate. The redeeming of the pledge to reinstate the National Assembly in 1981 was one response to these anxieties.[84] An additional consequence was a Kuwaiti retreat into rigid Pan-Arab orthodoxy that occasionally bordered on anti-Americanism, without resolving the dilemmas confronting the Kuwaiti government.

One dispute between the embassy and the Kuwaiti authorities that arose during this delicate period grew out of a child custody case in nearby Saudi Arabia. It resulted in the American consul in Kuwait, Robin Bishop, being declared persona non grata.[85] Although the Kuwaiti desire to mollify their Saudi neighbor was understandable, the announcement omitted an essential fact—the two minors were born in the United States while the father was a student and, consequently, were U.S. citizens. The mother, unable to leave Saudi Arabia without the permission of her husband, had accompanied him to Kuwait where he was to speak at Kuwait University. She brought with her valid U.S. passports for the children but her own passport was held by the husband. The consul's "crime," therefore, was issuing a replacement passport to an American citizen in good standing. Ambassador Dickman informed the Ministry of Foreign Affairs consular section of the case, and nothing more was heard until he was summoned several weeks later to the ministry to receive a protest. The consul's expulsion was announced in the media. The Department of State decided not to retaliate, but the Consular Section was shorthanded for a time. Three months later, the Saudi husband succeeded in locating the children in Aurora, Colorado, and kidnapped them to Saudi Arabia. The mother later went back to that country to seek custody of her children but was rebuffed by a Saudi court.

Developments in other parts of the Middle East also took a toll on the content and tone of bilateral relations during this period. The Israeli attack on Lebanon in June 1982 ushered in a particularly difficult time for the embassy in Kuwait. The Kuwaiti government had expended a great deal of time and diplomatic effort trying to end the civil strife in Lebanon and to facilitate the extension of the Lebanese government's authority over all its territory. During this time, President Reagan's personal emissary, Ambassador Phillip Habib, succeeding in establishing a cease-fire along Israel's northern borders. Nevertheless, Israel seized on an assasination attempt against the Israeli ambassador in London by anti-PLO Palestinians to launch an invasion into southern Lebanon with the announced objective of occupying the area from which rockets could be launched into its territory. President Reagan called again on Habib, who was attending a conference at Ditchley Park in Oxfordshire, England, to deal with the situation.[86] Following meetings at Versailles with Secretary of State Haig and President Reagan, Habib's small party proceeded to Tel Aviv where it met with Prime Minister Menachem Begin and Defense Minister Ariel Sharon. The Israelis restated their limited objectives and agreed they did not seek a war with Syria which had forces south of Beirut but north of the declared Israeli "red line." Ambassador Habib immediately flew to Damascus where President Assad concurred in a ceasefire. While still in Syria, it was clear from the launching of military aircraft that Syria was on a war footing. Before Habib could return to Tel Aviv, the Israeli forces had passed their self-declared objective and were engaging Syrian troops. Within hours, we learned that the Israelis were in the outskirts of Beirut and shelling the vicinity of the Presidential Palace. When Habib asked Begin and Sharon why he was sent to Damacus believing that Israel supported a cease-fire, the reply was as simple as it was disingenuous: "We said we wanted a cease-fire but we didn't say a cease-fire was in place." Habib's credibility with Hafez al-Assad was completely destroyed by the cynical Israeli word game.

Israel's advance on Beirut confirmed the Kuwaiti government's suspicion that Secretary Haig had given his approval to the Israeli actions.[87] Ambassador Dickman denied the Secretary's involvement, but notes that in late June he received a "very tough" instruction from Haig to inform the Kuwaitis that the PLO was finished in Beirut and that Kuwaitis should convey that message to the Palestinian leadership. The ambassador, a conscientious officer, chose not to carry out Haig's instruction because he was convinced the arrogant tone would infuriate the Kuwaitis.[88] The issue became moot when several days later President Reagan replaced Haig with George Shultz. It may never be proved that Haig colluded in the Israeli plan, but his behavior as the Israeli plan unfolded did nothing to disprove this widely held suspicion.[89]

The political and emotional aspects of the shelling of Beirut infuriated the Kuwaiti government and citizens, particularly as footage of the damage and the massacre of Palestinian noncombatants in the Sabra-Shatila refugee camps by Lebanese Maronite militias allied with Israel was aired across the Arab world.[90] There were, however, practical internal security concerns as well. The embassy reported that the Kuwaiti authorities staged several rallies with an anti-American tone at sports clubs to vent popular anger and distance itself from events unfolding in Lebanon. A large demonstration where American flags were burned in protest against uncritical U.S. support for Israel was permitted not far from the American Embassy compound.[91] The overriding fear, however, was that Palestinian fighters being forced out of Beirut could try to regroup in Kuwait. Strict new visa procedures were established by Kuwait to meet this threat and media coverage of disturbing images from the Israeli operation were curtailed to avoid further inflaming public anger. The embassy's reporting about these measures was leaked to the press in Washington, adding to bilateral frictions.[92]

While Kuwait's reactions to the tragic events in Beirut were understandable, other irritants in the relationship seemed gratuitous—except in terms of an effort to needle the United States. In light of the Soviet occupation of Afghanistan, a USSR-Kuwaiti joint statement opposing foreign military bases in the Gulf region rang especially hollow.[93] Some months later, the amir himself told the media that he planned to ask other states of the Gulf Cooperation Council (GCC) to establish diplomatic relations with the Soviet bloc to "balance" their foreign relations.[94] The historical record does not indicate whether he followed up on this idea. In any case, there was no rush among other Gulf states to follow Kuwait's lead, which was regarded as wrongheaded. The prevailing view among diplomats of Kuwait's GCC allies was summed up in the phrase "Kuwait thinks there are three great powers—the United States, the Soviet Union, and Kuwait."[95]

Minister of Defense Shaikh Salem al-Sabah, in particular, seemed to believe that the Soviet card was trump, and used it frequently in public declarations about private negotiations. In August 1981, for example, he announced that Kuwait had "rejected" an American offer to sell it Hawk anti-aircraft missiles.[96] The common theme of his pronouncements was that, in contrast with Washington, Moscow was "denying us nothing in their arsenal."[97] Ambassador Dickman, who had known Shaikh Salem when he was the Kuwaiti Ambassador in Washington, now found him no more accomodating in private. Although U.S. Navy ships had been making port calls in Kuwait since the 1940s, the Minister refused every request for a friendly visit.[98]

Ambassador Dickman concluded his four-year term on the same sour note that characterized his tenure during one of Kuwait's most turbulent and dangerous periods. In August 1983, the Kuwait government refused to grant *agrément* to his successor, Brandon Grove.[99] Dickman's last official act in Kuwait was to submit Grove's biography to the Foreign Ministry. He was summoned to see Under Secretary Rashed al-Rashed, who informed him that Grove was unacceptable because his last post was Consul General in Jerusalem and would be criticized by many Kuwaitis and the large Palestinian community. To no avail, Dickman explained that the United States had maintained a consular presence in Jerusalem for more than a century and that it did not imply recognition of the city as Israel's capital. His appeals for reconsideration during farewell calls on the Foreign and Oil Ministers convinced him that the decision had been taken by the ruler. By the time he returned to Washington, he discovered that the Kuwaiti rejection had been leaked publicly. Small wonder that Dickman looked back to his ambassadorship in Abu Dhabi with nostalgia.[100]

Kuwait was clearly within its rights to refuse agreement, as Dr. Mohammad al-Rumaihi, one of Kuwait's leading intellectuals, argued in a comtemporary article.[101] His conclusion that the Kuwaiti action was dictated by an Arab League decision "years ago" not to accept diplomats on direct transfer from Israel is less compelling since it implies that the Arab League members had recognized Jerusalem as an integral part of Israel, which the United States had not. The more fundamental issue is whether it was wise to exercise the "right" of refusal. The upshot of this episode was to antagonize senior elements of the U.S. government and forego the presence of an American Ambassador for an extended period at a critical juncture in Kuwait's history.

Ambassador Dickman would not be replaced for one year. In the interval, Phillip Griffin, who had replaced Brooks Wrampelmeier as Deputy Chief of Mission, headed the American Embassy. He was chargé d'affaires when the devastating truck bomb attack struck the Embassy in December 1983.

13

Tentative Alliance

The atmosphere in Kuwait began to change for the better in the mid-1980s. The war between the Iraqis and the Iranians had settled into a grinding stalemate of massive artillery barrages and human-wave attacks by the more populous Iran. It was now a conflict that Iraq was not going to win, at least not with conventional weapons. Following initial Iranian advances in the direction of Basra, determined Iraqi resistance stiffened along the Shatt al-Arab line.[1] For a time, there was concern in Kuwait that an Iranian breakthrough could bring the Iranians to Kuwait's northern border. In fact, Iranian forces on a probing operation against the al-Fao Peninsula in 1985 encountered so little Iraqi resistance that they were able to consolidate their positions there. From al-Fao, Chinese-made Silkworm anti-shipping missiles were capable of reaching Kuwait City and its environs. The residents of Kuwait, particularly along the Gulf Coast where the American Embassy was located, had grown accustomed to the rumble massed artillery that rattled their window panes.

The bombings of December 1983 and the attempt on the life of the amir drove home to Kuwaiti authorities the gravity of the internal security threat posed by Iran and its regional allies and surrogates (including a limited number of Kuwaiti nationals). The Kuwaiti regime had regained its footing and was vigorously pursuing a menu of measures to forestall, contain, and prosecute elements prepared to commit acts of violence and terrorism. Relatively minor incidents continued into 1987[2], and the Kuwaiti public was often critical and impatient. The Kuwaiti government and security forces, however, were acting with increasing confidence and effectiveness against perpetrators inside the country.

Security was not the sole concern of Kuwaitis in the mid-1980s. During the final months of Ambassador Dickman's term, the economy had suffered a self-inflicted wound. In October 1982, an informal trading market, Suq al-Manakh, crashed when the government felt compelled to ask the approximately seven thousand traders to declare their positions. The *Suq*, which was housed on the ground floor of a parking garage on the site of an earlier camel market, had developed over several years to facilitate the purchase of shares in local firms with few, if any, assets. Share prices were bid up using postdated checks that frequently were endorsed and reused many times. Dickman, whose speciality was economics, described the *Suq* as "an unofficial futures market using deferred payments."[3] Huge paper profits were made on paper companies. Dickman reportedly pointed out the inherent dangers to bankers and Ministry of Economy officials but a decision to intervene was not taken until the speculation reached such proportions that it could no longer be overlooked. By that point, accumulated debt was astronomical and, when it could not be covered, the bubble burst with serious consequences. Despite government efforts and bailouts of some of Kuwait's most prominent citizens, retail activity slumped for the next several years and the otherwise healthy economy was temporarily crippled.[4]

A new U.S. ambassador, Anthony Quainton, arrived in Kuwait during the summer of 1984 and presented his credentials to the amir in September, almost one year after his predecessor's departure. "Tony" Quainton was a career Foreign Service officer who had previously been the U.S. ambassador to Nicaragua. He had been given several months of substantive briefings and an intensive introduction to the Arabic language, but was in no sense a Gulf or Middle East specialist. He did bring useful past experience in counterterrorism to the Kuwait assignment.[5]

From the outset, Ambassador Quainton could hear audible reminders of the war as gunfire some fifty miles distance reverberated in the residence rooms overlooking the Gulf. "Frequently one heard flying overhead, Iraqi planes on (sic) route to attacking Iranian targets.... There were often sonic booms as the planes went over."[6]

Among his initial priorities was dealing with the residual

trauma of embassy staff and resident Americans still struggling with the effects of the truckbomb attack nine months before. Physically, the compound was strewn with equipment needed for repairs and enhancements to perimeter security. The ambassador's Residence, which had not been seriously damaged, housed the health unit in the master bedroom, the motor pool was operating out of the library, and other functions that had been located in the partially collapsed administrative building were scattered about the house. Tony Quainton and his family waited several days before moving into their new quarters. Eventually, tents occupied by various offices were replaced by prefabricated buildings and the compound adjusted to the new "normal."

More difficult was the challenge of the anxieties of personnel and their families who continued to associate the Embassy grounds with the bombing. Many parents refused to bring their children to swim in the Embassy pool or attend social events at the Residence. It required "a very concerted effort" by Ambassador and Mrs. Quainton—and the passage of time—to restore the confidence of the shaken community.[7]

The tone of working relationships between the embassy and the Kuwaiti authorities improved markedly in 1984. There were undoubtedly a number of reasons for the improvement, not least a dawning realization that "positive nonalignment" was not a reliable source of security in the raw and menacing atmosphere prevailing in the Gulf. Small Arab neighbors and natural allies had never shared their enthusiasm for a nonaligned posture or relations with the Soviet bloc. Quainton believed they were trying to balance relations between the United States and the USSR, but he was not exposed to the period in which Kuwait was fulsome in its criticism of Washington yet pulled its punches in dealings with Moscow.[8] Nevertheless, a surprising level and frequency of bilateral consultations, including a number of senior-level visitors, took place even in the most difficult of times.[9] The Kuwaitis extended an especially warm welcome to Andrew Young, the former American ambassador to the UN, who made a private visit in March 1980. Ambassador Young had been compelled to resign when his meeting with a PLO representative the previous year was made public in the miasmic atmosphere of Washington politics.[10]

The creation of the Gulf Cooperation Council (GCC) was a measure on which there was substantial congruence between Kuwaiti and U.S. views, although the embassy was careful not to be overly supportive in public to avoid providing its enemies a pretext for opposing the organization.[11] The concept was not completely new but had been held in abeyance because the Iraqis had insisted on becoming a member. Once Iraq was otherwise engaged in a war with Iran, Shaikh Sabah al-Ahmad, Kuwait's Foreign Minister, shrewdly revived the proposal for an association of the other Arab states in the Gulf. The GCC, which comprised Bahrain, Kuwait, Oman, Qatar, Saudi Arabia, and the United Arab Emirates, was established at a meeting of rulers at Abu Dhabi in May 1981. The organization's headquarters and secretariat were set up in Riyadh, and Abdullah Bishara, Kuwait's former ambassador at the United Nations, was tapped to be its first Secretary General. The GCC not only provided the American diplomats with a noncontentious topic for private exchanges, but closer Kuwaiti interaction with its more traditional regional "allies" was probably one of the factors moderating the more grating aspects of Kuwait's "nonalignment."

Other key issues on the agenda between Kuwait and the United States included the need to invest accumulated oil revenues and the price and supply of petroleum itself. Much of the discussion was technical and noncontroversial, but differences of analysis or policy did occur and external considerations, including public opinion in both countries, could sometimes complicate relationships. Kuwait, for example, had begun to seek profitable investments abroad in the 1970s when essential infrastructure projects were completed. In late 1974, the Kuwait Investment Company purchased Kiawah Island off Charleston, South Carolina. They planned to develop the island as a resort.[12] The United States government welcomes foreign investment and saw no problem with this private sale, but the news of the Kuwaiti purchase set off reactions among a small number of xenophobes and individuals with dubious agendas. Ambassador Dickman, who was assigned to Washington at the time, recalled a spate of "silly" media stories and letters that congressmen sent to the State Department for reply. One of the letters stood out for its outlandishness: the island had been acquired, according to the writer, as a base for missiles aimed at the United States![13] Over the years, the Kuwaitis, who prefer to invest profitably and quietly, learned to accomodate occasionally raucous reactions in the United States, realizing that they did not reflect an official viewpoint or that of the vast majority of Americans.

Nearly a decade later, Kuwaiti investment in the United States and other developed economies was considerably more substantial. The leadership prudently created the Fund for Future Generations, a portfolio designed to prepare for the time when petroleum reserves had run out or were no longer in demand. In the spring of 1982, Kuwaiti holdings in America became an issue once more. A column by Dan Dorfman in May 1981 had included a list of U.S. stocks owned by the Kuwaiti government and managed by a major U.S. bank. The total value exceeded $7 billion and included minority stakes in approximately 150 blue-chip corporations.[14]

Representative Benjamin Rosenthal of New York, with whom the purloined list had been shared, was quoted in the article as raising the fear that Kuwait would gain control of major American companies.[15] Of course, the congressman should have known that if Kuwait, or any foreign investor, had a controlling interest in a company that would have triggered reporting mechanisms and it would not have been necessary to steal the list. Kuwait simply changed its account to another institution that could better safeguard the confidentiality of their transactions and continued to build the Fund. Like American diplomats in Kuwait, the Kuwaitis were becoming adept at working around such mischief and distractions. Ironically, these investments abroad would be tapped in the 1990s to offset a substantial portion of the costs incurred by the United States and other Western countries to liberate Kuwait from the Iraqi occupation.

There would be more. Kuwait also devised an innovative strategy in the petroleum sector during the 1980s, using its accumulated reserves, to invest "downstream" in both Europe and the United States. It pursued a cutting edge policy among oil-rich states to break out of the traditional role of producer of crude and a limited range of refined products; instead it intended to share in operations from wellhead to consumer.[16] The Kuwait Petroleum Company (KPC) acquired a refinery in Amsterdam from Gulf Oil, and with it, a string of service stations in Europe.[17] KPC also formed a joint venture in the United States with an American agribusiness company. The move that unleashed a storm in the United States, however, was KPC's public announcement of its intention to buy Santa Fe International, based in California, at a premium on its listed share price. The attraction from Kuwait's viewpoint was the acquisition of the capability to explore for oil throughout the world. Criticism erupted in Congress, led by Congressman Rosenthal, who seemed to have been the "designated hitter" regarding Kuwait. For the first time in its six years of existence, the interagency Committee on Foreign Investment in the United States was convened to fuel the political controversy. The purchase was facilitated in the spring of 1982 by KPC's agreement to exclude the Braun Construction Company, a Santa Fe subsidiary that had once performed engineering at a sensitive U.S. government site. To further strengthen its case, Santa Fe added former President Gerald Ford to its board of directors.[18] In Kuwait, the Santa Fe acquisition had its political analog. The National Assembly took to task the clever and visionary oil minister, Shaikh Ali Khalifa al-Sabah, for overpaying as well as subjecting Kuwait to Congressional pressures.[19]

Quite apart from political storms of this kind, oil had been, and would continue to be, a staple of the American dialog with Kuwait. Fundamentally, the U.S. government sought access to petroleum from the Gulf producers at "reasonable" and stable prices.[20] Whether the American ambassador was experienced in oil affairs, like Fran Dickman, or a relative newcomer, like Tony Quainton, petroleum matters were always high on his agenda and that of the Embassy Economic Section. At the time when Ambassador Dickman arrived in Kuwait, oil prices were extremely high, largely as a consequence of the turmoil in Iran where production had fallen from five to one million barrels per day, resulting in gas lines reminiscent of 1973 in the United States and elsewhere; prices on spot markets had risen to more than $30 per barrel. In his discussions with Kuwaiti authorities, the ambassador argued vigorously for moderate prices, as his counterparts in Saudi Arabia, the UAE, and other moderate producers were also doing. Whether as a result of these demarches or other considerations of self-interest, the moderates sought to counter the price hawks, such as Libya, Iran, Venezuela, and Indonesia, within OPEC. The December 1979 meeting of the cartel in Caracas ended in unprecedented discord due to the high demand.

By late 1980, just as oil prices began to moderate somewhat, Iraq invaded Iran, setting off a further round of international angst. At the time, Iraq was producing about 3.5 million barrels a day and Iran had boosted its output to approximately 2.5 million. Uncertainty regarding the effect of the war on the production of the two belligerents and concern about assuring the secure passage of tankers through the Gulf raised worries in the industrialized world that new shortages were likely. Naval powers from the United States to Australia initiated intense consultations about possible combined operations in support of freedom of navigation.[21] The shortfall crisis, however, never materialized. In spite of the efforts of Iraq and Iran to destroy or damage one another's oil infrastructure, prices did not again reach the levels recorded in 1980.[22] In 1982, prices actually began to fall and OPEC efforts to prop them up through assigned quotas were unsuccessful. Saudi Arabia, by far the world's largest producer, was given a "swing" role, lowering its output if world demand fell below 17.5 million barrels/day.

For the United States, OPEC was anathema because, as a cartel of oil producers, it was seen as keeping prices artificially high. The Reagan Administration favored allowing the free market to set prices and Ambassador Quainton was under instruction to reiterate this position to the oil minister. On one occasion when the ambassador was sent in to brace Ali Khalifa in connection with an upcoming OPEC meeting in Vienna, the minister delivered a "sermon" on market forces and concluded by suggesting that the U.S position was unsound. A free market, he argued, would be more harmful to the United States because Kuwait could produce a barrel of oil for slightly more than one dollar.[23] Noting that analogous costs in west Texas were almost $10/barrel, Ali Khalifa suggested that what was needed was a stable price in the range of $17–18 per barrel. Shortly thereafter, OPEC failed to reach agreement on national quotas, and Kuwait, Saudi Arabia, and others began to increase production. The world price fell to $7–8 a barrel, an uneconomical level for producers in the United States and other areas. Once quotas were set and prices rose to a range that satisfied producers worldwide, the embassy ceased to receive instructions to hammer the Kuwaitis on the virtues of the free market.[24]

The international petroleum market is extremely complex and prognostication is tricky, even without taking into consideration variations in the composition and sulphur content of different crudes. In the years following the oil embargo of 1973, all participants in the international market faced a steep learning curve. On the one hand, the United States and other industrialized countries came to understand that extremely low prices are a two-edged sword. For their part, low-cost Gulf producers gained a more sophisticated appreciation of the tradeoffs for them of extremely high prices. As their investments in the economies of the West grew, pricing policies that harmed those economies not only triggered production in marginal areas but adversely affected the return on their invested profits. In the late 1980s it was estimated that Kuwait's income from international investments was roughly equivalent to profits from petroleum sales. This equation and growing familiarity created a basis for a more harmonious relationship on oil matters.[25]

The American community weathered the dangers and apprehensions generated by the Islamic revolution in Iran and the major war between Iraq and Iran, as well as subversion and terrorist attacks within Kuwait, without flight or panic.[26] At the embassy, the trauma caused by the 1983 bombing had moderated as a consequence of measures to create a more secure environment and the normal turnover of personnel. The watchword of the new normalcy was vigilance. An impressive new wall, highly resistant to hostile penetration, girded the compound.[27]

The American community continued to grow in size as well as diversity. Representatives of the Federal Highway Works Administration (FHWA) joined the embassy staff to advise and assist the Kuwaitis in the construction of a first-class network of highways and ring roads. One element of the community that had virtually disappeared was the employees of operating oil companies in Kuwait. Long gone were the rough but amiable drillers and construction workers of the early days of the oil boom, replaced largely by company executives and engineers of more mature industries. As the operating companies were nationalized,[28] even these Americans were replaced by Kuwaitis. A contingent of Americans working for Texaco was producing oil along Kuwait's southwestern frontier with Saudi Arabia. Under arrangements negotiated with the Saudis when the former Neutral Zone was divided between them, American personnel worked on both sides of the border and lived in residences technically within Kuwait.[29] Socially, they were members of the American community in Kuwait.

Aside from the looming security threat, life in Kuwait for citizens and Western expatriates was increasingly pleasant. In addition to restaurants and other amenities, taxation was unknown. Hospitals were well-equipped and staffed, with the significant exception of nursing care, and health care was free. Education for Kuwaitis was free and public schools were supplemented by private institutions that taught a variety of national curricula; there were three high schools accredited in the United States. Gasoline and other fuels were cheap by world standards and water and electicity were subsidized. Almost any food desired, with the exception of alcohol and pork products, was available at premium prices in modern supermarkets.[30] Housing was uniformly good and Kuwaiti citizens received substantial state assistance to purchase or build a residence.[31] The societal atmosphere in Kuwait was open and liberal for the region. Women could not vote, but they were unveiled, drove automobiles, studied and worked openly, and held responsible positions in business, education, and government. A Catholic cathedral and several churches were integrated into the community.

In spite of troubled security conditions, the American and other Western expatriate communities found opportunities for lighter moments. As Brooks Wrampelmeier recalled:

> *The PAO (Public Affairs Officer, Ray Peppers) was a former opera singer and aspiring thespian. There was an active little theater group, of which he was president, that put on quite good productions of Death of a Salesman ... and Love of Four Colonels .... Plays were presented in the theater of the old television studio near the Kuwait Towers.*[32]

The Residence of the Embassy Marines, which was located at the time near the Qabazard compound across the street from the embassy, offered another center for community entertainment. Pickup volley ball games were held on Thursday afternoons and the embassy fielded a softball team.[33]

In retrospect, problems the embassy encountered with the clearance of diplomatic pouches is mildly amusing, but they were more than an inconvenience. Kuwaiti customs officials, possibly motivated by growing security concerns, were "getting very sticky about the size, weight, and content of (diplomatic) pouches. Finally, they refused to clear a large incoming shipment at the airport. For more than two days, embassy officials shuttled to the airport in shifts to maintain custody of the shipment until a courier arrived to escort it back to Athens. It turned out the shipment included "classified operations manuals" for the Hawk ground-to-air missile system the Kuwaiti armed forces had purchased. The embassy informed the military of the reason for the delay. On another occasion, the embassy managed to clear a large shipment of office supplies and equipment by informing the Kuwaiti authorities that the consular section was almost out of visa application forms and would soon have to cease issuing visas. Thereafter, the embassy requested that the Department of State include a box of these forms in each large shipment.[34]

Whether the average American was apprehensive about future developments to the north or not, the embassy staff certainly were. Ambassador Quainton cited three areas of immediate concern: a possible breakthrough by Iranian forces that might see a flanking movement through Kuwaiti territory as a way to break the stalemate on the war front; success of strong Iraqi pressure tactics against the Kuwaiti authorities to acquire the "use" of Kuwaiti territory and the low-lying islands of the Khor Abdallah that Baghdad had long coveted; or Moscow finding a means to parlay the tensions and uncertainties of the conflict to increase its presence and influence in the Gulf region.[35] The Kuwaiti government unquestionably shared at least the first two concerns as well as a growing understanding of the role both belligerents played in directing or inspiring internal security threats. At the same time, caught between two hostile neighbors with their own agendas, Kuwait knew better than to publicly air its grievances over their behavior. In spite of Iran's sponsorship of subversion within the country and the unrelenting rhetorical attacks of Tehran's propaganda machine, Kuwait tenaciously maintained "correct" diplomatic relations with Iran,[36] even as it gave way to Iraq's demands for massive financial assistance, unsupervised access to dedicated Kuwaiti piers, and overflight rights for Iraqi aircraft bombing Iranian targets in the Gulf. The Kuwaitis had little basis for trusting either belligerent given their past actions, but probably calculated that acceding to some Iraqi demands was the preferrable course if it kept the Iranians at bay, secured Iraq's good behavior, and allowed them to hold the line regarding territorial concessions.

When Iranian forces captured the Fao Peninsula opposite Bubiyan Island, in February 1986, it appeared that the first of the feared scenarios was unfolding. Prime Minister Rafsanjani underlined the implications, gloating, "These countries should remember that we are now on their borders."[37] For reasons that had nothing to do with Iraqi pressure, intimidations, or "charm," the United States government was acting in ways that favored Iraq tactically in the conflict as well.[38] As the Iraqi attacks against Iran faltered and Iranian armed forces and their allied militia (Basij) began to recover their natural advantage in population base, Baghdad sent signals that it was interested in ending the war. This had always been an objective of U.S. policy and signs of change in the Iraqi position were welcomed in Washington. Iran, by contrast, gave every indication of determination to continue fighting until "victory"; as the tide turned and Iran recaptured lost ground and later pushed the Iraqis back into their own country, regime leaders in Tehran seemed intent on pursuing a total, existential war. Iran rejected UN Security Council efforts, spearheaded by the United States, to end the fighting until the summer of 1988.

Iraq adopted more moderate public positions regarding relations with both the United States and Western-oriented Arab countries. The conflict between Iraq and Iran lasted so long that most analysts and commentators lost sight of the conditions prevailing in the Middle East at its beginning. Egypt, for example, was largely isolated and shunned in the Arab world as a result of the peace treaty it had concluded with Israel and progress toward a political solution to the Palestinian plight was at a standstill. It was Iraq, undoubtably out of necessity and desperation, that led the reintegration of the largest Arab state into the regional fabric.[39] Saddam Hussein's embrace of Egypt at peace with Israel raised an intriguing question: did this signal that Iraq, long among the loudest and most hardline "rejectionist" states, might now be prepared to align itself with a serious peace process? Given these considerations, it was felt that the United States should position itself to "test" Saddam's newfound "moderation." There were few illusions about the nature of the man and his regime, but some basis for hope that he had the capacity to learn from his mistakes. In the final analysis, it became clear that his learning curve was extremely flat, but the testing phase continued until 1990. Nevertheless, the perception that the United States was "on the side of the Arabs in what was seen as an Arab-Iranian war was certainly a positive dimension for our bilateral relations with the Kuwaitis and other Gulf Arabs."[40]

The United States and Kuwait were poised to enter a period of closer consultation and cooperation on shared security concerns, even if this was not clear to casual observers. Kuwait was under pressure from Iraq and under explicit threat from Iran; it had to wonder whether its traditional strategy of playing off more powerful states against one another was still an effective policy. It had not, after all, preserved Kuwait from the subversion and terrorism of Iran and its regional surrogates, or the playing out of the Iraq-Iran conflict in the streets of Kuwait. Increasingly effective security measures and counterterrorism forces had been the factors that improved domestic security, although small incidents continued to disturb the peace periodically. Kuwait's very success in identifying, apprehending, and prosecuting perpetrators had the potential to generate further violence by elements seeking to free their "colleagues." Still Ambassador Quainton could opine at the conclusion of his tenure (1984–87): "There was, in fact, almost no violence in Kuwait in the period that we were there. There may have been one or two small bombings but no major terrorist incidents."[41]

The GCC, touted at the outset as a forum for economic cooperation among the Arab states of the Arabian Peninsula, nevertheless provided Kuwait with important psychological assets—strategic depth and a mechanism through which the new, likeminded "allies" could cooperate on common concerns. Almost from its inception, the rulers of the GCC states, the majority of which were unambiguously pro-Western in orientation, engaged on issues of internal and external security. With a periodic nod in the direction of Moscow, Kuwait now opened a new and more routine chapter in its relationship with the U.S. Embassy and Washington.[42]

U.S. weapons systems were, of course, already in the inventory of the Kuwaiti armed forces and more were in process of delivery. The associated training and logistics train was large enough that military specialists (USLOK) had been assigned to the embassy to provide training, supply, and support functions. From the mid-1980s, more regular and sustained exchanges on security cooperation and Kuwait's arms procurement requests were initiated in a businesslike atmosphere. Unresolved or controversial issues still became public but without the barbs and recriminations that had poisoned the atmosphere previously. In mid-1984, for example, media in the United States reported that Kuwait had asked informally for Stingers (shoulder-fired anti-aircraft missiles)[43] and that the U.S. government had replied that the system was not available. The request was sufficiently important to Kuwait that Foreign Minister Shaikh Sabah al-Ahmad appealed for approval of the sale at a press conference, at which he also revealed that Kuwaiti air defense had a real-time link for data from U.S. AWACs aircraft operating out of Saudi Arabia. At the Department of State, it was confirmed that Kuwait had been informed that the Reagan Administration could not approve export of Stingers because of Congressional opposition and was looking at "immediate and effective" ways to enhance Kuwait's air defense capabilities. Within ten days, the Defense Department formally notified Congress of an intent to sell air-defense systems valued at $82 million.[44] Plans to train 150 Kuwaiti pilots were announced in Washington by the Department of Defense in July 1984.[45]

Even as Kuwait improved its defense against potential air attacks, the Iranian threat to Kuwaiti interests took another ominous turn. Toward the end of 1986 there emerged a clear pattern of attacks by the Iranian Navy and Revolutionary Guards on tankers and other shipping of Gulf nonbelligerents.[46] Mining of sea lanes and approaches to Kuwait harbor and the harrying of ships by Iranian small boats posed a very serious challenge to Kuwait, whose total oil exports were transported through the Gulf waters by tanker. Iran targetted vessels carrying Kuwaiti cargos, reportedly striking three tankers flying Kuwait's flag and ten others under neutral flags during 1986. Some ships were no longer willing to sail to Kuwait.[47] Urgent countermeasures, including assistance from one or more major powers, were vital if the country's economic lifeline was not to be choked off.

Tracing the evolution of the Tanker Protection Regime, as it came to be called, is complicated by the fact that early discussions were confidential and took place through several channels. The announcement in Washington during March 1987 that the U.S. administration had responded positively to a Kuwaiti request for armed protection of Kuwaiti-owned ships seems to have been the first official statement on the matter.[48] Even that disclosure, however, gave little indication that a full-blown operational concept was in play in U.S.-Kuwaiti talks. The U.S. Navy had escorted U.S.-registered vessels since the Iraq-Iran war began and the implication of the March report appeared to presage little more than an extension of escort services to ships flying Kuwait's flag. Another source, however, suggests that the idea of transferring Kuwaiti-owned tankers to the U.S. registry was under consideration as early as December 1986.[49]

Whatever was in the Kuwaiti government's mind initially, it is reasonably certain that discussions explicitly centered on reflagging Kuwait's tankers commenced in the spring of 1987. On April 21, Assistant Secretary of State Richard Murphy publicly confirmed that the United States and Kuwait were "consulting" on the possibility of registering Kuwaiti ships under the American flag.[50] The actual negotiations were conducted principally in Kuwait, directly between the ambassador, the prime minister, and the minister of defense "over a number of months."[51] Embassy expertise was supplemented during the bilateral discussions by senior visits from the Pentagon, U.S. Central Command (USCENTCOM), and other interested agencies.[52] Specialists on the technical aspects of the reregistration of Kuwaiti tankers also traveled to Kuwait for brief periods.

Public awareness of the proposal to place Kuwaiti-owned tankers under the American flag generated concern and outright opposition among elements in both countries.[53] Joe Twinam pointed out the irony of the effort to pass off this groundbreaking arrangement as consistent with nonalignment:

> *It is remarkable how various Gulf Council states, including Kuwait, tried at the political level to strike public postures of noninvolvement with the massive Western military engagement that the Kuwaiti initiative had brought forth. Kuwait officials denied any intent to give the Western powers use of military facilities and even suggested that now the United States and Britain, not Kuwait, were solely responsible for the safety of the reflagged tankers.*[54]

In fact, Kuwait and its Gulf allies favored the U.S. Navy commitment and took action behind the scenes to support naval and aviation operations. As Twinam observes, American spokesmen fended off critics in their own country with vague assurances that the GCC states were making contributions to the reflagging project.

Whatever the obfuscations, the Kuwaiti turn to the United States was a decisive departure from the state's traditional posture of nonalignment and balance. Despite the efforts of the regime to distance itself publicly from the consequences of the process it had set in motion,[55] some in Kuwait saw through the effort to obscure the implications and reacted negatively. In the United States, elements opposed to the proposal felt that Kuwait's history of nonalignment and criticism of U.S. policies made the country an unreliable partner. The concern that Kuwait might "invite" the Soviets to establish a military presence in the Gulf reinforced the force of the opponents' argument.[56] Other American critics questioned the wisdom of assuming an obligation in the Gulf that could draw the United States into the ongoing conflict there. Ultimately, longer term interests, including long-standing opposition to an enhanced Soviet (i.e., Russian) strategic role in the vital Gulf region, overcame American doubts and reservations. U.S.-Kuwaiti agreement on the Gulf Protection Regime was announced on May 19 1987.[57]

Work quickly began on the remaining practical aspects of the reflagging. Formal title for the eleven tankers was taken from the Kuwait Oil Tanker Company (KOTC) by an American company

(Chesapeake Shipping, Inc.) that Kuwait chartered for the purpose in the state of Delaware.[58] The ships were renamed using a map of small towns across the Delaware River in southern New Jersey.[59] Inspections were conducted by the United States Coast Guard and repairs and modifications required to meet American standards were carried out in port where possible, or while the ships were underway when necessary. Because the reflagged tankers would be sailing to Europe or the Far East, some requirements concerning manning and other matters for vessels operating in U.S. waters, were waived. Only the Master and radio operator on each ship had to be Americans.[60]

Plans were already being made for protection of the American-flag vessels by MIDEASTFOR headquartered afloat in Bahrain, as well as for augmentation of U.S. Navy assets in the Gulf.[61] In August 1987, the Defense Department created a new command—Joint Task Force Middle East (JTFME).[62] Commanded by Rear Admiral Dennis Brooks with the carrier battle group in the Gulf of Oman, JTFME was directly subordinate to the CINCCENT (Gen. Crist) and responsible for the entire transit of the tankers, including the 550 mile run between the Straits of Hormuz and Mina al-Ahmadi in Kuwait.[63] The plan called for ships entering the Gulf to assemble off Khor Fakhan, a UAE port on the Gulf of Oman. From there, the convoy with U.S. Navy escorts passed through the Straits; vessels departing Kuwait gathered in a designated area near Mina al-Ahmadi and reversed the route. In addition to surface combatants, the ships were provided air support during the passage.

Implementation of the plan required an augmentation of military support personnel at the embassy, but many in Kuwait were at the time "allergic" to the presence of foreign military on their soil. A solution was devised to bring in small groups on a rotating basis to conduct the necessary coordination with KOTC and other Kuwaiti agencies involved in the operation.[64] With that issue resolved satisfactorily, cooperation between Americans and Kuwaitis was exceptionally close and productive.

In late July 1987, after weeks of negotiations and preparations, the first escort mission got underway at Khor Fakhan. As the single file of ships passed Bahrain and neared Kuwait on the morning of

July 24, the reflagged tanker Bridgeton struck a mine. The ship sustained minor damage but was able to continue on to Kuwait.[65] It was not determined when the mine was sown, but events would later demonstrate that, with sufficient notice, the Iranians had the capability to plant naval mines clandestinely.

As fortune would have it, the incident occurred on the same day that the Senate Committee on Foreign Relations held hearings on my nomination as the next American ambassador to Kuwait. I learned of the mine incident only when I arrived at the committee hearing room.

14

Prelude to Disaster

Operation "Earnest Will" was in full swing when I arrived in late August 1987. Sustained and effective coordination with Minister of Oil Shaikh Ali Khalifa al-Sabah, the chairman of Kuwait Oil Tanker Company (KOTC), Abdul Fatah al-Bader, and other involved Kuwaiti officials, were at the top of the embassy's agenda.[1] Changes and adaptations had been made to deal with the threat of mines since the incident of late July, and further refinements were in process with the assistance of Kuwait. Both Americans and Kuwaitis were acutely aware that the tanker protection regime was in the public eye and that critics on both sides were looking for further failures. The tower of the Hilton Hotel across the street from the embassy was filled with American reporters.[2]

The American Embassy, led by DCM James Hooper between ambassadors, was a medium-sized mission of about ninety-five Americans from the State Department and a mix of other U.S. government agencies along with another sixty Foreign Service Nationals (FSNs). Morale appeared to be good, with little indication of the trauma that Ambassador Quainton had found on his arrival. Although Kuwait continued to be plagued by internal security challenges until late 1988,[3] the incidents did not reach the level of the earlier embassy bombing. The embassy staff and families, as well as the larger American community, were wary and vigilant but seemed to have made a good adjustment to the situation. The Embassy grounds themselves showed little evidence of the destruction suffered in 1983. The former administration building was rebuilt and had been converted into a residence for the Marine Security Guards assigned to the mission. Administrative offices as well as other functions (e.g., the Commercial Office) were installed in new temporary buildings, and an impressive new wall encircled the entire five-acre compound. The installation bore almost no resemblance to the desolate, sandy lot of the early 1960s. The embassy grounds, in fact, now were a verdant oasis featuring well-tended trees and lawns. The city had long since expanded past the embassy property and grown up around it.[4]

Kuwaiti authorities greatly expedited the presentation of credentials, first to the minister of foreign affairs, and then to His Highness the Amir. Normally, new ambassadors may not engage formally before this presentation, but pressing issues involved in implementing the protection of tankers tested the letter, if not the spirit, of diplomatic protocol. While formal calls on Kuwaiti officials had to wait, I found ways to slip discretely into the building where the Ministry of Oil and the KOTC were located for working sessions. These early consultations laid the foundations for productive relationships with Shaikh Ali Khalifa and Abdul Fatah al-Bader. It was fortuitous that a good rapport be established immediately, because Kuwait and its tanker fleet and the U.S. naval vessels escorting them very quickly faced a new and dangerous threat.

In early September 1987, with the convoying of Kuwaiti shipping beginning to hit its stride, a missile streaked past the city and impacted in a deserted area in the south. Amazingly, the million-dollar projectile caused no injuries, although it spooked a nearby flock of goats. It was quickly determined, from fragments recovered at the scene, that it was a Chinese-made "Silkworm" missile fired by Iranians from recently consolidated positions on the al-Fao peninsula.[5] While ineffectual in this case, the introduction of the Silkworm menace set off alarm bells among those responsible for the defense of Kuwait and neutral shipping. In an exercise that would be repeated several times over the fall of 1987, Under Secretary Sulaiman al-Shaheen summoned ambassadors of the permanent members of the UN Security Council to the Foreign Ministry, where he passed around fragments of the missile bearing clear Chinese markings. While he called for support at the UN and elsewhere, the Chinese ambassador "pretended" not to be able to read Chinese. In truth, he was in a delicate and difficult position, and there was a degree of professional understanding of his charade. It was clear to all participants that the problem would not be solved at the UN where the Iranians were stonewalling efforts by the United States and others to bring the Iraq-Iran conflict to a negotiated conclusion.[6]

U.S. Navy authorities in the region engaged KOTC and other Kuwaitis in a project to devise a way to neutralize the Silkworms, but there would still be several months of tension and tragedy. As I pondered the threat posed by the relatively primitive Silkworm guidance systen, I considered the possibility that they might, by accident or design, target the massive distillation plants on which Kuwait depended for potable water. The Embassy compound already had a number of large fiberglass tanks to store water. I ordered that they be augmented subtantially with additional tanks, little realizing how crucial they would be in the future.

Until a solution to the challenge of the Iranian missiles was found, the residents of Kuwait, and the merchant mariners serving them, would remain exposed to the threat. The launchers at al-Fao continued to lob the missiles periodically and, in October 1987, they found targets with tragic results. That month, the Liberian-registered tanker, Sungari, was hit in the offshore area where the tankers were loaded. On October 17, an even more devastating attack struck the reflagged tanker, Sea Isle City, blinding Captain John Hunt, the American master.[7] In retaliation for this blatant attack on an American ship, U.S. naval forces in the Gulf exacted a heavy price. The Iranian Navy and militias were using an artificial platform, "Rashadat," in international waters to monitor shipping in the waterway and to resupply the small craft used for raiding. After warning the armed Iranians on the platform to leave, U.S. warships destroyed the platform, as well as the Iranian military who had not heeded the warning.[8] A second Iranian oil platform was knocked out in the same operation.[9]

The Kuwaitis deployed radar assets and a Hawk missile battery to Failaka Island to detect Silkworm missiles after launch and attempted to shoot them down as they traveled south over the Gulf. Nevertheless, the Iranians were able to hit the Kuwaiti Sea Isle oil loading terminal, inflicting substantial damage.[10] The definitive answer, however, lay in a crash project at the U.S. Navy Research laboratory financed by Kuwait. In record time, and at relatively low cost, the lab produced a template for "metal grid radar reflectors" that could be mounted on a small barge for about $40,000 each. The trick was to convince the Silkworm's on-board guidance radar that the decoy barge was much larger than anything else around it. As soon as the problem was solved, the first barges were fabricated in Kuwait.

The climax of Iran's Silkworm campaign arrived quickly, scarcely noted by the media or the international community. So unremarkable did the event appear that even experienced observers missed the real story.[11] I was in the VIP Lounge at the Kuwait airport on the morning of December 7, 1987, with a number of senior Kuwaiti officials, including the minister of oil. One of the Kuwaitis took a telephone call and announced that a Silkworm launch at al-Fao had been confirmed and the missile was being tracked as it approached the loading facilities offshore. Shortly thereafter, the phone rang again with very welcome news: The Silkworm had headed straight for a decoy barge!

Later that day, the five ambassadors were summoned by the Foreign Ministry Under Secretary once again. He was scarcely able to conceal his elation as he reported that the strike was a total failure. The Chinese ambassador was more than normally engaged as he sought to learn what had caused the Chinese-manufactured weapon to malfunction. He got almost no satisfaction during the brief meeting and tried once more as the group was getting into their cars. "Oh," one of the Western envoys said before driving away, "barges." A European colleague later quipped, half seriously, that perhaps the Chinese ambassador was going to ask the head of the Kuwait News Agency (KUNA) for an explanation, since his name was Barges al-Barges.

In the late 1980s, life for Western expatriates (including Americans) was unexpectedly easy, despite the struggle being waged at sea and occasional acts of arson and bombing at oil facilities. With more than twenty-five hundred citizens in residence, the American community had achieved sufficient mass to support a range of institutions, activities and events—either independently or in association with Kuwaitis and other national communities. The reasons for their relative indifference to unexpected violent attacks were complex. There seems little doubt that the example set by Amir Shaikh Jabir al-Ahmad was a factor in public attitudes. His demeanor following the abortive assassination attempt may, in fact, have marked a psychological turning point in the struggle against domestic terrorism. Within hours of his narrow escape in May 1985, and even before the security services could be certain that additional plots were not under way, the ruler appeared briefly on Kuwaiti television—in bandages—to reassure the population that he was well and determined to carry on. As a man who was quiet and modest in his personal habits, it was easy for ordinary Kuwaitis and others to identify with his experience and sangfroid.[12] The inner fortitude he exhibited in the face of personal danger had the effect of reinforcing popular support for his leadership.[13] Success of the security services in preventing further terrorism akin to that of the mid-1980s also bolstered public confidence.[14]

A range of amenities and activities were available to American residents; excellent housing was plentiful, and interaction with both Kuwaitis and other expatriates was easy for those willing to seek them out. There were good restaurants, especially in the hotels, and an increasing selection of fast-food franchises with familiar names and logos—KFC, Pizza Hut, and Hardee's.[15] Modern supermarkets, including Safeway, offered almost any foods desired, from Washington state apples to Australian kiwis.[16] Outlets for a French department store and high-end clothing and shoes from well-known European boutiques could be found in modern shopping malls. Americans working for private companies enjoyed not only forgiveness of U.S. taxes on part of their income, but housing and educational allowances, generous leave, and paid travel back to the United States on an annual basis.[17]

Fully accredited American schools offered a U.S curriculum through high school for community children, as well as Kuwaitis and others interested in further study in the American system.[18] Two of them had great success in placing graduates in universities and colleges in the United States. Activities included sports teams that competed against American high schools across the Middle East and class trips abroad. The fact that the Kuwaiti Ministry of Higher Education had adopted the American collegiate system made these schools attractive to applicants of Kuwait and other nationalities interested in further study in the United States. Equally important, the availability of education for their children was of immense comfort to resident Americans.

The size and stability of the resident American community provided a foundation not only for schools but for other institutions and activities as well. A large informal association of women—the American Women's League (AWL)—brought together ladies from the United States, including those married to Kuwaitis, other Arabs, and South Asians. AWL sponsored a sizeable holiday bazaar at a local hotel during the Christmas season, as well as fashion shows and other activities to benefit local charitable causes, such as the Kuwait Handicapped Society. They also represented the United States with a booth in international charity fairs organized periodically. By tradition, the honorary president of the AWL was the spouse of the American ambassador.

An international softball league played at a field near the police training facility on Sixth Ring Road each Friday during the season (the local weekend was Thursday and Friday, the Muslim holy day). An American Embassy team was part of the eight-team league.[19] The Kuwait Little League played simultaneously on an adjacent field under the tutelage of several dedicated adults. One team, "Ambassadors," was sponsored by the embassy but the players included a number of young Kuwaitis who had learned the game while their families were in the United States for education or military training. A T-ball league for beginners began in the late 1980s.

Recreational facilities on the American Embassy grounds included a full-size swimming pool with an adjacent snack bar, two clay tennis courts, and grassy areas for picnics and volleyball.[20] Embassy personnel and families were free to use these amenities outside of working hours and others were invited for special events or as guests of employees. On Thursday afternoons there were regular volleyball games, often featuring matches with other embassies.[21]

On July 4th, the grounds were opened to the American community for a traditional cookout. Kuwaiti firms representing U.S. franchises supported these activities; "Hungry Bunny," the local name for an American fast-food chain, erected inflatable trampolines and other attractions. The Embassy compound was also used to entertain crews of U.S. Navy ships visiting Kuwait, which offered little activity for "liberty" parties. The ships usually provided food and soft drinks, and the arrangement avoided the possibility of incidents in the city.[22]

The area immediately behind the Ambassador's Residence was used for more formal receptions, such as those on the Fourth of July, and the children's Christmas party which was attended by the families of the American and FSN staff. Through careful tending over the years, the space had become an attractive garden with a lawn dominated by two regal Bir'i date palms and surrounded by a six-foot wall. The central area was paved and covered by a canvas pavillion under which fans were installed to circulate air. In 1989, the embassy restored a traditional heavy wood Kuwaiti door and installed it as the entrance to the Residence garden. In a ceremony in which Dorothy Scudder took part, the new entry was named "Scudder Gate" as a tribute to the dedicated staff of the American Mission Hospital. The new gate allowed guests to enter the garden directly without having to pass through the residence. Among the events held in the garden were a large themed reception each September, the annual celebration of the Marine Corps birthday in November, and special appearances of American performers, such as the "Sun Rhythm Section" (who backed Elvis Presley during his early days at Sun Records in Memphis) or Michael Doucet and "Beau Soleil" (a well-known Zydeco ensemble), sponsored by the U.S. Information Service (USIS).

Americans and other Western expatriates, as well as Kuwaitis, had a growing menu of entertainment options to choose from in the late 1980s. Hotels, commericial firms, and other embassies presented a range of events such as Disney on Ice, the Harlem Globetrotters, and the Vienna Boys Choir.[23] Local theater enthusiasts from the American, British, and other communities staged plays and musical revues, and American jazz and swing were performed by an international group of musicians led by the headmaster of the American Community School, a talented trumpeter.[24] The annual raft race at the Misilleh Beach Hotel drew a large international crowd as well as scratch-built rafts from the American embassy and other organizations for a day of picnicking and cheering on the shores of the Gulf. In addition, several ethnic groups among the British community—Scots, Welsh, and Irish—held elaborate celebrations on their national days. I was an honorary member by heritage of the Kuwait Cambrian Society (Wales) and regularly attended the dinner on St. David's Day, as well as Robbie Burns Night with the Kuwait Caledonians (Scotland). The British ambassador, Sir Peter Hinchcliff, and I were routinely asked to speak at these events because we could be counted upon to "roast" one another in good humor.

It was in fact possible for an American in modern Kuwait to immerse himself almost exclusively in familiar American or international cultures. At the American Embassy, however, the emphasis stressed interaction with the Kuwaiti people. The opportunities to do so were unquestionably greater than at any post where I served during my Foreign Service career. At least two evenings a week were routinely reserved for visits to Kuwaiti *diwaniyyas*. The host families were uniformly warm and welcoming. One or two embassy officers usually accompanied me and sat among the attendees so that two or three conversations were carried on during a visit of thirty minutes. In that way, several *diwaniyas* could be visited each night. The individual venues varied in subject matter and in style; some focused on a single conversation, others broke up into smaller groupings around the room. Sometimes the attendees wished to elicit my views on current issues or events—commerical, cultural, or political—that concerned them. On other occasions, they merely carried on the discussion. Nevertheless, the proceedings offered an unparallelled window into a broad cross-section of Kuwaiti preoccupations and worries, especially when embassy visits were made on a regular basis. I was at a loss to understand why more diplomats did not avail themselves of this rare opportunity.

The future of the Embassy complex assumed a higher priority as the end of the lease in the 1990s approached. The location, barren and relatively isolated when it was selected, was in many ways ideal now that the city had embraced it. Situated on the Gulf, not far from the Ministry of Foreign Affairs and other Kuwait government agencies, new roads had opened good access in several directions, while quiet residential streets inland added a layer of security against a repetition of threats such as the earlier truck bombing.[25] The location of the compound had many advantages.

Standing in the way of remaining and constructing new permanent facilities were two factors. The first was the interest of the Bahraini owners in regaining control of the property for commercial development. Periodically, agents of the Bahraini ruling family met with American Ambassadors and other administrative officers in the hope of terminating the lease early, or, at least, raising the rent that had been negotiated in the late 1950s. They were, of course, unsuccessful on either count, but, conversely, it was not prudent to make major improvements in embassy structures until the long-term future of the property was clarified. The second obstacle confronting the State Department's Foreign Buildings Office (FBO) regarded the security of any new structure, particularly with tall buildings such as the hotel tower across the street.[26] Ongoing discussions with FBO turned to designing a new embassy without windows facing outward, covered walkways, and other modifications to protect against snipers and other potential terrorist threats. The embassy was resigned to incorporating elements of modern penal architecture if the issue of extending the lease or purchase could be resolved.

On the night of September 21–22, 1987, U.S. forces in the Gulf scored a dramatic success in their campaign to protect neutral vessels.[27] An Iranian ship, later identified as the *Iran Ajr*, was detected and Army helicopters based on a guided missile frigate were launched to keep it under observation. When the helicopters, equipped with sophisticated night observation capability, witnessed the crew of the ship launching sea mines in international waters in the vicinity of Bahrain, they were ordered to "stop the mining." Fire from the helicopters killed several of the crew and drove the rest overboard.[28] A Navy SEAL team boarded the craft and confirmed the presence of mines in the cargo well. The SEALs also took the surviving twenty-six Iranian crewmen into custody. Under questioning, the Iranians admitted that they were laying mines and provided information regarding the location of the mines they had already deployed. Charts found on the ship indicated the mining plan and facilitated the retrieval and disarming of seven mines that the ship had planted in the Gulf.[29] On September 26, the naval units scuttled *Iran Ajr* in international waters; the detained members of its Iranian crew were quietly repatriated to Iran through Oman. The Iranian flag that the ship was flying when captured was sent to the U.S. Navy Museum.

The Iranian regime, predictably, claimed that the vessel was a merchant ship and that charges of mine laying were "lies." The Iranian news agency reported the ship was engaged in transporting foodstuffs to the port at Bushire.[30] But the photographic and other evidence gathered by the attacking helicopter and boarding parties quickly exposed the duplicity of the Tehran regime.[31] To this point, Iran had sought to achieve its designs without leaving evidence of its culpability. *Iran Ajr* had their fingerprints all over it and, henceforth, the gloves were off.[32]

Mines were the most persistent and difficult threat to "Operation Earnest Will," and considerable effort and ingenuity were applied to neutralizing it. Many of the precautions and measures taken were unpublicized at the time and some remain secret today, but the broad outlines are clear. The U.S. Navy began the tanker protection regime with a serious deficit in coastal mine-sweeping capabilities.[33] A number of World War II, vintage wooden minesweepers were mothballed at Charleston, South Carolina and were quickly commissioned and rushed to the Gulf. The more immediate solution, however, was to fashion sweepers from assets already in the Gulf. In a characteristic collaboration between the Navy and Kuwaiti oil officials, two 150-foot commercial tugs were made available by the Minister of Oil and minesweeping cable was flown in from the United States. Suspended between the two tugboats, now known as "Hunter" and "Striker," the cables cleared a swath of sea about 1,200 feet wide.[34] The Government of Japan, which was greatly dependent upon oil from the Gulf, purchased a state-of-the-art navigation system based on a series of towers as its contribution to the protection of commercial shipping. When finally installed, the system made it easier for tankers to stay within lanes swept of mines and also facilitated accurate surveys of the sea bottom.[35]

The U.S. Navy was the lead service during "Earnest Will," and engaged in conventional naval tasks. But the operation was, in a real sense, a hybrid; drawing upon several armed services as well as commercial assets in the region, as illustrated. The task was without precedent or a "school solution" in the parlance of the

American war colleges. Unlike other likely missions, there was no preconceived Operations Plan (OpPlan) for the contingency when USCINCCENT was assigned the job. The broad outline of the OpPlan was hammered out over several sessions at U.S. Central Command Headquarters in Tampa, Florida in which I participated as Command Political Advisor (POLAD), and adaptations were made as needed in the Gulf. The fact that it succeeded was a testament to the flexibility of Americans, Kuwaitis, military services, and civilian agencies.

The concept of a "mobile sea base" to meet the requirement for surveillance and deterrence near the center of the route through the Gulf was probably the best example of the ingenuity and flexibility of the operation. Outside the small circle of American and Kuwaiti participants, it remains the least known aspect of the tanker protection regime. Few close observers were fooled by the efforts of Gulf states to distance themselves from the operation, but their public posture severely limited the kinds of support they could provide.[36] All were extremely sensitive to the stationing of American forces in their territory. While this sensitivity was understandable in light of domestic and regional politics of the time, their unwillingness to host military personnel who were protecting their interests complicated the U.S. Administration's ability to sell a policy that also served American interests.[37] A practical solution to the need for additional assets to cover the central portion of the Gulf presented itself when the President of the Kuwait Oil Tanker Company agreed to a long-term lease of two large commercial barges from Brown and Root.[38] Lashed together and positioned off Bahrain, the newly created sea base was quickly modified to add electronics, helicopter landing pads, launchable small boats, and integral anti-aircraft and anti-surface armament. With the capability of relocating fairly easily, and close-in defenses that included frogmen and other elements that have not been publicly disclosed, the mobile sea base confronted potential Iranian attackers with a formidable and unpredictable menace.

In one sense, necessity became a virtue during the conflict in the Gulf. When the *Iran Ajr* was detected and captured, it gave a boost to the morale of Gulf Arabs and seemed to disconcert the Iranian leadership, which was at a loss to understand how it had happened. A historian of the tanker war believes the deterrent effect of that single incident was sufficient to prevent the Iranians from undertaking further mining until the spring of 1988.[39] The Iranian naval forces would eventually regain some of their balance and aggressiveness shortly before the tragic shootdown of an Iranian commercial Airbus by the guided missile cruiser USS *Vincennes*. The circumstances of this accident by the cruiser, which was maneuvering in a battle with Iranian surface forces, have been investigated and reviewed exhaustively by the U.S. Navy and others without great satisfaction. What is not in doubt was the great sadness the loss of innocent lives engendered in the region.[40] Shortly thereafter, the Iranian regime, which had steadfastly rejected UN efforts to bring the war with Iraq to an end, reluctantly accepted a truce. The tanker war was over for the moment.

The Iraq-Iran conflict was one of the longest and most destructive wars of the twentieth century. When a truce was declared, the forces on the opposing sides found themselves essentially where they had stood when it began eight years before. The exception being that Iraq had lost the use of its major port at Basra due to silting and unexploded ordnance, including gas shells, that fell into the Shatt al-Arab. The tanker war, minor by comparison in terms of casualties, was nonetheless very destructive, especially for Iran. About 440 vessels took hits, several on multiple occasions. Of that total, over half (239) were oil tankers. Insurers and/or owners sank or wrote off 115 vessels, including several Iranian warships. Shipping losses totaled approximately $2.5 billion. Ship attacks by Iraq took over three hundred lives, while Iran killed about sixty, exclusive of injuries.[41]

A measure of peace came to Kuwait, and the seas around it, for the first time in eight years with the declaration of a ceasefire between Iraq and Iran on August 20, 1988.[42] In the sealanes and elsewhere in the Gulf, no new mines were sown after the truce but sweeping operations continued apace to locate and explode mines moored in the period of active combat.[43] Within Kuwait, security forces saw a substantial tapering off of acts of terrorism and sabotage committed in support of Iranian interests.[44]

Over the period leading up to the tanker protection regime, and during its prosecution, the country experienced a sustained campaign directed primarily at oil handling facilities seemingly designed to complement the assault on tankers serving the country. Resident Iranians and Shi'a from Lebanon constituted an internal security threat throughout the Iraq-Iran conflict, and an unknown number in those categories had been denied work permits, deported, or tried as part of Kuwait's countertettorism strategy. In 1984, for example, the Ministry of Interior accused four Iranian expatriates with forming a network for sabotage and acquiring bomb-making materials.[45] Several months later, in January 1985, five Iranian suspects were tried for "subversive activities," including plotting attacks against broadcasting stations.[46] The most troublesome aspect of this and subsequent attacks was the growing involvement of a small cadre of Kuwaiti Shi'a in domestic plots and violence. Over the period until the Iraq-Iran ceasefire, the role of Kuwaitis in attacks on oil facilities in particular became clear from the access required to well-secured sites.[47] Targets of these attacks were the offshore terminal at Ahmadi, a well in Maqwa, and a collecting facility in the same area. All were heavily protected and open only to credentialed employees. Responsibility for the arson and other incidents was claimed by a previously unknown group—"the Revolutionary Organization of the Prophet Muhammad in Kuwait"—in an unsuccessful attempt to draw attention away from the real perpetrators.[48] The circumstances of the crimes, and the subsequent involvement of Iranian assets among the Shia community in Lebanon, stamped the incidents as the work of Kuwaiti Shia elements serving Iran's interests.

The collusion of a small band of Kuwaiti Shi'as in actions against the security interests of their own country was as much a shock as it was a threat. The old Shi'a merchant families, including those of Persian origin, were well established and integrated into the Kuwaiti community; as a group, Kuwaiti Shi'a enjoyed acceptance and freedoms unique in the Arab world, with the possible exception of Lebanon.[49] To the extent that the Shi'a leadership felt apprehensive in the past, they and other minorities traditionally supported the amir in rivalries with the Sunni merchant community. The new circumstances threatened to upset long-held assumptions and societal mechanisms.[50]

Evidence of disloyalty among the Shi'a minority confronted the Kuwaiti authorities with the dilemma that all relatively transparent governments face when confronted by unreliable elements. The delicate issue is how to deal with the miscreants without punishing, and thereby alienating, the larger community. Few regimes get the balance right, particularly when they are under threat—as Kuwait was in the late 1980s.[51] Kuwait, which had quietly initiated a program of easing Kuwait Shi'as out of sensitive military and security positions, extended the policy to the oil sector.[52] Whatever their sense of grievance, the larger Shi'a community identified their interests with Kuwait and did not support or sympathize with acts of bombing and arson which were committed in pursuit of Iranian interests rather than the welfare of coreligionists in Kuwait. Nevertheless, precautionary measures taken by the Kuwaiti authorities could only deepen perceptions of prejudicial treatment.[53] The longer the campaign of homegrown terrorism continued, the more poisonous the atmosphere would become.

The continuing series of minor attacks took on anti-American overtones as the tanker protection regime was successfully implemented. Members of the American community in Kuwait were not explicitedly targeted, and none were injured, but the sites selected were increasingly identified with the United States. In late 1987, for example, a small bomb was planted at the office of the agent for Pan American Airlines.[54] A month later, in November, a small incendiary bomb started a fire in the building housing the American Life Insurance Company office, and the following spring the Avis rental car agency was bombed, injuring one person.[55] The terrorists likewise struck out in ways that threatened civilians. Two perpetrators accidentally blew themselves up attempting to plant a bomb in Salihiya in July 1987, and in September fires were set in three areas of Kuwait University and the Shamia secondary school for boys.[56] In November of the same year, an explosive was detonated under a police van parked near the Interior Ministry at a time when American and Kuwaiti officials were meeting inside to consider the threat posed by Iranian Silkworm missiles.[57] The unfolding pattern of attacks, as well as the identity of suspects, provided convincing evidence of the culpability of the Iranian regime and its Kuwaiti supporters.[58]

Perhaps surprisingly, the crisis-weary population of Kuwait, including the American community, refused to be cowed by the violence as they pursued their lives.[59] The American Embassy hosted meetings for wardens and other leaders more frequently than in quieter times. As well as confirming and updating the warden system, the ambassador and other senior officers shared their assessment of developments and answered questions. These exchanges offered opportunities for the embassy to know the issues concerning the American community and to judge the prevailing mood.

In 1988, the end of the vicious eight-year conflict between Iraq and Iran was greeted in Kuwait with immense relief and a hope that life would quickly return to a scarcely remembered normalcy.[60] For a time, there was optimism as well. Relative calm returned to Gulf waters, except for the constant search for old mines and a wary eye on Iranian naval forces. Conditions, however, were not normal. Divisions and tensions, regionally and within Kuwait, born of history and the wrenching experience of the 1980s, persisted well into the postwar period. No one in 1988 could imagine how short the interlude of "peace" would be.

The National Assembly had been dissolved two years earlier. That Assembly, elected in February 1985, had initially appeared to many to be an improvement over its predecessor, which was heavily weighted with Islamic fundamentalists. The government's hope to balance the fundmentalists with newly elected "nationalists" was an apparent success.[61] Contrary to those hopes, however, the nationalists in the Assembly coalesced with the remaining fundamentalists to attack the government on issues ranging from the practice of renaming the crown prince to also serve as prime minister, and the representation of parliamentarians in the cabinet. As contentious and distracting as these confrontations were to those wrestling with internal and external security challenges, it was probably the tendency of both factions, whose views were linked to regional movements, to criticize Kuwaiti foreign policy decisions that tipped the balance for the amir.[62] According to a prominent Assembly "nationalist," Ahmad al-Khatib, the parliament was suspended in 1986 to quiet criticism of disputed foreign policies.[63] It is a measure of the extent to which his estimate of the Assembly's performance was shared by the Kuwaiti public, that its suspension was greeted with widespread indifference at the time.

One area where Kuwait had cautious hopes for improvement was in its historically turbulent relationship with Iraq. In the years after its war turned defensive, Baghdad had adopted a posture of moderation which the Kuwaitis and other Arab states in the Gulf, as well as the United States, hoped signaled a fundamental change in Saddam Hussein's world view.[64] Indeed, in the immediate postwar period, the atmosphere between Kuwait and Baghdad was publicly cordial and optimistic. There was bilateral talk of finally demarcating Kuwait's northern border and massive schemes to exchange water from Iraq for excess electrical power in Kuwait. A joint commission to define and mark the frontier was announced, but never proved fruitful. Privately, Kuwaiti officials confided that there was no way they would entrust control of their water supply to the Iraqis. In any event, the Shatt al-Arab was a less desireable source of fresh water than it had been before the conflict. The channel to the port at Basra was unusable because the constant dredging required to maintain it before 1980 had been in abeyance for the eight years of war. A further complication was that tons of unexploded ordnance, including chemical and other dangerous shells, had burrowed into the silt.

Kuwait had supported Iraq with loans of as much as $20 billion to help fund its war effort and provided port facilities to compensate for Baghdad's loss of the use of Basra and Umm Qasr.[65] As months passed without movement on the commitment to ratify the border, the atmosphere began to sour. The Iraqis had never indicated publicly where they were prepared to draw the frontier and it was evident that they continued to covet Bubiyan and Warba. Kuwaitis were reluctant to discuss their exchanges with Iraq in detail, but help they requested for assistance in researching geographic aspects of the area clearly pointed to contentious exchanges. When Shaikh Sa'd al-Abdallah, the crown prince/prime minister made a "friendly" visit to Baghdad in February 1989, he found no give in Iraq's position on territorial disputes. Since Kuwait held the territory at issue, they decided not to raise the issues until the Iraqis did.[66] Far from agreeing that Iraq had a valid claim to additional Kuwaiti land, the British government appears to have concluded that Iraq was already occupying territory that was rightfully Kuwait's. A "Note on the Safwan-Khor Abdullah section of the Kuwait-Iraq Frontier," of November 1941 contains the following historical citation:

> That the definition of the Kuwait boundary contained in Lorimer's Gazetteer was by no means acceptable to Shaikh Mubarak of Kuwait is apparent from contemporary correspondence. The Shaikh claimed that Safwan and Um Qasr (the latter place being the original home of the Shaikh's ancestors) were undoubtedly his; and Captain Shakespear, Political Agent, Kuwait, in the 'Note on the Boundaries of the Kuwait Principality' which formed an enclosure to his letter No. C 62 dated 12th August 1912 to the Political Resident in the Persian Gulf, gave the strong support of his expert knowledge to the Shaikh's claim. His Majesty's Government were not, however, prepared to make any substantial alteration to the definition of the Kuwait boundary which had already been proposed to the Turkish Government....[67]

A senior Kuwaiti minister confirmed to me in 1990, when the frontier and Kuwaiti loans had again become issues, "Um Qasr was an 'Uthbi (i.e., Kuwaiti) town and we are not ready to cede more territory."

The bilateral cooperation that seemed feasible in 1988 faded over succeeding months, surviving only in the occasional public statement. Many Kuwaitis shed any optimism they had and reverted to the cynicism regarding the regime in Baghdad they had acquired in decades of bitter experience. Many regularly watched Iraq television in diwanniyas and homes for comedic relief. The evening fare was predictable: Saddam Hussein, the quintessential "talking head," pontificating about everything from animal husbandry to military tactics, while captive audiences struggled not to nod off. One of the favorite bits in Kuwait were the periodic military awards ceremony that continued long after the fighting ended. To the guffaws of the audience in Kuwait, Saddam bestowed racks of medals so large they had to be hung from brackets affixed to the chests of the recipients.[68]

***

Kuwait and the United States had developed a close and cooperative working relationship in the crucible of the tanker protection regime, which carried over into the postwar era. Despite the carping of critics and naysayers in both countries, a valuable measure of trust and confidence had grown among those most closely involved in Kuwait, Washington, and Tampa, where USCENTCOM was headquartered. In the spring of 1989, when it was clear that Iranian attacks would not resume, Kuwait informed the United States of its decision to begin deflagging its tankers. This logical request retriggered critics in the United States who had always maintained that the reflagging had been a scheme to "rent" the U.S. Navy. The removal of Kuwait-owned vessels from the U.S. registry had the potential to undermine the cooperation and comraderie build up during the struggle at sea.[69]

The initial response from U.S. authorities was ambiguous—in part no doubt because of the multiplicity of agencies and interests now seeking a role. Some Kuwaitis were inclined to interpret the muddy reply from Washington as "evidence" that the United States intended to keep control of the Kuwaiti-owned vessels. To support this concern they brought up an obscure World War I regulation. At the Embassy in Kuwait, it appeared unlikely that this bureaucratic tussle would be resolved quickly and cleanly enough to prevent a souring of important bilateral relationships.

The basic tradeoffs required for a constructive solution were clear; Kuwait needed to establish the principle that they could deflag their ships when they chose, and the United States needed to establish that the U.S. Navy had not been "used" as a convenience and discarded lightly. I was also aware that the real interest of the U.S. military was in the product carriers and not the crude tankers. Armed with this knowledge, I met with a senior Kuwaiti minister and suggested that Kuwait request the return of six crude oil carriers to the Kuwaiti flag and leave the five vessels capable of transporting refined products under the U.S. flag. The Kuwaitis readily agreed and a prolonged diplomatic dispute was short-circuited. In April 1989, five American-flag tankers were reregistered in the United States to the Glen Eagle Company.[70]

Crown Prince and Prime Minister Shaikh Sa'd al-Abdallah al-Sabah undertook an important official visit to the United States in the spring of 1988 where he met with President Reagan, Vice President Bush,[71] and other key officials. The major substantive accomplishment of the visit was the finalization of strategy for the sale of F/A-18 aircraft and associated armaments to Kuwait to replace the aging A-4 as its first-line fighter. Kuwait's request was reasonable considering the advanced aircraft in the inventories of its larger neighbors, but it was anticipated that the sale would face predictable opposition of some elements in the U.S. Congress.

Gen. Colin Powell, the White House national security advisor, headed the Reagan administration's effort to obtain authorization for the sale. In mid-June 1988, the administration's notification to Congress became public. The proposed package, valued at $1.9 billion, included F-18s, Maverick air-to-ground, Sidewinder heat-seeking air-to-air missiles, and an assortment of compatible bombs.[72] Almost at the same moment that opposition to the sale surfaced in Congress, Kuwait, in a move characteristic of its approach in such circumstances, announced the signing of an arms agreement with the Soviet Union.[73] Despite the apparent impasse regarding the proposed sale to Kuwait, the skillful efforts led by General Powell broke the logjam at the beginning of August. In an essential reversal of its earlier position, the U.S. House of Representatives approved the proposed sale with face-saving modifications. With uncharacteristic frankness, U.S. media reported that the reversal resulted from negotiations not only with the Reagan administration but "American Jewish groups" as well.[74] A prolonged and potentially harmful interruption in military-to-military cooperation with Kuwait was avoided by the determined administration push, and the delivery schedule for the F-18s was accelerated following Kuwait's liberation from Iraqi occupation in 1991.[75] American and Kuwaiti officials signed the formal agreement for the sale at the end of August.[76]

A relatively new area of bilateral consultation was the rising challenge of state-supported terrorism. During the war between Iraq and Iran, Kuwait had not only been the target of attacks by groups directed or inspired by Iran, but also by terrorists serving Iraqi objectives. The perpetrators included not simply Iranians,

Iraqis, and Kuwaitis susceptible to their influence, but also revolutionaries from Lebanon and the renegade Palestinian leader, Abu Nidal (Sabri Khalil al-Banna).[77] American citizens and interests in Lebanon and elsewhere were being targeted by the same elements. and exchanges with Kuwait on the shared threat were a logical response.[78] Washington was especially impressed by Kuwait's policy of refusing to release terrorists convicted of crimes in that country, even under extreme pressure and intimidation.

Kuwait's resolve was severely tested in April 1988 when a Kuwaiti airliner flying from Bangkok to Kuwait was hijacked by Shi'a terrorists demanding the release of colleagues imprisoned in Kuwait, including those convicted of the December 1983 bombings at the American Embassy and other sites.[79] The aircraft was forced to land in Mashad, Iran where some female passengers and one man with a heart condition were released.[80] From there, the pilot was directed to Larnaca, Cyprus, where two Kuwaiti passengers were murdered. The aircraft ended the sixteen-day ordeal in Algiers, when the remaining passengers and crew, including two members of the al-Sabah family, were released.[81] What is certain is that the Kuwaitis refused to cave to the main demand of the terrorists; the release of convicted terrorists.[82] In addition to regular consultations and U.S. training for Kuwaiti security personnel, the FBI provided forensic and other expertise during and after the 1988 hijacking.

Bilateral relations between the United States and Kuwait were positive and productive as the decade of the 1980s drew to a close. Both parties had come to appreciate that their interests were best served by working together, even if some differences, such as the Palestinian question, persisted. The fact that both had found ways to work around critics and impediments, like the objections in both countries to the reflagging of Kuwaiti tankers or opposition in the U.S. House to the F-18 sale, indicated that each side had come to regard the other as a reliable partner that had to contend with its own political environment.[83] The decade of the 1980s was a crucible in which much of the innocence and illusions of the past were destroyed; Kuwait and the United States were strangers to one another no longer.

***

December 1989 would prove to be a watershed for Kuwait and its friends both, domestically and internationally. The world's attention was riveted on unfolding events in Romania where longtime strongman, Nicolae Ceaușescu, was overthrown in a popular uprising. Television images of his public appearance on December 21, and the look on his face as the crowd turned hostile, were dramatic and unforgettable. Within days, Ceaușescu and his wife were executed in one of the opening phases of the liberation of Eastern Europe from decades of dictatorship. Momentous developments were also beginning to unfold that December much closer to Kuwait and the Gulf.

Within Kuwait, a campaign to reinstate the National Assembly, suspended three years earlier, began to gather steam.[84] Little was said publicly, but in early December I was informed by Kuwaiti friends and contacts that the issue was the focus of a series of special diwanniyas and that the authorities were working to prevent the emergence of a strong consensus.[85] Dr. Shafeeq Ghabra, one of Kuwait's premier political scientists and the former head of the Kuwait Information Office in Washington, has written about the period with unique insight:

> *Beginning in December 1989, a public meeting was held every Monday involving several thousand citizens who expressed popular demand that the country's National Assembly be restored. This diwaniya [sic] represented the new cooperation between the various forces of society....*[86]

During each session, the site of the succeeding meeting was announced. Government efforts were ineffective in interrupting the gathering of several thousand very vocal Kuwaitis. The meetings were held in residential *diwanniyas* which could not accomodate crowds of such size; accounts received by American diplomats indicated that the proceedings were broadcast so that Kuwaitis in the immediate vicinity could listen over their car radios. In any event, the movement had reached proportions that the Kuwait government could not ignore. This was no longer agitation by former parliamentarians with personal interests involved, but a movement representing a broad slice of Kuwaiti society.

The regime responded with a harshness uncharacteristic of traditional Kuwaiti political behavior. Whether the leadership had been under challenge so continually over recent years that it lost sight of the distinction between criminal acts and legitimate political opposition, or it was lulled by the mild public response to the 1986 dissolution,[87] the government took up the cudgels for a confrontation it could not win. On December 28, it issued a pronouncement that forbade the discussion of "national" issues in *diwanniyas*, a position at variance with a lengthy tradition of the free exchange of views in these settings.[88] When this failed to squash the weekly meetings, the Interior Ministry employed the police to disperse the attendees by force, initially at a gathering in al-Farwaniya.[89]

By February, cooler heads prevailed. Although some clashes and arrests continued, the crown prince/prime minister, a genial and popular figure, met with twenty-eight former deputies to discuss their demands.[90] In April, he announced that parliament would be restored, but conditioned the resumption of parliamentary life on agreement of new regulations and procedures. The ruler issued a decree later that month creating a transitional "National Council" that would be tasked with evaluating the country's "parliamentary experience" and proposing regulations consistent with "stability and national unity." The council would have fifty elected members, twenty-five appointed by the government, and an indeterminate number of cabinet ministers.[91]

The government's proposal failed to mollify many of the those pressing for reinstatement of the National Assembly or unify a divided population. At least twenty-five former members announced their rejection within days, arguing that they would boycott the National Council because it violated the constitution. Several arrests were made during the first half of May and dispersal of gatherings continued. [92] The proposed resolution of the dispute, however, was not universally rejected and seemed to draw off some of the support for the hardline former MPs. Elections for the National Council were hastily arranged and a reported 62 percent of the voters participated in the voting.[93] The amir announced his twenty-five appointees at the end of June, permitting the National Council to hold its first meeting in early July. The government's speedy action and the participation of a subtantial proportion of Kuwaiti electors made further debate academic, at least in the short term. It did not, however, heal the divide that had opened within the body politic:

> *The crisis was deeper than many in Kuwait's past because it had the effect of reshaping established political foundations within society and politics.*[94]

One can only speculate about how the council experiment would have played out. By the time the new body was called to order in Kuwait's modernistic parliament building, a looming deterioration in relations with Iraq overshadowed normal political activity within Kuwait and would soon suspend it completely for a number of months.

At the end of 1989, at the very time when agitation to restore the Assembly was gathering steam, an abrupt change in Iraqi rhetoric and behavior became evident. Saddam Hussein had welcomed American power and influence in the Gulf when the outcome of his war with Iran was uncertain and he was almost frantic to end it. By 1990, however, the old strut was back and he denounced U.S. presence.[95] He also antagonized Egypt, which had provided Baghdad with vital material assistance and intelligence, by his treatment of Egyptian guestworkers who had come to Iraq to take up the slack in the economy created by the massive mobilization of Iraqi manpower for the war. He also resumed threats against Israel, including an obscure reference that many took to hint at the use of binary chemical weapons. The real focus of his venom, however, was reserved for Kuwait and, later, the United Arab Emirates.

Diplomatic observers of Saddam's aboutface were not privy in real time to Iraqi statements in bilateral or Arab fora, but sensed that something sinister was afoot. Only half in jest, diplomatic circles in Kuwait speculated that footage of the downfall of another strongman, Ceauşescu, had spooked the Iraqi dictator. In actuality, Iraq's weak financial situation was probably the prime motivator. An equally plausible consideration was his "need" for an identifiable "enemy" to distract his broken people, including unemployed former soldiers, from the disastrous consequences of his leadership.

The embassy in Kuwait was convinced that it was essential to make sense of Iraq's radical new behavior. Although American embassies in the region shared their perspectives by cable, it was clear that none of the posts had enough of the pieces to make sense of the emerging puzzle. I proposed, by telegram to counterparts in the Gulf and in Baghdad, that the regional ambassadors meet in Kuwait to compare notes. The Department of State was naturally an info addressee because it would be invited to send participants.[96] Ambassadors in the region enthusiastically concurred and a target date was set. As Embassy Kuwait was preparing to host the conference, word was passed to me that this initiative had offended Assistant Secretary of State Kelly, who believed he was being usurped. That, of course, was not the intent but it also was not my chief concern in light of increasing unease in the area. The conference of posts most concerned and knowledgeable in the matter, in any case, never took place because the assistant secretary preempted it with a hastily arranged conference of the entire NEA Bureau—from Morocco to Pakistan—near Bonn in April 1990. Whether a smaller, more focused conference of experienced Gulf diplomats would have been able to tease out the strands of Saddam's motivations and intentions cannot be known. But, it is certain that Bureau's conclave in Germany, while a pleasant interlude, offered little opportunity to consider the subject of developments in the Gulf in depth in the midst of sessions devoted to the Arab-Israeli dispute, North Africa, South Asia, and the full span of Middle East issues.

Kuwait was no stranger to Iraq's intimidation.[97] With Iraq facing an estimated $80 million in debt to Western and Arab states to finance its war of choice with Iran, Kuwait was viewed in Baghdad as the weak link in the phalanx of debt holders. Iraq owed $10 –15 billion to Kuwait and was pressing hard for Kuwait to "forgive" Iraq's debt and ante up more. Kuwait refused to write off the debt, but there is little evidence that it was pressing for repayment. Despite its financial problems, Iraq, far from demobilizing its massive military machine, was actually building up its armed forces and pursuing the technology for weapons of mass destruction.[98]

We in Kuwait understood that Kuwaitis regarded the Iraqi debt as the one card it held in relations with a much more powerful Iraq. The debt was Kuwait's ace, to be played, if at all, only in return for the country's overriding objective—a final demarcation of the border with Iraq and a definitive recognition of Kuwait's independence, sovereignty, and integrity.

As June turned to July, the price of oil began to fall, partially because Kuwait, the United Arab Emirates, and possibly other OPEC members were producing above the quotas they had been given.[99] This behavior infuriated Saddam Hussein who was almost completely dependent upon oil revenues and exhibited little understanding of complex concepts such as elasticity of demand. It further fed Saddam's conspiratorial mindset, confirming in his thoughts that he was the victim of a plot to which Kuwait was a party. In his traditional public address on the occasion of Iraq's national day, July 17,[100] the Iraqi leader castigated Kuwait for overproducing and suggested it was related to a plot with the United States to harm "Arab" (read Iraqi) interests. He hinted that if his warnings were not sufficient, Iraq would take further action.[101]

Tensions continued to build and elements of the Iraqi army began to redeploy to the vicinity of the Kuwait's frontier to underscore harsh Iraqi rhetoric. The Kuwaitis took Saddam's words seriously enough to lock down a base where American personnel worked in support of U.S.-origin equipment when it declared an alert. The alert was short-lived as Kuwaitis were advised by President Mubarak and other concerned Arab leaders that Saddam was assuring them that he did not intend to use force and urged the Kuwaitis to take no action, including alerts, that might provoke the unpredictable Iraqi strongman. No one saw the logical inconsistency of their reassurances and their cautions.

The Iraqis accused Kuwait of conspiring to damage Iraq, of acting with the UAE to produce more than their OPEC quota, and of slant drilling in northern Kuwait into Iraqi oil structures. American companies were drilling in that area under contract with the Kuwait Drilling Company and I had visited them prior to the crisis. To my knowledge, no proof of Saddam's assertion that Kuwait was tapping anything other than a geologic structure that may have straddled the undefined border was ever produced, even after Iraqi forces exercised full control of the area.[102] In any event, Kuwait and the UAE agreed in late July to limit their production to their OPEC quotas, thereby eliminating one of the major pretexts of the case Iraq was building.

By July 25, the day Kuwait's agreement to reduce production was made public, Iraq had amassed more than one hundred thousand men on the border near Kuwait.[103] The same day, Saddam Hussein, who met with ambassadors to Iraq very infrequently, summoned Ambassador April Glaspie to an impromptu meeting. The story of that conversation, for which the ambassador had no specific instructions from Washington, has been rehearsed, debated, and misrepresented ad nauseum, and bears only tangentially on this narrative. The text of Ambassador Glaspie's report of that conversation, which was also received in Kuwait, has been widely circulated on the web.[104] I read the Baghdad cable immediately in my office and looked up to see my deputy chief of mission, Barbara Bodine, standing in the doorway with her copy.

"Are you thinking what I am?" I asked Ms. Bodine, who had served previously in Baghdad when we had both observed the buildup for Iraq's invasion of Iran in 1980.

What bothered us both was not so much Ambassador Glaspie's words; no American ambassador can threaten or commit the United States to the use of force without very explicit instructions to do so. The Iraqi president had stated that he would not employ armed force, at least until after he had met with the Kuwaiti crown prince/prime minister in Baghdad, a commitment he did not honor. The element that troubled us was the eerie parallel of Saddam's case of victimization and lack of "choice" to the justification he had spun in 1980 just before invading Iran. There was less inclination to believe or trust Saddam Hussein in the Kuwait Embassy than was apparent in either Baghdad or Washington.

That same day, we sent a cable we coauthored to Washington, Baghdad, and other involved posts.[105] The cable explained these haunting parallels in Saddam's performance with that in September 1980 and concluded with the judgment that the Iraqis would cross the border and probably occupy Kuwaiti territory as far as the Mutla Ridge. No one at that point realized the enormity of Saddam's intentions—the occupation of the entire country.[106] It seemed in Kuwait that the Iraqis were leaning too far forward militarily to accept a humiliating stand down. No comment or reply to the cable was ever received by the embassy in the week before Iraq struck.

The claim, frequently asserted, that the United States, in Ambassador Glaspie's meeting with Saddam Hussein or otherwise, gave Iraq a "green light" to attack or swallow up Kuwait is, in my judgement, an absurd conceit. It is not the role of the U.S. government to dispense permission to any state to violate constraints imposed by the United Nations Charter or, in this instance, the Charter of the League of Arab States as well.

There was enough substance in U.S. public statements and the history of American support for the independence and welfare of Kuwait and the other small states of the Gulf to give pause to any prudent and rational regime even in the absence of formal treaty commitments. The United States responded promptly to the request of the less exposed UAE for a small joint exercise.[107] In Kuwait, I was unsuccessful in stimulating an invitation for a U.S. Navy ship visit.

The embassy in Kuwait hosted an extraordinary meeting of wardens the week of July 30, both to share its views on the situation with a relatively calm American community and to be certain that the warning system was fully functional. It was midsummer and many American expatriates, as well as Kuwaitis, took leave to escape the worst of the heat. It was essential to be certain that, where necessary, replacements had been designated in the telephone tree. As the embassy ended its normal work week, except for duty personnel who would cover the local weekend (Thursday and Friday), the embassy staff were instructed not to travel outside the city and to be able to report to the Chancery within one hour of notification.

15

Besieged but Not Beaten

The telephone at my bedside rang at about 2 am on the morning of August 2, 1990, in Kuwait. The embassy officer who maintained liaison with Kuwaiti intelligence asked me to come to the Chancery several hundred feet away. A few minutes later, he reported that his Kuwaiti counterpart had called to inform him that Iraqi forces had crossed Kuwait's northern border in the last hour and were "rolling up" the Kuwaiti border posts. I immediately called the Department of State Operations Center on the newly installed "secure" phone to report the Iraqi incursion.[1] The OP Center would relay the report to senior department officials, the White House, and key U.S. government agencies. This was the first confirmed report Washington received of the launch of Iraq's invasion. In Baghdad, Chargé Joseph Wilson learned of the embassy in Kuwait's report from Sandra Charles, a staffer on the National Security Council at the White House.[2] It would be several hours until daybreak when satellites could assess the situation on the ground.[3]

Sergeant Paul G. Rodriguez was the Marine Security Guard (MSG) on duty at Post One that fateful morning. One of the best of a tiny, hand-picked unit, the sergeant had witnessed the urgent proceedings as I was summoned. He later recalled overhearing me informing the embassy duty officer, Kevin Briscoe, of the Iraqi sweep into Kuwait and seizure of Kuwaiti oilrigs. On instuctions, he phoned the Marine House on the compound and ordered Cpl. Daniel K. Hudson to turn out the MSGs. Detachment Commander SSgt. Jimmy Smith and Regional Security Officer (RSO) Michael Bender were already enroute to the Embassy and soon joined the cadre in the Chancery.[4]

As the duty officer and other key personnel reported to the embassy, three priority tasks faced the post: assuring the security of the Embassy compound, including classified files and communications gear that could compromise the worldwide network; accounting for official Americans and their families; and establishing sustained communication with embassy wardens and the wider American community. Consul Gale Rogers, who had arrived in Kuwait just days before the invasion, quickly began the task of contacting resident Americans with whatever assistance could be given as more personnel arrived from their homes. An Australian who was in touch with the embassy throughout the occupation observed:

The US Embassy... had been frantically calling its registered nationals, telling them to stay at home. It was largely because of this quick action that the only Americans captured on the first morning were those on desert oil rigs in the path of the advancing troops, or on BA149.[5]

When the embassy staff turned to this laborious task, they had reason to be thankful that the crisis occurred in August when many Americans were out of Kuwait on leave. Nonetheless, the post was still responsible for more than two thousand citizens and dual nationals.[6]

The perfidious Iraqi attack on its sovereign neighbor augered ill for their adherence to international norms regarding diplomatic missions and their expatriate citizens. Embassy planning, therefore, was based on the assumption that Iraq's word could not be trusted and that they were capable of almost anything, including a forcible breach of the compound wall. A team of embassy communications personnel, including all secretaries, had immediately begun the destruction of sensitive files, beginning with the highest classification and working down.[7] Meanwhile, a separate staff group was contacting official employees living throughout the city. It was quickly decided to instruct them to make their way to the embassy with their families, valuables, and as much food as they could carry. There was the sound of fighting from north of the embassy in the vicinity of Dasman Palace (the residence of the Amir), but conditions in other parts of town were unclear.

Therefore, incoming employees were told not to take risks but to seek safety if they encountered fighting or other disturbances, and to contact the embassy for further instructions.[8]

In the first days of the invasion, the embassy's window on the wider situation in Kuwait was confined to: what could be seen from the compound; what could be gleaned from employees arriving at the embassy; and reports from private citizens contacted by the consular office.[9] Although active fighting was audible initially only from the north, it was soon clear that some Iraqi forces had bypassed the city on the highspeed Ring Roads and were already south of us on the road to Saudi Arabia.[10] Sgt. Rodriguez and other Marines at Post One became a clearinghouse for information on the invading Iraqi forces. From this position in the Chancery, they were able to monitor developments around the compound perimeter over closed-circuit cameras located on the walls. Information was also being collected by members of the local contract guard force stationed at the front and back gates. The supervisor of these guards, Ghazi Hamdan, was set up in the rear gatehouse where he had a view of traffic along the Corniche and provided hourly summaries of his observations. The data collected on Iraqi units, equipment and insignia was provided to an officer in touch by radio with USCENTCOM Headquarters in Tampa.

Without better information on Iraqi dispositions and intentions at the time, planning for an evacuation convoy southward in the direction of Saudi Arabia was problematic.[11]

From the embassy's limited vantage point, sights and sounds of war were noteworthy. As the fighting at the Dasman Palace continued throughout the morning, it was evident that the small Kuwaiti force there was mounting a valiant—but ultimately hopeless defiance—of the now-empty palace. A wheeled, light armored vehicle drove past the embassy firing its small-bore gun at the attacking Iraqis. It was quickly knocked out, probably by a tank round, and stood at the side of the road for several weeks, mute testimony to the small nation's defiance of the invaders. By 2 p.m. in the afternoon, the Palace had fallen.[12]

The National Guard unit quartered at the Embassy was observed capturing several stray Iraqi soldiers, who were stripped to their underwear and marched away. Later in the day, the men of the unit changed into civilian clothes and melted away, either on orders or out of a reasonable assessment of their situation. Many of them likely joined the internal resistance or made their way to Saudi Arabia where remnants of the Kuwaiti armed forces would eventually regroup.

From their southern airbase, Kuwaiti aircraft roared overhead on several sorties against Iraqi ground forces and helicopters. They flew into the following morning and then, as their last base south of Kuwait City was overrun, flew to Saudi Arabia to fight another day.[13] By the strange chemistry that bonds humans sharing a traumatic experience, the Kuwaiti planes were "ours" as well. I was summoned to the USLOK offices, where the teletype had stuttered into life. As I watched the message unroll, it turned out to be a request from Brig. Gen. Ghazi al-Abdul Razzak, director of Technical Affairs of the Kuwaiti Armed Forces, containing a list of needed spares and munitions. This was the ultimate act of positive thinking. Ominously, the machine stuttered into silence in midmessage. "What cheek!" If the Kuwaitis were determined to take on the world's fourth largest army in defense of their homeland and freedom, I reflected, they deserved all the help the world could give them.

North of the city, several Kuwaiti officers of the 35th Armored Brigade managed to assemble a force of approximately battalion-size, despite the absence of an alert. The force departed its base about twelve kilometers from Ali Salem airbase and headed for Jahra. Col. Salem Al Srour led this pickup unit in a delaying action just in front of the Armed Forces Headquarters, engaging elements of two elite Iraqi Republican Guard divisions. Deploying his small group of old British Chieftain tanks, Col. Srour and his men engaged the Iraqi invaders for several hours before running out of ammunition and being almost encircled.[14]

Reports and rumors began to trickle in as Kuwaitis and expatriates alike awoke to their worst nightmare. The Iraqis had occupied the Sheraton Hotel beyond the old American Mission compound and were setting up a headquarters there. The Iraqi army had executed a number of officers and men who balked at firing on the Kuwaitis, according to a rumor that was never confirmed. South Asian parishioners of the National Evangelical Church called in to detail Iraqi occupation and wanton trashing of the Church compound. The embassy could only advise them not to take unnecessary risks. Patients were being compelled to leave Kuwaiti hospitals according to several reports that turned out to have a basis in fact. It was very difficult to form an accurate overall assessment from the mix of information and misinformation—characteristic of such confused and emotional situations.[15]

One report that turned out to be true was the Iraqi storming of a camp south of the city near Fahaheel, where British military personnel serving with the Kuwaiti armed forces and their families lived.[16] Commanded by Col. Bruce Duncan, the British Liaison Team (BLT) consisted of seventy-seven officers and senior NCOs from the British Army and Royal Air Force (RAF) whose task was to maintain British tanks and aircraft in the Kuwaiti inventory. They were "seconded" to the Kuwaiti Armed Forces and wore Kuwaiti uniforms, but had no combat role.[17] The men found there were seized by the Iraqis and many of their families were brought to the International Hotel (formerly the Hilton) across from the American Embassy, having elected not to try to drive the short distance to the Saudi border.[18] The American Embassy staff gathered toothbrushes, toiletries, and other items that might be needed by the detainees and delivered them to the hotel.[19] Although American military personnel in USLOK, by contrast, were not an integral part of the Kuwaiti Armed Forces, no one believed that the Iraqis would be constrained by such niceties, and concern grew for the safety of the embassy's active duty military. Getting them to safety as soon as possible became an additional priority. The British dependents in the hotel were moved by bus to Baghdad shortly thereafter.

At midmorning, Under Secretary of Foreign Affairs Sulaiman Majed al-Shaheen phoned to convey a message for me from the foreign minister, Shaikh Sabah al-Ahmad: "Now is the time for the United States to come to the assistance of Kuwait."[20] Al-Shaheen was an extremely capable diplomat with whom I had worked closely in difficult times over the previous three years. He would understand my frank reply: "Last week may have been the time for an American gesture of support, and the time probably will come again in the future, but right now is not the time." I pointed out that American forces were far away and it would take time to mount an effective military effort, if the president decided to intervene. At the moment, Kuwait could not even assure that it would control ground for a landing. We hung up after wishing one another well.[21]

Practical issues related to survival claimed priority attention as the reality of the unfolding situation sank in. The population of the compound, normally the ambassador's household and six Marines, swelled manyfold. Sleeping accomodations were carved out in the Residence, the Wyden House adjacent to the swimming pool, the Marine House, and assorted offices in buildings scattered throughout the central area. Regular meals were served in both the Residence and Chancery and pens for pets were built in the large warehouse. Children and young people were given responsibility for their pets' care and feeding or entertained with videos and Mickey Mouse. Quarters were tight but workable as the essential work of destruction files continued. Consular officers, and others enlisted to assist them, worked telephone connections with the American community.

It was not deemed safe for several days to leave the compound unnecessarily. Around the embassy and elsewhere throughout the city, however, acts of defiance and incipient resistance were taking place. Several sources reported that individual Kuwaitis were targetting the tank trucks transporting water for the large invading force (a single hole from small arms could put the tanker out of action in the oppressive heat and humidity). The embassy inhabitants were getting their first glimpse of the Iraqi juggernaut on the roads around the compound. In contrast to the Republican Guard that spearheaded the attack, the occupation troops were a sorry lot of conscripts: ill-fed; indifferently-equipped; and unmotivated.[22]

Aside from their ill-disciplined, and desperate conscripts, the Iraqi occupation troops contributed to the prevailing anxiety and uncertainty by their bizarre behavior. No effort was made to contact embassies as Iraqi soldiers moved about, and it was impossible to ascertain whether they even knew that the compound was a diplomatic mission. Iraq's intentions toward American and other expatriates was an even bigger question mark. Anxiety within the compound was raised further by rumors and threatening phone

Besieged but Not Beaten 327

calls claiming that the embassy was to be attacked by men dressed in civilian Arab clothing.[23] Many a sleepless night was passed inside the American Embassy, watching small military units prowl about with aid of night-vision cameras mounted around the walls. Their purpose was not easy to discern and it seemed conceivable that they might try to infiltrate the embassy grounds. If they were successful, Iraqi troops could be upon the occupants with little or no warning.[24] Vigilance was the order of the day and night.[25]

By the afternoon of the first day, the embassy had canvassed the network of wardens and, through them, the private American citizens who were registered with the Consular Section. Contacts were maintained as long as the phone system was operational.[26] In the confusion of the moment, there was little practical advice that the consular officers could offer anxious citizens besides cautioning against unnecessary travel in the city and recommending that they prepare for an evacuation convoy should it be safe to organize one. Later, as urban clashes came to an end, we organized several meetings of wardens at the Consulate. It was important to assure the community that the embassy was continuing to function and would not abandon them. Many appeared to have taken some comfort from that certainty in the midst of so many unknowns. As Maureen Aldakheel, an American married to a Kuwaiti engineer, wrote following the final meeting:

> ...our acting AWL warden, went to a warden meeting at the embassy on the 18th and said that Nat seemed very calm and confident of a positive outcome, and that it made everyone feel a lot better.[27]

This reaction was all the more remarkable considering that one of the topics covered in the August 18 meeting was elemental precautions in the event the Iraqis used chemical agents, as they had in the past.

The potential contingencies confronting the embassy and the community were three in number. Most desireable would be a political solution and an Iraqi unilateral withdrawal, or Iraqi acquiesence in a convoy of Americans overland, preferably to Saudi Arabia. Rumors of expatriates arrested attempting to drive south on the highway, or families stranded and dying trying to cross unmarked desert routes made this an unattractive option for hundreds of Americans. One American family, dressed as Kuwaitis, attempted to use a desert track with a group of Kuwaitis and were arrested and turned back in August. Their American nationality was not discovered.[28] Nevertheless, serious planning was initiated to prepare for a convoy in case one became possible, or if the situation in Kuwait deteriorated to a point where there was more risk in remaining than in making a run for safehaven. In cooperation with embassy administrative officers, several logisticians from USLOK performed yeoman service in readying all serviceable vehicles on the compound. Since there would be no possibility of arranging an orderly assembly point, potential routes through the city were selected that could be communicated to private citizens wishing to join the convoy or needing transport on the fly. Plans were laid for marking the convoy vehicles with distinctive tape designs. The embassy was as ready for the dash as it could be, but I quietly prayed that there would be no need to implement this plan, for it was unavoidable that some would be left behind.[29]

The second possibility was that those on the Embassy compound would have to survive an extended period on their own resources. By late August, there were almost two hundred people sheltering in the Embassy, including both embassy staff and their families as well private citizens. Clearly, additional supplies would be essential to support such a population for a period of weeks or even months. As soon as it became possible to move outside the compound, a provisioning program, spearheaded by Chief Warrant Officer 4 David L. Forties and supported by Major Fred L. Hart, Jr., was implemented amid the chaos. Arrangements were made with a major Kuwaiti food wholesaler to pick up foodstuffs from his underground warehouse—dubbed "Aladdin's Cave"—in exchange for a verbal commitment that the U.S. government would reimburse him outside the country. Many times until late August, the embassy's five-ton truck made its way to the "Cave," which had not been discovered by the Iraqis. The elaborate debris which camouflaged the entryway was moved while it drove inside to load.

In this way, tons of canned tuna and other long-life foods, as well as diapers, baby bottles and other items needed by the diverse compound population, were transported to the Embassy snack bar, which had been designated the food store under the management of the general manager of a hotel in Kuwait. Meanwhile, Sergeant First Class (SFC) Laurens C. "Dutch" Vellekoop made the rounds of pharmacies, hospitals, and clinics seeking first aid supplies, as well as specific medications required by the embassy nurse, Mary A. Bender, R.N. and individuals on the compound. "Dutch" found many items in short supply due to early Iraqi looting expeditions and evaded Iraqi troops already within the facilities he visited. Eventually the Iraqis stripped medical facilities of most of their specialized equipment and pharmaceuticals.[30] As the "shopping" was under way, I, widely known for smoking a pipe, was surprised to see several locally hired embassy security guards enter the Chancery grinning and carrying several large cardboard boxes. Inside were dozens of mismatched packets of pipe tobacco. Asking what I owed for this treasure trove, the guards replied that the merchants gave them away to keep them from being stolen by Iraqis. One hoped that was a truthful reply.[31]

Along with official Americans and dependents, every American citizen or legal resident wishing to take refuge on the premises, was welcomed.[32] Many others calculated logically that they would be less vulnerable remaining elsewhere in the city than at the embassy. The Residence and the Marine House had become dormitories, and individuals and families were stuffed into every available space, including offices, where they often spread bedding atop unused desks. The wife of the NCOIC, who commanded the Marine Guards, took on the job of finding space for new arrivals as they came, and the spouse of the Regional Security Officer, a registered nurse, assumed charge of the health unit with great skill and reliability.

One specialized segment of the American community was of particular interest to the embassy leadership, and strong efforts were mounted to get them into the compound or otherwise assure their security from Iraqi searches. These individuals were employees of American companies providing technical support to the Kuwaiti armed forces on advanced U.S. weapons systems. Engineers with Kay and Associates, for example, were serving as advisors to the Kuwait Air Force.[33] Even more useful to the Iraqis would have been the engineers employed by Raytheon Corporation, with expertise on the Improved-Hawk ground-to-air missiles in the Kuwait air-defense system. Iraq was believed to have captured at least some of these missiles intact, and it was essential to prevent them from using them:

> *Five of these men, Felipe Alayon, Lloyd Culbertson, Tal Ledford, Bennie Mitchell, and his wife and infant son, and Guy Seago reported to the embassy.... In the embassy, the five men were told to destroy any documents... which could link them to Raytheon or the Kuwaiti forces. They were given replacement embassy IDs....*[34]

While all of them did not remain on the compound, those that did became valuable members of the community in the embassy.

In early August, the diplomatic community discovered that the Iraqi ambassador, now sporting a military uniform, was in town and working out of the Iraqi Embassy. Since there had been no contact with the Iraqis since Iraqi national day celebration in July, I decided to beard the lion in his den and try to arrange an orderly evacuation of American citizens. An appointment was set up by telephone, surprising the Iraqis, who were under the impression that the ambassador had departed and were expecting to deal with Chargé Barbara Bodine.[35] With some trepidation, the embassy watched me, accompanied by an Arabic-speaking officer, leave in the limousine, uncertain whether we would be allowed to return. Henry, the driver, was in his element; he had both flags flying. As a precaution, the radio in the vehicle was left open so that the Marine at Post One (and, hence, Washington) would know immediately if something untoward occurred.[36]

The meeting at the Iraqi Embassy was correct, even cordial, but two things became clear. First, the Iraqis were stalling on evacuation and insisting that all departures be through Iraq. The second conclusion was even more ominous. Although the Iraqi ambassador sat at the big desk, he was not in charge. At several points, his phone rang for brief exchanges. Someone elsewhere in the building was monitoring the meeting and giving him instructions regarding his replies. The conversation ended without a definitive answer and our small party returned to the Embassy, to the relief of all.[37]

I made another call on the Iraqis several days later, again with no success regarding an evacuation. On August 16, the Iraqis took the initiative to ask me to come to their Embassy. The previous evening had been an active one for the Kuwaiti resistance, who reportedly killed a number of Iraqi soldiers with small arms and rockets. Again, the Iraqi ambassador adopted a cordial tone, expressing concern for the safety of Americans and other expatriates. He brushed aside the retort that the local situation was all the more reason for an orderly evacuation of foreign nationals. Getting to the point of the meeting, he said the occupation authorities wanted the embassy to order the American community to report to local hotels (the Kuwait International for Americans), where the Iraqis could "protect" them. I said that I would convey the Iraqi "request," but that the Iraqis should understand that Americans are free and independent people: "I don't know what kind of authority you have over Iraqis in Kuwait, but I can't order my community to do anything!"

The dialogue between Iraqi officials and Western ambassadors seeking the freedom and safety of their communities was a deadly serious exercise disguised as a diplomatic minuet. Based on his interviews with many of the attendees at these conversations, John Levins captured the character of the the thrust and parry involved:

> *The Iraqi insisted that he wanted everyone. When he asked US Ambassador Nat Howell to tell him where all the Americans were, 'so that we may protect them', Howell replied 'America is not a police state; it does not keep track of its citizens in that manner. I would not be at liberty to tell you where the Americans in Kuwait are, even if I wanted to. This order is not only a practical impossibility: I have no power to order my people to move.*
>
> *The Iraqi replied to the effect of 'Come off it! Even we know where 90 percent of your citizens are.' Howell shot back, 'Then could you please give me your list so that I can contact them.' The Iraqi's bluff had been called, but his men would soon start hunting down recalcitrant Americans and other Westerners.*[38]

Although I had no intention of helping the Iraqis capture American citizens, the request opened the possibility of incremental "victories." I was able to secure agreement that the International Hotel would be the assembly point for Americans; its proximity to the Embassy would facilitate efforts to wave off any arrivals. It was also possible to have Embassy phone service restored, ostensibly to carry out the Iraqi demands.

On the way back to the Embassy and afterwards, I mulled over the Iraqi move. Clearly, the Iraqis were a greater menace to Americans than the current disorder, and the community knew that as well. There was enough evidence of Iraqi perfidy for all but the densest expatriate to recognize the crocodile tears. At the same time, the community needed to know of this shift in occupation tactics. In the end, a carefully worded statement was crafted to the effect that any American citizen who thought he or she would be safer in Iraqi hands than at their current location, could report to the Kuwait International Hotel. The Voice of America (VOA) and the BBC broadcast the message on August 17. So far as I was aware, no American citizens showed up for the party the Iraqis had arranged for them.[39] The agreement to pass on the Iraqi request not only alerted the community to a dangerous change in the Iraqi game plan but opened a small window to rescue those Americans already staying in hotels. Embassy vehicles were dispatched to the Meridian, SAS, and other hotels where Americans were known to be while embassy officers phoned to warn them to be ready.

> *The Meridian Hotel bus arrived with a load of American businessmen and the American manager of the hotel with his family in tow. An American consul who arrived at the SAS Hotel one step ahead of the Iraqis crammed too many people in a car too small. There would be no second trip. Unloading at the embassy, they were like endless clowns coming out of a circus Volkswagen.*[40]

Jack Rinehart, a businessman from Missouri, was one of the passengers during the embassy's ingathering of the most vulnerable citizens.

> *Early on August 18, officials from the US Embassy arrived at the SAS (hotel) and announced that the troops were taking Westerners at gun point... The officials offered refuge in the embassy to all*

Americans and we gladly accepted. Eleven Americans... quickly crammed into a small diplomatic car.... [41]

The number on the Embassy compound now surpassed 170 persons, although some private citizens declined the offer of hospitality and a few already there departed because of Saddam Hussein's threat to close embassies in Kuwait. After casting about for a pretext for his invasion, Iraq declared that Kuwait was the 19th province of Iraq, now renamed Khazima. Iraq's earlier claim that it had acted in support of a Kuwaiti "opposition" coup, and, then, the fiction that its forces were assisting a "provisional" Kuwait government, had foundered on the refusal of any credible Kuwaiti citizen to cooperate with the occupation.[42] Forced to fall back on Iraq's long-standing claim to Kuwaiti territory, Saddam exposed his motive as naked aggression. Noon on August 24, 1990 was set as the deadline for all embassies to close and withdraw, and threats of varying severity were circulated through the diplomatic community. Diplomats of several smaller nations were reportedly told that the penalty for disobedience could be death. The U.S. Embassy did not receive so menacing a message directly, although it was clear to all that, after the deadline, diplomats would lose their diplomatic status and "immunity."[43]

Following the transparent effort of the occupation authorities to have American, British, and other expatriates assemble at hotels to simplify the task of collecting human shields, it was no longer safe for private Americans to move outside their homes and safe havens; their personal sieges began on or about August 18. Because of the changed circumstances, members of the American community were cautioned against attempting to reach the Embassy compound.[44] Henceforth, private citizens would be dependent upon support and assistance from Kuwaitis and others who were constantly warned that harboring "foreigners" was a capital offense. At the embassy, it was judged, correctly, that the Iraqi authorities were counting on their threats to solve the problem of the embassies, and would not take hostile measures before their unilateral deadline. Foodstuffs and other necessities continued to be collected, and rudimentary plans for communicating with the local resistance and other contacts were laid.[45]

With the Iraqi deadline for embassies to close looming, important decisions could not be postponed. The Iraqi ultimatum implied that departing diplomatic personnel would be accorded safe passage out of the country, but there was still no indication the occupation authorities would allow nonofficial expatriates to depart. Indeed, holding national communities as hostage was now assumed to be part of the Iraqi strategy for deterring the American and other military forces beginning to arrive in the region. For me and other senior officers in the American Embassy, the idea of "abandoning" American citizens in Kuwait was more odious than the potential consequences of defying Saddam Hussein's fiat. Some staff would be staying!

Fortunately, the Department of State concurred with our position. Equally important for me personally, the administration in Washington agreed that as ambassador I should be among the group staying behind.[46] With this point settled in a telephone conversation, attention turned to deciding the number and identities of the "hardcore" that would staff the mission when the deadline passed. "Choose fifteen people to stay with you," the department representative said, ending the exchange. DCM Bodine and I then met in the executive office to implement that instruction. For more than an hour, we considered how many people and with which skills would be needed to run the five-acre compound around the clock. At the outset, it was decided to pare the list to the absolute minimum number consistent with the revised embassy mission, including maintenance of contact with American citizens now in hiding. Military personnel, who were considered to be at greatest risk, were first excluded.[47] A conscious effort was likewise made to eliminate persons with young dependents. Finally, a list of twelve officers embodying the requisite skills—program direction, administrative and security support, communications, and consular experience—was compiled.[48]

When I contacted the Department Task Force again to deliver the list, the response gave me a rude shock. I had hardly begun explaining that we felt we could operate with twelve persons, rather than the fifteen specified a little over an hour before, when the task force interlocutor interrupted with an abrupt "You can have eight." No amount of explanation of why eight was an insufficient complement could shake the department's new diktat or elicit an explanation of what had changed in the brief period between conversations.[49] With the newly imposed limitations, the DCM and I went back to the drawing board, but with a diminished desire to bring the Department of State into our internal deliberations in the future.[50] Whatever the conventional wisdom in Washington, the group in the embassy meant to succeed if at all possible.[51]

Several days before the expiration of the Iraqi deadline, a final meeting at the Iraqi Embassy was arranged to make preparations for the evacuation of embassy personnel and dependents. There was no reason to alert the Iraqis to the U.S. intention to keep limited staff on the compound[52] because that might have made them less cooperative with the evacuation scheduled for August 22, two days before their deadline. The ride to and from the Iraqi mission was through streets increasingly trash-strewn as a result of Iraqi neglect and depredations, a sad departure from what some had described as "the cleanest city in the Arab world." In the driveway of the Iraqi embassy, canvas bags, clearly marked as Kuwaiti diplomatic pouches, were lined up, filled with what was probably loot. At one point, I passed an Iraqi television crew filming "imported" Iraqi citizens in what would be portrayed as a demonstration by "Kuwaitis" in favor of union with Iraqi.[53]

My final effort to make arrangements for an orderly evacuation of private American and other foreign citizens fell on deaf ears at the Iraqi Embassy. The Iraqi ambassador, and his handlers listening in elsewhere in the building, were much more accomodating regarding the official evacuation on August 22, although they insisted that the evacuees leave by way of a grueling overland route to Baghdad. Citing the Iraqi ambassador's claim at the previous meeting of insecurity in the city, I insisted that the convoy have an Iraqi escort to the border. That way, I explained, Iraqi responsibility for the welfare of the evacuees would be clear all the way to their capital. It was quickly agreed that an Iraqi escort would arrive at the back gate of the Embassy compound at 3 a.m. on the morning of August 22.

There was much to be done to prepare the convoy which would be under the direction of Economic Counselor Emil M. Skodon, now that we knew the departure must be overland. Emil Skodon was a capable officer who had already demonstrated superior leadership skills during the crisis. It was he who informed the embassy on the first day of the invasion that staff in Jabriya were unable to make their way safely to the compound because of clashes in the streets. Told to seek sanctuary at the Japanese Embassy, he sucessfully led a group of sixteen that included, in addition to his family, Colonel John Mooneyham, chief of USLOK and his family; three other USLOK employees and families; a civilian from USLOK and his wife; a Navy enlisted man; and a civilian teacher. When, after two weeks of tension and uncertainty, the embassy was able to bring the group into the compound, Emil immediately became a key part of our operation. We had complete confidence in designating him to take charge of the convoy.[54] The Embassy in Baghdad had sent an experienced officer, Charlie Sibel, to accompany the exodus. With his Iraqi diplomatic credentials, and knowledge of that country, he was welcomed as an escort and guide.[55]

> *We assembled in the parking lot at 2:30 A.M., cars gassed up and ready, food packs in each vehicle—a case of tuna, bottles of water, crackers, canned beans, peanut butter and chocolate bars. It was a memorable picture; that dark early morning with vehicles of all types piled high with luggage; of dogs and cats in their carriers, of people standing around, quietly talking, taking the last message or letter home for those staying... and of the strange, somber unlit silhouettes of the proud Kuwaiti towers looming ahead of us like markers from a distant future or forlorn past. I had been so happy here.*[56]

The mood as people assembled in the darkened parking lot was somber and almost surreal. Those who would be leaving faced an uncertain and arduous journey; those who would not or, in the case of private citizens, could not, go with them also faced an unknowable future and were at some level a little bit envious.[57] Nevertheless, everyone hoped that these travelers would be the first wave to reach safety. The pets, in cases and crates, were unusually subdued as if they sensed the gravity of the occasion.[58]

Several Iraqi officers arrived somewhat after 3 a.m. When they saw the obvious—that the embassy was not evacuating its entire complement, they took the position that only fifty of the more than one hundred waiting to depart were authorized to leave. Informed that this change was unacceptable to the embassy, they melted away. After instructing that the convoy be reconfigued to include all minors among the first fifty in line, I went inside to consult the Department of State. The Iraqi reaction was conveyed to the Task Force and the reliability of Iraq's word (nil from the embassy's viewpoint; more generous on the part of State) was discussed. In the end, agreement was reached to attempt to send the entire convoy despite the restriction imposed by the officers of the "escort."[59]

> Four hours later, we were told we were all going and to get out to the parking lot. The convoy had been arranged in two groups with all the children in the first group of fifty people. The rest of us will try to push our way through when we reach the border. There were twenty-nine cars in all.[60]

With all flags flying and looking as official as possible, my Cadillac led the convoy out of the compound in the light of early morning. DCM Bodine would remain in charge of the embassy in my absence, but it would be essential to stop short of the no man's land between Abdali and Safwan; lest I be compelled to have continued on to Baghdad as the Iraqis obviously wished. While traffic was not heavy, the drive was tortuous as the driver picked his way around impassable roads and the hulks of wrecked and looted vehicles. As the head of the convoy reached the Mutla' Ridge, it joined a procession of heavy trucks overloaded with scores of Filipino and South Asian day laborers, sweltering without cover in the late-August sun. I took notes of interesting sights, such as the fact that most of the Iraqi tanks had colorful 55-gallon oil barrels welded behind the turrets. While this arrangement extended the range of the Iraqi armor, it also made the tanks vulnerable to a well-placed rifle round. At last, the first unit of the convoy reached Abdali and joined the slow-moving line passing through the first Iraqi check point. The limousine pulled onto the median strip to watch the convoy pass through. My driver, Henry, was not convinced that it was wise to park there with the American flag flapping in the face of Iraqi columns still moving into Kuwait, but as always, he accepted the risks of his position. I couldn't help but wonder what the arriving Iraqi troops thought of invading another Arab state, and the first thing they saw was the flag of the United States.

Long minutes passed without any sign of the second section of the convoy. Just as concern was turning to anxiety, several cars bearing our distinctive tape design on their doors hove into view and pulled up behind the line. Michael Capps jumped out and quickly came across to the median. He explained that the lead vehicle of that group inexplicably paused at the embassy gate, losing sight of the lead section. Later after reaching the highway, one of the American cars collided with another vehicle, badly injuring Odessa Higgins, an employee of the General Services Section. She and her husband, Bobby, were transferred to the "drag" car by LTC Thomas G. Funk and Sgt. Dan Hudson, and raced back some twenty miles to a hospital in Kuwait for treatment of shock and serious injuries.[61] The courageous men who took them back, Michael explained breathlessly, planned to race back to try to rejoin the convoy. At the rate the traffic was moving forward, they just might make it.

One by one, the vehicles of the convoy edged forward, disappearing from view on the Iraqi side of the border post:

We stream through the Kuwaiti side of the border and wave goodbye to the ambassador. He gives us the thumbs-up sign.[62]

Just as the last American car was passing the check point, the good samaritans who had rescued the accident victims roared up and, with a wave, drove out of sight.[63] There was no indication that the Iraqis at the border had stopped any of the evacuees! So far, so good.

The drive back to the embassy was uneventful, providing time to review the challenges that had been overcome and to consider those likely to lie ahead. In the context of crises as massive as the Iraqi aggression, ordinary daily problems lose much of their capacity to daunt. Two days before the convoy, for example, the water distribution system on the compound suffered a potentially devastating failure. A one and one-half inch polyethylene pipe bringing water onto the compound burst, permitting water to escape at an alarming rate. Unless it was repaired quickly, much of the stored supply would be lost. Private citizens in the compound managed to stem the flow and repair the line with the help of a former Palestinian employee who was contacted.[64] Disaster was averted, and the temporary patch proved serviceable for the duration of the siege. An equally serious breakdown took place on August 8 when the RSO misunderstood my order to "disable all excess weapons on the compound." By the time the instruction reached the Marine Guards, it had been transformed into "Destroy all weapons!":

> *After several Marines questioned the order, Staff Sergeant Smith snapped to the Marines, "Just do it." Sergeant Rodriguez and the other Marine Security Guards then began to systematically "smash all 870P Shotguns, all .357 pistols, all .38 pistols, 1 Uzi 9mm,... and also destroyed the Ambassador's personal Colt .44 Magnum Python."*

Staff Sergeant Jimmy Smith later told interviewers that the detachment was authorized to use deadly force at outset but later I changed the rules of engagement to require my verbal order. He recalled that this change, combined with accidental destruction of weapons, depressed unit morale. Sergeant Rodriguez added that "the RSO misread the ambassador's order that read 'to render all weapons inoperable and not to destroy them, as Staff Sergeant Smith ordered the Marines to do on the morning of the 8th."[65]

The first indication that something had gone terribly awry was when my personal weapon, a gift from my father, was brought to my office in several jagged pieces rather than missing the firing pin and other key components. Further investigation revealed that the Marines' weapons, definitely not excess, had received similar treatment with a maul. The embassy was one week into the crisis and effectively disarmed. Working with the pieces, we were able to reconstruct one shotgun from cannibalized parts and DCM Bodine bravely went out to collect a handgun donated, if memory serves, by our colleagues at the Turkish Embassy.

Pondering the future, the large number of chemical and decontamination units was a worrying feature of the ghastly parade at the border. It was impossible to locate the wrecked Higgins car amid the other detrius of flight and war on Kuwait's excellent roadways.⁶⁶ One block from the Embassy, our car was waved to a stop by a scraggly group of Iraqi soldiers manning a check point by the traffic circle. Henry stopped, as he'd been instructed, and a nattily attired lieutenant of the elite Republican Guard rose from the stolen desk chair in which he was lounging. As he approached, I cracked the rear door and told the officer in Arabic that he was impeding the ambassador of the United States of America. In excellent English, he said he only wished to remind the ambassador that he must leave Kuwait by August 24, two days hence. A noncommittal "I have heard that" was the response. With that, the car was waved forward to the Embassy and an unknown future.

The audacity of Saddam Hussein's sudden invasion of neighboring Kuwait surprised Western intelligence analysts⁶⁷, and stunned world capitals. While the horizon of Kuwaitis and expatriates grew increasingly constricted, the wider international community began to deal with the enormity of Iraq's attack. Baghdad's blatant aggression, violating not only Saddam's promises to President Mubarak, but Iraq's commitments under the charters of the United Nations and the League of Arab States, was easy to condemn. Deciding what to do about it would take several more months. This process lies beyond the thread of this narrative, except to note that without the firm leadership of President George H. W. Bush and Prime Minister Margaret Thatcher of Great Britain, the skills of diplomats like Ambassador Thomas Pickering, the American permanent representative at the United Nations, and the courageous refusal of the Kuwaiti government and people to accept the fate that Saddam had decreed for them, Iraq's coup might well have gone unchecked.⁶⁸

The initial UN Security Council Resolution was standard fare, condeming Iraq's invasion and demanding that it withdraw without condition. There would be additional resolutions in coming weeks but it was far from inevitable that they would eventually adopt one putting teeth in the demand. Iraq's defiant response was to announce the annexation of Kuwait on August 8, 1990. The following day, the first U.S. troops arrived in Saudi Arabia, and military aircraft were deployed to Turkey, on Iraq's western flank.⁶⁹ Their arrival was very good news to the American community in Kuwait and for Kuwaitis subjected to the harsh occupation, although few probably realized how long it would take to build up an American military force capable of taking offensive action against the hundreds of thousands of Iraqis consolidating positions in Kuwait. From service with U.S. Central Command, I knew that the group at the Embassy compound would have to survive on its own resources for a minimum of sixty days.

Around the embassy, individual Kuwaitis and some expatriates began to resist the invaders almost as soon as they recovered from their initial shock. Shots and bursts of automatic weapons fire could be heard from time to time, even as a herd of prize camels from the fallen Dasman Palace was driven south along the corniche, probably to augment the meager rations of the Iraqi conscripts.[70] Reports of looting and wanton destruction at the Evangelical Church and the American Mission compound were received from Filipino and other non-Western parishioners who undertook to watch over the premises. Eventually, a handwritten report of depredations, including the trashing of the residence and personal effects of Dorothy Scudder, was passed to the embassy.[71] The area in the vicinity of the embassy was not especially active, but occasional firefights between the Kuwaiti resistance and Iraqi troops surrounding the embassy broke out, as occurred in the early evening of August 8.[72] While the the Marines conducted themselves with admirable professionalism, the reaction of a few members of USLOK raised concerns. Some, who had been relatively idle for days, were heard discussing manning the Embassy walls Beau Geste style.[73] The idea of individuals firing from the Embassy was alarming, as it would undoubtledly draw Iraqi counterfire, including mortars and artillery. It was to eliminate this possibility that I decided to disable excess weapons on the compound. While the episode was unfortunate, wit and good fortune—not weapons—had to protect the embassy against the Iraqi forces now in control.

As the Iraqi occupation unfolded, observers within the embassy walls were struck by two incongruous impressions. Aspects of the invasion were well-planned and supported the conclusion that Iraq had been contemplating a move against Kuwait for some time. At the elite Kuwait Foundation for the Advancement of Sciences (KFAS), for example, Kuwaitis were surprised at the arrival of Iraqi "colleagues" who had previously worked there. The Iraqis carried with them lists of equipment and laboratories that had obviously been compiled years earlier with looting in mind.[74] Similarly, the Iraqis contacted the Kuwait National Petroleum Company (KNPC) a year and a half before the invasion, expressing interest in purchasing surplus equipment. They made detailed surveys and submitted a nominal bid, which was refused. The implication was that "they were simply compiling their own inventories to make the process of looting more efficient."[75] On the other hand, many of the troops roaming around appeared lost, disoriented and unfamiliar with the city they were attempting to control. However long Saddam and his colleagues had the rape of Kuwait in mind, it seemed likely that their plans were tightly held until the last minute.[76]

A striking anomally was that the Iraqi invasion assumed the aspect of an underdeveloped society taking over a more advanced one, a huge military machine overwhelming a much smaller, but more sophisticated, neighbor. The Iraqis, for example, were reportedly surprised and disappointed that much of Kuwait's wealth was not held in gold in bank vaults. In fact, the Iraqi occupation authorities proved incapable of operating the banking system until they could round up Indian, Filipino, and other expatriate clerks and computer technicians. Similar difficulties were encountered when the Iraqis took over the modern Kuwaiti oil complex in and around Ahmadi. Dependent upon Kuwaiti technicians to operate the system, the Iraqis unwittingly allowed the resistance based in Khafji, Saudi Arabia to play a role in mitigating damage to pipelines, wellheads and other key facilities.[77] Likewise, the fax machine was apparently an enigma to the massive internal security contingent that accompanied the occupying army. The Kuwaiti Resistance sent faxes to and from Kuwaiti authorities in Saudi Arabia whenever they had access to an international phone connection. Among the besieged embassies inside Kuwait, faxes were exchanged, including several issues of a semihumorous broadsheet entitled "The Hostage Journal" with locally produced cartoons ridiculing Saddam Hussein.

While telephone lines were assumed to be monitored, it was a bit surprising that the Iraqis apparently could not intercept fax transmissions. In this respect, the occupation authorities were apparently victimized by their own repressive culture. In a country that tightly controlled even typewriters, they were simply overwhelmed by new technology that was common in more open societies.

There was little doubt among Americans in Kuwait that Saddam Hussein and his regime were capable of unimaginable brutality; the atmosphere in occupied Kuwait was already somber and oppressive even though the full extent of Iraqi barbarism was not yet known. More surprising than the behavior of the Iraqi leadership was the readiness of some commentators, observing the situation from afar, to seize on any pretext to minimize the mistreatment of Kuwaitis and expatriates alike.[78] The Iraqis made a great show at the outset of the occupation to control looting, possibly to prevent freelancers from getting a jump on their state-sponsored effort. The widely circulated photograph from the Iraqi-published newspaper of an unidentified man hanged from a tall construction crane, set the tone. The victim was said to have been caught looting, but his identity and details of his alleged crime were never disclosed. Meanwhile, word of early incidents of excess was soon circulating thoughout the society:

> *Ahmed Mahmoud Qabazard was a 33-year-old police captain abroad on vacation. Leaving his wife and children in safety, he made his way to Kuwait speaking Farsi and posing as an Iranian laborer. He joined the resistance and was arrested by Iraqi secret police on September 4, 1990. After twelve days the Iraqis brought him home and burned his home. They shot him in the driveway.*[79]

Similar stories were very much on the minds of the Americans in the embassy, as well as those in hiding throughout the city, as they settled down for the siege that lay before them.[80]

With the convoy on the road, the last full day before the impending Iraqi deadline was consumed with preparations for whatever contingencies might be faced. Some additional supplies, including a very welcome shipment from Kuwait Danish Dairy[81], were stowed away, water tanks were topped up, and brains were wracked trying to imagine anything that had been forgotten or overlooked. Fuel for the emergency generator was recognized as a potential vulnerability, but the fuel tank and every possible container was already full. The only way to stockpile additional diesel was to "borrow" the tank truck in which it was delivered from the distibutor. When the supplier agreed to the plan, knowing that the Iraqis would steal his trucks anyway, a delivery the following morning, August 24, was arranged. The driver, who was not let in on what was afoot, was instructed to drive the tanker onto the Embassy compound, park it, and make his way back to the company. After full consideration, it was felt that he would be safer if he were truly "innocent" of the plan. Unfortunately, this plan could never be implemented.

The most gnawing worry facing me and the DCM was the one created by the Department of State's curious insistence on reducing the Foreign Service staff below a sustainable threshhold. There was only one way to make up for the deficiency—enlist some of the private citizens among the complement of about seventy remaining. These Americans were under no obligation to help, but survival is a great motivator. Some had already proved their value in dealing with the water leak and other problems. A few of them would respond to our requests for their cooperation.

The collection of individuals who inhabited the island the compound had become in a sea of hostility, faced a daunting task: creating a working, thriving community from ground zero. Aside from the eight FSOs, almost no one knew any of the other residents; there were few bases for cohesion other than a shared future. Uncertainty was palpable in the eyes of many citizens as they looked at the small band of government officials. What were they thinking? "Can I trust these diplomats? Are they up to the situation?"

Doubtless many of the stereotypes the public applies to diplomats and "cookie-pushers" flitted through some minds. And, it must be said, some of their doubts were reciprocated. I have a vivid impression of passing Post One in the lobby of the Chancery. Where I was accustomed to seeing a reassuring Marine Guard, there now sprawled a young man with a bandana around his unruly red hair and what appeared to be a wild look in his eyes. That first impression proved to be highly misleading, but at that moment it was disheartening.

Nevertheless, a start had to be made. On the morning of August 24, as many of the compound residents as possible gathered in the Residence sitting room.[82] As the noon deadline neared, I faced what was arguably the most momentous address I had ever delivered. No transcript exists, but the brief statement began with an unambiguous assurance that the government personnel would not leave the compound voluntarily without all the others. To survive the coming test would require that each person in the room contribute whatever he or she could to the effort because the group was interdependent. There would be times when everyone would be required to follow orders of those in positions of authority because "this will not be a democracy. But if you are willing to accept these terms, we can deal with whatever the Iraqis throw at us." DCM Bodine and several others added their comments, including some practical advice and needs in the immediate future.

Jack Rinehart recalled his impressions of the meeting:

> ... the diplomats presented us with an orientation talk. They told us how to handle traumatic situations like incarceration. We learned a simple code for communicating without speaking.... We were told "do not resist if the Iraqis come into the compound...". By the time some of the attendees reached a point of near hysteria, the speech wrapped up with the diplomat telling us, "Don't worry though, everything will be OK."
> ... during our meeting to discuss survival plans, the lights went out and everything was still.[83]

The siege of Embassy Kuwait had begun.

Gallery D

Fireboats and other craft come to the assistance of a stricken tanker during Operation Earnest Will, the U.S. Navy's protection of Kuwaiti and other neutral shipping from Iranian mines and small boat attacks in 1987–88. *Howell photo*

U.S. Secretary of Defense Frank Carlucci discussing "Operation Earnest Will" with Minister of Oil Shaikh Ali al-Khalifa al-Sabah in 1988. The operation involved U.S. Navy protection of Kuwaiti tankers and neutral shipping from Iranian attacks while transiting the Gulf. At left are senior Pentagon official Richard Armitage and Ambassador Howell. *Kuwait Oil Company*

Kuwaiti Crown Prince and Prime Minister Sa'd Abdallah pays his respects at Arlington National Cemetery. His official visit in 1988 was a key building block in strengthening bilateral relations over the period leading up to the Iraqi aggression in 1990. *Department of State photo*

Putting aside concerns about their circumstances and prospects, the resilient group of Americans trapped on the Embassy compound took time out to stage a talent show in September 1990. With a flashlight in case of power failure and formal attire tailored to the lack of air conditioning, Ambassador Howell acted as master of ceremonies. *Jeff Jugar*

In October 1990, two months after Iraq's invasion and occupation of Kuwait, a unit of the Kuwaiti Resistance set off a bomb just outside the lower lobby of the Kuwaiti International Hotel. The Iraqi forces used the hotel to accommodate high-ranking officials and foreign guests; the Resistance targeted a reported meeting of key security personnel. This photo of the resulting fire was taken from within the Embassy compound, over the wall and roof of the Chancery. *Jeff Jugar*

The unexpected success of a well in the Residence garden gave new life to the Americans besieged by the Iraqis on the Embassy compound. Thanks to the vision and efforts of horticulturist Paul Brown, it became possible to cultivate a vegetable garden and to take warm showers. The photo shows the moment when a pump was connected to the well. Foreground from left: Sergio Ado; Jack Rinehart (peering into well); Ambassador Howell; Paul Brown (partially obscured bald head); and Ron Webster (in truck bending over generator). Because the water could not be tested, it was not used for drinking or cooking. *Jeff Jugar*

Mimi Logsdon, embassy secretarial assistant, and Sergio Ado, American businessman, perform mundane but critical tasks under difficult circumstances during the Iraqi siege of the Embassy compound, August–December 1990. Hygiene was a high priority to prevent sickness and contagion. *Jeff Jugar*

In November 1990, with the siege of the American Embassy in its fourth month and no end in sight, the Americans on the compound had to decide whether or not to celebrate Thanksgiving. In the end, they decided they had much for which to be thankful. Here, Ambassador Howell presides over the Thanksgiving meal, with the table set with the best linens and china. The main course was tuna fish molded in the shape of a turkey. *Jeff Jugar*

Some survivors of the siege of Embassy Kuwait gather for a reunion with Ambassador Howell (seated) at his home in Albemarle County, Virginia, in 1994. From left: Rev. Maurice and Laurie Graham and son of the Evangelical Church; Paul Brown, horticulturalist and the force behind the Embassy well; Jack Rinehart, businessman and technician; Mimi Logsdon, secretarial assistant; Wayne Logsdon, General Services officer; El Miloudi Hamid, businessman and chief gardener ("Mr. Greenjeans"); Ron Webster, businessman, engineer, and morale officer; and B. George Saloom, businessman and head chef. *Jeff Jugar*

The long-neglected Men's and Women's Hospitals of the American Mission were renovated by the Dar al-Athar al-Islamiyyah, Kuwait's outstanding national museum. Fitted out with spaces for offices, research, and outreach, the complex was designated the Americani Cultural Centre in recognition of the achievements and contributions of the American Mission personnel. These facilities opened to the public in 2011. *Claudia Farkas Al-Rashoud*

Ambassador and Mrs. Howell with Shaikha Hussah Sabah al-Salem al-Sabah, director of the Dar al-Athar al-Islamiyyah, Kuwait, on May 31, 2011. Ambassador Howell was honored to be invited to deliver the inaugural lecture in the auditorium of the Americani Cultural Centre. *Claudia Farkas Al-Rashoud*

16

The Valley of the Shadow

In 2001, I co-wrote an account of the ways in which the inhabitants of the Embassy compound forged a viable and dynamic community to survive the prolonged siege. While that book purposely omitted the political aspects of the situation, it is related primarily from the perspective of the Embassy leadership.[1] The account in the chapter that follows is based in large measure on the diaries and oral histories of ordinary American citizens within the Embassy and in hiding throughout the city of Kuwait.

Around 11 a.m. on the morning of August 24, as the Americans on the compound were meeting in the Residence, the Iraqis cut the municipal power to the American Embassy. The Iraqis had imposed their noon deadline using Baghdad time, which was one hour ahead of Kuwait. Although the emergency generator kicked in almost immediately, the tank truck bringing additional fuel for the generator was stopped and turned back within two blocks of its destination. The loss of those supplies was a great disappointment and underlined the urgent necessity of reducing the load on the generator to an absolute minimum.[2]

Ron Webster[3], a businessmen with electrical and many other practical skills, modified the circuitry in the generator control panel to power communications equipment and a limited number of refrigerators where food was stored.[4] "The only major problem we had early on," Jack Rinehart, another private citizen with a wide range of practical capabilities, observed, "was the kids continued to turn on air conditioners.... Wire cutters remedied the situation...."[5] There would be numerous modifications of the electrical, water, and other systems on the compound as the occupants perfected the art of conservation. The immediate necessity was to reconfigure the systems so that, for example, incoming water went to reserve storage tanks rather than refilling toilets. Ron Webster noted that one water pipe was cut off completely: The other source "continued to supply water for many days...."[6]

During this initial period of frantic activity, it was soon clear that many of the citizens who had sought refuge in the embassy brought with them vital skills that greatly improved the odds of survival. Embassy Administrative Officer Wayne Logsdon (code name: "Whiskey Tango"),[7] surveyed the population for expertise and found a treasure trove. The stars of this early surge were, in addition to Webster (code name: "Longhorn"), was Tony Mireles (code name: "Laredo"), who took charge of carpentry and built a deluxe outhouse over a sewer outlet; Rinehart, who assumed responsibility for plumbing modifications; and Charlie Carradine, who isolated the stored potable water from the system and created additional storage capacity in cardboard boxes lined with garbage bags.[8]

The besieged embassy had not yet settled into the studied routine that would sustain it over the months ahead. However, the joint efforts of these and other citizens and the Foreign Service contingent, headed by Logsdon and General Services Officer (GSO) Mark Herzberg (code name: "Clown"), to solve urgent problems were a good start toward breaking down the reserve that divided the two groups. The more practical-minded among the new arrivals had not wasted their time prior to the imposition of the siege. Ron Webster, for instance, had familiarized himself with the compound and its resources even as preparations for the evacuee convoy of August 22 were under way:

> *We 'vagrants' divided ourselves into predictable areas of technology (power, water, fuel, food, etc.) and endeavored to learn all we could.... There was enough food, assuming no spoilage, to easily last through the year and well into the next spring. There were over seven thousand cans of tuna alone.... Dozens of frozen turkeys, beef, bacon, seafood, etc., was scattered over some dozen freezers and even more refrigerators. The warehouse was full of*

paper goods, plastic utensils, soaps, toiletries, etc. There were some seven thousand gallons of potable water in reserve with some fifteen–twenty thousand gallons of "brackish" water for secondary use.... There were three generators at our disposal: a large Cat (360 kwa) and a 4 cylinder Detroit Diesel (50 kwa), as well as a very small (.65 kwa) gasoline Honda. All had full tanks and there was (sic) seven thousand liters of fuel in an underground tank. There was a major 'cache' of propane tanks in the corner of the compound providing sufficient alternate fuel for cooking....[9]

Armed with this knowledge, Ron and other "kampers"[10] were ready to attack urgent tasks and vulnerabilities from the outset.

The loss of air-conditioning after the cut of municipal power made buildings on the compound virtually uninhabitable. Most were constructed on the assumption that they would be cooled mechanically and had small windows that provided little prospect of natural ventilation. Security measures in the chancery and Residence further restricted the ability to even open windows. As a result of these constraints, the community adopted a new lifestyle centered on the Embassy swimming pool and the adjacent snack bar. With daily temperatures in excess of 130 degrees Fahrenheit, and humidity during the monsoon season at 100 percent, strenuous activity in the heat of the day was impossible. At night, there was little relief and individuals found places to sleep outside, learning by experience not to bed down near the eaves of structures. The humid air condensed on roofs and ran off like rain.

An adaptive routine evolved. Awaking at sunrise when swarms of flies made further sleep impossible, the kampers undertook morning chores, including garbage disposal and doing personal laundry in buckets. Paul Brown (codename: "Brownie"), an agronomist who was working on landscaping for the Kuwait government, could be heard trundling his garage cart to a far corner where trash was burned. Paul was not above using the trash fire to torment Iraqi guards on the other side of the compound wall; "at least two aerosol cans" exploded each day—startling the Iraqis. Webster was convinced that Paul kept a supply of used cans to add to the noxious smoke of burning garbage and circuit boards.[11] To the amusement of some, he then spent time each day digging a deep hole in the garden behind the Residence in the relative cool of the morning. Breakfast was served up by B. George Saloom (codename: "Ramblin' Wreck") and Sergio Ado (codename: "Frog") in the dining area set up outside the snack bar. This was also a time for conversation and a vigorous, but ultimately futile, effort to kill pesky flies before the rising sun compelled everyone to seek shelter from its withering rays.[12]

Lunch was a sluggish affair with individuals emerging from shelter for only the brief period required to collect and consume the increasingly monotonous fare. In the initial weeks, 3 p.m. was a time of resumed activity when the generator was started to power three hours of communications[13] with Washington and the preparation of the evening meal. This was the time when there might be messages from loved ones in the United States. During these periods, essential business was conducted with the Task Force in the Department of State and, periodically, I could consult with Secretary of State Baker or, occasionally, the president.[14] Within the strict three-hour time window, there was often time for me to speak briefly with my spouse, Margie Howell, who was a volunteer member of the Task Force and often served as the embassy's "voice" with the American media. It was a high point of the day for everyone, except for those who did not receive eagerly awaited messages from wives and families.

As critical as the Task Force was for the besieged Embassy, its services to families of Americans caught in Kuwait and Iraq were among its most important functions, offering them a point of contact twenty-four hours a day, every day. "The State Department's policy was to call families at least every 48 hours, even if there was no new information, just to keep in touch. Relatives of known captives and other special cases were called daily."[15] Service on such groups is far from pleasant, especially for consular and welfare specialists who deal with the anxious relatives of victims of crisis. Aside from the long grinding days and nights they must work, opportunities to improve the situation are more infrequent than the occasions on which they must absorb the anger and frustration of the public. It was in this context that my wife made, what has been characterized as an "invaluable" contribution:

In the United States at the time of the invasion, she was on the Task Force within a week. As a public figure in Kuwait for the previous three years, Margie Howell had excellent contacts among displaced Americans and Kuwaitis. She became a lightning rod for officials, business people, and displaced Americans alike. Most importantly for people with men trapped in Kuwait and Iraq, she could identify with them as her own husband was in the same situation.[16]

The hour between power shutdown at 6 p.m. and dinner, very quickly morphed into a "happy hour." A portable bar found in the Marine House was moved to the dining area and served drinks concocted from liquor supplies in the ambassador's storeroom or supplies brought in by others. As variety dwindled, the "handgrenade" made with packaged pineapple juice became the staple libation. By the time those involved with communications made their way to the pool area, "happy hour" was usually in full swing.

During dinner, a preselected list of films from the Embassy's video library was circulated, and the film of the evening was chosen by majority vote. While every effort was made to insure the integrity of this exercise in democracy, it did not escape the suspicion of some disappointed "kampers" that the voting was rigged.[17] Nevertheless, the evening film showing was a highlight of the day, providing an opportunity to relax in the relative cool of the evening in company with the entire community. Ironically, action films such as *The Alamo, The Great Escape,* or *55 Days at Peking* proved the most popular choices. Initially, there was some reluctance to show *The Alamo* in light of the siege of the Embassy. When it was pointed out that the situations were not analogous, reservations seemed to evaporate. "We are much more heavily outnumbered than the contingent at the Alamo," someone quipped with characteristic gallows humor. Similarly, when the 55th day of the siege of Embassy Kuwait passed in late October, exceeding the siege of the diplomatic quarter in Peking, the embassy cable incorporated a line reading: "Day 56. Eat your heart out, Charlton Heston."

Power for the VCR player and several lightbulbs (needed to clean up and wash dishes after dinner) was provided by a small Honda generator mounted on a movable cart. This generator, which ran on gasoline reclaimed from automobiles on the compound, was not in the embassy inventory. It had been purchased, like many other items, for the Embassy in Baghdad and was awaiting pickup when the Iraqi army invaded Kuwait. That was to prove extremely providential for it could be employed for many purposes, including powering an electric typewriter without drawing on the vital reserves of diesel fuel needed for communications.

Except for those who would be on duty in the compound's two guardhouses through the night, the conclusion of the film signaled the end of the day. "Lights out" had real meaning for the "kampers"; some read for a while by improvised lamps, but most went to their beds to get what sleep they could before the swarms of flies heralded another day.

When the siege began on August 24, there were more than seventy Americans within the Embassy walls, including older citizens with serious health problems and a number of children. A rudimentary "school" for younger "kampers" was set up in the small United States Information Service (USIS) Library under the tutelage of Reagan Miller (codename: "Grasshopper"), a teacher working in Kuwait. Birthday cakes and other treats provided the children with as much normality as possible. By using the large generator, small airconditioned areas were maintained for the elderly and medical cases, including one individual who was recovering from recent heart surgery. Stocks of foodstuffs were centralized and inventoried, and food preparation was consolidated in the snack bar area. While there was some possibility that the crisis might be resolved quickly through diplomacy, we worked on the assumption that the siege could last indefinitely unless the Iraqi Army, which isolated the compound from contact with the world outside, decided to invade the Embassy grounds.

The embassy's isolation was broken for the first and only time by a visit in late August from Reverend Jesse Jackson and an accompanying press group.[18] On August 31, he appeared at the back gate of the compound, escorted by an Iraqi "keeper"[19] and Vice Consul Melvin Ang from the U.S. Embassy in Baghdad. The occupation authorities denied him permission to enter the Embassy, so his brief conversation with me and the DCM took place through the chained pedestrian turnstile; Consul Ang memorialized the moment with a picture taken through the gate and later sent us a copy. Prior to Reverend Jackson's arrival, DCM Bodine and I decided to use this opening to push for the evacuation of the most vulnerable citizens among us—children, serious medical cases, and the elderly.[20] Jackson took this request to heart and promised to do what he could to take these groups with him when he departed Kuwait. He was as good as his word and over the next twenty-four hours arrangements were made for their evacuation. At almost the last minute, a private citizen on the compound confided that he had been diagnosed with HIV/AIDs. His name was quickly added to the list of evacuees and the Iraqi authorities, anxious to facilitate his departure, broke records adding him to the list.[21]

The next afternoon, the day appointed for the group's departure, Reverend Jackson came to the front gate of the compound to collect evacuees from the Embassy. He brought the welcome news that serious medical cases outside the compound, including the badly injured Odessa Higgins, had also been assembled. No one was permitted to enter or exit the Embassy except those who were leaving with Jackson. Through the door opened for them, however, Jesse Jackson asked that all present join hands for a prayer. This reasonable request presented a dilemma for me, as I was smoking a pipe and had no place to put it. Jack Rinehart, who was watching the proceedings from inside the compound, observed the departure:

> *The ambassador respectfully removed his pipe from his teeth, but had no free hand to hold it. He stuck the hot pipe under his left armpit and then did a (silent) separate prayer that Jackson's prayer would be brief. Being a very rugged individual, he patiently waited for the prayer to end. When he came back into the compound fanning his armpit, no one dared laugh. Unfortunately, after a few seconds, I lost control and laughed.... I felt we may someday become friends (and we did).*[22]

Unlike former Attorney General Ramsey Clarke and other supplicants who would parade through Baghdad over the coming weeks, Jesse Jackson earned the respect of ordinary Americans within the compound for his achievement.[23] Other commentators were not as charitable about Jackson's mission. Levins, for example, faulted him for not securing the release of a larger number of women, whom he believed had been cleared by Iraq for departure.[24] Whether true or not, we were overjoyed that Jackson took with him categories of hostages that were not covered and might not otherwise have had a timely chance to depart. In the compound, the sniping at Jackson's achievement was not shared. Every American who made his or her way to freedom was a "victory," and the departure of citizens with serious medical conditions was a particular relief. "Kamp Kuwait" had limited medical capabilities. It was fortunate to have a physician, Dr. Jim Carroll (codename: "Doc"), a pediatric specialist who had been teaching at the Kuwait University Medical School, but was equipped to deal only with advanced first-aid cases. The possibility of a serious injury, medical crisis, or communicable disease was a constant worry that haunted the leadership. Scrupulous attention to sanitation was a precaution against contagion, but avoidance of injury depended on good fortune as much as caution.

With the press contingent of Reverend Jackson lining the roof of the International Hotel across the street (they were permitted no closer), the small group of travelers moved down to the cars waiting to take them to the airport. Among them were Bonnie Anderton and her daughter, who were compelled to leave husband and father, Richard (codename: "Big Bird"), behind with the other "kampers." With them went the hopes that the Iraqis would keep their word this time rather than soil their copybooks with Jesse Jackson. In stark contrast, an attempt to bring additional stocks of diesel fuel into the compound during the hoopla surrounding the Jackson visit failed:

> *On the day that the Reverend returned, an(other) attempt at the delivery of additional diesel fuel was made.... It never got close. Assuming that the lights, cameras, and flux associated with the 'Jackson media blitz' would create some opportunity, it seemed like a good idea...*[25]

Meanwhile, forty-seven women and children from the Embassy

convoy of August 22 arrived at Andrews Air Base outside Washington D.C. on August 27. In violation of their promises, the Iraqis prevented male members of the group, including high school students and summer interns, from leaving Baghdad, apparently in an effort to compel Embassy Kuwait to close. Led by Luz Marina Colwell[26], the wife of the former American Consul in Kuwait, the refugees who deplaned at Andrews were met by Assistant Secretary of State John H. Kelly and Margie Howell:

> Mrs. Howell, who was not in Kuwait at the time of the invasion, said she was "very relieved on behalf of my husband that these women and children are out"[27]

She spoke for everyone in the besieged embassy. The number who reached safety in this operation was small in relation to the Americans still trapped in Kuwait, but their journey was the first of what was hoped would be a repatriation of the entire community. Preparations were already under way for an American flight to carry American and other expatriate women. As the group with Reverend Jackson disappeared from view, the large generator was shut down for the duration:

> The ambassador called for a complete shutdown of the large generator, since the need for air-conditioning was less due to the departure of several medical cases.[28]

The media coverage of Jesse Jackson's successful extraction illustrated a dilemma faced by the embassy in an age of instantaneous worldwide communication and news coverage. From the embassy perspective, the Iraqi Army and government were the primary enemy and target of its message—psychologically. In the early days of the siege, our priority was to prevent the Iraqi troops from forcing their way onto the compound. Even as preparations proceeded to survive a prolonged siege, every effort was made to "play the bird with a broken wing," to convince the Iraqis that the embassy was desperate and could not hold out long if they were patient. We reasoned that if they held off long enough, it would be increasingly costly to employ force against the compound, particularly as American and allied forces built up in Saudi Arabia and the Gulf region. In brief, it was desirable that they believe the embassy would quickly acknowledge defeat without the firestorm an attack would surely generate.

An important element of this strategy was to prevent the Iraqis from learning about embassy capabilities and assets for the long term. To that end, every American who was able to depart was briefed about the need not to reveal details of the true situation within the compound walls.[29] One individual, Lloyd Culbertson (76), who left with Jackson, took the coaching to heart. When he spoke with Western media, he spoke dramatically of the friends he left behind, drinking water from the swimming pool and breaking up furniture for cooking fires.[30] This was fine in terms of the impression provided to the Iraqis. However, it was not true! Nevertheless, the imagery was simply too good for the media to ignore. Years later, the idea that the "kampers" had to drink from the swimming pool remains such an inextricable part of the mythology that even direct denials by those who were there cannot extinguish it.[31]

The difficulty was that American press and networks picked up this tale and replayed such details to the families of those in the Embassy. It was a constant challenge, never fully resolved, to straddle a theoretical line between convincing the Iraqis that conditions were insupportable and assuring these families that their loved ones were not as desperate as depicted. One solution lay in almost daily phone conversations between the State Department Task Force, including Margie Howell, with the families out of earshot of the media.[32]

Survival was essential if the U.S. Embassy was to perform its two primary missions: constitute a physical rebuke to the Iraqi pretension of having absorbed independent Kuwait; and render all possible support and assistance to American citizens until they were able to depart the country. Both objectives were uppermost in the thoughts and actions of embassy leadership. The well-established warden system was activated on August 2 and continued to operate, often in the face of serious difficulties, throughout the siege.[33] Relying upon the telephone system, especially after it became impossible to leave the Embassy grounds, contact with citizens throughout the community was vulnerable to phone-line disruptions. As the Iraqi grip on Kuwait tightened, normal telephone lines began to fail:

> *The phone facilities were initially in disarray... all international lines were disconnected, whether on purpose or by general ineptitude. Efforts were made by the Iraqis to disconnect embassy phones but some 'communications types' at the embassy were able to isolate and rewire the system to provide some half-dozen serviceable 'outside' lines.*[34]

These "rescued" lines were routed to the gate houses and offices, and a hotline was positioned outside the snack bar where people tended to congregate. The restoration of telephone capabilities was spearheaded by Benny Mitchell (codename: "Chicken") and Mike Penniman (codename: "270"), who took charge of the switchroom and ferreted out several old phone connections which were no longer in service. Mitchell, one of the I-Hawk missile technicians, proved to be a wizard at rewiring the switchboard. By reconnecting them, the embassy reacquired local service and continued access to the community in Kuwait.[35] The interruption of consular operations was thankfully brief.

Exchanges with the widespread dispersed American community were continuous and productive, enabling the embassy to organize more than a dozen evacuation flights when they became possible, and to facilitate communication between fellow citizens in hiding and loved ones in the United States. For extended periods, the embassy could offer little more than "handholding," but this proved very important in times of despair.

In the immediate aftermath of the embassy siege, a book by Jadranka Porter included tendentious and erroneous criticisms of the embassy performance. Charging that the American Embassy was uninformed and indifferent to "the situation outside its own compound," she wrote that, well into the crisis, "the American counsellor, Barbara Bodin [sic], told Eoin the embassy was only then thinking of setting up its own warden system. It never happened, because events overtook them."[36] Ms. Porter was a British subject who had been working before the invasion for an English-language newspaper in Kuwait. She was not particularly well connected with the American Embassy before or during the Iraqi occupation, and her assertions in this rush-to-publication memoir betray a serious ignorance of what was going on around her.

The maintenance of round-the-clock access to the outside community was beyond the capability of the single Consul and other Foreign Service staff remaining at the compound. Private citizens on the compound pitched in and were given introductory guidance and training. Soon, most were functioning effectively in support of the consular operation:

> *Diplomats and those on guard duty monitored the phones twenty-four hours each day. Calls came in back to back from early morning to after midnight each day. We recorded information on dozens of note pads....*[37]

Representative excerpts of recollections by American citizens outside the Embassy in Appendix E provide insights not only into interactions with embassy staff but also the ebb and flow of anxiety and morale over the period from August to December 1990.

For most of the workday, contact was maintained over phone lines routed to the two guard houses that were manned at all times. Since they were concrete with bullet-resistant windows, making them habitable in extremes of the Kuwaiti summer was a challenge that was taken up by the problem-solver "kampers." Automobiles that were considered unsuitable for a possible evacuation convoy (should that become possible) were cannibalized for ventilation fans and glove compartment lights that could be operated on car batteries. The fans could not really cool the buildings but did keep the heavy, moist air moving. The portable lights proved to be ideal since they did not come on until lifted. For the most part, those on duty moved their phones and lights outside the guard houses during the hours of darkness.

In addition to learning about embassy consular functions, the civilians staffing these posts acquired a fine appreciation for the frustrations frequently faced by professional consuls in dealing with the public:

> There were several calls from people who had been evacuated earlier and drove back across Iraq from Jordan so they could retrieve more of their personal property. Other calls were taken in October and November from mothers requesting evacuation justified by newborn American children. Many of these women were evacuated on earlier flights and some were in America when Kuwait was invaded. They had traveled back to Kuwait to visit husbands or other relatives realizing they could be evacuated by the U.S.A.[38]

The phenomenon of "anchor babies" has become a controversial issue in the debate on illegal immigration in the twenty-first century, but its implications extend far beyond that issue. It likewise impacts crisis situations like that in Kuwait where there is a premium on space for evacuating American citizens in danger:

> ... the evacuations, of necessity, expanded to include American citizens and their immediate families. This could mean that an infant, born in the United States, could be accompanied by a mother, father, brothers and sisters, and, in some cases, grandparents. It was common for such situations to occur in which one such infant could provide passage, courtesy of the U.S. taxpayer, for nine people to the United States. It was ironic that a majority of these non-U.S. citizens were Palestinians, a group which Saddam was supposedly representing in the Arab stand against the infidel, Colonial West....[39]

A typical case of which I was aware involved an Egyptian woman who traveled without problems from Kuwait to the United States, where she remained for two weeks while she delivered her baby. Returning to Kuwait, the family called the embassy to arrange evacuation for the baby and seven other family members. Far from being appreciative, the family was extremely upset by the arrangement offered them; they had assumed, wrongly, that the U.S. government would also transport their car and household effects! As Webster summed up the experience, "The phone contact meant we would learn patience and constraint while even the eligible participants in the evacuation flights were difficult enough, many callers were simply not eligible, but persisted.... It was a considerable challenge to maintain civility."[40]

Issues regarding evacuation flights were only a small part of exchanges with remaining members of the American community. Until December, male citizens were not eligible for the flights under the conditions imposed by the Iraqi occupation authorities. The major effort made for those who were trapped was to provide them with a measure of companionship and a means for limited communication with family, friends, and employers at home. The initial device developed was the "message board" sent to and received from the Department of State Task Force. Briefly, Americans in hiding, as well as the occupants of the embassy, were allowed to submit several messages of three or four lines each, per week. Those received in Kuwait were incorporated by Mimi Logsdon of the embassy staff, in a cable for transmission when communications were available. In Washington, the messages were conveyed by phone to the addressee specified by the originator. Replies were consolidated by the Task Force into a cable that was sent to Kuwait the next time communications were up. Embassy staff separated the incoming messages and repeated them by phone to the originator. Then, the process would start all over again. This was a cumbersome and largely unsatisfactory procedure but most people agreed it was better than nothing.[41]

Quite early in the siege, the embassy sought to have the Voice of America (VOA) carry messages from families in the United States, as the BBC was doing for the British community in Kuwait. There was initial resistance in Washington based upon the differences in the charters and practices of the two broadcasting services.[42] Over succeeding weeks, the opposition within the U.S. government was overcome and VOA began to broadcast recorded messages to Americans under the Iraqi occupation. VOA's good-faith effort was subject to the same criticisms as the "message board."

Conversations between those manning the embassy phone lines and citizens seeking to elude detection by the Iraqis, often with the support and assistance of Kuwaiti and other neighbors, provided opportunities for the exchange of information about developments around town.[43] Since everyone had only a limited window on the environment, it was important to build up a larger picture based on multiple sources. The embassy was eager to help its citizens elude capture by the Iraqis, and, therefore, knowing which neighborhoods were being searched was essential. In the words of Jack Rinehart:

> ... the embassy was able, in some cases, to get supplies to those in hiding .... With the help of some very courageous friends throughout the city, some of the men in fairly dangerous locations were moved to safer areas in the city. We had no way to get them to the embassy, but we did what we could.[44]

Those individuals who could move about and help in the resupply and transport of Americans and others in hiding—Kuwaitis, Lebanese, Syrians, Australians, etc.—were indeed courageous; the Iraqis had announced that anyone caught harboring or assisting "foreigners" was liable to execution. Having set a rescue operation in motion, there was little that those in the embassy could do besides wait impatiently for it to unfold. Often, the operation was successful, sometimes it was too little, too late.

A major failure that resulted in the death of a British expatriate unfolded slowly as the embassy was organizing his move to an apartment where he would have security and the assistance of companions. Unbeknownst to those on the compound at the time, one of those also working on the case was an American banker whose Levantine background and Arabic capability gave him a measure of anonymity. Michael Kano, who was directly involved with the case, later wrote at some length about his role, including contact with Marthe, a German lady who was living near the man. Eventually, Marthe reported that she discovered "an English gentleman" whose condition concerned her; he was drinking and would not eat. When Kano and Moe, a Lebanese friend, called her again from another location, she was more alarmed: "This Englishman is passed out on the floor. He is vomiting blood and will not wake up." The two arranged for an ambulance. The crew, however, were denied entry into the building because they would not tell the Iraqi police who had sent them:

> The standoff lasted for over an hour until the British Embassy, through a neutral country, convinced the authorities to let the doctors in. It was too late. The man had bled internally for several hours and had died while the Iraqis obstructed the ambulance.[45]

At the Embassy, we knew that the building in question was a stone's throw away and that a "German lady" was the go-between, but little more. And Kano, for his part, was unaware that the embassy and others were working in parallel on the problem.[46] It mattered little that those working on such problems did not know the identity of one another; the less one knew, the less they could reveal if they fell into Iraqi hands. But it was emblematic of those dark days that apparently none of us knew the name of the British victim we were laboring to help.[47]

In early September 1990, the Iraqi regime decided that Western women and children could leave Kuwait and Iraq. The origins of this reversal of policy are obscure but some believe that a speech by British Prime Minister Thatcher accusing Saddam Hussein of hiding behind women's skirts stung him into this reversal of policy.[48] It is also probable that King Hussein of Jordan, and others who were pursuing a misguided policy of supporting Baghdad's aggression, were urging him to mitigate Iraq's treatment of Western expatriates. In any case, Saddam Hussein was well on his way to convincing himself that he could play the issue of hostages and human shields to make the major powers forget that the central issue was his seizure of Kuwait and its people.

With confirmation from the Department of State and Embassy Baghdad of the new Iraqi policy, preparations began in earnest within the compound for an initial evacuation flight on September 7, 1990. There were no precedents for the procedures that evolved under pressure of the approaching date. The Iraqi regime insisted that only Iraqi Airways could be used for the flight to Baghdad and onward to Europe. On the other hand, it was doubtful than any American carrier would have accepted the task even if the Iraqis agreed. An Iraqi aircraft was, therefore, chartered to fly to Kuwait on that date and return to Baghdad.[49] One or more consular officers from the embassy in Iraq would accompany the aircraft to provide an official presence once the passengers were embarked.

Consul Rogers (codename: "Gazelle") and those assisting her on the compound initiated contact with Americans in hiding to inform them of the opportunity and to confirm those women who wished to join the flight:

> ... a number of evacuation flights were administered from Camp Kuwait. Although physically confined and unable to physically attend to the departure of the flights, most arrangements were made by phone or facsimile machine and numerous campers were pressed into service to assist in the creation of the flight manifests.[50]

Once the list was collated, a flight manifest was prepared for transmission to Washington and Baghdad on a typewriter powered by the small Honda generator.[51] Great care was taken to assure that the whereabouts of every traveler was clear at all times and that a responsible American was with the passengers whenever possible.

An assembly point that would be known to members of the American community was needed, and the parking lot of the Safeway supermarket on Sixth Ring Road was an obvious choice. From there, hired buses would take the evacuees to the Kuwait Airport. Those departing were advised not to have husbands or other American or Kuwaiti males drive them to the Safeway because the Iraqi authorities were likely to seize them.[52] Since those in the American Embassy were unable to leave the compound, there were many aspects of this plan that depended on the resourcefulness and resilience of the private Americans, and the indispensible help of non-Americans who could move about. The embassy owed a debt of gratitude to those men, in particular Canadians Eoin MacDougal and Britt Mackridge, who met the arriving evacuees and assisted with the transfer to leased buses. The passengers would unavoidably be out of contact and dependent upon their own devices for a lengthy period. Many questions could not be answered; how, for example, would the women, some accompanied by children, handle their luggage and formalities at the airport now under Iraqi "management"? No one knew, although evacuees were advised not to bring more luggage than they could carry. The time between dropoff at the airport and the boarding of the aircraft, where an American consul could monitor the situation, was the most nerve-wracking part of the journey.[53]

Among those who signed up to take the first flight was a very capable lady from Missouri, who was married to a Kuwaiti engineer. Maureen Aldakheel, who is a good friend of my wife and me, also served as an educational counselor at the American Embassy. She was asked to assume a leadership role with the first tranche of evacuees and readily agreed. Her memories of the experience illuminate the initial evacuation flight:

> *I was in touch with the embassy during this time (August 2 to September 7). Margie's husband called every now and then to see how I was doing. In fact, when he called, he would identify himself as 'Margie's husband'.*
>
> *The drive to our rendezvous point for evacuation was eerie. My mother-in-law and sister-in-law drove me. (I was advised by the embassy not to have Lateef drive me because the situation was too dangerous for Kuwaiti men.)*
>
> *It took three days to reach the states.... I was able to send and receive messages from Lateef while our embassy was still open in Kuwait. That was how I learned of the death of my father-in-law in October.*[54]

Word that the first flight of evacuees organized by the embassy had reached safety was greeted with great relief among those who had worked so long and hard to make it happen.

The knowledge that the process devised had worked, and particularly that the Iraqi authorities had not interfered, unleashed another flurry of activity on the compound as preparations were made for further flights. Over the next three months, a dozen additional evacuations were organized along the same lines. Priority was accorded to American citizens who were allowed to leave by the Iraqis. The goal, however, was to load each aircraft fully, and when the number of Americans who elected to depart was less, space was allocated to evacuees from Britain and other friendly countries.[55]

Although there was now a general template for civilian evacuations, the individual flights never became routine. Occasionally, some details, such as the location of the assembly point, had to be altered. In early October, however, a major change occurred when the Iraqis ceased using the commercial airport for civil aviation. In a move that was not fully understood at the time, the flights were rerouted into and out of Ali Al-Salem Air Force Base, located between Kuwait and the Iraqi border. This change necessitated a further bus ride and additional baggage handling, lengthening the passengers' ordeal, but not stopping the flow.

The series of flights through the month of September occurred with such regularity, that some expatriates began to treat the airbridge as a regularly scheduled service. Individuals planning to depart would delay their departure until a "later" flight with the result that some aircraft were not as fully loaded as the embassy intended. Consequently, the flight of September 22 was advertised as the "very last one."[56]

A very special passenger on the September 22 flight deserves mention because her departure from Kuwait brought to an end an important chapter of the country's history. She was Dame Violet Dickson, widow of Colonel Harold Dickson and a lifelong resident. In her 90s, senile, bedridden, and hospitalized in the spring of 1990, Dame Violet was in such critical condition that the British Embassy had begun excavations for her interment on their compound.

Dame Violet's caretakers had become increasingly concerned, as her condition deteriorated, that the Kuwait Oil Company Hospital would not be able to provide adequate care, and contacted the British Embassy to make arrangements for her to be evacuated with a medical escort.[57] On the morning of the flight, Dame Violet was placed in an ambulance with two Indian nurses (Feky Rego and Veronica Bernard) and driven to the airport:

> *The British Embassy had arranged for only two seats, one for Dame Violet, and one for a companion, despite the old woman being bedridden. They had also made no provision for getting her to the aircraft. When the Americans discovered this, they blocked a whole row of seats for her to lie down on, and seats for two nurses and the attending physician, and arranged with the Iraqis to get her ambulance to the door of the plane.*[58]

Even with the ambulance permitted on the tarmac, there was still a logistics hurdle to surmount. The two nurses and the ambulance drivers had to wrestle the very large patient up the steep steps and into the plane.

It is questionable that the venerable Dame Violet was even

aware of what was happening to the Kuwait she loved; she was told only that she was being taken to England. The flight had a four-hour stop in Baghdad, where the British Ambassador, Sir Harold "Hooky" Walker, came to see Dame Violet.[59] She died January 4, 1991 in a nursing home at Goring-on-Thames.[60]

Only subsequently was it learned that the closure of the Kuwait International Airport in early October was not a case of Iraqi harrassment, but the result of Kuwaiti resistance activity. Organized spontaneously by former Kuwaiti military and police personnel, and loosely coordinated from Khafji on the Saudi side of the border by a group created by Shaikh Ali Sabah al-Salem al-Sabah, resistance began from the day of the invasion. By late September, the resistance was poised to make the Iraqis pay for their treachery.

> *On October 2, 1990, Athbi Fahad's group carried out one of the most audacious resistance attacks against the Iraqis... though news of the attack barely made it out of Kuwait. Hiding out near Kuwait's airport behind a block of flats, Athbi Fahad, along with two Bedouins and two other men, scanned the Iraqi jets preparing for takeoff. The group was armed with Stinger missiles obtained from the Kuwaiti storage units. As a plane carrying senior Iraqi military personnel ... took off, they hit it with two missiles.... Iraqis closed the airport citing "technical reasons."*[61]

Isolated behind the walls of the compound, embassy officers had only a vague appreciation of the struggle unfolding in the villas and streets of the city around them. Secondhand reports of atrocities being perpetrated against the Kuwaiti population were received and passed on to Washington, as were rumors of neighborhoods organizing to provide essential services and assistance to those in need.[62] Occasionally, documentary evidence was received by fax, such as the report prepared by South Asian parishioners of the mindless destruction and looting by Iraqi troops of the American Mission compound and the Evangelical Church premises.[63] The reality, however, was that the embassy had no "need to know" details that could be compromised if the Iraqis stormed the compound.

Most resistance activity took place out of sight and hearing of the embassy but occasionally the "kampers" had a front row seat. Sabotage and firefights often occurred in the early days in distant neighborhoods:

> *To counter the looting in some areas, the Kuwaitis organized vigilante groups... Leaflets were also distributed, appealing to Kuwaitis not to hoard, to be sparing with electricity and water and to ignore rumours put about by the Iraqis.*[64]

A resistance group in Kaifan was one of the first activated as it became evident that Kuwaitis were determined to resist and strike back.[65] As time passed, this and other resistance cells, became more organized and interconnected. At the same time, the Iraqis were slowly consolidating their control and tightening their grip on the smaller Kuwaiti society. Eventually, they were able to locate and eliminate visible sources of armed resistance, like that in Kaifan. "Passive" resistance, and the quiet circumvention of Iraqi control measures, stood a greater chance of long-term success.

On the night of September 2, one month after the Iraqi invasion, a chorus was heard from rooftops throughout the city, including neighborhoods adjoining the Embassy. It was the sound of Kuwaiti women shouting "Allahu Akbar!" ("God is Greatest") and ululation, the eerie sound with which Bedouin women traditionally cheered their men into battle.[66] The sound of thousands of unamplified voices was spine tingling and impressive; it panicked the Iraqi occupation troops who poured into the streets shouting and firing wildly. Without hand-held radios or night-vision devices, Iraqi officers and NCO's struggled to impose fire discipline over their badly trained and ill-equipped troops. It was a frightening exercise in futility.[67]

The September 2 demonstration, despite its effectiveness, was the last observed from the Embassy grounds. Kuwaiti and other contacts outside informed us that the Iraqi forces were increasingly frustrated and brutal, sparing neither women nor children. Whatever illusions they had entertained that they could enlist elements of the Kuwaiti population to support their objectives had long since dissipated. Baghdad had badly misjudged the politics of their more-open neighbor before the invasion.[68] As a matter of fact, there is little evidence that Baghdad wanted the city of Kuwait and its people, which raised the spectre of "ethnic cleansing" of a population so relatively small.[69] What the Iraqis indisputably valued was the port and unfettered access to the Gulf and the oil resources of Kuwait. It was not difficult, therefore, for Iraqi decision-makers in Baghdad and Kuwait to fall back upon their default tactics—brutality and intimidation with tragic implications not only for the Kuwaiti resistance but the civil population as well. The risks of casual resistance outweighed its benefits.

At the beginning of October, a final, audacious act of resistance took place in the vicinity of the American Embassy. Just before the scheduled opening of communications with Washington, the compound was shaken by a very large explosion at the hotel across the street. The hotel had become home for Iraqi officers, especially the Mukhabarat (secret police), as well as what appeared to be guests from other Arab countries. It also provided a vantage point for observation into the Embassy grounds. Ron Webster, who was on guard duty at the time, recalled:

> ... the Embassy literally shook from an explosion at the... hotel. Some five to seven cars were destroyed by the Kuwaiti resistance bomb or resultant fires as a car bomb in the parking lot ignited.... I was afforded a view of the ... autos as they were towed up Gulf Road.... We were all oddly disappointed that no real damage was done to the hotel ... and no secondary efforts were forthcoming.[70]

The bomb was planted under a covered driveway leading to the lower lobby of the hotel, and heavy black smoke poured forth for several hours. Details of the attack or the resulting casualties were never released, but the prevailing rumor was that the resistance had learned of an important meeting of Iraqi occupation authorities at the hotel and hoped to inflict maximum casualties. Although the hotel and driveway roof were not damaged structurally, the lower entry wiwth its burned-out escalator was closed for the duration of the occupation.[71]

The October bombing was reportedly conducted by a resistance cell subquently identified as "the February 25 Group" (Kuwait's

National Day). Those responsible for the successful counterstrike included Miss Suad Al-Hassan, Thamer Dokar, and Miss Wafa Al-Amer—all Kuwaitis. They were joined by Ashraf Abdullah, of Palestinian origin, and Abdulrahman Ali, an Iraqi resident of Kuwait.[72] They were probably disappointed that the act of resistance had not caught more senior Iraqi officials, but the psychological effects, bringing the struggle to the doorstep of one of Iraq's "most secure" sites, were substantial. Moreover, the incident at the Kuwait International Hotel underlined the extent to which Kuwaiti women and non-Kuwaiti residents were involved in opposition to the occupation.

Among the measures taken by Iraq to tighten their control over resistance activity within Kuwait was the importation of undisciplined Palestinian allies. Iraq had earlier formed a "Popular People's Army of Free Kuwait (PPA)" composed mainly of resident Palestinians to serve as auxillaries and assist in sweeps and searches.[73] The employment of these armed elements severely embarrassed the Iraqis on September 14 when they invaded the French Embassy, reportedly seizing four men inside.[74] Although the Iraqis probably found it prudent to exert more control over the "Popular Army" following that incident, their Palestinian minions continued "to swagger(ed) about the streets of the city, stealing cars and making Kuwaitis miserable." Their behavior was a major factor in shaping Kuwait's decisions on the fate of the Palestinians and Jordanians who remained in Kuwait following liberation.[75]

As Iraqi tactics against the Kuwaiti population became more effective in rooting out resisters, and more brutal in the treatment of civilians, a decision was made in October in both Kafji and Kuwait to downplay direct confrontations with the occupying troops in favor of intelligence collection, financial support for the Kuwaitis under occupation, and other less visible objectives:

> *In October, word went out to the resistance in Kuwait to cease armed resistance activity, in order to prevent more bloodshed or antagonising the Iraqis into carrying out retributive attacks against the Kuwaiti population.*[76]

Most members of the American community in hiding had only incidental contact with the Kuwaiti resistance, except in those instances where its members provided help in the form of resupply or movements to safer locations. Michael Kano was an exception to this generality. Living with Lebanese and Syrian friends who were assisting the Kuwaiti resistance, Kano provided unique insight into the world of the resistance fighters. In late September, for example, "... the Iraqi governor of the province announced that the border with Saudi Arabia would be open to Kuwaitis who wished to leave.... A friend phoned the next day and gave us some distressing news: the Iraqis were arresting all Kuwaiti men over the age of sixteen at the border. It had been a trap."[77]

One of Kano's primary activities was to assist his friends in selling a large stock of perfumes and toiletries that were stored when the invasion occurred. The trade in these commodities was unexpectedly brisk, generating large sums of Iraqi Dinars.[78] The Kuwaiti government in exile and the resistance organizers in Khafji had made an early decision to provide monetary and other support to needy members of the Kuwaiti population subject to the stringencies of the occupation. The large supply of currency amassed by Kano's group provided a ready source of funds for redistribution. The resulting transactions were so substantial that they were having a serious impact on the economy and currency supply in Iraq itself. "This has caused a problem in Baghdad," a contact explained to Kano. "So much cash has come to Kuwait that there is a shortage up there. The army hasn't been paid for two months and state employees get a receipt instead of cash. The government is thinking of printing more money."[79] Within the American community, information circulated widely of organized self-help measures within neighborhoods as economic conditions deteriorated. Local cooperatives (supermarkets), facing dwindling stocks of foodstuffs, resorted to "ladies" days to thwart Iraqi soldiers from buying up produce and other items when they were put on the shelves.

Anecdotes were plentiful as well regarding torture and brutality toward Kuwaiti civilians. Neighborhood schools had been turned into police stations complete with torture facilities; reports reaching the embassy told of torture victims dumped at their homes, or taken to be executed in front of their families who were required to pay for the bullets used to kill them. It was not possible to verify all of these incidents but they were too pervasive and persistent to be pure fabrications. Dr. Shafeeq Ghabra, a respected political scientist was a witness to these events:

> Beginning in September, anywhere from one to five Kuwaitis were executed in front of their houses every day, with their families watching. Abdullah al-Darmi, the owner of a travel agency, was executed for possession of a Kuwaiti flag and a few photographs of the Emir. Another case was that of an elderly director of a Kuwaiti food cooperative, who refused to display one of Saddam's pictures in the cooperative without first consulting his board of directors. Six Kuwaiti doctors were seized from hospitals and executed on charges ranging from hiding valuable equipment to providing medical care for Kuwaiti resistance members.[80]

For those who knew of Saddam Hussein's treatment of his own people, it was difficult to discount these reports.[81] Michael Kano too reported atrocities:

> For the next few months several houses were set afire each day by the Iraqi army. These were homes of suspected resistance members and of those who were found hiding weapons. The inhabitants of these houses were usually shot in front of their neighbors as an object lesson and a reminder.[82]

The Kuwaiti Resistance, which was making an effort to document deaths and casualties attributable to Iraqi troops and police, counted 142 citizens who were received in hospitals through the middle of September.[83] The casualties almost certainly grew substantially after that as the intensity of punitive measures increased, but even that figure was understated. With the Iraqis in control of hospitals and clinics, to seek medical assistance would be to surrender to the enemy. Understaffed and handicapped by the looting of basic equipment and medications, these institutions were no longer the refuge to which Kuwaitis were accustomed. Incubators, dialysis machines, and other advanced equipment had been removed for weeks; even routine care was increasingly problematic. Kano spoke with an exhausted Syrian physician who had stayed to do what he could for his patients. The doctor recalled that he was on duty in the emergency room when a mother came in with her little boy, only a few years old. He was having trouble breathing and the woman was afraid he had inhaled a piece of food at lunch. His windpipe was clear, so obviously it had reached his bronchial passages. "Usually, we have this simple instrument for removing these things and it takes only a few minutes, but the soldiers had taken it." The little boy died in his arms and, shortly thereafter, the helpless doctor returned to Syria.[84]

When the Resistance leadership ordered an end to armed resistance in October 1990, local cells complied. Kano was present when a Kuwaiti resistance leader came to the house of one of his Lebanese friends; his message was blunt:

> *Mike..., we've got to hide all our arms. The Iraqis have been killing dozens of Kuwaitis for each of their soldiers that we kill. We have been instructed to put our guns away for the time being.... We operated from here because there was less chance of them searching a Lebanese house.... We carried out several missions but now we have to stop.*[85]

Morale on the Embassy compound remained surprisingly high as the siege dragged on into its second and third month. As time passed without an Iraqi assault, it began to appear that direct action against the "kampers" was unlikely.[86] All members of the little community had been instructed to contact me immediately if the Iraqis made any move to enter.[87]

The real reason for the good spirits was not that prospects for the future had improved. It was, rather, a widely shared determination to take control of conditions and the environment within the walls. The overall situation was tenuous and beyond our control, but most members of the group were increasingly confident of their autonomy within the space left to us.

The inexorable depletion of fuel for the generator was a grim reality. By dint of experience, the engineers on the compound had calculated a usage factor from the daily soundings with a simple dipstick.[88] By late November, it was estimated that the fuel would run out on or about Christmas Day.

A better appreciation for the consumption factor of food and water was in hand by October, following the departure of those who had accompanied Jesse Jackson and others who were eligible for an evacuation flight. Basic food supplies would last until at least March of the following year, despite the loss of large quantities of frozen items after power supplies were cut.

> *Perishable food stores were centralized.... the eight-hour generator days and, eventually, the three-hour generator days were inadequate to keep food frozen.*[89]

Imaginative efforts were undertaken to save or preserve the turkeys and other items from spoilage. Portions were cooked for immediate consumption and other measures were tried. A "smoke house" was erected of plywood sheets on the children's playground in a vain attempt to produce "turkey jerky." Other turkeys were submerged in cooking oil at the suggestion of a French chef at a local hotel. Nothing, however, was effective in slowing the spoilage in the intense summer heat. Ultimately, there was no alternative but to bury the turkeys in the area behind the ambassador's Residence, resulting in much joking about what future archeologists would make of the mass burial site.[90] Potable water looked as if it would last until the following April. Status reports provided to the Department of State were, if anything, conservative.[91]

Some aspects of life actually improved with the passing of time. A substantial crop of dates was harvested from the two mature palm trees in the Residence garden. The greatest morale booster occurred on October 15:

> *One of the happier days was in late October when an Ohio man, Brownie, dug a water well on the compound. While I remained skeptical, Brownie continued to dig. One morning a small puddle of water appeared in the six-foot-deep hole. I dipped the water out but it reappeared immediately. By that afternoon, the hole was several feet deep and full of clean water. The well was lined with steel drums and an emergency fire pump rigged to pump water. Although nearly inconceivable, the well could yield 150 gallons of water per minute, continuously. Soon after observing officers in*

the hotel across the street had reported to Saddam Hussein that water supplies in the embassy were nearly depleted, we washed all the cars on the compound and refilled the pool. We played in the water like kids with a garden hose on a hot summer day."[92]

The new well was a major development with implications far more important than a boost in morale. There was no capability within the embassy to test the water it produced and, therefore, it was never used for drinking or sanitation. Nevertheless, it permitted the refilling of the swimming pool where water had been evaporating rapidly. Plastic pipe from embassy stores was run to the bathhouse in the Snack Bar area and painted black, to produce warm showers for the first time since August 24. Most important, the additional water supply made it possible to plant vegetables in the garden plot behind the Residence.[93]

El-Miloudi Hamid eagerly took charge of the new garden, more than earning his sobriquet, "Mr. Greenjeans."[94] He could be found there whenever he had a spare moment—planting, weeding, and watering his tender plants. I happily joined him when possible, deriving great satisfaction in coaxing new life from the baked and dessicated soil. Working together on the familiar task of gardening provided a welcome respite from other concerns. El-Miloudi had served in the Moroccan Army before he emigrated to the United States, and was concerned by the activities of Iraqi soldiers on the beach across the street from the Embassy. They appeared to be planting bundles of two kinds at sites along the beach; wires were then run to firing positions some distance away. Was it possible that they were preparing to use binary chemicals? In light of Iraq's history of employing chemical weapons, it was a troubling possibility.[95]

Special attention was accorded to the effort to grow tomatoes and peppers. The grapevine in the garden was long dead and the vines were stripped from the steel frame of the arbor. The structure, with additional framing and plastic sheets, was then used to create a greenhouse.[96] The tomatoes in large pots were progressing well and early crops of greens had been added to the compound's menu by the time the "kampers" left. The produce not only added variety but nutritional balance to the communal diet.[97]

With longer-term sustainability assured, attention turned within the compound to alternative scenarios and challenges. The possibility that the American community held in Kuwait might be permitted to depart by convoy had receded with the passage of time, but it could not be totally discounted. *"After prioritizing cars according to general condition and identifying 'convoy-worthy' candidates, we started cannibalizing the remaining cars. Twelve volt batteries and fans and lights were first priorities."*[98]

Vehicles designated for a convoy were kept fully fueled and serviceable. As confidence grew that the Iraqi forces were reluctant to invade the compound, the "kampers" played gently on the minds of the watchers, lining up cars as if for departure and then returning them to their storage places.

Most ominous to me was the possible shelling or other military operations around the embassy. As it became more likely that the Iraqis would have to be driven out of Kuwait, the need to provide as much security as possible for the inhabitants of the compound grew in priority.[99] After a survey of all buildings, the best site for a bunker was the half-basement of the chancery that had housed the U.S. Information Service offices. The lower portion was below ground level but a row of small windows lined the upper half of the space.

> *The first task was to place sandbags against the windows. The sandbags were canvas mailbags filled with sand from the parking lot. Ambassador Howell wanted to draw as little attention to this work as possible. The younger men, including the ambassador, met in the parking lot in the middle of the night and filled the bags under cover of darkness.*[100]

In three or four nights of "sand pounding," this initial phase was completed.[101]

Under the direction of Wayne Logsdon, the next step was to shore up the ceiling of the large central room that would be the heart of the bunker. The ceiling was a single, large concrete slab, but little was known about internal reinforcement. To create a reinforced column in the center of the room, four huge Mosler safes were manhandled down into the basement and welded together to form a massive base about four and one half feet tall. The remaining space between the top of the safes and the ceiling was filled with heavy steel pipes salvaged from a basketball goal and angle iron from the warehouse. Following a design sketched out by Tony Mireles, Ron Webster welded the parts together, wedging them under the ceiling.[102]

With the basic structure in place, power was run from the small generator to the bunker, providing both 110 and 220 volts capability. Gravity-fed water for drinking and medical requirements was piped from storage tanks through a garden hose inside a steel conduit—to protection it from shelling or shrapnel.[103]

Since access in an emergency would be by an outside staircase at the end of the chancery, the underground stairwell was roofed and reinforced to prevent debris from blocking it.

Wayne Logsdon and Mark Herzberg took charge of stocking and equipping the completed bunker, and spent hours transporting and arranging stored water, food stocks, military MREs (Meals Ready to Eat), flak jackets, helmets, gas masks, batteries, transformers, chemical toilets, stretchers, and medical supplies.[104] A redundant, backup lighting system was fabricated from car parts and small oil lamps made from baby-food jars. The lamps had wicks fabricated from web belts and burned diesel too dirty to be used in the generator. Given sufficient warning of a contingency, the small Honda generator would be positioned just outside the bunker.

The little community on the Embassy compound was briefed on the bunker and the necessity of proceeding there independently should fighting begin during the night when people were dispersed. I served as liaison with Department of State Security and others who would be involved in any operation to come to the assistance of the embassy. Descriptions of the facility and detailed directions were provided; in confidential exchanges over many days, questions about modifications to the building, specifications of reinforced doors, and other obstacles, as well as the precise location of the Americans, were received and answered to prepare for a potential extraction in a "nonpermissive environment." Over a period of several weeks, plans were refined for an operation all hoped would never be necessary.[105]

A powerful sound system which served several functions,

including entertainment, was set up in the snack bar area and was powered by the small Honda generator. While it provided hours of entertainment for the group and Western expatriates hiding around in the immediate vicinity,[106] it was conceived to serve a more serious purpose—providing sound cover for a helicopter-borne rescue mission. Ron Webster, who played a leading part in installing it, explained the concept:

> *As part of our preparations for contingencies, which, in our minds, meant invasion and rescue, the ambassador requested that we provide for some loud noise.... Rising to the occasion, we located two very large speakers with self-contained amplification.... They were wired and secured over the snack bar area, disguised as just another set of boxes on an already cluttered roof. The speakers were attached to an amplifier in the "bunker" for use in case of 'contingencies'. Considerable verbal effort went into an appropriate "selection" for the "jailers" outside—1812 Overture. My personal favorite was the helicopter passages from the* Apocalypse Now *soundtrack.*[107]

With the system in place, the "kampers" began to accustom the Iraqi forces outside to living with the sound it made. Later, they would be treated periodically to the helicopters from "Apocalypse Now" so that the noises from a real incoming rescue force would not startle them.

The embassy parking lot was expansive enough to accomodate several transport helicopters, but a few obstacles—especially a basketball hoop—constituted potential hazards. To cover the action, "some metal fabrication was staged on the lot and, at an appropriate moment, we cut through the base of the goal post crouching behind a van" to obscure the view from the nearby hotel.[108] The goal was left standing but could be collapsed quickly by a single individual. To further confuse those surveilling the compound, the parking lot was regularly inspected for FOD (Foreign Object Debris), damaging small objects that could be kicked up by helicopter rotors.[109]

As time passed, the group in the embassy "staged" very obvious FOD removal exercises, walking across the parking lot with all eyes riveted on the ground, to stimulate among watching Iraqis a periodic heightening and relaxing of tension.

By November, the temperatures fell significantly and the prevailing winds, which had brought the humidity from monsoons in the Indian Ocean to Kuwait, now came from the north—carrying dry, cooler air. Those besieged in the compound began to give thought to foraging for a winter wardrobe. The turn of the seasons was appreciated but also served to remind everyone of how long the siege had lasted and the fact that no end was in sight. Some spirits began to dip as Thanksgiving approached.

Most members of the group welcomed daily tasks and major projects as diversions, but also found a variety of ways to occupy their time. Several were working on novels or science fiction stories, others read or played chess around the pool, some attended interdenominational religious services in the evening, led by Rev. Maurice Graham, and all came to Happy Hour. In addition, communal celebrations and activities brought the entire community together and cemented the ties that bound all.

In the first days of the siege, a precedent was set with a talent show, organized by Charlie Carradine and Raymond Robertson (codeword: "Redwood"), with a cast of "kampers" and sets courtesy of the administrative officers.

> *A truly remarkable repertoire of talent was exhibited, complete with the embassy piano, strobe lights, decorations, and the PA system. It was a splendid night and I'm sure it was a source of bewilderment to the Iraqi hosts outside....*[110]

The high standard set by that performance carried through October, with a gala Halloween celebration. "*A Halloween costume contest was held and some considerable creativity was evident. I'm sure the watchful Iraqi eyes were surprised with the attendees at the pool party: Abe Lincoln, King Saud, Maid Marion, two Caesars, the Pope, the Statue of Liberty, an Army officer in desert fatigues, Harpo Marx and others.*"[111]

A highlight of the competition was the costume created by Tony Mireles, who appeared as "Super Hostage," complete with leotard and cape. Hanging from his belt was a string bag containing several cans of tuna fish, by that time a staple of our diet.

When Thanksgiving rolled around, the enthusiasm of the group was in a trough; a minority openly opposed a celebration. Undeterred, Mimi Logsdon and a few colleagues plunged ahead with planning a special dinner in the Residence dining room. Outright opposition weakened, and by the time of the dinner almost everyone was at the table.[112] That evening, a larger than normal group assembled for a prayer service. Each participant was given five grains of corn and asked to think silently about five things they were thankful for. The exercise seemed to be transformative as most attendees pondered the question. The community came out of Thanksgiving in a better frame of mind; planning for the celebration of Christmas began almost immediately.

For reasons that are still unclear, the Iraqi occupation chose this time to launch a strange initiative. An Iraqi colonel phoned the embassy and DCM Bodine took the call. He indicated that the Iraqis were prepared to provide some food to the embassy and wanted to know what was needed. Barbara told him she must consult with me and would call him back. Both of us suspected that the Iraqis were probing to see how desperate conditions on the compound were. It was decided, therefore, not to disclose our greatest needs. When the DCM contacted the colonel, she asked for fresh fruit, soft drinks, and cigarettes for the smokers. Her reply told the Iraqis exactly nothing—except that the embassy was ready for an extended siege.[113]

The following day, November 30, an Iraqi vehicle drew up to the embassy's front gate and delivered "eighty-nine small bruised apples, forty-five tangerines, eighty oranges, 155 cucumbers, and a case of cigarettes" as well as ten cases of locally bottled sodas.[114] Ron Webster, and others who stepped out of the gate to pick up the delivery, inadvertently allowed the door to close behind them. After a momentary panic that they were locked out of the Embassy, the door was opened from inside, and they hurried back inside with their booty.

And then, with surprising speed, the siege of Embassy Kuwait drew to a conclusion. On a morning in early December that began much as the one hundred that preceded it, groups were gathered around battery-operated radios by the pool to catch the international news. Suddenly, the news reader announced that Saddam

Hussein had decided that all expatriates in Kuwait and Iraq were free to leave. The group, which had survived so long both by their wits and by assuming the worst, was subdued as they listened. They would need more confirmation to believe what they were hearing. When subsequent broadcasts continued to carry the news, their hopes rose.

Later in the day, I confirmed with the State Department Task Force that the report was true. It was agreed that the embassy would run an evacuation flight for American men and any other citizens who wanted to depart in two days. All private citizens and three of the Foreign Service Officers on the compound—Gale Rogers, Mark Herzberg, and Mimi Logsdon—would join the flight. Along with myself, DCM Bodine, Wayne Logsdon, communicators Jeff Jugar (codename: "Jaguar"), and Connie Parrish (codename: "Scorpion") would remain with me for four more days to give all remaining citizens a final opportunity to join the exodus. In Washington, the State Department Spokesman issued the following statement:

> *With the legitimate government of Kuwait temporarily residing in Taif, the principle function of our embassy in Kuwait City has been to work for the safe release of all Americans in Kuwait.*
>
> *If Saddam follows through on his commitment to let all Americans depart from Kuwait, the embassy will have fulfilled its major remaining task. Thus, we expect that Ambassador Howell and his staff to depart after all Americans have departed.*
>
> *Our diplomats will remain accredited to the legitimate government of Kuwait and the embassy will remain open. However, the embassy will temporarily not be staffed because we would then have no business to do with the Iraqi occupation forces.*
>
> *We will expect Iraq to safeguard the premises until the legitimate government of Kuwait and our embassy staff return.*[115]

There was no time for celebration. Almost everyone scrambled to the phones to notify the wider community, prepare the passenger manifest or to gather their few possessions for the trip home. On the morning of December 9, those leaving were ready near the front gate of the compound. It was a bittersweet gathering for many; Jack Rinehart expressed their ambivalence:

> *Ambassador Howell had said on several occasions, 'We are one. If they (Iraqis) come for anyone, we all go.' Saddam threatened at one point to take the nondiplomats out of the compound. Nat was prepared to defend us but now the tables turned. We were leaving the Ambassador and the other diplomats behind. We also knew he would not allow any of us to refuse to leave.*[116]

It began to appear that no one would leave that day; as the time for the aircraft's departure drew near, the Iraqi transport had appeared but the commander of the troops around the embassy had not received orders to let anyone leave the compound.[117] When it turned out that the impasse could not be broken without intervention of a higher level, I hurried across the street to the International Hotel, where senior intelligence officers were quartered. The scene in the reception area was surreal. While I waited for a senior officer to appear, I realized what I had just done and wondered if the Iraqis would hustle me onto the bus or allow me to return to the Embassy. The lower lobby with its escalator was charred and abandoned, the result of the resistance bomb in October. Incongruously, the sound system was playing "If I said you had a beautiful body, would you hold it against me?" When the colonel appeared, he quickly unsnarled the situation, and I returned to the Embassy as the departees filed out and boarded the bus.

John Levins, who was present, recounts these events from the viewpoint of onlookers:

> *Eventually the major was made to undertstand that Saddam had said that the Americans could go. But first, the Ambassador himself had to come out, go over to the International Hotel, and phone an Iraqi MFA official.*
>
> *This little visit by Ambassador Howell to the hotel caused a minor panic in Washington and the embassy. It was the first time he had been off the compound since August. He came out onto the road, spoke to the major, and then strode over to the hotel. Suddenly, the implication of the situation hit the diplomats. The ambassador was off the compound, alone, and in Iraqi custody. The satellite phone generator was fired up, and a message flashed to Washington. There was nothing the diplomats or the State De-*

partment could do other than pray that the Iraqis were acting in good faith....

Fortunately, the Iraqis had no ulterior motives, and so Howell returned to his much relieved subordinates, carrying a small camel whip which the MFA man, who turned up full of apologies, had given him as a gift.[118]

As the group outside the Embassy gate began to carry the baggage to waiting vans for the trip to the airport, John Levins suggested that it would be easier if the vehicles could be brought up to the gate.[119] Focused on getting the evacuees underway with as little delay as possible, I replied it would be quicker just to carry them. Levins winked and mouthed, "It's not what we want to get out, Sir, it's what we want to get in." With a look from others in the party, the intended ploy became clear. Suddenly, the luggage became too heavy to carry the distance to the vehicles.

Howell put on a consumate performance. The soldiers were displeased at having to open the barriers, but obliged. We drove the car around, the diplomats distracted the Iraqis, and we slipped the food and beer into the compound under cover of the outcoming cases. It was one small, final delicious victory.

The next four days until the final evacuation flight on December 13 were extremely busy for the five individuals now alone in the compound. In addition to making sure that every American that could be reached had an opportunity to join the flight, plaques, awards and other significant parts of the post's heritage were gathered and packed for departure; equipment that had been taken from the warehouse over recent months was returned and stowed. The last evening, the group met at the flagpole and hauled down the flag that had flown during the siege, and a larger garrison flag replaced it. To make it more difficult for anyone to remove that flag, the halyards were cut and knotted.[120]

On the morning of December 13, the bus arrived at the Embassy. My final act was to lock the front door of the chancery and twist two electrical wires together; the wires were connected to nothing but might give anyone entering the compound pause. The ride through Kuwait to the airport was sad and depressing. Iraqi troops were digging in for a war, one group having constructed an ineffectual redoubt from glass bricks. Uncollected garbage was smouldering everywhere and the normally pristine landscape was marred by ubiquitous mock-heroic pictures of Saddam Hussein. The airport was little better, largely deserted and stripped of almost everything that could be moved to Iraq. After a brief delay, the bus continued on to Ali Al Salem Airbase which was being used as a bare-bones civilian aiport.

While waiting in Baghdad for the onward flight to Frankfurt on an Iraqi plane, we were surprised to see a figure familiar to both me and Barbara Bodine strolling confidently into the restricted waiting room. Under one arm was tucked a case of beer, and the other clutched box lunches. It was the American Embassy's Kurdish driver.

"How does he do that?" the British ambassador to Baghdad, "Hooky" Walker, asked.[121] No one could answer his query, but the unexpected lunches were consumed with gusto.

After one night in a Frankfurt airport hotel,[122] the embassy group flew on to Washington on an Air Force transport, part of the gigantic airbridge ferrying troops and material to Saudi Arabia as part of the buildup for the liberation of Kuwait. Secretary of State James Baker headed the official welcoming party, which included my wife, at Andrews AFB outside Washington. After a blessedly brief ceremony in the biting December cold, the last of the "kampers," together for so long, dispersed for long-anticipated reunions with family members and friends who had come to greet them.[123]

Six months later, on June 7, 1991, those who had staffed Embassy Kuwait during the 110-day siege came together once again. It was the eve of Washington's tribute to the Armed Forces who had performed so admirably in liberating the Kuwaiti people. The occasion was a discreet awards ceremony at the Department of State, not far from the military parade route. Acting Secretary Lawrence S. Eagleburger[124] captured the moment:

> It so happens that tomorrow, just one block from here, the nation will pay tribute to the men and women of the Armed Forces who

won the great victory in Desert Storm. Let me take nothing away from our splendid military forces: they deserve all the attention and more. But today we acknowledge the contributions of a group of people, mostly Foreign Service officers, who could imagine a parade in their honor only if it was about to come over the wall. They are the men and women of the U.S. embassies in Baghdad and Kuwait.

17

Troubled Dawn

The war to liberate Kuwait from the Iraqi occupation commenced with airstrikes in mid-January 1991, one month after the American Embassy was vacated. The details of military operations by American and coalition forces have been recounted elsewhere and fall outside the scope of this narrative. During the fall of the previous year, the Americans under siege followed the deployment of the Iraqis and the coalition with great interest and, occasionally, unrealistic expectations. Saddam Hussein showed no interest in withdrawing his troops despite a mounting list of United Nations resolutions—which eventually authorized the use of force to dislodge him. Many of the "kampers" worried that their freedom would be won only by military action.

I urged patience. From my service with U.S. Central Command, including a number of massive military exercises, I was familiar with timelines for deployment of American forces to the area. I cautioned that, barring an Iraqi provocation, such as a move against the Embassy, it was unrealistic to expect offensive coalition operations for a minimum of sixty days.[1] As it turned out, the deadline for Iraqi withdrawal set by the UN Security Council was January 15, 1991.

It did not escape the notice of even the civilians on the compound that as the Iraqis deployed to the Saudi border they were uncovering their western flank. At an early poolside breakfast session, Felipe Alayon,[2] who had served with the 82nd Airborne as a young man, voiced the growing consensus of the group: "Pin the Iraqis along the front line and pinch them off from the flank." The famous "Hail Mary" flanking maneuver of the ground war in February thus came as no surprise to the novice strategists in the Embassy.

A number of members of the American community, primarily women married to Kuwaitis, had elected not to join the final two evacuation flights in December, and remained in Kuwait throughout the war. An unknown number of other Americans who were embedded in the local society, like Michael Kano, also chose to see the occupation through to its end. All of them came out of the experience unscathed, although several hundred unfortunate Kuwaitis were picked up and taken to Iraq in their final panicked retreat. Some of them have never been accounted for.[3]

The suffering and trauma experienced by the Kuwaiti people and expatriates alike, as a consequence of Saddam Hussein's aggression and brutality, is difficult to exaggerate. Their deadful experience was not well known to international audiences for most of 1990, however. There were some anecdotal hints that trickled out and the Kuwaiti Resistance made herculean efforts to spread the word, but by and large, the Iraqi effort to shield their crimes from public view succeeded for several months, permitting some in the West, including those who opposed the "liberation" of Kuwait by force of arms, to pretend that a potentially genocidal policy was not being pursued, that Saddam was being "demonized" and that, in any case, Kuwait's heritage and society was not worth defending.

John Levins, who lived through the tragedy, moved about more than most expatriates, and conducted years of reseach and interviews after the liberation, had this to say about elements in the United States who opposed military action almost to H-Hour:

> *Most of these individuals—described in the United States as liberals—were intelligent people of great integrity. They could not be dismissed easily, especially as they were particularly influential. The challenge was thus to turn their views around so that they would support the war. The Kuwaitis never had complete success with this, but with the news of the atrocities and Saddam's weapons programmes, a significant proportion of these individuals came to see war against Iraq as the lesser of two evils.*[4]

This is a charitable characterization of those who, indifferent not only to the fate of average Kuwaitis but their own countrymen and women, did not want to see coalition military action. Certainly, there were no "doves" on the Embassy compound, despite the high probability that some of them might not survive the beginning of hostilities.

Levins was considerably less generous in his appraisal of the performance of the international media during the crisis. It was not, of course, the fault of the media that the Iraqi authorities erected a giant media screen to shroud their behavior and allowed only carefully selected reporters into Iraq and occupied Kuwait. In general, however, whatever the Iraqis decided to put out or allowed to be seen, such as "costumed" Iraqis portraying Kuwaitis demonstrating for unity with Iraq, were broadcast without little explanatory comment. When, in October 1990, word of atrocities committed against Kuwaiti infants and children became known in the West: *"The Iraqis took CNN to Kuwait to film the Al-Adan Hospital which had been especially spruced up for the trip, with babies in incubators."*[5]

He points out that the film crews were not allowed to visit other hospitals or report on anything else in occupied Kuwait. "They (CNN) sold their credibility to the Iraqi propaganda machine and its charades," he concluded.

In fact, the cable network faced a genuine dilemma; serve Iraq's propaganda interests or lose its access to the country. It was much criticized in Kuwait and the United States for what it did not report as much as for what it did air.

The absence of media representatives in Kuwait meant that the atrocities being committed by the Iraqi occupation authorities could continue, for a time, undisclosed. All too frequently, reporters do not seem to realize, whether out of ignorance or indifference, the harm they can do to civilians in dangerous and delicate situations. Caryle Murphy of the Washington Post was the only American reporter in Kuwait when the Iraqi invasion took place and did some good reporting before she departed during the first days of the crisis. She eventually made her way to the embassy where, like all citizens who sought it, she was offered refuge. It soon became obvious, however, that she intended to come and go frequently to file reports, including her observations of conditions on the compound. To safeguard information that would be valuable to the Iraqis, DCM Bodine correctly gave her the choice of remaining on the compound, or departing and not returning. She chose the latter option. As Levins summed up:

> ... like many of her colleagues...Murphy seemed to have little concept of her power to put people at risk. Among other things, she tried to ascertain the number of people in the U.S. Embassy and their status as diplomats or otherwise. The United States did not want the Iraqis to know this in case they had to pass off the civilians and military in the compound as diplomats.[6]

Reporters in the United States were often no less careless. My wife, Margie Howell, was approached by a journalist who had obtained a panoramic photograph of the Embassy compound. He asked that she identify the various structures and point out where the occupants were located. She naturally refused to provide information that would have been of value to Iraqi occupation authorities. Other expatriates, including some who had escaped Kuwait or evaded capture, were not always aware of the need to safeguard details of escape routes, contacts, etc.

The problem with the media is not malice but, rather, that many contemporary reporters lack experience and cultural awareness, the critical context to assess what they are seeing. For the first part of my career, overseas bureaus of the major print media were staffed by seasoned journalists with years of residence in Beirut, Cairo, Athens, and other locations. Some were as knowledgeable about their "beat" as the diplomats with whom they exchanged views.[7] In the wartorn Beirut of the 1970s, there were strong bonds of trust and even friendship. At the same time, the handwriting was on the wall, even then. Television crews flew in and out, taking their pictures without connecting with the culture or people on the ground. On one occasion, the staff of the American embassy in the Lebanese capital observed a crew from a major U.S. television network encouraging the local guards outside to draw fire from a troublesome sniper in a tall building nearby. From inside the embassy, the incident was filmed with an 8mm movie camera; the offending television crew was then informed that, if they didn't leave immediately, the embassy would give the film to competing networks.[8]

A more complete appreciation of the brutality of the Iraqi occupation, as well as the means by which American, British, and other expatriates were able to elude capture for many long weeks, began to come into focus in December when Western residents were released.⁹ Suddenly, reporters, including those at hometown newspapers and stations, had access to a wide selection of evacuees who could provide the kind of "color" and specifics that had been missing since September 1990. Best of all, the anecdotes and commentaries could be connected to real people. Although the harrowing experiences of Kuwaitis and expatriates were difficult to weave into a comprehensive tapestry, they made the victims real and helped increase public understanding of the stakes in the effort of the international coalition to liberate the captive country.

Media reportage ranged from the staid pronouncements of the US government[10] to the more emotional outpourings of private American citizens who were coming to terms with the realization that they survived a lengthy ordeal that could have ended tragically. New details of how many of them were able to hide from searching Iraqis added human texture to what had previously seemed just another Middle East crisis. Dennis and Mary Ann Mosher, to cite one example, disclosed how one American citizen had given himself up when the Iraqis entered his building in order to divert their attention "while other Americans hid in the shower."[11] In relating these stories, a clearer picture began to emerge of the critical role ordinary Kuwaitis and others played in supporting expatriates in hiding: "He (Dennis Mosher) saw Kuwaitis being chased and shot. He also saw them make heroic trips to deliver food to trapped foreigners."[12]

The creation of a widespread and intricate support network—linking American and British fugitives, the American Embassy, the vestiges of the British warden system, the Kuwaiti Resistance, and others like John Levins (Australian) and Eoin MacDoughal (Canadian) who could move about at their own peril—in dire and threatening conditions is one of the most improbable stories of the Iraqi occupation. It is a testament to the indomitable spirit of Kuwaitis and the resilience and ingenuity of the men and women of the American and other foreign communities. Because so many aspects of the networking were diffuse and spontaneous, the Iraqi authorities and secret police had limited success in finding threads that would unravel more than tiny bits of the overall fabric. These same characteristics, on the other hand, make the network and its operation almost impossible to summarize.[13]

One journalist who sought to encapsulate the flood of anecdotes and information that burst forth in December 1990 wrote:

> *Many of the newly freed foreigners last week were adding their own graphic accounts to longstanding rumors of often heroic resistance to the Iraqi Army's brutal occupation. For more than four months, Kuwaitis and other Arabs, acting both individually and a part of organized underground networks, kept hundreds of Americans and other foreigners safe... they provided food, money and safe houses, even forged identity papers and Iraqi visas that a lucky few were able to use to make their escape. Rooted in the mosque, extended families and the divan—informal gatherings of neighborhood men—the underground runs clandestine medical clinics and food depots, even arranges basic services like collecting trash. And with foreign hostages now gone, resistance members are free to concentrate on collecting intelligence or harassing Iraqi troops—a role that will become all the more crucial if and when allied forces finally invade. 'The whole country is networked now, from the 70-year-olds to the young kids,' says Joseph Lammerding, 35, a California engineer freed this month.*[14]

Among the numerous Kuwaiti residents whose activities went beyond protecting expatriates on the run, was Jehan Rajab.[15] During the occupation, she and her son, Nader, hid an American in the nearby home of another son who was in England: "Through a network of Kuwaitis and expatriates, the resourceful Englishwoman was also smuggling tapes and letters detailing Iraqi positions in the surrounding area to the British Ministry of Defense."[16]

The Kuwaitis involved in these humanitarian activities were fully aware of the penalties they risked. Bethen Hanken, an American who was evacuated on one of the embassy flights in September 1990, was even more graphic in her description; "I don't think American people understand how many Kuwaitis put their lives on the line for Americans."[17] Countless acts of courage and kindness assured the survival and well-being of American and other expatriates, as well as Kuwaitis in financial and other difficulties. Regrettably, most will never be known except by those directly involved.

The relationship between Kuwaitis and sympathetic foreign communities was not always a one-way street. Many expatriates were more than eager to share relevant expertise with the Kuwaiti Resistance. Donald Latham, an American engineer from Albuquerque, revealed that a group of Germans were constructing precision timers; "We were teaching them how to use the timers with explosives."[18] Although there is no indication that members of the American or other European communities took part in actual resistance operations, an unknown number of Levantine Arabs (Lebanese, Palestinians, and Syrians) volunteered to the use skills they had developed in strife-torn Beirut to instruct Kuwaitis in urban warfare; several such individuals were associated with resistance strikes against occupation targets.[19]

Despite undeniable hardships and associated terror, the American community survived the occupation unexpectedly well. There was one known death as a result of Iraqi actions (see Chapter 15, supra). Miles Hoffman, an American banker, suffered a gunshot wound in an attempt to escape Iraqi agents invading his residence in Jabriya on September 4, 1990.[20] As the Iraqis burst into his home, Hoffman leapt out a window to reach a nearby apartment. He was shot in the left arm, setting off alarm bells in the embassy and throughout the expatriate community. He was, however, taken to a hospital and given the best available treatment before being moved to Baghdad. The embassy in Kuwait was contacted and FSNs on the embassy staff were permitted to visit him in the hospital before he moved.

The Iraqis were never able to pick up as large a number of American hostages as they wished. A few Americans and others may have found their situations untenable and given themselves up, but intimidation, neighborhood sweeps, and other methods were seldom productive. In an unusual departure, the Iraqis mounted an elaborate deception against the Arab-Americans on the American Embassy compound in late November. "One of the few categories of Western men allowed out of Iraq early," John Levins recalled, "were those who had been born in an Arab country, spoke Arabic, and had an Arabic name."[21] El-Miloudi Hamid ("Mr. Greenjeans") who was born in Morocco, took advantage of this opening to negotiate his way out of the embassy, fully expecting that he would be permitted to return to the United States. Shortly after El-Miloudi's departure, the Iraqi officer with whom he negotiated, phoned and asked by name for two others, Sergio Ado and B. George Saloom.[22] Both were born in the United States and neither spoke Arabic, but the Iraqi contact convinced them that they would be freed. Following agonizing consideration, they accepted the opportunity and were picked up by the Iraqis a day or so later.[23]

Saloom and Ado, it was subsequently learned, were lightly interrogated about people and conditions within the embassy (the Iraqis were particularly interested in knowing code names on the internal radio network) before joining several British men in detention. They were still unaware that they would not be free to depart Iraq. They encountered a local employee of the American Embassy in Baghdad at the airport but were hustled off to the Mansour Melia Hotel, used to receive "Human Shields." Only when they met a surprised El-Miloudi Hamid there did they realize that they had been duped.[24] Fortunately, Saddam Hussein's decision to allow all detained expatriates to depart came a few days later.

Many American residents had proved themselves highly resilient during the dark days of the occupation; the eighty-year heritage of the community would live on. Some of those who departed on the evacuation flights in 1990 decided not to return, as did a portion of those who were outside the country on summer leave when Iraq attacked. However, as many as five hundred Americans, largely women married to Kuwaitis, remained in place through the liberation in February 1991. They had ringside seats for the final paroxysm of gratuitous destruction visited by the Iraqis on the Kuwaiti people and their unfortunate land. On February 17, for example, even as the air-war raged, the occupation authorities inexplicably began a campaign to destroy monuments to Kuwait's history and heritage: "The first to go was the old city gate from the wall that surrounded Old Kuwait City as recently as the 1920s. They used a bulldozer to flatten an artifact which was to the Kuwaitis what the Statue of Liberty is to Americans, or Big Ben is to the British."[25] Similarly, the world-class Kuwaiti Museum, already looted of its Islamic treasures, was burned; a howitzer was set up in the affiliated planetarium to blow holes in the dome. This was wanton destruction of absolutely no military utility. The horrifying spectacle of burning oil wells was the final straw.

The ground war, once it began, was blessedly brief and overwhelming. Military superiority and excellent intelligence made short work of the overbearing but mediocre Iraqi military. On February 12, a coalition missile took out the room in the Kuwaiti communication center that had linked occupation forces and their Baghdad headquarters. "The accuracy was incredible. The destruction was total."[26] Increasingly isolated and facing certain defeat, the Iraqis panicked and were soon in headlong flight for the Iraqi border, pausing only to grab seven hundred Kuwaiti civilians off the streets as hostages. On a subsequent visit to Kuwait, I was taken to see the shambles on the road north where it crests the Mutla' Ridge. It has since been cleaned up, but at the time a long line of bombed and burned-out vehicles—fire engines, milk trucks, and family sedans interspersed with military trucks and tanks—remained as mute rebuke to the evil and overreach of Saddam Hussein and his minions.

Only in retrospect did the symbiotic relationship between the American Embassy and expatriate communities under stress stand out in bold relief. In spite of the limitations on what it was capable of doing for Americans and others in hiding, the embassy had become the major link with the outside world. The small community on the inside had been aware from the outset of the siege that fuel for its communications was limited. As the ordeal wore on, a realization of the fragility of that link became more widespread.[27] In late November, the embassy confronted a looming fuel shortage that no amount of ingenuity and expertise could overcome. Although these difficulties were never discussed over the phone, it was impossible to conceal them completely from the American community and the wardens of other communities, as the frequency and volume of their traffic was progressively reduced.[28]

The limited communications facilitation that the embassy was able to provide had become a vital constant in the otherwise unstable and threatening atmosphere. As it dawned on active and knowledgeable individuals like John Levins, the reality struck hard:

> For Westerners in Kuwait, this was serious. The US Embassy was the only reliable means of secure communication out of Kuwait. The French had left a couple of weeks earlier, and the

> British Embassy had a voice link to Abu Dhabi which could be
> eavesdropped on by the Iraqis, and serviced only the British....[29]

If the problem was generator fuel, the small multinational group of movers and shakers outside wondered whether an alternate electrical source might be run to the embassy? When the possibility was broached cryptically with DCM Bodine, she agreed it was worth exploring, provided Levins and his colleagues did not take undue risks. Mike Pennimann was designated the embassy liaison for the project.[30] The concept which appeared to have the best chance of success involved running an electrical cable from the backyard of one of the residences across a narrow road from the embassy. Several of these houses had been rented for embassy staff and were known to be unoccupied, although Iraqi foragers had occasionally entered them in search of food or loot. A small party actually visited the backyards one night, concealed by the wall that surrounded them. They felt they could find an electrical cable below the ground. The main problem remaining was to run the cable the fifty of more feet, under a roadway, into the compound. Noise and disturbance of the ground would give the project away and thought was given to attempting to drill a horizontal channel several feet below ground under the two walls separating the backyards and the compound. Water pressure seemed the quietest and least disruptive method. Ultimately, the solution had to be abandoned because the reinforced concrete of the compound wall extended down at least six feet. There was no alternative to trying to nurse the remaining generator fuel as long as possible.

Many of the U.S. citizens who had escaped the nightmare of the occupation chose to return as conditions permitted.[31] The American Embassy, now headed by Ambassador "Skip" Gnehm, was reoccupied and functioning immediately after liberation. Those who had occupied the Embassy compound during the siege did not envy their successors the task of undoing the extensive modifications to the electrical and water distribution systems made during the siege.[32] In spite of physical conditions and challenges, however, both the embassy and the larger community soon exhibited signs of recovery and a more normal routine. Maureen Aldakheel, who was a leader of the first group to fly out the previous September, wrote a year later:

> AWL (American Women's League) has gotten under way—we almost managed to do the Bazaar, but there are just not enough people back as vendors with their stuff here to get it all together fast enough. All the AWL material that was over at the International Hotel was looted, so they are having to reinvent the wheel in some cases. BUT there is tremendous enthusiasm and it will work out. They elected a new board two weeks ago, and we had a board meeting last week. None of the previous board members are here, so they really had to start again. Izy Al-Fulaij agreed to be president with several newcomers pitching in on some of the other positions....
>
> Last night (November 9, 1991) was the Marine Ball. I think everybody had a good time—it felt as much a celebration of the end of the fires as it did the classic ball. They had it catered by KIH (Kuwait International Hotel) around the pool with a dance floor built over the baby pool.[33]

The invasion and occupation constituted an existential trauma for Kuwaitis as well as other inhabitants of the small country. Happily, their government possessed the resources to provide critical financial support to those inside Kuwait during the occupation and to repair, restore, and rebuild the country physically following liberation.[34] While the material recovery did not occur quickly enough for many who had suffered anxiety and deprivation under Iraq's control, neither did they experience the prolonged economic distress typical of other societies subject to analogous disasters. Nevertheless, the restoration of infrastructure and services could not erase the severe psychological wounds inflicted by the shock and brutality of Iraq's betrayal. The continued existence and belligerence of Saddam's regime in Baghdad—a constant reminder of what had happened and could happen again—prolonged individual and collective trauma, denying victims the safe environment needed to deal effectively with the posttraumatic situation.[35] Only since the fall of Saddam's regime in 2003 has a necessary precondition for full individual and societal recovery been established.

Kuwait was understandably in the international spotlight during the Iraqi occupation and after liberation. Almost totally absent from Western commentary and analysis, however, was recognition of the deep psychological factors now at work within Kuwaiti society. This omission is perhaps unavoidable because most academics and pundits possess little experience in or empathy with societal trauma. Nevertheless, the resulting analysis is almost entirely mechanistic, as if the trauma had never taken place. Anger, for example, is a universal aspect of the posttraumatic state. Individuals and large groups under extreme and prolonged stress not only harbor deep anger but seek an accessible receptor against which to direct it safely. More often than not, the target is not the cause of their distress but authority figures or even one another.[36] And, thus, the anger and criticism directed by Kuwaitis toward their government following liberation was commonly interpreted solely as a continuation of preinvasion politics rather than a reflection of the inability of the Kuwaiti authorities to relieve the distress as quickly and completely as sufferers wished or outside observers expected.

Liberation, when it came in February 1991, did not and could not, deliver the immediate relief and gratification the traumatized population craved. Ambassador Joseph Twinam, one of the few commentators to consider psychological factors, assumed that serious societal tensions were to be expected among a people "subjected first to the horrors of the Iraqi occupation, then to the devastation of war and malicious Iraqi acts of destruction, and finally to the herculean tasks of reconstruction."[37] Life in liberated Kuwait was not easy during the initial six or more months. In addition to the deliberate desolation caused by retreating Iraqi troops, months of neglect of infrastructure had taken their toll. Hundreds of thousands of landmines remained throughout the country and massive ammunition dumps dotted the landscape, making travel off primary roads hazardous.[38] Six years after liberation, in June 1997, Shaikh Salem al-Sabah, Minister of Defense, summarized the damage inflicted by mines and explosives abandoned by the Iraqis: 1,700 civilians, many of them children, killed and 2,300 injured. Of the large number of explosive ordnance specialists who came from around the world to locate and defuse hazards, dozens died in accidental detonations and a further two hundred suffered injuries.[39]

A thick pall of heavy, oily black smoke from more than seven hundred sabotaged oil wells overhung their world for seven months, blotting out the sun, changing day to night and raising concerns for the health of residents, especially children and the elderly.[40] While there were no instances of starvation and massive imports of bottled water and supplies met basic needs, the newly freed Kuwaitis lived in an environmental disaster zone that magnified discontent.

With the pressure exerted by the Iraqi occupation removed, very real societal tensions and unresolved issues quickly asserted themselves. At the same time, Kuwait faced an unprecedented range of antisocial behaviors incubated during the occupation. During 1991, the Hospital of Psychological Medicine saw 150–180 outpatients per day, described by staff clinical psychologist Dr. Buthayana A. Mughawi, as a noteworthy increase especially given the reduced population.[41] Most of these patients needed not just medication but longer term psychological therapy. Such cases were more than an individual affliction; their inner torments often played themselves out in uncharacteristic public behavior—"fast driving, bouts of anger for trivial things, and general laxity in social behaviour"— viewed as outward manifestations of internalized anger.[42]

Incidents of violence in schools, in the streets, and in the political arena, practically unknown in preinvasion Kuwait, suddenly became common. Social Worker Latifa Al-Rageeb noted that the crime rate increased 48 percent following liberation. Even more troubling, the nature of crime in the country grew more serious, with growing incidents of murder, arson, theft, and possession of weapons.[43] According to one of Kuwait's most capable psychiatrists, the extraordinary number of deaths from single-vehicle highway "accidents" were privately classed as suicides.[44]

Against this backdrop of personal and corporate suffering, Kuwaitis confronted a number of divisive fault lines, including individual and family losses; an inevitable divide between those who had endured the occupation inside Kuwait and others, sometimes within the same family, who were abroad when Iraq invaded; the lingering strain between Sunnis and Shi'as from the period of the Iraq-Iran conflict; and, of course, the issue of those residents, primarily Palestinians and "stateless" residents (bidoons), suspected of collaborating with the Iraqis. The society had scant time to begin to mourn its losses before it was compelled to confront these very concrete issues.[45] With many hundreds of their fellow citizens carried off during the disorganized Iraqi retreat or otherwise unaccounted for, these losses were a source of national, as well as individual and familial, sorrow. Given the country's relatively small population base, almost every Kuwaiti family was touched and traumatized.[46]

The issue of the escape of the amir and senior members of the Kuwaiti government illustrates the interplay between traumatic regression and rational calculation that characterized much of the early popular reaction. In the American Embassy, there was relief that the Iraqi troops had not captured the state leadership.[47] The establishment of a government-in-exile in Saudi Arabia robbed Iraq of the opportunity to create a puppet regime in the country with any pretense to legitimacy, and, thus, simplified the effort to develop a broad consensus within the United Nations regarding the illegality of Baghdad's position. In a sense, the formation of the Kuwaiti government in Taif was a key building block in the process of liberation. To the extent that public opinion of the issue can be gauged, most Kuwaitis understood this consideration intellectually. At the same time, the emotional response to the departure of the leadership among those stranded inside Kuwait was understandably primitive: abandonment by the nation's father figure! It was not always easy to reconcile these conflicting perspectives.[48]

On a political level, the Iraqi effort to destroy the unique Kuwaiti identity, threw into doubt the attitudes and assumptions that had governed the state's approach to its regional environment. The resulting reorientation and adjustment is reflected in analyses by some of the country's leading thinkers. In the words of Prof. Badr Jassim Al-Yacoub, Minister of Information in 1992:

> ...the experience has changed Kuwait and its people.... Kuwait's culture was heavily targeted by the Iraqi forces intent on destroying all symbols of our nationhood. After stealing most of its contents, they set fire to our National Museum. They even burnt to the ground a beautiful "boom," the Al-Muhallab, which was built in 1937 and was one of the finest sail-trading vessels to work out of Kuwait in this century.[49]

Small wonder that anger and a sense of vulnerability was overwhelming among those who had survived the onslaught. Nor were these emotions focused exclusively on the Iraqi perpetrators. Arab regimes who had supported Saddam Hussein's aggression, Pan-Arab movements, Islam, and even their own leaders who did not meet expectations, were targets of their frustration and rage[50]. The picture of a society cut adrift from its recent heritage was echoed by Ahmed Bishara:

The occupation also brought about the demise of many strongly held beliefs and dogmas. Among the affected associations and groups were the Arab nationalist movement, the intellectuals, the political parties, the so-called human rights organizations, and the so-called parliament or pro-democracy movement in the Arab world. We saw them on television. We saw them in the press whenever possible. We heard them all the time on the radio supporting Saddam Hussein. They showed no regard whatsoever for what was happening to the Kuwaiti people, the brutality of the occupation, and the destruction of Kuwait.[51]

Shafeeq Ghabra paints the public mood following liberation in much the same terms. The sustained effort to destroy the independent Kuwaiti state created a "societal vacuum" into which all Kuwaitis were drawn:

Everything Kuwaitis had believed in during the preceding decades regarding Arab nationalism and their Islamic identity suffered a blow. This crisis in belief created the conditions for a further Westernization of Kuwaiti society.[52]

Such a trend was anathema to conservative Islamic elements which mobilized opposition with some success to "moral and behavioral changes" by capitalizing on the credibility the Islamists had gained in opposing the Iraqi occupation and by exploiting remaining alienation among some parts of Kuwaiti society. In this way, liberation provided tinder for future political and ideological struggles.

On the other hand, the Iraqi attack and occupation had the effect of unifying the vast majority of the Kuwaiti people, including those in the "opposition" who put aside their demands for the reinstatement of the National Assembly and other reforms to confront the more immediate threat posed by the common Iraqi enemy. The nation achieved a rare degree of national unity as previously resentful or outlying groups took leading roles to keep the society operating and to organize various forms of resistance.[53] One of Kuwait's leading political observers characterized the situation as follows:

> *Ironically, groups which had become the most politically marginalized in the power structure of the country since 1986—the opposition, the Shiite community, and the commercial class – tended, somehow, to be the most loyal and steadfast in terms of the crisis. The response of the Kuwaitis was both rapid and broad. The Islamic movement, particularly the Social and Heritage Societies, which controlled many of the elected boards of the cooperatives, played a key role in organizing and directing cooperatives.*
>
> *The open Arab secular force, the pan-Arab secular forces, Nasserites, Arab nationalists, Islamic forces, Shiite, the Heritage Society, and the Social Reform Society, all formed the educational, medical, and other voluntary committees. In sum, hundreds of young Kuwaitis volunteered to do what they could to assist. During occupation, these forces were strengthened, and their roles were enhanced.*[54]

In putting aside grievances and aspirations for the duration of the struggle for survival, these elements reaffirmed their loyalty to the amir and the shaikhly form of government, without abandoning their desire for eventual reform within that framework. Participatory government remained an integral part of the Kuwaiti identity. The broadly representative national unity conference held in Jeddah on October 13, 1990 implicitly confirmed that a revised national compact would be considered in the country after liberation.

In one sense, the government and people of Kuwait resumed control of their destiny following liberation, "with the task, and opportunity, of starting over."[55] It could not, however, be regarded as a clean start because the society continued to be influenced by its experiences prior to and under Iraq domination. The occupation experience fundamentally affected the pre-invasion balance among the several components active in political life; "(t)he roles of the local resistance in organizing political and civil disobedience during the invasion created the necessary foundation for changes in the arrangement between state and society in Kuwait."[56] Many Kuwaitis had risen to the occasion under occupation, joining armed and civil resistance and providing essential services. Their contributions in time of national crisis, they felt, entitled them to an enhanced role in the governance of the state. This sense of increased involvement carried over to the election of October 5, 1992:

> *A broad spectrum of the population, including naturalized Kuwaitis and women, participated in the campaign, and many concerned themselves with the debates; it was one of the most inclusive election campaigns in the history of the state.*[57]

The newly reinstalled Kuwaiti government responded to the physical chaos and sociopolitical flux by instituting martial law, with Crown Prince and Prime Minister Shaikh Sa'ad al-Abdallah as governor.[58] The experiment, however, was short-lived and the martial law regime and associated military courts were abolished on June 26, 1991.[59] Nevertheless, it appeared that the Kuwaiti public was more prepared to accord "the authorities significant latitude in cracking down" on domestic violence.[60]

Kuwait had survived the most serious threat in its often troubled history, and was now poised to resume its course. It was perhaps naive to anticipate, as some did in the euphoria of liberation, that so vibrant, outspoken, and (sometimes) a disputatious a people had embarked upon a period of serenity. Nevertheless, Kuwait was indisputably changed by its brush with extinction, especially in its perspective on its regional relationships. Particularly affected were groups reflective of pan-Arab nationalism and Islamic trends. All were chastized for "their prior identification with groups and forces in the larger Arab world that ultimately did not sympathize with Kuwait during the the Iraqi occupation. In reaction, such elements tempered their approach to political and social issues with "a more Kuwaiti flavor."[61]

At least as long as memories of the occupation remained vivid, the trends, movements, and ideologies of the larger Middle East would no longer color thought and actions in Kuwait's political arena as they had previously. And, Kuwait faced the future with a recognized northern border for the first time in its history. The frontier with Iraq was demarcated by a United Nations Commission that included American legal experts following liberation, fulfilling a long-standing Kuwaiti foreign policy objective.[62]

The physical toll exacted on Kuwaitis by Iraq's malicious attack and occupation was extremely heavy, particularly when weighed against a citizen base of well below one million persons. By conservative estimate, about three hundred Kuwaitis died as a "direct result" of the attack, primarily on the first two days when the Kuwaiti armed forces mounted defensive operations and fought an armed withdrawal toward Saudi Arabia.[63] Several thousand Kuwaitis died, were maimed by torture, or disappeared during the seven months of Iraqi control.[64] About seven hundred ordinary Kuwaitis were victims of random kidnapping by the fleeing Iraqi forces, and some have never been accounted for. According to the latest figures compiled by the Kuwaiti Martyrs Bureau, the remains of 469 Kuwaits have been found in mass graves in Iraq and identified by DNA testing; 190 missing persons have not been found and are presumed dead.[65] An unknown number of residences, buildings, and institutions were looted and burned—either in retaliation for acts of resistance or for the demonstration effect on the society. And, even after the aggressors had left, deliberately sabotaged oil well fires continued to consume national wealth and poison the air.[66] Hundreds of thousands of mines and huge munition dumps left in the deserts of Kuwait made travel off of cleared roads hazardous and continued to inflict casualties.

This was the visible legacy with which Kuwaitis faced the future that liberation had won for them. The personal and societal trauma that had been visited on them was no less real, although it could not be seen and was barely acknowledged. Scarcely a single Kuwaiti family had not lost relatives and friends in a tragedy as much personal as national. Kuwait had rebounded from disaster before, but it had never had to face a challenge of this magnitude.

18

Legacy of Pride and Suffering

Within several years after Kuwait's liberation in February 1991, most of the visible damage wrought by the Iraqis was repaired.[1] The veneer of recovery was occasionally interrupted in residential neighborhoods by heavily damaged villas. Some were shelled in firefights when members of the Resistance were located and cornered by occupation forces. Others, especially along the coast and at other strategic locations, had been fortified after the owners were evicted; their windows were filled in with bricks and cinder blocks to create firing positions. Many of the residences that appeared outwardly sound were looted, trashed or burned inside. The renowned national museum, the Dar al-Athar al-Islamiyyah, also lay in ruins; its stolen treasures yet to be recovered from Iraq.[2] Nevertheless, it was still possible for newcomers, including a substantial number of American visitors and residents, to conclude that the months of occupation had not been as devastating as they in fact were.

This delusion was facilitated by widespread unfamiliarity with Kuwait's history and society, as well as the tendency of international media to focus on the military aspects and the experiences of expatriate communities caught up in the occupation (see Chapter 17 supra). American wives of Kuwaitis evacuated to the US and others, among them Kuwaitis studying in American universities,[3] struggled valiantly to counter misinformation disseminated by "instant experts" recruited by the media with little or no qualifications. The National Organization for Women (NOW), for example, adopted a resolution lumping Kuwait and Saudi Arabia together as "despotic monarchies" guilty of practicing "gender apartheid" and therefore not worth defending.[4] After repeated rebuffs by the Los

Angeles office of NOW, a group in Washington was successful in meeting with NOW President Molly Yard, who privately acknowledged that the resolution was a mistake, although the organization never publicly retracted the errors and continued to quote from the original resolution. The damage had been done.

As individuals and a society, Kuwaitis had much reason for satisfaction and pride in their response to the overwhelming force deployed against them by their much more powerful neighbor. They had unanimously refused to accept the occupation and annexation as *faits accompli* when the situation appeared hopeless. They had organized themselves to support the less fortunate of their own people and the expatriate communities living among them. Within the limits of their circumstances, they had resisted the superior Iraqi forces, where possible, at the risk of life and family. And, finally, they had come together as a people unified by a shared sense of Kuwaiti identity and uniqueness. These were powerful assets with which to face the future.

On the negative side of the ledger, the psychological scars of the occupation experience continued to condition the behavior and responses of many Kuwaitis. In a society which had little prior experience with psychological counseling and treatment, the government and medical establishment faced an educational challenge roughly similar to what their ancestors had confronted in promoting inoculations against smallpox.[5]

Nevertheless, the Kuwaiti authorities deserve credit for recognizing the need and creating a supportive infrastructure for residents, Kuwaiti and expatriate alike. Uniquely in the region, the Kuwaiti authorities recognized that something transformative had happened to their people, something that demanded a therapeutic response. Thus, Kuwait public life and politics in the period since liberation reflect a continuing tension between contending hopes, aspirations, and challenges exacerbated by feelings of anger, anxiety, and depression.

Two basic political parameters of Kuwait's public life received decisive confirmation in the darkest hours of the occupation. The National Kuwaiti People's Congress that met in Jeddah October 13–15, 1990, brought together a broadly representative group of approximately 1,300 Kuwaitis to declare their dedication to the liberation of their country. With much of the population under occupation and the remainder widely dispersed, convening such an assemblage was a major undertaking. The effort, however, was well worth it. Putting aside the political and sectarian differences that preoccupied them before the invasion, the delegates reached consensus on the shape of a free Kuwait:

> ... the primary significance of this conference was first and foremost, the genuine recognition that there is a reality to the concept 'Gulf people.' The political and personal tragedy which Kuwait has suffered has brought an awareness of unity which previously existed more at the official level. The conference provided an instructive lesson in that it demonstrated a commitment to democracy concurrent with strong support for the ruling family.[6]

Support for the amiri form of government was reaffirmed, as well as continued development of Kuwait's representative institutions. It was a formula that marginalized the extremes on both wings of the society's habitual political divide.

Kuwait City was retaken by coalition forces, including Kuwaiti units, on February 26, 1991, and the ruler immediately imposed martial law for a period of three months.[7] Predictably, the city was in disorder and lacking many normal services, including an organized police force. While coalition troops had vanquished the occupying army, they were neither prepared nor configured to restore municipal administration or provide immediate security in the chaotic conditions they found there.[8] Those in authority had little appreciation for what they would find once they took control and assessed the situation. They did know that the country was full of weapons and explosives, both those acquired by the resistance and those abandoned by the fleeing Iraqi army. Many were in the hands of loyal Kuwaitis who were not prepared, or psychologically able, to give up the weapons they associated with a sense of security. Others who might be heavily armed could not be determined immediately. Had the Iraqis left behind agents provocateurs or non-Iraqi collaborators to undertake acts of sabotage and sow dissension?[9] It would take time to sort out these questions; martial law, including a nightly curfew[10], were prudent first steps.

By March 3, a day before conditions were judged secure enough for the prime minister to return, the international media, essentially mute for months of Iraqi occupation, found its voice. That same day, for example, the *New York Times* reported that members of the Kuwaiti resistance were in control of the city and had executed "a number" of Iraqi secret police. Kuwaiti soldiers, presumably part of the coalition forces, allegedly cordoned off predominantly Palestinian neighborhoods to search for weapons and individuals who had collaborated in the occupation, arresting several hundred Palestinians and confiscating hundreds of weapons.[11] There was, however, minimal media attention to the Iraqi destruction of effective institutions and the situation of ordinary Kuwaitis and their emotional distress during this chaotic transition.

Without question, incidents and revenge slayings occurred during the early period between the sudden departure of Iraqi occupation forces[12] and the time it took to reestablish an organized police force, court system, and other institutions. It is no apology for these reprehensible acts to note that they are characteristic of almost every collapse of an authoritarian regime, when individuals who previously have been among the hunted suddenly find themselves in a position to strike back. Few specifics came to light, probably because no one in authority was yet in a position to record them. Nonetheless, the Kuwaiti authorities distanced themselves from such behavior. On April 19, responding to an Amnesty International report the previous day, Planning Minister Sulaiman Mutawa acknowledged that Kuwaiti citizens might have abused suspected collaborators during the period immediately following the end of the occupation, but denied that such human rights violations were continuing.[13] Presumably, credible reports of extrajudicial incidents were investigated and prosecuted where confirmed. In December 1993, for instance, a court sentenced Jabar Abdallah Umayri, a former employee of the Interior Ministry, to life in prison for killing a man and his son that he accused of assisting the occupation.[14]

Meanwhile, the newly restored Kuwaiti government faced increasing dissatisfaction with its efforts to resolve practical problems from a Kuwaiti public that had endured the violence and rigors of the occupation and were impatient for a return to more normal conditions.[15] By March 19, criticism of the pace of reconstruction had mounted to a pitch that compelled the cabinet to submit its resignation. Nonetheless, protest demonstrations about the program of recovery continued.[16] Even the announcement of a new cabinet was greeted with further protests.[17] While the impatience of the stressed population was real and understandable, its reaction to the massive and complex task that would confront any regime was demonstrably unrealistic and reflected regression within a deeply traumatized people. It was an early indicator that governing post liberation Kuwait would not be an easy task.

Despite the criticism and demonstrations, Kuwait chipped away steadily at the accumulated problems of the period. The port at Shuaiba was cleared of mines and reopened on March 12, permitting U.S. and other ships carrying water and fuel to land their cargoes.[18] Later that month, banks in Kuwait reopened and new currency, uncompromised by the Iraqis, was issued. An American crew successfully capped the first of an estimated eight hundred damaged and burning oil wells.[19] By June, the petroleum infrastructure was sufficiently repaired to permit the export of the first tanker load.[20]

Restoration of the political life of the nation was a major priority of the Kuwaiti people, who were eager to implement the consensus achieved in Jeddah the previous October. Minister of State Abd al-Rahman al-Awadi promised in March that new elections would take place within six months, once the approximately four hundred thousand Kuwaiti citizens in exile were able to return.[21] In his first formal address to the nation since his return from Saudi Arabia, Amir Jabir al-Ahmad promised elections "during the coming year," and called for a review of the issue of voting rights for women and "second-class" citizens.[22] At the beginning of June, he set the elections for October and called for the National Council, which had been the subject of much contention before the Iraqi invasion, to convene in order to begin preparations.[23] The slippage apparent in these announcements was not well received by many Kuwaitis, already dissatisfied with the speed of physical recovery. The resurrection of the National Council had the unintended effect of reminding the "opposition" of past grievances and reviving the dysfunctional dynamics of the preoccupation period.

***

When the sun rose on a newly freed Kuwait in late February, members of the American community were there, as they had been for every sunrise since the American Mission took up residence eighty years earlier. A new U.S. Ambassador, Edward W. "Skip" Gnehm, formally reoccupied the Embassy compound, unstaffed since December 13 of the previous year, on March 1, 1991.[24] Most American residents, as well as many Kuwaitis, remained in evacuation status abroad, but several hundred American expatriates had never left. They were primarily American wives of Kuwaitis and their dual national children, as well as a tiny contingent of American and European men, such as Michael Kano (see Chapter 17), with deep roots and local support systems. Yet the community, in one sense, had never been more numerous given the tens of thousands of soldiers and Marines of "Desert Storm" who had fought their way into the country.

Firsthand accounts of the experiences of Americans who lived through the two months leading up to liberation are rare. Sandy Shinn was one of those intrepid individuals who remained in Kuwait for the entire occupation. With her husband, Bader al-Baijan[25], and twin teenage daughters, Dina and Dalal, she coped with the dangers and deprivations of that period. Through the last weeks of the occupation, the inhabitants were without running water or municipal electricity, challenges that were met by occupation-hardened residents with ingenuity and cooperation:

> Bader hooked up the generator and ran extensions to neighboring houses. We also shared the water that we had in our swimming pool, although it was just used for washing. The resistance brought us bottled drinking water and so did the American soldiers when they arrived.[26]

The day following Kuwait's liberation the family was surprised by an unexpected visit:

> The Kuwaiti son of a close American friend...had volunteered to join the Kuwaiti army and was liaisoned to the U.S. Marines as

a translator. He arrived at our door in a Humvee with a group of Marines and you can't imagine how happy we were to see them! They were all such wholesome, really nice, clean-cut young men. I remember that they were all from different parts of the United States.[27]

The meal that she and her daughters served the liberators was a sumptuous one by occupation standards: roast chicken with stuffing, mashed potatoes and gravy, topped off with a berry pie. The chicken and other frozen items had been distributed by members of the resistance once the cooperative supermarkets lost electricity. Sandy recalls that the garden was covered with dust from the recent bombing and "oil residue from the hundreds of burning oil wells...." Despite this, the family and their guests happily dined outside, enjoying the special meal and the renewed freedom that accompanied liberation.

By May 1991, the Kuwaiti authorities determined that, irrespective of the unhealthy situation resulting from burning oil wells, they could no longer fend off pressures to allow Kuwaitis and others to begin returning to the country. While many with young children continued to delay out of health concerns, the first returnees began to trickle into the devastated state. American wives of Kuwaitis were among those who were torn by the dilemma of when to come "home." One of the very first to return was Maxine al-Refai, principal of the elementary division of the American School of Kuwait (ASK). She was asked by the American Embassy to assess conditions at the school and the possibility of reopening the school in time for the fall 1991 semester. Along with the principals of the ASK Middle and High Schools, she found both the elementary school campus in Salwa and the upper school campus in Surra in "shambles."[28]

The Salwa campus had been commandeered by the occupying Iraqi forces and, aside from generalized vandalism, was filled with live ammunition and other hazards. Working with great care, Ms. al-Refai sorted through the salvageable books in the library which had been strewn all over the floors. Moving the books to the Surra campus where the elementary school would be located temporaily presented its own challenges: *"At that time we didn't even have any boxes in which to put the books. And there were no labourers around, and no trucks or other transportation."*[29]

The American military came to the rescue. A human chain of soldiers passed armloads of books out of the dangerous structure and salvaged whatever furniture they could find. Military trucks carried the precious loads to Surra, where the furnishings were thoroughly washed down. The school principals worked for a month to save whatever useable equipment and supplies they could, compiling lists of items to order so that school might reopen in September. The small group traveled briefly to the United States and returned in July to prepare for the school year.[30]

Even vivid descriptions of the devastation in Kuwait could not prepare American wives and others for the environmental "hell" into which their flights descended on return.[31] Often their first sight of the country was an afternoon sun blotted out by thick black smoke and vast lakes of oil dotting the desert.

The nightmarish atmosphere dictated significant adjustments of daily routines. Claudia al-Rashoud explained:

> *... once school started again my daily morning ritual was to go out on the roof of our house and check on the black oil pollution clouds which fluctuated according to the wind. If the smoke was too thick I would keep my boys home from school. Otherwise I sent them to school wearing protective face masks. Many other parents did the same. We weren't sure how much difference it made but we were determined to take all conceivable precautions.*[32]

Air purifiers and air conditioning filters were snatched up in local stores as soon as new shipments arrived.

Airborne oil particulates are particularly troublesome, especially when mixed with sand or in conditions of high humidity.[33] For many months, Kuwait was covered in sticky oil residue, deposited in tiny back droplets on everything, especially the white dishdashas worn by Kuwaiti men. Supermarkets carried a special spray to remove spotting on clothing and cars.

Landmines and unexploded ordnance left behind by the Iraqis constituted an even more lethal hazard for civilians in postliberation Kuwait. An explosive ordnance disposal (EOD) specialist provided an indication of the magnitude of the problem in 1992: *"Ten million tons of munitions were used to destroy Hiroshima. It is believed that five hundred million tons of munitions were laid in Kuwait. Many of them are still out there."*[34]

The sounds of numerous EOD teams destroying mines and other explosives became a regular accompaniment to everyday life; particularly loud explosions could still cause inhabitants to flinch. When crossing open ground, they tried to walk in tire tracks, and habitual family visits to the beach or the desert had to be curtailed for a number of years to avoid live explosives concealed by drifting sands.

The abandoned explosives represented more than the detritus of warfare. The Iraqi occupation troops had, for example, mined not simply the beaches and other possible lines of approach by coalition forces, but urban areas and residential neighborhoods as well. When some families returned to Kuwait after May, they discovered armed hand grenades (i.e., with their pins pulled) had been buried in the February mud of their gardens. If there was any doubt that the Iraqi intention was to cause innocent civilian casualties, their motives were confirmed at Entertainment City, an amusement park between the city of Kuwait and Jahra. The location had been extensively mined, including explosives carefully planted beneath the tracks used to move the boats for the jungle ride. The Entertainment City staff reported that five large truckloads of ordnance had been located and removed from the popular attraction.[35]

A particular concern for the authorities, as well as parents and families, was the fact that many of the explosive devices discovered were fashioned from colored plastic and resembled toys. Tragically, a number of unwary children picked them up and were killed or horribly maimed. The danger was so acute that the American Women's League (AWL) organized special presentations by EOD experts designed for American and other children. The attendees were shown and permitted to handle samples of deadly devices that had been deactivated with the strict admonition not to touch similar items encountered outside. They were then asked to repeat the mantra "If I didn't drop it, I won't pick it up!"[36] The presenter, Bill Wilk, an American EOD Quality Assurance Advisor to the Ministry of Defense, noted "I have seen more people killed and wounded here than I did during two and a half years of duty in Viet Nam."[37]

The return of Kuwaitis and Americans was a bittersweet and somber experience. The joy of being reunited with families and close friends was often tempered by sadness as they learned that people they had known well had been killed, tortured, or were still missing.[38] For long months, the effects of burning oil wells and the threat from mines and other explosives constricted their lives and prevented a resumption of normal routines. Nevertheless, there was nowhere else that the former exiles would rather be. As the well fires were extinguished and the skies began to clear and the EOD teams steadily extended areas cleared of hidden ordnance, it became thinkable to consider celebrating the deliverance of their country from its darkest hours. Two events of great significance and poignancy to the Kuwaiti people stand out.

The visit of former President George H. W. Bush in April 1993 provided a welcome interlude of good will amidst the frustrations and angst of the postliberation recovery. Popularly regarded as the liberator of Kuwait, the mood as he arrived by KAC jumbo jet the morning of April 13 was captured by the *Arab Times*, one of Kuwait's English-language dailies: "Welcome home, George and Barbara. We wish you all the best."[39]

At least two hundred thousand Kuwaitis, including school children given the day off, lined the route of the presidential motorcade as it made its way from the airport to the Bayan Palace where the Bushes were accommodated. American and Kuwaiti flags, normally reserved for serving heads of state, adorned the highways and streets. Reuters news agency reported:

> *An adoring Kuwait was in a carnival mood as it played host to Gulf War saviour George Bush. Kuwait City was decked out with paintings and cutouts of the former U.S. President who literally put the country back on the map. Motorists raced through the streets with portraits of Bush and the amir fixed to car roofs. Children released doves and coloured balloons as Bush addressed parliament on Thursday (the second day of the visit).*

In a large city square, hundreds of Kuwaiti men in flowing dishdashas danced with ceremonial swords to the beat of drums and rhythmic clapping reminiscent of long-gone performances in the historic al-Safat.[40]

Kuwait's seven daily newspapers published columns of tributes to the visitors in their pages. Among them was the following sampling culled from various sources:

> *It gives me great honor to heartily welcome George Bush between us. Mr. Bush has a very high place in the hearts and minds of the Kuwaiti people. During his presidency he planned, managed, and executed diplomatic and military battles which ended successfully in the return of our country and our liberty.*
>
> *His efforts are already part of the history of the State of Kuwait, the history of the UN, the history of justice and international cooperation, and the history of his own country. We will remember his favours and we will tell future generations: 'The United States of America has been a real friend for a long time and now it has become a reliable and strategic ally'."* Dr. Abdallah Rashed al-Hajri, Minister of Commerce and Industry.
>
> *George Bush not only liberated Kuwait, but also paves the way for the democratization of our country... He is our hero and the whole country is anxious for him to be here so that we can embrace him. Words alone can never express our real feelings...."* Ahmad al-Baquer, Member of Parliament and Secretary General of the National Assembly.
>
> *Like any Kuwaiti citizen I feel we are all indebted to the thirty-eight countries of the coalition headed by the U.S. under the umbrella of the United Nations. We feel strongly for George Bush because he expressed his feelings on the illegal occupation of Kuwait and as a president of a super power country he became emotionally involved with our cause.*
>
> *Kuwaitis were looking for a savior and found him in George Bush. He saved our country, our dignity, and our place within the international community. We also feel very close to the American people who sent their sons to fight a war to liberate us.* Ms. Badriya al-Awadi, attorney.

The late Dr. Saif Abbas Abdallah, Chairman of the Department of Political Science at Kuwait University, expressed his feelings in poetic form:

> As we, the Kuwaiti people, young and old go out to greet George Bush and his wife, Barbara Bush, we look around us and count our blessings. The Almighty Allah must have been kind to us that in our time of crisis George Bush was there.
>
> For me, every day when I see the clear waters of the Gulf rushing to the free shores, I see George Bush;
>
> When I see mothers visiting the gravesites of their beloved children I know they did not die in vain because George Bush chose that the lives of these martyrs should not go in vain;
>
> When I see a newlywed couple beginning their new lives with renewed hope of raising a new, free generation of Kuwaitis, I see George Bush;
>
> Every morning when I see the beaming smile on the face of my young son who was born during the early hours of the liberation of Kuwait, I see George Bush;
>
> For all these beautiful moments that I live to see, I am thankful for God Almighty that on August 2, 1990, George Bush was there;
>
> From the bottom of our hearts we welcome you Mr. President, and we wish you and Mrs. Bush, happiness always, good health and longevity so that you may visit us again and again. Indeed this is your second home and you have a very special place in our hearts. May God bless you and America.

In the course of his event-packed visit to Kuwait, President Bush was presented with the country's most prestigious decoration, the Mubarak al-Kabir (Mubarak the Great) Medal of Honor. Concluding his remarks at the presentation ceremony, Amir Shaikh Jabir al-Ahmad observed that "... the real decoration which surpasses any tangible expression of gratitude is the love and sincere affection that Kuwaitis harbour for you deep in their hearts."[41] In addition, the former president was awarded an honorary doctorate at Kuwait University before a very enthusiastic audience; mingled freely with Kuwaiti and American guests at a reception at the American Embassy; and reviewed and talked with U.S. troops at Camps

Doha and Jouan, sharing with them the warm appreciation of the Kuwaiti people.⁴²

One of the most significant points of the Bush visit came when he addressed the Kuwaiti National Assembly, the mother of Gulf parliaments.

Paying tribute to Kuwait's parliamentary experience, he took the occasion to encourage continued perfection of participatory government:

> *Your shoulders bear a great responsibility. The world respects this National Assembly. You have taken an important step. You understand that the hard work of governing a free society requires good will and the spirit of cooperation. By doing so, you are setting the foundation of a stronger nation where future generations of Kuwaiti men, women, and children can enjoy the blessings of peace, prosperity, and freedom....*
>
> *My friends, today Americans and Kuwaitis share a special bond. We hold our freedom dear. When Almighty God called on us to defend that principle, we joined hands. And the world joined with us.*⁴³

The Bush visit of 1993 offered an important opportunity for unalloyed enjoyment amid the challenges, that included continued Iraqi provocations in the border regions and a reported Iraqi plot to assassinate the visitor. For George H. W. Bush, the tributes were a vindication of the dark hours and difficult decisions necessitated by Iraq's aggression and occupation. For a brief several days, the Kuwaiti people could push aside the difficult business of physical and emotional recovery to relive the unity and euphoria of liberation. For the peoples of Kuwait and the United States, the celebration was a milestone in their relationship, a confirmation of how far they had come together in less than one hundred years.

The point was driven home shortly after the departure of President Bush when a further 191 American guests, ranging in age from six to seventy-four, arrived in Kuwait to an equally warm welcome. Although they held no high public office, it would be incorrect to characterize them as "ordinary Americans" for they were family members whose loved ones had made the ultimate sacrifice in the process of liberating Kuwait. Their visit was hosted by the American Women's League (AWL) in cooperation with the Kuwaiti government. Crown Prince and Prime Minister Shaikh Sa'd al-Abdallah al-Sabah personally underwrote the visit.[44] Shaikh Sa'd entertained the families at the Shaab Palace and the visitors were received in the homes of Kuwaiti families, many of whom were also grieving losses during the Iraqi occupation.[45]

These encounters between Kuwaiti and American families served a clear therapeutic purpose for both. Dubbed "Desert Peace" by the organizers, the visit was recognized as an important factor in facilitating their common mourning process. Fareed al-Anzi,[46] a Kuwaiti coordinator, spoke of the occasion to express emotions that "had still been kept inside these last two years. This was an opportunity for all of us to let our feelings out." Nancy Ray, an American coordinator, stressed the significance for fellowship across cultural boundaries:

> Until they came here, most American families had no idea how the Kuwaitis felt. Many thought that their loved ones who sacrificed their lives had been forgotten, but now they know that their memory will always live on.
>
> When American mothers and fathers saw grown Kuwaiti men cry, when they heard the story of how their son or daughter had died for Kuwait, they were deeply touched. They have been so impressed with the warmth and sincerity of the Kuwaiti people that now they can really feel that this country deserves to be free.[47]

Among the American guests were William and Marsha Connor, whose son's aircraft went down near Failaka Island during "Desert Storm." They were impressed with the resilience of the Kuwaitis and the rapidity with which they had repaired the physical damage of the occupation and liberation. "In fact, there is hardly any evidence of the war," Mr. Conner observed, "until you start talking to the people and you learn about the emotional damage they have suffered." Marsha Connor was struck by the personal relationships developed in the margins of formal banquets and other program events:

> *There is a six-year-old girl in our group who is here with her mother. Like our son, her father was on the USS Roosevelt and was lost when his plane went down. He is still listed as MIA. At the lunch, the little girl got together with a Kuwaiti girl about her age, whose father was killed by the Iraqis, and they were singing and dancing and playing together like they were dear friends. They are symbolic of our common bond, and they are our future."*[48]

"Desert Peace," with few precedents in the annals of international relations, was replete with special events, including a tree planting at the Embassy compound that withstood the Iraqi effort to strangle it. The most precious tributes to the families of American casualties, following all the hospitality and ceremonies, was the heartfelt outpouring of Kuwaiti affection and solidarity in their shared grief. In speeches, interviews, and letters in local newspapers a wide segment of the society expressed the prevailing view summed up by Eman Hussein al-Qallaf of the Ministry of Communications:

> *Every Kuwaiti welcomes you here in Kuwait, in your country and among your family. Those martyrs, God bless their souls, are alive among us, and are awarded eternal happiness in Paradise. The blood that had been shed never went in vain, those martyrs have spared their valuable lives for the sake of peace and justice. This unity for fighting evil just gave us hope in life once again after being shocked by the barbaric invasion of our so-called brothers and neighbors. No matter what we do, we can never repay your favour back. Thank you so much, dear friends.*[49]

The departure of Iraqi forces from Kuwait did not end Baghdad's threats and provocations against the country. Even while the Kuwaiti authorities were occupied attempting to locate and apprehend Iraqi "sleeper" agents left behind and Saddam's regime was carrying out a bloody campaign to put down an uprising by Iraqi Shi'a in the south, Iraq continued to probe the Kuwaiti frontier. In mid-June, a Kuwaiti border partrol reportedly killed one Iraqi and wounded three others trying to infiltrate Kuwait.[50] Within two years, similar incidents had become more or less routine. In November 1993, a

Kuwaiti surveyor working within the Kuwaiti border recently demarcated by a United Nations commission, killed an Iraqi policeman and wounded a second when they attempted to arrest the six-man survey team.[51] Less than a week later, the Kuwaiti Interior Ministry reported a firefight between Iraqi and Kuwaiti troops at an outpost east of Abdali.[52] On November 15, 1993, a reported 350 Iraqi troops in civilian clothes entered Kuwaiti territory near al-Mazari and fired on a Kuwaiti police post.[53] The following week, approximately five hundred Iraqis crossed the border in the vicinity of Umm Qasr to protest against the demarcation of the frontier by the United Nations.[54] A four-man EOD team locating mines and munitions in the northen desert areas disappeared; they later were found to have been captured by the Iraqis and held in Iraq.[55] Clearly, it was the policy of the Iraqi regime to keep the frontier region on edge. Among the measures taken by the Kuwaitis to stem the flow of infiltrators and smugglers was the construction of a formidable barrier along the entire 215 kilometer frontier. The installation consisted of a deep, wide trench and an electrified fence supported by nineteen Kuwaiti observation posts.[56]

Two factors probably accounted for the crescendo of border violations at this time. First, the Baathist regime, which feared the worst when Kuwait was liberated,[57] had survived and was regaining its footing. Employing the armored forces of the Republican Guard which had been spared by the ceasefire on February 27, 1991, and the armed helicopters that he had been permitted to use for "humanitarian" purposes under the terms of the truce negotiated at Safwan on March 3, 1991, Saddam's army had ruthlessly quashed the Shi'a uprising and other challenges to his rule. Saddam Hussein was beginning to feel confident that he had weathered the "Storm." Secondly, the Iraqi leadership had one eye on what was happening at the time in Kuwait, where an active investigation into an Iraqi plot to assassinate former President George Bush during his April 1993 visit was in progress.[58]

In the afterglow of that visit, reports emerged that the Kuwaiti security services had thwarted an Iraqi plot to assassinate the former president while in Kuwait. A vehicle carrying a number of Iraqi men was found to contain a large volume of sophisticated explosives that were allegedly to be used as car bombs during ceremonies at Kuwait University. On April 26, the Interior Ministry confirmed that it had detained "Iraqi-supported terrorists" but stopped short of verifying press reports that the infiltrators were carrying explosives and had admitted plans to assassinate President Bush.[59] The next day, however, a Ministry of Defense source announced that Kuwait had filed charges against seventeen suspects intending to destabilize Kuwait as part of a plot against the former president, adding that one detainee had confessed to planning to attack him.[60]

The Kuwaitis, who had maintained close working relationships with the FBI and other U.S. security agencies dating to the aircraft hijackings and terrorist incidents in the1980s,[61] naturally briefed and cooperated with American counterparts on a plot involving the former head of state. U.S. officials conceded on May 7 that they had received credible, if not conclusive, evidence that the Iraqi regime had plotted an attempt on the life of George Bush.[62] Several days later, the United States disclosed that they had been given access to the explosives being transported into Kuwait and found the explosive agents and the bomb designs to be consistent with Iraqi devices obtained from previous incidents.[63]

The Kuwaiti government decided that the suspects would be tried in Kuwait rather than be extradited to stand trial in the United States, but nevertheless granted free access to the accused for questioning by the FBI. On May 19, an FBI spokesman said the suspects had confessed to colluding with the Iraqi Intelligence Service (IIS) in the failed assassination attempt.[64] Fourteen individuals charged with conspiracy went to trial on June 4, 1993. During the opening day, Walid Abd al-Hadi Ghazali testified that he had been sent to Kuwait by an IIS agent to carry out the assassination and Raad al-Assadi, the putative leader of the group, claimed not to have known that President Bush was their target until after he was arrested. Other members of the group said they had gone along with the plot out of fear of the IIS. A defense attorney argued that the accused had had insufficient time to consult with their appointed counsel and the trial was continued until June 26.[65] The trial resumed on the appointed day with the testimony of the two accused principals.

The U.S. government announced in early June that it would decide the issue of retaliation only after the end of the trial and determination that the proceedings were deemed fair. By June 27, the Clinton Administration apparently decided that it had learned enough to act. On that day, U.S. Navy vessels launched twenty-three Tomahawk missiles against the Baghdad heaquarters of the IIS in the early hours of the morning to minimize civilian casualties. The objective was not to flatten the building but to render it unusable. According to the *Washington Post* journalists, who were extensively backgrounded:

> Clinton was persuaded to act by three kinds of evidence, a senior intelligence official said.... First, key suspects in the plot confessed to FBI agents in Kuwait. Second, FBI bomb experts painstakingly linked the captured car bomb to previous explosives made in Iraq. Third, unspecified intelligence assessments concluded that Saddam meant seriously the threats he has made against Bush. Other classified intelligence sources supported this analysis, the official said.[66]

American intelligence officials concluded that "key suspects" were recruited by an Iraqi intelligence officer in Basra, but admitted that no direct evidence had yet been found linking the plot to Saddam Hussein personally.[67] As frequently occurs in such cases, several of the accused retracted their confessions once they were in the courtroom, claiming they had been coerced, and set off a contentious debate.[68] In response to the issues raised, extensive internal reviews were conducted within U.S. government agencies[69] confirming the initial conclusion—the Iraqi regime attempted to assassinate former President George H. W. Bush in April 1993.

Iraq's resumption of harrassment operations was of more than passing historical interest as evidence of the incorrigibility of the Baathist regime. By design or not, the provocations and implied threats had important implications for the recovery of traumatized Kuwaitis. The first imperative in treating post-traumatic stress disorder (PTSD) mandates that the victims be removed to a "safe" environment isolated from the source of the trauma. With the Saddam Hussein regime still in power in Iraq and increasingly emboldened to test Kuwaiti defenses, that precondition of recovery could not be established; the pathology of those suffering was prolonged or even exacerbated. As this narrative will discuss, this invisible illness had the capacity to seriously affect individual and corporate behavior and responses in negative ways.[70]

The massive military force the United States and other coalition members had assembled to liberate Kuwait began its withdrawal almost as soon as the guns fell silent. Most of the troops involved in "Desert Storm" could be moved relatively quickly; the armor and material that had required four or more months to reach the theater would require almost as long to withdraw.

As the U.S. and host governments considered the regional situation following Iraq's defeat in Kuwait, it became clear that elements of instability remained at work. Within a short time, the Iraqi regime had put down uprisings by its Shi'a population and remained in power despite overly optimistic assumptions that Saddam Hussein was unlikely to survive his record of damage to his own country, as well as his neighbors. Kuwait, in particular, remained vulnerable because of its location and small size. As early as May 1991, Secretary of Defense Cheney introduced a note of caution. On a visit to Kuwait, he announced that approximately four thousand U.S. troops would remain in the country indefinitely.[71]

The decision made by Cheney, following consultations with his Kuwaiti hosts, reflected an evolution in Kuwait policy brought on by the shock of the Iraqi attack. In postwar circumstances, the leadership overcame its long-held aversion to the presence of foreign troops on their soil. Iraqi behavior confirmed their fears that Baghdad would remain both hostile and dangerous. Within months, Kuwait was ready to institutionalize the new dynamic; on September 4, the Kuwaiti cabinet approved a ten-year defense pact with the United States, permitting the prepositioning in the country of vehicles and equipment, while providing a framework for joint exercises with the Kuwaiti military.[72] This arrangement also suited Washington which had little interest in stationing large numbers of U.S. ground forces in the region.[73] Kuwait and the United States signed the pact in Washington on September 10, 1991; it has since been renewed.[74] Kuwait also signed defense agreements with Britain, France and Russia without provisions for prepositioning.[75]

Over the remaining years of the century, Iraqi behavior, including delays and obstructions in the implementation of the cease-fire agreement, progressively drew the United States and Britain into closer military involvement to force compliance and counter threatening Iraqi maneuvers.[76] In 1992, the United States declared a no-fly zone covering southern Iraq to curb the use of armed helicopters used to massacre Iraq's Shi'a population, and to extend the buffer zone between Iraq and Kuwait. Over the next two years, the Iraqi regime drained the marshes in the south, destroying the way of life the Shi'a "Marsh Arabs" had followed since time immemorial.[77] The United States decided in July 1994 to counter Iraq's growing assertiveness by beefing up its military assets in Kuwait. Military hardware, including tanks, armored personnel carriers, and artillery, was shipped to Kuwait as a permanent contingency arsenal in the country.[78]

The American precaution proved timely when, in October 1994, Iraq began to deploy elements of the elite Republican Guard divisions in the direction of the Kuwaiti border.[79] In response to this action, a sizeable number of U.S. troops was dispatched as a deterrent force.[80] The UN Security Council immediately adopted Resolution 949 of October 15, 1994, condemning "recent military deployments by Iraq in the direction of Kuwait," demanding an immediate withdrawal and full cooperation with UN respresentatives (UNSCOM), and forbidding Iraq to move surface-to-air missiles into the southern no-fly zone. Saddam's menacing move was perhaps a consequence of his frustration with UN sanctions and other pressures to comply with his ceasefire agreement, including the return of stolen Kuwaiti property, account for missing Kuwaitis kidnapped by occupation forces, and cooperate with the destruction of Iraq's weapons of mass destruction. Nevertheless, Saddam soon backed off when confronted, and adopted a more moderate line. In his report in 1995, the UN Secretary General was able to overlook previous Iraqi behavior and conclude:

> *In November 1994, the Government of Iraq took an important step forward by affirming its recognition of the sovereignty, territorial integrity, and political independence of Kuwait. The United Nations Iraq-Kuwait Observation Mission (UNIKOM) has continued to operate within the demilitarized zone established on both sides of the border between Iraq and Kuwait. In December 1994, Iraq formally recognized the international border demarcated by*

the United Nations in 1993. The situation has been calm in the Mission's area of responsibility.[81]

Iraq did not repeat an armored feint in the direction of Kuwait, but the tensions on the frontier continued.[82] A detailed account of U.S. military engagement, which increasingly involved aircraft rather than ground forces, is beyond the scope of this history.[83] A northern no-fly zone was declared to protect Kurdish regions from Baghdad's depredations. Iraq's on-again, off-again cooperation with UN inspectors charged with finding and eliminating Iraqi WMDs began to figure more decisively in military calculations. UN Chief Weapons Inspector Richard Butler, for example, reported on December 15, 1998, that the Iraqi regime was not living up to its promises of cooperation. The next day, the United States and Britain launched four days of intensive air strikes on command centers, missile factories, and airfields with the object of destroying Iraqi weapons stores.[84] Beginning in January 1999 and continuing regularly over succeeding years, American and British warplanes pounded Iraqi targets in the Kurdish north; more than one hundred sorties were flown in 1999 alone.

Kuwaitis prepared to resume parlimentary government against the backdrop of trials of individuals charged with collaboration with the Iraqis during the occupation. The number of accused, especially among Kuwaitis, was small. The Ministry of Justice gave notice in April 1991, while the country was still under martial law, that it intended to hold war crime trials for 628 Iraqis and other nationals in Kuwait's prisons.[85] A few cases were prosecuted the following June with Mankhi al-Shimaari (sic) convicted of joining the Iraqi army and receiving the first death sentence handed down by the martial law court.[86] Fatima Tafla, a Lebanese married to a Kuwaiti, was sentenced to death ten days later.[87] Shortly thereafter, five men and one woman of Palestinian, Kuwaiti, and Lebanese origins received death sentences for working for al-Nidaa, the Iraqi propaganda broadsheet during the occupation. Eight defendants in the proceeding were acquitted and ten others were given ten-year prison terms.[88] At the end of June 1991, however, Crown Prince and Martial Law Administrator Shaikh Sa'd al-Abdallah al-Sabah commuted all twenty-nine of the death sentences passed until that time.[89] A year later, during which martial law was lifted, collaborationist trials resumed in regular courts with the conviction of two Iraqis, Mohsin Shawkhat Tahir and Ghalib Turki, on charges of collaborating with the Iraqi military.[90] Thereafter, the Kuwaiti judicial system seems to have continued to try those accused of committing crimes during the Iraqi occupation, but the proceedings were neither numerous enough or sufficiently dramatic to merit publicity. In May of 2000, however, it was reported that 'Ala' Husayn, a Kuwaiti, was convicted of treason and sentenced to death.[91]

Just as the brutality and atrocities committed by the Iraqis during the occupation seem to have avoided coverage by international media, trials of individuals accused of collaboration in the torment of the Kuwaiti civilian population received scant attention. A search of information about Iraqi war crimes on the Internet is revealing and disturbing. The majority of items turned up are diatribes about U.S. "war crimes" against the aggressor—from flaky accusations by Ramsey Clarke and others suggesting that the Iraqi military personnel and looters killed on the "Road of Death" were attempting to comply with UN Security Council resolutions rather than constituting an armed mob driven out by coalition forces—to a bizarre resurrection in 2011 by Presidential candidate Ron Paul of the canard that the United States tricked Saddam Hussein into attacking Kuwait. It is an immensely sobering exercise in twisted reasoning and misinformation. With "friends" like these, who needs enemies!

In spite of pressures to restore the National Assembly and the country's dogged pursuit of effective representative government, the cabinet did not set assembly elections before October 1992.[92] On October 5, 278 candidates vied for fifty assembly seats in the first parliamentary election since 1986.[93] With over 80 percent of those eligible to vote participating in most districts, opposition candidates won between thirty and thirty-five of the seats. The new National Assembly began its session on October 20 with Shaikh Sa'd al-Abdallah in the familiar role of prime minister.[94]

In practice, the restored parliamentary system would prove to be more a continuation of the politics of contention and obstruction than the brave new beginning conceived in the depths of the occupation experience. Much of the goodwill and empathy engendered by the shared national tragedy had been dissipated by that time; Kuwait's parliamentary experience had always been about the distribution of power and influence. Very quickly, the opposition began to delineate issues it would pursue, such as a demand that the roles of crown prince and prime minister be separated. A running theme of the conservative Islamist opposition became the insistence on segregating males and females in the classrooms, libraries, and cafeterias at Kuwait University. The Assembly defeated a bill to this effect in December 1994[95] but passed a similar bill in July 1996.[96] Much of the energy of the opposition appeared to be absorbed in such marginal special-interest issues, perhaps as part of a strategy for discomforting the government. The significant turnover of parliamentarians from election to election seemed to indicate that the general electorate was unimpressed by their performance.

The 1992 Assembly, nevertheless, lasted until the end of its term. New elections, in which about 75 percent of the electorate voted, were held on October 7, 1996.[97] Preliminary analyses suggested that government supporters had gained seats at the expense of the Islamist bloc. Despite these optimistic predictions, however, relations between the government and the Assembly again proved unproductive. The Islamic bloc remained strong enough to challenge the cabinet on issues of interest to them. Their preferred tactic, which has become familiar, was to target individual ministers in an effort to force their resignation. The object of their attention at this period was the Information Minister, Shaikh Saud Nasir al-Sabah.[98]

On March 16, 1998, the amir accepted the resignation of the cabinet to short-circuit a building parliamentery fight between loyalists and Islamist members over a no-confidence vote directed at the Information Minister. Shaikh Sa'd al-Abdallah was reappointed Prime Minister with instructions to form a new cabinet.[99] The new cabinet was soon caught up in a renewed struggle with the opposition, this time over an attempt to question the Interior Minister Shaikh Mohammad Khaled al-Sabah about drug traffic and human rights. The cabinet boycotted the parliamentary session in June 1998 over the issue.[100] The stalemate was complete.

The amir dissolved the National Assembly on May 4, 1999, on

the basis of the political deadlock. This was the third dissolution since 1963, but, in contrast to the two previous occasions, he called for new elections within the two-month period specified by the constitution.[101] He took advantage of the period between assemblies to issue numerous amiri decrees, including one granting women in Kuwait full political rights. Support for women's suffrage was not a sudden conversion for Amir Jabir al-Ahmad:

> *Numerous statements by the amir and the crown prince have put the family on the 'right,' or pro-democracy, side of the issue, implicitly putting the National Assembly on the 'wrong' side, given the vote against women's rights by the 1981 parliament. ... In 1992, the secular opposition challenged the amir's right to change the law unilaterally, despite the risk that this might alienate women and their supporters.*[102]

Assembly elections were conducted on July 2, 1999. Circumstantial evidence lent credibility to the assessment that the electorate voted in part against the chronic wrangling between the government and the parliamentarians. Less than one-half of incumbents were reelected, leading Kuwaiti analysts to conclude that the electorate had voted out of dissatisfaction with both the administration and the legislature.[103]

Shortly after the new Assembly was seated, Prime Minister Shaikh Sa'd called upon the parliamentarians to approve the more than sixty amiri decrees that had been issued between sittings, foremost among them was women's suffrage.[104]

There was some support for the suffrage amendment among moderates and liberals in the Assembly, but they showed a proprietary reluctance to achieve the objective through ratification of the amiri decree. Supporters within the legislature, therefore, decided to garner the credit for themselves by introducing a bill in the assembly.[105] A vote on the measure was first postponed on November 9 and then taken on November 23.[106] The bill was defeated and was placed before the house once again a week later. Although the numbers of supporters was greater on the second vote, they fell short by one vote of the thirty-three affirmatives required for measures with constitutional implications.[107] The parliament's failure to act on this issue of growing salience was emblematic of the ineffectiveness of Kuwait's parliamentary system as the twentieth century drew to a close.[108]

An historic era for Kuwait and American residents also ended in 1996 when the compound that had housed the U.S. Embassy since Kuwait's independence was abandoned. After liberation, there were no serious efforts to extend the lease on the property. Instead, a new and elaborate Embassy compound was contructed inland in Mishrif through the generosity of the Kuwaiti Government. On March 23, 1996, the new Embassy was dedicated with the participation of the prime minister, former President George H. W. Bush, and Ambassador Ryan Crocker.[109] This rite of passage was viewed with mixed feelings by generations of Foreign Service personnel who served on the old site, both because the move broke the longstanding linkage with the waters of the Gulf and because the formidable security barriers built into the new facility significantly compromised interaction with the American community and Kuwaitis.[110]

Like the new embassy, the American community at the end of the millenium was larger, firmly planted, and expansive—as befitted the wide range of areas of Kuwaiti-American cooperation. The military presence was substantial, the U.S. Army Corps of Engineers oversaw many of the projects associated with reconstruction, and private American companies such as Bechtel, TCOM, and the oil industry benefitted from preferences in contracting for goods and services.[111] The contrast with the tiny group of Americans who took up residence in Kuwait at the beginning of the century could not have been more stark. And yet, the debt of the contemporary community to the patient and involved service of the missionaries and other early pioneers in winning the trust and respect of the Kuwaiti people was immense. What they lacked in numbers, they more than made up in their immersion in Kuwaiti society and success in turning "strangers" into friends.

19

Friends and Allies

Kuwait celebrated the twentieth anniversary of its deliverance from the Iraqi occupation in February 2011. While the residents weathered further difficulties during the 2003 invasion of Iraq to achieve it, their nemesis, Saddam Hussein, was overthrown, tried, and executed. They had survived him and the continuing threat he represented. A cardinal condition for fuller recovery was achieved. The invisible effects of the trauma he had inflicted on Kuwaiti society, however, still affected individual Kuwaitis, as well as their corporate behavior, in significant ways.

According to Dr. Abdallah al-Hammadi, a Kuwaiti psychiatrist working with patients suffering from PTSD, at least 20 percent of the population still exhibited symptoms of the condition in 2012.[1] The condition was particularly acute among survivors of torture. In general, however, it may affect anyone who "experienced intense fear, stress, helplessness, or horror."[2] Symptoms range from severe anxiety, depression, irritability, and aggression to emotional withdrawal, loss of memory, and the sense of a foreshortened future. Untreated, this can become a chronic disabling condition.

Dr. al-Hammadi attributes the increase in societal problems, such as violence or divorces, to the effects of PTSD. He notes that the disease can also affect the patient's work, leading to a rise in the rate of early retirement: "Since Kuwait is a small country and we are losing a significant number of people who were trained in specific jobs" the quality of the national workforce is affected. Experience has shown that individuals with PTSD often suffer other health problems, such as diabetes, high blood pressure, and substance abuse. "Although the consumption of alcohol is not usual in our society," Dr. al-Hammadi explained, "it is significant and proven that those with PTSD are more in contact with alcohol and with drugs."

The Kuwaiti authorities showed unusually good judgement in establishing programs to deal with the physical and psychological effects of the occupation experience from the early days after liberation. A number of new agencies, such as the Social Development Office within the Amiri Diwan (amir's office), were created to identify the residual effects on the society and to design programs to deal with them. In 1993, when the al-Riggaee Center[3] completed its initial screening for instances of PTSD, it was determined that the problem was more widespread than originally anticipated.[4] A major difficulty facing the Kuwaiti medical community is the reluctance of many sufferers to acknowledge their condition. According to Dr. al-Hammadi:

> *Many don't want to come for treatment simply because it involves recognition of the traumatic issue that is causing them so much pain and distress. When someone is suffering from PTSD, that person seeks to avoid thoughts, feelings, or conversations that arouse recollections of the trauma.*[5]

Others recoil because of the social stigma involved and fear of consequences in their life and work.

Due to delayed onset and dormant PTSD among untreated individuals, the incidence of chronic symptoms seems to have increased with the passage of time. Successful treatment does not involve erasing the trauma but assists the patient to confront the experience and integrate it into his or her life narrative. The late Dr. Jaafar Behbehani, one of Kuwait's leading psychologists, noted that some individuals make a "spontaneous recovery"[6] but others go on to develop debilitating symptoms.[7] A peculiar complication in Kuwaiti efforts to deal effectively with this national epidemic was, at least until 2003, the continued existence of the Saddam Hussein regime and its continuous provocations:

> *...every time Saddam Hussein begins one of his frequent bouts of saber-rattling, the population suffers from worry, fear, and*

insecurity. The painful and intrusive memories are made to recur time and time again.[8]

While individuals may be in denial regarding the psychological damage inflicted by the Iraqi occupation, the Kuwaiti government is in no doubt. An elaborate support infrastructure created in 1991 continues to minister to Kuwaitis and others who suffered harm and loss. A centerpiece of this comprehensive system is the Martyrs Bureau established by Amiri Decree in August 1991.[9] When it opened, the bureau identified 191 martyrs killed by Iraqi forces; today it serves the families of 1,332 individuals, defined as "anyone who gave his or her life for Kuwait, irrespective of nationality...." Almost 250 of the families receiving benefits include Indians, Iranians, Egyptians, Lebanese, Bahrainis, Saudis, Omanis, Jordanians, and bidoon (stateless). There are even a few Iraqis "who were living in Kuwait at the time of the invasion and fought against Saddam Hussein's regime."

The number of confirmed "martyrs" has grown over the years as bodies of the missing were found and identified. After the collapse of the Saddam Hussein regime in 2003 it became possible to search for the hundreds of civilian men, women, and children[10] who were seized by the fleeing Iraqi Army and taken to Iraq. None were found alive, but the remains of 469 Kuwaitis categorized as "missing" were discovered in mass graves and identified by DNA testing. At the bureau's information center in the suburb of Yarmouk, there are three large photo albums containing photographs of torture victims of both sexes and all ages. Used for documentation purposes and to support claims with the UN's compensation bureau, these gruesome exhibits are now locked away. Nevertheless, the bureau makes every effort to keep the memory of those who made the ultimate sacrifice alive through outreach programs and a museum open to the public. One wall in the museum is covered with small illuminated photographs of all martyrs above the Kuwaiti skyline. "They are our brave martyrs," Public Relations Manager Nabil al-Baijan explains. "They will forever shine like bright stars over Kuwait, and we will never forget them."

The Martyrs Bureau, headed by Ms. Fatima al-Ameer, the general manager, has seventy-five fulltime employees and more than

150 volunteers. It offers a comprehensive program of support and services—recreational, psychological, educational, legal, financial, religious, and social welfare—to the families of the deceased free of charge. The menu is constantly evolving to meet changing needs; in recent years, for example, a new health care program for those over the age of sixty was added to deal with the needs of aging beneficiaries.

Kuwait has made a major investment of talent and finances to deal with the trauma of the occupation experience. As noted, however, there is a limit to what government programs can accomplish, even with the best of intentions, for individuals who cannot or will not acknowledge their PTSD-related disabilities. While it is not possible to quantify the extent of dysfunction within the greater society, it appears to have at least some effect on public life and attitudes—demonstrated by indecisiveness, heightened anger, violence, and risk aversion. Without probing the underlying causes of Kuwait's malaise, the chairman of the Political Science Department at Kuwait University, Professor Abdallah al-Shayji, has accurately described the result:

> ... (T)his endless bickering between the cabinet and a determined parliament has derailed Kuwait's ambitious plans for development and becoming a major regional financial and services hub.... The endless bickering and continuous conflicts, which keep coming like waves, have taken their toll on the psyches of Kuwaitis.... This Byzantine politics has beseiged and brought Kuwait's political system to a screeching halt."[11]

On January 15, 2006, Amir Shaikh Jabir al-Ahmad al-Sabah died in Kuwait. He had ruled for nearly thirty turbulent years, including his country's gravest period during the Iraqi occupation.[12] His passing was deeply felt among Kuwaitis for whom it represented a break in the continuity he had epitomized for so long. Thousands of them pressed into the Sulaibikhat cemetery where he was buried, as tradition dictated, in a simple, unmarked grave.[13]

Crown Prince Sa'd al-Abdallah al-Sabah was named to succeed hum, despite deep concerns about the state of his health.[14] The Cabinet resolved these concerns within a week, declaring Shaikh Sa'd too ill to rule on January 23 and asking the National Assembly to remove him from power.[15] Kuwait was spared a possibly contentious succession crisis when it nominated Shaikh Sabah al-Ahmad al-Sabah, a brother of the deceased amir, who had replaced Shaikh Sa'd as Prime Minister, to be the new amir on January 29. But it bought an easy succession at a price.

Shaikh Sabah al-Ahmad was a plausible, even logical, choice. By selecting him, the Assembly opted for a conservative solution. Shaikh Sabah is a highly experienced figure and had been the world's longest serving minister of foreign affairs before becoming prime minister. He was, however, only about two years younger than his brother. Unlike other Gulf states which had already transitioned to a younger generation of rulers, Kuwait kicked that challenge down the road. Likewise, incapacity of Shaikh Sa'd had the effect of breaking the tradition of alternating, in senior positions, members of the two main lines of the al-Sabah family. The takeover was sealed when the new amir promoted his half-brother, Shaikh Nawwaf al-Ahmad al-Sabah from interior minister to crown prince, thus locking the al-Salem out of the next round of leadership changes. Only time will tell what effect this narrowing of the support base within the family may have.

By separate decree, Amir Sabah al-Ahmad appointed his nephew, Shaikh Nasir Mohammad al-Ahmad al-Sabah, as prime minister.[16] The separation of the positions of crown prince and prime minister responded to an issue that had been raised by the "opposition" and probably smoothed the way for a majority in the Assembly to approve the new crown prince.[17] The stage was thus set for future rivalries within the ruling family and, as Ghanim al-Najjar observed: *"Past experience shows that differences between ruling family members have proved to be helpful to enhancing democratic processes, and not the other way around."*[18]

For the third time in twenty-five years, the winds of war swirled around Kuwait and its inhabitants in early 2003. On March 20, 2003, the United States, Britain and smaller coalition partners launched "Operation Iraqi Freedom," the invasion of Saddam Hussein's Iraq. Kuwaitis were ambivalent about the implications of another massive military conflict, but, on balance, had decided that they would never have security and peace of mind as long as Saddam ruled Baghdad. In the context of increasing military cooperation with the United States, the small country opened up its territory and facilities to support the buildup of allied forces and the logistics train required to support operations in Iraq.[19] In the buildup before the war, Kuwait made "a full 60 percent of its total land mass" available to coalition forces for this purpose.[20] Access to and through Kuwait was critical to the ability of the United States and its allies to pursue their offensive against the Iraqi regime and to sustain their presence in that country for almost eight years.[21] In December, 2011, the last American combat forces in Iraq conducted an orderly withdrawal through a Kuwaiti border crossing.

Unlike the Iraqi aggression in August 1990, the 2003 conflict did not come as a surprise. During the weeks before March, expatriates and others in Kuwait had time to consider their situation and leave the country; many took advantage of this opportunity. The U.S. Embassy travel advisory of March 16, 2003 encouraged American citizens to evacuate:

> *On March 16, the Department of State ordered all family members and non-emergency personnel to depart the country as a result of a deteriorating security situation in the region. U.S. consular personnel remain available to provide emergency information and services to American citizens....*
>
> *U.S. citizens who remain in Kuwait despite this Travel Warning are encouraged to register at the consular section of the U.S. Embassy and enroll (sic) in the Embassy's warden system (emergency alert network) in order to obtain updated information on travel and security in Kuwait. Please note that although commercial air service is currently available, there remains the possibility of commercial flight disruptions should there be military action in Iraq. In the event of military action in Iraq, there is a risk that Iraq or terrorist organizations may use chemical and/or biological materials which could affect the region. Americans in Kuwait should exercise caution and take prudent measures to maintain their security. These measures include being vigilantly aware of their surroundings, avoiding crowds and demonstrations, keeping a low profile, varying times and routes for all required travel, and ensuring travel documents are current.*[22]

As the conflict in Iraq unfolded, the embassy continued to update its advisories in Kuwait as well as other Middle Eastern states. On March 20, a "Worldwide Caution" was released counseling American citizens to take precautions.[23] Most expatriates and some Kuwaitis had heeded the embassy's recommendation to evacuate over the days and weeks before the attack on Iraq commenced. There was a grand scramble for available seats on regularly scheduled planes leaving Kuwait, and it was frequently necessary to make several attempts to depart, especially once the military action began. One Kuwaiti-American family attempted to fly out three times "just before the war broke out" and was frustrated every time by flight cancellations. The last time, the first morning of the war, "... they were on the plane when the air raid sirens went off, and they were told to disembark." By the time the passengers had gathered their belongings and were leaving the plane, the "all-clear" was sounded. The flight was cancelled nonetheless, and the family returned home.[24]

Most of the Americans remaining in place during the conflict were veterans of the Iraqi occupation of 1990–91, although few of their children had vivid memories of that nightmare. As a consequence, they required little coaching regarding survival under dangerous circumstances. In any case, before the beginning of the war, the Ministry of Information distributed a "Safety Guide for Emergency" to every household in the country. Printed in Arabic and English, the pamphlet used cartoons to convey frightening guidance in the least alarming way possible. Included were types of sirens, shelter construction, what to do in case of fire or chemical attack, how to fit gas masks, and the elements of first aid. The message was so effective that it led to humorous incidents as people digested the warnings. One Kuwaiti lady shopping in a supermarket when the sirens first sounded threw herself face down on the floor and covered her face with her arms. When the "all-clear" came, she looked up to find she had attracted a curious crowd, mainly Egyptian workers, standing in a circle looking down at her.[25]

A major difference was that in 2003 Kuwait was the target of Iraqi missiles.[26] The remnants of the American community and their families went about the business of preparing themselves to the extent they were able for whatever was in store for them:

> *Just yesterday my mom & I did the last grocery shopping & stocked up on some more canned goods & nonperishable food items. We already had extra water, batteries, flashlights, etc. For the last few days we've been taping some of the windows and sealing them with plastic sheeting. We were advised to prepare safe rooms both for conventional and bio/chemical weapon attacks, so we secured all the basement, for conventional and then did an upper floor room with bathroom for bio/chemical. They say that gas/chemical weapons are heavier than air, so they sink, so in that case you should go to an upstairs room. The problem is, when the sirens go off, no one knows what kind of attack it is, but since there has been no evidence of any chemical warheads used so far, we've been going to the basement.*[27]

Although chemical/biological warheads were never employed, the visible preparations for such a contingency added to the ominous atmosphere in wartime Kuwait. Kuwaiti Special Forces had dug in along major roads and highways and supported police units manning checkpoints. Special German and Czech chemical/biologicial vehicles roved Kuwaiti neighborhoods sniffing for trace elements; in case of an incident, the units were equipped to set up treatment stations for victims. At the Radisson SAS Hotel, entry was through a small side entry; the main doors were locked and sealed with plastic sheeting and duct tape. A "decontamination unit" was set up in front of the hotel. The numerous foreign journalists who had flocked to the area were seen all over town with gas masks always strapped to their belts. Kuwait was on alert and on edge.[28]

One American who remained in place was Jane Hassounah, a longtime resident and teacher at the American International School (AIS). Although most schools had closed well before the emergency, she and the remaining staff returned to make certain the seniors could complete the requirements for graduation. One day the maintenance man ran in shouting "Evacuate! Evacuate! Bomb! Bomb!" With others she organized the exit of the students to an area being cordoned off by Kuwaiti Special Forces. A search revealed that the bomb alert had been a false alarm.[29] On the last day of school, reporters converged on the campus in search of a story. What they saw was children coming in from recess with one little girl crying as a result of a schoolyard altercation with classmates. The film was reportedly shown on American television, with dramatic music, as if it was somehow related to the approaching war.[30] If the anxiety affecting children was not visible to eager reporters, it was nonetheless real. Mrs. Hassounah recalled saying goodbye to one of her students, adding "I'll see you after the break." The boy replied: "Yes, Mrs. Hassounah, if I'm still alive!"[31]

With talk and warnings of missiles and suicide bombings, nerves were stretched taut even among the most experienced of Kuwaiti residents. Jane Hassounah herself experienced a tragicomical episode one early evening as she walked her dog. A Kuwaiti man standing nearby said to her "Excuse me, madam, but I am going to make a big boom." Distressed thoughts passed through her mind as she tried to pull the recalcitrant pet along. It was at that instant that she noticed two young children nearby eagerly waiting for their father to set off some fireworks. He waited patiently until she and her dog had cleared the area before treating the children to a small fireworks show in their garden.[32]

U.S. Embassy communication with the American community sought to provide reliable information about Iraqi missile attacks which could often be heard throughout the city. On March 20, Consul Sean Murphy reported that:

> ... the Iraqi regime has fired several missiles at Kuwait during the course of the day. All missiles have fallen north of Kuwait City and none have impacted populated areas; no chemical or biological agents have been detected. We are unaware of any casualties or property damage.[33]

The Iraqi missile barrage continued and, four days later, Consul Murphy confirmed that some of them had begun to creep closer to populated areas of the city: "*The Iraqi regime has fired missiles at Kuwait during the past 48 hours. No chemical or biological agents have been detected.... A missile that landed in the water near Fahaheel, south of Kuwait City, on March 20, caused minor property damage.*"[34]

Later that month, one of the last missiles the Iraqis were able to fire scored a hit on the Souq Sharq, a seafront shopping center favored by American families for an outdoor breakfast or lunch overlooking the Gulf. Fortunately, the missile impacted after 1:30 a.m. when the mall was largely deserted, although the explosion rattled windows in many residential neighborhoods. A pier and parts of the shopping center were damaged and two people were reportedly injured.[35]

The Iraqi regime employed a range of missiles in its ill-targeted and largely ineffective campaign. Aside from the familiar Silkworms, Soviet-origin SCUDs and indigenous "Ababeel" and "Al-Samoud" missiles with longer ranges were hurled at Kuwait. The latter varieties had been ordered destroyed by the United Nations and were not supposed to be in Iraq's inventory.[36] American forces in Kuwait deployed Patriot missile systems with some effect to shoot down incoming fire while the Iraqis were depending upon luck to hit important targets. As a result, their missiles proved to be more a terror weapon and nuisance than an effective military tool. In general, while those in Kuwait suffered loss of sleep between constant missile alerts and efforts to follow the conflict on CNN, the BBC, and other satellite channels, they were spared loss of life and serious destruction of property and infrastructure.

Broadcasts from Iraq found appreciative audiences among those in Kuwait who had suffered so heavily from Saddam Hussein's depredations. Viewers were elated by the sight of the destruction of the massive statue of Saddam in Baghdad's main square.[37] Television footage of the inhabitants of the Iraqi border town of Safwan methodically tearing down omnipresent pictures of Saddam Hussein provoked a moment of typical Kuwaiti humorous relief. One joke making the rounds had Saddam declaring that the pictures were not of him but his body double.[38] Television broadcasts also showed antiwar demonstrations in Arab and other capitals which people in Kuwait watched with skepticism.[39] One Kuwaiti happened to see his housemaid in Cairo participating in a demonstration there. When he called her to ask why she was demonstrating, she replied that she had been given $10 and a free meal in return.[40]

As the missile attacks tapered off as a result of the overrunning of their launch sites, Kuwaiti residents concluded that it was safe enough to resume some normal activities. As Claudia al-Rashoud wrote at the time:

It was our weekend and since we hadn't had any sirens for a while, families were beginning to go out to the beach again and to restaurants. But it looks like it won't be safe for quite some time and we'll just have to live with the situation. We'll still try and go about our business as close to normal as possible, but we'll also be as cautious as we can. People have to go to work—they can't afford to just stop everything and stay at home.[41]

Most of the American schools had fortuitously been on spring break when the conflict began. A major problem facing families compelled to stay inside their homes was the issue of keeping children and young persons occupied.[42] Kuwait high schools reopened March 29 and others somewhat later. In addition to vicious sandstorms, those venturing outside still had to cope with a plague familiar to veterans of the postliberation era in 1991. As part of his defenses, Saddam Hussein had created vast lakes and trenches of crude oil which he had ordered lit. Kuwaiti oil firefighters working with American counterparts in Iraq were quickly extinguishing the fires, but not before prevailing northerly winds blew huge columns of oil smoke, carrying carcinogens and other toxins, into Kuwait.[43] Those venturing outside were advised to strictly limit their exposure.

From the outset of the crisis, Kuwaitis were involved with American and British forces as well as in civil defense operations. Kuwaiti volunteers went into Iraq with combat forces to serve as guides and translators, as they had done during Kuwait's liberation. Firemen and other emergency personnel also provided auxillary resources, and volunteers within Kuwait provided translation and other assistance to Americans and other expatriates in need.

Kuwait, with its extensive system of medical facilities, was ideally situated to serve as a massive receiving station for military and civilian casualties from Iraq:

Here in Kuwait, the focus is very much on what can be done to help the Iraqi people and there is a massive campaign going on to ease the humanitarian crisis. From the Kuwaiti government and the Kuwait Red Crescent to local charities and religious, cultural, & women's groups—many people are involved in the effort. Kuwaiti

> doctors are ready to go to Iraq and we have had more Iraqi war casualties arriving for treatment in our hospitals, especially the very difficult cases and children.... Kuwaiti doctors have lots of experience treating these kinds of horrific injuries (loss of limbs and severe burns caused by explosions & penetrating shrapnel) because of the large number of casualties from unexploded ordnance & all the mines planted by the Iraqis during their occupation of Kuwait.[44]

Private Americans who remained in Kuwait contributed in various ways. Some students and others, for example, volunteered with UNICEF in programs to assist Iraqi refugees. The remaining members of the British Ladies Society (BLS) continued to meet during the critical days and undertook public service projects such as making "distraction activity packs" for Kuwait Action for the Care of Children in Hospital (KACCH). The group, headed by Margaret al-Sayer, a British woman married to Dr. Hilal al-Sayer (subsequently the Minister of Health), was preparing to extend their activities to Iraq, beginning in the south, as soon as the areas were declared safe to enter.[45] They welcomed the participation and support of American women still in the country.

Members of the American and other Western communities who braved the worst days of the crisis were frequently surprised by the warmth of the feelings that other Kuwaitis showed for them. Much as during the Iraqi occupation, ordinary Kuwaitis were appreciative of those who stayed with them under difficult conditions. Many expatriates received calls from Kuwaiti neighbors offering any needed assistance.[46]

By mid-April, the first of the evacuees had begun to return. American, British, and Canadian teachers were back in connection with the reopening of many private schools in the country. Others had enrolled their children in the United States and elsewhere and would not return until the end of the academic year. Traffic jams were almost back to normal and stores and restaurants were open for business.[47] The population of the resurgent city was swollen by an increased American and British military presence.[48] Residents became accustomed to sharing shops and restaurants with young men and women in uniform, and the streets and roadways with military vehicles. Claudia and Salah al-Rashoud were on a visit to Ace Hardware when they noticed a convoy including camouflaged ambulances on the side of the road. Several soldiers, from what they assumed was a routine convoy, were attempting unsuccessfully to communicate with Iranian laborers at the side of the road. Abandoning their errand, the couple turned around and asked the soldiers if they were lost. As Salah began explaining where the hospital they were seeking was, the soldiers explained they were coming from Iraq with badly wounded men:

> *So Salah said, 'Why didn't you say so?! Follow me!' They were actually only about ten minutes away from the hospital but they were headed in the complete opposite direction, so we got turned around and with them following us, Salah took all the shortcuts he knew and got them to the hospital in no time. We were just going to drive away when one of the soldiers yelled for us to stop. He came over and introduced himself, thanked us, gave us his address and invited us to come visit him and his family the next time we're ever in Ohio.*[49]

The fact that this kind of interaction with the American military could take place in a country that adamantly rejected the notion of foreign troops on its soil only two decades before speaks volumes about the evolution of relations between the Kuwaiti and American peoples.

Kuwait had experienced and surmounted another traumatic episode in its modern history. It was less traumatic than the Iraqi occupation to be sure, but the American commitment was more prolonged. Kuwaitis were relieved with the collapse of Saddam Hussein's regime, since they had never been quite certain that he would never return. Sheltering in their homes at the beginning of the conflict, they were more connected with one another and the outside world because of recent technological advancements such as email and satellite television. With the fall of the Baathist regime, hopes soared that several hundred Kuwaitis seized by the Iraqi army in 1991 might miraculously come home. In this, they were destined to be disappointed, although the remains of many were identified, again through new technology (DNA testing). But this more recent experience also exacted its toll on the inhabitants of the small country, arousing memories and feelings they had hoped were behind them: *"After all of this, we are all feeling drained, physically and emotionally, but very grateful that Kuwait managed to escape the conflict with just a few physical scratches."*[50]

The terrorist threat of which the U.S. Embassy warned in 2003 at the beginning of Operation "Iraqi Freedom" did not materialize in earnest for two more years. As 2004 drew to an end, however, the embassy and Kuwaiti government began receiving credible reports that Islamic militants were planning to launch attacks in Kuwait. Kuwait announced a high security alert that included patrolling armored vehicles and enhanced protection of oil installations and Western diplomatic missions.[51] In January, 2005 the U.S. Embassy warned its citizens that individuals in a black vehicle intended to attack Westerners at random in the city. Americans and other Western expatriates were now on notice that they were potential targets by terrorists still at large.

The day after the special alert was lifted, January 10, 2005, Kuwaiti security forces caught up with suspects they were seeking in the suburb of Hawalli. In the ensuing shootout, one suspect and two policemen were killed and two others were wounded.[52] An indeterminate number of suspected militants, including Kuwaitis, were arrested in Jaber al-Ali and other neighborhoods and held for questioning in connection with the clash.[53]

The Kuwaiti public, including representatives of the Islamist factions in the National Assembly, were shocked by the revelation of Kuwaiti participation in the terrorist cells, and condemnation of their actions was universal. There had been indications of Kuwaiti involvement in groups plotting violence, and Shaikh Saud Nasir al-Sabah, the former Minister of Information and of Oil, went further, charging that "sleeper cells" had been operating under cover: *"Extremist groups here are like fire under the ashes. There are sleeper cells... in the security and military agencies of this country."*[54]

Veterans of the American community took sensible precautions. Having survived the Iraqi occupation and missile attacks, however, there was little undue alarm. As the security search for suspects (who were now on the run) continued, Peter Menting, an eleven-year resident from New York, spoke for most when he expressed confidence that the authorities had the situation under control. Linda Steffen, marketing manager for a shipping company from Salt Lake City, concurred: "We have come to realize that it is a very safe country... I love Kuwait. I go to sleep at night without worrying about my safety."[55]

The Kuwaiti manhunt came to its apparent end in February, 2005, when Kuwaiti state security and special forces arrested two brothers without firing a shot in the Andalus suburb.[56] The identity of the final suspects was disclosed by previously arrested terrorist suspects in Sulaibiya and Jahra. In retrospect, it was clear that this was an organized terrorist group with assets in many parts of the country. Once alerted, the security apparatus acted with professionalism and courage to roll up the cell, including operations and gun battles in several locations. The United States appropriately expressed admiration for the operation which prevented the group from carrying out any of its plans. In one of the raided safe houses, chemicals and instructions for making bombs were discovered. In the end, some forty individuals were referred to state prosecutors for trial. The operational group was reportedly comprised of twenty-four persons, including Jordanians, Saudis, and bidoon (stateless residents). In December, 2005, a Kuwaiti court sentenced six of those charged to death.[57]

After 2003, Kuwaitis were at peace with their neighbors, but less so with themselves and one another. Relationships between the Prime Minister and his Cabinet, and the increasing vocal "opposition" with the National Assembly, remained sour at best, ushering in an unprecedented era of revolving door governments and deepening the gridlock on projects and programs. Hardly had Iraqi missiles stopped falling when a pattern was set. The elections of July, 2002 produced an Assembly with twenty-one Islamists, almost assuring stalemate on important substantive issues. The parliament was able, somehow, to pass legislation granting Kuwaiti women the right to vote and stand for election (over the objections of the Islamists), but the government would be constantly on the defensive otherwise.[58]

To challenge the government position, the opposition settled on a strategy of undermining Prime Minister Shaikh Nasir whenever possible, and attacking members of his cabinet when that failed. Their goal was to compel the prime minister to appear in the National Assembly in order to be questioned. The amir chose to short-circuit this maneuver through a combination of Cabinet resignations or dismissals of the parliament for new elections. In 2007, the opposition target was Shaikh Ahmad Abdallah al-Sabah, followed by Minister of Health Massouma al-Mubarak (the first woman minister appointed in 2005) and Oil Minister Bader al-Humaidhi. It was increasingly difficult to govern. Street demonstrations and government dependence on the security forces became a more frequent accompaniment to the maneuvers of the politicians. New elections took place in: July 2003; June 2006; May 2008; May 2009; February 2012; and December 2012.

The ultimate target of the parliamentary opposition remained the prime minister, the amir's nephew. In December 2009, Shaikh Nasir felt strong enough to subject himself to a no-confidence vote which he survived.[59] By January 2011, the prime minister was again before the National Assembly for another no-confidence vote following questioning regarding a police crackdown on opposition MPs and their supporters. He once more escaped a crucial vote, but the margin had narrowed ominously. The chamber split 25 to 25, thereby failing to garner a majority.[60] With its back against the wall, the government suffered a further wound in February when Minister of Interior Shaikh Jabir al-Khaled Al Sabah was compelled to resign over the death of a prisoner in police custody. Shaikh Jabir was scheduled to appear in parliament to address the alleged torture of a man arrested for selling illegal liquor. The amir replaced him from among the narrowing circle of close relatives.[61]

Several hundred Kuwaitis staged a protest in March 2011 to demand greater political freedoms and the resignation of the besieged prime minister.[62] Riot police used tear gas to quell a gathering of some two hundred demonstrators.[63] Such measures, however, proved ineffective in ending the crisis. As the National Assembly moved to summon three ministers (all were members of the al-Sabah family) for questioning, the amir accepted the Cabinet's resignation on March 31.[64] The nub of the standoff between rigid government and opposition positions was: *"a running, five-year-long struggle to oust the prime minister, the amir's nephew, who opponents say has mismanaged Kuwait's economy and helped erode such core values as freedom of speech."*[65]

The familiar parry and thrust of recent Kuwaiti politics, however, no longer had the power to bring even momentary relief from the tensions. Small but persistent demonstrations continued on by those demanding the resignation of the prime minister and other reforms[66]; other groups with causes unrelated to the central controversy took advantage of the disorder to press their agenda[67]; and groups of public sector employees (90 percent of the workforce) chose the period of government vulnerability to stage strikes welcomed by the "opposition" in pursuit of higher wages and greater benefits:

> *A deeper crisis in the entire country was expressed by a series of strikes in 2011. Teachers, customs workers, jurists, and other professionals organized these protests, which prompted major losses for merchants; the government had no choice but to agree to most of the demands of the striking sectors.*[68]

With Kuwait already locked in internal political conflict, and while development and other affairs of state were in abeyance, a bombshell was dropped into the mix in early September. Allegations of serious acts of corruption involving up to fifteen members of the National Assembly threatened to send the country into deeper crisis.[69] The affairs emerged when officials of two Kuwaiti banks noted large unexplained transfers of funds into private accounts abroad and alerted the public prosecutor.[70] The Kuwait daily, *al-Qabas*, speculated that the deposits were possibly funds paid to MPs to buy their support during voting on crucial issues.[71] Even though the results of a thorough investigation into the accusations had not been concluded, the revelations gave new energy to the campaign for the prime minister's resignation, including continuing demonstrations by youth movements. On November 16, 2011, young activists, egged on by opposition leaders, pushed their way past police and National Guardsmen protecting the parliament building and entered the main chamber where they chanted, sang the national anthem, and departed. A number of the young demonstrators were arrested.[72]

From that moment, the fate of Prime Minister Nasir Mohammad was likely sealed. He had withstood a drumbeat of criticism for most of the six years he had served, but his room for maneuver had run out. In October, his cabinet had suffered the resignation of Shaikh Mohammad al-Salem al-Sabah, the respected minister of foreign affairs and the only senior representative of the al-Salem branch. Discovering that the facilities of his Ministry had been used to transfer illicit funds without his knowledge, he resigned.[73] At the beginning of December, the amir conceded the obvious and accepted Shaikh Nasir's resignation; First Deputy Prime Minister and Minister of Defense Shaikh Jaber al-Mubarak al-Hamad al-Sabah was tapped to form a new government.

The consequences of the lengthy standoff were not the victory the opposition anticipated. The bickering had tarnished the public's view not just of the Cabinet but the Assembly as well, for reasons that informed Kuwaiti observers explained:

> *An embattled prime minister, a senior member of the ruling Al Sabah family, which garners much legitimacy and popular support, has finally succumbed to the popular pressure, led by the determined opposition and strengthened by the youth movement. Shaikh Nasser (sic).... stepped down after six years, having led seven cabinets....*
>
> *Although it is true that the forces of change were able to topple the controversial and beleaguered cabinet and force the upending of the bruised and much-despised parliament, leadership is still lacking.*[74]

Political scientist Shafeeq Ghabra offered a grim analysis of "a steady deterioration in governance, priorities, and vision." Specific areas where there have been deficiencies, he wrote, were energy, education, health care, and the economy: "... *despite women's right to vote in Kuwait since 2006, as well as wider freedoms and human rights compared to other Gulf nations, Kuwaiti youth see wealth being spent without much to show for the effort.*"[75]

All indicators suggest that the public was exasperated and disgusted with the quality of leadership offered by all participants in the debacle. As an experienced observer of Kuwaiti politics concludes, "While previous dissolutions resulted from MP-government showdowns, this most recent election was a result of popular demands to disband both parliament and the government."[76] When the electorate went to the polls in early December, 2012, a mere 40.3 percent (lowest in Kuwaiti history) cast ballots. The opposition, which called for a boycott, claimed that the number was even lower. It remains to be seen whether the struggle for power can be resolved in the near term, but in the meantime, Kuwait is no longer the shining beacon it once was.

It is probably not an accident that the evolution of the political process toward stalemate and ineffectual bickering coincides closely with the postliberation period. The trauma responses implanted in the national psyche by that existential experience undoubtedly affect individual behavior and the tone of public discourse. At the same time, measureable societal changes have helped create a new and unfamiliar paradigm. Long gone are the days when politics were determined by the competition between the ruling family and the wealthier merchant class. In those terms, the ruler could more or less count on the support of minorities and the tribal areas of the desert hinterland to balance the merchants.[77] The relationship with the tribal elements, however, has changed significantly as they have acquired wealth, more education, and residences in the city.[78]

Shafeeq Ghabra flagged the implications of these changes—which he called "Desertization"—in an astute analysis in the 1990s. He noted that oil wealth had lifted Kuwaiti society out of its "traditional economic environment" very rapidly.[79] The process, Ghabra argued, "brings into the urban milieu the ultraconservative values of the desert, which are often mixed with Islamist popular beliefs":

The process destroys those aspects of urban life that allow for the assimilation and acculturation of newcomers and new ideas. It puts the national, civil framework at risk and prevents it from maturing and coalescing. Religious fervor, in addition to creating divisiveness based on values, can also highlight sectarian (Shi'a-Sunni) and societal (bedouin-urban) differences....[80]

In terms of practical politics and governance, the phenomenon transforms the bedu into a relatively "poor" and resentful urban sector even more receptive to the call of Islamist groups and opposition to a system in which they believe they have little stake: *"The ground was laid for the penetration of Islamic fundamentalism and fanaticism into tribal areas. The outcome was apparent in the 1992 election to parliament of an Islamist and fundamentalist majority."*[81]

Ghabra sees the scenario he foresaw more than a decade ago playing out in the current political crisis, with the resettled tribes providing a "strong base" for opposition candidates.[82]

Since their emergence on the political scene in the 1980s and 90s, the Islamists have promoted an agenda at variance with historic trends in Kuwaiti society. Having successfully achieved segregation of the sexes in government schools, for example, the regulation was extended to private universities in 2000.[83] Unable to stop the Assembly's decision to grant the vote to Kuwaiti women, they sought to undermine the measure in other ways. In June, 2007, the parliament adopted a law forbidding women to hold jobs that required them to work between the hours of 8 p.m. and 7 a.m. or in places with an all-male clientele.[84] In 2008, they turned their attention to female members of the Cabinet. In October, the Legal and Legislative Committee of the Assembly sought unsucessfully to block the appointment of two ministers—Education Minister Nuriya al-Subayh and Minister of State for Housing and Administrative Development Mudi al-Hamoud—for violating the constitution because they did not wear the hijab (head covering).[85] The following year, a petition was submitted calling for the annulment of the election of two female members of parliament on the grounds that they refused to wear the hijab. The Constitutional Court, in rejecting the petition, ruled that the constitution, which guarantees personal freedom and freedom of worship, is superior to any other law, including religious tradition. For good measure, the court also struck down the 1962 requirement that Kuwaiti women have their husbands sign applications for passports.[86] To date, the Islamist challenges have constituted nuisances rather than serious assaults on longstanding values. Time will tell whether, having attained the powers and responsibilities of office, the Islamists will modulate their positions or, perhaps, feed cultural conflict.[87]

Closely related to these demographic trends in the minds of many urban Kuwaitis is the issue of the bidoun, "stateless" bedu

Friends and Allies 459

living in Kuwait. While a small number who could satisfy authorities of their historic connection with Kuwait have been given Kuwaiti nationality, the government and most Kuwaitis believe the majority of these people are Iraqis, Saudis, or Syrians who hide their nationality "to gain entitlement to superior Kuwaiti economic, social and political rights."[88] Public protests of the kind staged by bidoun in 2011 do not present a serious challenge to the government but serve to keep the issue before the nation. It is a safe bet that the authorities will consider the balance between urban and desert elements in deciding how to deal with this irritant.

Whatever the character of the Kuwaiti government, it will have to cope with regional politics and security. Development projects may be delayed, social policies may be the subject of endless contention, and political campaignng can become a semipermanent feature of the local scene. But threats of terrorism, tensions with and between neighbors, and other urgent matters demand attention. With the exception of the contentious question of Iran's nuclear ambitions and its potential "fallout" for other nearby states, Kuwait is not under serious external threat today. Nevertheless, no Kuwaiti administration can ignore relations with Baghdad, the small country's historic nemesis.

Relations with Iraq have improved markedly since the overthrow of Saddam Hussin in 2003. Kuwait not only supported the replacement of his regime but moved to normalize relations with successor authorities through financial support for reconstruction, commercial activity and humanitarian assistance. Within the limits imposed by disorder and murky lines of authority, cooperation was pursued on issues like accounting for Kuwaitis taken in 1991 and indemnification for the crimes of Iraqi occupation forces.

In 2008, the two countries began the move toward normalizing diplomatic relations through the exchange of ambassadors. Ambassador Ali al-Mo'men (appointed July, 2008) took up residence in Baghdad and Ambassador Mohammad Hussein Bahr al-Uloom arrived in Kuwait on July 30, 2010.[89]

Despite the efforts of the diplomats, the Kuwait-Iraqi relationship is laden with decades of baggage and took a worrisome downward turn during 2011. The proximate cause was a Kuwaiti decision to build a new port on Bubiyan Island not far from Iraq's al-Faw Peninsula. Opposition to the project was strong among unreconstructed Iraqis who once again detected plots and schemes against Iraq unfolding. Professor al-Shayji outlined the early stages of unofficial Iraqi reactions from a Kuwaiti perspective:

> *Iraqi officials made xenophobic and inflammatory statements depicting this Kuwaiti project as part of a conspiracy to undermine Iraq and negatively affect traffic at its ports, especially the Faw Port which Iraq is considering building not too far from Kuwait's Mubarak Port. This touched off anti-Kuwait demonstrations in Iraq and calls to expel the Kuwaiti ambassador.*
>
> *Iraqi views over the sensitive issue could not be more divergent. The new Iraqi ambassador to Kuwait, Mohammad Bahr Al Ulum, expressed satisfaction after the meeting of the visiting Iraqi joint committee with the Kuwaiti side over the port, describing the meeting as 'very reassuring and comprehensive as it tackled all questions posed by the Iraqi side, and answered professionally and accurately by the Kuwaiti side.*[90]

With an exquisitely inept sense of timing, the Iraqi government chose August 2, 2011, the 21st anniversary of Iraq's invasion, to ask officially that Kuwait halt development of the new port.[91] Intentionally or not, the Iraqi demarche was punctuated by the launch of three rockets from Basra. An Iraqi official hastened to explain on August 26 that the rockets were not fired at Kuwait or the site of the new port, although a Shi'a militia had threatened an attack if Kuwait did not stop construction at Mubarak Port. The official claimed, somewhat lamely, that the target of the rockets was a former prison being "used by foreign companies."[92] It was even less coincidental that Kuwait chose September 4 to reveal the arrest of an Iraqi accused of providing the Iraqi government with sensitive classified information about key installations in the country.[93] These were, unfortunately, not isolated incidents; underlying feelings of anxiety and hostility are easily triggered. For Kuwaitis, lingering trauma was stoked once again. Abdallah al-Shayji once more described the mood:

Friends and Allies 461

It (Iraq's reaction) reminds Kuwaitis their problem was not with Saddam Hussain, who is long dead and buried, but rather with Iraq as a system, entity, neighbour, and people. This is unfortunate, especially with the seeming thaw of tensions and high-level visits by officials of both countries in the last few months. Kuwait's Prime Minister Shaikh Nasser Al Mohammad Al Sabah visited Iraq in January (2011) and Iraq's Prime Minister Nouri Al Maliki visited Kuwaitt in a symbolic gesture to mark Kuwait's celebration of its 50th anniversary of independence and, more importantly, the 20th anniversary of liberation from Iraq's occupation.

... attacks by rogue Iraqi militia (later the Mahdi Army claimed responsibility) targeting the Kuwaiti Embassy in Baghdad with Katyusha rockets last week forcing Kuwait to pull out all of its diplomats who returned to Kuwait; that was followed by menacing threats by another Iraqi rogue militia (Iraq Hezbollah) threatening to target the South Korean firms building Kuwait's Mubarak Kabeer Port on the northern Boubyan Island close to Iraq's Shatt Al Arab causeway. Iraqi parliamentarians claim the port will suffocate Iraq and deny it access to the Arabian Gulf and negatively affect the Grand Faw Port under construction. On the other hand, Iraq points to the Kuwaiti port as a manifestation that Kuwait is back to its old tricks to keep Iraq shackled in hardship and has conspired against Iraq to thwart its prosperity.[94]

Bilateral relations with Iraq are an unavoidable priority for Kuwait now as throughout its modern history. Neither nation has an interest in open conflict and there are many inducements to cooperation, but recent events have underlined the unhealthy nature of their interaction. The first visit of the Kuwaiti Prime Minister in 2011, for example, took place two days after a clash between the Kuwaiti coast guard and Iraqi fishermen resulted in the death of one Kuwaiti.[95] It would be surprising if Kuwaitis did not distrust Iraq, given their historic experience, and many, if not most, Iraqis resent Kuwaiti independence and prosperity. Recently, exchanges appear to have been more restrained and professional; Iraqi officials announced in March, 2012 a number of agreements settling longstanding disputes growing out of the 1990 invasion and occupation.[96]

Kuwait has exhibited enormous reserves of resilience and restorative capabilities. If it is threatened today, it is not by neighbors, but from within. As Kuwaitis contemplate their dysfunctional political system, they would do well to recall the factors that have enabled them to survive multiple crises in an unstable neighborhood. Unity and a high degree of openess and tolerance have been key attributes in preserving their unique social and political heritage.

20

Snapshots at Age One Hundred

The American community now enters upon its second century of unbroken residence in Kuwait. It is, of course, no longer the tiny coterie of Americans who unpacked their worldly goods and ideals at the American Mission compound in 1911, but neither is Kuwait the same society that first accepted, and then embraced, these new strangers. Both the guests and the hosts evolved and grew in magnitude over the intervening decades in a symbiotic tandem. In the process, their governments and their peoples have progressed from wary interactions to friendship, tolerance, and cooperation. In the crucible of threat and crisis, friends became allies in many areas of shared concern. This progression has been, in many respects, unique in the history of relations between widely separated and culturally diverse societies.

Unlike the normal progression of the colonial era, it was private American citizens who pioneered the relationship with the Kuwaitis. The American community resided there for forty years before there was a U.S. government presence. In a sense, this sequence provided time and space for Americans and Kuwaitis to learn to appreciate one another's personal qualities without the frictions and power disparities inherent in government-to-government dealings. The early American missionaries, who failed in their hope to convert Kuwaitis to Christianity, would not have realized how revolutionary was their achievement—the opening of minds and hearts to mutual acceptance and respect.

Missionaries from New England and the Midwest; oilmen from Texas, Louisiana, and Oklahoma; diplomats from the Middle Atlantic states; naval personnel from Hampton Roads and California;

and young women from universities and college towns across a continent—all left their imprint on both the American community and Kuwait over the years of the twentieth century. As always, these residents brought with them material and philosophical elements from their regions. In the beginning, they carved out homes and compounds that were American in character and atmosphere. When the oilmen began to arrive in the 1930s, these aspects of life—square dancing, beach excursions, religious services—were replicated in the oil camps and towns. With the arrival of the American Consulate in the 1950s, the official offices and residences likewise served as American community centers in Kuwait. With rare exceptions, however, there is no evidence in the record to indicate that these small spaces of Americana were ever regarded as enclaves shutting out the Kuwaiti society around them. The high standards of service and social engagement set by the American Mission personnel from the outset constitute a legacy that continues to resonate in a tradition of community involvement today.

Some Americans, like the missionaries, came to Kuwait to serve, to understand and interact with local society over an extended period. Others came to do a job of limited duration, although a notable proportion of them ended up extending their stay or taking opportunities to return. As Kuwaitis studying in the United States returned with American wives and children holding U.S. passports, the roots and permanence of the community were extended and reinforced. Today, the next generation of these hybrid families, straddling Kuwaiti and American culture, is growing into adulthood. To a surprising degree, Kuwait is a place where expatriates come to stay rather than visit.

It is not easy to enumerate all the factors that make Kuwait attractive as a residence for expatriates from half a world away. Even before the first missionary doctors planted their tiny community, Kuwait had established a reputation for commerce and reliability that was essential to a city-state that supported itself by trade and shipping. Kuwaitis were thus accustomed to dealing with other cultures, although their experience with Europeans was limited. While the local population was primarily Sunni Arab, it had incorporated other belief systens (Shi'a, Judaism) and ethnic groups (Persians) within the close-knit town. Acceptance of the Christian newcomers was not inevitable, but it was at least conceivable. The ultimate embrace of the American Mission was the breakthrough that opened the way for mutual tolerance and understanding.

Under continuing threat from neighbors and marauding tribes, the Kuwaitis survived by developing a strong sense of corporate identity, a shared vision of who they were and who they were not. This self-awareness, which strikes a responsive chord among many Americans, gave Kuwaitis the confidence to engage the Americans among them with openness. As the growing number of Americans in Kuwait brought with them their own little pieces of America, Kuwaitis, including those who had studied in the United States, took those elements they liked and adapted them to the local market—everything from restaurants (sliders, bagels, cupcakes, frozen yoghurt, pizza) to interior design, architecture, fashion, spa and salon services, and all sorts of technology. As Claudia al-Rashoud, a resident for more than thirty years, explains:

> ... Kuwaitis do not just indiscriminately copy all things American. They take only what they like and often give it a uniquely Kuwaiti flair. Kuwaitis have always been great entrepreneurs. They have always welcomed and embraced new products and innovations like no other people I can think of.... The underlying fabric of the society is something uniquely Kuwaiti, still deeply rooted in a moderate Islamic heritage with a close community. Americans are welcomed into this community and as a result, many American expats really enjoy the friendly, cosmopolitan, casual lifestyle where people still have time for each other. Yes, life in Kuwait has definitely become much more fast-paced, but we don't have quite the rat-race, nor the impersonal lifestyle that exists in many big cities in the United States. There is something very attractive and comfortable about Kuwait that keeps many Americans here long-term, and perhaps the successful blend of East and West has something to do with it.[1]

Like any fine blend, the ambiance that American expatriates find so congenial was long in the making. It does not hurt that Kuwaitis and Western communities alike enjoy upscale lifestyles made possible by oil wealth. In fact, it was the advent of that wealth that gave Kuwait the possibility of adapting Western technologies and outlooks. The amalgamation of the latter, however, gathered real momentum following the end of the Iraqi occupation in 1991. The fact that the Americans were widely seen as key to Kuwait's liberation facilitated an openness to things American that concerned some observers at the time. Alarmed by the possibility that the much larger American culture might overwhelm and swallow up Kuwait's, one of Kuwait's most influential thinkers gave voice to these misgivings:

> On the cultural level, influence is moving essentially only in one direction—from the United States to Kuwait. CNN, NBC, America Plus, videos, movies, the Internet, cafes, schools, department stores, and fast-food restaurants all symbolize the process of Americanization of the younger generation. Kuwaitis realize this is part of the globalization process and, therefore, are not erecting barriers to this cultural interaction, but they must be wary of losing their own cultural identity as well as making sure this aspect of the relationship is more of a two-way street.[2]

Fortunately, these worries reckoned without a full appreciation for the vitality and resilience of the Kuwaiti ethos, which flirted in the 1950s and 60s with the siren call of Pan-Arabism and other ideological currents and, then, shook them off to reaffirm the essentials of their unique indigenous culture.

At various periods in its history, the American community in Kuwait was a small minority dependent upon centers and institutions to sustain its identity and links with the United States—(the American Mission compound, widely dispersed oil camps, the American Consulate and Embassy). Today, however, a "critical" mass seems to have been achieved. Organizations like the American Women's League (AWL), which was once crucial to wives and other newcomers as an American haven in an unfamiliar environment, no longer possess the centrality of the past. Elements of the American lifestyle—in shopping, business, education, dining, and entertainment —are not difficult to find. Emphasis has shifted to "interest" associations that attract both Americans and Kuwaitis in shared activities. The Embassy, now a much larger institution in an isolated and heavily fortified new location, no longer has the capacity or the need to serve as an informal gathering place for Americans and their Kuwaiti friends.

The American experience in Kuwait coincides neatly with the age of photography. With increasing frequency over the years, photographs augment the documentary record of that experience. For much of this history, it was feasible to frame all, or most, of the community in a single photograph. In the second decade of the twenty-first century, the American community has become too large, too diverse, and too dispersed to do so. It no longer gathers en masse to renew its ties with the United States at Independence Day and other occasions, nor does it need to do so. Americans and aspects of American culture are around them in the larger society, blended harmoniously with elements of Kuwait's unique charm and culture.

Since it is no longer possible to pose the American community in one physical location, a series of verbal snapshots must suffice to depict the depth and breadth of community life. Contemporary freeze-frames inescapably capture comfortable interaction and the extent to which former strangers have become friends.

Dr. Ghabra's concerns regarding the potential dominance of American influence following liberation were shared initially by others. With Kuwait more vulnerable as a consequence of the dislocations and doubts created by the Iraqi betrayal, many felt it important that Kuwait reaffirm its strong cultural identity as it had many times in its history; that the synthesis of new influences and long-standing heritage be carefully crafted.[3] Later tensions involving Muslim extremists highlighted the importance of orienting newcomers to their new environment. Among those committed to a respectful exchange of views and experiences between Kuwaitis and expatriates was a small group of Kuwaitis and American Muslims. They were disturbed by stereotypes and misunderstandings following the extremist attacks in the United States in 2001 and the American-led invasion of Iraq two years later. In 2003, they established AWARE (Advocates for Western-Arab Relations), a private nonprofit with a center in Surra.[4]

AWARE's goal is to provide a cultural gateway for Westerners to explore Arab and Islamic culture through social encounters, educational activities, dialogue, cultural exchanges, and friendships across cultural lines. One of its most popular regular events is the open diwanniya held every Tuesday night. Kuwaitis and Westerners can take advantage of these typically Kuwaiti venues to discuss a range of topics and form relationships. General Director Dr. Ibrahim al-Adsani and Hassan Bwambale, the education manager who hosts the diwanniya, eschew proselytizing and politics to offer a forum for explaining Kuwaiti culture. The AWARE Center is supported by memberships, paid events, field trips, and other activities and donations from Kuwaiti companies and foundations.

Kuwait was, of course, a very different place in the mid-1950s when the number of long-term residents of American origin began to grow significantly. The country was not well known in the United States and was only starting to experience the marked changes that accompanied independence and development. The American Womens League (AWL), the first community institution, was conceived toward the end of the decade to provide a forum for fellowship, the exchange of ideas and interests, social and cultural activities, and familiarization with Kuwaiti customs and culture.[5] Maxine al-Refai, AWL's longest serving member, recalls that the nonprofit, nonpolitical association began with a small number of members, but soon grew. Initially confined to Americans or the wives of Americans residing in Kuwait, the rules were later amended to include certain categories of non-Americans.

The AWL held monthly meetings which featured guest speakers or special events like cultural evenings, travel fairs, or seasonal celebrations at a time when such diversions were rare in Kuwait. A Children's Activities Committee sponsored celebrations of American holidays like Halloween, Christmas, and Easter for children of members and their guests. An Adult Activities Committee organized tours of places of interest to help members become more familiar with Kuwaiti culture. A Newcomers Group met monthly to offer a wide range of informative and recreational activities, and the Mothers of Young Children group gathered weekly.

American women married to Kuwaitis, a group that grew significantly as young Kuwaitis returned from studies or extended military training in the United States, became an important constituency and many recall AWL as a lifeline during the early years of life in a strange society. As Jerry Ismaiel, who moved to Kuwait with her husband in 1972, noted: "We needed a link to home and that's what AWL gave us." Debbie Bourahmah, a resident for decades, joined the Mothers of Young Children group and fondly recalls informal gatherings with other American mothers and children at playgrounds in gardens or by the beach:

It was usually a potluck occasion and something we really looked forward to, especially since in those days there were no cafes or public places where you could sit and have a conversation. Many of us who were married to Kuwaitis and had young children lived in small apartments or with our in-laws, so entertaining at home was difficult.

For American wives whose husbands' work brought them to Kuwait, AWL offered early contacts and a softer landing in an unfamiliar environment. Patricia Wyss was one such expatriate who was unprepared for her arrival in 1982. She enjoyed her initial contact with fellow members but she soon found that work and new friendships with Kuwaiti women left her little time to attend AWL functions. At that point, Dorothy Scudder (supra) counselled her to make time for the association's activities:

[She] reminded me that first and foremost I was, as she had been, an American married to an American in Kuwait. As much as we shared our love for the people, language, and culture of Kuwait ... we would never be Kuwaiti... I would be a better, balanced, lifelong friend to Kuwait if I would reengage with my American culture by reengaging with AWL. AWL means a reality check.

When I had a child, AWL became a lifeline for me and a conduit for my daughter to bond her with American culture. AWL event photos when she was a toddler at the Christmas party at Camp Doha, the Easter egg hunts, the Halloween parties, to hosting U.S. military for dinner are all testimonials of how integral AWL activities were in helping me, my husband and our daughter embrace our American culture. AWL, besides meaning friends and grounding me in my culture, grew to mean family, a sense of belonging for my entire family. AWL gave me, an American, a tangible sense of being American—allowing me to integrate and be part of Kuwaiti society.

The links established in more normal circumstances carried over into the terrifying days of the Iraqi occupation, imparting strength and coherence to the American community. Many AWL members and their children were among those evacuated on the flights arranged by the U.S. Embassy during the fall of 1990. Besides providing support to one another during the trip and after resettlement in the United States, some of them became active in the "Free Kuwait" movement on the home front. They published newsletters, supported demonstrations and spoke to civic and other interested groups. Given their personal familiarity with Kuwait and connections with loved ones still detained by the Iraqis, they were able to provide the American public with informed commentary to counter widespread ignorance and the frequent misinformation in media reporting. A group of mostly blonde women, wives of Kuwaitis, was approached by a curious Latino while attending a birthday party for their children in a California public park. "How come all your kids look like Mexicans?" he inquired innocently. The American public had much to learn about the country its fellow citizens would soon be fighting to liberate.

After liberation, the evacuees returned to Kuwait and their husbands and quickly resumed AWL activities (see Chapter 16). Many were surprised at the extent of the warmth and respect shown to them by the Kuwaiti people. In April 1995, Shaikha Latifa Fahad al-Sabah, wife of the crown prince and prime minister, was the featured speaker at an AWL meeting. She recognized the role these women had played in Kuwait's brush with Iraqi designs:

I would like at the outset to convey the deep appreciation of Kuwaiti women to the American people, who not only stood by us firmly and strongly against the treacherous Iraqi invasion and occupation of our country...but also sent American young men and women to fight with us against the forces of evil aggression until Kuwait was liberated. In this connection I would like to pay tribute to the active participation by American women in the battle for Kuwait. Such participation will always be remembered with esteem by all of us in Kuwait.

The Kuwaiti people have always harboured feelings of admiration and appreciation towards the United States, not only because it is a big power but also because it is a great nation that honours and upholds high values and noble ideals in which we too strongly believe. The Kuwaiti people share the American people's commitment to the principles of right, justice, equality, and rejection of aggression. It was not unusual that the United States stood by our cause and led the international coalition that undertook to defeat Iraqi aggression.[6]

In her remarks, Shaikha Latifa placed recent events in the context of the historic relationship between Kuwait and the American community. She pointed out that Kuwaitis had direct contact with American residents since the arrival of the American Mission hospital in the early years of the century. "Thanks to their noble character, humane behaviour, and valuable help, American doctors, of both sexes, had won the hearts of Kuwaitis so much so that the latter gave them new names—Kuwaiti names—to show that they considered them to be actual members of the Kuwaiti community."

Paradoxically, at the heighth of its reputation, AWL entered a period of change. The organization continued many of its traditional social and other activities including fundraising events and volunteer services at the orphanage, the Kuwait Handicapped Society, and special needs schools and institutions. But the AWL seemed no longer the centerpiece of American women's lives as it once was. The evolution of the iconic "Annual Charity Bazaar" tells the tale.

For many years, the AWL Bazaar in the pre-Christmas season was considered "the shopping opportunity of the year and the social event of the season." The second year (December 1992) after liberation, the event took up where it had left off with what was advertised tongue-in-cheek as "the mother of all bazaars." For two decades beginning in the early 1970s the event offered a rare opportunity to purchase seasonal items such as handmade Christmas decorations, home-baked holiday treats, and traditional favorites such as stockings and candy canes brought from the United States. "With the vendors' booths in the hotel ballroom all beautifully decorated, piped-in Christmas music playing in the background, and the hustle and bustle of friendly and eager shoppers, the event truly put people into the festive spirit and was enjoyed by Kuwaitis just as much as expatriates."[7]

The last grand Bazaar was sponsored by AWL in 2006. Since then, two veterans of the organization, Karla Khaja and Kim al-Yousifi, have taken over management of the bazaar as a personal enterprise and sponsor two bazaars each year.

The reason for this decision was, in part, that AWL had discharged its function too well. Membership was declining rapidly from its peak of over 350 to fewer than twenty members by 2011. A membership drive increased the numbers to just over fifty by the spring of 2012, but expectations are that it will continue to operate as a significantly smaller group than in its heyday.

Why was AWL contracting? This issue is often discussed among longtime AWL members who have come up with a long list of reasons, the main one being, they just don't need AWL like they did in the old days. Gone are the times when there was nothing "American" in Kuwait, when there were no suitable places for ladies to gather, when AWL members exchanged recipes for unattainable American food items like pumpkin pie or pancake syrup, or when their children would have had little exposure to American holiday events or popular American culture.

Contemporary Kuwait has modern shopping malls with American franchise stores; they are filled with Starbucks and other American coffee shops and restaurants. American foods fill supermarket shelves and frozen food sections. There is no longer any shortage of seasonal items and decorations for all the American holidays. Parents can take their children to a Halloween party at TGI Friday's or any number of American chain restaurants and they can admire Christmas trees and other festive decorations when they do their holiday shopping in the mall.[8]

Just as the atmosphere in Kuwait has changed, so too have many of the American women living in the country. Employment and commercial opportunities have burgeoned and many women now work fulltime or run their own businesses. Most of those married to Kuwaitis have moved from the homes of their in-laws or small apartments into spacious homes purchased or built with the assistance of the government's housing authority. Entertainment at home or in public accomodations is much easier than in the past. Most larger companies with significant numbers of American employees provide their own social activities for employee families.[9] As former AWL members have concluded, "Nowadays there is just too much to do in Kuwait and not enough time to do it in."

AWL filled a deep chasm when there were few, if any, alternatives. Whatever form the association takes in the future, its legacy is a positive one that lives on in the spirit of camaraderie and friendship which manifests itself at important junctures in the life of the American community and its individual members. When someone faces a personal crisis—when there is a birth, a marriage, a serious illness, or a death—AWL veterans come together, to celebrate or commiserate or offer support, as the occasion demands. An American woman mourning the death of her father in the United States recently received friends for condolences in her home. As she looked around her large multipurpose room filled with alumnae of AWL, she was moved to say: "It's so good to see you all but we've got to get together more often that just at weddings and funerals."

With the expansion of the resident American community, the members have many opportunities to interact with one another—and with Kuwaitis—in schools, shopping centers, and the restaurants they favor. An important manifestation of the embedded American community is the system of private American educational institutions. From very modest beginnings in 1963, American schools today constitute an important resource not simply for children in the community but also for Kuwaitis and others interested in pursuing studies in the United States. Maxine al-Refai, who was instrumental in this development, recalled its simple origins:

> *In September 1964 we opened the school (ASK) with seventy-five students, with two girls graduating that same year. We were housed in one of Sheikh Jaber's houses that were used for the diplomatic corps, in the Dasman Area of Sharq. We were right next to the Russian Embassy and during recess we had to be careful not to let the children play ball on that side of the school so their ball wouldn't hit the windows of the Embassy. I remember we often had little Russian children peeking at us from over the wall.*[10]

Originally named the International School of Kuwait (ISK), the institution enjoyed the support of the Kuwait Oil Company (KOC), the U.S. Embassy, and the American Mission. Teaching a curriculum from kindergarten through grade 12, the school accomodated students from several countries. In 1969, this school relocated to larger facilities in the suburb of Surra and changed its name to the American School of Kuwait (ASK); Mrs. al-Refai was named Elementary School Principal and served in that capacity until her retirement in 1995.[11] Formally recognized by Kuwait's Ministry of Education, ASK was granted accreditation from The Middle State Association of College and Secondary Schools in the United States in 1971.

ASK made a second move to its current site in Hawalli in 1995. Today it has been joined by more than a half-dozen other accredited American schools (e.g., the American International School and the Universal American School), as well as several bilingual schools, such as the American Baccalaureate School, that offer American and Arabic curricula. In 2003, the American University of Kuwait (AUK) was established in association with Dartmouth College in New Hampshire.[12] Other private institutions of higher education based on the American model, such as the Gulf University of Science and Technology (GUST) and the American University of the Middle East (AUM), followed.

The commercial facet of U.S.-Kuwaiti relations falls under the purview of the American Business Council of Kuwait (ABCK).[13] Organized in the 1980s, the Council is a nonprofit that operates under the auspices of the Commercial Section of the American Embassy to promote and develop American businesses and their interests in Kuwait. Executive Director Muna al-Fuzai assumed the position in 2008 and has concentrated on enhancing services, including organizing focus groups and providing information on issues such as foreign investment, local labor laws, the role of sponsors, and other rules and regulations. She has articulated her philosophy of creating greater cultural understanding and linkages by fostering closer business ties.

ABCK is particularly useful to small and medium-size American companies which are new to the Kuwaiti market. As Ms. al-Fuzai explains:

The American company may never have done business outside of the United States and the Kuwaiti company might not have any experience in international business, but by giving them the right advice we can help them begin a successful business relationship.[14]

She is very pleased with the interest and receptivity of both Kuwaiti and business leaders to the efforts of the Council.

The dynamic Kuwait Little League (KLL) continues after thirty years to provide recreation for Americans as well as many Kuwaitis and other nationalities.[15] Dependant on the voluntary efforts of parents and coaches and the generosity of companies, KLL fielded twenty-seven teams with 350 players in its most recent season. It is easily the largest organized children's sport in Kuwait.

At the opening ceremony on the Martyr Fahad al-Ahmad al-Jaber al-Sabah Baseball and Softball Fields within the premises of the Hunting and Equestrian Club, the American ambassador, Matthew Tueller, observed that more than twenty nationalities were represented on the teams. The KLL pledge was recited in five languages and the anthems of Kuwait and the U.S. were performed. A color guard posted the flags of the United States, Kuwait, KLL, and the U.S. Baseball League.[16]

To many families in Kuwait, and especially Kuwaiti-Americans, KLL means fun, fellowship, and capturing a bit of small-town America. Sheryll Mairza, whose son, Mahdi, played in the League, is a good example:

Mahdi played only four seasons but loved every minute of it. He attended a private Arabic school during those years which offered little to no extracurricular activities for students. Each week as Mahdi's team gathered at the fields we saw him come alive. The fresh air and sunshine, as well as the other ballplayers and their families cheering on both their own kids and their friends' kids as they played the all-American game of baseball, brought a healthy slice of 'home' for all of us.

Mahdi loved the game enough that he never missed a practice during the week and even when he was sick refused to miss a game. Time spent and relationships developed at the Kuwait Little League fields are some of our fondest memories from when our son was a teenager. Our daughter, who was afraid of a moving ball, chose not to play, but sat in the stands with us each week or played at the KLL playground with friends she made there.[17]

Snapshots of the American community at age one hundred must go beyond highly visible institutions if it hopes to capture the reach and diversity that characterize it. Over the preceding century, literally thousands of Americans have come to live in Kuwait. Some have come on government assignments or to accept lucrative contracts—they remained for a few years and then departed.[18]

Others have come and made their homes in the country for long periods or stayed permanently, like the members of the American Mission hospital or those who married Kuwaitis. The growing number of the latter, and their offspring, constitute an increasing part of the entire community and play a disproportionate role in knitting the American and Kuwaiti people together. Like the original cadre of Americans in the American Mission, they are of the society and not merely in it, making important contributions and are affected by—as well affecting—their adoptive home. In this group are three individuals selected to give detail and texture to this snapshot in time.[19]

Sheryll Mairza, a native of Illinois, arrived in Kuwait with her husband, Hussein, on the eve of the Iraqi invasion. She was active in the charitable activities of the American Women's League (AWL) and founded her own charity in 2004, Operation HOPE Kuwait (OH). Since that time the organization has blossomed into a leading force of Kuwaiti and expatriate volunteers working for the well-being of poor third-country nationals who make up the menial workforce in Kuwait.

The impetus for Operation HOPE was the sight of a Bangladeshi cleaner working on a cold November day in a thin yellow uniform and oversized shoes without socks. Unable to get the disturbing image out of her mind, Sheryll and Hussein returned to the shopping area where the man was working to give him winter clothes and proper shoes. That Christmas, she asked family and friends to consider distributing winter clothing to needy workers as a way of marking the "season of giving." The response was overwhelming and, within three weeks, she and her new volunteers collected and distributed more than a thousand "winter gift bags" containing a water-resistant coat, hat, gloves, and socks. Operation Hope was born and more than twenty thousand warmth bags have been distributed since.

Funds needed to sustain the charity are collected through a range of creative fundraisers, including bake sales, rummage sales, booths in local bazaars, and admission to sponsored events. The centerpiece of her fundraising is the Annual Mother's Day Breakfast each spring. OH's goals include helping individuals in need on a case-by-case basis; providing opportunities for families of Kuwaiti and expatriate communities to work in cooperation; to provide at least five thousand needy workers with warm clothing each year; and to stock embassy shelters with clothing, blankets, and other basic necessities.

From its simple beginnings in an act of individual charity, Operation Hope has mobilized a highly effective corps of workers with a wide variety of volunteers from private schools, the Girl and Boy Scouts, the American Women's League, the British Ladies Society, and a Spanish-speaking women's group. Sheryll's vision is broad and long-term:

> *Almost every English-language school in the country has become involved with Operation Hope. We would like to see the involvement of students from the local government schools and hope this is something that will happen in the future. If young people become entrenched in community service then many problems and issues will be resolved. After all, today's students are tomorrow's leaders.*[20]

Recently, OH has expanded its concerns to third country nationals who are diagnosed with tuberculosis after arriving in Kuwait. TB patients are automatically deported after proving positive for the disease. Operation Hope assists them with repatriation and provides seed money to resume life in their home countries. Expatriate families who are experiencing temporary difficulties from the death or illness of the head of household may also apply for help.

Well-established as an institution, OH has constructed a HOPE House in the garden of the Mairza home. It replaces the leaky tent in which volunteers have gathered, sorted, and packed donations for distribution, as well as housing the latest fundraising venture, Esther's Attic, the first secondhand charity boutique in Kuwait. By blending American and Kuwaiti traditions of private charity, Operation Hope is making an important contribution.[21]

John Peaveler came to Kuwait in 2000 with the U.S. military. Four years later, he returned as a contractor and met Ayeshah al-Humaidhi, the founder and director of a private nonprofit group dedicated to the welfare of animals. The Kuwait Society for the Protection of Animals and their Habitat (K'S PATH) relies largely on volunteers and donations for its operations. In 2006, the couple was married and decided to devote full time to their animal shelter and the promotion of animal welfare programs and policies.

Ayesha established the organization in 2005 when she returned from pursuing a Master's degree in Public Policy and Management at Carnegie Mellon University in the United States. As she explains:

In the United States I spent six years working with animal shelters and animal rescue organizations. When I came back to Kuwait I found there was a need in these areas that had to be filled. I also believed it was important for there to be an animal welfare organization run by a Kuwaiti, someone who can speak the language of the local population and understand how they think and feel about relevant issues. In my case, this is my country so I have a vested interest in animal welfare in Kuwait. It is an issue that has a direct influence on my quality of life and that of my children.[22]

John and Ayesha have a young daughter and an infant son who are growing up around the animals at K'S PATH shelter in the desert town of Wafra. The proud parents point to research showing that children brought up around animals are generally happier and more content and less likely to suffer from allergies and asthma. In her pioneering work in Kuwait, Ayesha is uniquely qualified to argue her cause in a context other Kuwaitis will appreciate:

First of all, Islam stresses the importance of animal welfare and there are many mentions in the holy Koran clearly stating that animals must be treated humanely. The holy Koran and the Hadith, the recorded sayings of the Prophet Mohammed, make it clear that our treatment of animals will eventually determine our fate in the hereafter. All Muslims know the Hadith in which the Prophet Mohammed told his companions of a woman who was destined to hell because of incarcerating a cat in a cage and never feeding it nor releasing it. On the other hand, a man was forgiven his sins for giving water to a thirsty dog. These are just two examples in the Islamic code of conduct which states that animals should be treated with kindness and consideration but which unfortunately is all too often violated or ignored."

About two hundred rescued animals are cared for by the organization staff at the shelter. They include pets as well as farm animals and more exotic creatures, like baboons, that are unsuitable as pets. A major concern of the organization is the increasing number of endangered, protected, or illegal species smuggled into Kuwait for sale. While the government has acceded to the Convention on International Trade in Endangered Species of Wild Fauna and Flora (CITES), enforcement measures are not commensurate with the extent of the problem. Recently, K'S PATH has begun a wildlife program, a marine conservation program, and Kuwait's first humane animal population control program. Sponsored by the Kuwait Oil Company, the policy has been succesfully implemented in the town of Ahmadi. It is hoped that these initiatives will spur the government to adopt and implement these programs nationwide.

Kuwait, which has a full slate of fast-food and other franchise restaurants, also boasts a unique American eatery thanks to the vision and hard work of a young woman from California. Bianca Simonian has lived in Paris, London, Costa Rica, and Armenia, but it was not until she visited Kuwait at the invitation of a friend that she found what she was seeking. Noting the substantial American presence and the lack of authentic American breakfast offerings, she returned to Los Angeles, put her affairs in order and returned in 2008 to open The Early Bird in the southern suburb of Fahaheel: *"Going out to breakfast is so American. That's what we Americans do. We love it, and that's why back home you find a breakfast place on almost every corner."*

Drawing upon culinary school in Pasadena and an internship in

London, Bianca left her high-end work among the glitterati in Beverly Hills and Bel Air and traded a clientele of stars and beautiful people for a hungry crowd of American oil workers, military personnel, teachers, and other expatriates. Regular customers include many Kuwaitis who studied or worked in the United States where they developed a taste for French toast, waffles, fluffy pancakes with maple syrup, omelettes, hash browns, biscuits and gravy, and eggs with bacon and sausage.[23]

The Early Bird, which opens six days a week at 5:00 a.m. has been a popular sensation, serving clients nostalgic for a taste of "home." Bianca has progressed in a few short years from a one-woman show to an established institution with twenty employees. A second restaurant has opened in Jabriya and a third outlet is in the offing.

Whatever the limitations of this effort to convey the richness and texture of the progession from strangers to friends, nothing symbolizes the culmination of the process as much as the circle closed by one of Kuwait's iconic institutions—the Dar al-Athar al-Islamiyyah (DAI). The facilities of this world-class Islamic museum were devastated by the Iraqis during the occupation. Although many of the priceless treasures in its collections have been returned from Iraq, the preinvasion buildings are still in the process of restoration:

> ... despite the absence of a permanent home, as well as the many challenges the institution has had to face, DAI has made a strong postwar comeback. As the museum staff expected, the restoration of the artifacts damaged by the Iraqis has neccessitated a major ongoing effort... But besides restoring and recataloguing the artifacts returned from Baghdad under the auspices of the United Nations, the DAI plays an active role in the local cultural scene. The institution has expanded its lecture and concert series by inviting distinguished musicians and some of the world's most eminent experts in the fields of Islamic history, art, architecture, and archaeology. It has renovated the Abdullah Al Salem auditorium and rendered it Kuwait's most technologically sophisticated and accoustically perfect community theater.... The DAI also produces special publications, presents local courses on Islamic history and

art, and organizes international conferences, seminars, and exhibitions."[24]

Under the inspired and dedicated leadership of Shaikha Hussah Sabah al-Salem al-Sabah, the Director General, the Dar's vision went far beyond restoration. Through her persistence, the DAI gained ownership of the men's (c. 1954) and women's (c. 1930) hospitals of the American Mission[25] and incorporated them into the museum complex. After a period of careful reconstruction and remodeling, the buildings were reborn as the administrative offices of the DAI. An impressive interactive exhibit details the history and contributions of the mission to the people of Kuwait. In May of 2011, my wife and I were invited to Kuwait to take part in the DAI's annual lecture series. I was honored to deliver a lecture on the research for this book in a newly completed auditorium at the rear of the Mylrea Memorial Hospital building. How fitting that these structures, which were built by Americans to serve the Kuwaiti people, are once more in service to these goals and values.

Appendices

Appendix A

RULERS OF KUWAIT

Shaikh Sabah Al-Ahmed Al-Sabah (Sabah IV)	2006–present
Shaikh Jabir Al-Ahmed Al-Sabah (Jabir III)	1977–2006
Shaikh Sabah Sabah Al-Salem Al-Sabah (Sabah III)	1965–1977
Shaikh Abdallah Al-Salem Al-Sabah (Abdallah III)	1950–1965
Shaikh Ahmed Al-Jabir Al-Sabah (Ahmed I)	1921–1950
Shaikh Salem Al-Mubarak Al-Sabah (Salem I)	1917–1921
Shaikh Jabir Al-Mubarak Al-Sabah (Jabir II)	1915–1917
Shaikh Mubarak Al-Sabah Al-Sabah (Mubarak I)	1896–1915
Sabah Muhammad Al-Sabah Al-Sabah (Muhammad I)	1892–1896
Shaikh Abdallah _____ Al-Sabah (Abdallah II)	1866–1892
Shaikh Sabah Al-Jabir Al-Sabah (Sabah II)	1859–1866
Shaikh Jabir _____ Al-Sabah (Jabir I)	1814–1859
Shaikh Abdallah Al-Sabah Al-Sabah (Abdallah I)	circa 1756–1814
Shaikh Sabah bin Jabir [Muhammad]* (Sabah I)	circa 1752–1756

* Local traditions identify the father of Sabah I as either Jabir or Muhammad. See Rush, *Al-Sabah*, p.193.

Appendix B

ARABIAN MISSION AGREEMENT WITH THE BRITISH

Undertaking with the British Government

We the undersigned, Directors in the Persian Gulf of the Dutch Reformed Church Mission in Arabia, recognizing the special position on the British Government at Kuweit, hereby undertake—in the event of our obtaining from Sheikh Mubarek with British consent, a site in Kuweit, on lease or purchase, for the permanent establishment of our Mission—that while it will always be our endeavour to carry on our work and arrange any little difficulties that may arise from time to time, with the Sheikh direct, should we find ourselves unable to adjust our differences in that manner, we will refer them for the arbitration or good offices of the British representative alone, or, in his absence, of the British resident in the Persian Gulf. The Kuweit establishment will be entirely independent of the branch of our Mission at Busrah and in no circumstances will we, directly or indirectly, seek the intervention of Turkish authorities, or of Consular officials accredited to Turkish territory.

(Signed) Jas. E. Moerdyk
D. Dykstra

At Bahrein
November 18th 1910

Reproduced in Abu Hakima, *Modern History of Kuwait*, p. 201.

Appendix C

AMERICAN CHIEFS OF MISSION IN KUWAIT

Enoch Duncan	Consul	October 15, 1951–
Harrison M. Symmes	Consul	1953–1955
William A. Stoltzfus	Vice Consul	1954–1956
William D. Brewer	Consul	1955–1957
Talcott W. Seelye	Consul	1957–1960
	Vice Consul	1956–1957
Dayton Mak	Consul	Diplomatic relations established
	Chargé d'Affaires	September 22, 1961–January 7, 1962
Parker T. Hart	Ambassador	January 7, 1962–July 13, 1963
	Resident at Jidda	
William A. Stoltzfus	Chargé d'Affaires	Summer 1963–between ambassadors
Howard Rex Cottam	Ambassador	October 24, 1963–July 6, 1969
John Patrick Walsh	Ambassador	November 5, 1969–December 19, 1971
William A. Stoltzfus	Ambassador	February 9, 1972–January 6, 1976
	Also acredited to Abu Dhabi, Doha, Manama, and Muscat	
Frank E. Maestrone	Ambassador	June 13, 1976–July 5, 1979
François M. Dickman	Ambassador	November 24, 1979–August 8, 1983
Philip J. Griffin	Chargé d'Affaires	August 8, 1983–September 1984
Anthony C. E. Quainton	Ambassador	September 19, 1984–August 14, 1987
W. Nathaniel Howell	Ambassador	September 2, 1987–February 1991

Following Iraqi Invasion, the Embassy was evacuated, but not closed, on December 13, 1990; it was reoccupied on March 1, 1991.

Edward William Gnehm   Ambassador   April 2, 1991–
April 1, 1994

Liaison to the Kuwaiti Government-in-Exile during the Iraqi occupation, arriving, in Kuwait following liberation

Ryan Clark Crocker	Ambassador	September 7, 1994–December 4, 1997
James A. Larocco	Ambassador	December 16, 1997–May 17, 2001
Richard Henry Jones	Ambassador	October 1, 2001–July 26, 2004
Richard B. LeBaron	Ambassador	October 12, 2004–July 11, 2007
Deborah K. Jones	Ambassador	2007–2011
Matthew H. Tueller	Ambassador	September 23, 2011–

Key members of embassy staff (identified in the text but not by name)

John Edward Cunningham (Vice Consul) 1951–54
Robert L. Gordon (Vice Consul) 1956–59
Lucien L. Kinsolving (Vice Consul, later Consul) 1957–58
Lancelot P. Olinde (Vice Consul) 1958–60
J. Bruce Scrymgeour (Vice Consul) 1959–61
William H. Bartsch (Vice Consul) 1960–61
Robert O. Manon (Vice Consul) 1960–62
Richard P. Mitchell (Consul) 1960–63
Paul J. Hare (3rd Secretary, later Deputy Principal Officer) 1961–63
James A. May (Counselor) 1963–64
John N. Gatch, Jr. (Counselor, later Deputy Chief of Mission) 1964–68
John W. Vonier (Public Affairs Officer) 1965–68
Frank A. Mau (Counselor) 1974–76
Peter A. Sutherland (Counselor and Deputy Chief of Mission) 1976–80
Phillip J. Griffin (Counselor)1982–85

Robert Holliday (Counselor) 1984–87
Joan C. Donahue (Executive Secretary) late 1980s
Patricia Heller (Executive Secretary) late 1980s

Appendix D

U. S. NAVY SHIP VISITS

Date	Year	Vessel	Port	Comment
Unknown	1948	*Greenwich Bay*	Kuwait	Hosted by H.H. Shaikh Abdallah
Unknown	1953	*Duxbury Bay*	Kuwait	
4–6 Dec.	1955	*Duxbury Bay*	Kuwait	
13–16 Dec.	1957	*Duxbury Bay*	Kuwait	
16–19 Dec.	1957	*Duxbury Bay*	Mina al-Ahmadi	
19–23 May	1959	*Valcour*	Kuwait	
Unknown	1960	unknown	Mina al-Ahmadi	
Unknown	1961	unknown	Kuwait	
November	1962	*Greenwich Bay*	Mina al-Ahmadi	
Unknown	1963	unknown	Kuwait/Ahmadi	
Unknown	1964–5	unknown	unknown	CMEF records incomplete
14–16 Mar.	1966	*Greenwich Bay*	Kuwait	
11–13 May	1966	*Greenwich Bay*	Kuwait	
16–19 Sept	1966	*Valcour*	Kuwait	
19–23 Mar	1967	*Beatty*	Kuwait	
21–23 Mar	1967	*Valcour*	Kuwait	
18–21 May	1968	*O'Hare*	Kuwait	
20–22 Oct.	1968	*Strickfell*	Kuwait	
11–13 Jan.	1969	*R. E. Kraus*	Kuwait	
28 Sept. – 1 Oct.	1969	*Valcour*	Kuwait	
11–13 May	1971	*Valcour*	Kuwait	
4–9 Aug.	1971	*Valcour*	Kuwait	
4–7 Aug.	1971	*R. E. Kraus*	Kuwait	
22–17 Oct.	1971	*Power*	Kuwait	
Unknown	1973	unknown	Kuwait	
Unknown	1974	unknown	Kuwait	CMEF records incomplete

19–21 Feb.	1977	*Lasalle*	Kuwait	
13–15 June	1977	*Lasalle/Trippe*	Kuwait	Took part in search for Kuwaiti helicopter
Unknown	1977	*Sellers*	Kuwait	
12–13 Dec.	1978	*Lasalle*	Kuwait	
Unknown	1985	*Klakring*	Kuwait	
4–6 Jan.	1987	*Sampson*	Shuaiba	
Aug	1987			Operation "Earnest Will" begins
13–16 Mar.	1988	*Reuben James Garcia*	Shuaiba	Bell chronology
17–20 Nov.	1988	*Lasalle*		CKTFME embarked, Bell chron.
May	1989	*Curts*	Ahmadi	Margie Howell memo, June 1
May	1990	*Reid*	Shuaiba	Arab Times, May 23, 1990

Source: Middle East Force records, additional sources as indicated

Appendix E

SELECT EXCERPTS FROM DIARIES OF CITIZENS IN HIDING, AUGUST–DECEMBER 1990

"The American Embassy called on request of Tom Hinds to make sure we were safe." (August 2)[1]

"Iraqi radio warns that the severest penalties will be visited upon any Iraqi citizen who harbors foreigners. It also states that diplomats refusing to close their Embassies in Kuwait will lose their diplomatic immunity and be treated like any other foreign citizen. Hussein has declared that all foreign Embassies should close in Kuwait since they are superfluous due to the fact that Kuwait, according to Hussein, is now part of Iraq."[2]

"Jack called the American Embassy and they gave us a telephone number to call. We couldn't get in touch, and Jack finally called the Embassy back and they gave us another number to call. He gave us directions to his flat."[3]

"We've learned that Randel is our Embassy Warden.... He's constantly in touch with the Embassy so we're going to be well informed.... The American Embassy says they aren't moving out unless it's threatened at gunpoint by Iraqi soldiers." (August 21) [4]

"The American Embassy has kept in close contact with Randel and other wardens despite the fact that they are surrounded by soldiers." (August. 25)[5]

"The Iraqis haven't made a move to oust the Embassy staff out by force.... The Embassy still has their phones connected and are in touch with the Wardens...." (August 26)[6]

"After Iraqi officials detain several husbands and teenage

sons, an exhausted group of 47 American women and children are allowed to leave Iraq and Kuwait. Cheers break out as they arrive at Andrews Air Force Base near Washington."[7]

"According to U.S. Ambassador W. Nathaniel Howell and Deputy Chief of Mission, Barbara Bodine conditions at the U.S. Embassy in Kuwait are getting worse and worse. In an emotional meeting with the Reverend Jesse Jackson, they have requested a medevac plane, fresh water and fuel. The Ambasssador says the food is rotting, there is no electricity, no working water line, no plumbing and no air conditioning in the over 100 degree weather. Bodine said bad telephone lines make it impossible to stay in touch with the 2000 U.S. citizens living or hiding throughout the country. Howell said there are at least 11 sick Americans requiring immediate evacuation and medical attention." (August 30) [8]

"We had a phone call from the American Embassy this afternoon that swung our pendulum of emotions high. They told Judy about a list our names would be placed on and that the Embassy is pushing for a plane for women and children that would leave out of Kuwait." (September 2)[9]

"Judy called the American Embassy and they've sent the list with our names to the Iraqis and probably won't have a reply for 3 days as to whether we can take a flight out of here." (September 4)[10]

"Jack greeted me with some wonderful news! The American women and children will be leaving by Iraqi Airways some time next week and fly to Baghdad and on to Amman after we receive our exit visas, etc. We've been waiting for this, and I'll believe it's all true once we arrive in Amman and board the plane out. It scares me thinking about it...."

"There was a report on BBC that an American was shot at the American Embassy. They haven't been able to find where he was taken. Everyone is playing dumb. Received a call from the Embassy. It's a go for sure. Yea! We're to drive to Safeway and from there we'll go to the airport." (September 6)[11]

"The embassy told us on the telephone that night that we were not to take a male driver to the pickup point which would be at the Safeway parking lot, the reason being that the husbands of the British ladies (that had left previously) all came out of hiding to take the wives to the pickup place. And as soon as the buses left, all of those husbands and fathers were picked up and taken to be used as human shields at the military installations." (September 6)[12]

"On the eighth (sic) of September, 1990, the Iraqi government announced that all of the hostage women and children could leave the country. After checking with the Resistance, and our Embassies, we decided it was not a trick. I dressed as an Arab, and loaded the car after it was dark. We definitely did not want to expose our house to the Iraqis who were in the neighborhood. My wife and Mother, dressed in Abayas, and with my wife driving, they went out of our area by using the back way. My wife then removed the Arabic clothing, and drove to the meeting place which was the old Safeway store on Sixth Ring Road.... From there they were driven to the airport, and eventually, flown to Amman Jordan and then home to freedom."[13]

"The American Embassy called and asked how we were. We said we were ready to go home. There are two women at the Embassy that I know of. You have to take your hat off to them for staying. All women were authorized to leave. I wish to God someone would tell me that I could go if I wished." (September 26)[14]

"I sent a message to Bert today. Could only send two lines, but that's better than nothing I guess. The embassy said I could receive a reply in a few days." (October 2)[15]

"VOA has a new service, that is people back home can leave a call and VOA will broadcast the message five minutes prior to the hour. We heard this from another hostage, and sure enough we tuned in and they were relaying messages. Randel overheard one message saying something sent from Rick to Jack. Maybe it wasn't Rick, anyway it made me feel good." (October 5)[16]

"We are told that a bomb went off in the Hilton Hotel a few days ago. They said it took an hour to get the fire dept. there." (October 7)[17]

"One month since the ladies left. It does feel good that they are being spared this ordeal. The worst part is the not knowing what is really going on. Even the US Embassy has been asking us for the news when we call in for our morning check. It seems that they have no news from the TV or anything as they don't have the fuel to use for their generator. They did have some news for us this morning though. It seems that the Kuwaiti resistance had word of a meeting of the Iraqis being held at the International (Hilton) hotel and put a car bomb in front. The Embassy had a front row seat for the results. Lots of ambulances and confusion. Hope they killed a lot of them." (October 7)[18]

"The Embassy still has no news on evacuation of the old and sick. As a matter of fact, they don't seem to be getting any news at all. When I call in the morning, they always ask what is going on in the world. Probably don't have enough gas to run their generator and pick up anything. The man I talk to still says that they think they can last another month. I hope so as it will be a definite blow to our morale to have them leave." (October 13)[19]

"The embassy called today about 10:30 a.m. with a message from Bert! I at least know she is safely home. That's the most important thing. She said happy birthday and that there was a great deal of support for the people over here." (October 14)[20]

"We listened to the 8:00 a.m. VOA 'Messages From Home' but the reception is so bad it was difficult to hear clearly. But at 12:00 p.m. I heard Bert! Yea! Yes, everything is fine I guess. Lots of yellow ribbons and support. I hope the people back home continue. It will be tough on everyone here. Anyway, to hear Bert was a real treat!" (October 17)[21]

"The Canadian Embassy closed today. That leaves just a few:

the U.S., Britain, Bahrain, U.A.E., and the French. They too must be almost out of stocks of food and will leave soon. I hear the U.S. people are eating just tuna, because that's all they have."

"I called the Embassy this morning and they were a little worried because I was late." (October 17)[22]

"The American Embassy called and asked me about my asthma and high blood pressure, so at least they are concerned. Those people have nothing themselves. No food or much water from what I hear. They can't last much longer." (October 20)[23]

"The American Embassy called today and asked about my medication. Said they would try to help me. That was nice, if unexpected." (October 25) [24]

"More good news. As everyone knows, the water and electricity were cut to all embassies at the very beginning of the siege. Guess what? The American Embassy has dug a well. It is not good for drinking, but they can use it for washing and such. To goad the Iraqi troops around them, they all went out and washed their cars. I imagine it really frosted the Iraqis good. The British may drink champagne by candle light, but now the Americans have their car wash. Good on them." (October 25)[25]

"Dad got a call from Gail (sic) at the embassy today also. The French are pulling out this afternoon, or in the morning, and they will supply French travel papers to a few Americans. She wanted to know if Dad wanted to try. I didn't say much, but he decided not to chance it." (October 27)[26]

"The Embassy called last night and wanted all our ages, weight loss figures, and health statistics." (October 31)[27]

"The American Embassy called, wanted to know how old we are, any problems, and how much weight loss. Nice of them to be interested, but nothing much they can do." (November 1)[28]

"From now on I will try to get a message out on Monday and Dad will send on Tuesday.... I've already written a three liner for transmission. The American embassy only allows us three lines a week, as they are running out of fuel for their generator." (November 2)[29]

"The American Embassy called today, had a message for Randel and one for me from Bert. She said they are tryng to save the property, all are fine and don't worry.... I guess she doesn't know that 'trying to save the property' and 'don't worry' are not the same. I guess she doesn't realize what she sent was really upsetting. Well, I have less that a 50-50 chance of coming out of this thing alive anyhow, so I guess the property should be the least of my worries." (November 7)[30]

"I gave him (Embassy representative) my parents' phone number and some other details before he wished me luck and hung up. There had been little the Embassy staff could do other than organize lists and offer moral support, but they had done their best. Throughout the occupation they had kept in touch regularly. They checked on our mental and physical states and sent messages to our families confirming they had been in touch with us. Now they would be gone." (undated)[31]

"Ramsey Clark is in Baghdad today. The first thing he did was say President Bush is wrong in his approach to the crisis, and the troops in Saudi Arabia are a threat to peace. This scumbag should be jailed, but I guess that's not possible.... Let's see how many people he takes out. If he doesn't get any out, no one else will try. Even if he got me out I would still dislike him." (November 11)[32]

"Just heard on VOA that the Iraqis delivered fresh produce and misc. supplies to the U.S. Embassy in Kuwait. And more deliveries tomorrow! The comment from Pres. Bush was that he didn't know if the Iraqis were trying to prevent the embassy from becoming a tripwire for war, but he was grateful for the action." (December 1)[33]

"We have also heard from the embassy here, that the Iraqis gave them some fresh fruit and a case of cigarettes yesterday. This was before the announcement by Bush. The embassy people have mixed feelings about accepting the gifts. They wanted the world to know that there are a lot of things they need more than smokes, and for everyone to understand that this does not constitute a resupply by the Iraqis. If the Iraqis wanted to make a gesture, all they would have to do would be to turn on the electricity and water.... The embassy is down now to transmitting and receiving messages Monday, Wednesday, and Saturday, and they say the messages are getting real messed up. They have to conserve fuel if they want to last out the problem." (December 1)[34]

"Sent the message to Bert. Embassy says cutoff of 'Messages' will be before Christmas, so soon we will be out of service and disconnected, further narrowing our little world. The electric generator is almost out of fuel." (December 5)[35]

"Just received a call from the embassy. Bert said she is concerned she has not heard from me. Our messages must have passed each other as I sent one out to her yesterday. 'AT 3:05 P.M. BBC ANNOUNCED THAT ALL HOSTAGES ARE FREE TO GO HOME! PRAISE GOD!' (December 6)[36]

"The embassy called this a.m., said to pack our bags and stand by. Said we could take the same amount of luggage as a normal flight anywhere. Said to stay indoors for now. I packed two bags, did my laundry, and I'm ready." (December 7)[37]

"Dad just called the embassy, and they told him that they were already working hard on a blanket visa for all the Americans. Apparently the embassy staff is going to be going with us on the flight. They are only figuring on about 150 Americans form [sic] Kuwait being on the flight. A lot of them are staying behind to sit this out. Most of them are married to Kuwaitis, and lot more Americans got out than they originally thought....

"The embassy called back later tonite and told us to saddle up and be ready to meet at the Airport by 0900 hrs in the morning.... They are convinced that it is not a trick. We were not easily convinced but, as a matter or fact, about half of the embassy crew are going to be on the same flight with us. (December 8)[38].

Bibliography

Books

Atlas al-Kuwait. Kuwait: Al Jahra Press Co., n.d.

Abu-Hakima, Ahmad Mustafa. *Eastern Arabia: Kuwait—Historic Photographs 1900–1936*. Special Revised Edition. Cambridge: Probsthain, 1986.

———. *History of Eastern Arabia, 1750–1800: The Rise and Development of Bahrain and Kuwait*. Beirut: Khayats, 1965.

———. *The Modern History of Kuwait: 1750–1965*. London: Luzac & Company, 1983.

———. *Tarikh Al-Kuwait ([History of Kuwait)*. 3 vols. Kuwait, 1968, 1970, and n.d..

Alani, Mustafa M. *Operation Vantage: British Military Intervention in Kuwait 1961*. Surbiton, Surrey: LAAM, 1990.

Allison, Dr. Mary Bruins. *Dr. Mary in Arabia*. Austin: University of Texas Press, 1994.

Allison, Robert J. *The Crescent Obscured: The United States and the Muslim World, 1776–1815*. New York: Oxford University Press, 1995.

Assiri, Abdul Reda. *The Government and Politics of Kuwait: Principles and and Practices*. Kuwait: n.p., 1996.

Awadi, Sulaiman Abdullah Ali Mohamed Al-. *Kuwait al-Maadi*. Kuwait: Al-Khat Press, 1987.

Bader, Bader Khaled al-. *Ma'raka Al-Jahra, Maa Qabilha wa maa Ba'dha (The Battle of Jahra, What Preceded and What Followed It)*. Kuwait: Dar al-Qabas, 1980.

Barger, Thomas C. *Out of the Blue: Letters from Arabia—1937–1940—A Young American Geologist Explores the Deserts of Early Saudi Arabia*. Vista, CA: Selwa Press, 2000.

Boghardt, Lori Plotkin. *Kuwait Amid War, Peace and Revolution: 1979–1991 and New Challenges*. In association with St. Antony's College, Oxford. New York: Palgrave MacMillan, 2006.

Bryson, Thomas A. *Tars, Turks, and Tankers: The Role of the United States Navy in the Middle East*. Metuchen, NJ: The Scarecrow Press, 1980.

Busch, Briton Cooper. *Britain and the Persian Gulf, 1894–1914*. Berkeley and Los Angeles: University of California Press, 1967.

Butt, Gerald. *The Lion in the Sand: The British in the Middle East*. London: Bloomsbury Publishing, 1995.

Calverley, Eleanor T., M.D. *My Arabian Days and Nights*. New York: Thomas Y. Crowell, 1958.
Carter, J. R. L. *Merchant Families of Kuwait*. London: Scorpion Books, 1984.
Childs, J. Rives. *Foreign Service Farewell: My Years of Service in the Near East*. Charlottesville: University of Virginia Press, 1969.
Chisholm, Archibald. *The First Kuwait Oil Concession: A Record of the H. T. Negotiations, 1911–1934*. London: Frank Cass, 1975.
Crowe, Adm. William J., Jr. *The Line of Fire: From Washington to the Gulf, the Politics and Battles of the New Military*. New York: Simon & Schuster, 1993.
Crystal, Jill. *Oil and Politics in the Gulf: Rulers and Merchants in Kuwait and Qatar*. Cambridge Middle East Library: 24. Cambridge: Cambridge University Press, 1990.
Culbertson, Roberta, and W. Nathaniel Howell. *Siege: Crisis Leadership—The Survival of U.S. Embassy Kuwait*. Charlottesville: Virginia Foundation for the Humanities and Public Policy, 2001.
Daniels, John. *Kuwait Journey*. Luton: White Crescent Press, 1971.
Dar al-Athar al-Islamiyyah. *Conversion of the American Mission Hospital into the Dar al-Athar al-Islamiyyah*. Kuwait: Ministry of Information, November 1996.
Darwin, Alex. *The Edge of War: Kuwait's Underground Resistance Khafji 1990–1991*. Foreword by George H. W. Bush. London: Gulf Museum Consultancy Company, 2011.
Daugherty, Leo J. III. *The Marine Corps and the State Department: Enduring Partners in United States Foreign Policy, 1798–2007*. Jefferson, NC: McFarland & Co., 2009.
Dickson, H. R. P. *The Arab of the Desert*, Third Edition. Edited and abridged by Robert Wilson and Zahra Freeth. London: George Allen & Unwin, 1983.
———. *Kuwait and Her Neighbours*. London: Allen & Unwin, 1936.
Dickson, Dame Violet. *Forty Years in Kuwait*. London: Allen & Unwin, 1978.
Ebraheem, Hassan A. Al-. *Kuwait: A Political Study*. Kuwait: Kuwait University, 1975.
Ebraheem, Hassan Ali Al-. *Kuwait and the Gulf: Small States and the International System*. Center for Contemporary Arab Studies. London: Croom Helm, 1984.
Field, Michael. *The Merchants: The Big Business Families of Saudi Arabia and the Gulf States*. Woodstock, NY: The Overlook Press, 1985.
Freeth, Zahra. *Kuwait Was My Home*. London: George Allen & Unwin, 1956.
Fuccaro, Nelida. *Histories of City and State in the Persian Gulf: Manama since 1800*. Cambridge: Cambridge University Press, 2009.

Gardiner, Stephen. *Kuwait: The Making of a City*. Essex: n.d.
Ghabra, Shafeeq N. "Kuwait and the United States: The Reluctant Ally and U.S. Policy toward the Gulf," in David W. Lesch. *The Middle East and the United States*. Boulder: Westview Press, 1999.
———. *Palestinians in Kuwait: Family and the Politics of Survival*. Westview Special Studies on the Middle East. Boulder: Westview Press, 1987.
Ghunaim, Prof. Abdullah Yusuf al-, Supervisor. *Kuwait-Iraq Boundary Demarcation: Historical Rights and International Will*. Kuwait: Center for Research and Studies on Kuwait, 1994.
Hanioglu, M. Sukru. *A Brief History of the Late Ottoman Empire*. Princeton: Princeton University Press, 2008.
Harrison, Ann M. *A Tool in His Hand: The Story of Dr. Paul W. Harrison of Arabia*. Weybridge, VT: Cherry Tree Books, 2004. reprint of 1958 book.
Harrison, Paul W., M.D. *The Arab at Home*. New York: Thomas Y. Crowell Co., 1924.
———. *Doctor in Arabia*. New York: The John Day Company, 1940.
Hart, Parker T. *Saudi Arabia and the United States: Birth of a Security Partnership*. An ADST-DACOR Diplomats and Diplomacy Book. Bloomington: Indiana University Press, 1998.
Hewins, Ralph. *A Golden Dream: The Miracle of Kuwait*. London: W. H. Allen, 1963.
Hijji, Yacoub Y. Al-. *Old Kuwait: Memories in Photographs*. Kuwait: Center for Research and Studies on Kuwait, 1997.
———. *The Story of Al-Muhalab*. Privately printed, 1983.
Hogarth, David George. *The Penetration of Arabia: A Record of the Development of Western Knowledge Concerning the Arabian Peninsula*. New York: Frederick A. Stokes Company, 1904.
Hogan, Roberta and John. *Trapped in Kuwait: Countdown to Armageddon*. With Linda D. Meyer. Lynnwood, WA: Chas. Franklin Press, 1991.
Holden, David. *Farewell to Arabia*. London: Faber & Faber, 1966.
Howard, Roger. *The Oil Hunters: Exploration and Espionage in the Middle East 1880–1939*. London: Hambleton Continuum, 2008.
Ismael, Jacqueline S. *Kuwait: Dependency and Class in a Rentier State*. Gainesville: University Press of Florida, 1993.
———. *Kuwait: Social Change in Historical Perspective*. Syracuse: Syracuse University Press, 1982.
Jastrow, Morris. *The War and the Bagdad Railway: The Story of Asia Minor and its Relation to the Present Conflict*. Philadelphia: J. B.Lippincott Company, 1917.
Joyce, Miriam. *Kuwait 1945–1996: An Anglo-American Perpective*. Portland, OR: Frank Cass, 1998.

Kabeel, Soraya M. *Source Book on Arabian Gulf States: Arabian Gulf in General, Kuwait, Bahrain, Qatar, and Oman.* Kuwait: Libraries Department, Kuwait University, 1975.

Karsh, Efraim, and Inari Karsh. *Empires of the Sand: The Struggle for Mastery in the Middle East, 1789–1923.* Cambridge: Harvard University Press, 1999.

Kirsch, Gaby. *Prigioniera in Kuwait.* Firenze: Edizioni Valle, 1991.

Kuwait Foundation for the Advancement of Sciences. *Kuwait in World Maps: Facts and Documents.* Kuwait Documents Project. Kuwait: KFAS, 1992.

Kuwait Historical Preservation Study. Vol. 1: *Old Kuwait Town.* Kuwait: Kuwait Municipality, 1988.

Kuwait News Agency (KUNA). *A Twenty-Five Year Era of Kuwait's Modern Advancement.* Kuwait: Information and Research Dept., 1986.

Latham, Don. *Occupation Diary: The Diary of an American in Kuwait, August 2, 1990, until December 10, 1990.* Kuwait: Noureya Al Saddani, 1992.

Levins, John. *Days of Fear: The Inside Story of the Iraqi Invasion and Occupation of Kuwait.* Dubai, UAE: Motivate Publishing, 1997.

Lewcock, Ronald. *Traditional Architecture in Kuwait and the Northern Gulf.* London: Art and Archaeology Research Papers, 1978.

Lienhardt, Peter. *Disorientations: A Society in Flux—Kuwait in the 1950s.* Middle East Cultures: Kuwait, Edited by Ahmed Al-Shahi. Reading, U.K.: Ithaca Press, 1993.

Locher, A. *With Star and Crescent: A Full and Authentic Account of a Recent Journey with a Caravan from Bombay to Constantinople, Comprising a Description of the Country, the People, and Interesting Adventures with the Natives.* Philadelphia: Aetna Publishing Company, 1891.

Loeffler, Jane C. *The Architecture of Diplomacy: Building America's Embassies.* An ADST-DACOR Diplomats and Diplomacy Book. New York: Princeton Architectural Press, 2011. paper.

Longhurst, Henry. *Adventures in Oil: The Story of British Petroleum.* London: Sedgwick & Jackson, 1959.

Mansfield, Peter. *Kuwait: Vanguard of the Gulf.* London: Hutchinson, 1990.

Marafie, Abdul Husain Rafie, Comp. *The Construction of Al Hashemi II: A Voyage through the History of Wooden Ships.* A Concise History of Kuwait; The Art of Making Traditional Vessels. Kuwait: Alfain Printing Co., 2002.

Meyer, Karl E., and Shareen Blair Brysac. *Kingmakers: The Invention of the Modern Middle East.* New York: W.W. Norton & Co., 2008.

Miles, Col. S. B. *The Countries and Tribes of the Persian Gulf.* London: Harrison and Sons, 1920. 2 vols.

Ministry of Foreign Affairs State of Kuwait. *Diplomatic and Consular Corps in Kuwait.* Kuwait: Deparment of Protocol, January 1987.

———. *Diplomatic and Consular Corps in Kuwait*. Kuwait: Deparment of Protocol, January 1988.

———. *Diplomatic and Consular Corps in Kuwait*. Kuwait: Deparment of Protocol, January 1990.

———. *Prominent Personalities of the State and Official National Corporations*. Kuwait: Department of Protocol, April 1990.

Ministry of Information, State of Kuwait. *Kuwait, Facts and Figures 1988*. Kuwait: Ministry of Information, 1988.

Monroe, Elizabeth. *Britain's Moment in the Middle East, 1914–1956*. Baltimore: The Johns Hopkins University Press, 1963.

Moore, Molly. *A Woman at War: Storming Kuwait with the U.S. Marines*. New York: Charles Scribner's Sons, 1993.

Motter, T. H. Vail. *The Persian Corridor and Aid to Russia*. United States Army in World War II: The Middle East Theater. Washington: Center of Military History, United States Army, 1952.

Mylrea, C. S. G. *Kuwait before Oil*. Privately printed, 1952.

National Republican Institute for International Affairs. *Political Participation and Constitutional Democracy in Kuwait*. Edited transcript of a conference, Washington, 1991.

Oren, Michael B. Power. *Faith, and Fantasy: America in the Middle East 1776 to the Present*. New York: W. W. Norton, 2007.

Palmer, Michael E. *Guardians of the Gulf: A History of America's Expanding Role in the Persian Gulf, 1833–1992*. New York: The Free Press, 1992.

Panaspornprasit, Dr. Chookiat. *US-Kuwaiti Relations, 1961–1992*. London: Routledge, 2005.

Philby, H. St. J. B. *Arabia of the Wahhabis*. London: Frank Cass, 1977.

Porter, Jadranka. *Under Siege in Kuwait: A Survivor's Story*. Boston: Houghton Mifflin,1991.

Rashoud, Claudia Farkas Al-. *Dame Violet Dickson: "Umm Saud's" Fascinating Life in Kuwait*. Updated Second Edition. Kuwait: n.p., 2007.

———. *Kuwait: Before and After the Storm*. Kuwait: The Kuwait Bookshops, 1992.

———. *Kuwait: Before and After the Storm*. Updated Second Edition. Kuwait: The Kuwait Bookshops Co., 1999.

———. *Kuwait's Age of Sail: Pearl Divers, Sea Captains, and Shipbuilders Past and Present*. Foreword by Husain Mohammed Rafie Marafie. Singapore: Marafie, 1993.

———.` *Kuwait Kaleidoscope*. Kuwait: Kuwait Bookshops, 1995.

Records of Kuwait, 1899–1961. 7 vols. *Vol. I: Internal Affairs, 1899–1921; Vol. II: Internal Affairs, 1921–1950; Vol. III: Internal Affairs, 1950–1961; Vol. IV: Economic Affairs; Vol. VI, Foreign Affairs I; Vol. VII: Foreign Affairs II*. Selected and edited by A. de L. Rush. Trowbridge, U.K.: Archive Editions,1989.

Rihani, Ameen. *Around the Coasts of Arabia*. London: Constable, 1930.
Royal Scottish Museum. *The Evolving Culture of Kuwait*. Edinburgh: Her Majesty's Stationery Office, 1985.
Rumaihi, Muhammad. *Beyond Oil: Unity and Development in the Gulf*. Trans. by James Dickins. London: Al Saqi Books, 1986.
Rush, Alan. *Al-Sabah: History & Genealogy of Kuwait's Ruling Family, 1752–1987*. London: Ithaca Press, 1987.
Ruthven, Malise. *Freya Stark in Iraq and Kuwait*. The St. Antony's College Middle East Archives. Reading: Garnet Publishing, 1994.
Sandwick, John A., ed. *The Gulf Cooperation Council: Moderation and Stability in an Interdependent World*. Boulder: Westview Press, 1987.
Sanmiguel, Msg. Victor. *Pastor in Kuwait, 1966–1978*. Kuwait: privately printed, 1978.
Sayre, Joel. *Persian Gulf Command: Some Marvels on the Road to Kazvin*. New York: Random House, 1945.
Schofield, Richard. *Kuwait and Iraq: Historical Claims and Territorial Disputes, A report compiled for the Middle East Programme of the Royal Institute of International Affairs*. 2nd. edition. London: R.I.I.A., 1993.
Shamlan, Saif Marzook al-. *Pearling in the Arabian Gulf: A Kuwaiti Memoir*. Trans. from the Arabic by Peter Clark, London: The London Centre of Arab Studies, 2001.
Shaw, Ralph. *Kuwait*. London: Macmillan, 1976.
Shiber, Saba George. *The Kuwait Urbanization – Documentation – Analysis – Critique*. Kuwait: n.p., 1964.
Sindelar, H. Richard III , & J. E. Peterson, eds. *Crosscurrents in the Gulf: Arab, Regional and Global Interests*. For the Middle East Institute. New York: Routledge, 1988.
Smith, Maurice L. *Diary in the Sand; Events Recorded by an American Military Advisor*. San Antonio: Leland's Publishing, 1992.
Smith, Simon C. *Kuwait, 1950–1965: Britain, the al-Sabah, and Oil*. Oxford: Oxford University Press, for the British Academy, 1999.
Stegner, Wallace. *Discovery: The Search for Arabian Oil*. Beirut: Export Press, 1971.
Stanton, Martin. *Road to Baghdad*. New York: Ballantine Books, 2003.
Stevens, Richard P., ed. *The Iraqi Invasion of Kuwait: American Reflections*. Washington: International Education and Communications Group, 1993.
Storm, W. Harold. *Whither Arabia? A Survey of Missionary Opportunity*. London: World Dominion Press, 1938.
Thompson, Eric V., comp. *Major Oil Companies Operating in the Gulf Region (by Country)*. Charlottesville: Petroleum Archives Project, Arabian Peninsula and Gulf Studies Program, University of Virginia, 1995.

Trench, Ralph. *Arabian Travellers*. London: Papermac, 1987.
Tuson, Penelope. *India Office Records: Guides to Archive Groups: The Records of the British Residency and Agencies in the Persian Gulf*. London: India Office Library and Records, Foreign and Commonwealth Office, 1979.
Twinam, Joseph Wright. *The Gulf, Cooperation and the Council: An American Perspective*. Washington: Middle East Policy Council, 1992.
U.S. Department of State, Office of the Historian. *Principal Officers of the Department of State and United States Chiefs of Mission, 1778–1986*. Washington: GPO, 1979.
———. *United States Chiefs of Mission, 1778–1982*. Washington: GPO, 1982.
U. S. Navy, Hydrographic Office. *Persian Gulf Pilot: The Persian Gulf, The Gulf of Oman and The Makran Coast*. H.O. No. 158. First Edition. Washington: Government Printing Office, 1920.
Van Ess, Dorothy. *Fatima and Her Sisters*. New York: John Day, 1961.
Van Ess, John. *Meet the Arab*. New York: The John Day Company, 1943.
Villiers, Alan. *Sons of Sinbad: An Account of Sailing with the Arabs in their Dhows, in the Red Sea, around the Coasts of Arabia, and to Zanzibar and Tanganyika; Pearling in the Persian Gulf; and the Life of the Shipmasters, the Mariners and Merchants of Kuwait*. New York: Charles Scribner's Sons, 1968.
Vine, Peter, and Paula Casey. *Kuwait: A Nation's Story*. London: Immel Publishing, 1992.
Viorst, Milton. *Sandcastles: The Arabs in Search of the Modern World*. New York: Alfred A. Knopf, 1994.
Winkler, David F.. *Amirs, Admirals & Desert Sailors: Bahrain, the U.S. Navy and the Arabian Gulf*. Annapolis: Naval Institute Press, 2007.
Winstone, H. V. F., and Zahra Freeth. *Kuwait: Prospect and Reality*. London: George Allen and Unwin, 1972.
Yahya, Mohammed Abdulrahman al-. *Kuwait: Fall and Rebirth*. London: Kegan Paul International, 1993.
Zahlan, Rosemarie Said. *The Making of the Modern Gulf States: Kuwait, Bahrain, Qatar, the United Arab Emirates, and Oman*. London: Unwin Hyman, 1989.
Zatarain, Lee Allen. *Tanker War: America's First Conflict with Iran, 1987–1988*. Philadelphia: Casemate, 2008.

Newspaper, Journal, and Internet Articles

Abercrombie, Thomas J. "The Persian Gulf: Living in Harm's Way." *National Geographic Magazine* 173, no. 5 (May 1988): 648–71.
Al-Najjar, Ghanim. "Is Kuwait Out of the Impasse?" *Sada*, Carnegie Endowment for International Peace (Mar 2012). http://carnegieendowment.orgsada/index.cfm?fa=show&article=47427&soir_hillite

———. "The Challenges Facing Kuwaiti Democracy." *Middle East Journal* 54, no. 2 (2000): 242–58.

Anderson, N. "Give Us More American Education: How the Persian Gulf Command Made Mechanics of Teenage Peasants." *Survey Graphics*, no. 35 (January 1946): 13–14.

Apple, R. W., Jr. "52 Americans Freed: But Baghdad Prevents 3 From Exiting – Long Standoff is Feared." *New York Times*, Aug. 27, 1990.

———. "Big Gain for Bush: U.S. Sees U.N. Backing for Force in Embargo as More Likely." *New York Times*, Aug. 25, 1990.

———. "U.S. Keeps Kuwait Mission Open." *New York Times*, Aug. 23, 1990.

Arias, Ron. "Held Hostage; In Baghdad, Three U.S. Students Are the Reluctant 'Guests' of Saddam Hussein." *People Weekly*, October, 1990, 46 ff.

Armerding, Dr. Paul. "A Doctor Remembers." *Gulf View* (Dubai), n.d.: 34–36.

Asrati Information Center. "Ousat Awwal Sa'ih Amreeki Zaaran Al-Kuwait Qabil Akthar Min Ma'a wa Ashreen Aman." Asrati, n.d.

Assiri, Abdul-Reda. "Kuwait's Political Survival in the 1980s and Beyond: Small-Nation Response to Regional Pressure." *American-Arab Affairs*, no.30 (Fall 1989): 27–35.

Baker, James A., III. "Why America Is in the Gulf." *World Affairs Journal*: A Compendium, Los Angeles World Affairs Council, Speaker Season, 1990–91, Vol. 3, no. 1: 61–66.

Balz, Dan. "Getting By on Tuna Fish and Rice; U.S. Diplomats in Kuwait Fight Deteriorating Conditions." *Washington Post*, Nov. 30, 1990.

Balz, Dan and Al Kamen. "Bush Maintains Pressure on Iraq; 'I Have Had It' with Hostages' Treatment." *Washington Post*, Nov. 1, 1990.

Bejec, J., R. K. Gang, and A.R. Lari. "Post Gulf War Explosive Injuries in Liberated Kuwait." *Injury* 24, no. 8 (September 1993): 517–20.

Bibby, Geoffrey. "Looking for Dilmun." *Aramco World* 21, no. 1 (1970): 24–29.

Birnbaum, Michael. "Battle to Oust Kuwait Premier Gains Urgency." *Washington Post*, Mar. 7, 2011.

Bishku, Michael B. "Iraq's Claim to Kuwait: A Historical Overview." *American-Arab Affairs*, no. 37 (1991): 77–88.

Bloom, Johnathan M., and Lark Ellen Gould. "Patient Restoration: The Kuwait National Museum." *Saudi Aramco World* 51, no. 5 (2000): 10–21.

Bodine, Barbara K. "Saddam's Siege of Embassy Kuwait: A Personal Journal." In Joseph G. Sullivan, ed. *Embassies Under Siege: Personal Accounts by Diplomats on the Front Line*. An Institute for the Study of Diplomacy Book. Washington: Brasseys, 1995, 112–31.

Bondarevsky, G. L. "Iraq, Kuwait and Nazi Germany." Lecture, October 23, 1998. *Hadeeth ad-Dar* (Kuwait 28 (2008): 54–59.

———. "Kuwait and the Gulf States during the Second World War." *Bareed ad-Dar* (Monthly Newsletter of the Friends of Dar al-Athar al-Islamiyyah, Kuwait). Annual Edition 1999–2000: 5.

Bonner, Raymond. "Report from Kuwait: A Woman's Place." *New Yorker*, Nov. 16, 1992.

Boustany, Nora. "Bush Calls Americans Held By Iraq 'Hostages.'" *Washington Post*, Aug. 21, 1990.

Brewer, William D. "Yesterday and Tomorrow in the Persian Gulf." *Middle East Journal.* 23, no. 2 (1967).

Broder, John M. "U.S. Embassy's Water, Power Cut Off By Iraq." *Los Angeles Times*, Aug. 26, 1990.

Brodie, Ian, and Michael Smith. "The Middle East: Westerners in Kuwait Told to Remain Hidden." *Daily Telegraph* (London), Dec.8, 1990.

Burns, John F. "Iraq Backs Off Its Threat to Execute Diplomats Who Hide Civilians." *New York Times*, Sep. 28, 1990.

Busch, Briton Cooper. "Britain and the Status of Kuwayt 1896–1899." *Middle East Journal* 21, no. 2 (1967): 187–98.

Butt, Gerald. "Iraq, West in War of Nerves." *Christian Science Monitor*, Aug. 24, 1990.

Butt, Gerald, and Wendy Holden. "Life Sentence Threat to Hostages Found Fleeing." *Daily Telegraph* (London), Sep. 8, 1990.

Caverley, Edwin E. "Kuwait Today, Yesterday and Tomorrow." *Muslim World*, January 1962.

Cary, Peter. "Librarian to Human Shield." *U.S. News & World Report* 109, no. 25 (Dec. 24, 1990).

Case, Paul Edward. "Boom Time in Kuwait: An Obscure Persian Gulf Shaikhdom, Enriched by Oil, Uses Its Wealth to Improve the Lot of All Its People." *National Geographic* 102, no. 6 (December 1952): 783–802.

Chen, Edwin, "Hostages Return, Tell of Ordeal at Embassy." *Los Angeles Times*, September 3, 1990, A1.

Chin, Paula, and Bill Hewitt. "Home for Christmas." *People Weekly*, 34, No. 25 (December 24, 1990): 30–36.

Clancy, Ray. "UK Fugitives Await All-Clear from Embassy." *Times* (London), December 8, 1990.

Cockburn, Patrick. "Union Flag Flies in Kuwait as Envoys Follow Hostages Out. *Independent* (London), December 17, 1990.

"Commencements: At Notre Dame, a Call to 'Be Informed'." *New York Times*, May 20, 1991.

Curtiss, Richard H. "Fawzi Dalloul: A Palestinian from Kuwait." *Washington Report on Middle East Affairs*, February 1991, 21 ff.

"Daily Struggle of Survival: Water in Kuwait defore the Oil." *Kuwaiti Digest*, July–September 2002: 33–37.

Dar al-Athar al-Islamiyyah. "Dar al-Athar al-Islamiyyah's New Home." *Bareed ad-Dar* (Monthly Newsletter of the Friends of Dar al-Athar al-Islamiyyah, Kuwait) 9, No. 2 (2007): 11.

———. "The American Mission Hospital. Part I." *Bareed ad-Dar* (Monthly Newsletter of the Friends of Dar al-Athar al-Islamiyyah, Kuwait) 1, No. 3 (November, 1998): 2.

———. "The American Mission Hospital, Part II." *Bareed ad-Dar* (Monthly Newsletter of the Friends of Dar al-Athar al-Islamiyyah, Kuwait) 1, No. 4 (December, 1998): 2.

———. "The American Mission Hospital, Part III." *Bareed ad-Dar* (Monthly Newsletter of the Friends of Dar al-Athar al-Islamiyyah, Kuwait) 1, No. 5 (January/February, 1999): 2.

———. "The American Mission Hospital, Part IV." *Bareed ad-Dar* (Monthly Newsletter of the Friends of Dar al-Athar al-Islamiyyah, Kuwait) 1, No. 6 (March and April, 1999): 2.

"Diwaniyyahs—Cultural Fora or Social Heritage." Translation of a series of articles published in *al-Qabas* (Kuwait), May 1988.

"A Donkey's Tale." *Kuwaiti Digest*, July–September 2000: 21–22.

Downs, Natasha. "Diary of a Hostage: Escaping to Freedom." *McCall's*, May 1991: 42.

Duncan, Col. B. A. C. "Cruelty and Compassion: An Englishman in Kuwait." *Army Quarterly and Defence Journal* (London) 121, no. 2, Gulf War Issue, 1991.

Earle, Sylvia A.."Persian Gulf Pollution: Assessing the Damage One Year Later," *National Geographic* 181, No. 2 (February 1992): 122–34.

Ebraheem, Hassan Al-. "Interview." *American-Arab Affairs*, No. 34 (Fall 1990), 8–11.

Eddy, William A. "King Ibn Saud: Our Faith and Your Iron." *Middle East Journal* 17, no. 3 (Summer 1963).

Eilts, Hermann Frederick. "Ahmad Bin Na'aman's Mission to the United States in 1840: The Voyage of the Al-Sultanah to New York City." Reprinted by Petroleum Development (Oman) Limited with the kind permission and corrections of myself and the Essex Institute, Salem Massachusetts, in whose quarterly the article was originally published in October 1962. Beirut: Middle East Export Press, n.d.

"Embassy Security Not Beefed Up." *Denver Post*, December 13, 1983.

"Exploring Old Kuwait." *Bareed ad-Dar* (Monthly Newsletter of the Friends of Dar al-Athar al-Islamiyyah, Kuwait) 1, No. 4 (December 1988).

"Escape from Kuwait." *Reader's Digest*, December 1990.

Everly, George S., Jr. "Reflections on the Reconstruction of a Nation:

Rebuilding the National Identity of Kuwait." *International Journal of Emergency Mental Health* 3, no. 1 (Winter 2001): 1–3.

Facey, William. "Sons of the Wind." Photographs by Alan Villiers. *Saudi Aramco World*, 61, No.2 (March/April 2010): 8–17.

Fineman, Mark. "U. S. Hostage Dies, Iraq Claims." *Los Angeles Times*, August 28, 1990, A11.

Fisher, Marc. "Embassy Staff Leaves Kuwait; U.S. Ambassador, 4 Others End 4 Months Siege." *Washington Post*, December 14, 1990, A1.

Fordham, Alice. "Iraq reaches settlement with Kuwait on disputes: Baghdad continues regional charm offensive ahead of Arab summit." *Washington Post*, March 15, 2012.

Frazer, John E. "Kuwait: Aladdin's Lamp of the Middle East." *National Geographic* 135, No. 5 (May 1969): 636–67.

Friedman, Thomas L. "U.S. Set to Vacate Embassy in Kuwait" *New York Times*, December 8, 1990.

Friend, David. "America Abroad: Embassy on the Front Line of Terror." *Life*, December 1985, 130–36.

———. "Embassy on the Front Line of Terror." *Life* 8, no. 13 (December 1985): 130–36.

Fromkin, David "How the modern Middle East map came to be drawn." *Smithsonian* 22, no. 2 (May 1991): 132–48.

Gerstenzang, James. "Bush Says 3,000 Americans are 'Hostages' and Warns Iraq." *Los Angeles Times*, August 21, 1990, A1.

Ghabra, Shafeeq N. "Balancing State and Society: The Islamic Movement in Kuwait." *Middle East Policy* 5, no. 2 (May 1997): 58–72.

———. "Democratization in a Middle Eastern State: Kuwait, 1993." *Middle East Policy* 3, no. 1 (1994): 102–19.

———. "Kuwait and the Dynamics of Socio-Economic Change." *Middle East Journal* 51, vol. 3 (Summer 1997): 358–72.

———. "Kuwait's Democracy is Challenged by Pressure for Reform." The Washington Institute for Near East Policy, Policy Watch # 1897, July 2, 2012.

———. "The Iraqi Occupation of Kuwait: An Eyewitness Account." *Journal of Palestine Studies* 20, No. 2 (Winter 1991): 112–25.

Ghanim, Dalal al-. "History of Water in Kuwait." *Dinar* (Commercial Bank) 1, No. 5 (1984): 32–38.

"Going Down Deep: Pearls of History." *Kuwaiti Digest*, October–December 2001: 41–44.

Goldman, John J. "U.N. Demands Resupply of Embassies in Kuwait." *Los Angeles Times*, October 30, 1990, A6.

Gorman, Tom. "Hoping, Praying, Waiting for a Husband Left Behind." *Los Angeles Times*, December 23, 1990, A1.

Goshko, John M. "Iraq Accused of Erecting Red Tape to Block Exit of U.S. Women and Children," *Washington Post*, September 1, 1990, A18.

Hajji, Dr. Yusuf Al-. "The Art of Building Sailing Ships in Kuwait." The Newsletter of Dar al-Athar al-Islamiyyah, Issue 10 (2001):, 11–13.

Harrigan, Peter. "The Captain and the King." *Saudi Aramco World* 53, no. 5 (September/October 2002): 12–21.

"Healing the Scars of the Past." *Majalla*, September 1, 2010. <<http://www.majalla.com/eng/2010/09/article55122465/print/>>

Hessler, William H. "By the Shores of Araby: The Persian Gulf Command." *U.S. Naval Institute Proceedings* 82, No. 10 (October 1956): 1027–41.

Hewitt, Bill. "Our Flag was Still There ... A Stubborn Diplomat Wouldn't Abandon Kuwait." *People Weekly* 35, No. 17 (May 6, 1991): 52–53.

Hijji, Yacoub Yusuf Al-. "In Memory of Kuwait's Masts and Sails: The East African Voyage." Abridged from a Lecture. *Hadeeth ad-Dar* (periodic journal of the Friends of Dar al-Athar al-Islamiyyah, Kuwait) 18 (2004) 18 (2004): 30–32.

Hobson, Richard, Jr., and John Lawton. "New Battle in an Ancient War." *Aramco World Magazine* 38, No. 3 (May–June 1987), 6–13.

Hoffman, David. "Besieged Embassy Given Food." *Washington Post*, December 1, 1990, A22.

———. "Diplomacy Shifting Western Debate From a Stick to a Carrot." *Washington Post*, December 7, 1990, A28.

———. "U.S. Orders Iraqi Embassy To Cut Staff by Two-Thirds." *Washington Post*, August 28, 1990, A1.

———. "U.S. to Evacuate Kuwait Embassy." *Washington Post*, December 8, 1990, A1.

"The Hostages' Tale." Editorial. *Washington Post*, December 16, 1990.

Howell, W. Nathaniel. "In the Wake of the Storm: Kuwaiti Society Following Liberation." *Middle East Insight*, March–April 1995.

———. "'The Evil That Men Do...': Societal Effects of the Iraqi Occupation in Kuwait." *Mind & Human Interaction* 6, No. 4 (November 1995): 150–69.

Hughes, Colin, and John Lichfield, "Marines Withdrawn from Mission." *Independent* (London), August 24, 1990.

Ibrahim, Youssef M. "Mitterrand Irate: French Ask U.N. Council to Extend Its Embargo to Include Flights." *New York Times*, September 16, 1990.

"Images from the Past." *Kuwaiti Digest*, July–September 1997: 25–28.

"In Search of Water." *Kuwaiti Digest*, July–September 2000: 23–25.

"Islamic Art and Its Patronage: Treasures from Kuwait: Ten Years around the World." *Bareed ad-Dar* (Monthly Newsletter of the Friends of Dar al-Athar al-Islamiyyah, Kuwait), Annual Edition 1999–2000.

Jehl, Douglas. "52 Americans Leave Iraq." *Los Angeles Times*, August 27, 1990.

Jordan, Mary, and Peter Baker. "Hostages' Joy Tinged with Fear; Nine Bring Home Concern for Others." *Washington Post*, October 26, 1990, D1.
Kamen, Al. "U.N. Declares Annexation of Kuwait 'Void'; Iraq Closes Borders, Bars Exit of Foreigners." *Washington Post*, August 10, 1990, A1.
Kamen, Al, and Keith Kendrick. "Saddam's Human Bargaining Chips." *Washington Post,* August 12, 1990.
Kamen, Al, and Patrick E. Tyler. "3–4 Weeks of Food Left in Embassy." *Washington Post,* November 1, 1990.
Kaplan, Marion. "Twilight of the Arab Dhow." *National Geographic* 140, no. 9 (September 1974): 330–51.
Kelley, Jack. "Ex-hostage: Our People Are Starving." *USA Today*, September 4, 1990.
Kempster, Norman. "U.S. Diplomats to Leave Kuwait." *Los Angeles Times*, December 8, 1990.
Kennet, Derek. "Failaka Island: Centre of Kuwait's Archaeological Heritage." *Arab Times* (Kuwait), May 7, 1990.
Khouri, Rami G. "Kuwait's Heritage House." *Aramco World* 41, No. 6 (November–December 1990): 30–37.
Kifner, John. "An Ambassador-in-Waiting Takes Office in Washington." *New York Times,* November 6, 1990, A14.
Kinzer, Stephen."Last Flight of Hostages, Envoy Aboard, Gets to West." *New York Times,* December 14, 1990, A14.
Krauss, Clifford. "Embassy Gets Food: Iraq's Troops in Kuwait Deliver Some Supplies to the U.S. Mission." *New York Times*, December 1, 1990.
———. "Envoy to Kuwait Is Greeted in U.S.: Ambassador and Party, Met by Baker, Saw No Sign of Iraqi Desire to Leave." *New York Times*, December 15, 1990.
———. "Foreigners Warned: Iraqis Order Americans and British to Gather at 2 Kuwait Hotels." *New York Times*, August 17, 1990.
———. "Only 4 Embassies Hold Out in Kuwait as Food Dwindles." *New York Times*, October 12, 1990.
———. "U.S. Unlikely to Use Force to Resupply Embassy." *New York Times*, November 7, 1990.
"Kuwait's Developments Marvelled at...46 years ago." *Kuwaiti Digest*, January–March 2001: 48–51.
"Kuwait's Residential Architecture." *Kuwaiti Digest*, April–June 1995: 16–19.
Leff, Lisa, and John Lancaster. "Quiet but Happy Scene at Andrews as Last of Embassy Staff Arrives." *Washington Post*, December 15, 1990.
Lippman, Thomas. "The Pioneers," *Saudi Aramco World* 55, No. 3 (May/June 2004): 14–21.

Lorch, Donatella. "Old Glory Returns to Kuwait Capital," *New York Times*, March 2, 1991.
Mallakh, Ragaei El-. "Economic Development Through Cooperation: The Kuwayt Fund." *Middle East Journal* 18, no. 4 (Autumn 1964): 405–20.
Mandaville, Jon. "Rahmah of the Gulf." *Aramco World Magazine* 26, No. 3 (May–June 1975): 12–13.
Mann, Jim, "Iraq Surrounds U.S. Embassy in Kuwait, Detains Evacuees." *Los Angeles Times*, August 25, 1990.
Masland, Tom. "Underground in Kuwait." *Newsweek*, December 31, 1990, p. 43.
McAllister, Bill. "U.S. Resists Iraqi Deadline on Embassy." *Washington Post*, August 23, 1990.
Monroe, Elizabeth. "Across the Rub' Al-Khali: H. St. John Philby's Great Arabian Journeys of Exploration, Part one, 1932." *Aramco World Magazine* 24, No. 6 (November–December 1973): 6–13.
———. "Kuwayt and Aden: A Contrast in British Policies." *Middle East Journal* 18, no. 1 (Winter 1964): 63–74.
Morganthau, Tom, et. al. "Waiting, Hoping, Praying." *Newsweek*, August 20, 1990, p. 28.
"Mr. Ezzat Jaafar Looks Back on the Dawn of Kuwait's Modern History." *Kuwaiti Digest*, July–September 1996: 24–26.
Munro, John, with Martin Love. "The Nairn Way." *Aramco World Magazine* 32, No. 4 (July–August 1981): 18–23.
Muehring, Kevin. "The Struggle over Kuwait's Money Machine." *International Investor*, August 1988, 44–54.
Mulligan, William. "Air Raid! A Sequel." *Aramco World Magazine* 29, no. 4 (July–August 1976), pp. 2–3.
Murphy, Caryle. "Power to U.S. Embassy in Kuwait Is Cut Off." *Washington Post*, August 26, 1990.
Mylrea, C. Stanley G. MD. "Kuweit, Arabia." *The Moslem World* 7, no. 2 (April 1917).
Naser, Fahad Al, George S. Everley, Jr., and M. I. Al-Khulaifi. "Overcoming the Effects of Disasters: A Rational for the Kuwait CISM Program." *International Journal of Emergency Mental Health* 3, No. 1 (Winter 2001): 11–12.
Nazar, Fatima, and Kamiar Kousekanani. "Attitudes towards Violence against Women in Kuwait." *Middle East Journal* 61, no. 4 (Autumn 2007): 641–54.
"New Discoveries of Ancient Cemeteries in Kuwait." *Kuwaiti Digest*, July–September 2004; 43–46.
Newton, Edmund "Iraqis were Brutal, Not Bright, Envoy Says." *Los Angeles Times*, March 15, 1991.

Oberdorfer, Don. "Missed Signals in the Middle East." *Washington Post Magazine,* March 17, 1991.
Park, Michael Y. "Former 'Guests' of Saddam Hussein Recall Days of Anguish in Kuwait." Fox News.com, August 1, 2000. <<http://www.foxnews.com/world/gulfwar/iraq_hostages_park.sml>>
Phillips, Don, and Dan Balz. "U.S. Warns Americans in Kuwait to Stay Away from Embassy." *Washington Post,* August 26, 1990.
Priest, Dana. "500 to Forego U.S. Evacuations; Many Are in Families with Mixed Citizenship in Kuwait, Iraq." *Washington Post,* December 12, 1990
———. "Hostages Pour Out From Iraq, Kuwait; 163 Americans among 950 Evacuated." *Washington Post,* December 10, 1990.
———. "Iraq Targets U.S. Public's Hostage Fears,. *Washington Post,* November 6, 1990.
———. "Saddam Orders the Release of All Hostages." *Washington Post,* December 7, 1990.
Putnam, John J. "The Arab World, Inc." *National Geographic* 141, no. 10 (October 1975): 494–533.
Quandt, William B. "The Gulf War: Policy Options and Regional Implications." *American-Arab Affairs,* No. 9 (Summer 1984): 1–7.
"A Quieter, Simpler Time: Life in Kuwait before the Discovery of Oil." *Kuwaiti Digest,* October–December 2001: 25–27.
Rashoud, Claudia Farkas Al-. "Hair comes down, feelings let out." *Arab Times,* May 1, 1993.
———. "'Hands-on' approach... so they'll stay on." *Arab Times,* November 10, 1992.
———. "Postcards from Kuwait." *Inland Empire Magazine* (Riverside, CA), January, 1991, p. 67. (This article was published anonymously to protect family still in occupied Kuwait.)
———. "Serving martyrs families and honor." *Arab Times,* February 22, 2012.
———. "Stay away from death traps, EOD advisor warns children." *Arab Times,* November 22, 1993.
———. "The war within ... get help: PTSD rampant in Kuwait." *Arab Times,* February 22–23, 2001.
———. "Tributes paid to American women." *Arab Times,* April 27–29, 1995.
"Retracing Old Streets of Kuwait." *Kuwaiti Digest,* July–September 2002: 40–44.
Rosenthal, Andrew. "Baghdad Warns Diplomats Against 'Act of Aggression'" *New York Times,* August 24, 1990.
———. "Threat in Kuwait: Barring Iraqi Violence, U.S. Fight for Mission Is Seen as Unlikely." *New York Times,* August 24, 1990. p. A1.

Rupert, James. "Diplomats Struggle On in Saddam's Capital." *Washington Post*, October 3, 1990.

Rumaihi, Mohammad al-. "Arabian Gulf Security." *American-Arab Affairs*, No. 23 (Winter 1987–88): 47–56.

———. "Kuwaiti-American Relations: A Case of Mismanagement." *American-Arab Affairs*, No. 9 (Summer 1984): 77–80.

Sabah, H.E. Shaikh Saud Nasir al-   "Developments in the Arabian Gulf: A View from Kuwait." *American-Arab Affairs*, No. 26 (Fall 1988: 92–95.

———., "Interview." *American-Arab Affairs*, No. 33 (Summer 1990): 1–5.

Saul, Stephanie, "For 47, a Long, Hard Journey Back Home." *Newsday*, August 29, 1990.

Schloesser, Maj. Jeffrey. "The Limits of Power: America's 20 Years in the Gulf." *Military Review* 72, no. 1 (January 1992):17–29.

Schmitt, Eric. "Iraqi Diplomat Vows to Release Kin of Envoys." *New York Times*, August 26, 1990.

Sciolino, Elaine. "As 700 Hostages Fly to Freedom, There Is Relief but Little Rejoicing." *New York Times*, September 3, 1990.

"A Seasonal Tradition: Desert Camping in Kuwait." *Kuwaiti Digest*, January–March 2002: 22–25.

"The Second Liberation: Bringing Back the Sun." *Kuwaiti Digest*, October–December 2001: 20–24.

Shayji, Abdullah al-. "Kuwait-Iraq: Cold war brewing." *Gulf News*, July 25, 2011

———. "Kuwait in midst of its own Arab Spring," *Gulf News* (Dubai), December 12, 2011.

Shenon, Philip. "For Freed U.S. Families, a Tearful Homecoming." *New York Times*, August 29, 1990.

Tétreault, Mary Ann. "Autonomy, necessity, and the small state: Ruling Kuwait in the twentieth century." *International Organization* 45, no. 4 (Autumn 1991): 565–91.

———. "Civil Society in Kuwait: Protected Spaces and Women's Rights." *Middle East Journal* 47, no. 2 (Spring 1993): 275–91.

———. "Kuwait: The Morning After." *Current History* 91, no. 561 (January 1993): 6–10.

———. "Kuwait's Unhappy Anniversary." *Middle East Policy* 7, no. 3 (June 2000): 67–77.

Tétreault, Mary Ann, & Haya al-Mughni. "Modernization and Its Discontents: State and Gender in Kuwait." *Middle East Journal* 49, no. 3 (Summer 1995): 403–17.

"Timeline: Iraq's Invasion of Kuwait." Fox News.com. August 2, 2000. <<http://www.foxnews.com/gulfwar/timeline_invasion.sml>>

Toth, Jennifer,."U.S. Diplomat Howell Comes Home a Hero." *Los Angeles Times,* December 15, 1990.
Tracy, William. "A Talk with Violet Dickson." *Aramco World Magazine* 23, No. 6 (November–December 1972): 12–19.
Treaster, Joseph B. "Evacuation of Hostages Is Stalled As Iraqis Prohibit Foreign Flights." *New York Times,* September 4, 1990.
———. "Life in Emptied Kuwait City: Diplomats Long for Comforts." *New York Times,* September 1, 1990
Twinam, Joseph Wright. "America and the Gulf Arabs." *American-Arab Affairs,* No. 25 (Summer 1988): 126–56.
———. "America and the Gulf Arabs." *American-Arab Affairs,* No. 26 (Fall 1988): 107–24.
Tyler, Patrick E. "500 Gulf Hostages Flown to Safety: Only One American Shows Up in Kuwait for Final Flight." *New York Times,* December 12, 1990.
———. "Large Evacuation of U.S. Hostages Is Expected Today." *New York Times,* December 9, 1990.
———. "Relief, Tears and Hope at Hostages' Hotel." *New York Times,* December 8, 1990.
———. "Standoff in the Gulf." *New York Times,* December 8, 1990.
"US Ambassador Endorses American Mission Hospital Plan." *Bareed ad-Dar,* Year 9, Issue 3. 2007.
U.S. Department of State. "3 eyewitness accounts of the truck bombing at Embassy Kuwait/" Department of State Newsletter, No. 264 (February 1984): 2–8.
———. "3 national employees killed in Kuwait attack." Department of State Newsletter, No. 263 (January 1984): 8.
———. "Crisis in the Persian Gulf: Statements by President Bush, Secretary Baker and Ambassador to Kuwait Nathaniel Howell." *U.S. Department of State Dispatch.* 1, No. 17 (December 24, 1990): 347 ff.
———. "Evacuation from Kuwait." Department of State Newsletter (October 1990): 4.
———. "Extra! Envoy 'Escapes'!" Department of State Newsletter (January 1981): 10.
———. "Post of the Month: Kuwait." Department of State Newsletter, No. 265 (March 1984): 40–45.
———. "Terrorism." Department of State Newsletter, No. 265 (March 1984): 6–7.
"U.S. Diplomats Leave Kuwait." *Chicago Tribune,* December 14, 1990.
"U.S. Envoy Leaves Kuwait." *Los Angeles Times,* December 13, 1990.
"US Lecture Tour." *Bareed ad-Dar* (Newsletter of the Friends of Dar al-Athar al-Islamiyyah, Kuwait) 2, No. 2, 2001.

Van Pelt, Mary Cubberly. "The Sheikhdom of Kuwait." *Middle East Journal* 4, no. 1 (January 1950).
Viorst, Milton. "A Reporter at Large: Out of the Desert." *New Yorker*, May 16, 1988: 43–74.
Von Drehle, David, and R. Jeffrey Smith. "U.S. Strikes Iraq for Plot to Kill Bush." *Washington Post*, June 27, 1993.
Watson, Russell. "Crisis in the Gulf." *Newsweek*, November 12, 1990.
Wheeler, Deborah. "New Media, Globalization and Kuwaiti National Identity." *Middle East Journal* 54, no. 3 (Summer 2000): 432–44.
Williams, Daniel. "U.S. Hostage Mystery: How Many Are Left Behind, Facing What Perils?" *Los Angeles Times*, September 3, 1990.
Williams, Daniel, and Tamara Jones. "Last U.S. Envoys Leave Kuwait Post." *Los Angeles Times*, December 14, 1990.
Zaman, Amberin, and Wendy Holden, "Embassy Wives and Children Reach Safety." *Daily Telegraph* (London), August 28, 1990.
Zdanowski, Dr. Jerry. "King 'Abd Al-'Aziz in the Reports of the American Missionaries, 1901–1921. <<http://www.darah.org.sa/bohos/Data/15/06.htm>>

Documents and Unpublished Materials

Akins, James. Unpublished conversation. October 6, 1988.
Aldakheel, Maureen. "A Year in the Life of Maureen Aldakheel, August 1990–Present." Typewritten manuscript, 1991.
Allison, Mary. "Health Care in Kuwait in the 1930s." Lecture delivered at the Medical Faculty of Kuwait University. Soundtrack of video recording. Transcribed November 4, 1988.
American Embassy in Kuwait. "American Embassy Kuwait – Quick Reference Tel. List by Section, November 1989." Typewritten.
———.Telegram 05334 to Department of State listing personal effects of Amb. and Mrs. Howell, partially packed in July 1990, October 22, 1990.
———. Telegram 05779 (USIS) reporting English translation of article in Kuwait daily, *Al-Siyassah*, about Embassy reception on Kuwaiti-American Educational Exchange, October 3, 1988.
———.Diplomatic Note No. 359, announcing the departure of Amb. W. Nathaniel Howell, July 25, 1990.
———. "Diwaniyas in Kuwait, 1994." Typewritten list of *diwaniyas* by time of sitting, with locations and contact information.
———.Guest List, Independence Day Reception, July 7, 1990. Typewritten.
———. "History of American Diplomatic Representation in Kuwait." Kuwait, June 22, 1981. Typewritten.

———. Itinerary for the Visit to Kuwait of the Hon. Frank C. Carlucci, Secretary of Defense, December 6–7, 1988.

———. Record of visits to diwaniyyas during Ramadan (April–May 1989). Typewritten.

———. Reproduction of map of the Bnaid Al-Gar area, annotated to show residences of American employees on the Embassy Compound and surrounding neighborhood, 1990.

———. "A Short History of Kuwaiti-American Relations." Prepared for the Occasion of the Fifteenth Anniversary of the Opening of the American Consulate in Kuwait, October 1964. Typewritten.

———. Telephone List, dated November 1989. 2 pages. Typewritten.

———. Press release entitled "Embassy Kuwait Honors Longest American Resident," August 10, 1989.

———. Program for the Community 4th of July Party, July 6, 1989.

———. "Visit of The Honorable George Bush, 41st President of the United States, March 22–24, 1996." Typewritten agenda.

Bell, Col. James. "Kuwait Chronology — July '87–July '89." Typewritten, July 21, 1989.

Bosch, Dr. & Mrs. Don. Correspondence with author, 1993.

Brewer, William D. Correspondence with author, 1991–92.

———.. The Foreign Affairs Oral History Collection of the Association for Diplomatic Studies and Training, August 2, 1988. http://www.adst.org/OH%20TOCs/Brewer,%20William%20D.toc.pdf

Campbell, Kay Hardy. "The History of United States Consulate General Dhahran, Saudi Arabia." Unpublished monograph, March 1988.

Cecil, Amb. Charles. Correspondence with author, February 1989.

Claussen, Paul. Letter from Office of the Historian, Department of State, regarding the establishment of a Consulate in Kuwait (with attached documents.), November 29, 1988.

Cottam, Mrs. Howard. Correspondence with author, 1993.

Dar Al Athar Al Islamiyyah. Plans, drawings, schematics, and text prepared by Ghazi Sultan, Architect/Planner in connection with the "Conversion of the American Hospital." Produced by the Ministry of Information, State of Kuwait, November 1996.

Dickman, Francois M. Correspondence. July, 1988.

———. The Foreign Affairs Oral History Collection of the Association for Diplomatic Studies and Training. http://www.adst.org/OH%20TOCs/Dickman,%20Francois%20M.toc.pdfbin/query/r?ammem/mfdip:@field(DOCID+mfdip2004dic02)>> February 9, 2001

Eagleburger, Lawrence S. Text of remarks at Awards Presentation. Department of State, June 7, 1991.

Edwards, Lovelyn. Transcription of cassettes recorded in September 1988.

Bibliography

Gatch, John N., Jr. Correspondence, 1988.

Geerhart, Mrs. Wilton. Recorded recollections of resident of Kuwait (Bechtel), 1948–1981, December 4, 1988.

Griffin, Philip J. Correspondence, 1988.

Handwritten report of Iraqi vandalism and theft at the compound of the Evangelic Mission, dated October 31, 1990. Received by fax at the American Embassy, Kuwait, on November 4, 1990. Marked "CHALOUB Inc." 3 pages.

Haroon, Abdul Muti Abdul Rahman. Transcription of interview in Arabic. Recorded November 9, 1988.

Hart, LTC Fred L., Jr. "The Iraqi Invasion of Kuwait: An Eyewitness Account." Personal Experience Monograph (PEM) prepared for the U.S. Army War College, Carlisle Barracks, Pennsylvania, n.d. Available in the internet at <<http://www.sault.corn.com/~danvaught/eyewitness01.html>>

Hart, Parker T. Correspondence, October 25, 1988.

"Historical Overview of GSA/FHWA in Kuwait." Typewritten manuscript.

Howell, W. Nathaniel. Letter to General Alfred M. Gray, Commandant, USMC, May 13, 1991.

———. Contemporaneous Notes and Chronology, 1987–1991.

———. Remarks at Embassy Reception (September 28, 1988) celebrating educational cooperation.

Jaafar, Ezzat M. Ezzat Gaafar Visits California, August 1948. Photocopy of bound photographs of Mr. Jaafar's visit to the United States.

Jones, Hugh B. Memories of U.S. Federal Highway Administration official assigned to Kuwait 1977–1988. Transcribed by author from cassette, January 1989.

Kano, Michael. "Hiding from Saddam: An American in Occupied Kuwait. "Typewritten manuscript, 1998.

Keene, Douglas R. The Foreign Affairs Oral History Collection of the Association for Diplomatic Studies and Training. http://www.adst.org/OH%20TOCs/Keene,%20Douglas%20R.toc.pdfbin/query/r?ammem/mfdip:@field(DOCID+mfdip2010kee01)>> February 2, 2007.

Lawn, Elizabeth Calverly. Correspondence with author, 1995.

Lisle, Leslie. Correspondence, January 21, 1989.

Lowrie, Arthur L. The Foreign Affairs Oral History Collection of the Association for Diplomatic Studies and Training., December 23, 1989. http://www.adst.org/OH%20TOCs/Lowrie,%20Arthur%20L%20.toc.pdf

Lumsden,George Quincey. The Foreign Affairs Oral History Collection of the Association for Diplomatic Studies and Training, January 11, 2000.

http://www.adst.org/OH%20TOCs/Lumsden,%20George%20Quincy.toc.pdf

Maestrone, Frank E. The Foreign Affairs Oral History Collection of the Association for Diplomatic Studies and Training, June 6, 1989. http://www.adst.org/OH%20TOCs/Maestrone,%20Frank%20.toc.pdf

Mak, Dayton S. Correspondence with author, 1988. Oral memories transcribed from cassette, June 8, 1988.

———. The Foreign Affairs Oral History Collection of the Association for Diplomatic Studies and Training, August 9, 1989. http://www.adst.org/OH%20TOCs/Mak,%20Dayton%20S.toc.pdf

Maqamis, Khaled M. Al-. "The Kuwaiti Diwaniya and its Influence on Parliamentary Life." Kuwait – Keifan 1986. Computer printout.

Materials Relating to the Official Visit to the United States of His Highness Shaikh Sa'd Al-Abdullah Al-Salem Al-Sabah, Prime Minister and Crown Prince of the State of Kuwait. Washington, DC, July 11–13, 1988.

McClelland, Walter M. The Foreign Affairs Oral History Collection of the Association for Diplomatic Studies and Training, November 20, 1995. http://www.adst.org/OH%20TOCs/McClelland,%20Walter%20M.toc.pdf

Miller, Ardith H. Correspondence with author, November, 1988.

Mishari, Abd al-Aziz Thunayan al-. "From the Legacy: The American Hospital." The Weekly *Al-Qabas*, January 28, 1985. Photocopy.

Mutawa,. Faisal Al-. "Origins of Modern Education in Kuwait and Kuwaiti-American Educational Exchange." Typewritten summary, September 12, 1988.

Mylrea, Dr. C. Stanley G. "Kuwait Before Oil: Memoirs of Dr. C. Stanley G. Mylrea, Pioneer Medical Missionary of the Arabian Mission, Reformed Church in America." Written between 1945 and 1951. Typewritten manuscript, 162 pages..

National Evangelical Church in Kuwait. Order of Worship, Funeral of Dr. Lewis R. Scudder, April 5, 1975.

Quainton, Anthony. The Foreign Affairs Oral History Collection of the Association for Diplomatic Studies and Training, November 6, 1997. http://www.adst.org/OH%20TOCs/Quainton,%20Anthony.toc.pdf

Rashoud, Claudia Farkas al-. "American Business Council of Kuwait." March 2012, typewritten manuscript, March 2012.

———. "American education in Kuwait." Typewritten manuscript, March 2012.

———. "American Womens League (AWL)." Typewritten manuscript, March 2012.

———. "AWARE Center." Typewritten manuscript, December 2011.

———. "Contributiing to Kuwait."Ttypewritten manuscript, March 2012.
———. Interview with Abdallah al-Hammadi, M.D. February 2012.
———. Interview with Maxine al-Refai. February 2012
———. Interview with Sandy Shinn. February 2012.
———. "Kuwait Little League." Typewritten manuscript, February 2012.
———. "Return to Kuwait." Typewritten manuscript, February 21, 2012.
Rinehart, Jack. Typewritten manucript on the siege of the Embassy. 1993.
Sakhleh, Suleiman N. "Notes to Ambassador Howell." Summary information about Little League in connection with effort to fund new facilities, 1989.
Scudder, Dorothy B. Handwritten letter. June 15, 1989.
———. "The Beginnings of Medical Work in Kuwait. "Paper presented April 4, 1976, at a seminar sponsored by the Family Development Society at the Sheraton Hotel, Kuwait, April 4–6, 1976.
———. Notes of conversation, March 4, 1989.
———. Slide lecture delivered January 25, 1988, to the American Women's League. SAS Hotel, Kuwait.
Scudder, Dorothy B,. with L. R. Scudder, Jr. "Kuwait in Recollection and Prospect." Monograph, November 7, 1983.
"The Scudder family of missionaries in India." <<http://en.wikipedia.org.wiki/Thr_Scudder_family_of_missionaries_in_India>>
Seelye, Talcott W. The Foreign Affairs Oral History Collection of the Association for Diplomatic Studies and Training, September 15, 1993. http://www.adst.org/OH%20TOCs/Seelye,%20Talcott%20W.toc.pdf
Smith, Maurice L. Correspondence with author, 1991.
Stammerman, Kenneth A. The Foreign Affairs Oral History Collection of the Association for Diplomatic Studies and Training, July 28, 2000. http://adst.org/wp-content/uploads/2012/09/Stammerman-Kenneth-A.toc_.pdf
Stoltzfus, William A., Jr. The Foreign Affairs Oral History Collection of the Association for Diplomatic Studies and Training, May 18, 1994. http://www.adst.org/OH%20TOCs/Stoltzfus,%20William%20A.%20Jr.toc.pdf
Symmes, Harrison M. Correspondence with author, August 1988.
———. The Foreign Affairs Oral History Collection of the Association for Diplomatic Studies and Training, February 25, 1989. http://www.adst.org/OH%20TOCs/Symmes,%20Harrison%20M%20.toc.pdf
Undeland, Richard E. The Foreign Affairs Oral History Collection of the Association for Diplomatic Studies and Training, July 29, 1994. http://www.adst.org/OH%20TOCs/Undeland,%20Richard%20E.toc.pdf
U.S. Department of State. "Highlights of Relations Between the United States and Kuwait, 1909–1987." Unpublished compilation prepared

by the Office of the Historian at the request of the American Embassy, Kuwait, November 1987. 12 pages.

———, Bureau of Near Eastern Affairs. Background Note: Kuwait, December 27, 2011.<<http://www.state.gov/r/pa/ei/bgn/35876.htm>>

———, Office of Historian. "Chronology" prepared at request of Embassy Kuwait, 1987.

U.S. Senate. "Persian Gulf: Report to the Majority Leader, United States Senate, from Senator John Glenn and Senator John Warner on Their Trip to the Persian Gulf, May 27–June 4, 1987." Committee Print, June 17, 1987. Washington: GPO, 1987.

Webster, Ron. "The Innocent Period (An Innocent Abroad?)." Typewritten and annotated manuscript incorporating notes kept by an American businessman during the Iraqi siege of the American Embassy in Kuwait, n.d.

Wrampelmeier, Brooks. Correspondence with author, 1988 and 1994.

———. The Foreign Affairs Oral History Collection of the Association for Diplomatic Studies and Training, March 22, 2000. http://www.adst.org/OH%20TOCs/Wrampelmeier,%20Brooks.toc.pdf

Notes

1 An Incidental Encounter

1. By the mid–1850s American trading vessels were not uncommon within the Gulf and the United States began to seek a commercial agreement with the Persian Empire. In December 1879, the *U.S.S. Ticonderoga* became the first American warship to enter the Gulf. It called at Bushire and Basra, and penetrated the Shatt al-Arab to a distance of seventy miles. Michael E. Palmer, *Guardians of the Gulf: A History of America's Expanding Role in the Persian Gulf, 1833–1992*, New York: The Free Press, 1992, pp. 9–10.
2. See A. Locher, *With Star and Crescent: A Full and Authentic Account of a Recent Journey with a Caravan from Bombay to Constantinople, Comprising a Description of the Country, the People, and Interesting Adventures with the Natives*, Philadelphia: Aetna Publishing Company, 1891.
3. Ibid., pp 62–63.
4. Alan Rush, *Al-Sabah: History & Genealogy of Kuwait's Ruling Family, 1752–1987* (London: Ithaca Press, 1987), p. 141. Rush places this visit in 1868 but does not provide the rationale for this choice of dates. The weight of evidence appears to argue against his conclusion. The account was not copyrighted until 1888 and Rush, who may have based his conclusion on an Arabic translation of 1958, misidentifies the author as "Luther" rather than Locher.
5. The term, "dhow," which we use generically to describe a variety of lateen-rigged vessels used in the Gulf and beyond has no meaning for Kuwaiti and neighboring seamen. They know these vessels by their local designations, such as *sambuk* or *jalbut* thought to be an adaptation of the English jolly boat. Locher mentions seeing "bagalows" on the local waters, which was almost certainly his adaptation of *baghala*, one of the indigenous classes. The vessel most identified with Kuwait, however, is the *Boom*, a cargo vessel normally rated according to the bales of dates it could carry. Several examples of the *Boom*, including two huge reproductions built by the Marafie family, whose forefathers were prominent in the country's maritime commerce, may be seen in Kuwait today.
6. Locher, *With Star and Crescent*, p. 55.

7   During the winter, long-distance trading voyages were the primary economic activity. Sailing first north to load bales of dates in the Basra area, the vessels then fanned out to "the Makran coast, Karachi, Cochin and Calicut," as well as Zanzibar to exchange the dates for timber, coffee and other goods required in Kuwait. *Records of Kuwait, 1899–1961* (hereafter referred to as "Records"), A. de L. Rush, editor, vol VII p. xxii. At other times of the year, the Kuwaitis took to smaller craft in pursuit of pearls.
8   Locher, *With Star and Crescent*, p. 54.
9   Ibid., pp. 64–65.
10 Kuwaiti men wear the traditional *dishdasha*, a loose robe, and covering *thob*, while in the country. In the late 1950s and early 1960s, some had begun to wear western sports coats in response to the massive influx of Westerner influences. A conscious decision was reportedly made to reverse this trend which is observable in other Middle East societies. Travelling abroad, they easily transition into Western suits, although several friends confided that they must exercise care in Kuwait because the loose-fitting garments allow their waists to expand beyond the capacity of their tailored trousers.
11 To an important degree, diversity is mirrored in Kuwaiti society itself. Essentially comprised of families that migrated to the area within the last three hundred years, Kuwait is made up of Arabs who originated in central Arabia, as well as Arabs from Mesopotamia (Iraq) and Arabs and Persians from Persia. Predominantly Sunni Arab in composition, the country has a significant Shiite minority and a tiny Arab Christian community. Until the late 1940s, a small Jewish minority more or less monopolized the textile trade; it voluntarily emigrated to Israel following the founding of that state. An early American visitor to Kuwait opined that the Jewish community chose to live there and "are in no sense discriminated against." John Van Ess, *Meet the Arab*, New York: he John Day Company, 1943, p. 142.
12 Locher, *With Star and Crescent*, p.68.
13 Ibid., p. 66.
14 Kuwait's climate is very hot during most of the year, but the extent of humidity varies with the direction of prevailing winds. Northerly winds normally bring dry conditions, although they may also pick up and carry sand in their journey across Iraq, accelerating desertification in Kuwait. During monsoon season in the Indian Ocean, however, the southerly winds are heavy with moisture, adding extreme levels of humidity to the heat.

Particularly, in the latter case, sleeping inside is all but impossible without air conditioning.
15 Locher, *With Star and Crescent*, p.73. In contrast, his impression of Kuwait, based on an afternoon hike around the town was positive: "We found the town greatly resembling Muscat, but differing advantageously from that city in regard to cleanliness; Kuwait being remarkably clean for an Arab town, though up to the time of our visit it had scarcely ever been visited by a European...." (ibid., p. 61).

2: From Fishing Village to Commercial Port

1 "Kuwait" is the diminutive form of the Arabic term "kut," or fort, suggesting that a minor fortification may have predated the establishment of a noteworthy settlement in that location. The origin of "Grane" is more obscure. It is apparently a diminutive of "Qarn," the Arabic word for "high hill" and therefore a misnomer, given the flat character of the terrain. See also Ahmad Mustafa Abu-Hakima, *The Modern History of Kuwait*, 1750–1965, n.p.,1982. In any case, the Danish traveller, Carsten Niebuhr employed both names to designate the town on the map he created in 1765.
2 Ralph Shaw, *Kuwait*, London: Macmillan, 1976. p. 12.
3 Ibid. Shaw argues that the migrants discovered "a good supply of sweet water," but that is highly unlikely. Kuwait possesses no sources of fresh water, although there are a small number of sites with brackish water. As late as the first half of the Twentieth Century, drinking water for the growing town had to be brought in by dhow from the Shatt al-Arab and distributed to homes by donkeys.
4 Peter Mansfield, *Kuwait: Vanguard of the Gulf*, London: Hutchinson, 1990, p. 18.
5 Subsequent investigation has disclosed that the area had been the site of several settlements dating from antiquity. Earlier civilizations had settled offshore islands (Failaka and Akkaz off Kuwait, as well as Bahrain, Kharg off Iran and Umm al Nar near Dubai) probably to avoid the menace of desert raiders. Geoffrey Bibby, the Danish archeologist who excavated the Dilmun civilization (circa 2000 BC) found its northernmost outpost at Failaka. Geoffrey Bibby, "Looking for Dilmun," *Aramco World*, Vol. 21, No. 1, January–February 1970. p. 24. Failaka was apparently the southernmost extent of the empire of Alexander the Great (circa 300 BC) based on discoveries there of Greek temples, wine vessels and art

works. About 600 AD, a Nestorian Christian community occupied the island and built a large church before they were expelled by the Byzantines. Derek Kennet, "Failaka Island: Centre of Kuwait's Archaeological Heritage," *Arab Times* (Kuwait), May 7, 1990.
6   Abu-Hakima, *Modern History of Kuwait*, p. 2.
7   The apparent origin of this name is not ethnic but descriptive, deriving from the Arabic verb *'ataba*, meaning to move from place to place. Lt. Col. H. R. P. Dickson, the British Political Resident most closely identified with modern Kuwait, wrote that the ruler, Abdallah al-Salem, told him his people were given that name following their move north from Najd and the vicinity of Qatar. See Dickson, *Kuwait and her Neighbours*.
8   Abu-Hakima, *Modern History of Kuwait*, p.4.
9   Ibid., p. 6.
10 Rush, *Al-Sabah*, p. 2.
11 "The wealth of the Shaikh (and consequently the town) can perhaps be judged by his refusal of the Baron's [Kniphausen, head of the Dutch mission] offer of 1,000 piastres when he had asked for 2,000 ...." (Abu-Hakima, *Modern History of Kuwait*, p.7.
12 Quoted by Rush, *Al-Sabah*, p. 195.
13 Carsten Niebuhr, *Description de l'Arabie, faite sur des observations propres et des avis recueillis dans les lieu me*, Amsterdam, 1774, p. 296. Niebuhr's estimate does not differentiate between cargo and fishing vessels, and should probably be treated with some scepticism. Manning so large a fleet would require a population larger than Kuwait's in that era. Still, it is clear that the Kuwaitis were essentially a maritime people.
14 Abu-Hakima, *Modern History of Kuwait*.
15 On the occasion of the Eid, for example, there is an long-established protocol setting the order in which the leading families are visited. The British, American and Saudi ambassadors, whose missions are the only ones ever located within the walled city, begin their calls with the Emir immediately following morning prayers, and continue with families that once resided in Sharq, ending with lunch with the Al-Rashed family. The following day, they visit families originally associated with Qibla.
16 See Rush, *Al-Sabah*, p. 195.
17 Ibid. The reference to *Safat* offers, perhaps, a clue to the shape of the town in the 18th Century. There is still a Safat Square in Kuwait, although it is no longer the "open space" it was even in the early years of the 20th Century. Buildings, parking garages and souks or markets have made it one of the major shopping centers

near the center of the city. Rush places it "behind the town" indicating that the walled area was initially substantially smaller than it later became when the walls were extended to incorporate *Safat* as a central square.

18 Abu-Hakima (*Modern History of Kuwait*, p.11) lists "the Shahs of Persia, the Ottomans in 'Iraq or Mesopotamia, Bani Khalid and the Arab tribes in Eastern Arabia, and the European trading companies" as factors with which Kuwait and other sheikhdoms had to deal in maintaining their identity and well-being.

19 Rush, *Al-Sabah*, p. 185.

20 The Al-Khalifa were cousins of the Al-Sabah and the ancestors of present-day rulers of Bahrain. Although relations between the two branches of the family remained cordial, Abu-Hakima (op. cit., p. 9) suggests that an element in the Al-Khalifas' departure from Kuwait was disappointment that one of their number was not selected to succeed Sabah 1st.

21 Rush, *Al-Sabah*.

22 Ibid.

23 The Beni K'ab became an increasing menace to Gulf shipping by the 1760s. Sallying forth from their base at Fawraq, they attacked not just Kuwaiti vessels but those of the East India Company. The Persians tried unsuccessfully to suppress them in 1759 and a British-Ottoman expedition in 1765 was equally non-productive. See Abu-Hakima, *Modern History of Kuwait*, p. 18.

24 The fortifications of Kuwait were exclusively oriented to landward and the threat of raiding tribes, including the increasing menace of the Wahhabis who were engaged in a war of domination with the Kuwaitis' former overlords, the Beni Khalid. The wall, in its several expansions, always formed a crescent anchored on each end in the waters of the Gulf.

25 In 1789, Shaikh Abdallah decided to grant asylum in Kuwait to the leaders opposed to Ottoman rule in Basra. Suleiman Pasha, the Ottoman Governor in Baghdad, strongly sought the return of the fugitives according to a contemporary British source, but Abdallah declined to comply. This skillful act of independence was apparently one of the factors that led the British East India Company to resume operations through Kuwait for a time in the 1790s. Rush, op. cit., p. 186. Difficulties with the authorities in Basra were another factor; the choice of Kuwait strongly suggests that the city was independent from the Ottomans (Abu-Hakima, *Modern History of Kuwait*, p. 42).

26 The tiny original wall enclosing the town was apparently replaced

about 1811 by a new wall that more than quadrupled its area. The walls had been tested by bedu tribes of central Arabia and proved their value. In the 1790s, the Wahhabis, having eliminated the power of the Bani Khalid, launched significant attacks on Kuwait. In 1793, and again in 1797, they defeated determined Kuwaiti resistance in front of the town but were unable to follow through when the defenders withdrew behind their fortifications (Abu Hakima, *Modern History of Kuwait*, pp. 46–47).

27 Rush, *Al-Sabah*, p. 187.
28 Ibid., p. 173. Abdallah's preference for another son, possibly Duaij, may have been at the root of the discord, but Duaij was killed in 1809. A cousin, Muhammad Salman, a son of Sabah I, seems to have assumed power initially but when the population urged Jabir to return to Kuwait and welcomed him enthusiastically, he bowed to Jabir's popular mandate.
29 Ibid., p.176.
30 Ibid., p.174.
31 These twists and turn of Kuwaiti policy in the first half of the nineteenth century are documented in ibid., pp. 174–75.
32 S. Hennell, secret report of 24 April 1841 to the Court of Directors of the East India Company, (Bombay Government, *Selections from the Records of the Bombay Government*, Vol. XXIV, Bombay, 1856), quoted in Rush, *Al-Sabah*, p. 174.
33 Rush, *Al-Sabah*, pp. 153–54.
34 This gesture probably also mollified Kuwait's merchants since it eliminated steamships competing in the India trade with their sailing ships.
35 See Chapter I. Rush, *Al-Sabah*, p. 239, gives the date of this visit as 1868 but there is no confirmation One can only speculate about how so careful and valued a chronicler introduced these errors into his account. A possible clue, however, is Rush's reference to a version "translated and published in Arabic" in 1958. Rendering "Locher" into Arabic could produce the "Luther" variant. It seems possible that Rush relied exclusively on the Arabic translation. If so, this could also explain his placing the visit in 1868 and resolve the apparent anomalies of Locher's description of opulence at a time of "severe economic crisis" in the period 1868–71 as well as Abdallah II's advanced age.
36 Rush, *Al-Sabah*, p. 140.
37 Ibid., p. 141.
38 Ibid., p. 140. Over one hundred years later, Kuwait experienced similar threats during the 1980s war between Saddam Hussein's

Iraq and the Ayatollah Khomeini's Iran. While avoiding involvement in the fighting, Kuwait ceded Iraq control of several piers to receive imports and unimpeded transit to Iraq.

39 Simon C. Smith, *Kuwait, 1950–1965: Britain, the al-Sabah, and Oil*, Oxford: Oxford University Press, for the British Academy, 1999, pp. 46–47. These date groves became a continuing source of friction between the al-Sabah and the Iraqi successors of the Ottomans and a constant headache for the British trying vainly to resolve the dispute.

40 Rush, *Al-Sabah.*, p. 119.

41 Zahra Freeth, the daughter of the British political agent, who grew up in Kuwait in the 1930s, characterizes the prevailing political situation under Muhammad I as follows: "During the years before Mubarak's reign the internal affairs had been allowed to lapse into utter confusion by his predecessor, the ill-advised and incompetent Shaikh Muhammad. The Arabs of the desert, always impatient with authority, found that under the weak rule of Muhammad they could with impunity engage in their traditional pursuits of raiding and casual warfare. They blatantly disregarded the Shaikh's authority and complete lawlessness reigned among them in Kuwaiti territory, At the same time Shammar and Dhafir tribesmen entered and raided Kuwait from Najd, and in the north Turkey gradually encroached into the realm of her small neighbour-state, so that Kuwait's frontiers were virtually nonexistent." (Zahra Freeth, *Kuwait Was My Home* [London: George Allen & Unwin, 1956], p. 26.)

42 See Rush, *Al-Sabah*, p 101 ff. The heirs of Muhammad and Jarrah made their way to Ottoman Iraq following their deaths. Rush suggests that they were "exiled" by the new ruler, while some older Kuwaitis claim they escaped. In a private conversation on November 7 1988, a knowledgeable Kuwaiti told the author that the children were taken to Basra on a *boom* belonging to a prominent Kuwaiti Shi'a family, the Marafies, that was engaged in shipping and had connections with the Shi'a community in Basra.

43 Although it was not a factor in British calculations at the end of the Nineteenth Century, the Gulf was soon to assume additional importance for London. In the early years of the new century, Britain began converting its naval vessels from coal to oil. For a discussion of the considerations determining the character and timing of Britain's assumption of responsibility for Kuwait's security, see Briton Cooper Busch, *Britain and the Persian Gulf, 1894–1914* (Berkeley: University of California Press, 1967).

44 Hassan Ali al-Ebraheem, *Kuwait and the Gulf: Small States and the International System*, Center for Contemporary Arab Studies (London: Croom Helm, 1984), p. 42. Al-Ebraheem's account, based on a 1916 source, gives 1899 as the date of these events. Morris Jastrow (*The War and the Bagdad Railway: The Story of Asia Minor and its Relation to the Present Conflict* [Philadelphia: J. B. Lippincott Company, 1917], p. 83) places the German cruiser's voyage in 1898.
45 Records, Vol. I, p. 245.
46 Rush, *Al-Sabah*, p. 103.
47 Shaikh Khaz'al, whose state did not survive the rise of Iranian nationalism and Britain's policy of protecting its oil interests at Abadan and elsewhere in Persia, was given permission to build a palace in Kuwait. The ruins of that structure, now reportedly being rehabilitated, could be viewed directly behind the present British Embassy in the late twentieth century.

3 The Coming of the American Mission

1 The "Arabian Mission," frequently referred to unofficially as the American Mission, was established at the beginning of the 1890s and formally dissolved in 1973. It comprised a cadre of dedicated Protestant evangelists, doctors and educators who staffed mission posts throughout the western littoral of the Gulf, from Iraq to Oman. Though the original expectation of spreading Christianity in the Islamic heartland had to be tempered by experience, Mission personnel nevertheless gave witness to the best of Christian compassion by bringing modern medicine and education to the Arab societies among whom they lived, raised their families, and often died there. When the Mission at last folded its tents, its members left behind the respect and fond memories of those whose lives they touched and successor institutions like the Evangelical Church in Kuwait.
2 Lewis R. Scudder, *The Arabian Mission's Story: In Search of Abraham's Other Son*, The Historical Series of the Reformed Church in America No. 30 (Grand Rapids: Wm. B. Eerdmans, 1998), p. 99. According to Scudder, Kuwait had two primary "virtues" that made it attractive. First, it was relatively clean and healthy, as compared to other Gulf ports. Although its population suffered from tuberculosis, syphilis, scurvy, and fly-borne eye diseases, it escaped widespread Malaria. Second, as a thriving commercial center, the town offered easy access to the interior of the peninsula. Scudder

was born in Kuwait in 1941, the son of medical missionaries, and followed in their footsteps. His book is the definitive history of the Arabian Mission in Kuwait and elsewhere in the Gulf.

3   Scudder, *The Arabian Mission's Story*, p.177.
4   The term *colporteur* was used freely in the writings of Mission personnel, to designate local workers, usually (but not exclusively) Arabs and Christians, who supplemented the American cadre and made important contributions to medical and other activities. The term is of French origin and was used to describe individuals who sold or distributed religious literature.
5   Quoted in Scudder, *The Arabian Mission's Story*.
6   Nonmedical missionaries also grasped the power of simple first-aid skills in an area completely devoid of modern medicine and ministered to those they encountered to the best of their capabilities. As late as the 1970s, many Bedouin in remote locations were convinced that most Westerners were *hakims* or doctors. When camping along the TAPLINE road in Saudi Arabia, my companions and I always packed aspirin, antiseptic, tongue depressors, and bandages to "treat" desert herdsmen who came into camp for help. Preoccupied with the need to "do no harm," Western visitors were deeply touched by the gratitude their "patients" showed, usually in the form of fresh goat's milk.
7   Scudder, *The Arabian Mission's Story*.
8   According to Mgr. Sanmiguel who served in Kuwait, Dr. Zwemer brought with him in 1903 "his *coadfutor* (colporteur) Salomi and his family. They rented a bible shop which was closed after about six months." Mgr. Victor Sanmiguel, *Pastor in Kuwait, 1966–76*, Bishop's House, Kuwait, 1978, p. 144.
9   Scudder, *The Arabian Mission's Story*.
10 Abu Hakima, *Modern History of Kuwait*, p. 123. Scudder (*The Arabian Mission's Story*, p. 84) also credits Shaikh Khaz'al with playing "a critical mediatorial role in launching the mission's medical work in Kuwait."
11 Scudder, *The Arabian Mission's Story*, pp. 178–79.
12 Abu Hakima, *Modern History of Kuwait*, p.123.
13 Ibid., pp. 124–24. Abu Hakima reports finding in contemporary files archived in the India Office Records in London evidence of British suspicion of the energetic young Americans who made a practice of touring throughout the Gulf region.
14 Van Ess participated in the selection of the site for the new Mission station and continued to visit the Mission into the 1920s. William D. Brewer, one of the first American Consuls to Kuwait,

married his daughter who could remember "trips to Kuwait in the late Twenties when she played freely with Kuwaiti children, including Jabir al-Ahmad, and saw nothing but 400–500 camels crouched on the Safat" (Brewer letter to the author, dated July 10, 1991).

15 The arrival of the three American missionaries in 1911 quadrupled the European population of the town. Bennett later recalled that when he visited shortly before that he and the British political agent, Captain Shakespear, frequently dined together. He adds, "I always had to dress. In spite of the fact that we two men were the only Europeans in the City." Quoted in Scudder, *The Arabian Mission's Story*, p.180, note 145.

16 Ibid., p. 181, footnote 149. Perhaps fittingly, the Mission also used it for worship services until a chapel was built in 1931.

17 The British agent reported that the ruler "has placed at the disposal of Dr. Bennett a big house the property of one of his nephews and close to his palace, where a medical dispensary is being opened. Dr. Bennett and his friends with a few Baghdadi Christians had a small religious meeting on Sunday the 13th March at the premises of Messrs Gray Paul & Co's agency in Koweit" (Records VII, p. 703).

18 Ann M. Harrison, *A Tool in His Hands: The Story of Dr. Paul Harrison of Arabia* (Weybridge VT: Cherry Tree Books, 2004), p. 41. This is a reprint of a book published originally by Dr. Harrison's wife in 1958. While useful for the personal impressions it presents, it is relatively weak regarding timelines. The author had the benefit of her husband's recollections, although they did not marry until after his tour in Kuwait. For that reason, the account by Dr. Scudder, which was written with access to the records of the Reformed Church and its Arabian Mission, must be considered authoritative.

19 Saba George Shiber, *The Kuwait Urbanization – Documentation – Analysis – Critique* (Kuwait: n.p., 1964), p. 75.

20 H. R. P. Dickson, *The Arab of the Desert*, Third Edition. Edited and abridged by Robert Wilson and Zahra Freeth. London: George Allen & Unwin, 1983, p. 12.

21 Shiber, *The Kuwait Urbanization*.

22 Scudder, *The Arabian Mission's Story*, p. 96.

23 Among the trades mentioned in contemporary memoirs were gunsmiths, tinkers, weavers, tailors, sandal-makers, leather workers, saddle-makers, jewelers, etc.

24 As we shall see, the Wahabbi *Ikhwan* of Central Arabia were to

menace Kuwait within ten years of the arrival of the new American community. Among their reported demands were an end to prostitution, smoking, and the brewing of alcoholic beverages by the small Jewish community. Nor was this the first effort to stamp out these practices. Sheikh Salim, shortly after he became ruler in 1917, forbade the Jewish community to distill liquor in Kuwait and decreed that prostitutes could not reside within the city. Rush, *Al-Sabah*, p. 81.

25 Ralph Shaw, *Kuwait*, Ministry of Information, 1976. p. 18.
26 Eleanor T. Calverley, M.D., *My Arabian Days and Nights* (New York: Thomas Y. Crowell, 1958), p. 146.
27 Scudder, *The Arabian Mission's Story*, p. 64.
28 Ibid., p. 264. Scudder writes: "Kuwait, unlike the other stations, began specifically as a medical mission. The clergymen who accompanied the doctors were adjuncts to the effort in a professional sense and, to a certain extent, in a vocational sense as well. That is *not* to say that there was no attention paid to the evangelistic effort—Mylrea himself would not have tolerated such an interpretation. It was simply a matter of priority in the public eye—the mission *was* the hospital; it came first. On its shoulders all the other activities rested."
29 Harrison, *A Tool in His Hand*, p. 41.
30 Ibid., p. 42
31 Typewritten memoir quoted in Scudder, *The Arabian Mission's Story*, pp. 184–85. Dr. Mylrea had, as we shall have occasion to see later, a hot temper and was given to frankness.
32 John Van Ess, *Meet the Arab* (New York: The John Day Company, 1943), p. 116.
33 Ralph Hewins, *A Golden Dream: The Miracle of Kuwait* (London: W.H. Allen, 1963), p. 162.
34 The text of this agreement is at Appendix B.
35 Scudder, *The Arabian Mission's Story*, p. 75.
36 Safeguarding Britain's "special" position in Kuwait and the rest of the Gulf remained a preoccupation over succeeding decades and would arise once more when the United States sought, after World War II, to establish a consulate in Kuwait. In fact, as late as 1972 when I was assigned to open an embassy at Abu Dhabi in the newly independent United Arab Emirates, the majority of British diplomats were warm and welcoming, but there was a distinct minority who resented the American presence.
37 Communication, dated February 20, 1919, to the British Civil Commissioner in Baghdad (Records I, p. 515).

38 Edwin and Eleanor Calverley had three daughters, one of whom was born in India in 1912 (Calverley, *My Arabian Days and Nights*, p. 59). They incidentally introduced the first baby carriage in the town.
39 Scudder, *The Arabian Mission's Story*, pp. 264–65. The author, son of the last head of the Kuwait station, grew up in this house, which his mother continued to occupy until 1990, when she left for home leave shortly before the Iraqi invasion. Unfortunately, she passed away in 1991 before she could return to Kuwait. At the time, some critics charged that the site of the Mission compound "was too far out of town" (American Embassy, Kuwait, "A Short History of Kuwaiti-American Relations," "prepared for the Occasion of the Fifteenth Anniversary of the Opening of the American Consulate in Kuwait," October 1964, p. 2).
40 Record VII, pp. 694–96. The British political officer's report of these singular events, dated February 17,1914, is contained in Records VII, p. 709. The Mission's house on the hill itself became a landmark for mariners before Kuwait's skyline grew after oil. The U.S. Navy cited it as a navigational reference point in the first half of the Twentieth Century. See U. S. Navy, Hydrographic Office, *Persian Gulf Pilot: The Persian Gulf, The Gulf of Oman and The Makran Coast*, H.O. No. 158, First Edition (Washington: Government Printing Office, 1920), p. 158.
41 Dar al-Athar al-Islamiyyah, "The American Mission Hospital," Part I, *Bareed ad-Dar* (Monthly Newsletter of the Friends of Dar al-Athar al-Islamiyyah, Kuwait), Vol. 1, No. 5 (January/February, 1999), p. 2.
42 Scudder, *The Arabian Mission's Story*, p. 190. The first hospital was built by Charles Shaw and Philip Haynes, two non-resident civil engineers with the Arabian Mission.
43 Harrison, *A Tool in His Hand*, p. 53.
44 Calverley, *My Arabian Days and Nights*, p. 147.
45 Ibid., pp. 147–48.
46 The British Political Agency also ran a charitable dispensary, staffed in this period by Assistant Surgeon C. C. Kelley, probably an Anglo Indian (Records I, p. 510).
47 "The American Mission Hospital," Part IV, *Bareed ad-Dar* (Monthly Newsletter of the Friends of Dar al-Athar al-Islamiyyah, Kuwait) Vol. 1, No. 6 (March and April, 1999). p. 2.
48 Calverley, *My Arabian Days and Nights*, p.100.
49 Scudder, *The Arabian Mission's Story*, pp. 182–83.
50 The Mission compound seems to have acquired adjacent land in

the 1920s as a gift from Manad Abdallah al-Saqr and Abdal Latif Al-Jalil. A letter of appreciation, dated December 24, 1925, was reproduced in *al-Qabas* (Kuwait), June 6, 1994.

51 A substantial part of this practice until the 1930s was the treatment of pearl divers of whom there were about 10,000 in the first decades of the century. As Paul Harrison recalled, "In winter the usual influx of sick pearl divers increased his workload. No occupation was so costly to health as theirs. The high pressure of the water at great depths frequently burst their eardrums and caused chronic running ears. There was much tuberculosis among them. Their diet on the boats was so poor that many of them had gums bleeding from scurvy." Harrison, *A Tool in his Hand*, p. 83.

52 Scudder, *The Arabian Mission's Story*, p.196. Dr. Mylrea purchased a horse in 1916 for outpatient calls. Dorothy B. Scudder, "The Beginnings of Medical Work in Kuwait," a paper presented April 4, 1976 at a seminar sponsored by the Family Development Society at the Sheraton Hotel, Kuwait, April 4–6, 1976. According to Dorothy Scudder, the Mission's first church was behind Gray McKenzie downtown and the Yacoub Shammas family lived in it.

53 "Mission homes were designed with a separate *majlis* or *diwanniya* (sitting room) for women with entrances isolated from those used by men." Thus, traditional Kuwaiti features were incorporated in Mission housing to facilitate contacts (Scudder, *The Arabian Mission's Story*, p. 204). A member of the community who is often overlooked was Iva Robertson, a nurse, who came as a teacher for the Calverley girls. She taught the Illinois curriculum and remained for 5 1/2 years (Calverley, *My Arabian Days and Nights*, p. 126).

54 Miriam Joyce, *Kuwait 1945–1996: An Anglo-American Perspective* (Portland, OR: Frank Cass, 1998), p. xvii. Another graduate was Majed al-Shaheen, the father of Suleiman al-Shaheen who was the very capable Deputy Minister of Foreign Affairs in the late 1980s and early 1990s. Conversation with the author, April 26, 1990.

55 To finance his diplomatic and military gambits, he erred in levying a series of taxes on imports, pearling, houses and the Hajj. These taxes offended many Kuwaitis, including some of the wealthier merchants. Led by Hilal at Mutairi, a number of these prominent citizens sailed secretly to Bahrain with most of their assets. When Shaikh Mubarak annulled the taxes, they happily returned. Joyce, op. cit., p. xii. For contemporary British reporting on the "merchants revolt," see *Records* I, pp. 543–61.

56 Scudder, *The Arabian Mission's Story*, p, 100.

57 Dr. Jerry Zdanowski, "King 'Abd Al-'Aziz in the Reports of the American Missionaries, 1901–1921, <<http://www.darah.org.sa/bohos/Data/15/06.htm>>
58 The article entitled "Sheikh Sir Abd-El-Aziz Ibn Saoud, K.C.I.E." appeared in *The Near East*, May 11, 1917.
59 Records I, p. xxiii. The Convention, under negotiation between London and Constantinople for several prior years would, among other things, have defined the frontier between the Vilayet of Basra and the areas owing allegiance to the Kuwaiti ruler. Seeking to balance their obligations under their agreement with Shaikh Mubarak and to strengthen relations with the wavering Ottoman state, Britain tried to thread the needle in the draft Convention. The evolving position was summarized as follows by the secretary of state for India in 1912:

> As regards Koweit, His Majesty's Government are concerned to ensure the continuance of local government of the Sheikh of Koweit, so defined in their Memorandum of 29th July 1911. His Majesty's Government would be fully prepared to recognise Turkish suzerainty over Koweit and to recognise Sheikh as Turkish Kaimmakam, but they attach cardinal importance to the islands of Warba and Bubiyan being admitted by Turkey to be within the confines of Koweit, and to the withdrawal of the Turkish military post on Bubiyan....(Records I, pp. 365–66).

The draft Convention, never ratified, was overtaken by Turkey's alliance with Germany. The Turks had been testing the autonomy of Kuwait over the early years of the century. As early 1901–02, Turkish warships made excursions monitored by the British into Kuwaiti waters and, in 1912, a Turkish fort was established at Safwan, just north of Abdalli, the current Kuwaiti border post with Iraq (Records I, pp 156–62 and 45–6).
60 Records I, p. 383.
61 Ibid., p. xxiii.
62 Harrison, *A Tool in His Hand*, p. 84. Victims were so numerous and deaths so relentless that there were no able-bodied people in the mosques to wash the bodies in accordance with Islamic practice. "Finally, the ruler [Abd al-Aziz al-Saud] had ordered trenches dug for the dead, but he had difficulty in getting enough able men to do the job."
63 Rush, *Al-Sabah*, p. 94.
64 Ibid., p. 95.

Notes

65 Shaikh Kha'zal, as we have seen, was a frequent visitor to Kuwait and maintained an elaborate residence in Kuwait.
66 Scudder, *The Arabian Mission's Story*, pp. 103–04.
67 Paul Harrison, who had been posted outside of Kuwait for many years, called on Ibn Saud much later and was reportedly told: "You may find some of my Bedouin hostile, but that needn't trouble you. You are a guest in my house, and no harm can come to you. I know you are a Christian, but honorable men are friends though they differ in religion. I met your fellow doctor in Kuwait years ago when he treated some of my men" (Harrison, *A Tool in His Hand*, p. 78).
68 Scudder, *The Arabian Mission's Story*, p. 104.
69 Ibid., pp. 80 and 186.
70 Records I, pp. 646–47.
71 Scudder, *The Arabian Mission's Story*, p. 104. Many Kuwaitis reportedly faulted the influence of Ibn Saud with the British for this stern measure. See also reports of the Political Agency of September 4 and 19, 1918 regarding Shaikh Salim and discontent by merchants and others (Records I, pp. 691–95).
72 'The Ajman were emboldened by Ibn Saud's defeat by the Al-Rashid Shammar tribesmen, allied with the Ottomans in January, 1915. In the fighting, Captain William Shakespear was killed helping to serve a Saudi field piece. By the end of the year, Ibn Saud was besieged in the city of Hofhuf by Ajman forces and appealed to Kuwait for help and the ruler. Shaikh Mubarak sent a force under Shaikh Salim to lift the siege and scatter the Ajman force. Scudder, *The Arabian Mission's Story*, p. 103.
73 Rush, *Al-Sabah*, p. 94. Whatever the rationale for Kuwait's grant of sanctuary to elements of the Ajman tribe, the gesture was not out of character for Kuwait, whose recorded history contains many instances of such hospitality, including, of course, the fleeing Ibn Saud and his father. It is also relevant to recall that traditional Bedouin practice tends toward the granting of protection to persons who reach their camp or territory. Kuwait's action may not have been wise, given Ibn Saud's great ambition, but it was not alien to the Peninsula.
74 No less astute an observer than Dr. Stanley Mylrea evidently believed that Ibn Saud had his eyes set on incorporating Kuwait in his empire. He argued, "It is certain that Ibn Saud coveted the province of Kuwait with its excellent deep-water port. The possession of this port would make a superb outlet for his newly won empire. The great Shaikh Mubarak of Kuwait, the one man

Notes   539

who could have handled Ibn Saud and avoided war with him, had been in his grave more than four years" (Records I, p. 704).
75 Scudder, *The Arabian Mission's Story*, pp. 104–05.
76 Royal Scottish Museum, *The Evolving Culture of Kuwait* (Edinburgh: Her Majesty's Stationery Office, 1985), p. 30.
77 By far the most detailed account of the events at Jahra, and in Kuwait itself, during this critical period are to be found in a typewritten article, entitled "The Enemy at the Gates" which is included among official British papers (Records 1, pp. 703–17). Although unattributed or identified by the editor of the Records volumes, the account is a chapter from an unpublished memoir by Dr. Mylrea entitled *Kuwait Before Oil, Memoirs of Dr. C. Stanley G. Mylrea, Pioneer Medical Misssionary of the Arabian Mission, Reformed Church in America*, written between 1945 and 1951. The reference to penicillin for the treatment of infections confirms the date of writing. Although penicillin was known as early as the 1920s, it was not proven and placed into mass production until about 1942.
78 Records, Vol. I, p. 706.
79 Ibid.
80 Ibid., pp. 706–07.
81 Ibid., p. 707.
82 Rush, *Al-Sabah*, p. 81.
83 Records I, p. 708.
84 Ibid. After pointing out the reluctance of the Ikhwan, in their fanatical religious zeal, to take cover with disastrous results, Dr. Mylrea concludes that "there can have been few more bloody fights in the history of Arabia. The Ikhwan, who went into action with some thirty-five hundred men, lost about eight hundred killed and as many more wounded—nearly half their total strength. Their wounded, with no skilled medical attention, died like flies."
85 An exact count of the casualties at Jahra is impossible to compile. The "Red Fort" in that oasis has been preserved and today is a tourist attraction as well as a memorial to the heroic stand by the Kuwaiti defenders. There are graves of many who died there around the fort, but other corpses were dumped unmarked down wells due to the heat and the threat of disease. Freeth, *Kuwait Was My Home*, p. 94. While most of the Kuwaiti casualties had family in the town who could at least make known the fact that a relative was "missing," the Ikhwan kept no records of their losses.
86 Records I, p. 709–10.
87 Ibid., pp. 709–10.

88　Ibid., p. 711.
89　Ibid., p. 713.
90　Ibid., p. 714.
91　Scudder, *The Arabian Mission's Story*, p. 105.
92　Records I, p. 714.
93　Ibid., p. 715.
94　Ibid., p. 716. Dr. Calverley recalls that British machine guns were set up on the roofs of Mission buildings, but she may have been mistaken (Calverley, *My Arabian Days and Nights*, p. 122). The *Ikhwan* delegation reportedly did not leave Kuwait until October 24. It is not clear why they stayed on several days after Dawish's ultimatum was rejected, but the British authorities were probably happy for them to observe the arrival of warships with their heavy guns, as well as naval detachments and airplanes.
95　Records I, p. 716. Rumors circulated in late November that the Ikhwan had materialized in Wafra, but this turned out to be untrue. The last British warship sailed from Kuwait on November 6.
96　Records I, p. 717.
97　Ibid.
98　Scudder, *The Arabian Mission's Story*, p. 186.
99　A term used in earlier times to describe Kuwaitis involved in trades related to the sea, including shipwrights, deep-sea sailors, and pearlers. This element, very large at the time when Kuwait was one of the premier maritime centers in the region, possessed a distinct subculture. As Zahra Freeth, the daughter of British Political Agent Harold Dickson, recalled, one of the Baharna beliefs was that a woman who managed to step over the keel laid down for a new ship, would conceive a child. The ship, however, would be cursed and one of its crew would die. To forestall this, the keelboards of ships which once covered the foreshore of the town, were closely guarded until the sides grew high enough to prevent this practice. Freeth, *Kuwait Was My Home*, p. 107.
100　The Kuwaiti practice of linking full citizenship to ancestry in 1920 does not seem to have excited much controversy prior to the beginning of the oil era in the 1940s. When oil revenues financed extensive medical, educational and other benefits for Kuwaiti citizens, the exclusionary aspect of the policy became controversial for some commentators.
101　William Tracy, "A Talk with Violet Dickson, *Aramco World Magazine*, Vol. 23, No. 6, November–December 1972, p. 14.
102　Records VII, pp. 512–17.
103　Records, II, p. 14.

104 Calverley, *My Arabian Days and Nights*, p. 106.
105 John Munro, with Martin Love, "The Nairn Way," *Aramco World Magazine*, Vol. 32, No. 4, July–August 1981. pp. 18–23. A problem encountered with tires on this difficult desert run led to the development by the Firestone Tire and Rubber Company of a more durable tire incorporating rayon produced by DuPont.
106 Letter to author, January 11, 1992. Shaikh Ahmad also Westernized portions of his palace. With the help and advice of the political agent and the Calverleys of the American Mission, he furnished a drawing room and dining room in Dasman Palace with European-style furniture brought from India (H. V. F. Winstone and Zahra Freeth, *Kuwait: Prospect and Reality* [London: George Allen and Unwin, 1972], p. 89)

4 Decade of Austerity and Promise

1 Scudder, *The Arabian Mission's Story*, p. 187.
2 Ibid., p. 266.
3 Rush, *Al-Sabah*, p. 51.
4 Winstone and Freeth, *Kuwait*, p. 99.
5 Rush, *Al-Sabah*, p. 55. note 2. Rush intimates that "Kuwaiti delegates" were present, but it appears more likely that Kuwait's "interests" were represented by the British political agent, who would have been much the junior participant. According to Dr. Hassan El-Ebraheem (*Kuwait: A Political Study* [Kuwait: Kuwait University, 1975], p. 61), the composition of the delegations was as follows: "The Saudi delegation was headed by Ibn Saud and his aides. The Iraqi delegates were headed by Sir Percy Cox and included Sabih Beg, minister of communication and works. Kuwait was represented by Major J. C. More, the political agent in Kuwait. p. 61. See also Scudder, The Arabian Mission's Story, p. 106.
6 Rush, *Al-Sabah*, p. 55. note 2, describes the lost territories as "desert" which of course they were. But such a description understates their real significance. Despite their aridity, these areas were part of the vast grazing grounds required to support the herds and flocks of Bedouin tribesmen. Without them, tribes that had formed an important part of Kuwait's defense were not able to remain loyal to Kuwait and were compelled to come to an accommodation with Ibn Saud instead.
7 David Fromkin, "How the modern Middle East map came to be drawn," *Smithsonian*, Vol. XXII, no. 2 (May 1991), p. 148. Ibn Saud

was unlikely to recognize this as an important concession, however, since he now claimed, with characteristic grandiosity, all of Kuwait to the walls of the city,
8 H. R. P. Dickson, *Kuwait and Her Neighbours* (London: Allen & Unwin, 1936), p. 276.
9 Ibid.
10 Michael Field, *The Merchants: The Big Business Families of Saudi Arabia and the Gulf States* (Woodstock, NY: The Overlook Press, 1985), p. 196.
11 Peter Lienhardt, *Disorientations: A Society in Flux: Kuwait in the 1950s*, Middle East Cultures: Kuwait, edited by Ahmed Al-Shahi (Reading, U.K.: Ithaca Press, 1993), p. 55.
12 Winstone and Freeth, *Kuwait,* p. 90. Philby, who explored the Rub' al-Khali in 1930s, visited Kuwait with his wife, Dora, in 1935. He arrived by car and stayed with the Dicksons, suffering a fever during his stay (Elizabeth Monroe, "Across the Rub' Al-Khali: H. St. John Philby, Great Arabian Journeys of Exploration, Part one, 1932," *Aramco World Magazine*, Vol. 24, No. 6, November–December 1973, p. 13).
13 Simon C. Smith, *Kuwait, 1950–1965: Britain, the al-Sabah, and Oil* (Oxford: Oxford University Press, for the British Academy, 1999), p. 15.
14 Records II, p. 423. A listing of numerous incursions into Kuwaiti territory in the years 1921–29, provided to the British by the ruler is at pp. 423–28. This record, which is divided between apparently freelance tribal raids and attacks by the *Ikhwan* and elements owing allegiance to Ibn Saud, appears to have been an enclosure to a letter, dated August 3, from Shaikh Ahmad al-Sabah to Colonel Dickson, the British political agent at the time. Attacks and incursions occurred in every year of the period covered.
15 Records II, p. 375. A report of May 8, 1924, for instance, notes that "The people of Kuwait are now getting over their panic caused by Dhaidan al-Hithlain's raid, but the town wall is still manned to some extent at night, and the country is still patrolled daily between Shu'aibah, Subaihiyah and Jahra."
16 Dickson, *Arab of the Desert*, p. 125. The Saudi boycott had the effect of disrupting historic migratory patterns among Najdi tribes who traditionally traded at Kuwait seasonally. "The inconvenience and hardship caused by the King's prohibition roused bitter feelings among the bedu, and it was an important cause of the build-up of dissatisfaction which was to culminate five years later in the Ikhwan rebellion." Winstone and Freeth, *Kuwait*, p. 90.

17 Scudder, *The Arabian Mission's Story*, p. 107.
18 Records VI, p. 328.
19 "The British East India Navigation Company introduced its first steam service between India and Basra in 1862 and began calling at Kuwait in 1904. One year later, its steamers were reported to be transporting more than half of Kuwait's imports—a loss only partly offset by a large increase in the overall volume of imports which, in 1905, were valued at Rs 4,818,929. By 1936, the degree of outside competition had reached serious proportions." Records IV, pp. xxii–xxiii.
20 One measure of the slim margin on hospital operations was the frequent acceptance of matchboxes and bottles (for dispensing medicines) and food as payment from patients. Calverley, *My Arabian Days and Nights*, p. 74.
21 Ibid., p. 103.
22 Abd al Aziz Thunayan al-Mishari, "From the Legacy: The American Hospital," *Al-Qabas* (Kuwait), January 28, 1985.
23 A British survey report in 1927 includes the following notation: "At present, *The American Mission* gives by far the best education in Kuwait, particularly as regards English, but it only has twenty boys—which is about all it can accommodate." Records II, p. 60.
24 Records VII, pp. 724–27. The Jewish community also maintained a school of almost equal size. A single teacher instructed 15 young men in Hebrew reading and writing, according to Dr. Calverley in "Education in Kuwait," *Neglected Arabia* (circa 1929), cited in Records VII, p. 725.
25 Scudder, *The Arabian Mission's Story* pp. 253–54. Dr. Mylrea went even further in his praise for the influence of Calverley's educational efforts, crediting the school with being the catalyst for the initiative of Kuwaitis to create a parallel institution, the Mubarakiyya School, which operated into the 1950s, not far from the Mission compound.
26 Ibid., p. 254. After the closure of the school, Donald MacNeil occasionally tutored students in English. One of this small group was a young Palestinian electrical engineer working for the Kuwaiti government; his name was Yasir 'Arafat." Ibid., p. 324.
27 Peter Mansfield, *Kuwait: Vanguard of the Gulf* (London: Hutchinson, 1990), p. 109. The magazine lasted only two years and Kuwait did not have a printing press until the government installed one in 1947. The first magazine printed in the shaikhdom, *Al-Kazima*, appeared in 1948.
28 Author's conversation with Amb. Faisal al-Mutawa, September 12, 1988.

29 A British report in 1938 noted: "The only hospital in Kuwait is that of the American Mission to Arabia (sic), which has 12 beds for males and 12 for females." The facility boasted an electrically lit operating table, but no X-ray capability (Records II, p. 42).
30 Dr. Mary Allison, "Health Care in Kuwait in the 1930's," lecture delivered at the Medical Faculty of Kuwait University in the 1970s. Transcribed from the soundtrack of video recording, November 4, 1988.
31 ".... recently Arabs have started to bring their male children to qualified doctors instead of to traditional practitioners for the operation (circumcision), resulting in a much more rapid recovery" (Dickson, *Arab of the Desert*, pp. 115–16).
32 The clinics had neither running water nor bathrooms and depended upon a small sterilizer heated by a Primus stove to prevent infections. Allison, "Health Care in Kuwait."
33 Miriam Joyce, *Kuwait 1945–1996: An Anglo-American Perspective* (Portland, OR: Frank Cass, 1998). p. xviii. Dame Violet Dickson, the wife of the British political agent at the time, recorded her firsthand impression of the epidemic: "In the first ten days of the epidemic over 4,000 persons died. It was a terrifying sight to see the corpses being carried daily to their last resting place. But so great was the secrecy that we could not find out if cases had occurred in the houses of our own servants.... Among (those) who fell victim was Nazaal, the ruler's chief guide and falconer, and great was Shaikh Ahmad's distress. The primitive Arabs knew only one supposed cure; they believed that one particular smell, different in every case, had the power to cure, but the problem was to find the one and only smell which would be effective. In Nazaal's case every possible thing was brought before him, fruit, flowers, vegetables, cooked food, etc. Then children, young women, and old women were made to pass before him...." (cited in Winstone and Freeth, *Kuwait*, p. 194).
34 Records II, p. 4. Much of the growth seems to have been in the Shuwaikh area, near the American Mission compound.
35 In the second half of the 1940s, a former British resident returning for a visit, wrote: "Among the features of old Kuwait which are still to be seen is the town wall, which remains, somewhat incongruously, to encircle the new Kuwait. It stretches in an arc from sea to sea on the town's landward side, and along its four and a half mile length crenellated mediaeval towers stand at regular intervals, and traces of a firing-platform are still visible in the rain-eroded mud of the inner side." (Freeth, *Kuwait Was My Home*, p. 49).

36 Ibid.
37 Ibid., p.11; Dame Violet Dickson, *Forty Years in Kuwait* (London: Allen & Unwin, 1978, p. 89).
38 Dorothy B. Scudder, slide lecture delivered January 25, 1988, to the American Women's League, SAS Hotel, Kuwait.
39 Dorothy B. Scudder, with L. R. Scudder, Jr., "Kuwait in Recollection and Prospect," monograph, November 7, 1983.
40 Records II, p. 22.
41 The battle of Riqa'i is noteworthy as the first use by indigenous forces of motor vehicles in the Arabian Peninsula. The political agent wrote that ".... at 4.30 p.m. on the 28th January fifteen cars out of twenty five which had left Kuwait arrived at Riqa'i -- a very criedtable [sic] performance in view of the fact that there is no road beyond Jahrah, and all the cars were grossly overloaded, some carrying as many as nine men. Although only numbering about 75 rifles, the Kuwait force was very much better armed than the raiders, to whom the motorcar was an entirely new factor in war. The result was that the Kuwait force inflicted very heavy casualties on the enemy, and forced them to abandon a considerable portion of the booty." (Political Agent, February 7, 1928, in Records VII, pp. 108–9.)
42 At least one knowledgeable observer believes that Ibn Saud began to entertain doubts about the utility of employing the Ikhwan as a tool earlier, when they failed in their attack on Jahra (Scudder, *The Arabian Mission's Story*, p. 70). These doubts could have only grown in light of Ikhwan behavior during the conquest of the Hejaz.
43 Winstone and Freeth, *Kuwait*, p. 97.
44 Glubb, better known to the world as "Glubb Pasha" and to the Arabs as "Abu Hnaich," became the legendary commander of the Arab Legion of Transjordan (afterwards Jordan), one of the finest forces in the modern Middle East. He later authored several books on his experiences in command of bedouin troops.
45 Rush, *Al-Sabah*, note 2, pp. 55–56.
46 Records, II, p. 414. This statement, attributed to the Kuwaiti Ruler, is a rare bit of evidence of the fact that the disregard for Kuwait's interests at 'Uqair continued to rankle and color Shaikh Ahmad's attitude toward Ibn Saud and, more importantly, Great Britain seven years after the fact. The Ruler's anguish at being compelled to turn his back on the Mutair was also occasioned not only by the violation of the bedouin tradition of *dakhala* (or sanctuary); it was correct that Kuwait's historic links with this tribe had been

severed after World War I by British mapmakers and Ibn Saud's manipulation: "Kuwait territory has long been part of the Mutair tribal *dira*, and from as far back as they can remember this tribe had acknowledged the authority of the Sabah until, on the death of Shaikh Mubarak, Ibn Saud enticed them to switch their allegiance to himself. When the Mutair rebelled against Ibn Saud from 1928–9 and sought refuge in Kuwait they pleaded—without avail—to be allowed to return to their traditional loyalty to the Sabah. Another tribe, the Awazim, occupy the territory which stretches down the coast south of Kuwait, now lying in Saudi Arabia, though many of them consider the ruler of Kuwait their true overlord." (Winstone and Freeth, *Kuwait*, p. 56.)

47 "Dr. Mylrea incidentally in discussing causes, asked me if I thought H.M.'s Government would really defend Kuwait if it were suddenly attacked by Bin Saud. He also asked whether it had struck H.M.'s Government that all past attacks were done by bin Saud's orders. He then said 'Of course, H.M.'s can stop every single raid, if it chooses, by a firm threat to break with Bin Saud from the start.'" (Political Agent to Political Resident, January 1, 1930 in Records II, p. 444.)

48 Records II, p. 445.

49 A detailed recapitulation of the *Ikhwan* surrender is found in Winstone and Freeth, *Kuwait*, pp. 100–106.

50 Scudder, *The Arabian Mission's Story*, pp. 71–72. The author concludes that the attack on the American party was deliberate and targeted: "Charles Crane or Henry Bilkert or both." Ann Harrison (*A Tool in His Hand*, p. 97), who was the widow of Rev. Bilkert and subsequently married Paul Harrison, provides a somewhat different conclusion, attributing the death to "some unknown Bedouin who was demonstrating against the new boundary line determined by the king of Iraq."

51 Winstone and Freeth, *Kuwait*, p. 105.

52 Ibid., p. 111. The co-author of this book is the daughter of Col. Dickson, who not only grew up in Kuwait but had access to his personal papers that may not have found their way into official compilations.

53 Ibn Saud rid himself of the offending Ikhwani leaders through an act of treachery, violating the Bedouin code of hospitality (Winstone and Freeth, *Kuwait*, p. 100).

54 Freeth, *Kuwait Was My Home*, p. 41. The decision of whether to land in Kuwait was left up to the pilot making the service so un-

predictable as to be undependable even for mail (Residency Bushire, 4 December 1935, Records IV, p. 38, and Political Agency Kuwait, November 30, 1935, Records IV, p. 3). Kuwait's first landing field was just outside one of the manned gates in the town wall.
55 The chapel is now the sanctuary of the National Evangelical Church in Kuwait. By tradition, the American Ambassador is invited to read the President's Proclamation at the annual Thanksgiving Day service.
56 Scudder, *The Arabian Mission's Story*, pp. 265–66.
57 British Political Resident, Manama, in Records II, p. 103
58 Freeth, *Kuwait Was My Home*, p. 77.
59 A curious footnote to relations with Saudi Arabia took place in the mid-1930s, years before Ibn Saud's embargo was lifted. Col. Dickson reportedly learned that the ruler had received a message from King Ibn Saud on 19 February (probably 1933). Shaikh Ahmad subsequently made two secret journeys to the south. "The first was on 20 February and the second... on 27 February. Both journeys started late at night.... On his return, the shaikh announced that he had been on hunting trips." Dickson believed that the ruler had met Ibn Saud, at least on the second trip, and that the discussion focused on the King's urgent need for money—and oil, Winstone and Freeth, *Kuwait*, p. 151
60 Responsibility for the post office in Kuwait bounced around like a rubber ball until it was finally turner over to Kuwaiti administration in the 1950s. Prior to World War I, it was operated by the Government of India and during the war it was transferred to the civil administration, later the military, of the Iraq Mandate. In 1942, the Post and Telegraph of India was given charge and replaced by Pakistan following partition. The British General Post Office assumed responsibility in April 1948 and held the reins until it became part of the Kuwait government. (Records IV, p.50.) Postage stamps were frequently India issue with a "Kuwait" overprint.
61 The idea of a consultative council was raised as early as 1918, and endorsed by the British as a device for constraining Shaikh Salem. Rush, *Al-Sabah*, p. 54.
62 Ibid., p. 55.
63 Elizabeth Monroe, "Kuwayt and Aden: A Contrast in British Policies," *Middle East Journal*, Vol. 18, no. 1 (Winter 1964), p. 64. Monroe argues that Kuwaitis were "more thrusting and hardier" than most coastal societies and "had made more of the Gulf's scanty resources than had its other inhabitants...."
64 Field, *The Merchants*, p. 192. The al Sabah were "perpetually in

debt" to the prominent merchants (Miriam Joyce, *Kuwait 1945–1996: An Anglo-American Pesrpective* [Portland, OR: Frank Cass, 1998], p. xvi).
65 Lienhardt, *Disorientations*, p. 62.
66 One specialist argues that some Kuwaiti merchants, faced with depressed economic conditions of the 1930s, invested in real estate and thus established links that facilitated "intrigue with Iraqis" (Jill Crystal, *Oil and Politics in the Gulf: Rulers and Merchants in Kuwait and Qatar* [Cambridge Middle East Library: 24, Cambridge: Cambridge University Press, 1990], p. 39).
67 Ibid., p. 36.
68 For official British reports of Iraqi agitation against Kuwait, see Records VI, pp. 373–82.
69 Records II, p. 608.
70 It is difficult to comprehend today the wonder with which many Kuwaitis regarded their "modern" neighbor at that time. As they experienced the early strains of great change without the rewards it would ultimately bring, at least some elements of the Kuwaiti population looked on Iraq as a source of many good things. In a conversation with an older Kuwaiti friend, he recalled with childlike joy the first time he had seen red tissue paper imported from Basra. In the fullness of time Kuwait would far surpass Iraq in terms of modernity. When the Iraqis occupied Kuwait in 1990, for example, this disparity rapidly became clear. The Iraqi occupiers did not comprehend the fax machine and could not operate the computerized banking system until they had rounded up Filipino and Pakistani technicians. But in the mid-1930s this reversal of fortunes was well in the future.
71 Rush, *Al-Sabah*, p. 52.
72 Winstone and Freeth, *Kuwait*, p. 118.
73 G. L. Bondarevsky, "Iraq, Kuwait and Nazi Germany," lecture presented October 23, 1998 (*Hadeeth ad-Dar* (Kuwait), Vol. 28, 2008, p. 54).
74 Ibid., p. 55.
75 Among other Iraqi tactics, a sustained effort was mounted, apparently headed by the Governor in Basra, to induce Kuwaitis to accept Iraqi citizenship, using both persuasion and property owned by Kuwaitis within Iraq. Kuwaiti students enrolled in Iraqi schools were targeted as well. See Records II, p. 132.
76 Joyce, *Kuwait 1945–1996*, p. xv, and Rush, *Al-Sabah*, p. 52.
77 Records II, pp. 193–94. The assessment judged that at least half the population opposed the Council, including the Al-Sabah family

and their tribal allies; former officials who had been replaced by Council supporters; notables and merchants whose interests had suffered at the hands of the Council; and "ten thousand or more Shias" who felt marginalized and threatened by a Sunni Council.

78. Crystal, *Oil and Politics in the Gulf*, p. 54.
79. Records II, p. 216. Political Agent de Gaury adopted a strictly hands-off posture regarding the evolving power struggle, although both the ruler and his opponents appealed for British support. His governing principle seems to have been to come out on the side of the winners.
80. Records II, p. 255.
81. The events of March 1938 are seldom discussed in contemporary Kuwait, in large part because the dispute pitted prominent families against each other and even members of the same family against one another. This account is pieced together from contemporaneous documents, published sources, including memoirs, and several conversations with older Kuwaiti friends.
82. Records II, pp. 258 and 264. See also Joyce, *Kuwait 1945–1996*, p. xv.
83. Records II, p. 258.
84. Ibid., p. 285.
85. Ibid., p. 319.
86. Winstone and Freeth, *Kuwait*, p. 121.
87. Scudder, *The Arabian Mission's Story*, p. 107. In a letter to the DeJongs written from India, Dr. Mylrea wrote in 1942: "If Lew [Scudder—the author's father] would visit my friends in prison some time & give them my salaams, I should be much obliged:- Yusuf Marzuk, Suleiman Adasani, Masalaam Khuthair, & the rest of them. I know they will be sorry to know that Bess has gone."
88. Dickson, *The Arab of the Desert*, p.119.
89. Apparently, Shaikh Ahmad favored American cars. See Alan Villiers, *Sons of Sinbad: An Account of Sailing with the Arabs in their Dhows, in the Red Sea, around the Coasts of Arabia, and to Zanzibar and Tanganyika: Pearling in the Persian Gulf: and the Life of the Shipmasters, the Mariners and Merchants of Kuwait* (New York: Charles Scribner's Sons, 1968), p. 333.
90. Winstone and Freeth, *Kuwait*, p. 196. The Palestinians who came to Kuwait before the advent of the oil era (working in education, creation of a police force and army, etc.) are regarded by Kuwaitis through a significantly different lens. In contrast with the much larger numbers who migrated from Palestine in the late 1940s after oil revenues began to flow and the establishment of the state

of Israel had displaced them, these early pioneers are recalled as persons "who came to help us when we had almost nothing." A number of families from this group were accorded Kuwaiti citizenship. Author's observations and conversations with Kuwaitis during 1987–90.
91 Winstone and Freeth, *Kuwait*, p. 194.
92 The ruler began to receive payments for the oil concession in 1935, years in the advance of the proving of the first producing well. But, while significant, the annual payments were less than half the proceeds of customs duties. Crystal, *Oil and Politics in the Gulf*, p. 55.

5 World War II Comes to Kuwait

1 Villiers, *Sons of Sinbad*, p.330.
2 Daniels, *Kuwait Journey*, p. 17.
3 Villiers, *Sons of Sinbad*, p. 340.
4 In the early 1970s, a film produced by a young Kuwaiti captivated the former pearling communities. Entitled *Bas Ya Bahr* ('Enough Oh Sea'), the dramatic evocation of the rigors of pearl diving left audiences deeply moved, "purged by feelings of pity and pride. The film they had seen was about *their* past and *their* suffering." (Field, *The Merchants*, p. 177.)
5 Villiers, *Sons of Sinbad*, p. 323–24.
6 Crystal, *Oil and Politics in the Gulf*, p. 39. Villiers added that if Kuwait had not been able to shift to fill the void in shipping, it would have suffered economically even more that it did. Villiers, *Sons of Sinbad*, p. 351.
7 Daniels, *Kuwait Journey*, p. 20. The appetite for gold in India is remarkable. During my time in the United Arab Emirates at the beginning of the 1970s, Dubai was reportedly the fourth largest gold market in the world. A planeload of gold was flown in monthly to provide cargoes for dhows, by then greatly upgraded with powerful marine engines. This trade was open and legal in Dubai, but frowned upon by the Indian Coast Guard. Commercial contacts who offered an opportunity to buy into the trade said they lost one in four vessels. The trade from Dubai was curbed when India established a Consulate on the "Creek" where they could monitor sailings. The rumor, at the time, was that departures were then moved up the Gulf to Umm al-Qaiwain and other more secluded ports.
8 Tracy, "A Talk with Violet Dickson," pp. 15–16.

9   Kuwait's closest brush with combat operations occurred in 1940 when three Italian bombers from Rhodes overflew Kuwait on their way to bomb Bahrain, and Dhahran (Dickson, *The Arab of the Desert*, p. 451).
10 The sole exception to this statement, well remembered because it was atypical, was the Italian bombing mission in October 1940. The aircraft flew at night across the Arabian Peninsula from the Italian-occupied Dodecanese Islands in the eastern Mediterranean to target the new American oil town of Dhahran in Saudi Arabia and the refinery at Sitra in Bahrain. Dhahran suffered minor damage but the bombs in Bahrain were released harmlessly in the desert. This attack on American targets occurred more than a year before the United States entered the war. (Field, *The Merchants*, pp. 204–5.) Dickson reports that some attacks on Kuwaiti facilities were fended off. While the Rashid Ali revolt was under way in Iraq, British women at KOC were evacuated to India. American women remained and worked throughout the war (Dickson, *The Arab of the Desert*).
11 Scudder, *The Arabian Mission's Story*, p. 107. For the Mission hospitals, shortages of key medications, such as sulphur and penicillin, were a persistent problem. Dorothy B. Scudder, "The Beginnings of Medical Work in Kuwait," a paper presented April 4, 1976 at a seminar sponsored by the Family Development Society at the Sheraton Hotel, Kuwait, April 4–6, 1976.
12 Crystal, *Oil and Politics in the Gulf*, p. 74.
13 Ibid.; Winstone and Freeth, *Kuwait*, p. 171. In a 1943 document, the Political Agent reported that large profits were realized due to price controls and the shortage of consumer goods.
14 Scudder, *The Arabian Mission's Story*, p. 328. Dr. Lew Scudder was the father of the historian of the Arabian Mission, who was born in Kuwait during World War II.
15 Field, *The Merchants*, p. 205.
16 Ibid., p. 207. A similar phenomenon occurred in Kuwait following the 1991 liberation from the Iraqi occupation. A number of Kuwaiti newborns were named "Boush," at least provisionally, in honor of President George H. W. Bush.
17 Winstone and Freeth, *Kuwait*, pp. 170–71.
18 Records II, p. 363. Kuwait was also considered briefly as a site for assembling military trucks (ibid., p. 354).
19 Ibid., p. 365.
20 Ibid., p. 367. Possibly in connection with consideration of sheltering ships at Kuwait, an undated port survey of the time included a

brief synopsis of medical facilities: "There is one hospital and two outpatient dispensaries in the town. The hospital is the American Mission Hospital and consists of two sections, men and women. Both these sections cater for Arabs only, and have no suitable accommodation for Europeans, but the latter can be admitted in an emergency. Number of beds –25." "The Kuwait Oil Company have two rooms (one air-conditioned) for the use of their employees near, and under the care of the Mission Hospital." (Ibid., p. 369.)

21 Field, *The Merchants*, p. 122.
22 Daniels, *Kuwait Journey*, p. 16.
23 Joel Sayre, *Persian Gulf Command: Some Marvels on the Road to Kazvin* (New York: Random House, 1945), p. 6.
24 Sayre, *Persian Gulf Command*, pp. 99–100.
25 The following account of the barge assembly facility at Kuwait is drawn from T. H. Vail Motter, *The Persian Corridor and Aid to Russia* (Washington: Office of the Chief of Military History, Department of the Army, 1952), pp. 109–112.
26 In 1941 the British military had extended the existing pier at Ahmadi and installed associated water tanks because the pier at Shuwaikh was deemed too close to populated areas for handling ammunition and other hazardous cargoes (Records II, p. 347).
27 Paul Edward Case, "Boom Time in Kuwait: An Obscure Persian Gulf Shaikhdom, Enriched by Oil, Uses its Wealth to Improve the Lot of all its people," *National Geographic*, Vol. 102, no. 6 (December 1952), pp. 783–802.
28 It is not clear from other sources what the "stone buildings" referred to actually had been used for. There are no references to any hospital other than that at the American Mission, which was in the town not far from Shuwaikh, although inside the town walls. It is possible, although undocumented, that victims of smallpox, etc. were isolated there during epidemics such as those in the 1930s. They do not appear to have been affiliated with the American Mission Hospital.
29 The British political agent reported July 28, 1942, on the American operation at Shuwaikh noting that they were using the water tank there for themselves and the Kuwaitis in their employ (Records II, p. 356).
30 Higgins Industries is best known for its production of the landing craft used in the Normandy and other amphibious landings. These versatile boats were so identified with the company that they were known popularly as "Higgins boats."

31 Records II, p. 316.
32 Ibid., p. 317 (May 17, 1942).
33 Ibid., p. 318.
34 Having chronicled the many threads of Kuwait's experience over the last thirty years in which Dr. Mylrea's played a part, it first appeared that he had not been associated with the exploration for petroleum. Then, there he was in a photo of the ruler's party at Bahrah, where a dry hole was drilled in 1936. Winstone and Freeth, *Kuwaut* p. 169.
35 Scudder, *The Arabian Mission's Story*, p. 267, footnote 27.
36 "The Scudder family of missionaries in India," <<http://en.wikipedia.org.wiki/The_Scudder_family_ of_missionaries_in_India>>
37 The memoirs that follow are drawn from transcriptions of slide presentations in Kuwait by Mrs. Scudder on March 24, 1987, and January 25, 1988.
38 The city gates continued to be secured at night at least until 1949. Gerald Butt, *The Lion in the Sand: The British in the Middle East*, London: Bloomsbury Publishing, 1995, p. 98.
39 Scudder, op, cit., p. 268.
40 There is some confusion in the literature as to whether the x-ray unit was installed in 1943 or 1945.
41 Scudder, January 25, 1988 The telephone system served only 400 subscribers in 1953. Records IV, p.71.
42 A merchant, Yusuf al-Ghanem, had a generator of limited capacity and a small associated ice factory. The Mission received a 2'x2' block every day. D. Scudder, January 25, 1988.
43 The hospital was finally air-conditioned in 1952 when relatives sent a unit intended for the Scudder bedroom. It was instead installed in the OR, allowing the staff to take mid-day naps there in relative comfort.
44 Dorothy B. Scudder, "Kuwait in Recollection and Prospect," monograph, November 7, with L. R. Scudder, Jr., 1983
45 Lewis R. Scudder, Jr., "Celebration in Crisis Land," *fromthemideast* (2005) <<http://fromthemideast.livejournal.com/13227.html>>
46 Ibid.
47 D. Scudder, January 25, 1988.
48 Scudder, *The Arabian Mission's Story*, p. 270.
49 See, for example, Archibald H. T. Chisholm, *The First Kuwait Oil Concession: A Record of the Negotiations, 1911–1934* (London: Frank Cass, 1975), and Henry Longhurst, *Adventures in Oil: The Story of British Petroleum* (London: Sedgwick & Jackson, 1959).

50 Daniels, *Kuwait Journey*, p. 23.
51 Winstone and Freeth, *Kuwait*, p. 125. It is one of the ironies of Middle Eastern oil development that, in spite of British solicitude for Ibn Saud and his ego, the Americans stole a march on them in winning Saudi concessions.
52 Freeth, *Kuwait Was My Home*, p. 35.
53 To cite one example, "In 1934, the Political Agent in Bahrain received a telegram from the British consul in Basra informing him that he had granted an entry visa to Bahrain to a Mr. Harding of American Express. The agent panicked when he read the telegram; he did not want any Americans in Bahrain. He therefore decided to prevent Mr. Harding's entry. He went to the airport and prepared to send him back immediately after his plane landed, but to his surprise and relief, Mr. Harding turned out to be an Englishman; he was allowed in." (Rosemarie Said Zahlan, *The Making of the Modern Gulf States: Kuwait, Bahrain, Qatar, the United Arab Emirates, and Oman* [London: Unwin Hyman, 1989], p. 14.)
54 Winstone and Freeth, *Kuwait*, p. 36.
55 Ibid., p. 37.
56 Ibid., p. 150. About ten days earlier, the two companies came to a separate agreement to work together rather than compete. This book, a collaborative product of Col. Dickson's daughter and an oil specialist, provides a good brief account of Kuwait's oil development and includes insights regarding Dickson's views not available in other sources.
57 Ibid., p. 140.
58 Freeth, *Kuwait Was My Home*, p. 37.
59 Winstone and Freeth, *Kuwait*, p. 168.
60 Ibid., p. 165.
61 Zahlan, *The Making of the Modern Gulf States*, p. 18.
62 Winstone and Freeth, *Kuwait*, p. 171.
63 The agreements included an Agreement of Friendship and Neighbouring Relations, an Extradition Agreement and a Trade Agreement. Negotiations leading to the agreements began in 1934 and, "By mutual arrangement between the two countries," their provisions were observed since March 1940. (Report from the Political Agent in Kuwait to the Political Resident in Bahrain, dated June 3, 1942, Records VII, p. 312.)
64 The first American aircraft, a Fairchild 72, overflew Kuwait in 1934 on its way to the oil camp at Dhahran, Saudi Arabia to assist in exploration operations. Shipped to Alexandria, Egypt, the aircraft followed a route that took it to Cairo, Gaza, Rutbah Wells,

Baghdad, Basra, Kuwait, Bahrain, Dhahran. The Royal Air Force at Basra apparently warned the pilots not to overfly Kuwait, but the advice was ignored. To assist in the aerial exploration, Eastman Kodak developed a film that could be developed in the high temperatures of the Arabian Peninsula. (Wallace Stegner, *Discovery: The Search for Arabian Oil* [Beirut: Export Press, 1971].)

65 Michael E. Palmer, *Guardians of the Gulf: A History of America's Expanding Role in the Persian Gulf, 1833–1992* (New York: The Free Press, 1992), pp. 40–41.
66 Records VII, p. 655.
67 Ibid., p. 659.
68 Palmer, *Guardians of the Gulf*, p. 29.
69 Ibid., p. 45.

6 From Boom Port to Boom Town

1 John Daniels, *Kuwait Journey* (Luton: White Crescent Press, 1971), p. 20.
2 Freeth, *Kuwait Was My Home*, p. 54.
3 John E. Frazer, "Kuwait: Aladdin's Lamp of the Middle East," *National Geographic Magazine*, Vol. 135, No. 5 (May 1969), p. 638.
4 Joyce, *Kuwait 1945–1996*, p. 2.
5 Freeth, *Kuwait Was My Home*, p. 45.
6 Winstone and Freeth, *Kuwait*, p. 171.
7 Harrison M. Symmes, Correspondence with the author, August 1988. See also Mrs. Wilton Geerhart, Recorded recollections of a resident of Kuwait (Bechtel), 1948–1981, December 4, 1988. Kuwait's first airport was just outside the gate.
8 Winstone and Freeth, *Kuwait*
9 Ibid.
10 According to Zahra Freeth, *Kuwait was My Home*, p. 38, "The Kuwait oilfield would have been producing by the early 1940s, had not the outbreak of war in Europe delayed its development. From the beginning of the war all drilling was suspended, the wells were closed, and only a skeleton staff of oil company personnel was left in Kuwait." Rightly or not, some Kuwaitis still contrast the British decision to mothball operations in their country unfavorably with continued development by ARAMCO in eastern Saudi Arabia.
11 Freeth, *Kuwait Was My Home*, 38. As the petroleum pioneers were discovering, Kuwaiti crude oil is among the least expensive in the world to produce.

12 Winstone and Freeth, *Kuwait*, p. 171. Among the amenities that the management procured for their employees was a war-surplus mobile military hospital purchased from the U.S. Army. When the crates in which the components arrived were unpacked, one was found to contain a massive supply of canes, which were resold elsewhere. (Ibid., p. 172.)

13 When I arrived in Abu Dhabi in 1972 to open the American Embassy there, I was astonished to find on the shelves of the small "supermarket" many varieties of hot sauce as well as black beans and other staples of Southwestern cuisine.

14 Winstone and Freeth, *Kuwait*, p. 172. In their relatively large numbers, the American oilmen engendered among many Kuwaitis and other Gulf Arabs a misimpression regarding of American speech patterns and accents. Many later arrivals, including the author, who did not have southwestern accents, found it difficult to convince their interlocutors that they were indeed Americans too.

15 Joseph Wright Twinam, *The Gulf, Cooperation and the Council: An American Perspective* (Washington: Middle East Policy Council, 1992), p. 79.

16 Ibid., p. 78. In Saudi Arabia, for example, a number of loan words entered the local language, such as *"shawwal"* for shovel. Even verbs were not immune; Americans instructing local workers to tighten a bolt spawned the verb *"tayyit."*

17 Scudder, *The Arabian Mission's Story*, p. 108. Wilton Geerhart was Bechtel's project manager for the south pier, refinery and associated construction. He and his wife first arrived November 18, 1948 and returned periodically in the employ of Abdallah al-Rayes until the early 1980s. Mrs. Geerhart provided unique perspectives on Kuwait and expatriate life during that era (Geerhart, recorded recollections).

18 Freeth, *Kuwait Was My Home*, p. 39.

19 Winstone and Freeth, *Kuwait*, p. 173.

20 Ibid., p. 174.

21 Ibid., p. 175.

22 Freeth, *Kuwait Was My Home*, pp. 38–39.

23 Ibid., p. 38. The capacity of the south pier also permitted ships taking oil from Abadan to move to Kuwait as berths intended for dry cargo were converted to oil (Geerhart, recorded recollections).

24 Geerhart, recorded recollections.

25 There were approximately 1,000 British and American personnel (330 of them with wives and families) working for KOC at the time (Freeth, *Kuwait Was My Home*, p. 39).

26 By the time of Kuwait's full independence in 1961, the student body numbered 401.
27 Winstone and Freeth, *Kuwait*, pp. 184–85.
28 Freeth, *Kuwait Was My Home*, p. 39.
29 Eric V. Thompson, comp. *Major Oil Companies Operating in the Gulf Region (By Country)* (Charlottesville, VA: Petroleum Archives Project, Arabian Peninsula and Gulf Studies Program, University of Virginia, 1995), p. 6 The American Independent Oil Company was a joint venture of Phillips Petroleum, Signal Oil and Gas, Ashland, J. S. Abercrombie, Sunray Mid-Continental Oil Company, Globe Oil and Refining Co., and Pauley Petroleum Inc.
30 Freeth, *Kuwait Was My Home*, pp. 39–40. Pacific Western became Getty Oil Company; Winstone and Freeth, *Kuwait*, p. 180.
31 Freeth, *Kuwait Was My Home*, p. 40. Pacific Western subsequently built its own separate terminal further south in Neutral Zone, which it named Mina Saud.
32 Interestingly, at least a few Americans who first came to Kuwait in connection with the jobs of their parents would decide on careers that brought them back to work in Kuwait or elsewhere in the area.
33 Geerhart, recorded recollections. Mrs. Geerhart was chairman of the Ahmadi women's group.
34 The introduction of Kuwaitis to the benefits of modern medicine is the most obvious legacy of the Mission's work, but there are other influences, less easy to quantify, that can be adduced. For instance, the American Mission included a long line of compassionate professional women who must have had an effect on the evolving attitude toward the capable and increasingly well-educated women of Kuwait — Dr. Eleanor Calverley (1912–29); Dr. Ester Barney (1930–37); Dr. Mary Alison (1934–1940) and (1946–63); Dr. Ruth Crouse (1940–46); Miss Mary Van Pelt "Khatun Miryam" (1916–38), and Mrs. Dorothy Scudder, RN (1939–90) (Scudder, *The Arabian Mission's Story*, p. 270).
35 Ibid., p. 108.
36 Ibid., footnote 104.
37 In the years after 1947 four state hospitals, two general and two specializing in treating TB, were opened. Since then, of course, the number and sophistication of Kuwait's medical facilities have increased. Freeth, *Kuwait Was My Home*, p. 45.
38 Scudder, *The Arabian Mission's Story*, p. 388. Building materials were still scarce because of the lag caused by the wartime economy and the demand for available supplies to fuel the massive projects of the oil industry and other public works projects.

39 At its creation in 1949, the command was officially designated Commander Persian Gulf Area.
40 The three seaplane tenders that served COMMIDEASTFOR in rotation were U.S.S. *Duxbury Bay* (AVP-38), U.S.S. *Greenwich Bay* (AVP-41), and U.S.S. *Valcour* (AVP-41). These vessels were distinctively painted white or very light gray because of the extremes of heat in their area of responsibility (AOR). Air-conditioning was installed in the crew spaces as soon as practical.
41 Thomas A. Bryson, *Tars, Turks, and Tankers: The Role of the United State Navy in the Middle East* (Metuchen, NJ: The Scarecrow Press, 1980), pp. 142–43.
42 William D. Brewer, Correspondence with the author, 1991–92.
43 Harrison M. Symmes, Correspondence with the author, August 1988.
44 Records II, p. 180.
45 Joyce, *Kuwait 1945–1996*, p. 7. Ironically, parts of the crew working a drilling rig are known as "roughnecks" in the industry.
46 Records II, pp. 330 and 337.
47 An analogous arrangement was in force, with somewhat better results, in the former Trucial States until 1972, when Bahrain, Oman, Qatar and the United Arab Emirates gained full independence from Britain. The American Consulate General at Dhahran in Saudi Arabia was responsible for services and protection in those sheikhdoms. Consuls from Dhahran made periodic visits to provide routine services and emergency trips to handle formalities in cases of death, for example. In addition to necessary forms and supplies, they carried a hand seal that had to be safeguarded even while sleeping. In the spring of 1972, before embassies were established in Abu Dhabi, Manama, and Muscat, I took part in the final consular circuit.
48 Joyce, *Kuwait 1945–1996*, p. 8. Well-supplied with data by the State Department Secretary Jones bolstered the case with the British Foreign Office. Joyce summarizes the elements of the American presentation: "Americans in Kuwait had become involved in litigation and criminal processes. The United States had earlier agreed to the trial of American citizens before the British Political Agency Court; however, it was the right of the accused to have convenient access to an American representative. There were also issues regarding seamen and shipping. Annually, more than 100 American tankers picked up petroleum products in Kuwait harbor, and as oil production increased so too did the number of such tankers. In addition, a large number of American-registered mer-

chant ships called at Kuwait. The consul at Basra was unable to provide needed services. He could not examine ship papers, or issue visas. Neither was he available to pay discharged seamen the wages deposited by the master."

49 Ibid., p. 9.
50 From the time of its establishment until Kuwait achieved full independence in 1961, the U.S. Consulate in Kuwait was formally accredited to the British government and fell organizationally under the State Department's Bureau of European Affairs rather than its Middle Eastern counterpart. Except for the prohibition of direct contact with the Ruler of Kuwait and his government, the arrangement permitted the consulate to discharge its responsibilities to American citizens, seamen, and others. Communication with the Ruler, when necessary, was conducted through the British political agent (ibid., pp. 13–14).
51 Ibid., p. 14. In the early 1970s, in anticipation of the British withdrawal from the Trucial States, a similar situation arose. Before any serious analysis was done regarding proposed new embassies in Abu Dhabi, Manama, and Muscat, a State Department official testifying before Congress was caught off guard when asked the cost of the three new missions. Off the cuff, he replied that it could probably be done for $ 200,000 each. Regardless of his intention, the casual remark became the base figure for the first year of operation for all three embassies.
52 Records III, p. 3.
53 Scudder, *The Arabian Mission's Story*, p. 108.
54 Rush, *Al-Sabah*, p. 53, ".... after the sunset prayer, 'he complained of feeling cold, then began to shiver and said his eyesight was failing'." Other sources give his age as sixty- nine.
55 Dorothy Scudder told the author in 1987 that she and her husband knew Jabir and Sabah well. As they were growing up, they frequently played at the Mission, which was not far from the ruler's palace. She described them as normal boys, who were occasionally "naughty." Shaikh Ahmad was survived by nine sons and fifteen daughters.
56 According to Rush, *Al-Sabah*, "The huge crowds that attended his funeral on the bitterly cold morning of January 30th and the grief of the mourners were clear signs of the extent to which he had maintained, or regained, the support of the people."
57 Crystal, *Oil and Politics in the Gulf: Rulers and Merchants in Kuwait and Qatar*, p. 64. To their credit, not all knowledgeable British officials foresaw this dire scenario. See, for example, Records II, p. 339.

58 Joyce, *Kuwait 1945–1996*, p. 12.
59 Crystal, "The Merchant Families and the Ruling Family," in National Republican Institute, *Political Participation...*, p 9.
60 Ibid., p. 1.
61 As Crystal accurately observes elsewhere, "The merchants, especially in Kuwait, maintained an unexpectedly strong corporate sense and continued to function, economically and socially, as a collective body. They did not simply disappear as a class" (ibid., p. 7).
62 Many of these new Persian expatriates, who constituted an element distinct from the old, well-established Kuwaiti families of Persian origin, came directly from Abadan following the expulsion of the Anglo-Iranian Oil Company by the Iranian government. Freeth, *Kuwait Was My Home*, p. 42.

7 Developers, Dissidents, and Diplomats

1 Records II, p. 344.
2 Ibid., p. 341.
3 British "recognition" of Shaikh Abdallah was delayed while the political agent pressured him to appoint British experts in key government departments, name his own successor, and dismiss Ezzat M. Jaafar from his entourage. Ultimately, he agreed to implement the first demand partially (Rush, *Al-Sabah*, p. 43). See also Political Agent's memorandum of February 16, 1951 in Records III, p. 8. The date of Shaikh Abdallah's accession has since been observed as the Kuwait National Day, perhaps indicative of a popular perception that the country's modern history began with his rule.
4 Records III, p. 12. USS *Maury* (AGS-16), a survey ship, made three eight-month deployments to the Gulf to create charts of the waters in 1949, 1950, and 1951 in company of two seagoing tugs (U. S. Navy website).
5 Lienhardt, *Disorientations*, p. 29.
6 The first radio station in Kuwait, for example, was established in 1951. It was a private venture that initially broadcast only two hours a day (Joyce, *Kuwait 1945–1996*, p. 4).
7 This contact with the next Kuwaiti Ruler did not violate the British prohibition on direct contact between the U.S. consul and the ruler strictly speaking because the British delayed Shaikh Abdallah's recognition as ruler until late February.
8 The account of Consul English's report is contained in Joyce, *Ku-*

wait 1945–1996, p. 12. English returned to Basra on February 2, as usual damaging the Consulate vehicle on the primitive desert track. In a footnote he complained of personnel shortages at Basra where four of six positions were unfilled.

9 Duncan was relatively junior for a chief of mission. He joined the U.S. Foreign Service in 1946 and had four years of service in Cairo under his belt. Joyce (*Kuwait 1945–1996*, p. 14) records that he spoke "a few words of Syrian Arabic," but if he picked up his Arabic in Egypt, it is unlikely that it was the Levantine dialect.

10 Ibid., p. 15.

11 Scudder, *The Arabian Mission's Story*, p. 236.

12 Scudder, Slide lecture delivered January 25, 1988. The photograph was probably destroyed during the Iraqi occupation of 1990–91.

13 It should be recalled that Shaikh Fahad Salem, the son of the ruler at the time, enrolled in Edwin Calverley's school at the American Mission compound in his youth. See Chapter III of this book.

14 Joyce, *Kuwait 1945–1996*, p. 16. Whatever his views on polygamy in general, a revealing anecdote was related to the author by several knowledgeable Kuwaitis. When the young Shaikh Sa'd Al-Abdullah, who was later to be crown prince and prime minister, asked to marry his daughter, Shaikh Fahad made it a condition of his consent that Shaikh Sa'd take no additional wives. He was also a strong advocate of education for women, including his own daughters.

15 Ibid.

16 Ibid. This trivialization of Shaikh Fahad's role is disingenuous. In addition to being the ruler's brother, Fahad held important positions in the development programs, frequently to the frustration of British officials as documented throughout declassified records. The primary British authority on the history of the Al-Sabah characterized Shaikh Fahad as "popular among the townspeople" and comfortable " in the new world of technology and international business and finance." See Records III, p. xvii.

17 Joyce, *Kuwait 1945–1996*, p. 17.

18 "Kuwait before the days of oil was a Muslim state barely touched by outside influences. The original population were all of the Sunni sect, but there was also a large Shia group, many of them of Iraqi or Persian origin. Together they formed a God-fearing community for whom religion coloured practically every thought and action of their lives, in a way that has something of a parallel in medieval Europe." (Winstone and Freeth, *Kuwait*, p. 49.)

19 Records II, p. 27. In January 1951 only 50 of the 9,000 employees of

KOC were American citizens but the number grew substantially in the 1950s as other American oil and construction companies began operations in Kuwait (Joyce, *Kuwait 1945–1996*,,p. 7).
20 Ibid., p. 15.
21 Records VI, pp. xxv–xxvi.
22 Personal conversations, 1987–89.
23 Shaikhs Jabir and Sabah Al-Ahmad, both of whom were to become Amir, toured the United States as young men with their tutor, Ezzat M. Jaafar, another British *bete noire*. The Political Agency appears not to have been aware of this visit until perhaps as late as May 1951. Jaafar had previously visited parts of the United States two years earlier. See Ezzat M. Jaafar, "Ezzat Jaafar Visits California, August 1948," photocopy of bound photographs of Mr. Jaafar's visit to the United States, given to me by Mr. Jaafar.
24 Joyce, *Kuwait 1945–1996*, p. 13.
25 Records III, p. 22. There are a number of references to Shaikh Fahad's dark complexion in contemporary British documents.
26 Ezzat Jaafar was another figure of whom the British had complained for years; increasingly he was accused of advocating for American commercial firms. The British political agent observed on January 2, 1949, that Jaafar was "a power in the Palace ... who is the influence behind the pushing of American interests with the Shaikh." As noted above, the removal of Jaffar was one of the conditions they sought to impose on Shaikh Abdallah al Salem as the price of his confirmation as Ruler a year later (Records II, p. 325).
27 Ibid., p. 33.
28 Rush, *Al-Sabah*, p, 40.
29 Ibid.
30 Ibid., p, 41.
31 Scudder, *The Arabian Mission's Story*, p. 109. One of his early acts was to invite displaced Palestinians to come to Kuwait to find employment. He likewise initially planned to establish elected councils to give the major families a voice in running the country, but was thwarted by other members of the Al-Sabah.
32 Paul Claussen, letter to the author from the Office of the Historian, Department of State, regarding the establishment of a Consulate in Kuwait (with attached documents), November 29, 1988. The clerk was possibly Pat Cunningham, who was recalled as working with Vice Consul Duncan by several older Kuwaitis in a conversation with the author in the al-Abdul Razzaq *diwanniya* on April 26, 1990. According to the same sources, Bader Saud al-Abdul Razzaq, who later joined the Ministry of Public Works, worked for

the American Consulate from 1951 to 1953. They last saw Enoch Duncan in 1971, when he returned to Kuwait for the tenth anniversary of Independence.

33 American Embassy Kuwait, "History of American Diplomatic Representation in Kuwait," June 22, 1981, typewritten. This and other accounts of the development of the diplomatic establishment in Kuwait are very useful in their broad outlines. Compiled long after the fact, however, specific details must be viewed with care. This source states that the first office was obtained "through the courtesy of the KOC," whereas contemporary accounts indicate that Shaikh Fahad and/or AMINOIL provided key assistance (see above).

34 American Embassy Kuwait, "A Short History of Kuwaiti-American Relations, Prepared for the Occasion of the Fifteenth Anniversary of the Opening of the American Consulate in Kuwait," October 1964, typewritten, p. 3; Memorandum of Conversation, April 26, 1990.

35 American Embassy Kuwait, "A Short History.." This document gives the date of the rental as late 1951, which seems to be an error. What is more certain is that these premises were occupied by the time Harrison M. Symmes arrived in 1953 to replace Duncan. Symmes, correspondence with the author, August 1988.

36 American Embassy Kuwait, "History of American....," pp. 1–2.

37 Vice Consul William A. Stoltzfus, Jr. was posted to Kuwait in 1954. Except as indicated, details of developments in 1953–55 are from Symmes, correspondence.

38 American Embassy Kuwait, "History of American....."

39 Ibid., p. 2.

40 Symmes, correspondence.

41 The majority of vehicles in Kuwait were manufactured by General Motors; and the agents, al-Ghanim, would grow to be one of the largest GM dealerships in the world.

42 "There were few Americans living in Kuwait Town in the early fifties. Those few in the American Mission, the American Independent Oil and Getty Oil Companies, and the American Consulate numbered fewer than twenty. The Americans working for the oil companies at Ahmadi or in the Neutral Zone kept to themselves and had little to do with the Consulate except for passports or other consular services. Visiting American businessmen frequently came by the Consulate for briefings but the lack of hotels and restaurants in Kuwait meant that social contact with them was usually in the home of their 'Kuwaiti Partner'." Symmes, correspondence.

43 KOC discreetly granted the consul access to its commisary and assistance in hiring servants. Symmes had the good fortune to engage in this way Gulzaman Khan, an imposing Pathan who had served for years as head bearer for the Australian high commissioner in India.

44 Symmes, correspondence. Blanket cuts and limits of this kind occur periodically. In 1973, during the early phase of establishing Embassy Abu Dhabi, the State Department placed a worldwide freeze on new hires. There were four Americans, including me, in the embassy and one Foreign National (FSN) driver, whose position at Dhahran was redundant. Interviews were in progress to fill three authorized FSN positions—a secretary, a commercial assistant, and a consular assistant. When queried, the State Department confirmed that the freeze also applied to the undermanned embassy, despite an imminent trade mission. The children and wives in the Embassy were mobilized to stuff envelopes and provide other support for the event.

45 The practice of sending Kuwait's diplomatic pouches via Dhahran seems to have continued into the early 1960s, according to Eugene H. Bird, The Foreign Affairs Oral History Collection of the Association for Diplomatic Studies and Training <<http://www.adst.org/OH%20TOCs/Bird,%20Eugene%20H.toc.pdf>>.

46 The consulate also had reason to avoid confidential cables because of the laborious encryption and decryption procedures.

47 William A. Stoltzfus, Jr. The Foreign Affairs Oral History Collection of the Association for Diplomatic Studies and Training <<http://www.adst.org/OH%20TOCs/Stoltzfus,%20William%20A.%20Jr.toc.pdf>>

48 Symmes, correspondence.

49 Stoltzfus, oral history.

50 The Consulate landlord, who was "friendly, gracious and accommodating."

51 Sympathetic to Americans and suspect by the British. He was married to Shaikha Badria who was a prominent and successful busineswoman before it became fashionable. Most of their children were educated in the United States with support and assistance of the American Mission. Shaikh Fahd periodically gave banquets for expatriates. Stoltzfus, himself the son of missionaries, remembered that at the beginning of one of these occasions the shaikh asked a missionary guest to say grace: "A number of his retainers, seated way down the long table, had already dived into the meat and rice. They certainly never had heard of saying

a prayer before meals. Under the sheikh's reproving glare they sheepishly sat back and submitted to the missionary's tactfully ecumenical blessing."
52 Welcomed visits by consulate staff to his garden north of the town at any time. "On one occasion, when he was in residence, the American visitors explained that they had brought their own picnic lunch and, as they ate, servants brought ... camel's milk, fruit, goodies of all sorts and a horse ... to ride." Shaikh Jabir, a popular figure who maintained relationships with the tribes, was still active and friendly to the United States in the 1980s when I was posted to Kuwait.
53 Symmes, correspondence. In the later years of the decade, as the society became more complex and the number of European expatriates increased, protocol inevitably grew more rigid and customary practices became more rare. Senior shaikhs no longer accepted invitations or made calls on holidays.
54 William D. Brewer, Correspondence with author, 1991–92, and The Foreign Affairs Oral History Collection of the Association for Diplomatic Studies and Training <<http://www.adst.org/OH%20TOCs/Brewer,%20William%20D.toc.pdf>> August 2, 1988. Except as otherwise noted, information in this section is drawn from these documents. The Consulate in Basra had donated a handsome louvered screen for the dining room behind which Gulzaman could stand to see to the needs of guests, only "the starched top of his pugarree" showing above the screen. Symmes, correspondence.
55 Travel within the country at this period could be hazardous. Abdul Muti, the long-serving driver of the Consulate and Embassy, remembers that Vice Consul Akins became stuck in sand driving to Wafra and was unable to dig his vehicle out before a sandstorm struck. Fortunately, he was found by a bedouin, who delivered him to the Consulate in his red pickup truck in the early hours of the following morning. The Consulate motor pool in the mid-1950s consisted of a Jeep, a 1952 Chevrolet, and a Morris Minor. Abdul Muti Abdul Rahman Haroon, Transcription of interview in Arabic recorded by the author, November 9, 1988.
56 Both AMINOIL and Getty began operations in Kuwait in 1953. Larry Ison, a veteran of ARAMCO, served for six years as vice president, general manager, and director of AMINOIL, Kuwait. He retired near my residence in Charlottesville, Virginia.
57 Scudder, *The Arabian Mission's Story*, p. 258. Three doctors from the American Mission Hospital—Mylrea (1952), Nykerk (1964), and Scudder (1975)—are buried in Kuwait. D. Scudder, "The Be-

ginnings of Medical work in Kuwait," April 4, 1976. Dr. Mylrea was laid to rest in the old Christian cemetery which is walled and closed to the public. Drs. Nykerk and Scudder were interred in a newer cemetery. Geerhart, Recorded Recollections.
58 Freeth, *Kuwait Was My Home*, p. 80. Mrs. Mylrea had passed away several years earlier in India, where they retired.
59 The Mission station in Kuwait frequently hosted meetings of Mission personnel in the Gulf and these conferences became such a fixture of the local scene that into the 1970s the landing cards used by Kuwaiti immigration authorities included not only the usual reasons for visiting but a separate option, "Mission meeting" (Scudder, *The Arabian Mission's Story*, p. 328).
60 Ibid., pp. 265–66.
61 Mission personnel had long since come to terms with the resistance of local Muslims to conversion to Christianity and decided that living their spiritual values was adequate testimony of their faith. However, Church authorities in the United States seemed, in the main, incapable of overcoming their disappointment and frustration with the lack of converts.
62 Scudder, *The Arabian Mission's Story*, p. 274, note 31.
63 Ibid., note 33.
64 Ibid., p. 259.
65 Ibid., pp. 272–73. Among the distinguished attendees were Mr. and Mrs. Jordan of KOC; Mr. Witherspoon, Manager of AMINOIL; British Agent Bell; Consul and Mrs. Brewer; Harold and Violet Dickson; and Mrs. Van Ess, widow of John Van Ess and mother-in-law of Bill Brewer. D. Scudder, loc. cit., March 24, 1987. The cornerstone was laid by the ruler, Shaikh Abdallah al Salem, and Dr. L. R. Scudder in November 1954.
66 Scudder, *The Arabian Mission's Story*, p. 274, note 32.
67 Ibid., pp. 265–66.
68 Ibid., p. 274.
69 Mustafa M. Alani, *Operation Vantage: British Military Intervention in Kuwait 1961* (Surbiton, Surrey: LAAM, 1990), p. 191.
70 In 1950, Iran was the largest producer of petroleum in the Middle East and the major oil asset of the Anglo-Iranian Oil Company. When the Iranian oil industry was nationalized in 1951 by the Mossadegh government, "a world fuel shortage threatened and Kuwait became, suddenly and acutely, the centre of international attention." In the crisis that followed, "Kuwait and KOC rose to the occasion with a combination of enthusiasm and enterprise that produced some remarkable results, and handsome rewards.

In the next two years the production of crude oil was doubled, reaching 37 million tons in 1952. By 1953, Kuwait was the second largest exporter (behind Venezuela and 4th overall producer." Winstone and Freeth, *Kuwait*, p. 177.
71 Simon C. Smith, *Kuwait, 1950–1965: Britain, the al-Sabah, and Oil* (Oxford: Oxford University Press, for the British Academy, 1999), p. 25.
72 Political Agent, November 19, 1953, Records III, pp. 101–7.
73 Records VI, p. xxv. The compiler summarizes the British outlook as follows: "The year 1953 was the time when Britain made a determined bid to boost her alliance with Kuwait and tighten her control over the state." Since Kuwait had overtaken Bahrain in importance, it was recommended that Kuwait's Political Agency should no longer be subservient to the Residency in Manama. Although this change was not made, the grade of the political agent was raised to enable direct communication with the Foreign Office. At the same time it was decided to attempt to extend British influence inside the shaikhdom. "Her Majesty's Government cannot now disinterest themselves from such features of Kuwait's internal affairs as may directly or indirectly affect their wider interests."
74 Abu Dhabi and the other northern emirates confronted analogous challenges when development took off in the 1970s, and planners there often told me that they had taken note of Kuwait's pioneering experience and were determined to avoid problems, such as the plague of rats that arrived in the Kuwaiti port aboard the many ships.
75 Winstone and Freeth, p. 204.
76 British Resident, March *Kuwait,* 19, 1953. Records III, p. 538. The interior masonry had to be furrowed out to provide channels.
77 Records III, p. xix.
78 The longtime administrator of the American Mission Hospital, Haidar Mohammed Al-Khalifa, offered anecdotal evidence of the effects to a reporter: "In 1949, my father bought a plot in the capital for $ 1,260 and built a house on it for $ 4,200. In 1961 the government bought the house and land for $105,000." Frazer, "Kuwait," pp. 636–47. See also Zahlan, *The Making of the Modern Gulf States*, pp. 34–35.
79 Political Agent, August 2, 1952, in Records III, p. 58.
80 Ibid., pp. 556–57.
81 British Agent, 19 December 1952, in Records III, p. 71.
82 Rush, *Al-Sabah*, p. 41. In the same period, the British Treasury was

attempting to ban the export of Kuwaiti oil outside the Sterling area and opposing the founding of a Kuwaiti national bank.

83 Harry Symmes, the U.S. consul, reported on the situation on March 20, 1953, noting that the Britons responsible for the Development Plan were "turning Kuwait into an Anglo-Indian rest camp. They are living like spoiled aristocrats in luxurious houses...built... from State funds while the average Kuwaiti finds it impossible to get a power allocation which would give him a single electric bulb in his house." Quoted in Zahlan, *The Making of the Modern Gulf States*, p. 33.

84 British Resident, Manama November 28, 1952. Commenting on a local magazine that charged that Kuwait was being flooded with British employees, that the only work going on was for their comfort, that they were pushing Kuwaitis out of scarce housing and engaging in riotous living, the resident admitted, "There is a substratum of truth in this in that the first thing that has to be done is to build accommodation for these employees, that meanwhile they are taking up much of the available accommodation in the town and that they are indulging in large and noisy cocktail parties whenever occasion arises" (Records III, p. 529).

85 Ibid., p. 549. He added, without offering supporting evidence, "It is said that [Majdud Din] Jabri [Shaikh Fahad's choice for Chief Engineer] is connected with American contracting interests and is here to assist their entry into Kuwait."

86 See preliminary report on development prepared for the ruler in February 1952 in Records III, pp. 515–19.

87 August 9, 1953. Records III, p. 568. The evaporators in Distillation Plant "A" were supplied by Westinghouse but those for Plant "B" went to G. and J. Weir (Records III, p. 414).

88 Reporting a conversation with Shaikh Fahad Al-Salem on September 9, 1953, the British political agent dismissed the shaikh's frank expression of grievances as demented (Records III, pp. 90–93).

89 Early in his rule, a British assessment concluded, "Abdulla Salim aged 55 has no great ability and his younger brothers Fahad and Subah have no good reputation" (ibid., p. 3).

90 Crystal, *Oil and Politics in the Gulf*, p. 67.

91 Rush, *Al-Sabah.*, p. 41.

92 British Political Agent, April 6, 1952 in Records III, p. 507.

93 Ibid., p. 613. Harrison M. Symmes, who had a distinguished diplomatic career including several ambassadorships in the Middle East, was the U.S. consul from 1953 to 1955.

8 Road to Independence

1. Western commentators on this and later periods of Kuwait's evolution tend to apply their own cultural paradigm to its experience, demonstrating little appreciation of the effects of the "trauma" of rapid, concentrated change. On this scale, it is easier to find Kuwaitis wanting than to recognize their success in navigating these troubled waters or grasping the indigenous timeline for modernization.
2. Dr. Lewis Scudder was asked years later to recall what Kuwait was like when he arrived: "'It was a very simple little town when I came here in 1939,' said the American physician, who still lives in the hospital compound. 'The wall gates were locked at night, and you had to get a watchman up to let you through.'" Frazer, "Kuwait," p. 650.
3. "Preliminary Report on Development of Kuwait State, Accepted by His Highness February 1952,"Records II, pp. 515–16. In 1953 the village of Dimna was absorbed into Kuwait and renamed Salmiya. Today it is a fashionable shopping suburb (Royal Scottish Museum, *Evolving Culture ...*, p. 31.
4. "Development of Kuwait," 1954 in Records III, p. 590.
5. Ibid., pp. 515–16.
6. Lienhardt, *Disorientations*, p. 32. One of Kuwait's traditional rituals was lost with the development of the *Safat*, now covered with shops, parking garages, pavement, and other modern accouterments. In times past, senior shaikhs and others performed the *ardha*, or sword dance on the Eid and other occasions. Zahra Freeth provides a graphic account of one of the last performances in the late 1940s. The dancers performed much as their ancestors had for generations, except for one jarring modern innovation. "Some of the badu were wearing coloured coats adorned with gold braid, and as they passed us we could read on their cuffs the names of American hotels and cinemas. For America exports to Arabia large quantities of secondhand commissionaire's coats, which are much sought after by the badawin." Freeth, *Kuwait Was My Home*, pp. 113–14.
7. Dorothy Scudder remarked in one of her slide lectures (March 24, 1988) that the wall was torn down in 1958. Consul Brewer, however, recalls its being razed in the spring of 1957. William D. Brewer, Correspondence with author, 1991–92.
8. Freeth, *Kuwait Was My Home*, p. 48.
9. Lienhardt, *Disorientations*, p. 49.

10 Scudder, *The Arabian Mission's Story*, p. 235.
11 Ibid., p.109.
12 Al-Ebraheem, *Kuwait and the Gulf*, p. 122.
13 Scudder, *The Arabian Mission's Story*, p. 110.
14 Smith, *Kuwait, 1950–1965*, p. 70.
15 Joyce, *Kuwait 1945–1996*, p. 24.
16 Ibid.
17 Records III, p. 169.
18 Crystal, *Oil and Politics in the Gulf*, p. 82.
19 Ibid.
20 Records III, p. 197.
21 Ibid., p. xix. The British Political Agency was conscious of the potentially destabilizing influence of the large numbers of expatriate Arabs brought in to staff the expanding school system, hospitals and clinics. On April 9, 1956, the Agency placed the numbers of senior staff in Kuwaiti institutions at 240 Kuwaitis, 350 Egyptians, 865 Palestinians and Jordanians, and 135 British. Records II, p. 189.
22 Daniels, *Kuwait Journey*, pp. 45–6.
23 Except as noted, the following outline of events in connection with the Suez crisis is drawn from a confidential British report covering the period October 28 to November 28 in Records III, pp. 219–22.
24 Joyce, *Kuwait 1945–1996*, p. 42.
25 The disorder in Kuwait in reaction to the Suez crisis apparently was the first development in Kuwait to attract widespread attention of the American media. In late November–early December 1956, Mr. Carruthers, a photographer from NBC; Mr. Smith of Fortune magazine; and Mr. Love from the *New York Times* arrived in Kuwait. Their presence was considered noteworthy by the British Political Agency. Records III, p. 231.
26 Ibid., p. 219.
27 Shortly after "severing" ties with Great Britain, the Education Department quietly purchased 300 cans of British paint on the local market (ibid., p. 222).
28 The other main goals of the club movement—subscription of funds for Egypt and registration of volunteers for military service in that country—impacted the Western expatriates less directly. By the end of November about £1 million was raised, one/fifth of the amount from the ruler. British employees in government departments were able to evade pressures to contribute but their Arab colleagues were not so fortunate and a number complained

in private about having to turn over up to one month's salary. Contemporary reports place the number of individuals who signed up for service with the Egyptian Army at between one and two thousand (ibid.).
29 Daniels, *Kuwait Journey*, p. 50.
30 Records III, p. 232.
31 Ibid., pp. 218.
32 ibid., pp. 230–31.
33 Joyce, *Kuwait 1945–1996*, p. 46–47. The commander of U.S. naval assets based in Bahrain offered to send two U.S. destroyers for a port visit but was advised not to do so.
34 Daniels, *Kuwait Journey*, p. 51.
35 Records III, p. 235.
36 An expatriate observer living in Kuwait during these events commented "even some Kuwaiti women demonstrated in support of Egypt" at a time when most of them were still veiled. Daniels, *Kuwait Journey*, p. 44.
37 Records III, p. xix.
38 Shaikh Fahad died in 1959 while on a visit to Saudi Arabia. Joyce, *Kuwait 1945–1996*, p. 65. Before he passed away he had given his consent for Shaikh S'ad al-Abdallah, later Crown Prince/Prime Minister, to marry his daughter.
39 Rush, *Al-Sabah*, p. 41. His relationship with the British was not without its strains. In late 1954, for example, the Political Agency reported its pique with Abdullah Mubarak. Records III, p. 143
40 Rush, *Al-Sabah*, p.141.
41 Alani, *Operation Vantage*, p. 24.
42 Brewer, correspondence with the author, 1991–92.
43 Joyce, *Kuwait 1945–1996*, p. 18. Some years earlier, when the ruler requested payment in U.S. dollars from Gulf Oil, Britain objected, and noted that the U.S. concessionaire in the Neutral Zone, AMINOIL, was already paying in dollars. The British were pressing the Kuwaitis to accept payment in Pounds Sterling in lieu of Indian Rupees, still in circulation in Kuwait and other parts of the Gulf. Smith, *Kuwait, 1950–1965*, p. 33.
44 Joyce, *Kuwait 1945–1996*, p. 53.
45 *Middle East Journal*, Chronology, Vol. 12, no. 1 (Spring 1958), p. 185.
46 Records III, p. 640ff.
47 Ibid., p. 652. American companies active in the bidding for this large project included Hawaiian Dredging Co, & J. H. Pomeroy, McWilliams Dredging Co., Zoetmulder & Van Winkel, Pacific Dredging Co., and Raymond Concrete Pile.

48 Lienhardt, *Disorientations*, p. 44.
49 Records III, pp. 26–27. Years later, the early arrangements at Ahmadi still rankle with Kuwaitis, including many too young to have experienced exclusion from this area of their country. Comingling carried risks but segregation made it easier to "demonize" expatriates in time of tension.
50 Ibid., pp. 652–3.
51 Alani, *Operation Vantage*, p. 24.
52 Some of these (Pan-Arab) feelings, and the desire to follow a more independent path, had rubbed off on some Kuwaitis who had returned from abroad, principally from Egypt, as well as those who listened to Cairo radio spreading anti-Western views (Daniels, *Kuwait Journey*, p. 45.
53 Smith, *Kuwait, 1950–1965*, p. 97. Whatever his other qualities, al-Khatib was no historian. His implication that the al-Sabah had somehow forced themselves on the Kuwaitis was highly misleading and ignored the fact that they had been chosen to provide administration by the notables in an early "social compact." Until oil revenues began to flow, the niche occupied by the al-Sabah was not a lucrative one. "The(se) merchants provided credit to the ruling family and the al-Sabahs were perpetually in debt to them." Joyce, *Kuwait 1945–1996*, p. xvi.
54 Rush, *Al-Sabah*, p. 41.
55 Joyce, *Kuwait 1945–1996*, p. 61.
56 Ibid., p. 62.
57 Safwan is a nondescript little oasis where Iraqi immigration and customs were located. In the late 1980s, I escorted a visiting Congressional Delegation to Basra and we paused at Safwan to complete formalities. As we waited in the little square surrounded by low, one-story buildings, one member of my Kuwaiti security escort read the slogans daubed in Arabic on the structures. He read one touting Iraq as the "Mother of Arabism," spat and muttered "Iraq—Whore of Arabism." Safwan would be the site of the capitulation of Saddam Hussein's generals at the end of Operation Desert Storm in 1991.
58 Winstone and Freeth, *Kuwait*, p. 213.
59 The anti-Soviet Pact grouped Iraq, Iran, Turkey, and Great Britain. Iraq withdrew in 1959 after the monarchy was overthrown and the alliance was renamed the Central Treaty Organization.
60 Records II, p. 540.
61 Records III, p. 406.
62 "Development Progress Report, February 1956 in Records II, p.

635. The output of distillation facilities was an estimated 2 million gallons per day by 1955. Freeth, *Kuwait Was My Home*, p. 45. Brackish water was added to the distilled water in small amounts "to provide minerals," according to Winstone and Freeth, *Kuwait*, p. 204. Local sources told the author in the late 1980s that brackish water was mixed in after Shaikh Abdallah complained that the distilled product had no taste.

63 It should be remembered that Washington supported the project, not on its merits or practicality, but because Secretary of State John Foster Dulles wanted to support Nuri Al-Said for his championing of the Baghdad Pact. To make certain that the Consulate in Kuwait was not dragging its feet, Ambassador Gallman was sent down from Baghdad, "ostensibly on leave." Brewer took Gallman to see the ruler with the acting political agent in tow: "Of course Abdallah Salem told him just what he'd told us. Washington usually is reluctant to deal in these realities." Brewer, correspondence.
64 Ibid.
65 Records VI, p. 128.
66 Shaikh Abdallah Salem was scheduled to visit Cairo following his state visit to Baghdad in May 1958 but cancelled the Egyptian visit for reasons that are not entirely clear (Chronology, *Middle East Journal*, Vol. 12, no. 3 (Summer 1958), p. 314). In August of the same year, the ruler made a state visit to Tehran, underlining Kuwait's relationship with that important regional power.
67 Records III, p. 266.
68 Winstone and Freeth, *Kuwait*, p. 214.
69 Saba George Shiber, *The Kuwait Urbanization – Documentation – Analysis – Critique* (Kuwait: n.p., 1964), p. 85.
70 Daniels, *Kuwait Journey*, p.58.
71 Records II, p. 592.
72 Shiber, *The Kuwait Urbanization...*, p. 85. Curiously, no figures are given for Egyptians who supplied a large proportion of teachers and Education Department bureaucrats, as we have seen.
73 Author's interviews, 1987–88.
74 Records III, p. 540.
75 Ibid., p. 691.

76 Ibid., p. 697.
77 Ibid., p. 706.
78 Joyce, *Kuwait 1945–1996*, p. 5.
79 Mary Ann Tétreault, "Civil Society in Kuwait: Protected Spaces

and Women's Rights," *The Middle East Journal*, Vol. 47, no. 2 (Spring 1993), p. 282.
80 In 1950, Kuwait had renegotiated its relationship with the oil companies to provide an equal division of profits.

Chapter 9: Independence

1 Daniels, *Kuwait Journey*, p. 92.
2 Rush, *Al-Sabah*, pp. 41–42.
3 Alani, *OperationVantage*, p. 53.
4 Ibid., p. 57.
5 The improvement in relations was not simply that Saudi Arabia and other area states had lost their appetite for expansion at their neighbors' expense. In 1949, for example, the Saudi King demanded a change in its frontier with the Shaikhdom of Abu Dhabi. On Saudi behalf, an armed group seized a village in the disputed area of the Buraimi oasis. Although Saudi Arabia agreed to international arbitration, the process broke down in September 1955. The following month, the British sanctioned the expulsion of Saudi forces from Buraimi. Smith, *Kuwait, 1950–1965*, p. 80. In the early 1970s, the officers' mess of the Trucial Oman Scouts in Sharjah displayed a small Saudi flag captured from the sedan of the Saudi general during the clearing operation.
6 Winstone and Freeth, *Kuwait*, p. 211; Smith, op cit., p. 115.
7 Alani, *Operation Vantage*, p. 55.
8 Daniels, *Kuwait Journey*, p. 60.
9 Joyce, *Kuwait 1945–1996*, p. 73.
10 Alani, *Operation Vantage*, p. 142.
11 Joyce, *Kuwait 1945–1996*, p. 124.
12 Parker T. Hart, *Saudi Arabia and the United States: Birth of a Security Partnership* (Bloomington: Indiana University Press, 1998), p. 78.
13 Protection of citizens in times of threat and instability is the ultimate responsibility of community leadership. In 1961, the American Embassy assumed this important function. As we have seen, however, the American Mission performed this duty during the turbulent decades of the 1920s and 30s in coordination with the British Political Agency. Dr. Mylrea was an active participant in Kuwaiti affairs at the time of the battle of Jahra (see Chapter 3) and later in the same decade, when the Ikhwan again threatened to attack Kuwait, Political Agent J. C. More assured Dr. Calverley that "during the present crisis American citizens are to be protected in exactly the same manner as British subjects." Records VII,

op. cit., p. 731. Organizationally, evacuees were to be split into two parties led by the Political Agent and Dr. Calverley. Records VII, p. 733.
14 Lienhardt, *Disorientations*, p. 44.
15 Kuwaitis consistently draw a distinction between Americans, Palestinians and others who came to assist them when their needs were many and their resources meager, and those who flocked to the country once the oil revenues began to flow. Many still speak with affection of the Mission personnel who shared their discomforts and dangers in more grim days.
16 Winstone and Freeth, *Kuwait*, p.195. Zahra Freeth, whose familiarity with developments in Kuwait encompassed decades, was unequivocal in attributing this success to the Mission: "The fact that today the Arab mother will voluntarily take her child to be vaccinated is one of the results of forty years of work and teaching on the part of the Mission hospitals." Freeth, *Kuwait Was My Home*, p. 80.
17 Joseph Wright Twinam, *The Gulf, Cooperation and the Council: An American Perspective* (Washington: Middle East Policy Council, 1992), pp. 76–77.
18 The account of this dramatic episode in the history of the American Mission is contained in Scudder, *The Arabian Mission's Story*, pp. 274–76.
19 The World Missions Board in the United States was clearly seeking a way to terminate the American Mission in Kuwait by this time and increasingly became a drag on its operations.
20 Lienhardt, *Disorientations*, p. 45. He also acknowledges that he found himself being drawn into Arab expatriate circles and away from Kuwaiti society with which the Arabs were out of touch.
21 Ibid. In 1972, I was in the U.S. Embassy in Beirut when I was assigned to establish the new American Embassy in Abu Dhabi. While I was excited at the prospect, local friends and contacts—Lebanese, Syrians and Palestinians—could not hide their horror and sympathy.
22 Villiers, *Sons of Sinbad*, p. 381.
23 Jacqueline S. Ismael, *Kuwait: Dependency and Class in a Rentier State* (Gainesville: University Press of Florida, 1993), p. 117.
24 A prominent Kuwaiti told the author that he had attended a year of secondary school in Fairfax County, Virginia, where he joined the football team, serving as one of the first soccer-style kickers. Indicative of the salutary effect of this experience is the fact that many of these Kuwaitis remain in contact with their "host families" in the United States.

25 Daniels, *Kuwait Journey*, p. 153.
26 Amb. Faisal al-Mutawa, typewritten summary of lengthy conversation with the author, September 12,1988
27 Ibid. The same source credited American Consul Talcott Seelye with resolving an early glitch in the project when he was able to obtain a waiver of the standard practice of fingerprinting applicants for U.S. visas. Meanwhile, the Kuwaiti authorities were seeking quality education for young women whose conservative families were unwilling to allow them to travel to America. The initial solution was matriculation at Beirut College for Women (later Beirut University College). Conversation with the author, December 6, 1988.
28 American Embassy telegram, dated October 3, 1988, reporting reception with the theme "Kuwaiti-American Educational Exchange."
29 Daniels, *Kuwait Journey*, p. 92.
30 "In Cairo, the Arab League, of which Kuwait had become the eleventh full member, described the Iraqi claim as a 'surprise'." Winstone and Freeth, *Kuwait*, p. 214. The Arab League admitted Kuwait as a full member on July 20 over Iraq's opposition. Al-Ebraheem, *Kuwait: A Political Study*, p. 131.
31 Joyce, *Kuwait 1945–1996*, pp. 102–3.
32 Alani, *Operation Vantage*, p. 55.
33 Ibid., p. 61. Qassem did not explain that his argument relied on the inversion of history. Kuwait's agreement with Great Britain was concluded in 1899. The country of Iraq was not created for twenty more years, following the defeat of the Ottoman Empire in World War I.
34 Joyce, *Kuwait 1945–1996*, p. 104.
35 Ibid,, p. 94.
36 Al-Ebraheem, *Kuwait*, p. 131.
37 Daniels, *Kuwait Journey*, p. 98.
38 Al-Ebraheem, *Kuwait: A Political Study*, p. 131.
39 Crystal, *Oil and Politics in the Gulf*, p. 59.
40 Records III, p. 242.
41 Joyce, *Kuwait 1945–1996*, pp. 59–60.
42 Alani, *Operation Vantage*, p. 46.
43 The following paragraphs draw heavily on the summary in Smith, *Kuwait 1950–1965*, pp. 119–20.
44 The British officials exhibited no awareness in the irony of their new anxiety to enlist the United States in intimate cooperation. For much of the preceding decade, at least some British officials

behaved on the assumption that the United States was seeking to usurp Britain's position in Kuwait. At several points from the time of the American Consulate's establishment, the British seem to have considered inconclusively bringing it into planning for Kuwait's defense. See, for example, Joyce, *Kuwait 1945–1996*, p. 72.

45 Ibid., p. 105.
46 Alani, *Operation Vantage*, p. 88
47 Ibid., p. 91.
48 Ibid., p. 89.
49 Joyce, *Kuwait 1945–1996*, p. 106. Given the time difference between Kuwait and Washington, it is likely that British troops were actually landing by the time the U.S. was informed.
50 It would seem that Washington wished to be absolutely certain, in lending its support to British operations, that it was acting in conformance with the wishes of the Kuwait government. The American Consulate in Kuwait reported that it had found no evidence that the British had pressured Amir Abdallah to accept the troops. Ibid.
51 Winstone and Freeth, *Kuwait*, p. 215.
52 Daniels, *Kuwait Journey*, p. 97. At least one source suggests that, following a visit to Kuwait by the head of the Saudi army, some Saudi troops crossed into Kuwaiti territory and the Saudi border with Iraq was closed. Winstone and Freeth, *Kuwait*, p. 215.
53 Quoted in Alani, *Operation Vantage*, p. 212.
54 Behind the scenes, a virulent propaganda struggle was being waged. Baghdad media, with a long tradition of unconcern for veracity, reported that masses of Kuwaitis demonstrated in support of inclusion in the Iraqi state. Joyce, *Kuwait 1945–1996*, p. 94. They would repeat these falsehoods in the age of television when Iraq occupied its smaller neighbor in 1990. More worrying were Cairo's call for the withdrawal of "foreign" (i.e., British) troops. Moscow, which played no constructive role in the crisis, echoed the demand that British forces be withdrawn, possibly in the hope that this would ingratiate them with radical Arab nationalist elements. Winstone and Freeth, *Kuwait*, p. 216.
55 Alani, *Operation Vantage*, p. 207.
56 Cited in ibid., p. 182.
57 On July 6, Iraq was reportedly continuing to build up its border forces and the commander of the British 24th Infantry Brigade believed that the possibility of an attack had increased. Winstone and Freeth, *Kuwait*, p. 215.
58 Joyce, *Kuwait 1945–1996*, p. 107–8.

59 Ibid., p. 108.
60 Ibid. Libya and, initially, Sudan were unwilling to contribute troops, while Lebanon and Yemen were reluctant. The UAR supported the replacement of British forces with Arab troops but didn't want to send its own army. Jordan agreed to participate but didn't want its troops to risk hostilities with the Iraqis. Small wonder that at the beginning of September no date for the arrival of the Arab League force had been established and a commander had not been named.
61 Al-Ebraheem, *Kuwait: A Political Study*, p. 132.
62 A less publicized factor in the unfolding of the crisis was the position of the Iranian government. Reportedly, Iranian craft ferrying supplies to Kuwait were attacked by Iraqi patrol boats. Winstone and Freeth, *Kuwait*, p. 215. More generally, Iran has always been concerned by the possibility of a stronger regional rival gaining control of Kuwaiti territory and strategic islands in the northern Gulf. According to Rush (Records VI, p. xxviii), "In the crisis of 1961,... Shah Muhammad Reza was fully prepared to deploy his forces in defence of Kuwait. Knowledge of this possibility is known to have weighed heavily in Qasim's decision to cancel his invasion plans."
63 Smith, *Kuwait 1950–1965*, p. 129.
64 David Holden, *Farewell to Arabia* (London: Faber & Faber, 1966), pp. 155–56.
65 Ambassador to Kuwait, 1972–76, and also accredited to Bahrain, the United Arab Emirates, Qatar, and Oman upon their independence.
66 Joyce, *Kuwait 1945–1996*, p. 132.
67 Ibid., p. 127.
68 Even before a resident consul was assigned to Kuwait, British documents show the close attention paid to visiting consular staff from Basra. In 1948, for example, the political Agent found time to worry about whether U.S. warships had rendered gun salutes to American vice consuls: "I heard ... that the United States Vice Consul Mr. Jova received a salute when he paid his call on the U.S.S. *Greenwich Bay*, but I have been unable to confirm this report. However, Mr. McKillop, United States Consul at Basra, definitely received a seven-gun salute after paying his call on the U.S.S. *Pocono*, and also received a similar salute from *Siboney*, although I personally did not hear it." Political Agent, September 11, 1948 in Records VII, p. 660–61. The Foreign Office actually instructed its embassy in Washington to raise the matter with the Department of State.

69 Dayton Mak, the first head of the American embassy, looked back at the early 1960s in a 1988 interview: "We got along very well with them (British diplomats), socially and in every way, and in a way I think they knew that they had a problem of getting out of their obligations gracefully. They knew that there was no choice but for us to take over (security responsibilities)... And that was a bitter pill, but they knew that it was one they had to swallow because the orders came from London that they had to cut down on their expenditures, which would certainly reduce their privileges in the area. So it was a period of transition for the British, definite transition, that was hard for them to take, and they did it gracefully." Dayton S. Mak, The Foreign Affairs Oral History Collection of the Association for Diplomatic Studies and Training, August 9, 1989. Available at <<http://www.adst.org/OH%20TOCs/Mak,%20Dayton%20S.toc.pdf>>

70 Author's conversations 1987–90. The shower and changing rooms built at this period were still present but used for storage since direct access to the beach was no longer possible.

71 Akins served on the consulate staff from 1958 to 1960 and was the U.S. ambassador to Saudi Arabia 1973–75 before leaving the Department of State to pursue a career in the energy sector. He died in 2010.

72 Author's conversation with James Akins, October 6, 1988. Wags in the U.S. Foreign Service joked that the FBO economized by using architects from the Bureau of Prisons when they were not designing penitentiaries.

73 The American Embassy moved in that year to a new compound, paid for primarily by Kuwait, in Mishref.

74 Joyce, *Kuwait 1945–1996*, pp. 110–11.

75 By the late 1950s, the majority of trucks and noncombat vehicles serving with the Kuwaiti military were of American manufacture, purchased commercially. Ibid., p. 25.

76 Ibid., p. 109.

77 Ibid., pp. 124–25.

78 Shafeeq N. Ghabra, *Palestinians in Kuwait: The Family and the Politics of Survival*, Westview Special Studies on the Middle East (Boulder, CO: Westview Press, 1987), p. 43. Ghabra's study provides useful insights into the experience of Palestinians in Kuwait. The first Palestinians, an education team, arrived in Kuwait in 1936 and was led from 1938 to 1942 by Muhammed Najem who earned the respect of Kuwaitis by his contributions to the emerging educational system.

79 Shafeeq Ghabra, "Democratization in a Middle Eastern State: Kuwait, 1993," *Middle East Policy*, Vol. III, no. 1 (1994), p. 103.
80 Shafeeq Ghabra, "Democratization...," p. 102.
81 Crystal, *Oil and Politics in the Gulf*, p. 86.
82 Dr. Khatib was such a well-established thorn in the side of the British and the Kuwaiti authorities in the 1950s that the British Agency attributed to him Kuwaiti hesitancy to send more students to the American University and other institutions in Beirut. With unconcealed satisfaction, the Political Agent wrote: "We have not heard of many Kuwaitis going to Beirut recently ... The well-known example of a Kuwaiti who has been there, Dr. Ahmad Khatib, does not suggest that that is a particularly good place for the further education of Kuwaitis. I believe that it is recognized that there is a communist influence in the American University and certainly there is a strong communist party in the Lebanon." Political Agent, July 11, 1955 in Records III, p. 710.
83 Winstone and Freeth, *Kuwait*, p. 212.
84 Rush, *Al-Sabah*, p. 39.
85 Ibid.
86 Ibid., p. 42.

10 Growing Pains and Engagement

1 Shaikh Sabah commanded the Kuwait police from 1938 to 1959, playing a leading part in developing the country's internal security forces. He was head of the Department of Public Health until October 1961 when he resigned to establish the Department of Foreign Affairs. In January 1962, he became Kuwait's first minister of foreign affairs and deputy prime minister. Named heir apparent in October, he replaced Amir Abdallah as prime minister in January 1963. Rush, *Al-Sabah*, p. 27.
2 Ibid., p. 29.
3 This paradigm was considered in effect until 2006 when Shaikh Jabir al-Ahmad, who had become the amir, died. Shaikh Sa'd Abdallah, of the Salem line, was named amir but was unable to serve because of incapacitation. Shaikh Sabah Ahmad, brother of the deceased amir, became the ruler. In the period following Sabah's accession, the Salem branch was effectively excluded from senior positions, narrowing the base of family cohesion.
4 Twinam, *The Gulf, Cooperation and the Council*, p. 181.
5 Rush, *Al-Sabah*, p. 29.
6 "With few exceptions, during this period, Kuwaiti associations

continued to be influenced directly and indirectly by Arab nationalists' grass roots movements. The Labor Unions' Association of Teachers and Students, the Literary Club, and the Independence Club, all called for Arab unity, total independence from foreign rule, the liberation of Palestine, and a socialist-based society." Shafeeq Ghabra, "The Democratic Movement in its Historical Context," in National Republican Institute for International Affairs, *Political Participation and Constitutional Democracy in Kuwait*, Edited transcript of Conference, Washington, 1991, p. 13.

7 *Middle East Journal*, Chronology, Vol. 18, no. 3 (summer 1964), p. 334. It was reported from Kuwait that the Foreign Minister summoned the Soviet ambassador to issue a formal protest, Kuwaiti Officials were said to have commented that diplomatic relations would be broken off unless there was "a satisfactory apology." Whether accurately reported or not, there is no record of a Soviet retraction of Khrushchev's highly offensive remarks.

8 In the judgment of Jill Crystal, *Oil and Politics in the Gulf*, the Assembly was able to remove the cabinet only because "the cabinet itself defied the tacit rules of Kuwaiti politics: merchants were to stay out of formal politics."

9 Rush, *Al-Sabah*, p. 29.

10 Crystal, *Oil and Politics in the Gulf*, p. 88.

11 Rush, *Al-Sabah*, p. 29.

12 The Kuwaiti authorities were concerned by Egyptian activities and intentions but constrained by the regional environment. The senior American diplomat at the time recalled that the Egyptians "were the element that was considered to be the most disruptive in Kuwait while we were there. It was the Kuwaitis who were keeping an eye on them." Dayton S. Mak, Oral History.

13 Rush (*Al-Sabah*, p. 29) observes that the reverses were so devastating that "most people were sure the elections were rigged," although he leaves no doubt that majority opinion had swung decisively against the most radical activists in the previous Assembly.

14 Dayton Mak's recollections of his service in Kuwait are recorded in The Foreign Affairs Oral History Collection of the Association for Diplomatic Studies and Training.

15 In addition to his accreditation to Saudi Arabia, Parker Hart was also minister to the Yemen and became increasingly preoccupied with affairs there following the uprising against the government of Imam Ahmad and the intervention of the United Arab Republic in support of the new "republican" regime.

16 Parker T. Hart, correspondence with the author, October 25, 1988.

17 It is important to recall that this extraordinary degree of hospitality was feasible when the number of diplomats in the country was very small. As the diplomatic corps grew, this informality had to be discontinued. Some readers familiar with stereotypes about the attitudes of Gulf Arabs toward women should know that this openness to Western women is not unique. In 1972, I was deputy principal officer in Abu Dhabi shortly after independence. When our three-man embassy made its first Eid call on the ruler and UAE President Shaikh Zayed bin Sultan al-Nahayyan, a colleague told the shaikh that our children would be thrilled to meet him. Without hesitation, Shaikh Zayed said, "Tonight" and specified the informal palace where he relaxed. "Bring your wives," he added. The evening, complete with bandoliered guards, falconers, coffee, and sweets, was one of the highlights of our tour. There were no more than twenty diplomats of all nationalities in country at that time.

18 At that period there were several Palestinians in the Foreign Office "as assistants to the foreign minister and with the deputy emir." They were also useful contacts.

19 The managing director of KOC in the late 1960s was James E. Lee, an American. Frazer, "Kuwait," p. 662.

20 Nancy Chippendale and Virginia Cheslick were young stenographers in the Embassy. Mak recalls that they were practically adopted by several Kuwaiti families ("the Marzouks and the Al-Mullahs and the Al-Ghonims"). "The wives and mothers of the Sheikhs and their children really considered them as their daughters. They would send their chauffeur-driven cars to pick up the girls to take them to their homes and they would be given dinners and lunches, the run of the whole household with their swimming pools and so forth. These girls really introduced the Consulate, and later the Embassy, to many of these Kuwaiti families, all of whom had the utmost respect for these very highly intelligent and respectable young women." Mak, Oral History.

21 Dayton Mak was the first occupant of the new facilities and has left a vivid picture of the compound upon his arrival: "There was hardly a blade of grass—in fact there was no grass. There were some palm trees that were perhaps a foot high and some tamarisks ... a little taller that had been ... planted throughout the compound, but other than that there was no greenery whatsoever. There were three structures on the ... property; one was the Embassy residence which was about twenty-five yards from the water. A square building, large enough, it had five bedrooms,

... three baths, a nice reception room, a dining room, a small library or study, a kitchen and appurtenances. In addition there was the Consulate building, later the Embassy Chancery, about twenty-five yards back from the Residence .... To the left of that as you faced the water there was a large apartment house structure which was the staff apartments." Ibid.

22 American embassies in the Gulf region face a dilemma with regard to Independence Day. Because of the withering heat in July, it is not always practical to hold outdoor receptions on July 4. One solution some adopted was to shift the celebration to George Washington's Birthday, which falls in February.

23 The Consulate compound was built by Abdul Ali Reza, a prominent Kuwaiti businessman of Saudi origin. While certainly the first Fourth of July celebration in the new premises was particularly noteworthy for its guest list, it was not the first in the country. We know from surviving photographs taken in the early 1950s that modest Independence Day events were hosted at the club in Ahmadi and perhaps elsewhere. Members of the American Mission are shown in attendance.

24 The former Consulate, which the new compound replaced, had no capability for entertaining or large gatherings. Chargé Mak was the last American to serve there for a very brief time and described it as "... an Arab-style building of stucco type over some sort of brick ... with a roof that was apparently either of reed or palm frond ... that let in the water when you had the periodic deluges of Kuwait." Mak, Oral History.

25 British schools of the era, whether in Beirut, Abu Dhabi, or Kuwait, extended only to the third grade, after which children were sent to boarding schools in the United Kingdom. It seemed to work reasonably well for most British families but was anathema to American families.

26 Mak, Oral History.

27 The children of the American Mission personnel had attended schools in the hill stations of India where there was a large and well-established missionary community and associated infrastructure: "Our children went to school in Kodekanu, South India, up in the hills; they went through high school there. When they had to go by ship it took two weeks ... to get to Bombay and two weeks to get home. ... Flying it was much better." D. Scudder, Notes, March 24, 1987.

28 Consul Harry Symmes sent his young daughter to the Shuwaikh British school with satisfactory results; but it could not accommodate older students. Symmes, correspondence.

29 American Embassy Kuwait, "A Short History of Kuwaiti-American Relations," p. 4.
30 D. Scudder, Notes, March 24, 1987. The American Community School in Abu Dhabi (ACSAD) had similar humble beginnings in 1972. Phillips Petroleum made available two small buildings (three classrooms and an office/library on their compound. A teaching couple completing their contract in Dhahran was engaged and supplemented by qualified spouses. The author's wife served on the first school board, taught sixth, seventh and eighth grade science, and was the school nurse.
31 Twinam, *The Gulf, Cooperation and the Council*, p. 77.
32 Scudder, *The Arabian Mission's Story*, p. 415.
33 Ibid., p. 227 footnote 55. Dr. Lewis Scudder died on April 3, 1975; more than 1300 persons attended his funeral. Abd al Aziz Thunayan al-Mishari, "From the Legacy: The American Hospital," *The Weekly Al-Qabas*, January 28, 1985.
34 Joseph Wright Twinam, "America and the Gulf Arabs," *American-Arab Affairs*, No. 25 (Summer 1988), p. 132. Joe Twinam was one of a small group of Foreign Service officers with extensive experience in the Gulf region. An alumnus of the University of Virginia, he served not only in Kuwait but also as ambassador to Bahrain and deputy assistant secretary of state responsible for Gulf affairs before retiring. In retirement he continued his involvement in the area as a professor at The Citadel in Charleston, South Carolina.
35 In December 1960, for example, a US-Kuwaiti agreement on nonimmigrant visas was concluded, as the two countries tackled bilateral issues that had been superfluous as long as Britain was responsible for Kuwait's foreign relations.
36 Mak, Oral History. This was a fairly common progression for "Gulf hands," as the pioneering Foreign Service officers were styled. When the author was involved with opening the Embassy in Abu Dhabi in 1972, communication was by Telex machine in the Chancery until Department of State communications were eventually installed.
37 *Middle East Journal*, Chronology, Vol. 17, nos. 1 & 2 (Winter–Spring), p. 121.
38 In April, the Assembly was still dealing with a motion to terminate the 1961 agreement with Britain and initiate talks with the UAR, Syria and Iraq for a federal Arab state. *Middle East Journal*, Chronology, Vol. 17, no. 3 (Summer 1963), p. 302.
39 Hart, *Saudi Arabia and the United States*, pp. 80–81. During the Iraqi visit, a substantial Kuwaiti loan to Iraq was announced.

40 Joyce, *Kuwait 1945–1996*, p. 145. A little more than one year later, in February 1966, the British informed the Amir that ground forces would not be available under any circumstances.
41 The British previewed this decision with its NATO allies at the North Atlantic Council in Brussels in late 1967. I had been assigned to the U.S. Mission to NATO when the United Arab Republic severed diplomatic relations with Washington in June 1967. The British permanent representative's announcement was received with surprise. When he was asked what would remain once the withdrawal was complete, he responded with characteristic British humor. "Oh, I suppose two men, a boy, and a dog."
42 Smith, *Kuwait 1950–1965*, p. 134.
43 In May 1958, for instance, two Soviet warships called at Iraq's new port at Umm Qasr. This incursion marked the first Russian naval presence in Gulf waters for over sixty years. The flotilla then visited Bandar Abbas, "recalling the *Glysk* voyage...." William D. Brewer, "Yesterday and Tomorrow in the Persian Gulf," *Middle East Journal*, Vol. 23, no. 2 (Spring 1967). p. 153.
44 Rush, *Al-Sabah*, p. 29.
45 On June 5, 1967, the government declared the country to be at war with Israel, placed all oil companies in Kuwait under the control of the military governor, and banned all demonstrations. *Middle East Journal*, Chronology, Vol. 21, no. 4 (Autumn 1967), p. 516.
46 Charles Cecil, correspondence with the author, February 1989. Kuwait was very good to Chuck Cecil. It was there that he met and married his wife, Jean, a newly arrived teacher at the American School. He is an accomplished photographer who has been published in *Saudi ARAMCO Magazine* and spent much of his free time in Kuwait honing his skills at sites like a large open space near the new Sheraton Hotel, where traditional singing and dancing took place on Fridays.
47 There was no shore road at the time and the Hilton Hotel had not been completed.
48 In addition to Ambassador Cottam, the American staff included John Gatch, deputy chief of mission, political officer, econ-commercial officer, vice consul, administrative officer, public affairs officer, a JO (Cecil), and four secretaries. A general services officer was added shortly thereafter, and April Glaspie was transferred from Amman as a result of the 1967 War.
49 "During the early days of that week there was a sense of controlled panic among the expatriate community as many left and there was a scramble for seats on airlines." Cecil, correspondence. As other

posts in the Arab world drew down staff, the Embassy staff read the reporting cables with interest, getting a much-needed laugh from Beirut's recording that it was paring down to "a skeleton staff of 32."

50 While the U.S. government unquestionably supported Israel's right to defend itself, much of the damage to the American position and anger among Arab publics can be attributed to the "Big Lie" concocted by the Nasser regime. I was posted in the Cairo Embassy during the war and watched Egyptian television commentators announce aerial victories for several days after the Egyptian Air Force had been devastated, largely on the ground. When the truth could no longer be concealed, UAR authorities explained their defeat by claiming that they faced U.S. and British, as well as Israeli, air forces. Returning to his residence one day, the building *sofragi* (doorman) asked why the United States was attacking Egypt? When the author replied that it wasn't, he added, "But they shot down a U.S. plane today!" Unfortunately, he said, it fell into the Suez Canal and couldn't be recovered.

51 Rush, *Al-Sabah*, p. 30.

52 *Middle East Journal*, Chronology, Vol. 22, no. 1 (Winter 1968), p. 66.

53 The amir's state visit to the United States December 10–16, 1968, included visits to Annapolis, Maryland, Cape Kennedy and Palm Beach, Florida, and New York City, in addition to Washington. He met with President Lyndon Johnson on December 11. One remarkable aspect of the general Arab reaction to the events of 1967 was the complete absence of pique with France. France had, of course, joined Britain in the Suez invasion in 1956 and the Israeli Air Force that humiliated the UAR and other Arab air forces in 1967 was equipped with warplanes of French origin. Israel did not begin to receive modern U.S. warplanes until *after* the conflict. Yet, France somehow managed to escape the Arab condemnation that was directed toward Washington, London, and even Bonn, a true act of diplomatic legerdemain.

54 The commander of the Middle East Force at Bahrain immediately after the 1967 War was Marmaduke G. Bayne (d. 2005), later vice admiral and commandant of the National War College in Washington. The U. S. naval presence in Bahrain was extremely discreet. On his first visit to Manama in 1972, the author paid a courtesy call on Admiral Bayne. The taxi driver took him to a modest house and indicated that the admiral was there. Through the screened front door it was obvious that this was a residence rather than a military installation. When the admiral appeared,

he was clutching a towel around his waist, having just come in from tennis. He was gracious, nonetheless; and it turned out that he was raised in Norfolk, Virginia, just across the Elizabeth river from my hometown.

55 François M. Dickman, The Foreign Affairs Oral History Collection of the Association for Diplomatic Studies and Training Available,February 9, 2001, at http://www.adst.org/OH%20TOCs/Dickman,%20Francois%20M.toc.pdf. Dickman occupied a senior position in the Department of State at this time.
56 Thomas A. Bryson, *Tars, Turks, and Tankers: The Role of the United States Navy in the Middle East* (Metuchen, NJ: The Scarecrow Press, 1980), p. 203.
57 Adm. William J. Crowe, Jr., *The Line of Fire: From Washington to the Gulf, the Politics and Battles of the New Military* (New York: Simon & Schuster, 1993), pp.169–70. An account of the entire episode is contained at pp. 162–71.
58 Ibid., p. 171. In 1979, it was named Administrative Support Unit (ASU) Bahrain, carefully avoiding the use of the toxic word "base." Since that date, its area and functions have been expanded substantially with the full agreement of the Bahraini and other emirates.
59 Joseph Wright Twinam, "America and the Gulf Arabs," *American-Arab Affairs*, No. 25 (Summer 1988), p. 144.
60 Kuwait responded to Iraq's bellicosity in March 1973 by requesting a U.S. military survey team.
61 According to the *Washington Post* of May 23, 1972, Kuwait was expected to order a package valued at about $500 million, including 160 tanks, 32 Crusader fighters, and anti–aircraft missiles. *Middle East Journal*, Chronology, Vol. 27, no. 4 (Autumn 1973), p. 492.
62 Twinam, *The Gulf, Cooperation and the Council*, p. 85.
63 In October 1963 the prime minister addressed the National Assembly on behalf of the amir. The key foreign policy statement declared that his government would follow a policy of non-alignment, support all efforts to prevent war, and oppose racial discrimination. He added that the government would work to strengthen bonds among Arab states and the Arab League and support "Palestinian integrity." *Middle East Journal*, Chronology, Vol. 18, no. 1 (winter 1964), p. 91.
64 Rush, *Al-Sabah*, p. 30.
65 A British UN resolution recognizing Kuwait's independence was vetoed by the Soviet Union in July 1961 (*Middle East Journal*, Chronology, Vol. 15, no. 4 [Autumn 1961]), p. 434. Again, in Novem-

ber, the USSR vetoed a UAR-sponsored resolution proposed to admit Kuwait to the United Nations. The UN General Assembly unanimously voted to admit Kuwait in May 1963. *Middle East Journal*, Chronology, Vol. 16, no. 1 (Winter 1962), p. 71. In March 1963 a joint communiqué, issued in both Moscow and Kuwait, announced the exchange of ambassadors. *Middle East Journal*, Chronology, Vol. 17, nos. 1 & 2 (Winter–Spring 1963), p. 121. Relations with the People's Republic of China followed in December. *Middle East Journal*, Chronology, Vol. 18, no. 1 (Winter 1964), p. 91.

66 Mak, Oral History.
67 When I was nominated to be ambassador to Kuwait in 1988, a senior State Department official suggested that one of my key assets was the fact that I was as outspoken and disconcerting as the Kuwaitis. That may well have been true because I never found it impossible to deal with Kuwaitis even when there was disagreement on a particular issue. When a prominent Kuwaiti repeated, on the eve of the Iraqi invasion of 1990, the familiar mantra of nonalignment, the author replied: "Oh, I understand that. You sell your oil, produced with Western equipment and expertise, in the West. When you want to invest your oil revenues safely, you invest in the West. You purchase your cars and other goods from the West. And, when you want to educate your children, you send them to Western institutions. I can see that you're 'nonaligned' and that's fine with me."
68 William A. Stoltzfus, Jr., Oral History. I was chargé d'affaires at the American Embassy in Abu Dhabi when the 1973 Arab-Israeli war occurred. The UAE government was genuinely upset, especially by the massive U.S. military resupply operation for Israel. A senior Foreign Ministry official summoned the chief of mission several times at the height of the crisis. He would begin by observing that the chargé surely knew why he had been called in. The author replied that he did and that the official knew how he would respond. "Good," the official said, "let's have tea." After a suitable period, the author took his leave, and the local media dutifully reported that the American chargé had been suitably upbraided.
69 These subtleties are not always understood or appreciated in Washington, unfortunately. Reflecting on his experience in Kuwait in this period, Economic Officer Richard Bogosian explained: "If you're living there and working with them, there are two things. First of all, you're not trying to trick each other. On the other hand, you're living in a context where the more positive parts

of the relationship are out there as well. But on the other hand, they would say to me things like, 'Don't you want us to be frank' and the short answer was no, we'd rather you didn't, actually." Richard W. Bogosian, The Foreign Affairs Oral History Collection of the Association for Diplomatic Studies and Training, April 1, 1998, at http://www.adst.org/OH%20TOCs/Bogosian,%20Richard%20W.toc.pdf

70   "Our relations with Kuwait were good. Kuwait did not break relations with us as did a number of other Arab states after the June 1967 war. While Kuwait never wanted to appear to be in our pocket, as a very small state it has had to rely on others for its security —first the British and then us." Stoltzfus, Oral History.

71   It was announced in the summer of 1968, scarcely a year after the June War, that the amir would make a six-day state visit to the United States the following December. *Middle East Journal*, Chronology, Vol. 22, no. 4 (Autumn 1968), p. 485.

72   Howard Rex Cottam presented his credentials as the first resident ambassador to the State of Kuwait on October 24, 1963. Vice President Spiro Agnew, Secretary of State William P. Rogers, Chairman of the Senate Foreign Relations Committee William Fulbright, Deputy Assistant Secretary of Defense James Noyes, and Treasury Secretary William Simon were among the senior officials who visited at the time.

73   *Middle East Journal*, Chronology, Vol. 28, no. 3 (Summer 1974), p. 293. Similar training and extended interactions would be required for maintenance, munitions, logistics and other functions to support the program.

74   Rush, *Al-Sabah*, p. 30.

75   Ibid.

76   Twinam, *The Gulf, Cooperation and the Council*, p. 85, and "America and the Gulf Arabs," p. 135.

77   Ibid., p. 136.

78   Rush, *Al-Sabah*, p. 30.

79   David Rockefeller visited Kuwait in the late 1980s with several colleagues. This was clearly not his first such visit. I first encountered Mr. Rockefeller in Abu Dhabi in 1973 and accompanied him and his party to Dubai, where Chase Bank was a partner in the Commercial Bank of Dubai. It was striking that when Rockefeller called on Shaikh Jabir al-Ahmad, who was by then the amir, on the later visit, they greeted one another as old friends.

80   Field, *The Merchants*, p. 134.

81 Author's personal observations. I was invited by the Ford agent, Arabian Motors, to take part in the festive inauguration of Ford's return at one of Kuwait's most luxurious hotels.
82 Twinam, *The Gulf, Cooperation and the Council*, pp. 85–86.
83 Ibid. Twinam was no less critical in his analysis of the positions of Western officials and commentators on the evolution of the Gulf states. "Western critics of the current state of affairs should keep in mind the tribal and Islamic traditions of Gulf Council societies. The concepts of consultation and consensus are deeply imbedded, and it can be argued that they are a more stately approach than the rough and tumble of open executive-legislative struggle with the up-or-down voting on issues inherent in Western systems of representative government. Peninsula defenders of the present order often stress the concept of 'tribal democracy,' manifested in the *majlis* system. By and large the governed in Gulf Council states do have access to the governors and can express their grievances and opinions with a freedom not found in many parts of the world."

11 A Bad Neighborhood

1 *Middle East Journal,* Chronology, Vol. 16, no. 2 (Spring 1962), p. 199.
2 Ibid. As the new year began, Iraq seized three Jordanians from a medical unit serving with the Arab League peacekeeping force. They had allegedly strayed across the unmarked border.
3 *Middle East Journal,* Chronology, Vol. 16, no. 3 (Summer 1962), p. 356.
4 Mak, Oral History.
5 The turbulent history of Iraq during the remainder of the 1960s is beyond the scope of this study. Suffice it here to note that by July 1968, the Baath was in control under General Ahmad Hassan Al-Bakr. Saddam Hussein emerged as the regime's strongman and, in 1979, institutionalized his primacy by pushing Al-Bakr aside.
6 *Middle East Journal, Chronology,* Vol. 17, no. 4 (Autumn 1963), p. 430.
7 Fran Dickman, who had extensive experience in Gulf affairs, later observed that "Under Abd al Latif al Hamid, the Kuwait Fund for Arab Economic Development had become second only to the World Bank in the number of low interest loans made to developing countries. Initially, the loans had been extended to poor Arab countries, but by 1979, that restriction had been removed.

The Kuwait government supported this institution for very good political reasons since they generated interest and support in the Third World for Kuwait's continued existence, particularly when Kuwait was faced with periodic threats from Iraq." Dickman, Oral History.

8   *Middle East Journal,* Chronology, Vol. 18, no. 1 (Winter 1964), p. 91.
9   Ibid.
10 Ibid.
11 Ibid., no. 2 (Spring 1964), p. 224. The arrangement had an announced duration of ninety-nine years.
12 Ibid., no. 3 (Summer 1964), p. 333.
13 However attractive the proposal to pipe water from the Shatt al-Arab may have been in theory, Kuwait's need for fresh water was less urgent than it had been in the past. In addition to the increasing capacity of Kuwait's massive distillation units, potable water had been discovered at Rawdatain fifty miles north of Kuwait City. Estimates placed the capacity of the underground springs there at up to 7 million gallons per day. A pipeline to carry 5 million gallons daily was placed in operation in late 1962. Ibid,, Vol. 17, nos. 1 & 2 (Winter–Spring 1963), p. 120.
14 Ibid., no. 3 (Summer 1963), p. 302.
15 During the visit instruments of ratification were exchanged for the economic cooperation agreement that had been negotiated between the two states. Kuwait had already approved loans to Iraq (ibid., Vol. 20, no. 4 [Autumn 1966], p. 503).
16 Ibid.,Vol. 24, no. 3 (Summer 1970), p. 364. Doubtlessly, Qadduri's primary purpose was to collect the payoff for Baghdad's reasonableness.
17 Ibid.,Vol. 25 no. 1 (Winter 1971) p. 72
18 Ibid., 27, no. 3 (Summer 1973), p. 363. The Iraqi foreign minister told *al-Sayyad* (Beirut) that Iraq would only demarcate the boundary with Kuwait if the tiny islands of Bubiyan and Warba were transferred to Iraq. The islands are located in the Khor Abdallah, which provides access to the Iraqi port at Umm Qasr.
19 Stoltzfus, Oral History Stoltzfus had a uniquely broad experience in Kuwait. Prior to becoming ambassador in 1972–76, he served as Vice Consul from 1954 to 1956 and was sent from Washington as chargé d'affaires ad interim (1963) between the Hart and Cottam ambassadorships.
20 Walter M. McClelland, The Foreign Affairs Oral History Collection of the Association for Diplomatic Studies and Training, November 20, 1995, at http://www.adst.org/OH%20TOCs/McClelland,%20Walter%20M.toc.pdf

21 Dickman, Oral History.
22 In the end, the Kuwaitis chose to purchase thirty-eight more sophisticated Mirages from France.
23 Much more controversial in the U.S. Congress than the aircraft themselves were Sidewinder air-to-air missiles to make them effective. With substantial effort, the U.S. administration succeeded in winning approval for a limited number of missiles.
24 Stoltzfus, Oral History. The 1973 war did abort plans for a visit to Kuwait by Under Secretary Rush, and placed consideration of the sale of F-4 Phantom aircraft to Saudi Arabia or Kuwait on indefinite hold. Dickman, Oral History.
25 Jacqueline S. Ismael, *Kuwait: Social Change in Historical Perspective* (Syracuse, N.Y.: Syracuse University Press, 1982), p. 91. I was in Abu Dhabi at the time, and early in 1974 a friend there asked me why the United States was depriving Abu Dhabi of gasoline. The UAE at the time did not have refinery capability. I explained that because the Gulf states had cut off supplies of crude for refining and bunkering for the tankers, there was no way to provide gas to them.
26 *Middle East Journal*, Chronology, Vol. 29, no. 2 (Spring 1975), p. 191.
27 Abdul Mu'ti, a Palestinian, was hired by the then-consulate in 1954 and chauffeured ambassadors until his retirement in the 1980s. Ambassador Stoltzfus recalled that he first arrived unwashed and in rags but later was never less than impeccably turned out in his uniform. Stoltzfus, Oral History.
28 Gulzaman was hired by Consul Harry Symmes (1953–55) and was suggested by L. T. Jordan, the manager of the Kuwait Oil Company (KOC), where he was employed. Gulzaman was a six-foot-tall Pathan who cut an impressive figure in white shirt, baggy trousers and *pagri*, or turban. Stoltzfus characterized Gulzaman as "the epitome of a British Raj's butler, discreet, imperious, skillful, reliable." Ibid.
29 George Quincey Lumsden, The Foreign Affairs Oral History Collection of the Association for Diplomatic Studies and Training, January 11, 2000, at<<<<http://memory.loc.gov/cgi-bin/query/D?mfdip:4:./temp /~ammem_FLbG::>> ; and my correspondence with Mrs. Howard Cottam, 1993.
30 William D. Wolle, The Foreign Affairs Oral History Collection of the Association for Diplomatic Studies and Training, March 6, 1991, at http://www.adst.org/OH%20TOCs/Wolle,%20William%20D.toc.pdf .

31 A somewhat more positive assessment of Ambassador Walsh's tenure is provided by Ardith Miller, who served as the ambassador's secretary from October 1969 to November 1971. The Embassy swimming pool built in 1967 was still a novelty in Kuwait and Ambassador Walsh contributed to community morale by opening it to all American residents one or two days a week. One day was set aside for high school students from the American school. Ardith H. Miller, Correspondence with the author, November, 1988. Other secretaries in the Embassy at this time included Catherine Postupack, June Kimura, and Florence Hall.
32 Lumsden, Oral History.
33 Wolle, Oral History. Wolle reports several examples of idiosyncratic behavior, including a tendency to keep others waiting, for no good reason.
34 Embassy Kuwait underwent its first departmental inspection about 1970. Since it is always assumed that inspectors are under pressure to reduce post allowances, there was concern about the retention of Kuwait's 15 percent differential. The inspection team sent to Kuwait was composed of two officers from the European Bureau who were so laid low by the extreme heat that they recommended that the differential be raised because of the "hellish" climate. There is no record of their findings regarding post morale.
35 Chookiat Panaspornprasit, *US-Kuwaiti Relations 1961–1992* (New York: Routledge, 2005), p. 53.
36 McClelland, Oral History.
37 Stoltzfus, Oral History. See also Lumsden, Oral History.
38 Stoltzfus, Oral History. Among the alterations at this time was the installation of floor-to-ceiling windows and sliding doors facing the Gulf. The original dining room, for example, was a medium-size room but had small windows near the top of the wall. The effect of the changes was to open up the areas used for entertaining. Two bedrooms with a bath in between were included in the guest wing. On the second floor, in the family quarters, there were three large bedrooms, a small bedroom, three baths, and a small lounge area.
39 To house the growing staff, the embassy leased in early 1967 a four-unit building built by Mohammed Qabazard across the street from the compound and slightly to the west of the Hilton site. The four units were allotted as a Marine House and quarters for the gunnery sergeant in charge and one of the junior officers. Cecil correspondence. The Marines were relocated to the compound in the mid-1980s when the bombed administrative building was rehabilitated.

40 Lovelyn Edwards, transcription of cassettes recorded for the author in September 1988. The area created was partially underground and was converted into a redoubt during the Iraqi occupation of 1990–91.
41 Stoltzfus, Oral History. Ornamental iron grills were installed over the windows in the permanent structures on the compound, and it was probably at this time that a steel door was added at the top of the stairs to the family quarters on the second floor of the ambassador's residence. It was bolted nightly to create a safe haven.
42 Historically, the U.S. Consulate-General in Dhahran, Saudi Arabia, provided consular services to Americans in Bahrain, the Trucial States, and Oman through periodic visits by a consular "circuit rider." In the case of a death of an American citizen there, a consul and mortician from Dhahran (ARAMCO) traveled down to the appropriate city to complete formalities necessary to repatriate the body of the deceased. Under a long-standing agreement between the United States and Great Britain, the United States assumed responsibility for British nationals in Eastern Saudi Arabia in the event of emergency or evacuation and the British provided reciprocal services to American citizens in the remainder of the lower Gulf.
43 It was assumed that Oman would be an independent state, but the British encouraged the formation of a single state comprised of Bahrain, Qatar, and the seven Northern shaikhdoms (Abu Dhabi, Dubai, Sharjah, Ajman, Umm al-Qawain, Ras al-Khaimah, and Fujairah). In the end, Bahrain and Qatar withdrew. After exploring the possibility of independence, Ras al-Khaimah joined the other six to form the United Arab Emirates (UAE).
44 The embassy in Abu Dhabi, for example, was initially composed of the chargé, commercial officer, and an officer to handle administration and communications. They were supported by a driver, a consular assistant, and a secretary. Both the chargé and the commercial officer were accredited as consuls.
45 While the U.S. government intended to eventually establish an embassy in Doha, the Qatari government very quickly established its embassy in Washington, forcing the State Department to set up a one-man embassy in Qatar. In the summer of 1973, when the incumbent left the post on leave, I was sent up from Abu Dhabi to take charge. The staff consisted of an Indian clerk and an assistant of Palestinian origin. It was nonetheless a very enjoyable experience. In Doha at that time it was possible to meet all the important personages in a short time and the tiny American community

could be accommodated for a July 4th barbecue in a garage. My two sons were excited to raise and lower the American flag each day.
46   The choice of Kuwait to oversee the new embassies probably reflected a judgment that it would be more acceptable than Saudi Arabia in states like the UAE, which had a history of troubled relations with the Saudis over Buraimi Oasis and other Saudi territorial claims.
47   Richard W. Bogosian, Oral History. One of the author's vivid memories of the period was the arrival in Abu Dhabi of a wooden crate from Kuwait. Morale skyrocketed as we imagined the typewriter ribbons, paper and other desperately needed items inside. When the top was finally prised off, the contents included a crowbar, several flashlights and sufficient Dixie cups to supply the post for a decade. After an interminable period of being directed to reconsolidate the post supply needs—for three months, then for six months, or for one year—we could not decide whether to laugh or cry. Likewise, the consular section had none of the red ribbon required for official documents including those attached to coffins of deceased American citizens. Embassy wives scoured the markets of Abu Dhabi and Dubai but could find only bright orange ribbon of the size needed.
48   The U.S. government leased the upper floor of a three-story, octagonal building on the coast. The space was available and relatively inexpensive because the previous tenants had moved out hastily, believing the structure to be unsafe. The staff was convinced that Ambassador Stoltzfus never entered the Embassy premises when in town because he did not consider them appropriate for an embassy.
49   The commercial officer in Kuwait assumed a "regional" title but was a supernumerary, because each post had its own independent commercial officer who neither needed nor recognized his "supervisory" function. The assignment of a U.S. Information Service (USIS) FSN and vehicle to Abu Dhabi was predicated on the assumption that, in the absence of a USIS Officer at post, I would add the information and culture portfolio to his other duties. When a disagreement arose over accountability for the vehicle and other USIS assets, USIS Kuwait initially took the position that its FSN was in charge. Embassy Abu Dhabi successfully contested this unique interpretation.
50   Rush, *Al-Sabah*, p. 30.
51   In my view, many Western commentators appear eager to criticize

Kuwait's parliamentary history, which has endured for more than five decades. Less apparent than the hiccups and imperfections of that history, is the fact that to sustain it the Kuwaiti authorities had to cope not only with those imperfections but with the chiding and disapproval of similarly situated neighbors who either fear the influence of Kuwait's example on their own populations or lose no opportunity to question why the Kuwaiti amir puts up with the institution. The reason, of course, is that the Kuwaitis chose the parliamentary route for their own reasons. It is a logical outgrowth of a strong tradition of consultation and compromise manifested in the historic *diwanniya* system.

52 Twinam, "America and the Gulf Arabs," *American-Arab Affairs*, No. 26 (Fall 1988), p. 110.

53 The involvement of other governments, including Iraq and Iran, was frequently a complication in proceedings in the State Security Courts. Their operation does not meet the highest juridical standards, particularly in terms of transparency. The Kuwaitis would argue, however, that the security courts allowed the government to prosecute individuals that posed a threat to public order and security without exacerbating relations with "friendly" states. What is observable is that some of the accused were regularly acquitted. In the fall of 1969, for instance, twenty-one individuals were tried on charges of seeking the overthrow of the government in connection with a bomb incident the previous year. Four were acquitted and seventeen were sentenced to one to seven years in prison. See *Middle East Journal*, Chronology, Vol. 24, nos. 1 and 2 (Winter and Spring 1970), p. 58 and p. 192.

54 McClelland, Oral History

55 According to Quincey Lumsden, who followed economic affairs at the U.S. Embassy from 1969 to 1972, "In the bureaucracy, [workers] were Palestinians and in the grunt jobs in the field, they were mostly Asian subcontinentals from Pakistan, India, and places like that." Lumsden, loc Oral History. There was at least one exception. In September 1975, Palestinians and Kuwaiti sympathizers staged a one-day work stoppage to protest the Egyptian-Israeli agreement on the Sinai. The government treated it as "unwarranted absenteeism." *Middle East Journal*, Chronology, Vol. 30, no.1 (Winter 1976), p. 70.

56 In 1971, for example, the Interior Ministry announced publicly that "communists" would not be permitted to operate in Kuwait. *Ibid.*, Vol. 26, no. 1 (Winter 1972), p. 46.

57 In 1973, my nine-year-old son observed an unknown man pho-

tographing homes of American diplomats in Abu Dhabi. He carefully wrote down the license plate number of the car the photographer was driving. The car turned out to be registered to the Iraqi "Trade Representative," and he was expelled from the country. At about the same time, when an Iraqi diplomatic pouch was dropped and broke open in Manama airport, Kalashnikov assault rifles spilled across the floor. Four years later, in October 1977, UAE Minister of State for Foreign Affairs Sayf bin Ghobash was killed by a gunman as he escorted Syrian Foreign Minister Khaddam to the airport VIP room for departure. Sayf was a very decent, capable man and a close friend of ‚mine. He was probably the victim of an attempt on Khaddam at a time of rivalry between competing Baathist regimes in Baghdad and Damascus.

58 Lumsden, Oral History.
59 *Middle East Journal*, Chronology, Vol. 29, no. 2 (Spring 1975), pp. 190–91.
60 *Middle East Economic Digest,* cited in *Middle East Journal, Chronology,* Vol. 31, no. 1 (Winter1977), p. 55.
61 *Ibid.*, no. 2 (Spring 1977), p. 196.
62 *Christian Science Monitor*, quoted in *ibid.*
63 *Ibid.* (Autumn 1977), p. 476.
64 *Ibid.*
65 Rush, *Al-Sabah*, p. 30. Kuwait's massive oil revenues and generous foreign assistance programs assured the attention of important Arab states such as Egypt. In April 1973 Kuwait pointedly let it be known that so long as the current confrontation with Iraq continued it would have to reconsider its policy of extending financial assistance to the "frontline" states facing Israel. *Middle East Economic Digest,* cited in *Middle East Journal, Chronology*, Vol. 27, no. 3 (Summer 1973), p. 363.
66 *Middle East Journal*, Chronology, Vol. 26 no. 2 (Spring 72) p. 298.
67 Rush, *Al-Sabah*, p. 30. Articles of the Constitution dealing with the press were also suspended. *Middle East Journal,* Chronology, Vol. 31, no. 1 (Winter 1977), p. 54.
68 Crystal, "The Merchant Families ...," p. 92.
69 In the late 1980s, my wife and I had the pleasure of visiting Dorothy Scudder in the home she had occupied since the departure of Dr. Stanley Mylrea (in the early 1940s).
70 Kuwait took control of AMINOIL in October 1977, reportedly after negotiations reached a stalemate. It is doubtful that Kuwait intended them to succeed. *Middle East Institute,* Chronology, Vol. 32, no. 1 (Winter 1978), p. 52.

598   Notes

71 Dickman, Oral History.
72 Several years earlier, in December 1969, Kuwait and Saudi Arabia agreed to divide the anomalous Neutral Zone between them. The Zone was partitioned leaving an undivided interest in the oil beneath it. Lumsden, Oral History By this action the two states promoted harmonious cooperation while eliminating vexing issues, such as whose laws were applicable in case of crimes or incidents. McClelland, Oral History
73 Lumsden, Oral History. Interestingly, the economic officers in the producing Arab states sensed long before the international companies that serious changes were in the offing: "We started to write despatches, I from Kuwait, François Dickman from Saudi Arabia, John Washburn from Tehran, saying, 'Look, Washington, something is happening here.... This is headed in a direction that could cause a big problem.'"
74 When the Iraqis invaded Kuwait in 1990, an American rig and drilling crew were working in Kuwait's northernmost oil field near the border with Iraq.
75 Stoltzfus, Oral History.
76 Bogosian, Oral History. Embassy economic and commercial officers at that time handled functions that were subsequently vested in the Foreign Commercial Service of the U.S. Department of Commerce.
77 The trend toward American university training was accelerated by Kuwait's adoption of the U.S system. A senior official of the Ministry of High Education explained to the author in the 1980s that an American education more closely matched Kuwait's needs than the British alternative. To paraphrase his explanation, if a Kuwaiti majored in biology in the United Kingdom he would return an authority on crayfish. The same student graduating from the United States could easily teach a range of biology courses.
78 Winstone and Freeth, *Kuwait*, p. 197.
79 Joyce, *Kuwait 1945–1996*, p. 152.
80 Some of the small cadre of Kuwaiti students who pioneered study in the United States in the 1950s and early 1960s recalled with good humor the puzzlement of Americans about who they were and where they came from. These earliest Kuwaiti students were generally placed in institutions near San Francisco and in the Southwest because that was where American oil companies were headquartered. Personal conversations, 1987–88.
81 Lumsden, Oral History.
82 See above. Lumsden, who was on hand for the Agnew visit recalls

that, despite the fact that the Vice President's stay was brief and short on substance, the Kuwaitis were flattered by his attention and valued his visit as confirmation of the country's significance to the United States. Lumsden, Oral History.

83 The "Rogers Plan," one of a series of American peace initiatives over the years, did not survive the obstacles raised by the parties to the conflict, partisan objections within the United States and the Yom Kippur war of October 1973.

84 Dick Bogosian, a control officer for the visit, provided an amusing vignette of Albert's visit: "Albert ... met with Abdul-Rahman Salim Al-Ateeqi, who was the minister of finance and oil and ... a man very passionate on the Arab-Israeli question. And as the Kuwaitis did, he just raked the Americans over the coals, and as he was leaving, Carl Albert said to us, 'I've never been through anything like that in my life.' So when he was leaving at the airport, I was with a colleague, Arthur Houghton, an Arabist accompanying him. They had been in Saudi Arabia. I said, 'Arthur, why is he so amazed? You know the Saudis feel the same way the Kuwaitis do.' He said, 'Yes, but, Dick, they [the Saudis] are so much more Olympian." Bogosian, Oral History.

85 *Middle East Journal,* Chronology, Vol. 27, no. 2 (Spring 73), p. 199.

86 Senator Fulbright visited Abu Dhabi while I was assigned there. I arrived at the old Al–Ain Palace Hotel to accompany the Senator to an appointment with Shaikh Zayed bin Sultan, President of the UAE, and discovered the UAE Foreign Minister with Algerian Foreign Minister Bouteflika who was being introduced to Senator Fulbright. I was immediately pressed into service to interpret from French to Arabic to English for the party during an interminable wait for the government interpreter and official cars to arrive. The experience was one of diplomacy's minor traumata.

87 Twinam, "America and the Gulf Arabs," p. 138.

88 After I returned from Kuwait in late 1990, my wife and I made a nationwide speaking tour sponsored by the American Foreign Service Association. In February 1991, before Kuwait's liberation, an older lady in the San Francisco audience stood and asked in a shrill voice why the United States should help free the Kuwaitis and concluded with her clincher: "They (Kuwaitis) don't even allow women to vote!" While I was carefully explaining that Kuwaiti women are very capable, that they already hold positions of responsibility, and that I had no doubt that women would some day get the franchise, my wife rose to deliver the ultimate stopper. "When my mother was born, women couldn't vote in *this* country!"

600 Notes

89 Bogosian, Oral History.
90 Rush, *Al-Sabah*, pp. 30–31.

12 Sea of Troubles

1. *Middle East Journal,* Chronology, Vol. 32, no. 2 (Spring 1978), p. 194.
2. Rush, *Al-Sabah*, pp. 15 and 17.
3. Discerning the trend in Iraqi policy during the late 1970s was difficult, perhaps because of rivalries within the Baathist leadership. At one point, Iraq and Syria, each ruled by a "Baathist" cadre, hinted at a rapprochement and potential unity. I attended a Syrian reception in Washington at the time where Syrian and Iraqi diplomats talked enthusiastically about unifying their missions (Iraq was at that time represented in Washington by an "Interest Section" under the Algerian embassy). To underline their point, they claimed that they had been instructed to inventory typewriters and office equipment to facilitate amalgamation.
4. Following the phone conversation, I contacted the American Mission to the United Nations and asked them to do what they could. Given the demands on the NYPD, we were gratified that a single police officer was stationed outside her hospital room. Iraqi diplomats called several times a day to complain that one policeman was not sufficient. Finally, in exasperation, I "explained" to them in a conspiratorial tone that the United States does not deal with security the way Iraqis do. They should, I urged, check regularly and call back *only* if they could detect other security personnel so we could discipline them for breaking cover. The phone calls stopped.
5. William B. Quandt, "The Gulf War: Policy Options and Regional Implications," *American-Arab Affairs*, No. 9 (Summer 1984), p. 1.
6. The Marine Guard unit in Kuwait was assigned circa 1967. Lovelyn Edwards, transcription.
7. Ambassador François M. Dickman, Oral History
8. *Middle East Journal,* Chronology, Vol. 34, no. 2 (Spring 1980), p. 173. Crystal "The Merchant Families . . .," p. 102, wrote that the Kuwaiti police did not hesitate to break up the crowd and arrest demonstration leaders. Kuwait's security forces had already clashed with elements responsive to Iranian manipulation. In March, Kuwaiti police had faced an estimated 10,000 demonstrators at the nearby Iranian embassy. Several persons were killed and dozens were injured. Lori Plotkin Boghardt, *Kuwait Amid War,*

Peace and Revolution: 1979–1991 and New Challenges, in association with St. Antony's College, Oxford (New York: Palgrave MacMillan, 2006), p. 30.
9. *Middle East Journal*, Chronology, Vol. 34, no. 2 (Spring 1980), p. 173. The secretary was accompanied by Assistant Treasury Secretary Fred Bergsten, NEA Deputy Assistant Secretary Joe Twinam, and a congressman.
10. Dickman, Oral History.
11. *Middle East Journal*, Chronology, Vol. 34, no. 2 (Spring 1980), p. 173. It can only be assumed that Minister al-Atiqi was similarly "outraged" by Iranian revolutionaries' blatant disregard for the conventions of diplomatic status and immunity, although the record does not reveal his "outrage."
12. By chance, a secretary from the Tehran Political Section was in Kuwait for a brief vacation when her Embassy was overrun. She volunteered to assist Gladys Chun, Dickman's secretary, in weeding out executive files.
13. With reference logs, it is possible to recall from the Department of State any hard copy needed. During the civil strife in Lebanon in the late 1970s, my colleagues and I in Embassy Beirut kept two days of cable traffic and relied on department facilities for any additional requirements.
14. "There was a main gate directly opposite the ambassador's office which opened onto the Hilton and all cars drove through that entrance and parked inside the compound." Lovelyn Edwards, transcription.
15. "Embassy Security Not Beefed Up," *Denver Post*, December 13,1983, p. 1A. The article in my possession includes a diagram of attack.
16. Personal observation.
17. *Middle East Journal*, Chronology, Vol. 38, no. 2 (Spring 1984), p. 298. The embassy placed a plaque in memory of killed and injured colleagues at the base of the compound flagpole; a memorial ceremony for all employees was held every year on the anniversary of the tragedy.
18. Evan Duncan, "Terrorist attacks on U.S. official personnel abroad, 1982–84," *US Department of State Bulletin*, April 1985. Transcript available on the Internet.
19. The bombing attacks of December 12, 1983 were carried out in the name of "Islamic Jihad." The driver of the truck bomb was subsequently identified as a pro-Iranian Iraqi. *Middle East Journal*, Chronology, Vol. 38, no 2 [Spring 1984] p. 298. Kuwait tried twen-

ty-five persons, predominantly Iraqis, for the crime in a Special State Security Court. Six (three in absentia) of the accused were condemned to death and fourteens others received sentences of between five years and life. At least some of the convicted were still incarcerated when Iraq invaded Kuwait in 1990.

20 Dickman, Oral History. At about the same time, the Grand Mosque at Mecca in Saudi Arabia was seized by Islamic extremists, who had to be dislodged forcibly by Saudi troops. In Islamabad, Pakistan, a mob incited by agitators attacked the U.S. Embassy compound there, setting fire to several buildings before being dispersed.

21 The embassy also took the precaution of setting up an alternate command post some distance from the Chancery itself. Dickman, Oral History. It is customary for embassies in times of heightened alert to intensify contact with resident American citizens through its system of community wardens.

22 The Embassy was located adjacent to Bneid al-Gar, a predominantly Shia neighborhood.

23 Boghardt, *Kuwait amid War . . .*, p. 37.

24 Dickman, Oral History.

25 Embassy dependents were evacuated several weeks before Christmas and not permitted to return to post until the early summer of 1980. Hugh B. Jones, Memories of U.S. Federal Highway Administration official assigned to Kuwait 1977–1988, transcribed from a cassette, January 1989. Foreign Service families are, in the main, an extremely hardy and resilient element of the community. Some wives in Kuwait were predictably unhappy at being ordered to depart but accepted "Service discipline." They were permitted to return on June 20, 1980 after a six-month absence. In the absence of dependents and non–essential staff, Ambassador Dickman promoted "victory gardens" at the Embassy Residence to occupy the remaining personnel. Dickman, Oral History.

26 Ibid.

27 Similarly, regular meetings for the community, organized by the heads of the Consular and Commercial Sections, were held at the Residence during my tenure from 1987 to 1990. Although any American resident was welcome, the primary attendees were wardens and heads of institutions with large numbers of American employees or clients. The gatherings were also useful for verifying the integrity of the warden system and associated telephone tree.

28 The Shia community held ten seats in the previous Assembly. Crystal, "The Merchant Families . . .," p. 101.

29 Ghabra, "Democratization in a Middle Eastern State...," p. 116.
30 The Assembly voted overwhelmingly in January 1982 to reject a proposal for female suffrage as Kuwaiti women demonstrated outside the parliament building. *Middle East Journal*, Chronology, Vol. 36, no 3 (Summer 1982). p. 405 A group of Kuwaiti women, including at least one shaikha from the al Sabah family, were actively agitating for voting rights during the 1980s. Ibid., Vol. 39, no 3 (Summer 1985), p.383
31 Kuwait confers citizenship to resident aliens sparingly and in instances where the beneficary has made significant contributions to society. Several Christian Palestinian families, who provided services in the days before oil wealth, have been accorded Kuwaiti nationality and Drs. Mylrea and Scudder of the American Mission hospital were reportedly offered citizenship.
32 Crystal, "The Merchant Families ... ," p. 103. Although the proposed bill failed, fundamentalist pressure to curtail Christmas trees in hotel lobbies and other public venues persisted into the late 1980s. Despite this current, however, some Kuwaiti families, especially those that had lived or studied in the West, adopted the practice of giving gifts at the Christmas season and even put up trees in their homes.
33 Boghardt, *Kuwait amid War* ... ," p. 51.
34 "The government, apparently confident that the Shia would be controlled by their established leading families, failed to anticipate and later assess the mass appeal of revolutionary Iran...." Crystal, "The Merchant Families ...," p. 101.
35 *Middle East Journal*, Chronology, Vol. 34, no. 3 (Summer 1980), pp. 334–35.
36 *Ibid.*, no. 4 (Autumn 1980), p. 479.
37 *Middle East Journal, Chronology*, Vol. 37, no. 1 (Winter 1983), p. 83. A Spanish court later convicted a Palestinian for the murder. *Middle East Journal, Chronology*, Vol. 37, no. 3 (Summer 1983), p. 460.
38 *Ibid.*, no. 2 (Spring 1983), p. 248.
39 To further complicate the picture, some Kuwaiti Shi'a are Arabs from Iraq who share the official faith of Iran, but not Persian ethnicity.
40 *Middle East Journal, Chronology*, Vol. 37, no. 2 (Spring 1983), p. 248.
41 "For eight long years there were intermittent Iranian pressures to scare the Gulf monarchies away from helping Iraq. While Iran at rare moments proffered the carrot of benign conduct to the non–belligerents, what was most frequently evident was the bran-

dishing of a collection of sticks. Iranian propaganda persistently called for the overthrow of the Arab monarchies across the Gulf. Iran is widely believed to have encouraged a variety of subversive or terrorist activities—the 1981 apparent coup attempt in Bahrain, the 1984 attacks against the American and French embassies and government facilities in Kuwait and the 1986 (sic) assassination attempt against the emir of Kuwait." Twinam, "America and the Gulf Arabs," p. 113.

42 Within days of the coordinated bombings of the American and French embassies and government targets on December 12, 1983, Kuwaiti authorities arrested ten Shi'a Muslims with links to the Iranian regime. One week later, seven additional suspects were detained. The group of 25, plus four individuals that eluded the police, were given a one-month trial in February 1984 and sentenced in March. *Middle East Journal,* Chronology, Vol. 38, no 2 (Spring 1984), p. 298, and ibid., no 3 (Summer 1984), p. 506.

43 "Their presence in Kuwaiti jails prompted continuing political violence, including the 1985 hijacking of a TWA flight, and 1984 and 1988 hijackings of Kuwaiti airliners." Crystal, "The Merchant Families ... ," p. 103.

44 Personal conversations with senior Kuwaiti officials, 1987–89. The heroic security personnel killed in the incident had been trained quietly in personal protection techniques by American experts.

45 *Middle East Journal,* Chronology, Vol. 39, no 4 (Autumn 1985), p. 812

46 The Ayatollah Khomeini characterized Kuwait's ruler, as well as those of other Gulf peninsula states as "mini-shahs," indicating that they were "legitimate" targets for Iran and its sympathizers. Boghardt, *Kuwait amid War . . .,* p. 29.

47 Seven years earlier, in July 1977, Kuwait suffered its first recorded airline hijacking. Twelve hijackers, later linked to a rogue Palestinian paramilitary organization, the Popular Front for the Liberation of Palestine – General Command (PFLP-GC), forced the plane to land at Kuwait for refueling. The passengers were released in return for safe conduct to the Peoples' Democratic Republic of Yemen. The aircraft was permitted to take off for Damascus where the perpetrators eventually surrendered to Syrian authorities. *Middle East Journal, Chronology,* Vol. 31, no. 4 (Autumn 1977), p 476.

48 The hijackers were never tried or apprehended. It seems incontrovertible that the Iranian regime, which reportedly supplied the hijackers with additional weapons after they landed at Tehran,

colluded with the perpetrators. The plane was returned to Kuwait more than a year later. See also Boghardt, *Kuwait amid War* . . ., p. 88.

49 In July 1985, bombs exploded at two popular restaurants in Kuwait, killing 9 persons and injuring 56 others in the vicinity. *Middle East Journal*, Chronology, Vol. 39, no 4 (Autumn 1985), p. 813. Several weeks later, a young Kuwaiti died of his injuries. Ibid., Vol. 40, no 1 (Winter 1986), p. 126.

50 Crystal, "The Merchant Families ... ," p. 104. Security was tightened so much that an American Wild West show touring the region at the time had to perform in Kuwait without its inoperable weapons.

51 *Middle East Journal*, Chronology, Vol. 39, no 4 (Autumn 1985), p. 812.

52 Ibid., Vol. 42, no 4 (Autumn 1988), p. 663.

53 Ibid., Vol. 41, no 4 (Autumn 1987), p. 606.

54 Kuwait had traditionally welcomed Palestinian refugees who had created there their most prosperous community in the Middle East. From the outset, however, it was made clear that Kuwait regarded their residency as "temporary," pending a resolution of the Palestinian question. In 1972, for example, Kuwaiti authorities stressed that Palestinians would not be permitted to settle permanently and would "return home eventually." This position was in accord with that of the Palestinian leadership and other Arab governments. *Middle East Journal*, Chronology, Vol. 26 no 4 (Autumn 1972) p. 438.

55 Ibid., Vol. 40, no 1 (Winter 1986) p. 126.

56 Ibid., Vol. 41, no 2 (Spring 1987) p. 269. The Iranian news agency claimed in August 1985 that 768 Iranians alone were deported in July. Ibid.,Vol. 40, no 1 (Winter 1986) p. 126.

57 Ibid., Vol. 39, no 4 (Autumn 1985) p. 812.

58 Ibid., Vol. 41, no 4 (Autumn 1987) p. 606.

59 The Special Security Court, administered by the Ministry of Justice, was abolished in 1995. Boghardt, *Kuwait amid War* . . ., p. 25.

60 *Middle East Journal*, Chronology, Vol. 42, no 1 (Winter 1988) p. 98. Only four of thirty individuals accused of "disturbing public security" in a related case were found guilty.

61 *Middle East Journal*, Chronology, Vol. 41, 41, no 3 (Summer 1987), p. 429. The saboteurs in a series of fires directed against the oil infrastructure were identified as Kuwaiti Shi'a of Iranian origin.

62 A Shi'a officer in the Kuwaiti armed forces was reportedly found guilty of advocating the overthrow of the regime on April 13, 1986 and sentenced to ten years in prison. *Middle East Journal, Chronology*, Vol. 40, no 4 (Autumn1986), p. 703.

63 *Middle East Journal, Chronology,* Vol. 40, no 4 (Autumn 1986), p. 703.
64 Ghabra, "Democratization in a Middle Eastern State: Kuwait, 1993," p. 15.
65 Crystal, "The Merchant Families ... ," p. 105. Senior Kuwaiti officials told me during the late 1980s that "irresponsible" statements and actions of parliamentarians were hindering efforts to maintain working relationships with both Iraq and Iran.
66 Boghardt, *Kuwait amid War . . .,* p. 108.
67 During the 1985 hijacking of TWA 847 to Algiers and ultimately Beirut, the Lebanese Shi'a highjackers collected the passports of passengers to identify Americans and singled them out for execution to enforce their demands. As deputy chief of mission in Algeria, I was the principal liaison with the Algerian *mukhabarat* during the aircraft's stops in that country.
68 *Middle East Journal, Chronology,* Vol. 39, no 4 (Autumn 1985), pp. 812–13.
69 Ambassador Dickman and his successors were provided with bodyguards and a security follow-car by the Kuwaiti CID whenever he left the Embassy compound.
70 Dickman, Oral History.
71 "On September 17, 1980, Saddam appeared on Iraqi television, tore up the 1975 Algiers agreement, and claimed sovereignty over the entire Shatt al-Arab." Lee Allen Zatarain, *Tanker War: America's First Conflict with Iran, 1987–1988* (Philadelphia: Casemate, 2008), pp. 1–2.
72 I was director of NEA/ARN (Iraq, Jordan, Lebanon, and Syria) at the time. After monitoring the rhetoric and maneuvering on September 21, I sent a cable suggesting that it would be prudent to withdraw Americans working on the petrochemical project near Basra, Iraq. About 5 hours later, at about 2 a.m. in Washington, the Department Operations Center called to inform me that a major Iraqi attack was in progress. The U.S. interests section in Baghdad and the embassy in Kuwait set the evacuation in motion, but it was not completed before Iranian aircraft struck Basra. I rushed to the Department of State and set up a Task Force. Because the Iranian Desk (NEA/IRN) was completely preoccupied with the Iranian hostage crisis, NEA/ARN was assigned the lead role regarding the new conflict. Embassy Kuwait received a Department Honor Award for assisting U.S. citizens to leave Iraq. Brooks Wrampelmeier, Correspondence with author, 1988 and 1994.
73 This is a favorite tactic of radio stations during a critical situation.

In Beirut during the civil conflict of the 1970s embassy officers learned to use the time delay in broadcasts to thwart the ploy, salting their comments with expletives that compelled the station to censor the entire broadcast.

74 Personal correspondence with Chargé Wrampelmeier, November 12, 1988. The Group Honor Award was carried to Washington when the Embassy was evacuated in December 1990, during the Iraqi occupation of Kuwait, and returned following liberation.

75 Not only had the Ayatollah Khomeini's regime decimated the shah's officer corps, but logistics were a shambles. The United States received reports, for example, that computerized spare parts lists had been destroyed and that Revolutionary Guards were going through boxes spread out in a large hangar to find urgently needed components for helicopters.

76 Personal conversations with senior Kuwaiti officials, 1988–89.

77 As early as 1974, Iraq concluded an agreement for the use of Kuwaiti ports to relieve shipping congestion in the Iraqi ports of Basra and Umm Qasr. *Middle East Journal*, Chronology, Vol. 29, no. 1 (Winter 1975), p. 74.

78 Dickman, Oral History.

79 The United States position, first enunciated by Deputy Secretary of State Warren Christopher at the beginning of October 1980, laid stress on several long-standing principles: the nonadmissability of the acquisition of territory by force, peaceful settlement of disputes, freedom of innocent passage in the Gulf, and respect for the neutrality of nonbelligerents. I was the principal drafter of the Christopher statement.

80 The Soviet Union's move into Afghanistan rang alarm bells in Washington also because it represented the first deployment of Soviet combat forces outside its sphere of influence for decades since the Second World War. Palmer, *Guardians of the Gulf*, p. 104.

81 Dickman, Oral History. Ironically, the Shah's regime in Tehran also opposed the projection of U.S. power into the Gulf region. At a 1972 press conference, the Shah declared: "Well, you know what we declared long ago that we should not like to see a foreign power in the Persian Gulf. Whether that power be Britain, the United States, the Soviet Union or China our policy has not changed." *Guardians of the Gulf*, p. 90.

82 Palestinians in Kuwait organized a large demonstration at the Embassy to protest the court's decision to extradite the accused bomber.

83 In his landmark book on Kuwait, Sir Harold Dickson wrote

decades earlier "the well-to-do from Kuwait imitate their nomad brethren and make for the high desert to enjoy four months of that badawin existence which they have so recently abandoned. Whole families take part in this spring migration from the city to the desert to live in black hair tents, while the poorer Arabs of the town plant themselves on kinsmen among the great Mutair, 'Ajman and 'Awazim tribes if they cannot afford tents of their own." Dickson, *The Arab of the Desert*, p. 20.

84 Dickman, Oral History.
85 *Middle East Journal, Chronology*, Vol. 35, no 4 (Autumn 1981), p. 608. The Kuwait News Agency (KUNA) claimed the Consul violated Kuwaiti law by issuing passports to two "Saudi" children to facilitate travel to US with their American mother.
86 When I was completing my tour as director of NEA/ARN, I was also at Ditchley and was asked by Habib to accompany him. The following account of the critical first two weeks of that mission is based upon my personal participation.
87 The Kuwaitis were not alone in this suspicion. Since Sharon met with Haig in Washington in May 1982, speculation had circulated within the Department of State that the purpose of the Sharon visit had been to obtain Haig's agreement to some Israeli action.
88 Dickman, Oral History. This uncharacteristic decision was the first time in Dickman's career that he had intentionally ignored a direct instruction.
89 Following separate briefings with the president and the secretary at Versailles, Habib told me that he had received entirely different instructions. The president had simply said "Stop it." And that was what he was going to try to do. During the initial meeting with Begin and Sharon, Sharon expressed surprise at Habib's mission, noting., "Your government knows about this." During Habib's shuttle to establish a cease-fire, he had several difficult phone conversations with the secretary. I was privy to only one side of the exchanges, but following an exchange at the U.S. Embassy in Damascus, Habib muttered that he was being "undercut."
90 It is indisputable that the Lebanese Phalange had carried out the massacre, but there has been some question about how much the Israeli forces allied with them knew and when they knew it. It strains credulity, on balance, to believe that the Israelis were unaware of the indiscriminate killing that occurred in the camp over several days. Israeli forces occupied the upper floors of two high-rise buildings overlooking the camp. The buildings, across a

traffic circle from the Kuwaiti Embassy in Beirut, were purposely constructed for Lebanese army officers to provide a commanding view of the low-rise Sabra-Shatila complex.
91 Boghardt, *Kuwait amid War ...*, p. 62.
92 Dickman, Oral History.
93 *Middle East Journal*, Chronology, Vol. 35, no. 3 (Summer 1981), p. 371.
94 Ibid., Vol. 36, no. 1 (Winter 1982), p. 72.
95 I and my colleagues in the Gulf heard these sentiments frequently during this period.
96 *Middle East Journal*, Chronology, Vol. 36, no. 1 (Winter 1982), p. 72. Kuwait subsequently purchased Hawk missiles.
97 Ibid., Vol. 38, no 4 (Autumn 1984), p.723.
98 Dickman, Oral History. Among the ambassador's other frustrations was the overruling at senior levels of a Kuwait Airways decision to purchase the Boeing 767 and rejection of a TWA application to initiate regular service to Kuwait because the airline had other flights that stopped in Israel. This consideration had not, of course, affected historic TWA service to Cairo or Saudi Arabia.
99 *Middle East Journal*, Chronology, Vol. 38, no 1 (Winter 1984), p. 108.
100 Dickman, Oral History.
101 Mohammad al-Rumaihi, "Kuwaiti-American Relations: A Case of Mismanagement," *American-Arab Affairs*, No. 9 (Summer 1984), p. 78.

13 Tentative Alliance

1 Shortly after the truce of 1988, I visited Basra to escort a congressional visitor to the nearby civilian airport. The city appeared largely deserted and the regime had lined the corniche along the western shore of the Shatt with crude Soviet-style statues of Iraqi generals killed in the defense of the Iraqi lines. Each was woodenly pointing east, toward Iran, and their number offered mute testimony of the extent of Iraqi casualties in the conflict. Saddam Hussein had no problem with dead "heroes" who could not challenge his rule.
2 Among these incidents, in February 1985, gunmen assassinated an Iraqi diplomat and his son in their home; "Islamic Jihad" claimed responsibility, *Middle East Journal*, Chronology, Vol. 39, no 3 (Summer 1985), p. 383; the editor of the Kuwaiti daily, *al-Siyassah*, was wounded in a machine gun attack in April 1985, ibid., no 4 (Autumn 1985), p. 812; the focus shifted to oilfields and

installations in June 1986 when explosions and arson damaged the Mina al-Ahmadi terminal and nearby al-Mukawa field, ibid, Vol. 40, no 4 (Autumn 1986), p. 703; the al-Mukawa field was again the target of arsonists in early 1987, ibid., Vol. 41, no 3 (Summer 1987), p. 429; and a car bomb exploded without casualties behind the Meridien Hotel in the center of town in January of the same year, ibid. Meanwhile, the State Security Court was in constant session trying suspects with a mixed record of convictions and acquittals.

3   Dickman, Oral History.
4   Although no Americans were involved in the Suq al-Manakh, the collapse nevertheless generated a further issue in bilateral relations. The embassy had reported the evolving crisis to the Department of State in a series of cables, highly classified to protect the identity of the "investors." The reports were nonetheless leaked in Washington and formed the basis of a May 1983 *Atlantic Monthly* article. The Kuwaitis were not amused. Ibid.
5   Ambassador Anthony Quainton, The Foreign Affairs Oral History Collection of the Association for Diplomatic Studies and Training, http://www.adst.org/OH%20TOCs/Quainton,%20Anthony.toc.pdf
6   Ibid.
7   Ibid.
8   Kuwait, for instance, was highly critical of the American decision to boycott the 1980 Olympics in Moscow in response to naked Soviet aggression in Afghanistan, but pro forma in its criticism of the aggression itself. Similarly, they clearly sympathized with the U.S. dilemma with the Iranian capture of its embassy staff in Tehran. It is understandable that Kuwait did not wish to antagonize the Iranians for seizing diplomatically protected persons, but they demonstrated no comparable restraint in attacking the U.S. decision to seize Iranian assets in America. Some years ago, a wise Arab diplomat told me that Arab criticism of American policy was actually a "compliment." They feel free to criticize not only because they believe the policies are wrong, but because they know they are unlikely to be slapped down for doing so. That was scant comfort.
9   The U.S. permanent representative to the United Nations, Ambassador Donald McHenry, visited in February 1980, *Middle East Journal, Chronology*, Vol. 34, no. 2 (Spring 1980), p. 173. Senator Charles Percy, chairman of the Foreign Relations Committee, arrived in January 1982, followed by Assistant Secretary of State for the Near East and South Asia Nicholas Veliotes in March, ibid.,

Vol. 36, no. 3 (Summer 1982), p. 405. Ambassador McHenry's son, a very capable young career officer, was later assigned to the Embassy in Kuwait.

10 Dickman, Oral History. The U.S. Congress had restricted contacts with the Palestine Liberation Organization (PLO) by American diplomats but members of Congress continued to meet Chairman 'Arafat and other PLO notables with alacrity. One of the minor pleasures of my posting in Beirut was responding to requests for arranging appointments for visiting congressmen, reminding them that the embassy was not permitted to deal with the PLO.

11 Ibid.

12 *Middle East Journal, Chronology*, Vol. 29, no. 1 (Winter 1975), p. 74.

13 Dickman, Oral History.

14 By the end of the decade, Kuwaiti investments in the American economy were estimated to be at least ten times the $7 billion figure.

15 Dickman, Oral History.

16 As early as 1966, the Kuwait National Petroleum Company (KNPC) bought a Danish subsidiary making Kuwait the first Middle East state to retail oil products in Europe. Crystal, *Oil and Politics in the Gulf*, p. 90.

17 Ibid., p. 96. KPC acquired hundreds of gas stations in Europes and began marketing Kuwaiti product under the "Q8" logo.

18 In 1982, former President Ford visited Kuwait. At Ambassador Dickman's invitation, he paid a visit to the Embassy compound and met with the Embassy staff on the Residence patio. Wrampelmeier, correspondence.

19 Dickman, Oral History.. Ali Khalifa had, early in his career, required oil companies operating in Kuwait to capture all the associated gas for conversion into valuable petrochemicals. It was several years before Saudi Arabia followed Kuwait's lead.

20 The United States itself was not a major importer of Kuwaiti crude oil. Kuwait was, however, the source of specialized refined products, such as "JP-5," an aviation gas used exclusively by U.S. Naval Aviation. On the other hand, Washington had to be concerned with anything that threatened the Gulf contribution to total world supply because of the effect of shortages on other countries, including its closest allies. Most Kuwaiti oil was shipped to U.S allies in western Europe and Japan. Quainton, Oral History.

21 My firsthand observation.

22 Dickman, Oral History. Among other factors cushioning the ef-

fects of the war were rising production levels in the North Sea oilfields, the end of the civil war in Nigeria, the beginnings of Alaska's north slope operation, the impact of conservation measures implemented by the administration of President Carter, and stockpiles amassed by oil companies during earlier panic buying.

23 Kuwaiti production costs are the lowest in the world.
24 Recounted in Quainton, Oral History.
25 As usual, some Arab regimes did not get the message. Saddam Hussein, for example, never grasped the intricacies of petroleum economics. Strapped for cash after the 1988 truce with Iran, he pushed relentlessly for higher prices, apparently convinced that every dollar increase meant an additional dollar of income. Although there were Iraqis who could have corrected his errors, if they dared, it is doubtful that he ever heard of elasticity of demand, or substitution. As the price rises, known oil from marginal sources comes onstream, thus decreasing demand and profits.
26 Ministry of Planning figures for Residence Permits issued to Americans, reproduced in Boghardt, *Kuwait amid War . . .*, p. 186) show general stability for the first part of the 1980s with a significant spike from 1983 to 1987.
27 Begun in December 1985, the Embassy wall was more than nine feet high topped with razor wire, and was reputedly the most expensive ever built. Quainton, Oral History. It enclosed an area of about 5 acres and was constructed of steel reinforced concrete set several meters in the ground. When I visited the Embassy with a U.S. Central Command delegation during construction, I observed the footings and noted a cantilevered arrangement that used the weight of any vehicle trying to ram the wall to further increase the resistance. The vehicular gate, commanded by a guardhouse with bullet-resistant observation windows, was heavy steel operated electrically, and accessed by narrow side streets. Some distance inside the gate were automatic "Jersey" barriers which rose out of the ground to create a "lock." A similar guardhouse protected the pedestrian entry near the Chancery, which was also served by a turnstile exit that rotated outward only. At one corner of the construction was a small, walled, but separate, compound that provided accommodations and working space for a Kuwait National Guard detachment, which provided perimeter security.
28 The last remaining American oil camp was dismantled following the take-over of the American Independent Oil Company (AMINOIL) in September 1977.
29 Quainton, Oral History.

30 Policy and practice with regard to Alcoholic beverages in Kuwait changed over time. "Alcohol imports were no problem. At the time the diplomatic missions still had permission to bring in and serve alcoholic beverages to their personnel and their guests, even in the hotels." Wrampelmeier, correspondence.
31 Quainton, Oral History. Kuwaiti officials involved in providing "public housing" to Kuwaitis told me in 1987 that the three major issues were the size of the *diwanniya*, or public sitting room; the amount of marble in the foyer; and the number of maid's rooms. Traditionally, *diwanniyas* existed only in the homes of wealthy merchant families. Housing and amenities, including air conditioning, for the large population of laborers from South Asia, the Philippines, or Iran did not meet these standards but was comparable to, or better than, accommodations in their home countries.
32 Wrampelmeier, correspondence. These productions continued a tradition of community performances. For example, Leslie Lisle, the PAO in the early 1970s, directed "a small madrigal group" that staged festive evenings while the American and British communities cooperated "to produce the musical '1776' in the Embassy auditorium to a sold-out house for five nights running." Leslie Lisle, Correspondence with the author, January 21, 1989. During my time as ambassador, plays including *A Christmas Carol* were held at the New English School and a "professional" musical revue featuring the talented daughter of an embassy official, Caesar Santucci, was presented.
33 Wrampelmeier, correspondence.
34 Ibid. As Wrampelmeier remembers, the Kuwait Air Force (KAF) had to send a special C-130 flight to Athens to pick up the elusive missile manuals.
35 Quainton, Oral History.
36 Kuwait's embassy in Tehran never closed even when attacked and damaged by a local mob and the Iranian embassy operated in Kuwait throughout the war. The Iranians sent a new ambassador to Kuwait in September 1989. *Middle East Journal*, Chronology, Vol. 44, no 1 (Winter 1990), p. 117. The Iranian ambassador lived no more than 250 yards from the American Chancery.
37 Quoted in Zatarain, *Tanker War*, p. 30.
38 I was director of the State Department office responsible for relations with Iraq until July 1983 and was thus privy to the reasons for this adjustment of policy. The original U.S. statement of policy in October 1980, including a firm rejection of the acquisition of territory by force, was issued at the time when Iraqi forces were driv-

ing into Iranian Khuzestan. It was not well received in Baghdad and was considered in some Arab circles as a "tilt" toward Iran.

39 As an added bonus, Iraq was able to purchase Soviet-made weapons compatible with those in its own inventory from Egypt, where they were surplus to Egyptian needs.
40 Quainton, Oral History.
41 Ibid.
42 Quainton (ibid.,) dates the pivotal period as 1986–87.
43 Stingers had achieved a high degree of notoriety as a "magic bullet" in the region after their employment by the resistance in Afghanistan succeeded in substantially neutralizing Soviet aviation. Reluctance to authorize their sale to Kuwait was not an isolated case. There was real concern in Washington at the time that these weapons could fall into the wrong hands and become a threat to commercial aircraft. It was only after Qatar managed to acquire a number of Stingers, probably from Afghani *mujahadeen* elements, that restrictions were relaxed for friendly governments.
44 *Middle East Journal*, Chronology, Vol. 38, no 4 (Autumn 1984), p.723. Kuwait's obvious concern was defense against potential Iranian aerial attacks. Three Iranian planes violated Kuwait's airspace in June 1981; Kuwait lodged a formal protest with the Iranian chargé, ibid., Vol. 35, no 4 (Autumn 1981), p. 608. When an unidentified (probable Iranian) aircraft overflew Kubbar Island in October 1986, Kuwait was in a position to fire two missiles with unconfirmed results. Ibid, Vol. 41, no 2 (Spring 1987), p. 268.
45 Ibid., Vol. 39, no 1 (Winter 1985), p.114. Interestingly, Kuwait publicized an agreement with the USSR for air defense improvements almost simultaneously. Minister of Defense Salem al-Sabah hastened to announce that "no more than ten" Soviet advisors would be stationed in the country in connection with the sale. Ibid., p.115.
46 Twinam, "America and the Gulf Arabs," p. 113.
47 Zatarain, *Tanker War*, p. 30.
48 *Middle East Journal*, Chronology, Vol. 41, no 3 (Summer 1987), p. 429. Since the beginning of the Iraq-Iran war, the Soviets had deployed additional warships to the Indian Ocean in connection with the transit of their arms shipments to Iraq. The warships occasionally entered the Gulf itself.
49 Palmer, *Guardians of the Gulf*, p. 122. Palmer writes that the Kuwaitis asked the U.S. Coast Guard for information on registration requirements on December 10. Whether the Coast Guard immediately recognized the importance of this request and shared the information with other interested agencies is unclear.

50 Ibid., p. 123.
51 Quainton, Oral History.
52 USCENTCOM, headquartered at McDill AFB in Tampa, Florida, was the successor to the Rapid Deployment Force (RDF) established during the Carter Administration. The new unified command's Area of Responsibility (AOR) at the time included the Gulf region as far east as Pakistan, the Middle East (except for Israel and the Levant), and the Horn of Africa. Prior to my assignment to Kuwait, I served as political advisor (POLAD) to the commander in chief (UNCINCCENT), a four-star flag officer. The CINC at in the period of the reflagging was Gen. George B. Crist, US Marine Corps, who was succeeded by Gen. Norman Schwarzkopf, US Army.
53 One historian of the Tanker Protection Regime was informed that when the concept was first broached with working levels of the U.S. government (presumably some months earlier), it was met with reluctance and "bureaucratic inertia." Zatarain, *Tanker War*, p. 34.
54 Twinam, "America and the Gulf Arabs," p. 139.
55 At about the same time that Kuwait initiated discussions with the United States, it also approached the Soviet Union. Although Moscow reportedly expressed interest in participating in the protection of Kuwaiti-owned tankers, in the end Kuwait merely leased three Soviet oil carriers that continued to sail under the Soviet flag. The gesture nonetheless set off alarm bells in Washington and provided ammunition for those opposed to, or dubious about, the reflagging.
56 Since the beginning of the Iraq-Iran war, the Soviet Navy had increased the operations tempo of its warships in the Indian Ocean, occasionally sailing into the Gulf. In January 1987, a Soviet naval vessel passed through the Straits of Hormuz for the first time to escort merchant ships. Zatarain, *Tanker War*, p. 31.
57 Palmer, *Guardians of the Gulf*, p. 123. Western powers had assumed access to the warm water ports of the Gulf to be an enduring goal of Moscow since well before the Soviet Revolution. Tsarist Russian vessels visiting these waters in the first decade of the twentieth century, as well as Russian interest in the proposed Berlin-Baghdad Railway with a potential extension to Kuwait's harbor at the time of World War I set off alarms and countermeasures in London. Britain, and later the United States, took seriously the provision of the Molotov-Ribbentrop Pact of August 23, 1939, when it became known, in which Soviet Russia and Nazi Ger-

many recognized Soviet territorial ambitions in the direction of the Persian Gulf.
58 Quainton, Oral History.
59 Zatarain, *Tanker War*, p. 64.
60 This might have created problems with American merchant mariners had the ships not been sailing in harm's way. Only once the danger was past did U.S. unions make it a serious issue.
61 Before departing USCENTCOM headquarters for Washington, I participated in the development of the operations planning for the tanker protection regime ("Earnest Will"). This proved extremely beneficial later when, as ambassador in Kuwait, I was in a position to fend off efforts by agencies in Washington to overload the operation with extraneous "requirements."
62 Palmer, *Guardians of the Gulf*, p. 132.
63 Zatarain, *Tanker War*, p. 65.
64 Quainton, Oral History.
65 The timeline for the convoy had been leaked in Washington, allegedly by a member of Congress who had been briefed confidentially by the administration. According to Zatarain (*Tanker War*, p. 74), Secretary of Defense Caspar Weinberger and Admiral Crowe, chairman of the Joint Chiefs of Staff, held a briefing for key congressional leaders some days before the sailing. The admiral stressed that the information was "sensitive." Nevertheless, immediately following the briefing, Congressman Les Aspin, chairman of the House Armed Services Committee, called a press conference in which he reportedly divulged the details of the initial convoy. His remarks were front-page news in the *Washington Post* the following morning.

14 Prelude to Disaster

1 To facilitate communication with the U.S. Navy in Bahrain, a small group of Naval technicians was attached to the embassy, where they maintained constant contact with COMMIDEASTFOR in Manama and JTFME afloat. The admiral in Manama was a colleague of mine from his time on the staff of USCENTCOM and relations were excellent.
2 One or two mornings after my arrival, and even before the presentation of credentials to the Amir, the embassy public affairs officer (PAO), Lee Irwin, reported that U.S media representatives had asked to photograph the outbound tankers where they assembled for the transit. This seemed a reasonable request and ar-

rangements were made for a photo op. Lee was back two days later with the same request. Since it seemed obvious that the goal was to determine when the convoy sailed, I denied the request explaining that the embassy was not going to help the media do Iran's intelligence work.

3 Among the more notable, a car bomb had exploded outside KPC offices without injuries in April 1987; another bomb went off in the city the following month hours before the arrival of Assistant Secretary Richard Murphy for talks on the tanker protection regime; and a fire was set at oil facilities at al-Mahri the same month. *Middle East Journal,* Chronology, Vol. 41, no 4 (Autumn 1987) p. 606.

4 The land on which the U.S. Consulate had been built was under long-term lease from the family of the ruler of Bahrain. The reasonable rent negotiated in the late 1950s was a measure of its isolation and desolation at that time. As Kuwait prospered and expanded, the commercial value of the land increased many times. Not surprisingly, the agents of the Bahraini Amir hoped that the U.S. would give up the property before the lease expired in the late 1990s. A previous Ambassador recalls the tenor of periodic visits from these agents: "Don't you think you'd like to move to some other place?" To which the response was invariably, "No, I don't think we would at all." Stolzfus, Oral History.

5 The Silkworm was a knockoff of a Soviet antiship missile, which was sold to both Iran and Iraq during their conflict. Although it had a range of 80–100 miles, it was a relatively unsophisticated radar-guided projectile that targeted the largest object in its path. The September attack attracted little media attention outside Kuwait at the time and it seems probable that this was not the first firing at Kuwaiti territory. The previous January a "shell" was reported to have fallen on the Kuwaiti island of Failaka. *Middle East Journal,* Chronology, Vol. 41, no 3 (Summer 1987). p. 429. This is now believed to have been a ranging shot of the Iranian Silkworms and predated the establishment of the U.S. Navy's role in protecting Kuwaiti tanker traffic. Zatarain, *Tanker War,* p. 35.

6 A fragment of the skin of the missile that landed in Kuwait in early September adorned the Christmas tree in the ambassador's Residence in 1987. When our household shipment failed to arrive before the Holidays, members of the Embassy quietly donated ornaments and surprised me and Mrs. Howell with the collection. It was a deeply touching gesture. When the decorations were placed on the tree for the children's Holiday party, one was found to be a piece of the Silkworm missile with "1987" painted on it. It was a

memorable tree, in a sense celebrating also our success in countering the Silkworm menace.
7. KOTC immediately took responsibility for Captain Hunt's medical evacuation to the United States and extended treatment and needs there.
8. Zatarain, *Tanker War*, p. 155.
9. Joyce, *Kuwait 1945–1996*, p. 162.
10. Kuwait quickly repaired the damage and purchased a spare single-point mooring buoy to provide backup loading capability.
11. Peter Mansfield (*Kuwait: Vanguard of the Gulf* [London: Hutchinson, 1990], p. 121) wrote simply that the missile "missed its target and fell into the sea...."
12. Mansfield, *Kuwait*, p. 122. The amir was widely known for his habit of rising very early to cultivate date trees on the palace grounds, sometimes giving the dates to others. Among his other "eccentricities" was his punctuality, which he shared with few of his fellow rulers in the Gulf. A well-connected Kuwaiti drew my attention to photographs of the amir at meetings of the GCC, where he invariably wore a stern countenance. The reason, he explained, was because the Amir was in his seat at the time for the meeting and then had to wait for his counterparts to gather at their leisure.
13. Boghardt, *Kuwait amid War...* , p. 89.
14. Kuwaiti security services eventually identified those behind the attack on embassies and the Amir, and arrested suspects still in Kuwait for prosecution. Many Kuwaitis, however, felt that the investigation was not pursued with sufficient urgency. Whether reasonable or not, frustration among the public reached such a level that the crown prince/prime minister took charge of security from the minister of the interior. Boghardt, *Kuwait amid War...* , p. 43.
15. McDonald's was late in the Kuwait market, insisting on adhering to its worldwide marketing plan. I was approached on several occasions by Kuwait businessmen seeking the agency and had to admit that among the many things an ambassador did not control were U.S. corporate decisions.
16. Kuwait's policy regarding alcohol evolved from the 1960s largely in response to pressures from conservative elements in the National Assembly. A law in 1960 eased conditions for consumption, including for Muslims who were permitted to drink in private. At the end of 1964, a new law was passed prohibiting the importation of alcohol except by foreign diplomats. Daniels, *Kuwait Journey*, p. 179. The ban was subsequently extended to diplomatic missions

Notes 619

as well, although liquor continued to enter the country in quantity and some expatriates resorted to "home brew," risking arrest for bootlegging.

17. American employees at the Embassy paid full federal and applicable state taxes and were entitled to home leave every two to three years.
18. There were also schools following other national curricula, including an excellent British school.
19. The Marines and other young Embassy players indulged me by permitting me to play and yelled lustily "Get the respirator!" whenever I got a hit. Softball also played a part in my welcome to Kuwait in 1987. Shortly after my arrival, the embassy staff informed me that I was expected to play in a game that had been arranged with the Japanese embassy. The problem, they explained gravely, was that the new Japanese ambassador had been a semi-pro softball player in Japan. The pressure was on. On the appointed day, my wife and I joined the game and, for a time, it seemed the warnings were apt. The Japanese jumped out to a quick lead. Ultimately, the American team prevailed but the embassy staff had had their fun with the new chief of mission.
20. Playground equipment for younger children had been constructed by the General Services section, incorporating slides, spirals, and ladders ordered from the United States.
21. On one occasion, the embassy made the mistake of challenging the Czech embassy, not realizing that Czechoslovakia provided the coaches for the Kuwait national volleyball team.
22. One planned party for a visiting vessel nearly came to grief. When an Embassy car and I visited the ship in the port to pick up supplies, a zealous port customs inspector waved the ambassador's limo through the port gate, but stopped the next car. When he saw that the packages of hot dogs listed ham as an ingredient, he refused to let them or the cases of root beer into the country. Happily, my sedan was crammed with enough provisions for the party to proceed. The director of Customs, a good friend, was more exasperated by the port guard's zeal than I was.
23. The first American performing group known to appear in Kuwait was a troupe of precision water skiers from Silver Spring, Florida. Brought in by a Kuwaiti who had seen them on a trip to the United States, they exhibited their skills offshore in the Gulf in the early 1950s.
24. An American-style big band practiced at the American School. I enjoyed playing alto in the saxophone section of the band. The other members of the reed section were all Polish.

25 A stylish beach road, or corniche, had been constructed along the entire coast in 1974–75, cutting off the direct access to the Gulf the embassy originally enjoyed when it functioned as a "family beach." The corniche had two lanes in each direction and a median strip with carefully tended palm trees. Somewhat ironically, the date palm seedlings had been imported from California, descendants of date palms from the Basra area.

26 The hotel tower offered panoramic views of the entire Embassy compound. Kuwaiti security, involving a permanent National Guard unit around the compound wall, did an excellent job, however, of surveilling higher buildings in the vicinity. The British ambassador informed me about the experience of a visiting British officer who was staying in the hotel tower. The visitor stepped out on the balcony of his room and snapped several photographs. Before he could even return to his room, there was a knock at his door. He was asked to surrender the film from his camera.

27 An American vessel was involved in an encounter with the Iranian Navy as early as May 1981 when Iranian naval forces seized a survey ship under contract to KOC. Iran claimed the ship was taken in their territorial waters. The ship was released after several weeks and returned to Kuwait. *Middle East Journal,* Chronology, Vol. 35, no 4 (Autumn 1981), p. 608.

28 *Iran Ajr* was a Japanese-built landing ship, with a ramp that could be lowered to load cargo or, in this case, deploy mines. It was purchased from Japan in the late 1970s.

29 See *Time* Magazine, October 5, 1987.

30 Ibid.

31 The incontrovertible evidence also quashed the campaign of a small group of "bottom-feeders" in the United States that was gearing up to accuse the United States of responsibility for the incident.

32 When the USS *Samuel B. Roberts* struck a mine in April 1988, the serial numbers of unexploded mines found in the vicinity were matched with those aboard the *Iran Ajr*. In retribution, U.S. naval forces in the Gulf sank several Iranian naval ships during what may have been the largest surface action since World War II. Wikipedia http://en.wikipedia.org/wiki/Iran_Ajr

33 U.S. naval assets were configured during the Cold War for combat at sea. It was apparently assumed that allies, such as the Netherlands, would assume responsibility for close-in minesweeping. "The damage by mines to merchant ship SS *Bridgeton* and frigate *Samuel B. Roberts* during 1987 and 1988 in the Persian Gulf

briefly focused the Navy's attention on mine warfare. As a result, the fleet refined mine hunting and sweeping tactics and procedures, and tested some new equipment. These efforts and the success of American counter mine actions during the last months of the Iran-Iraq War, however, fostered a complacent attitude in the Navy about its mine counter–measures capability. Consequently, the Navy was little better prepared in 1990 to deal with sea mines than it had been in 1987." Edward J. Marolda, Senior Historian, Naval Historical Center, "The United States Navy and the Persian Gulf," <<http://www.history.navy.mil/wars/dstorm/sword-shield.htm>>

34 Zatarain, op. cit*Tanker War*, p. 75. The tugs were partially manned by volunteer U.S. Navy seamen.
35 Palmer, op. cit., p. 133. The negotiation of the agreement with goverments on the western coast of the Gulf took longer than expected because, it was said, of a quirk in Japanese foreign assistance regulations. Recipients of assistance, according to Japanese practice, were expected to declare themselves destitute to be eligible for aid. Eventually a diplomatic formula was found that reconciled Japan's requirements and the self-respect of the Gulf states.
36 It is frequently axiomatic in the Arab world that the more secretive the cooperation, the greater the possibilities for collaboration. In fact, Kuwait offered landing rights for aircraft in distress, medical facilities, including access to its decompression chamber for injured divers, and one tanker load of JP5 aviation fuel per month for US Naval operations worldwide on condition that the US keep silent. On one occasion, I was braced by a visiting senator who fulminated about the absence of Kuwaiti contributions, especially staging for U.S. aircraft. It was obvious that the senator had made up his mind and, in any event, the cooperation the Kuwaitis were providing was more valuable than the satisfaction of deflating a blowhard.
37 Zatarain, *Tanker War*, p. 126.
38 Ibid., pp. 126–27.
39 Ibid., p. 124. A fundamental question facing operational planners from the outset was the type of mines being employed in the Gulf. Ultimately, it was determined that they were World War II–type tethered mines. Sometime referred to as "dumb" mines they were laid connected to cables on the sea bottom and detonated when a vessel struck them. Over time, the tethers rust and snap, permitting the mine to float free. To predict patterns of drift, the sand-table

model of the Gulf at the Kuwait Institute of Scientific Research (KISR) was used to model currents. The press at the time reported a series of meetings among Gulf states to consider "pollution" in the sea. "Pollution" in this instance was a code word for mines.

40 The incident on July 3, 1988, occurred on the eve of the Embassy's scheduled national day reception at the ambassador's residence. It was common knowledge that Kuwaiti Shi'a used this flight from Dubai to visit family in Iran; some of the victims indeed turned out to be Kuwaitis. At the Embassy, senior staff and I debated attempting to cancel the reception but couldn't figure a way to notify the invited guests in time. At about the same time, the floral arrangements sent by Kuwaiti families on such occasions began to arrive, many of them from Shi'a friends. One read "God Bless the United States." Touched by the gesture, I decided to proceed with the reception on a subdued basis and include a moment of silence in memory of the dead.

41 Considering Iraq's overwhelming advantage in the air, the Iraqi air force performed abysmally. One of the asymmetries of the conflict was that Iran offered a target-rich environment of vessels within its territorial waters and on offshore islands where oil handling and shipping facilities were located. Iraq, on the other hand, lost its offshore loading terminal in the Gulf early and thereafter exported oil by pipeline or tank trucks to Aqaba, Jordan. Iraqi pilots usually depended upon standoff missiles and infrequently were within sight of their targets. This timidity not only limited the effectiveness of their sorties but resulted in attacks on unintended targets. One of the most serious of these was the May 17, 1987, attack on the US guided-missile frigate *Stark*. The Iraqi pilot launched two French-made Exocet missiles at distances of 22 and 15 nautical miles. The *Stark* had identified the aircraft as Iraqi and was transmitting a warning to stand away when the missiles struck. The vessel was seriously damaged but later salvaged: 37 U.S. seamen were killed. In contrast to the Israeli attack on the noncombatant USS *Liberty* during the 1967 Arab-Israel war, it was plausible to attribute the Iraqi attack to incompetence and cold feet.

42 Since the truce was never superseded by a treaty of peace between the two belligerents, Iran and Iraq remain technically in a state of war to this day.

43 Zatarain, *Tanker War*, p. 387.

44 Boghardt, *Kuwait amid War...*, p. 124.

45 *Middle East Journal*, Chronology, Vol. 38, no 4 (Autumn 1984), p. 723.

46 Ibid., Vol. 39, no 3 (Summer 1985), p. 383. One Iranian and an associated Kuwaiti were convicted and sentenced to ten years; four others were acquitted.
47 In June, 1986, major fires were set at the Mina al-Ahmadi oil facilities. Zatarain, *Tanker War*, p. 30. In January, 1987, the Kuwaiti government disclosed the arrest of eleven persons suspected of setting these fires as well as similar incidents of arson the same month. In the resulting trial, six Kuwaiti Shia "of Iranian origin" (two *in absentia*) were sentenced to be hanged. *Middle East Journal*, Chronology, Vol. 41, no 3 (Summer 1987), p. 429.
48 Boghardt, *Kuwait amid War...*, p. 116. See also *Middle East Journal*, Chronology, Vol. 42, no 2 (Spring 1988) p. 293
49 Boghardt, *Kuwait amid War...*, p. 32.
50 In reality, this was not the first time that the Kuwaiti leadership had been compelled to recognize that elements, both Sunni and Shi'a, had been radicalized by external forces in the region. When, for example, Sunni extremists seized the Grand Mosque in Mecca, Saudi Arabia in November 1979, four Kuwaitis were found to be among the armed group and some of the leaflets they distributed had been printed in Kuwait. Ibid., p. 37–38. Similarly, ten years later, sixteen Kuwaiti Shi'a were accused of participating in bombings at Mecca during the Hajj in 1989 and were beheaded. *Middle East Journal*, Chronology, Vol. 44, no. 1 (Winter 1990), p. 117. More recently, a sprinkling of Kuwaitis have allied with Usama bin Laden and al-Qaeda in its campaign of international terrorism.
51 The Iranian regime did not make the task of the Kuwaiti leadership easier, nor was it Tehran's intention to do so. Aside from its surreptitious attacks at sea and sponsorhip of terrorism on land, Iran kept up a drumbeat of propaganda attacks and diplomatic demarches. For instance, in December 1986, the Kuwaiti Foreign Ministry felt it was necessary to deny Iranian allegations that Kuwait had provided refueling facilities for Iraqi jets attacking Iranian targets on Larak Island. *Middle East Journal*, Chronology, Vol. 41, no. 2 (Spring 1987), p. 269. The director of political affairs of the Iranian Foreign Ministry flew to Kuwait in March 1987 to accuse Kuwait of mistreating Muslims. Ibid., no 3 (Summer 1987), p. 429.
52 Joyce, *Kuwait 1945–1996*, p. 161.
53 Boghardt, *Kuwait amid War...*, p. 121.
54 *Middle East Journal, Chronology*, Vol. 42, no. 2 (Spring 1988), p. 293.
55 Ibid., and no 4 (Autumn 1988), p. 663.
56 Ibid., no 1 (Winter 1988), p. 98.

57 Ibid., no 2 (Spring 1988). p. 293. A further bomb, one of the last of the series, exploded in the Interior Ministry garage in April 1988. Ibid., no 3 (Summer 1988), p. 469.
58 Occasionally, Kuwaiti security services were unable to locate suspects who would then be tried *in absentia*. Habib Ghadanfari was one such fugitive who was believed to have sought sanctuary in the Iranian Embassy in Kuwait. Boghardt, *Kuwait amid War...* , p. 118. Despite their conviction that the Iranians were using their Embassy to protect key Kuwaiti assets and smuggle them out of the country, Kuwait elected not to challenge the Iranian regime for reasons of state.
59 My official vehicle had brackets on both front fenders for flags. Normally, only the American flag was flown on the right, but Henry, the Indian driver, loved to add the personal ambassadorial flag on the left fender. Whenever there was a Silkworm strike or particularly egregious bombing, however, I relented and allowed Henry to fly both flags for trips around Kuwait as a measure of personal defiance and, perhaps, reassurance that the United States would not be intimidated by Iran.
60 Iraq, and those like Kuwait that had supported its efforts to fend off the "fanatical" forces of Iran's revolutionary regime, had been ready for a ceasefire for years. I was constantly faced by Kuwaitis asking why the United States did not bring the war to an end. When I explained that the United States had acted to prevent an expansion of the conflict to nearby states and was pushing hard at the United Nations for a ceasefire resolution, they persisted. Asked what more they thought Washington could do, the answer was invariably the same: "We don't know. You are the Great Power and you must know."
61 Boghardt, *Kuwait amid War...* , p. 101. U.S. ambassador Quainton, who was in Kuwait during the 1985 polling, was satisfied that the elections were "free" and produced a legislature where there was a level of "genuine political debate" unrivaled in the Arab world. Quainton, Oral History.
62 Senior Kuwaiti officials told me on several occasions that statements and other actions by individual members of the Assembly created problems in steering a course in a hostile environment. They explained that at various times parliamentarians had complicated relations with Iraq and Iran, as well as Saudi Arabia.
63 Cited in Boghardt, *Kuwait amid War...* , p. 106. Boghardt notes the coincidence that General George Crist, Commander in Chief of U.S. Central Command, visited Kuwait several days after the As-

sembly had been suspended. I was a member of General Crist's party and know of no connection between the visit and circumstances leading to the dismissal of the Assembly. The visit, which was hosted by the commander of the Kuwaiti armed forces, not the amir, was one in a series of consultations between them. The Kuwaitis, for example, were invited to send observers to a major CENTCOM field exercise held the same year in the deserts and other areas of nine states in the western United States.

64 I was director of the State Department office responsible for Iraq until the summer of 1982. It was decided, without illusions about the Iraqi regime's nature, to test its new–found reasonableness. Saddam was known to be suspicious of Soviet flirtations with Iran and prepared to embrace Egypt, which had become a pariah in most of the Arab world for its peace treaty with Israel. The Iraqis even spoke guardedly of a negotiated solution to the Palestinian issue. Since the U.S. position supported the territorial integrity of both Iraq and Iran, it was judged worthwhile to make a few gestures to see Saddam's cards. I was transferred to another post before formal diplomatic relations with Iraq were restored.

65 Very senior Kuwaiti officials told me during the war, and *before* repayment became an issue between the two states, that Kuwait had been prepared to provide the requested funds as a gift. The Iraqis, standing on their "dignity," insisted that they be in the form of loans.

66 Twinam, "America and the Gulf Arabs, p. 144. Kuwaitis were united in believing that they had already conceded territory when the British granted lands inhabited by tribes loyal to Kuwait to Iraq at the 'Uqair conference in the 1920s (see chapter 4) and were resolved not to make further concessions.

67 Records VII, p. 418.

68 Author's personal observations.

69 One element contributing to the Kuwaiti decision was the maneuvering of the maritime union in the United States. Union leaders had maintained a very low profile during the period when the ships faced danger from Iranian attacks. As required by the U.S. Coast Guard, the master and radio operator were the only Americans on each ship and they served with distinction, in one case suffering serious injury. Once the dangers were passed, the union leadership began to try to require that more of the crews be American. KOTC was not willing to fire the crewmen of other nationalities who had served loyally through the war, but did indicate a willingness to hire some American seamen to fill its

needs. Reportedly, the union insisted instead that it would select crew members for six-month tours and rotate them among unemployed seamen. This curious alternative was not acceptable to KOTC.

70 Zatarain, *Tanker War*, p. 388.
71 In addition to scheduled appointments, an impromptu call on the vice president at his official residence on the Naval Observatory grounds was arranged. The vice president invited the crown prince to accompany him to Cincinnati for a baseball game. One member of the Kuwaiti official delegation and I accompanied the principals, who had relaxed talks on the vice president's aircraft.
72 *Middle East Journal*, Chronology, Vol. 42, no 4 (Autumn 1988), p. 663. Within several weeks, Congress adopted legislation barring the inclusion of the Mavericks.
73 Ibid. It is doubtful that this maneuver had a decisive effect on leading opponents in Congress whose position was determined by perceptions of Israel's interests.
74 Ibid., Vol. 43, no 1 (Winter 1989), pp. 92–93. Congressional modifications included extending the delivery date through 1994 instead of 1993, requiring the return of an A-4 fighter plane in the Kuwaiti inventory for each F-18 delivered; and substituting 200 Maverick-G missiles for the Maverick-Ds in the original package. The Kuwaitis had planned to get rid of their A-4s in any case and the United States undertook to help locate an approved purchaser for the mint-condition planes.
75 My wife and I had the opportunity to call on the Kuwaiti Air Force headquarters during a 1992 visit to the country. The Kuwaiti officers proudly displayed the newly arrived F-18s and we were invited to sit in the cockpit of one for photographs.
76 *Middle East Journal*, Chronology, Vol. 43, no 1 (Winter 1989), p. 93.
77 Abu Nidal lived in Iraq, where he received financial and other support from the government, from the early 1970s when he was expelled from the principal Palestinian organization, Fatah. Mainline Palestinians regarded him and his group as "mercenaries." He was assassinated in Baghdad in 2002.
78 When the internal situation in Libya deteriorated in March 2011 as a result of a popular uprising demanding that Colonel Qaddafi step down, at least one defecting official confirmed that Qadaffi had murdered the Imam Musa al-Sadr in 1978. Al-Sadr, an Iranian by birth, was the spiritual and titular leader of the large Shi'a community in Lebanon and a vocal opponent of the Ayatollah Khomeini in Iran. He "disappeared" on a visit to Libya, although

the Libyans maintained unconvincingly that he had departed by plane to Italy. During the civil strife in Lebanon during the 1970s, Al-Sadr founded the Amal militia, but kept the Shi'a strictly neutral, frequently facilitating the return of hostages. I was the Embassy Beirut liaison with the Imam's seat at Baabda, periodically meeting with his relative and chief of staff, an American. Had the Imam not disappeared at a critical juncture, the course of Shi'a politics in Lebanon would probably not have taken a turn congenial to Tehran.

79 Boghardt, *Kuwait amid War...*, p. 126.
80 Based on past experience, it is likely that additional hijackers and weapons boarded in Iran.
81 Although the terms of the agreement were not announced, there was a measure of relief when the plane was diverted to Algiers. Although the Algerians had workable relations with Iran, they had a tough, no nonsense attitude towards hijackers.
82 The Kuwaiti foreign minister had publicly denied speculation that Kuwait would release terrorists convicted two years earlier. *Middle East Journal,* Chronology, Vol. 41, no 2 (Spring 1987), p. 269. Kuwait did release two of the seventeen Lebanese Shi'a in prison (for the 1983 bombings) in February 1989, saying that their sentences of five years had been served. Ibid., Vol. 43, no 3 (Summer 1989), pp. 488–89. The remaining terrorists held by Kuwait were freed, by design or inadvertence, following the Iraq invasion of the country in 1990.
83 During this period, for example, I received an instruction to urge Kuwait to side with the United States in voting to "roll over" a loan to a major Latin American country that was not a good risk at the time. I went first to the finance minister, who responded that "Kuwait does not throw good money after bad."I then made the same case at the Foreign Ministry, stressing that this was very important to American banks that had overextended themselves. The reply ultimately received was that Kuwait would vote for the "rollover" as requested but wanted it clearly understood that it was doing so "for the United States" and not for the debtor state. Shortly thereafter, I visited the *diwanniya* hosted by the father of the finance minister. Somewhat surprisingly, the minister, who had been overruled on political grounds, was his usual cordial self.
84 Agence France Presse reported as early as February 1989 that petitions demanding reinstatement of the parliament were circulated in secret. If correct, the petitions had little effect.

85 Author's personal observation.
86 Ghabra, "Democratization in A Middle Eastern State: Kuwait, 1993," pp. 18–19, and *Middle East Journal*, Chronology, Vol. 43, no 3 (Summer 1989), p. 489. As Ghabra correctly observes, "When restrictions in Middle Eastern societies mount, much of the public debate is undertaken by non-associational groups such as the *diwanniya* or the Shi'i *husayniyya*, as well as within friendship and family networks." Idem, p. 15.
87 A distinction must be drawn between popular acceptance of the amir's decision to dissolve an Assembly that many believed had overreached itself at a time of serious danger and a permanent or long-term abandonment of the legislative experiment, which was intertwined with the country's sense of identity.
88 *Middle East Journal, Chronology*, Vol. 44, no 2 (Spring 1990), p. 300.
89 Ibid., no 3 (Summer 1990), p. 486. Boghardt (*Kuwait amid War...*, p. 140) in an exhaustive study of Kuwait's security challenges, regards the adoption of these countermeasures as the "turning point" in the confrontation, turning a political challenge into a law-enforcement problem and increasing popular sympathy for the protesters.
90 *Middle East Journal*, Chronology, Vol. 44, no 3 (Summer 1990), p. 486. The initial meeting took place on February 8, 1990. One can understand the reluctance of the government to a degree. Sessions of the National Assembly over the decades had been dominated by factions—Islamists, nationalists, etc.—who pursued their own agendas and did not distinguish themselves by their statesmanship. As an example, the one session spent much of its time and energy overturning Kuwait's tradition of coeducation at the university level. As in the United States popular government is not necessarily moderate government.
91 Ibid., no 4 (Autumn 1990), p. 692.
92 Ibid. As a general rule, those arrested were held for several days before being released without prosecution.
93 Voting was confined at that time to male citizens and it is not known how many stayed away from the polls because they opposed the Council concept.
94 Ghabra, "Democratization in A Middle Eastern State: Kuwait, 1993," p 19.
95 It was subsequently learned from informed Arab sources that Saddam astounded attendees at a February meeting of the Arab Cooperation Council (ACC) that Iraq had fought the war with Iran for the entire Arab world. The other Arabs now owed him

money, he asserted. He also reportedly also demanded that the U.S. Navy leave the Gulf. The ACC, which came to naught and which was often referred to among Gulf residents as "a beggars' league," was formed after Iraq failed to gain membership in the GCC. Saddam allegedly hinted that he would use force if the other members (Egypt, Jordan and Yemen) did not convince the Gulf emirates to pay up.

96 Regional Chiefs of Mission conferences are common in the U.S. Foreign Service. There had not, however, been a conference in the Gulf in the previous three years and for some time before.

97 Iraq frequently was a shadowy participant in attacks against Kuwaiti targets even while it was prosecuting its war with Iran. One authority, for example, believes Baghdad, probably through its instrument, Abu Nidal, was responsible for the 1981 bombings in Kuwait as well as the bombing of Kuwait's Embassy in Beirut to extort additional aid or control of Bubiyan. One of the perpetrators of the attack on a Kuwaiti diplomat in Madrid admitted to the Spanish that he was a member of the Abu Nidal gang. See Boghardt, *Kuwait amid War ...*, pp. 56 and 59.

98 In the spring of 1990 British Customs at Heathrow Airport seized a number of nuclear triggers on the way to Iraq. Consequently, Britain and the United States tightened controls on exports of "dual use" items to Iraq. In Kuwait, many citizens were surprisingly unconcerned about the Iraqi WMD programs. Not only did Baghdad's use of chemical agents against its own Kurdish citizens elicit little interest, but I met, as I occasionally did, with a political science class at Kuwait University. At the end of the discussion, several of the students referred to U.S. and British anti–proliferation policies and asked why the West was trying to deny the Arabs "modern technology"? I explained the basis for Western concerns and suggested that residents of Kuwait ought to share them. Taking the students to a balcony outside the classroom, I asked them to note the prevailing wind, which was blowing from the north. If Iraq acquired nuclear capability, I pointed out that even an accident would be a catastrophe for Kuwaitis.

99 Kuwait oil policy was predicated more on the maintenance of market share than price, although it recognized as well that high prices encouraged conservation, resort to alternative sources and technologies, and returns on its investments in industrialized economies. Whether its production decisions were wise or not given the tensions in the region, exceeding their OPEC quota was not something that bothered the United States, which opposed international cartels like OPEC.

630 Notes

100 The Iraqi National Day reception at the Sheraton Hotel in Kuwait was unusually well attended by senior Kuwaiti officials anxious not to give Saddam any offense, and by other invitees who wished to see what would transpire. Nothing untoward occurred but the tension could have been sliced with the elaborate cake. If Iraq was experiencing economic distress, there was no evidence of austerity observable at the expensive and elaborate "celebration."

101 Following his capture in 2003, Saddam admitted to his interrogators that his plan had been to drive up oil prices to pay off his debts and fund his weapons programs. Hindy, Lily (January 25, 2008), "Interrogator: Invasion surprised Saddam" (http://www.boston.com/news/world/middleeast/articles /2008/01/25/interrogator_invasion_ surprised_saddam/). *The Boston Globe* (Associated Press). http://www.boston.co

102 "Typically, participants in the same field share both production costs and revenues, using a formula that sets percentages of ownership. But Iraq refused to negotiate with Kuwait on such an agreement." Thomas C. Hayes, "Confrontation in the Gulf: The Oilfield Lying Below the Iraq-Kuwait Dispute," *New York Times*, September 3, 1990.

103 U.S intelligence on Iraqi troop movements was excellent. It was known, for example, that some logistics elements and support units needed for a large jump-off were not yet present. With the cooperation of USCENTCOM, the embassy in Kuwait arranged for a briefer to come to keep the Kuwaitis apprised of the evolving situation. What the available intelligence could not disclose was Iraqi intentions.

104 In the interest of full disclosure, I am an old friend of April Glaspie, an outstanding Arabist with a long record of service in the Middle East; she had served a tour in Kuwait in the 1960s. April had stayed with my wife and me in the spring of 1990 on a shopping trip to Kuwait and my wife and an old mutual friend (a retired Department of State geographer and his wife) had accompanied her on a recent excursion into northern (Kurdish) Iraq, which had previously been closed to embassies in Baghdad.

105 Somewhat inexplicably, this cable has never surfaced in all of the controversy surrounding U.S. policy on the eve of Iraq's invasion of Kuwait. The only public reference to the appraisal of Embassy Kuwait of which I am aware was a phone call I received in early 1991, after I had returned to the United States. The caller, Elaine Sciolino of the *New York Times*, was clearly aware of it, although it was not certain she had seen the entire text.

106 Interestingly, the Iraqi president does not seem to have ever listed Iraqi claims to Kuwaiti territory among his grievances.
107 "(T)he Kuwaitis, afraid that similar action on their part might provoke, rather than deter an Iraqi invasion, sent no requests for support to Washington." Palmer *Guardians of the Gulf*, p. 157.

15 Besieged but Not Beaten

1 The evening before, I had hosted a dinner in the Residence for unmarried embassy staff, including three summer interns who were taking time from their university studies to gain practical experience. Shortly before retiring, I was called by a senior Kuwaiti official with the news that the talks with Iraqi representatives in Saudi Arabia had failed but that negotiations would continue in Iraq. According to a subsequent reconstruction of events, LTC (then Major) Hart of USLOK recalled. "By 2300 hours 1 August 1990, the chief of USLOK, Col. John Mooneyham, began receiving telephonic reports from U.S. Westinghouse technicians manning a radar observation balloon position just north of Mutla ridge. Their reports were very pointed in that they described the radar paint as a mass armor formation resembling an iron pipe several kilometers long and rolling downhill. They were advised to cut the tether and move out smartly." See LTC Fred L. Hart, Jr., "The Iraqi Invasion of Kuwait: An Eyewitness Account," Personal Experience Monograph (PEM) prepared for the U.S. Army War College, Carlisle Barracks, Pennsylvania, n.d. available on the internet at <<http://www.sault.corn.com/~danvaught/eyewitness01.html>>, p. 8. If this timeline is accurate, the reports were not conveyed in real time to the ambassador or deputy chief of mission.
2 Joseph C. Wilson IV, The Foreign Affairs Oral History Collection of the Association for Diplomatic Studies and Training http://www.adst.org/OH%20TOCs/Wilson,%20Joseph%20C.%20IV.toc.pdf
3 After instructing the Marine at Post One to summon the DCM, the duty officer and other senior embassy officers, I returned to the Residence to dress for what promised to be a long and busy day. By the time I returned to the Chancery, it was evident that advance elements of the Iraqi army had reached the outskirts of Kuwait City; shortly thereafter a single artillery shell struck one of the tall buildings behind the Embassy compound. It was the last time I slept in the Residence.
4 Leo J. Daugherty, III, *The Marine Corps and the State Department:*

Enduring Partners in United States Foreign Policy, 1798–2007 (Jefferson, NC: McFarland & Co., 2009), p. 273.

5. John Levins, *Days of Fear: The Inside Story of the Iraqi Invasion and Occupation of Kuwait* (Dubai, UAE: Motivate Publishing, 1997), p. 52. John Levins was an Australian national who was accorded unusual ability to move about in occupied Kuwait. He was in touch with me and DCM Bodine and was very helpful to American and British nationals in hiding. His substantial book, based on a wide array of American embassy and other sources, presents an encyclopeodic account of events during that chaotic period. The occasional misinterpretations and errors that inevitably creep in to so ambitious an undertaking do little to detract from the value of his work. For example, he misreads the outside fires set to help destroy classified materials at the Embassy as the result of haste or chaos, when, in fact, they were set in chemical "burn barrels" designed for the purpose.

6. The absence of key Americans at companies and institutions also created some practical problems. The Embassy received informal permission, for example, to use the school busses belonging to the American Community School to transport Americans if it were possible to organize an evacuation to Saudi Arabia. The keys and papers for the buses, however, were locked away. Since the Iraqis had indicated that they would arrest drivers without registrations, and in one case hanged the body of a male they claimed had been caught with a "stolen" automobile from a construction crane, it was decided not to risk the lives of American citizens by operating the busses.

7. The destruction continued day and night for several days, although the most sensitive material was kept to an absolute minimum and was gone the first morning. Eventually, almost every piece of paper in the compound—Christmas and Eid card lists, guest lists, etc.—that might assist the Iraqi *mukhabarat* followed state papers into the giant disintegrators that turned paper into pulp. Based on experience with shredders during the takeover of the Tehran Embassy, the department had installed the rugged disintegrators.

8. Most of the employees were able to reach the Embassy during the morning without incident. One group, however, had to take refuge in the Japanese Embassy where the chargé, Akio Shirota, courageously gave them shelter for more than a week. When the American embassy was at last able to send cars to collect the group, the Japanese loaded about ten huge bags of rice in the trunks. Their assistance was typical of many acts of mutual cooperation

by Western embassies in the period until the end of August. The American embassy, for instance, provided the small Norwegian embassy with several cases of canned mackerel and arranged for a delivery of food to the Philippine Embassy, where hundreds of household servants had gathered without provisions.

9   Unknown to the embassy, which no longer tracked U.S.-flag vessels, the tanker *Chespeake City* slipped its moorings and sailed out of harm's way at 8:00 a.m. It was soon taken under escort by the USS *Robert G. Bradley*.

10 The amir, crown prince and other senior Kuwaitis departed for Saudi Arabia by automobile shortly before the Iraqis launched an attack on Dasman Palace to capture them. As the Iraqis attacked, remaining elements of the Amiri Guard mounted a desperate defense, joined by Shaikh Fahad Ahmad al-Sabah, a younger brother of the amir. Shaikh Fahad had a reputation as something of a maverick who had gone to Lebanon to fight with the Palestinians in the 1960s against the advice of his family. He was made head of the Kuwait Olympic Committee reportedly to confine his impulsiveness and was also elected head of the Asian Olympic Movement. See Jadranka Porter, *Under Siege in Kuwait: A Survivor's Story* (Boston: Houghton Mifflin Company, 1991), p. 18. I enjoyed Shaikh Fahad greatly and had paid a farewell call on him shortly before the invasion. At that meeting, Shaikh Fahad threw his support behind Atlanta, Georgia, to host the 1996 Olympics, assuring the success of its bid.

11 LTC Hart, "The Iraqi Invasion of Kuwait," p. 12.

12 Jadranka Porter, a British national working for a Kuwaiti English-language newspaper, wrote "I did not see a single Kuwaiti plane in the skies and neither, as far as I know, did anyone else" in a 1991 account of her experiences. See Porter, *Under Siege in Kuwait*, p. 40. This is not the only, or even the most egregious, inaccuracy in this hastily written little book.

13 LTC Hart, "The Iraqi Invasion of Kuwait," p. 9. An account of this gallant action is contained in Major Robert A. Nelson, "The Battle of the Bridges: Kuwait's 35th Brigade on the 2d of August 1990," *Armor* Magazine, September–October 1995, pp. 26–32. Colonel, later Brigadier, Srour successfully extricated his tanks and led them to Saudi Arabia, although he had to abandon much of his logistics train to save the tanks. See Darwin, *The Edge of War*, pp. 136–37.

14 I had learned to treat "eye-witness" accounts with skepticism during the civil strife in Lebanon in the late 1970s. A detailed

report would come in of the bombing of a specific building, down to the street address. When checked out later, either there had been no bombing or the target was a block away and on the other side of the street.

15 Hart, "The Iraqi Invasion of Kuwait," p. 13. This monograph is a useful document for the military aspects of the invasion but includes a number of inaccuracies, including accounts of meetings and other events of which the author had no direct personal knowledge.

16 Col. B. A. C. Duncan, "Cruelty and Compassion: An Englishman in Kuwait," *Army Quarterly and Defence Journal* (London), Vol. 121, no. 2, Gulf War Issue, 1991, p. 161.

17 Levins, *Days of Fear*, p. 64. Among other considerations was the lack of certainty regarding conditions on the route where Iraqi units were spreading out.

18 DCM Bodine, who oversaw the delivery of these items to the British refugees, also took the opportunity to borrow a Mickey Mouse costume from the hotel, which proved useful in diverting the American children on the compound.

19 Iraqi forces had overrun the ministry on their way to Dasman Palace early in the morning, but it is not clear that local commanders recognized its importance. They let the under secretary go. The minister by this time was at Khafji, Saudi Arabia, with the amir and other senior figures. Darwin, *The Edge of War*, p. xxviii.

20 During the 1980s, the United States and U.S. Central Command had been able to preposition materiel ("pre-po") for a rapid military response no closer than Oman. Kuwait and the other Gulf Arab states wanted American power "over the horizon." The sudden Iraqi seizure of Kuwait dramatized, as no amount of explanation could, how far away that horizon was. After liberation, the Kuwaiti and U.S. governments agreed to the stationing of vehicles and equipment for an armored brigade in country, thus shortening reaction time to that required to fly in brigade personnel.

21 On the second day, two Iraqi soldiers appeared at the back gate of the Embassy to offer their weapons and uniforms in exchange for food and civilian clothes so they could desert. Later the same day two more walked past sharing a single pair of boots. At the Turkish Embassy, the contingent was given several watermelons as their day's ration. They turned out to be Iraqi Turkomen and the Embassy guards gave them water. At the posh Meridian Hotel, American guests watched South Asian and Filipino workers

loot a high-end shoe store, exchanging their sandals and flip-flops for designer footwear. As they were doing so, a squad of Iraqis rushed at them causing the looters to flee. Rather than pursuing them, however, the Iraqis stopped and traded their ill-fitting boots for the discarded flip-flops.

22 Daugherty, *The Marine Corps and the State Department*, 374. Among the possible contingencies considered was the Iraqi use of such a mob to carry out an attack, for which they could deny responsibility.

23 On one especially eerie night, sounds were heard in the crawl space under the eaves of the Chancery roof. Sgt. Daniel Hudson hoisted himself into the crawl space with a flashlight and handgun. To the profound relief of all, he found only feral cats in the attic. This action was emblematic of the exemplary performance of the Embassy MSGs. I had only respect for their courage, reliability and devotion to duty. Late one afternoon, for example, a firefight broke out in the vicinity of the compound sending machine gun rounds in all directions. The Marine Guards stood to their posts; Sgt. Hudson, Sgt. Paul Rodriguez, and Cpl. Mark Royer rushed outside to scoop up children playing in the compound and to bring personnel housed in temporary buildings into the more substantial protection afforded by permanent structures.

24 The U.S. embassy had long operated an emergency network of handheld radios for the staff and had positioned transceivers at the British, Canadian, and other friendly embassies for just this kind of situation. They proved useful for checking on the well-being of the various posts but also had the potential to heighten anxiety. One evening, a routine check of the British Embassy elicited a garbled reply in very broken English. Concerned that the Iraqis had seized that embassy and were attempting to conceal the fact by faking the radio response, I asked to speak to the ambassador. The same non-British voice answered that the ambassador couldn't come to the radio because he was "tied up." It turned out that the British staff had gone to dinner or bed and left their Indian employees in charge. The British Embassy, in part because of its location closer to Dasman Palace, was unable to get adequate staff into the compound; their problems were compounded by the fact that none of the British or South Asians inside knew how to operate the telephone switchboard. Levins, *Days of Fear*, pp. 40–41.

25 Fox News Timeline, foxnews.com, August 2001. This source gives the number of Americans in Kuwait at 3,800; the embassy estimated the community, given summer absences, at 2,500. While

the embassy could not account for every American in the country, many of whom had not registered with the consular section, the only known missing were a dozen oil drillers working near the Iraqi border. For reasons that are best known to the Department of State, the department spokesman gave periodic updates that were immensely helpful to Iraqi authorities counting American noses in Kuwait. In late August, for instance, Richard Boucher, the deputy spokesman, announced that the embassy was in "contact with 1,982 of the 2,500 Americans believed to be in the country." Bill McAllister, "U.S. Resists Iraqi Deadline on Embassy," *Washington Post*, August 23, 1990, p. A1.

26 Maureen Aldakheel letter, August 22, 1990.

27 "Pawlowski family," Fox News Timeline, foxnews.com, August, 2001. Jack Rinehart, an American businessman who was to become one of the stalwarts of the besieged Embassy, was told while at a hotel that an Arab man made it to Saudi Arabia, but his wife and six children perished in the desert. Jack Rinehart, Typewritten manucript about the siege of the Embassy, 1993.

28 LTC Hart wrote in his post mortem, "In hindsight, we all know now that the border along Kuwait/Saudi remained porous until 11 August and we probably could have made it out." Hart, "The Iraqi Invasion of Kuwait," p. 10. While it is true that the Kuwaiti resistance continued to travel by desert routes with the help of local guides and specially modified vehicles, the suggestion that scores of passenger vehicles carrying hundreds of American men, women and children could "slip" through gaps in border control is too incredulous to merit further comment.

29 Prior to the invasion, Kuwaiti hospitals were well equipped with incubators, dialysis machines, operating room suites and all the paraphernalia of modern medicine. Kuwait maintained one year's supply of commonly used pharmaceuticals in its central warehouse. While there has been much debate regarding the widely circulated reports of infants taken from incubators in the first days of the invasion, what is not disputable is the massive looting that occurred during Iraq's control of the country. An American married to a Kuwaiti wrote that her father-in-law died in October 1990 because he "was unable to get his dialysis treatment since the machines had been taken from the hospitals." Maureen Aldakheel, "A Year in the Life of Maureen Aldakheel, August 1990 – Present," typewritten manuscript, 1991.

30 The local contract guard force manned gates and maintained security inside the compound. They were not armed. During the

first weeks of the Iraqi occupation, the guards continued to report to the Embassy and discharge their duties loyally. They were released shortly before the August 24 deadline for the Embassy to "close" so that they would not be caught inside. This guard force was the object of great curiosity among Kuwaitis because it consisted of Palestinians and Lebanese Shi'a. At a dinner a few weeks earlier, the host asked how could the embassy trust its security to this group. "Simple," I explained, "they have been with us for a long time, and, besides, the two groups watch one another."

31 According to LTC Hart ("The Iraqi Invasion of Kuwait," p. 24), "Small quantities of American citizens were allowed into the compound, primarily those with skills the embassy thought were needed to sustain embassy operations." Once again, his pen has outrun his personal knowledge. While the embassy was fortunate that many of those private citizens, especially those plucked from hotels before the Iraqis could round them up, possessed vital skills, the embassy had no way of knowing that beforehand. As DCM Bodine recalls, "There was never a question of accepting them, only where to put them and what sort of work to find for them." Barbara K. Bodine, "Saddam's Siege of Embassy Kuwait: A Personal Journal," in Joseph G. Sullivan, ed., *Embassies Under Siege: Personal Accounts by Diplomats on the Front Line*, An Institute for the Study of Diplomacy Book (Washington: Brasseys, 1995), p. 116.

32 Levins, *Days of Fear*, p. 121.

33 Ibid., p. 142.

34 In practice, DCM Bodine did most of the talking over the phone and radio net. She enjoyed using the phone and radio, but there was a more serious reason for the arrangement. Ms. Bodine could speak with authority, yet defer to the ambassador when faced with a question or circumstance that required consideration. This was useful in later contacts with Iraqi occupation authorities who would have expected immediate responses from the ambassador. Aside from their awareness that I was ending my tour, the Iraqis monitoring local embassy communications were probably misled by the radio traffic into concluding that I had already departed.

35 I was acutely aware that the failure to observe this elemental precaution in Beirut in 1976 meant that Ambassador Frank Meloy, Economic Counselor Bob Waring, and their driver, Zohair Mograbi had been taken from their vehicle and murdered before the embassy was aware that they had been captured.

36 In the corridor outside the Iraqi ambassador's office, I encountered

the Iraqi DCM, whom I knew from the diplomatic circuit. The Iraqi appeared genuinely shaken, explaining that he had been on the phone the night of August 1/2 trying to convince his wife and children to join him in Kuwait.

37 Levins, *Days of Fear*, pp. 171–72
38 Levins (p. 173) has a slightly different view: "A few Americans and several British families did report to the hotels, only to be told by the staff, and diplomats who had been posted there to receive them, that they were not expected." At least one non-American was nonplussed by the statements issued by the American and British embassies: "'Those who wish to go to the hotel should take their own food and one suitcase,' the announcement said. "What on earth did they mean by 'those who wish',″ I was shouting. I was furious. 'It is not what I wish. The question is, what is the safest thing to do? I want them to tell me what's *safe* for me to do!" Porter *Under Siege in Kuwait*, p. 68. Fortunately, the larger expatriate community was more perceptive.
39 Bodine, "Saddam's Siege of Embassy Kuwait," p. 120.
40 Jack Rinehart, typewritten manuscript, 1993. Rinehart had earlier called the embassy from his hotel, earning a scolding from the frazzled consul for not registering on arrival, as he humorously recalled: "'That's why we ask that you people register,' she said. 'How are we supposed to know who or where you are? Is there anyone else there with you that has not registered?' I told her about Ed. She calmed down and told me to stay in the hotel and keep a low profile until the military activity calmed down.... Later, the woman (Gale Rogers) came to be a very dear friend of mine and later, I found myself at the Embassy, answering the same questions with basically the same answer." According to John Levins, "The British embassy in Kuwait did not clear their nationals out of hotels before the Iraqis sealed them off. Those Britons who got out of the hotels in time did so on their own initiative." Levins, *Days of Fear*, p. 218.
41 "When the Iraqis announced the formation of an interim government, they said it was made up of Kuwaitis but conspicuously did not name them, and when the government was eventually named, nobody had ever heard of its members. Later I learnt that the Iraqis did try to recruit some prominent Kuwaitis among those who had stayed behind and those who were overseas, but were given short shrift. So they rounded up any Kuwaitis they could find to give the new government some semblance of credibility. They managed to find a Kuwaiti accountant with an Iraqi

mother and appointed him head of government. ... They were not recognised by the vast mass of Kuwaitis, who laughed at such inept tactics." Porter, *Under Siege in Kuwait*, p. 29. I am unaware of any case in which Kuwaiti citizens voluntarily cooperated with the Iraqi occupation. Boghardt, who conducted vigorous research in Kuwaiti security and demographic records after liberation, reached the same conclusion. Boghardt, *Kuwait amid War...* , p. 150. Shafeeq Ghabra provides a different perspective: "Six young men were appointed ministers, most of them lieutenants in the Kuwaiti navy; the new prime minister had the rank of captain. We learned that most of them had been taken prisoner during combat and forced to play these roles.... Since then, nothing has been heard of these young men." Shafeeq Ghabra, "The Iraqi Occupation of Kuwait: An Eyewitness Account," *Journal of Palestine Studies*, XX, No. 2, Winter 1991, p 115.

42 "Iraq warned the United States and more than two dozen other nations Thursday that if they challenged a deadline today and tried to keep their embassies in Iraq-occupied Kuwait open, as they have vowed to do, Baghdad would take it as an 'act of aggression'" (Andrew Rosenthal, "Baghdad Warns Diplomats Against 'Act of Aggression'," *New York Times*, August 24, 1990, p. A1).

43 "Because we do not know what instructions these guards have, American citizens should communicate with the embassy by phone, and should not, repeat should not, attempt to go to the embassy compound." Don and Dan Phillips, "U.S. Warns Americans in Kuwait to Stay Away from Embassy," *Washington Post*, August 26, 1990, p. A23.

44 The presence of foreign embassies in Kuwait was a continuing rebuke to and rejection of Iraq's pretension of annexing Kuwait. A further consideration in Baghdad undoubtedly was the ability for foreign diplomats to witness and report on the Iraqi rape of the country. Inside the Embassy, there was no interest in knowing the identity of individuals in the Kuwaiti resistance. Prudence and tradecraft dictated that the less Embassy personnel knew, the less they could reveal should they fall into Iraqi hands. Nevertheless, it was useful to have an ability to contact these elements from time to time. I discretely arranged a limited number of such blind contacts and basic passwords for this purpose.

45 As much as I would have preferred being elsewhere, I knew I could not leave and was worried that Washington might attempt to order me to join the evacuees, as it sometimes did in dangerous situations. Where this occurs, the withdrawal of the chief of

mission is based not on solicitute for the ambassador's person but on his or her symbolism as the personal representative of the president.

46 Several of the Marine Security Guards, who had proven so reliable and professional throughout the ordeal, came to me after the list was announced and asked to be allowed to stay. They were disappointed but accepted the final decision with characteristic discipline.

47 DCM Bodine, a key part of the new "team," described the criteria and deliberations in some detail at Bodine, "Saddam's Siege of Embassy Kuwait," pp. 118–19. Every person on the list was contacted individually and given an opportunity to opt out. To a man or woman, they expressed a willingness to remain.

48 "There is no guarantee that twelve to fifteen could have managed; it was certain that eight could not, whoever they were and whatever their mix of talents. By dictating this unrealistic number, the Department of State set up the embassy for failure.," Ibid., p. 119.

49 No satisfactory explanation for this sequence of events was ever received, even after the hardcore returned to the United States in December 1990. One Washington veteran speculated that the Department felt those who remained in the Embassy would be written off. By the peculiar calculus of Washington, D.C., media reportage would be less damaging if the loss of eight diplomats was announced rather than a group in double figures.

50 In Washington, "the impression ... Thursday night was that the United States and other countries believed that diplomats in Kuwait could only hold out for a matter of days under such circumstances." Andrew Rosenthal, "Threat in Kuwait: Barring Iraqi Violence, U.S. Fight for Mission Is Seen as Unlikely," *New York Times*, August 24, 1990, p. A1.

51 A meeting of Western chiefs of mission at a European embassy confirmed that almost all planned to defy the Iraqi edict by keeping staff in Kuwait. To their credit, many did make a valiant effort to remain, most with fewer personnel and resources than the Americans. One by one over the succeeding months, they were compelled to give up and leave the country. With one possible exception, the "cookie pushers" of Kuwait acquitted themselves with courage and distinction. One European diplomat was widely rumored to have trashed his chancery to simulate a mob attack and provide a pretext for withdrawing. In 1992, HH the amir decorated the chiefs of mission who had outlasted the Iraqis—Bahrain, the United Kingdom, and the United States.

52 At the Embassy, the satellite dish still received CNN and the Armed Forces Network and carried such "staged" local support for the Iraqi occupation. These manifestations were almost humorous to knowledgeable observers. While the "demonstrators" had been outfitted with Kuwaiti *dishdashas* and *gutras* [headresses], they wore them with none of the grace and elan of Kuwaiti men. The Embassy lost its satellite connection once electricity was cut and the dish no longer could track the satellite.

53 See Levins, *Days of Fear*, p. 53. FSO Skodon would not, in any case, have been a candidate for the "hard core" staying behind because of his young children.

54 Wilson, Oral History. The bedraggled convoy took more than a day to reach Baghdad, arriving at 3 a.m. the following morning, twelve hours after it was expected.

55 Natasha Downs, "Diary of a Hostage: Escaping to Freedom," *McCall's*, May 1991, p. 42. Ms. Downs, the wife of an embassy officer, was one of the evacuees. Each of the approximately thirty vehicles was marked with black tape, particularly on the roofs so that they could be tracked by satellite or identified by U.S. aircraft if necessary.

56 One of the most heart-wrenching aspects of the convoy was the "adoption" by embassy staff of two children of private Americans. These young people were documented as embassy dependents and traveled with their "new" families. Both arrived safely in the United States and were reunited with relatives there, but the scene of their farewell that August morning brought a tear to the most hardened eye. Whatever their individual emotions, everyone pitched in to prepare and load the convoy or dash off letters that would hopefully get through. Rinehart, typewritten manuscript.

57 The decision to provide for family pets, which is not always true of State Department evacuations, was a natural one for me; I had seen the anguish of evacuees at other posts forced to abandon part of their family. My Doberman, Jinn Roumi, was among them in the spacious wooden Lufthansa case that had been acquired years before to evacuate his mother from Beirut and Athens. He was a veteran of service in Algiers and frequently romped the compound in the evenings. His nose was cool as I said goodbye to him and Michael Capps, a summer intern from the University of Virginia, who had agreed to take care of him. The past weeks had been hard on Jinn without attention from his "family," and Michael took with him a handwritten note to Marge Howell explain-

ing that he would need special care. Jinn did not make it to the United States, or even Baghdad. On the way, the eleven-year-old veteran died in the crate in which he had been whelped. Word was passed to Kuwait from the embassy in Baghdad that an Iraqi employee, a Kurd, whom I knew well from visits there, had buried Jinn at a beautiful spot on the riverbank.

58 Once the Iraqi escort left, believing the embassy had given up the idea of sending the convoy that day, there was every reason *not* to call it back. The convoy would roll with the ambassador's official car leading as far as Abdali, the immigration post on the Kuwaiti side of the frontier. There was no way of knowing how much the Iraqi troops at the border knew of the arrangements. There was a better than even chance, given the level of efficiency observed during the occupation, that they would not be aware of the arbitrary fifty-person limit.

59 Downs, "Diary of a Hostage," p. 43. Each vehicle in the line was stocked with food, water, radio, and tools, and contained spare seats to pick up occupants of any car that broke down. Families were grouped together. The Embassy's five-ton stake truck, loaded with additional supplies and equipment for the travellers and Embassy Baghdad, was included to keep it out of Iraqi hands.

60 The "drag" car was assigned to bring up the rear of the convoy to deal with stragglers, breakdowns and other problems that might arise.

61 Downs,"Diary of a Hostage," p. 44.

62 Odessa Higgins received excellent care from Kuwaiti and other expatriate physicians and staff at the hospital. Bobby, although not seriously hurt, was admitted to the hospital for protection to hide his American nationality, reportedly heavily swathed in superfluous bandages. A Nordic colleague who was not under threat of detention agreed to check on them until a way could be figured to bring them to the Embassy or get them out of Kuwait safely.

63 Ron Webster, "The Innocent Period (An Innocent Abroad?)," typewritten and annotated manuscript incorporating notes kept by an American businessman during the Iraqi siege of the American Embassy in Kuwait, 199?, pp. 42–43

64 Daugherty, *The Marine Corps and the State Department*, p. 274. See also Levins, *Days of Fear*, pp. 149–50.

65 Odessa and Bobby were kept out of Iraqi hands and eventually flew to the United States, where she largely recovered. They returned to Kuwait following liberation. "Odessa and Bobby Hig-

gins are back. Odessa looks great! She has a slight limp, but otherwise, you wouldn't be able to tell that she had been (sic) such a horrible ordeal." Maureen Aldakheel, letter of December 2, 1991.

66 In retrospect, there have been unverified claims that individuals within the vast U.S. intelligence network forecast the move. The Iraqi forces near Kuwait were under close observation, seeking indicators their intent was more than intimidation. According to one study (Palmer, *Guardians of the Gulf*, pp. 158–59), the Central Intelligence Agency, the Joint Chiefs of concluded in the days immediately before August 2 that an Iraqi military action was imminent. The study concludes, however, that "no one in a position of responsibility in the United States seems to have considered the possibility that Saddam might attempt to overrun all of Kuwait." The problem was, however, that the cumbersome intelligence apparatus continued to supply the field with raw intelligence rather than an authoritative warning. A National Security Council (NSC) document, dated July 27, 1990 and subsequently declassified, captures the moment. It summarized the proceedings of the "Deputies Committee" meeting chaired by the deputy secretary of state that day: "Saddam apparently has increased his military force strength by one division along the border. He (and his people) are extremely bitter toward Kuwait, primarily because economically he is on the ropes. Analysts believe that a shallow incursion into the northen oilfields, Rumaylah, cannot be ruled out, while drastic military action is also possible if less likely.... There was a disjointed discussion on contingency planning. We need to talk Monday about where we are heading." By Monday, August 6, Kuwait would be up to its neck in Iraqi troops.

67 Almost a year later, after Kuwait's liberation, Acting Secretary of State Lawrence Eagleburger characterized the reversal of the Iraqi land grab as follows: "The fact of the matter is that the high water mark of the Iraqi expansion was reached on August 2. On that day, the flood tide reached as far as the gates of the American Embassy in Kuwait, and there it stopped... had they faltered, had they shown weakness to the Iraqis in their midst, President Bush's message of defiance and determination would have been attenuated at the very point of delivery." Transcript, June 7, 1991.

68 Fox News Timeline, foxnews.com, August 2001.

69 "By 4 August, the Resistance had started taking down street signs and house numbers to further confuse the Iraqi special units that were canvassing neighborhoods for westerners, high-ranking Kuwaiti officials, and military officers. The Kuwaiti resistance groups

were first organized by groups of Shiite Kuwaitis. Since these Shiites already had a somewhat underground bond and the Iraqis had inadvertently freed the leading Shiite radicals from Kuwaiti prisons, they naturally banded together and immediately began resisting...." "The Iraqi Invasion of Kuwait," p. 14.
70 A copy of this handwritten document is in my possession..
71 Hart, "The Iraqi Invasion of Kuwait," p. 19.
72 Among other things, senior officers discovered that the NCO responsible for administration "had failed to destroy and shred all the USLOK classified files." Ibid., p. 19. At about the same time LCRD Michael S. Schwartz and other military personnel, who went out to gather tactical "intelligence" for a battle that would not be fought for another six months, further compromised the Embassy radio network. Approached by Iraqis troops on one of their excursions, they threw the Embassy radio they had taken with them away.
73 My conversations with KFAS officials, 1992. The Iraqis systematically stripped Kuwaiti institutions, including the university and schools, of computers, office machinery, lab equipment, and other items of value. Thereafter, the process seemed to break down as complete laboratories were split up and parts sent to different universities in Iraq. By the Embassy, open semi-trucks passed on the way north with computer monitors, but the computers themselves were nowhere in sight. Whether they were ever able to marry up the parts of their loot is problematic.
74 Darwin, *The Edge of War*, p. 197.
75 A reliable British observer reports that he was told that "120 soldiers refused to start their tanks when told that Kuwait was the objective. Apparently they were lined up and executed on the Start Line as a brutal lesson to anyone else who chose to question the Orders." Ibid., p. 163.
76 For a discussion of Resistance work in the petroleum sector, see ibid., pp. 189–210.
77 Jacqueline S. Ismael, *Kuwait: Dependency and Class in a Rentier State* (Gainesville: University Press of Florida, 1993), p. 171, for example, maintains that "the real victims of Kuwait's occupation were the expatriate workers. The invasion had transformed them into either pauperized refugees of war or terrorized prisoners of occupation." A page later she decries "propaganda campaigns" in the West that, in her distant view, dramatized and magnified "Kuwaiti suffering and Iraqi brutality." There is no question that expatriates, in many cases, paid a heavy price

for Iraq's aggression—South Asians, Filipinos, Sri Lankans, and Palestinians. It is less clear that Ms. Ismael would include British, American, and Commonwealth nationals, including her fellow Canadians, in that number. Nevertheless, the actions of the Iraqi authorities during the occupation, and especially toward Kuwaitis, need no exaggeration to provoke revulsion.

78 Claudia Farkas Al-Rashoud, *Kuwait: Before and After the Storm* (Kuwait: The Kuwait Bookshops, 1992), p. 192. Mr. Qabazard was a member of the Kuwaiti Shi'a community and, according to an elderly eye-witness, bore the marks of torture during his detention— burns, shock treatment and beatings; his fingernails had been pulled out and holes drilled through his hands. Ms. Al-Rashoud is a photojournalist from California who has lived and worked in Kuwait since 1979. She and her two sons were evacuated in September 1990 on one of 13 flights the American embassy was able to arrange.

79 "During the third week of the occupation, the Iraqis unleashed a brutal offensive against Kuwaiti society. Special forces were brought into the city which took over all the checkpoints from the army. At the same time, the secret service and similar groups took over schools as headquarters. The policy of mass arrests, seizing young Kuwaitis at checkpoints, was intensified, and torture was practiced on a wide scale." Ghabra, "The Iraqi Occupation of Kuwait: An Eyewitness Account," p 118. Dr. Ghabra's wife and two American-born daughters departed on one of the embassy evacuation flights in September.

80 Kuwait Danish Dairy was operated by its managing director, Ezzat Mohammed Jaafar, who astute readers may recall, was frequently identified by the British as a "troublemaker" beginning in the 1930s. During the occupation, the seventy-year-old historic figure was arrested with his son and accused of being in contact with the amir and of helping finance the Resistance. They were held in Basra and Baghdad and badly tortured. On March 28, 1991, after having been told that they would be executed, Ezzat and Mohammed were unexpectedly released. Levins, *Days of Fear*, p. 561.

81 It was never possible to gather everyone at one time. At least two lookouts, who provided our only warning should the Iraqis decide to move against the Embassy, were constantly at the two armored gatehouses, designated "Falcon 1" and "Falcon 2" on the internal radio network.

82 Rinehart, typewritten manuscript. Elsewhere Rinehart recounts

the following vignette: "I overheard Ambassador Howell say, 'Who the hell does he (Saddam Hussein) think he is? We'll close the Embassy when we feel it is appropriate, not when he tells us to.'" The admonition not to resist an Iraqi incursion was related to the change in the rules of engagement that upset the Marine Guards earlier. The Marines always have the option on employing deadly force when they feel personally threatened. By August 8, two factors had changed. First, the Iraqis had consolidated their control around the Embassy to such an extent that any penetration was impossible without the active involvement of the Iraqi Army. Second, destruction of sensitive documents and communications gear had reduced the time needed to eliminate *all* remaining critical equipment to several minutes. Failsafe codes had been worked out with communicators inside the vault to signal the final irrevocable destruction. There was no point in sacrificing the MSGs or anyone else in a vain attempt to prevent the inevitable.

16 The Valley of the Shadow

1. See Roberta Culbertson and W. Nathaniel Howell, *Siege: Crisis Leadership: The Survival of U.S. Embassy Kuwait* (Charlottesville, VA: Virginia Foundation for the Humanities and Public Policy, 2001).
2. The Embassy's emergency generator was in the process of being replaced by a rebuilt generator when the Iraqi invasion occurred on August 2. The replacement had arrived but had not yet been moved across the compound. I ordered that work on the transfer be halted and the original generator restored to operation in case it was needed immediately.
3. Webster was in Kuwait to consult with the Environmental Protection Council (EPC) when the Iraqis attacked. Sadly, Ron passed away in Atlanta in June 2011, as this work was nearing completion. His skill and generosity, as well as an irrepressible sense of humor and a Texan's appetite for hot sauce, are greatly missed by those who had the privilege of serving with him.
4. Rinehart, typewritten manuscript (hereafter typescript).
5. Ibid.
6. Webster, "The Innocent Period," p. 45. The individual from the water company who accompanied the Iraqis to show them the water line was an Arab in western clothing, widely assumed to be a Palestinian. Inadvertently or by design, he closed the main pipe but left an older, smaller, line open for several days.

7   Wayne Logsdon and his wife, Mimi, arrived in Kuwait just days before the Iraqi invasion. Despite their rude introduction to Kuwait, Wayne performed heroically and both readily agreed to remain as part of the eight-person Foreign Service contingent. Mimi served as the executive assistant, preparing cables, flight manifests, and messages to and from citizens caught in Kuwait. In addition, she served as an unofficial morale officer, spearheading the Thanksgiving celebration, for example, when several inhabitants expressed ambivalence.
8   Rinehart, typescript, pp. 113–14.
9   Webster, "The Innocent Period," pp. 39–41. On his arrival at the Embassy, Webster was greeted by a daunting sight: "The Embassy was filled beyond its capacity with a large number of families, complete with pets.... It became clear why we had not been previously summoned.... Food was prepared in three different locations... ," p. 35. The overcrowding was eased by the departure of the convoy on August 23, but nearly one hundred persons, including women and some children, remained.
10 The Embassy was popularly known as "Kamp Kuwait" during the siege.
11 Webster, "The Innocent Period,," p. 67.
12 "In performing assigned tasks tools became too hot to hold if left lying on any exposed surface. In one instance, the wheels of a cart carrying water drums 'disappeared' into the asphalt..." Ibid., p. 45.
13 As the siege dragged on, communications were reduced to a three-hour period every three days to conserve generator fuel. It was not practical to reduce the frequency further because the batteries on the generator needed recharging. Elaborate calculations were constantly made to estimate when the fuel would be exhausted; the Residence dining room walls were eventually papered with graphs recording estimated fuel consumption and longevity.
14 The Task Force located in the Department of State Operations Center was directed by a succession of outstanding officers, many of whom were old friends and former comrades-in-arms of mine in earlier Middle East crises. When Ambassador-designate Edward "Skip" Gnehm left to liaise with the Kuwaiti government-in-exile, he was replaced by Ambassador David Ransom, a classmate at the National War College, and, later, by Ambassador Ryan Crocker. Eventually, Mary Ryan, an expert in consular affairs, became the embassy's principal interlocutor.
15 Levins, *Days of Fear*, p. 521.

16 Ibid. Margie Saunders Howell was subsequently awarded the Pamela Harriman Award by the American Foreign Service Association (AFSA), given annually to the ambassadorial spouse who has rendered exceptional service to the American community in their country of assignment.

17 One individual who held such suspicions was Ron Webster: "The movie scene was, in theory, a democratic process.... several of us suspected influence in the final tabulation, although it might have been merely the effects of an effective 'Ambassador lobby' that seemed to sway many voters. A theme was generally selected (westerns, musicals, 'oldies', Clint Eastwood, etc.) and many of us expressed apprehension upon the news of Mary Martin's death, as knowing the Ambassador's affinity for musicals and Mary Martin, that a 'Mary Martin night' might ensue." Webster, "The Innocent Period," p.47. Even the selection one evening of *Teenage Mutant Ninja Turtles* was not enough to shake the concern re undue ambassadorial influence.

18 Jesse Jackson was not a stranger to Kuwait. He had visited with his wife Jackie during Thanksgiving 1987. On that visit he attended and participated in the Thanksgiving Service at the Evangelical Church, where the American ambassador traditionally reads the President's Thanksgiving Day Proclamation.

19 John Levins (*Days of Fear, p. 462*) identifies this individual as Dr. Saadoun Joubaydi, Saddam Hussein's personal interpreter.

20 "The Iraqis have up to now denied visits to the American Embassy. But they made an exception today (Aug 31). After hours of negotiations with Iraqi officials, Mr. Jackson was permitted to talk to Ms. Badine [sic] and Ambassador W. Nathaniel Howell across a locked gate. Mr. Jackson was accompanied by this reporter.... The diplomats said that 11 Americans in Kuwait outside the compound needed medical treatment and asked that an evacuation flight be arranged." Joseph B. Treaster, "Life in Emptied Kuwait City: Diplomats Long for Comforts, *New York Times*, September 1, 1990. p. 1.

21 Sadly, he died in New York City in the late 1990s, presumably of the disease.

22 Rinehart, typescript. A photo later widely published showed me with an intense expression during the prayer. The source of the rhapsodic look was agony, not piety.

23 See, for example, Webster, "The Innocent Period,," p. 51.

24 Levins, *Days of Fear*, p. 253. He argues that an Iraqi decision had been announced but not tested. If his hypothesis is correct, Sad-

dam's decision had not been confirmed to the embassy by the Department of State. "His party was mainly from the US Embassy compound, Odessa Higgins with her dislocated hip from the American 'Convoy to Hell', Mr. Higgins, and Mrs. (Furiel) Allen. The reasons are still unclear."

25 Webster, "The Innocent Period," p. 52
26 The drama associated with the departure of this first tranche of Americans was also watched with intense interest by citizens who had chosen to hide in private residences throughout Kuwait. Unlike the Embassy, which lost its satellite connection when electricity was cut and the dish could no longer track the satellite, many of these Americans had access to international media. A journal kept by one such individual noted the successful rescue of this first group and the words of Mrs. Colwell from Washington: "Our hearts are left in Kuwait and Baghdad with all our husbands, members of our family, our private American citizens and members of the international community left behind." Roberta and John Hogan, *Trapped in Kuwait: Countdown to Armageddon*, With Linda D. Meyer (Lynnwood, Washington: Chas. Franklin Press, 1991), p. 44.
27 Philip Shenon, "For Freed U.S. Families, a Tearful Homecoming," *New York Times*, August 29, 1990, p. A16.
28 Webster, "The Innocent Period," p. 52.
29 "The Americans were particularly conscious of the security risk. They never, ever discussed over the phone the number of people in their compound, their roles, the names of their nationals in hiding, or their reserves of food or fuel. Later in the occupation, when the free nationals servicing men in hiding needed a list of Americans in Kuwait to ensure they were all covered if the diplomats were forced to leave, the US diplomats would not fax it out to us. Instead, it was encrypted, transmitted by satellite to their embassy in Baghdad, and brought back to Kuwait by Eoin MacDoughal. The British, however, were more open. This made things easier for those who needed help and for those helping them, but caused constant concern that security had been breached. It was a never-ending tradeoff between pragmatism and security." Levins, *Days of Fear*, p. 323.
30 Jack Kelley, "Ex-hostage: Our People are Starving," *USA Today*, September 4, 1990, p. 2A. Ed Johnson (62), another evacuee reinforced the dire picture of conditions in the Embassy and confirmed that Odessa Higgins had arrived at Dulles International Airport. Edwin Chen, "Hostages Return, Tell of Ordeal at Embassy," *Los Angeles Times*, September 3, 1990, p. A1.

31 Drinking water was never drawn from the swimming pool, although experiments were conducted, using sheets of clear plastic, to distill water. It was a slow and laborious process and was never needed. The pool served an equally essential purpose in providing relief from the grinding heat and humidity. "A chemical engineer 'adopted' the pool and all agreed the quality of the pool water rose significantly." Webster, "The Innocent Period," p. 46. The evaporation rate was calculated at two inches per day during the hottest period.

32 The true condition within the Embassy and what could be relayed to families of hostages were a routine topic in my occasional talks with my wife.

33 Before August 24, U.S. consular officers were able to travel cautiously to keep in touch with Americans outside. In the first days of the crisis, a hapless member of the Task Force contacted me to inform me that a citizen had phoned his congressman to say that he was unable to leave his residence. When his location was established, I informed the staffer that a consul had passed the location several times that day. Given his other concerns, I then asked that the Task Force forget the "Congressional Interest" tag for the duration of the crisis. "We will do everything in our capacity to help all American citizens," he continued, "but the intervention of some congressman will not buy any preference."

34 Webster, "The Innocent Period," p. 64.

35 Bodine, "Saddam's Siege of Embassy Kuwait," p. 170, note 9. These unlisted numbers did not pass through the Embassy switchboard, thereby confounding Iraqi ability to isolate and disconnect them. According to Levins (*Days of Fear*, p. 328), Benny Mitchell had "no previous training in phone systems, and had to teach himself as he went along." In addition, he was working without wiring diagrams.

36 Porter, *Under Siege in Kuwait*, p. 132. At another point, Ms. Porter writes: "Ski called Bill Van Rye, an American banker who took it upon himself to keep US citizens in touch with each other and their embassy." Porter, idem, p. 61. She appears completely unaware that Mr. Van Rye was an embassy warden!

37 Rinehart, typescript. The newly minted citizen-consuls sometimes went beyond strict procedures. As Rinehart recalls, "When they asked my opinion, I always made it clear that the Embassy was not to compel individual decisions or advise one way or the other. However, I usually added, 'Fortunately, I am not an Embassy official so I can say what I want. Pack your bags and get the

hell out of here. This is a war zone! If not for you, at least get your kids to safety.'"
38 Ibid.
39 Webster, "The Innocent Period," p. 69.
40 Ibid., p. 73. El-Miloudi Hamid provided essential Arabic capability when callers did not speak English. A patient and good-natured man, he developed a telephone relationship with an elderly Egyptian lady who knew she was not eligible for evacuation but called regularly, often in the wee hours of the morning, to chat. Whenever I visited Post 1 on my nightly rounds, Hamid often could be heard talking with "Ya Mamma" ("Oh, Mama"), who was simply lonely. Regrettably, Hamid passed away in August of 2014.
41 The failure to receive an expected message was a severe disappointment to individuals under great stress and often resulted in angry accusations that "someone" had failed to deliver the message. This was seldom, if ever, the case.
42 Historically, the BBC operated to inform and serve British communities throughout the British Empire. VOA from its inception was seen primarily as a news source for non-Americans and had no tradition of catering to American expatriates.
43 "Some callers provided local news which we could not obtain from our vantage points, such as periodic sweeps of Iraqi forces through neighborhoods. Sometimes our contacts would disappear only to be 'found' again later at a hotel awaiting transport to Baghdad." Webster, "The Innocent Period," p. 71.
44 Rinehart, loc. cit. Ironically, Jadankra Porter, who characterized the American Embassy as being out of touch and uninvolved, acknowledged at another point in her narrative that the Embassy had organized a "network of helpers" to assist trapped expatriates. See Porter, *Under Siege in Kuwait*, p. 108. It was only after Kuwait's liberation that the true identities of all those in the network were known. Levins confirmed in his interviews during and after the Iraqi occupation, the extent of the Embassy's hand in supporting trapped nationals. "Whereas the US Embassy arranged for medicine and food for those in dire need, or refuge for those with nowhere to go, it was the British wardens or free nationals helping them who did this for their people." Levins, *Days of Fear*, p. 339.
45 Michael Kano, "Hiding from Saddam: An American in Occupied Kuwait," manuscript, 1998, pp. 41–42.
46 "There had been little the Embassy staff could do other than

organize lists and offer moral support, but they had done their best. Throughout the occupation they had kept in touch regularly. They checked on our mental and physical states and sent messages to our families confirming they had been in touch with us." Ibid., p. 55.

47 He was subsequently identified as Norrie Atack, a Scotsman who died on 30 September of a perforated ulcer. "He had been living alone in the flat of the local Mercedes-Benz General Manager, Uwe Danzer, and consuming large quantities of home-made wine to ease himself through the crisis. He had actually called another Scotsman the night before his death to say he was coughing up blood. Tragically, the US embassy ... were making arrangements with a girl from the Kuwaiti Resistance to move him in with some other people who were prepared to care for him. Levins, *Days of Fear*, p. 346. The degree and speed of networking among various communities under Iraqi noses was one of the remarkable elements of the grave crisis.

48 Darwin, *The Edge of War*, p. 242. Saddam had previously tried to use the media to bolster his image with disastrous results when he was televised with a young British hostage, "Stewart," attempting to play the benevolent father figure. His perfomance proved the old saw that the only thing scarier than an Iraqi Baathist behaving normally was one attempting to be "nice."

49 Iraq was already subject to sanctions under United Nations Security Council resolutions, and the lease was technically a violation of those sanctions. Under the circumstances, there was no objection to the lease for humanitarian reasons. Still, the arrangement meant that the evacuees would be under effective Iraqi control until they reached Europe. In light of Iraq's record of reneging on its word, this was a troublesome development.

50 Webster, "The Innocent Period," p. 69.

51 Rinehart, typescript.

52 Getting to the Safeway parking lot created difficulties under the circumstances for many of the expatriate evacuees and the embassy provided assistance whenever it was able. Rita M. Hug, a library consultant at Kuwait University, later remembers: "I was reluctant to ask any of my Arab friends for a ride to the airport (September 6). So, the Embassy put me in touch with a Lebanese man who had volunteered to help and agreed to drive me, scoffing at the notion of possible danger as only someone who has lived much of his life in Beirut can! A friend from my apartment building gathered my things together as I dictated over the phone

and packed them for me, and another friend retrieved the suitcases and brought them to me..." Richard P. Stevens, ed., *The Iraqi Invasion of Kuwait: American Reflections* (Washington: International Education and Communications Group, 1993). pp. 14–15.

53 The evacuees on the September 7 flight spent "a tense nine-hour wait in the Kuwait airport" before they were allowed to board (ibid).

54 Aldakheel, "A Year in the Life of Maureen Aldakheel, August 1990 – Present.." Abdul Lateef Aldakheel, who met Maureen during his engineering studies in St. Louis, recently retired as chief highway engineer in the Ministry of Public Works.

55 "The Americans took out any other Westerners who wanted to go. With the exception of one special flight for the French, ... all other evacuations of Western women and children, regardless of nationality, were run by the Americans. There were twelve such flights prior to the release of their men in December: 10 in September, and one each in October and November. They became known as 'Air Rogers' flights after the US Consul in Kuwait, Mrs. Gale Rogers, who coordinated the Kuwait end of them." Levins, *Days of Fear*, p. 271.

56 A continuing issue during the stopover in Baghdad was the inclusion of dual national minors with their American mothers on the aircraft. The Iraqis initially took the position that these children were Kuwaitis ("Iraqis" in Baghdad's delusion) and, thus, not free to leave the country. This controversy caused delays but it is a tribute to the insistence, ingenuity, and dedication of personnel from Embassy Baghdad that it never halted the flow. A postcrisis accounting of the airlift credits it with the safe evacuation of more than 2,000 American women and children and related non-American family as well as nationals of some 30 other nations. Levins, *Days of Fear*, p. 271.

57 Claudia Farkas Al-Rashoud, *Dame Violet Dickson: "Umm Saud's" Fascinating Life in Kuwait*, Updated Second Edition (Kuwait: n.p., 2007), pp. 59–60.

58 Levins, *Days of Fear*.

59 "Hooky" Walker was himself something of a legend in the Gulf region. In diplomatic career that spanned the period 1956 to 1992, he had served as British Ambassador to Bahrain, the United Arab Emirates, Ethiopia, and Iraq. Both he and Dame Violet had certainly seen better times there.

60 Al-Rashoud, *Dame Violet Dickson*, p. 60.

61 Darwin, *The Edge of War*, pp. 290–91.

62 The anecdotal information received by the embassy was occasionally amusing. On August 24, some twenty-five embassies in Kuwait refused to obey the Iraqi order to close. See Clifford Krauss, "Only 4 Embassies Hold Out in Kuwait as Food Dwindles," *New York Times*, October 12, 1990. p.A13. Shortly thereafter, a diplomat in the Canadian Embassy heard small stones rattling against a second-floor window of their Embassy. When he looked out, he saw a small Kuwaiti boy in a *dishdasha* holding a tray of Hardee's hamburgers. After he had thrown the hamburgers up to the Canadian, the lad waved and scampered away before he was seen by an Iraqi patrol. The Canadian Embassy was forced to close about October 20. The Canadian chargé, William Bowden, was a steady and reliable colleague during troubled times, always ready to provide any assistance he could.

63 "The National Evangelical Church was badly affected (by the occupation), with one of its American pastors on leave outside Kuwait at the time of the invasion, another holed up in the US Embassy, and the Arab pastor too scared to come to the compound. It was kept going only by a few dedicated lay members," Levins, *Days of Fear*, p. 292.

64 Porter, *Under Siege in Kuwait*, p. 39.

65 Darwin, *The Edge of War*, p. 77. The Kaifan cell "specialized in gathering intelligence, direct action and transporting equipment and sensitive material."

66 "Allahu Akbar" has unfortunately been conflated in many minds with Muslim terrorism in recent years, but it is used by all Muslims as an expression of faith in God. Ululation has been described as a "long, wavering, high-pitched sound resembling the howl of a dog or wolf with a trilling quality." Anyone who has seen the scene from *Lawrence of Arabia* where the forces of the Arab Revolt set off for the attack on the Ottoman-held town of Aqaba will recall its eerie power.

67 The mass demonstration appears to have been inspired by Thuraya al-Baqsami, Kuwaiti artist and writer, and her husband Muhammad al-Qudeeri. Together, they published a clandestine broadside, called *Al-Smoud al-Shaabi* (The People's Steadfastness) on their computer, often urging civil disobedience and public demonstrations. The issue of August 27, 1990, called for unified action on September 2. Darwin, *The Edge of War*, pp. 167–68. Following liberation, Thuraya published a small book of sensitive and poignant poetry about the occupation experience entitled *Cellar Candles*. Another observer offers a dramatic account of the

event and its implications. "Word of this passed through whispers in co-operatives, mosques and *diwaniyas*. ... Just before midnight it all began. A sweep of a torch beam from a rooftop and a lone voice calling ... shredding the night silence to be followed by a deafening crescendo of voices 'Allah O Akbar' again and again, for one full hour. Some say Kuwait was born anew that night." Mohammed A. al-Yahya, *Kuwait: Fall and Rebirth* (London: Kegan Paul International, 1993), p. 88.

68 "The invasion temporarily overshadowed the confrontation between the government and the pro-democracy opposition. Iraq's claims to be acting on behalf of popular forces in Kuwait were unanimously rejected, and the legitimacy of al-Sabah rule in exile was affirmed by opposition leaders, all of whom refused to co-operate with Iraqi occupation forces. Ahmed Saddoun, the only opposition leader in Kuwait at the time of the invasion, refused to be associated with Iraq's efforts to set up a provisional government. Other opposition leaders appeared at the Kuwaiti embassy in London to swear allegiance to the emir." Ismael, *Kuwait*, p. 172.

69 Essential to the survival of the Kuwaiti society's integrity was the survival of the country's civil records in the face of Iraqi efforts to alter the composition of the population in their favor. For a discussion of resistance operations to preserve and smuggle out disks containing these records, see Darwin, *The Edge of War*, pp. 225–38.

70 Webster, "The Innocent Period,," p. 90. Whether purposefully or not, the fire department took an inordinate amount of time to respond. Hogan, *Trapped in Kuwait*, p. 100.

71 The Iraqis systematically eliminated all Kuwaiti flags, pictures of the Amir, and other manifestations of the country's heritage and separate identity. The covered portico of the hotel was rimmed by small flags of many nations; ironically, the Iraqis failed to notice that, among these flags, was one from Kuwait that continued to fly until the October bombing.

72 Levins, *Days of Fear*, p. 366.

73 Duncan, "Cruelty and Compassion," p. 172. Colonel Duncan is a friend of mine.

74 The Palestinian attack on the French Embassy compromised its ability to hold out and contributed to its eventual closure. "French officials said their diplomats in Kuwait had not fared nearly as well since Iraqi [*sic*] soldiers charged into the embassy compound last month, destroyed the main water pipe with a bulldozer and

plundered the ambassador's residence." Krauss, "Only 4 Embassies Hold Out in Kuwait as Food Dwindles," p. A13.
75 Kano, "Hiding from Saddam," p. 104. Other violations of diplomatic premises took place in the same time period. On September 13 occupation forces raided the Dutch Embassy, and Canadian and Belgian Residences the following day. These actions increased threat levels among the remaining diplomats and raised the question about future Iraqi intentions.
76 Darwin, *The Edge of War*, p. 414.
77 Kano, "Hiding from Saddam," p. 30.
78 The reason for the high demand for luxury goods under the dire conditions of the occupation was fascinating. A Jordanian told Kano "that the Iraqi troops at the border with Jordan stole cash, jewelry and electrical goods from each car that crossed their checkpoint. Many people were trying to leave Kuwait with some money in their pockets, so they bought perfume. It was easy to sell outside and could be used to bribe Iraqi border guards, who had little interest in taking the whole lot. In this way the refugees could preserve most of their capital." Kano, ibid., p. 34.
79 Ibid, p. 48.
80 Ghabra, "Democratization in a Middle Eastern State," p 119.
81 I was able to verfiy some of these anecdotal reports following liberation when I visited former torture chambers and spoke with Kuwaitis who had lived through the occupation. I led mixed teams of area specialists and professionals with psychiatric expertise that conducted about 150 in-depth interviews on behalf of the Social Development Office of the Amiri Diwan. A demonstration interview for the group of young Kuwaitis selected to work with the Americans had to be halted when the subject broke down. It turned out that his task with the resistance was to sneak into morgues to photograph the remains of torture victims before the Iraqis could destroy the evidence, and he had eventually been caught and tortured himself. His colleagues had not known of his experience.
82 Kano, "Hiding from Sadam," p. 36. Colonel Duncan and his family suffered a tragic loss of their own in the chaotic conditions created by Iraq. On October 22, Edward Heath (visiting Baghdad) had been able to arrange for the freedom of Duncan's two young sons in Kuwait. To permit the boys to reach Baghdad in time to depart on Heath's aircraft, they were required to surrender themselves at the Regency Palace Hotel. On the way to the Kuwait airport, the Iraqi driver collided with another vehicle, killing the elder

son, Alex, and four other passengers. The driver and the injured younger son, Rorie, were the sole survivors. Duncan, "Cruelty and Compassion," p. 176.
83 Darwin, *The Edge of War*, p. 262.
84 Kano, "Hiding from Sadam," p. 44.
85 Ibid., pp. 28–9.
86 The embassy, nevertheless, remained on alert for any sign of a change in the behavior of the troops posted around the compound perimeter. On one occasion, the sounds of digging were heard on the other side of the wall. Unable to see the source of the sound, the embassy requested that the satellite passing over Kuwait surveil the area as soon as it was light. The alarm was triggered by Iraqi troops fortifying firing positions in anticipation of a coalition attack. Tony Mireles was in charge of drawing up rosters for continuous coverage of the two guard posts.
87 Rinehart, typescript.
88 Amazingly, no one, including officials in Washington, could say what the total capacity, or even the shape, of the buried storage tank was. Those involved in estimating remaining supplies reported their findings in "goat bladders" rather than gallons or liters to confuse Iraqis monitoring the Embassy's handheld radio network. Locations on the compound were also designated by codenames, such as "Snake Pit," "Eagle's Nest," "Whisky Tango Bar and Grill" (outhouse), or "Big Cement Pond" for the same reason. Webster, "The Innocent Period,," p. 109.
89 Ibid., p. 53.
90 Within days the packaged turkeys began to explode, rattling the nervous Iraqi troops in the vicinity. Whether they ever figured out the source of this phantom "gunfire" is not known.
91 Private citizens in Kamp Kuwait had very quickly adjusted to consular work and adapted to other facets of the "bureaucratic" mindset. "Those estimating the supplies of goods necessary for survival were extremely conservative with the information reported to the State Department. We knew that if we told Washington we could survive for four months, they would leave us there for five." Rinehart, typescript.
92 Ibid. Despite the doubts and jibes of his comrades, Paul Brown had continued to dig daily for fresh water where none should have been. He was digging through beach sand where the Gulf shore had been before the construction of the Corniche. Nevertheless, the water he had found at about 13 feet was non-saline, possibly trapped runoff from heavy watering of the palms planted in

the median of the Corniche. The sides of the well were stabilized with a roll-down door. The steel drums referred to in the quotation above were actually a pontoon from the embassy's entry in the Mesillah Raft Race, an annual competition. Four drums welded end-to-end and fitted with mesh to filter out sand provided an ideal liner.

93 After the interruption of municipal power and water supplies on August 24, it was no longer possible to maintain the trees and shrubs so carefully nurtured by generations of embassy employees. Before the well came online, I passed time cutting and removing dead vegetation, which posed a fire hazard to the Residence and other structures.

94 "Mr. Hiloudi (sic)," Chattanooga, took refuge in the Embassy on August 18 and remained there until November 21. "Mr. Hiloudi spoke with pride about his association with the effort to keep the American flag flying over the compound and said he now regretted leaving his comrades in November, when Iraqi officials promised him a safe exit because of his Arab origin, then reneged." Patrick E. Tyler, "Relief, Tears and Hope at Hostages' Hotel," *New York Times*, December 8, 1990, p. 6.

95 One day, El-Miloudi was startled when he looked up to see a row of Iraqi heads watching him over a section of the perimeter wall. It turned out that a truck had been parked on the other side of the wall and they were standing on the truck bed. As the garden was in an isolated part of the compound, I was summoned to take a look. The Iraqis made no hostile move, and the truck eventually drove off. It seemed likely that the peasant draftees were merely gazing at the agricultural pursuits and thinking of the homes from which they had been torn.

96 Webster, "The Innocent Period," p. 79.

97 Unbeknownst to the gardeners, they were under observation by others besides the Iraqis outside. "The Ambassador continued his own exercise regimen in the garden, and I suspect it was also a mental health exercise, taking out frustrations through manual labor. ... The Ambassador deserved better. Under his insistence and support, his labor and the labor of others, the garden was a steady producer of 'greens' and other vegetables, a welcome nutritional necessity. For some reason, the circling proletariat (i.e., joggers) never noticed that the Ambassador didn't jog." Webster, "The Innocent Period," p. 121

98 Ibid., p. 62.

99 "The Ambassador identified the need for a 'safe haven' or

sanctuary for the campers in the event of military action." Ibid., p. 74.
100 Rinehart, typescript.
101 Webster, "The Innocent Period," p. 74. On the interior, the windows were sealed with plastic sheeting and duct tape.
102 At a critical moment, the oxygen cylinder feeding the acetylene torch ran out. When a search of the warehouse failed to locate another bottle, it appeared that the project might not be completed. Jim Carroll, the community doctor, came to the rescue, providing a small bottle of oxygen from the respirator in the Health Unit. Webster, "The Innocent Period,," p. 75.
103 Rinehart, typescript.
104 Webster, "The Innocent Period,," p. 76, and Rinehart, typescript. A communications room off the central space was outfitted with 24-volt short-range communications and spare automobile batteries. A separate room was set up for medical uses.
105 It was only prudent for me to make certain that DCM Bodine and other key officers were aware of everything of significance that I knew or did. Because of the precarious situation posed by the Iraqis, they had to be ready to carry on should I be killed or incapacitated. Operational planning for a military rescue and a few aspects of relationships with resistance "contacts" were the only exceptions to this rule.
106 "An Irishman who was hiding within sight of the embassy compound in Kuwait said Mr. Howell and his group of holdouts played Christmas carols over loudspeakers two nights ago as Iraqi soldiers maintained their cordon around the United States mission, which is still without electricity and basic services." Patrick E. Tyler, "500 Gulf Hostages Flown to Safety: Only One American Shows Up in Kuwait for Final Flight," *New York Times*, December 12, 1990. p. A1.
107 Webster, "The Innocent Period,," pp. 64–5.
108 The Iraqis had installed antiaircraft positions on top of the hotel and other civilian buildings, including the Kuwait Handicapped Society, in violation of the laws of war.
109 Levins (*Days of Fear*, p. 537) presents a concept of a rescue and extraction operation. While he includes elements that might be included in a "package," this description is both too specific and rigid to capture the flexibility built into any such effort. Clearly, there would be differences between a stand-alone operation and one launched in connection with the outbreak of general hostilities. In general, any such rescue would have been adapted to a

number of circumstances at the time. The fact that participating assets could launch in close proximity of the compound, facilitated this flexibility.
110 Webster, "The Innocent Period," p. 54.
111 Ibid., p. 93.
112 Hardline opponents took over duty in the guardhouses, and plates were sent out to them.
113 "(W)e weren't yet even close to the point of severe hardship, much less emaciation. This must have perplexed them and altered their almost assured conceptual view of Americans as spoiled aristocrats, especially at an Embassy." Webster, "The Innocent Period," p. 108.
114 Clifford Krauss, "Embassy Gets Food: Iraq's Troops in Kuwait Deliver Some Supplies to the U.S. Mission," *New York Times*, December 1, 1990, p. 1. The embassy did a careful inventory of the delivery and sent it to the Department of State so that the Iraqis would not be able to claim that they had "resupplied" the Embassy.
115 Transcript of State Department Press Briefing, December 7, 1990.
116 Rinehart, typescript.
117 I stepped outside the front gate to find out what the problem was. The Iraqi officer in charge of the bus was carrying a nice camel stick, which I admired, as I would not normally do with an Arab. When the officer offered the stick in accordance with local custom, I took it and kept it as a memento of my days as "a guest of Saddam."
118 Levins, *Days of Fear*, pp. 547–48. I had already concluded that the Iraqis were sincere when the officer handed over the camel stick in accordance with cultural norms.
119 When they arrived, they had been compelled by a barrier to park some distance down the road.
120 The group in the Embassy during the siege did not fully appreciate at the time how important it was for Americans, and Kuwaitis, to see the American flag flying during the occupation. As Ron Webster later remembered, "The entire local community (all nationalities) seemed to relish the sight of the American flag flying on the compound and many calls were received offering help and encouragement." Webster, "The Innocent Period," p. 70. According to at least one source, others entered the Embassy as liberation was underway to raise a flag. See Darwin, *The Edge of War*, pp. 422–23. If true, it means that the Iraqis had entered the Embassy and removed the flag raised on December 12. Reports I received

immediately after liberation, however, were clear that the Embassy had not been breached by Iraq in the interval.
121 The British ambassador and a number of Americans and others in Iraq shared our flight to Frankfurt.
122 Gen. Vernon Walters, the American ambassador to Germany whom I had known in Algiers and from other encounters, flew in from Bonn to greet the party on arrival in Frankfurt. His generous gesture was greatly appreciated.
123 Among those present were a number of individuals who had reached the United States on the December 9 flight and several members of the Marine Security Guard detachment of Embassy Kuwait. Evacuated in August, they had not been permitted to depart Iraq and served Embassy Baghdad with great distinction.
124 Eagleburger was named secretary of state in 1992. Following retirement, he moved to Charlottesville, Virginia, where he was my neighbor. He passed away on June 4, 2011.

17 Troubled Dawn

1   This calculation was based on the force of approximately 300,000 normally allotted to USCENTCOM. In the end, an estimated 500,000 American troops, including units stationed in Europe, were committed to the liberation of Kuwait.
2   Felipe was from El Paso, Texas and took a proprietary interest in the shower and other facilities in the snack bar area.
3   The American community in Kuwait was extraordinaily fortunate during the Iraqi occupation in terms of casualties. The only known American death (James Worthington) was one of three older men (the other two were British) who died of heart attacks while being held as hostages in Iraq. Levins, *Days of Fear*, p. 226.
4   Ibid., p. 512.
5   Ibid., p. 451. Levins correctly clarifies that tales of babies thrown on the floor were exaggerated; in fact, the newborns were removed from their incubators and handed to their mothers who had no means of ensuring their survival. Ibid., p. 515. Elsewhere, he relates an incident when the Iraqis seized the KOC Hospital in Ahmadi. "Two premature babies were on respirators in the area taken over by the Iraqis. Two hours later, they were dead. The Iraqis gave no explanation, and simply handed the bodies over to the Kuwaitis. It was never clear whether they simply did not know how to care for the babies in intensive care or had let them die, as such babies are allowed to in Iraq." Ibid., p. 118.

6   Ibid., p. 452.
7   In 1967, for example, I first met Joe Alex Morris in Yemen where a civil war involving the United Arab Republic was raging. I and several companions from Embassy Cairo had been transported to Taiz courtesy of the Egyptian authorities. How Morris managed to reach the isolated town was never completely clear.
8   Personal observations.
9   The Iraqis were especially eager to seize Americans and British citizens. Iraqi documents captured after Kuwait's liberation revealed the embarassment of those responsible for the "Human Shield" program that British hostages were so much more numerous than American. In September 1990, Iraqi Special forces were ordered "to conduct house-to-house searches and to concentrate specifically on the Americans as they had an insufficient number of them...." Levins, *Days of Fear*, p.210.
10 State Department spokesman Richard Boucher announced that 2,520 American citizens had been evacuated aboard 13 evacuation flights since September. An estimated 500 Americans elected to stay in Kuwait and Iraq, including 294 children, 100 women, and 115 men with dual citizenship. Jennifer Toth, "U.S. Diplomat Howell Comes Home a Hero," *Los Angeles Times*, December 15, 1990, p. A14
11 Dana Priest, "Hostages Pour Out From Iraq, Kuwait; 163 Americans Among 950 Evacuated," *Washington Post*, December 10, 1990, p. A1.
12 Ibid. One of the most debilitating aspects of dangerous and fluid crises for vulnerable populations is uncertainty regarding the safest course to take. Many Americans who chose to remain in hiding seem to have assumed that those who sought refuge in the Embassy were foolish because they were in plain sight. This was clear from the exchanges between them and fellow citizens on the compound. Jack Rinehart, whose *sang froid* seldom seemed to desert him, recounted one such conversation: "I told another man who was calling me from his air conditioner duct that he was crazy for not getting to the Embassy when he had the chance. He said, 'I'll be OK but they're going to hang you.'" Stevens, *The Iraqi Invasion of Kuwait*, p. 50.
13 Three non-Kuwaiti Arabs (Palestinian, Lebanese and Syrian) risked their lives time and again to assist Americans and others evading capture. When the Americans in the Embassy were finally free, these individuals accompanied them to the United States for their own safety and expeditious immigration. Despite

the recommendation and support of their applications by me and others, all three spent a year without governmental action in their cases. In the end, all became discouraged and decided to leave the United States. In retrospect, it probably would have been more effective to assist them to reach a neighboring country from which they could have walked in.

14 Tom Masland, "Underground in Kuwait," *Newsweek*, December 31, 1990, p. 43.
15 Jehan Rajab, born in Britain, is a long-term resident of Kuwait married to Tareq Rajab. They operate the premier British school in Kuwait and own a magnificent private collection of oriental treasures housed in the basement of their home. Fortunately, the museum was not discovered by the Iraqis and the Rajabs had used the time to secrete the most valuable items behind false walls.
16 Claudia Farkas al-Rashoud, *Kuwait Kaleidoscope*, Kuwait: Kuwait Bookshops, 1995, p. 44.
17 Russell Watson, "Crisis in the Gulf," *Newsweek*, November 12, 1990, p. 24. According to the same report a family of six, including two small children, was executed when a foreign passport was discovered in their home and a Kuwaiti accused of "feeding the enemies of Baghdad" was shot after his hand was lopped off.
18 Masland, "Underground in Kuwait."
19 The only American known to have been involved in the fighting was Tom Kreuzeman, an advisor to the Kuwaiti military. He was the only member of UKLOK to report for duty on the morning of August 2, 1990. When the Kuwaiti units he was advising withdrew before the Iraqi onslaught, Kreuzeman was escorted to his home by a Kuwaiti sergeant. Levins, *Days of Fear*, p. 73.
20 Ibid., p. 211.
21 Ibid., pp. 506–7.
22 Barbara Bodine and I were surprised that the Iraqis had their names because the Embassy had never revealed the names of private citizens in the Embassy. In his research on this episode, Levins concluded that El-Miloudi had identified them in an attempt to help the two return to the U.S.
23 Levins gives November 29 as the day of their departure. In the final analysis, the decision had to be left to each individual to make. El-Miloudi Hamid had been gone for two days and the embassy had received no indication that he had encountered problems. There was thus no basis, other than innate distrust of the Iraqis, to discourage the men from taking the opportunity.
24 Reconstruction of events by John Levins in *Days of Fear*. "Appar-

ently the Baghdad Embassy had sent a message to Kuwait saying that the release offer was a trick, but the Kuwait Embassy never received it."
25 Levins, *Days of Fear*, p. 587.
26 Ibid., p. 575. Shortly following my return to Washington, I was taken to a nearby military installation where I pointed out for targeters several key communications and electrical nodes. The Kuwaitis had shared this sensitive information during the 1987–88 concern about Iranian Silkworm missiles.
27 Near-disasters with the communications gear in the middle of the siege fortunately never became known outside a small group of Embassy staff. On one occasion, a communications element burned out. There was no redundancy in the system because of concerns that critical equipment not be compromised should the Iraqis enter the Embassy. In Washington, technicians took an identical unit, replicated the failure, and worked out a means of bypassing the failure. They then talked the capable and dedicated communicators in Kuwait, Jeff Jugar and Connie Parrish, through the repair. At another point, the fuel pump on the indispensable communications generator failed. A replacement was miraculously discovered on the new, uninstalled, generator. Through the skills of Ron Webster, Jack Rinehart and others, the part was cannibalized and adapted to the old unit.
28 John Levins (*Days of Fear*, pp. 317 ff.) observes that the Embassy's communications discipline was undercut by the State Department, which announced in Washington that fuel supplies were low..
29 Ibid.
30 Weeks earlier, Ron Webster and I discussed sources of municipal power that we might tap, such as a nearby streetlight, late one evening weeks before. Ron calculated that we could deal with issues of voltage and phases, but the idea died because the streetlights were in full view of the Iraqis guarding the compound. Levins and his companions would give us allies outside the walls, and so the idea gained new life.
31 Many returnees delayed until after the fires set by the retreating Iraqis in the Kuwait oil fields were extinguished and the resulting toxic pollution began to dissipate. Ultimately, the Kuwait Oil Company (KOC) secured and capped 727 sabotaged oil wells. Mary Ann Tétreault, "Kuwait's Unhappy Anniversary," *Middle East Policy*, Vol. VII, no. 3 (June 2000), p. 70.
32 American troops who first entered the compound set charges to

blow open a door to the executive suite of the Chancery, although Ambassador Gnehm was less than a day behind with the keys and combinations that had been carefully carried back to Washington and turned over to him. The explosion set fire to the curtains, doing unnecessary damage to the interior. At least, however, they had cranes and unlimited manpower to dismantle the bunker. We were later told that the four massive safes welded together to brace the ceiling were taken out to sea and dumped in the waters of the Gulf.

33 Letter to Margie Howell, dated November 10, 1991. The Marine Ball is held at the Embassy annually in November to mark the birthday of the USMC, America's oldest armed force, with a long history of association with the nation's diplomatic corps.

34 "On August 3, 1990, Kuwaitis had reason to be thankful that their government's policy over the years had been prudent enough to pile up as much as $100 billion in assets invested abroad—which the U.N. Security Council and industrial-country governments quickly protected from Saddam Hussein's grasp and soon made available for the needs of Kuwait's government-in-exile." Twinam, *The Gulf, Cooperation and the Council: An American Perspective*, pp. 194–95.

35 Ironically, the allied coalition to liberate Kuwait facilitated Saddam's survival, first by halting the war a day before the armor of the Republican Guard divisions pinned in southern Iraq could be destroyed or significantly degraded. This omission was followed closely by an ill-conceived "surrender" ceremony at Safwan on the Iraqi border. Rather than requiring Saddam to acknowledge defeat personally, he was allowed to send his hapless generals to sign the humiliating truce. In the flush of victory, none of the pundits who had castigated Ambassador Glaspie for her alleged lack of foresight before the invasion was inclined to question leadership failings at its termination.

36 In counseling embassy staffs and others on crisis leadership, I routinely caution that those in positions of responsibility during a crisis must anticipate that at least some of those they are endeavoring to assist will displace their anxiety and anger against their leaders, because it is both safe and cathartic to do so.

37 Twinam, *The Gulf, Cooperation and the Council*, p. 196.

38 An estimated 700,000 land mines were left behind when the Iraqis left. Despite extensive international minesweeping efforts, injuries are likely to remain a problem for decades to come. J. Bejec, R.K. Gang, and A.R. Lari, "Post Gulf War Explosive Injuries in

Liberated Kuwait," *Injury*, Vol. 24, no. 8 (September 1993), p. 517. Egypt still deals with a number of casualties each year from mines planted at al-Alamein during World War II.
39. Claudia Farkas al-Rashoud, *Kuwait: Before and After the Storm*, Updated Second Edition. (Kuwait: The Kuwait Bookshops Co., 1999) p. 214.
40. After seeing the hundreds of burning wells, the administrator of the U.S. Environmental Protection Agency (EPA) remarked. "If Hell had a national park, it would look like Kuwait." Quoted in Twinam, *The Gulf, Cooperation and the Council*, p. 197. Massive pools of crude oil covered much of the landscape even after the burning wells had been capped. An estimated five million people in Kuwait, Saudi Arabia and, to a lesser extent, Bahrain and the United Arab Emirates were exposed. The Kuwait Oil Company eventually recovered 24 million barrels of crude oil from pools in the desert. Kuwait did indeed record a reduced birthrate and unusually high complications in pregnancies. Rashoud, *Before and After the Storm*, op. cit., p. 215.
41. Al-Yahya, *Kuwait*, pp. 109–10. Except as otherwise noted, data in this section is drawn from this study.
42. "Mental health specialists add that their task is complicated by the traditional reserve towards mental health care among Kuwaiti nationals, although these reservations are receding. These unfortunate people suffer from depression, nightmares, anxiety, lack of concentration, nervousness, isolation from society and no interest in work or family life."
43. Many of the weapons in private possession were held by individuals who had been part of Resistance groups. Others who were determined not to be caught defenseless again in the future also held on to weapons easily available when the Iraqi army collapsed and fled.
44. Conversation with me, 1993.
45. A complete accounting of atrocities committed against Kuwaiti and other civilian residents can never be compiled, in some part, because of the reluctance of victims to discuss them. Nevertheless, confirmed incidents of summary execution and death and maiming under torture lend credence to numerous widely circulated anecdotes, such as the practice of killings in front of family members who were then required to pay for the bullets used. Familiar locations, such as neighborhood schools, were rendered "toxic" by their use as torture centers. Every effort was made to keep this fact from Kuwaiti schoolchildren and they

were extensively renovated before classes resumed, but, as usual, the children knew more than their parents suspected. If anything, statistics on Kuwaiti losses seriously understate the magnitude of the problem.

46 Twinam, *The Gulf, Cooperation and the Council*, pp. 196–97. A number of accused "collaborateurs" were tried in special courts and instances of extrajudicial murders were reported.

47 Subsequently, the Embassy used its communications to help facilitate the escape of several Kuwaitis whose capture might have given Iraq control over important Kuwaiti assets.

48 I and the University of Virginia teams that studied the societal effects of the occupation frequently encountered this unresolved duality among Kuwaitis interviewed. Typically, some young Kuwaiti students in dramatic recreations of the occupation vied to play the part of Saddam Hussein, because he was perceived as a "strong" figure.

49 Quoted in Peter Vine and Paula Casey, *Kuwait: A Nation's Story* (London: Immel Publishing, 1992), p. 7.

50 A prominent female artist told me in 1993 that at the extremes among Kuwaiti women were those who believed the occupation was punishment for not being good enough Muslims, on the one hand, and others who decided that both Arabism and Islam had failed them.

51 Ahmed Bishara, "Democratic Coalition of Kuwait," in National Republican Institute for International Affairs, pp. 26–7.

52 Ghabra, "Balancing State and Society: The Islamic Movement in Kuwait," *Middle East Policy*, Vol. V, no. 2 (May 1997), p. 58. "Kuwaiti society went through self-evaluation. Many young Kuwaitis looked toward the United States as a model for creating a new way of life. The country's liberation, their participation in it, and their contact with the U.S. army created among them a respect and fondness for Americans." Ghabra, idem, p. 63.

53 "Within Kuwait, [the occupation] also eradicated the traditional differences between ethnic, religious, and tribal groups because under occupation, all became as one to the Iraqi occupier. It did not matter if you were a Shiite or a Sunni or whether you were a Bedouin or a non-Bedouin. It did not matter whether you were a man or a woman. People had to help each other, work together, and endure...." Bishara, "Democratic Coalition of Kuwait," p. 27.

54 Shafeeq Ghabra, "The Democratic Movement in its Historical Context," in National Republican Institute for International Affairs, *Political Participation and Constitutional Democracy in Kuwait*, edited conference transcript, Washington, 1991, p. 20.

55 Twinam, *The Gulf, Cooperation and the Council*, p. 197.
56 Ghabra, "Democratization in A Middle Eastern State: Kuwait, 1993," p. 104–05. During the occupation, civil disobedience to "authority" was a civic virtue. The adjustment required by the reinstatement of legitimate Kuwaiti authority was not always easy or automatic. A Kuwaiti psychiatrist, for example, cited the case of a Kuwaiti woman who had become accustomed to driving the wrong way on a one-way street and continued to do so after liberation to the frustration of traffic police.
57 Ibid., p. 102.
58 Boghardt, *Kuwait amid War* . . . , p. 156.
59 Ibid. p. 165. Boghardt cites this as the first time in its history that Kuwait was governed under martial law. Jill Crystal ("The Merchant Families and the Ruling Family,," p. 10) argues, "Until the mid-1980s, with the political violence associated with the first Gulf war, Kuwait had no marshall (sic) law. Disappearances and the like were not on the ordinary political agenda." Whether or not the regime in the 1980s was formally martial law, there were special courts and other similar trappings.
60 Boghardt, *Kuwait amid War* . . . , p. 178. Despite widespread hopes that the new era would be characterized by a more peaceful and orderly political process, Kuwaitis were rudely reminded in late 1991 that some factions were still prepared to use violence. Incidents in which Islamists were implicated began then and continued up to the election a year later. As Ghabra reported, "Some Islamists were caught harboring large quantities of weapons and explosives. There were shooting incidents involving the Romanian circus, which was visiting Kuwait, and explosions occurred in several video stores." Ghabra, "Balancing State and Society," p. 63.
61 Ghabra, "Democratization in A Middle Eastern State," p. 111.
62 Mary Ann Tétreault, "Kuwait's Unhappy Anniversary," p. 68. The Commission's report confirmed that Iraq had steadily moved the de facto frontier southward and upheld Kuwaiti claims by reclaiming the purloined territory in its demarcation.
63 Levins, *Days of Fear*, p. 62. His estimate of military and police casualties—65 dead and 500 wounded—seems low, but counts only the set-piece battles at the Jiwan and Mubarak camps and not those suffered by military and police personnel who fought with the Resistance. Nevertheless, ... the dead represented about one-half of one percent of Kuwait's entire armed forces." Idem, p. 74.
64 Masland, "Underground in Kuwait," p. 43. Complicating the task

of compiling statistics in this category is not only the chaos in the country but the Iraqi practice of attempting to bury many torture victims clandestinely while the Resistance endeavored, at great risk, to document their number and photograph their remains.
65 Claudia al-Rashoud, correspondence with me, January 25, 2012.
66 " ...perhaps only a hundred wells were spared in Kuwait itself, outside of the Partitioned Neutral Zone. Over a thousand were blown up, with 737 on fire in Kuwait and 300 in Wafra." "The Second Liberation: Bringing Back the Sun," *The Kuwaiti Digest*, Vol. 27, No. 4, October–December 2001, p. 23. Control of the fires within eight months was a major achievement.

18 Legacy of Pride and Suffering

1 Claudia Farkas Al-Rashoud, an American photographer/writer resident in Kuwait with her husband and family since 1979, coauthored this chapter.
2 Al-Rashoud, *Kuwait: Before and After the Storm*, p. 202.
3 A substantial number of Kuwaiti students left their studies in the United States to serve as interpreters and pathfinders with military units of coalition forces in the liberation of their country. A smaller number actually joined the U.S. military, underwent basic training, and fought their way into Kuwait. One of these outstanding young men, Hazem al-Braikan, was a key associate and friend of mine and of others from the University of Virginia in the early 1990s. Following completion of his studies, he received an advanced degree in finance and became a leading practitioner in Kuwait. The last of his regular visits to see friends in Charlottesville took place the summer of 2008. Sadly, he reportedly took his own life in July 2009 in connection with a U.S. Securities and Exchange Commission investigation of alleged fraud. *Middle East Journal*, Chronology, Vol. 64, No.1 (Winter 2010), p. 119.
4 *Kuwait Notes* (Southern California), Issue 7, July 20, 1991. p. 3. NOW contended incorrectly that women in Kuwait were denied freedom of speech, dress, association, transportation, etc. The same issue also covered stereotyping and misrepresentations in articles written by Richard Reeves, Christopher Dickey, and Brian Michael Jenkins.
5 In its attitudes toward mental health services, Kuwait was by no means the most backward of the Arab states. Throughout the Arab world mental illness is widely regarded as a source of shame to be treated in secret. In otherwise sophisticated Beirut, offices of

mental health clinics had rear entrances so that patients could slip in unobserved. Many Kuwaitis suffered in silence and were reluctant to share their experiences and symptoms even with Kuwaiti friends. When the psychodynamic teams from the University of Virginia began their work in the early 1990s, they found many Kuwaitis anxious to talk with trusted outsiders, often beginning the conversation with the question "Where have you been?"

6 Hassan Al-Ebraheem, "Interview," *American-Arab Affairs*, No. 34 (Fall 1990), pp. 8–11.
7 *Middle East Journal*, Chronology, Vol. 45, No. 3 (Summer 1991), p. 488.
8 In May, two months after liberation, the United States agreed to provide 3,700 military policemen to help keep the peace until an adequate Kuwaiti police force could be reconstituted. Ibid., No. 4 (Autumn 1991), p. 667.
9 In early July, Minister of Interior Hamed al-Sabah declared that the greatest threat to Kuwait's internal security was posed by scores of Iraqi agents in hiding in the country. Ibid., p. 668.
10 A curfew during hours of darkness was imposed on March 5; it was lifted during Ramadan when *iftars* and mosque services required movement at night. Ibid.No. 3 (Summer 1991), p. 489.
11 Ibid.
12 The collapse of the Iraqis in Kuwait occurred in a period of several days between the launch of the ground war on February 23 and the entry of coalition forces into the city on February 26.
13 *Middle East Journal*, Chronology, Vol. 45, No. 4 (Autumn 1991), p. 666.
14 Ibid., Vol. 48, No. 2 (Spring 1994), p. 348.
15 The government refused to permit the substantial portion of the population still in exile to return to the country until May 11. Ibid., Vol. 45, No. 4 (Autumn 1991), p. 666.
16 Ibid., Vol. No. 3 (Summer 1991), p. 492.
17 Ibid., Vol. No. 4 (Autumn 1991), p. 666.
18 Ibid., No. 3 (Summer 1991), p. 491. U.S. and other coalition forces provided critical assistance with some of these projects.
19 Ibid., p. 493.
20 Ibid., No. 4 (Autumn 1991), p. 668.
21 Ibid., No. 3 (Summer 1991), p. 491.
22 Ibid., p. 495.
23 Ibid., No. 4 (Autumn 1991), p. 667.
24 Ibid., No. 3 (Summer 1991), p. 488. The British, French, and Canadian embassies also resumed operations.

Notes 671

25 Bader A. al-Baijan serves as the president of the Steering Committee of the Friends of Dar al-Athar al-Islamiyyah. He is a key figure in the activities of the national museum, including its move into the renovated buildings of the American Mission hospitals.
26 Claudia Farkas al-Rashoud, Interview with Sandy Shinn, February 2012.
27 Ibid.
28 Maxine al-Refai, interview with Claudia al-Rashoud, February 2012. Maxine has lived in Kuwait since 1956 and worked at ASK from its founding in 1964 (see chapter 10) until her retirement in 1994.
29 Ibid.
30 The ASK team stayed during the exploratory visit at the Safir International Hotel, across from the Embassy compound. Conditions at the former luxury hotel mirrored those they discovered at the school. "The Iraqis had occupied the hotel and left it in a terrible state. They pulled out the plumbing and the light fixtures, the tiles, handrails, most of the doors, etc. If your room had a door then it would have no lock, or even if there was a lock, then there would be no key. There was no hot water and just the very basic minimum of food services." al-Refai, interview.
31 Claudia al-Rashoud, one of these returnees, had consulted an environmental sciences professor at the University of California, Riverside, before departing California. Despite her eagerness to return to her husband and extended family in Kuwait, his advice was sobering. Noting that the air and soil were heavily polluted with carcinogens and other harmful substances, he advised her to "avoid eating any locally grown fruits and vegetables for at least the next four or five years" and to avoid lengthy exposure outside. Al-Rashoud, "Return to Kuwait," typewritten manuscript, February 21, 2012.
32 Ibid.
33 When I was assigned to Abu Dhabi, oil particles from Das Island often reached the city under normal circumstances. In the humid conditions there, it formed a thick, viscous film on the windshields of automobiles and other vehicles. Wiping the mixture with a clean cloth merely smeared the mixture making the car unusable. Veterans of the area, therefore, carried containers of clear water with them, even when going to a restaurant or movie.
34 Claudia Farkas al-Rashoud, "'Hands-on' approach ... so they'll stay on," *Arab Times*, November 10, 1992.
35 Al-Rashoud, "Return to Kuwait."

36 Claudia Farkas al-Rashoud, "Stay away from death traps, EOD advisor warns children," *Arab Times*, November 22, 1993.
37 Aside from the problem of hidden and attractive explosive devices, Wilk shared concerns about the stability of massive munitions dumps left by the Iraqis in bunkers and scattered across the desert. Winds, motion, and the extremes of temperature have the capacity to generate spontaneous explosions.
38 Al-Rashoud, "Return to Kuwait."
39 Betty Lippold, "Read our Lips: Welcome 'Home'," *Arab Times*, April 14, 1993.
40 Nirmala Janssen and Betty Lippold, "I have been welcomed in a way I will never forget," *Arab Times*, April 17, 1993.
41 Nirmala Janssen and Betty Lippold, "Together we made history," *Arab Times*, April 15–16, 1993.
42 Nirmala Janssen and Betty Lippold, "I have been welcomed in a way I will never forget," *Arab Times*, April 17, 1993.
43 Ibid.
44 Beginning in February 1992 and for a number of years thereafter, a ceremony honoring the American dead in Operation "Desert Storm" was held in the section of Arlington National Cemetery where the fallen were laid to rest. The annual ceremony was organized by a group called "No Greater Love," of which I was a board member. The Kuwaiti ambassador, Saud Nasir al-Sabah, financed the ceremony, Kuwaiti children in the Washington area laid floral tributes, and prominent public figures participated as the names of the deceased were read out. The military provided color and honor guards as well as musicians and ceremonial cannon. Family members from across the country were honored guests.
45 *Arab Times*, April 26, 1993; Kuwait News Agency (KUNA).
46 A member of the Kuwaiti Air Force, al-Anzi spent eight months as a prisoner of war in Iraq.
47 Claudia Farkas al-Rashoud, "Hair comes down, feelings let out," *Arab Times*, May 1, 1993.
48 Ibid.
49 "Hearts join in shared loss, collection of letters from Kuwaitis," *Arab Times*, April 26, 1993.
50 *Middle East Journal*, Chronology, Vol. 46, No. 4 (Autumn 1992), p. 676. In late August 1991, a group of armed Iraqis attempting to infiltrate Bubiyan Island were reportedly intercepted by Kuwaiti troops. *Middle East Journal*, Chronology, Vol. 46, No. 1 (Winter 1992), p. 89.

51 Ibid., Vol. 48, No. 2 (Spring 1994), p. 348.
52 Ibid. Iraq denied the report and a spokesman for the UN Iraq-Kuwait Observation Mission announced that the mission was not able to verify the Kuwaiti claim.
53 Ibid. No casualties were reported from this incident.
54 Ibid.
55 Claudia Farkas al-Rashoud, "Stay away from death traps...." I had the opportunity to overfly the border area on a UN helicopter in 1992 and visit several of the new observation posts. In the course of a brief flight, countless Iraqi munitions dumps, stacked and unprotected, could be seen dotting the ground.
56 Shafeeq Ghabra, "Kuwait and the United States: The Reluctant Ally and U.S. Policy toward the Gulf," in David W. Lesch, *The Middle East and the United State* (Boulder, CO: Westview Press, 1999), pp. 304–5.
57 According to credible reports, Saddam had an aircraft warmed up and waiting to make his escape when Kuwait was liberated. Most observers felt at the time that his regime, which had taken his people into two wars and lost both, could not survive.
58 High-profile incursions, particularly those involving large groups, are sometimes launched with no expectation of success but as a diversion to cover the infiltration of a smaller number of agents surreptitiously.
59 *Middle East Journal*, Chronology, Vol. 47, No. 4 (Autumn 1993), p. 686.
60 Ibid.
61 During the author's time as ambassador, the two countries had worked closely on aircraft hijackings and other terrorist incidents affecting their shared interests.
62 *Middle East Journal*, Chronology, Vol. 47, No. 4 (Autumn 1993), p. 686.
63 Ibid. A U.S. intelligence source later specified, "Certain aspects of these devices have been found only in devices linked to Iraq." David Von Drehle and R. Jeffrey Smith, "U.S. Strikes Iraq for Plot to Kill Bush," *Washington Post*, June 27, 1993, p. A1.
64 *Middle East Journal*, Chronology, Vol. 47, No. 4 (Autumn 1993), p. 686.
65 Ibid.
66 Von Drehle and Smith, "U.S. Strikes Iraq...." Reacting to allegations that the defendants had been tortured in detention, FBI agents active in the investigation said they had no reason to believe the accusation. Indeed the speed with which the defendants

were brought before the Kuwaiti court would seem to mitigate the possibility that they had been physically mistreated.

67 *Middle East Journal,* Chronology, Vol. 47, No. 4 (Autumn 1993), p. 687.

68 Later in 1993, for example, author Seymour Hersh published an article in the *New Yorker* in which he argued that there was no evidence directly implicating the Saddam Hussein regime in the assassination plot. Ibid., Vol. 48, No. 2 (Spring 1994), p. 348. The issue made of Saddam's involvement is an interesting one, given the ruthless control he exercised over his country. It is virtually inconceivable that a plot of such magnitude and critical implications for Iraq would have been launched by Iraqi "freelancers" without approval of the highest levels in Baghdad.

69 See, for example, the report of the FBI review of laboratory forensics at <<http://www.fas.org/irp/agency/doj/oig/fbilab1/05bush2.htm>>.

70 Ironically, many Iraqis today suffer from PTSD as a consequence of the brutality of the Saddam Hussein regime and the several major conflicts into which his regime led them. In 2003, following the overthrow of Saddam Hussein, I was involved with the project of a Kuwaiti charitable foundation to bring approximately twenty Iraqi psychiatrists and psychologists to Kuwait for a refresher course by American specialists on the treatment of PTSD.

71 *Middle East Journal,* Chronology, Vol. 45, No. 4 (Autumn 1991), p. 656.

72 Ibid., Vol. 46, No. 1 (Winter 1992), p. 89.

73 "Prepo" in the theater permitted a rapid response to contingencies since only the combat and armored personnel would have to be flown in to join the equipment in storage. The Kuwaiti agreement, which does not appear to have been released, provided initially for the tanks and other vehicles for an armored brigade and a limited number of American maintenance and security personnel. The armored brigade could be deployed in about twenty-four hours. I had an opportunity to visit Camp Doha where the prepo was located in 1992.

74 *Middle East Journal,* Chronology, Vol. 46, No. 1 (Winter 1992), p. 89.

75 Ghabra, "Kuwait and the United States... ," p. 304.

76 The U.S.-Kuwait military agreement contained provision for joint military exercises. The first of these took place in August 1992. Such exercises were useful in reminding Iraq of possible consequences of its adventurism but also served long-term goals,

including experience with interoperability, improving Kuwait's defensive capabilities, and providing familiarity with terrain local conditions for American troops. *Middle East Journal*, Chronology, Vol. 47, No. 1 (Autumn 1993), p. 106.
77 The extensive network of islets and waterways had been a thorn in the side of Iraqi governments, offering refuge to army deserters and opposition elements as well as the indigenous inhabitants. An unintended consequence of the drainage, as well as earlier conversions of wetlands to agriculture, has been to increase the exposed soil that is blown into Kuwait by prevailing northerly winds in winter. The net effect has been to increase desertification in northern Kuwait. On a more positive note, the destruction of their original habitat in the Iraqi marshes has led to a substantial increase in the number of Basra bulbuls (nightingales) and other birds living and breeding in Kuwait.
78 *Middle East Journal*, Chronology, Vol. 48, No. 4 (Autumn 1994), p. 709.
79 Saddam Hussein had been telegraphing his intentions for some time before the Republican Guard units made a move. On September 27 he told journalists that he would open to the Iraqi people "all the granaries of the world," He urged the journalists, "Tell the people that honor is more important than bread." A week later, an editorial in *Al Jumhuriya*, a government-controlled mouthpiece, warned, "The first and second world wars were caused by the imposition of borders on Germany without negotiations or German approval." True to his habit of casting his acts of aggression as being forced upon him, Saddam was laying the groundwork for a dramatic move. Cited in Elaine Sciolino, *New York Times*, October 11, 1994.
80 The rapidity of this deployment, in contrast with the weeks and months required to assemble a credible counterforce in 1990, confirmed the efficacy of "prepo" in erasing the geographic advantage enjoyed by Iraq.
81 Report of the Secretary General 1995 <<http://www.un.org/docs/SG/SG-Rpt/ch4d-13.htm>> Veteran Saddam watchers would not accept that so quick and complete a reversal of tone and policy heralded an end to the Iraqi menace. Successive Iraqi governments, dating from the era of the monarchy, have made similar "concessions" when forced to do so. Generations of Iraqi schoolchildren have been taught that Kuwait is an integral part of their country, detached by "imperialists." According to some sources, this indoctrination continues to this day.

82 In February 1998, for example, Kuwaiti forces deployed on the border to defend against a potential Iraqi incursion. *Middle East Journal*, Chronology, Vol. 52, No. 3 (Summer 1998), p. 434.
83 A Pentagon announcement in November 1996 reflected the change in tactics. More than four thousand American troops departed the following month; but a squadron of F-117 'stealth' warplanes, which arrived in September, remained indefinitely. Ibid., Vol. 51, No. 2 (Spring1997), p. 273.
84 The preplanned operation was dubbed "Operation Desert Fox."
85 *Middle East Journal*, Chronology, Vol. 45, No. 3 (Summer 1991), p. 495.
86 Ibid., No. 4 (Autumn 1991), p. 667. The accused (whose correct name was probably al-Shammari) had served as a radar technician with the Kuwait Air Force (KAF) before Iraq's aggression.
87 Ibid. Tafla reportedly informed the Iraqi occupation authorities of her husband's involvement in the Kuwaiti resistance, resulting in his death.
88 Ibid.
89 Ibid., p. 668. Actual executions in the Kuwaiti legal system are comparatively rare.
90 Ibid., Vol. 46, No. 4 (Autumn 1992), p. 676.
91 Ibid., Vol. 54, No. 4 (Autumn 2000), p. 638. Husayn was accused of agreeing to serve as the "Prime Minister" of the puppet government Iraq attempted to establish during the occupation. Three months later, an appeals court upheld his conviction and death sentence.
92 Ibid., Vol. 47, No. 1 (Autumn 1993), p. 106. In the meantime, the government had revived the National Council, conceived in controversy immediately before the Iraqi invasion and never universally accepted. Although the Council's composition was easier for the government to influence, it still had the capacity to embarrass the leadership. In June 1992, for example, the Council Speaker, Abd al-Aziz al-Musaed, gave an interview to *al-Majalla* (London) in which he singled out the American ambassador for criticism. Al-Musaed charged Ambassador Gnehm with encouraging the "opposition" and involving himself in Kuwaiti politics. Ibid., Vol. 46, No. 4 (Autumn 1992), p. 676. The ambassador, however, was simply enunciating the U.S. policy of supporting the democratic processes to which all Kuwaitis had subscribed during the occupation. Predictably, the Kuwaiti government quickly distanced itself from the Speaker's comments.
93 Ibid., Vol. 47, No. 1 (Autumn 1993), p. 106.

94 In an apparent bow to the Assembly, the prime minister–designate announced that six members of the cabinet would be drawn from among parliamentarians.
95 *Middle East Journal,* Chronology, Vol. 49, No. 2 (Spring 1994), p. 331.
96 Ibid., Vol. 50, No. 4 (Autumn 1996), p. 584.
97 Ibid., Vol. 51, No. 1 (Winter 1997), p. 113.
98 Saud Nasir, the former Kuwaiti ambassador to the United States, pursued his responsibilities at the Ministry of Information with energy and a determination to improve Kuwaiti media. He introduced, for example, a new morning format for Kuwait Television patterned on *Good Morning, America* early in his tenure. Sadly, he passed away in January 2012 at an early age. He was a friend of mine. His efforts in Washington during the Iraqi occupation greatly contributed to the liberation of his country. The action of some members of the Assembly in attacking his moderate views deprived Kuwait of his talents but cannot diminish his patriotic service.
99 *Middle East Journal,* Chronology, Vol. 52, No. 3 (Summer 1998), p. 434.
100 Ibid., No. 4 (Autumn 1998), p. 596.
101 Ghanim Alnajjar, "The Challenges Facing Kuwaiti Democracy," Ibid., Vol. 54, no. 2 (Spring 2000), p. 242.
102 Mary Ann Tétreault, "Civil Society in Kuwait: Protected Spaces and Women's Rights," p.289. The Amiri decree effectively amended the Kuwaiti Elections Law of 1962.
103 Alnajjar, "The Challenges Facing Kuwaiti Democracy," p. 246.
104 *Middle East Journal,* Chronology, Vol. 54, No. 1 (Winter 2000), p. 112.
105 Personal discussions with well-informed Kuwaitis, 1999.
106 *Middle East Journal,* Chronology, Vol. 54, No. 2 (Spring 2000), p. 287.
107 Ibid. Supporters within the National Assembly apparently miscalculated their capacity to pass their bill. In the aftermath of this disappointing result, the minister of education, Yusuf Mohammad al-Ibrahim, announced the appointment of Shaikha Rasha al-Sabah as undersecretary of education. Shaikha Rasha had previously held important posts at Kuwait University and within the Amiri Diwan. Following liberation, she hosted one of the few *diwanniyas* open to both men and women.
108 Kuwaiti women were very active in the 1999 election campaigns,

678   Notes

       demanding the right to vote. Some attended campaign rallies, traditionally confined to men. al-Rashoud, *Before and After the Storm*, p. 214.
- 109 President Bush's second visit after liberation took place between March 23 and 26. I was present at the dedication ceremony.
- 110 As seen in May 2012, the structures on the previous site had been flattened. A lone tiny palm tree broke the monotony of the empty site. Personal observation.
- 111 Ghabra, "Kuwait and the United States... ," p. 302. TCOM was awarded a contract in 1994 to maintain military and civilian surveillance systems and radar installations. *Middle East Journal*, Chronology, Vol. 49, No. 3 (Summer 1994), p. 502.

19 Friends and Allies

1. Unless otherwise noted, the information in this section is based upon Claudia Farkas al-Rashoud, Interview with Abdallah al-Hammadi, M.D., February 2012.
2. Although important strides have been made in diagnosing military personnel with PTSD, its influence on large groups, especially civilian populations, has not been well explored. A recent article in *The Economist* (Vol. 402, no. 8770 [February 4, 2012] p. 64) reports promising research by Brian Barber, a psychologist at the University of Tennessee, into the factors determining the severity of PTSD. He posits that the key is how the individual perceives the violence to which he or she is exposed. If they see themselves as engaged in purposeful activity rather than as helpless victims, they are more likely to process the experience positively. By this criterion, active members of the Kuwaiti resistance could be expected to suffer less enduring trauma. Intuitively, during the siege of the Embassy, great stress was placed upon assuring that each individual had tasks and responsibilities that impart a sense of autonomy, control, and connection with the group.
3. The al-Riggaee Center, now located in the Psychological Medicine Hospital, includes adult and pediatric psychiatrists, clinical psychologists, social workers, general practitioners, and nurses who treat PTSD victims.
4. Claudia Farkas al-Rashoud, "The war within ... get help: PTSD rampant in Kuwait," *Arab Times*, February 22–23, 2001. Approximately 15,000 Kuwaitis who survived Iraqi captivity and mistreatment and 6,000 prisoners repatriated from Iraq after liberation were prime candidates for treatment.

5   Ibid.
6   During my work with the Social Development Office in the early 1990s, I discovered a group of Kuwaiti men who had met frequently during the occupation and were imprisoned together. Following liberation, they transformed their informal *diwanniya* into an effective support group, which facilitated discussion of their trauma and recovery.
7   Al-Rashoud, "The war within ... "
8   Ibid.
9   Claudia Farkas al-Rashoud, "Serving Martyrs' Families and Honor," *Arab Times*, February 22, 2012. The information in this section is drawn from interviews and research contained in this article.
10 Bureau investigators have documented the fact that 10.5 percent of those killed were children.
11 Abdallah al-Shayji, "Kuwait in midst of its own Arab Spring," *Gulf News* (Dubai), December 12, 2011.
12 Shaikh Jabir al-Ahmad was a slight, taciturn figure who nevertheless projected great inner strength. On occasion, especially when encountering old friends, his severe demeanor gave way to a gentle smile with twinkling eyes. The occupation experience naturally drained him significantly.
13 *Middle East Journal*, Chronology, Vol. 60, No. 3 (Summer 2006), p. 559.
14 Ibid. Shaikh Sa'd was seventy-six years old and had been out of the public eye for some time. Periodically, he was in Britain for medical treatment over the preceding months; rumors abounded that he was suffering from memory loss and often was not sentient. He lived on until May 5, 2008. Ibid., Vol. 62, No. 4 (Autumn 2008), p. 687.
15 Ibid.
16 The new cabinet, including three more Islamists and two fewer liberals than its predecessor, was sworn in on February 11, 2006.
17 Parliament actively cooperated in the resolution of this potential constitutional crisis. This was probably motivation enough for most members, but for some, especially the perennial opposition, there were likely other calculations at play. The fact that the new prime minister was not the crown prince or an iconic member of the al-Sabah family meant, as later experience showed, that he was more vulnerable to parliamentary challenges. Further, the marginalization of the al-Salem branch of the family may have raised possibilities of future divisions or even a tacit alliance with the proponents of power-sharing within the National Assembly.

In any event, the advanced age of the new amir and crown prince assure that the country will revisit succession issues in the relatively near future.

18 Al-Najjar, "The Challenges Facing Kuwaiti Democracy," p. 257.
19 Symbolic of the robust agenda of consultations, exercises, and military sales, was the transformation of the military component of the U.S. embassy in Kuwait. In place of the relatively modest USLOK at the time of the Iraqi invasion in 1990, a U.S. Office of Military Cooperation in Kuwait (OMC-K) commanded by a brigadier general manages the relationship on behalf of U.S. Central Command. It consists of personnel from all four military services and civilian employees. U.S. Department of State, Bureaus of Near Eastern Affairs ("Background Note: Kuwait," December 27, 2011 <<http://www.state.gov/r/pa/ei/bgn/35876.htm>>).
20 Ibid.
21 In the summer of 2003, I had an opportunity to see the joint American-Kuwaiti logistics operation and other facilities employed to support the attack and subsequent occupation of Iraq. Working with a Kuwaiti humanitarian organization, I was transported to Baghdad by military air and spent two days in the recently liberated country. With the assistance and protection of a friendly Shi'a militia, I spent one night in Najaf, where I dined with Ayatollah Mohammad Bahr al-Uloom, a ranking member of the Iraqi Governing Council.
22 U.S. Embassy Kuwait email, dated Monday, March 17, 2003. This extremely strong travel advisory leaves little doubt regarding the prudence of departure. The reference to terrorist threats within Kuwait reflected concerns that Iraq might have assets in place inside the country. The availability of email provides embassies with valuable new tools for alerting and instructing the community. Emails also have the additional advantage of creating a written record that purely oral communications lack. These insights into conditions within Kuwait during this tense and dangerous period draw upon messages kept by Claudia al-Rashoud and others.
23 U.S. Department of State email, dated Thursday, March 20, 2003.
24 Claudia al-Rahoud, email, dated April 9, 2003. By March 20, all European airlines had suspended service to Kuwait and regional carriers had suspended or "severely restricted" scheduled flights. American Embassy Kuwait, Warden Notice 2003–10, dated March 20, 2003.
25 Claudia al-Rahoud, "Second Gulf War Experiences," typewritten manuscript, March 2012. Public reactions of this kind are

universal when people are severely stressed. During the 2001 anthrax scare in the United States, a Charlottesville housewife called the authorities to report that she had found a "suspicious white powder" while cleaning under her kitchen sink.

26 Not since the Iranian campaign of bombardment with Silkworm missiles in 1987 had long-range missiles targeted Kuwait.
27 Claudia al-Rashoud, email, dated March 20, 2003.
28 Claudia al-Rashoud, email, dated April 9, 2003.
29 Such false alarms were not unusual at private schools in the weeks before the war. Some high school students took exams at nearby mosques. Claudia al-Rashoud, "Second Gulf War Experiences."
30 The program greatly alarmed the families of some of the AIS teachers back in the United States.
31 al-Rashoud, "Second Gulf War Experiences."
32 Ibid.
33 American Embassy Kuwait, Warden Notice 2003–10, dated March 20, 2003.
34 Ibid. –12, dated March 24, 2003. A number of these missiles fell in Mutla, a sparsely populated area between Kuwait City and the border with Iraq. Claudia al-Rashoud, email, dated March 21, 2003.
35 Claudia al-Rashoud, email, dated March 29, 2003. No warning siren was heard and the Ministry of Information later explained that it was a low-flying, terrain-following Silkworm missile. Through April 3, there were an estimated 23 air raid alerts and 17 confirmed missile strikes. SCUDS fired following the impact on the shopping center were intercepted by Patriot batteries. Fortunately, a group of Filipino employees of the Subway sandwich shop narrowly escaped injury. They had just gotten off their shift and were awaiting transport next to the pier when the missile struck.
36 It is interesting to speculate whether those who claim to have known prior to the 2003 conflict that Iraq possessed no weapons of mass destruction (WMDs) also "knew" that Baghdad did not have the missiles designed to carry WMDs.
37 "After I watched the statue coming down on t.v. and people celebrating, it brought back such a flood of memories & feelings from the occupation that it was all going round in my head and I couldn't sleep." Claudia al-Rashoud, email, dated April 9, 2003.
38 Claudia al-Rashoud, email, dated March 27, 2003. Saddam Hussein was known to employ one or more look-alikes as part of his elaborate security precautions.

39 "I think we were not surprised to see anti-American demonstrations, and we could understand people demonstrating against the war (which we also desperately hoped wouldn't happen, but it did, because of SH), but what people were shocked to see were demonstrations supporting SH." Claudia al-Rashoud, email, dated April 16, 2003.
40 Ibid.
41 Claudia al-Rashoud, email, dated March 29, 2003.
42 Remaining inside during the critical phase of the period was somewhat easier because of weather conditions in the country. In late March, Kuwait suffered sandstorms that were "the WORST anyone can remember." Claudia al-Rashoud, email, dated March 26, 2003. The thoughts of many in Kuwait turned to "all the poor soldiers out in the desert."
43 Claudia al-Rashoud, email, dated April 3, 2003.
44 Claudia al-Rashoud, email, dated April 16, 2003. By this time, Kuwaitis were dismantling the safe rooms constructed in their homes against the missile threat.
45 Claudia al-Rashoud, email, dated March 29, 2003.
46 Claudia al-Rashoud, email, dated March 26, 2003.
47 Claudia al-Rashoud, email, dated April 16, 2003.
48 During my visit in July 2003, I visited a newly completed Hilton complex south of Kuwait City. The U.S. military had leased the entire hotel complex for housing.
49 Claudia al-Rashoud, email, dated May 20, 2003.
50 Claudia al-Rashoud, email, dated April 16, 2003.
51 Mansour al-Sultan, "Officers, gunman killed after U.S. warns Westerners of drive-by shooting threat," *Arab Times*, January 11, 2005.
52 Ibid.
53 Faisal al-Qahtani, "Still Dangerous... U.S. Embassy Restates Alert," *Arab Times*, January 12, 2005. A "reliable security source" was cited as saying that that the authorities were holding "a minimum of six Kuwaitis."
54 Remarks in *Al-Siyassah* newspaper by al-Qahtani, "Still Dangerous."
55 Quoted in ibid.
56 Mansour al-Sultan and Salem al-Ghusain, *Arab Times*, February 20, 2005. Andalus was the home of the al-Rashoud family at the time, and Claudia recalls how the security forces professionally cordoned off the neighborhood in preparation for the arrest.
57 *Middle East Journal*, Chronology, Vol. 60, No. 2 (Spring 2006), p. 351.

58 Ibid/, No. 1 (Winter 2006), p. 135. The controversy was inflamed by charges made by Shaikh Salem al-'Ali al-Sabah, the head of the National Guard, who charged that a small segment of the al-Sabah family was making decisions unilaterally.
59 This event marked the first time a sitting prime minister had subjected himself to such a vote. While thirty-five MPs voted against the motion of no confidence, this was in no way a victory for the government. *Middle East Journal,* Chronology, Vol. 64, No.2 (Spring 2010), p. 288.
60 Ibid., Vol. 65, No. 2 (Spring 2011), p. 316.
61 Ibid., No. 3 (Summer 2011), pp. 479–80. The amir appointed Shaikh Ahmad al-Hamoud al-Sabah deputy prime minister and minister of interior. Shaikh Ahmad served as interior minister in 1991–92 and as defense minister in 1994. BBC News, Middle East, "Kuwait interior minister resigns over custody death," February 7, 2011.
62 *Middle East Journal,* Chronology, Vol. 65, No. 3 (Summer 2011), p. 480. Emboldened by the sense of drift and disorder in domestic politics and, perhaps, by activism in other places associated with the "Arab Spring," some of the demonstrators reportedly questioned the role of the ruling family, and advocates of other unrelated "causes" also stepped up their protests.
63 Ibid.
64 Ibid. According to the Associated Press (AP), the handle chosen by the opposition to attack the three ministers was the failure of Kuwaiti troops to join those of Saudi Arabia and Abu Dhabi in Bahrain following challenges by that nation's Shi'a majority to the Sunni-dominated government. The likelihood is that this was more a pretext than a reason for the actions of the Kuwaiti opposition. Kuwait, which has largely escaped the kind of sectarian strife that has afflicted the neighboring states, has traditionally been extremely circumspect in such conflicts. See <<washingtontimes.com/news/2011/mar/31/kuwait-cabinet-resigns-over-bahrain-crisis/>>
65 Michael Birnbaum, "Battle to oust Kuwait premier gains urgency," *Washington Post*, March 7, 2011. p. A8.
66 The ranks of the "opposition" were swollen by the emergence of several youth movements ("Kafi," "Wall Five") that coalesced around the demand for the prime minister to resign and an end of corruption. Shafeeq Ghabra, "Kuwait's Democracy is Challenged by Pressure for Reform," Washington Institute for Near East Policy, PolicyWatch #1897, February 2, 2012.

67 In February 2011, for instance, approximately one thousand *bidoun* (stateless Arab residents) demonstrated in Jahra for the first time to press a disputed claim to Kuwaiti citizenship. Dozens were arrested and at least thirty were injured when the police dispersed them with smoke and water cannons. *Middle East Journal*, Chronology, Vol. 65, No. 3 (Summer 2011), p. 480.

68 Ibid. As Ghabra correctly points out, "Most Kuwaitis ... remain attracted by the government's relaxed working hours, along with its generous salaries and vacation policies."

69 *Middle East Journal*, Chronology, Vol. 66, No. 1 (Winter 2012), p. 139–140.

70 Liam Stack "Corruption Inquiry Rocks Kuwait," *New York Times*, Sept 21, 2011. A reported $350 million was involved in the transfers. Abdullah Al-Shayji, "Kuwait in midst of own Arab Spring," *Gulf News*, December 12, 2011. Al-Shayji is chairman of the Political Science Department, Kuwait University

71 *Middle East Journal*, Chronology, Vol. 66, No. 1 (Winter 2012), p. 139–140.

72 BBC News Middle East, "Protesters storm Kuwaiti parliament," November 16, 2011. <<http://www.bbc.co.uk/news/world-middle-east-15768027?print=true>>

73 Ghabra, "Kuwait's Democracy Is Challenged by Pressure for Reform."

74 Al-Shayji, "Kuwait in midst of own Arab Spring."

75 Ghabra, "Kuwait's Democracy is Challenged by Pressure for Reform," loc. cit.

76 Ghanim Alnajjar, "Is Kuwait Out of the Impasse?" (Sada, Carnegie Endowment for International Peace, Mar 8, 2012).<http://carnegieendowment.org/sada/index.cfm?fa=show&article=47427&soir_hillite=

77 A vestige of this relationship is the tendency of Shi'a MPs, including those of the Islamic bloc, to be less rigid in their opposition to the government. An unchecked Sunni majority is the last thing Shi'a Kuwaitis want to empower.

78 Traditionally, a senior member of the al-Sabah family performed the function of liaison with the desert-dwelling tribes that constituted Kuwait's defense in depth. In the late 1980s, Shaikh Jabir al-'Ali still played this role. Today, it is not possible to identify a go-between.

79 Shafeeq Ghabra, "Kuwait and the Dynamics of Socio-Economic Change," *Middle East Journal*, Vol. 51, vol. 3 (Summer 1997), p. 359. Of the tribes that came to Kuwait in the 1950s and '60s 66 percent

originated in the Saudi deserts, while 21 percent were of Iraqi origin and 3 percent came from Syria. p. 364.
80 Ghabra, "Kuwait and the Dynamics of Socio-Economic Change," p. 367.
81 Ibid.
82 Ghabra, "Kuwait's Democracy Is Challenged by Pressure for Reform." By his calculation, tribal elements make up as much as 65 percent of the total population.
83 *Middle East Journal, Chronology*, Vol. 54, No. 4 (Autumn 2000), p. 638.
84 Ibid. Vol. 61, No. 4 (Autumn 2007), p. 698.
85 Ibid., Vol. 63, No. 2 (Spring 2009), p. 303.
86 Ibid., Vol. 64, No.2 (Spring 2010), p. 288.
87 During my most recent visit to Kuwait in 2011, I spoke with several Kuwaiti friends who expressed the belief that many persons holding Kuwaiti citizenship but living in Saudi Arabia were skewing election results in Kuwait.
88 Mary Ann Tétreault, Mary Ann & Haya al-Mughni, "Modernization and its Discontents: State and Gender in Kuwait," *The Middle East Journal*, Vol. 49, no. 3 (Summer 1995), p. 408.
89 "Healing the Scars of the Past," *The Majalla*, September 1, 2010. <<http://www.majalla.com/eng/2010/09/article55122465/print/>> Ambassador Bahr al-Uloom is the son of Ayatollah Mohammad Bahr al-Uloom, a moderate Iraqi Shi'a scholar.
90 Abdullah al-Shayji, "Kuwait-Iraqi ties: The curse of history and geography," *Gulf News*, May 30, 2011. Al-Shayji continues to detail threats and fulminations against Kuwait by Iraqi politicians.
91 *Middle East Journal*, Chronology, Vol. 66, no. 1 (Winter 2012), p. 139.
92 Ibid.
93 Ibid. The accused spy was a former officer in the Iraqi army who entered Kuwait illegally and claimed he was "stateless." Kuwait had expelled an unknown number of Iranian diplomats the previous April on charges of spying for Iran since 2003. Ibid., Vol. 65, No. 3 (Summer 2011), p. 480.
94 Abdullah al-Shayji, "Kuwait-Iraq: Cold war brewing," *Gulf News*, July 25, 2011.
95 *Middle East Journal*, Chronology, Vol. 65, No. 2 (Spring 2011), p. 316.
96 Alice Fordham, "Iraq reaches settlement with Kuwait on disputes: Baghdad continues regional charm offensive ahead of Arab summit," *Washington Post*, March 15, 2012.

20 Snapshots at Age One Hundred

1. Claudia al-Rashoud, email to author, April 3, 2012.
2. Ghabra, "Kuwait and the United States... ," p. 303.
3. Many American and British "old Gulf hands" regret the changes they have witnessed in Kuwait and other regional shaikhdoms. Their nostalgia is a forlorn one as well. Change has been unavoidable as these states have modernized and entered the global economy. In addition, considerable benefits have accrued technologically and otherwise for the populations.
4. Claudia Farkas al-Rashoud, "AWARE Center," December 2011.
5. Claudia Farkas al-Rashoud, "American Women's League (AWL)," typewritten manuscript, March 2012. Except as otherwise noted, this discussion is based on a summary of interviews and other research into the history of AWL.
6. Claudia Farkas al-Rashoud, "Tributes paid to American women," *Arab Times*, April 27–29, 1995.
7. By custom, the American ambassador and his wife opened the Bazaar. This caused delays and frustration, because a Kuwaiti security team thoroughly swept the room before their arrival.
8. It is difficult to imagine that as recently as the late 1980s, Islamists in the National Assembly were still intent on banning Christmas decorations in the lobbies of Kuwait's major hotels.
9. American companies have long provided religious services and recreational activities for American and other employees on their compounds. An American secretary at the U.S. Embassy, for example, fondly recalls driving to the distant AMINOIL camp on Saturday nights (circa 1970) for square dancing. Miller, correspondence.
10. Claudia al-Rashoud, "American education in Kuwait," March 2012.
11. The elementary school building at the present location is appropriately named in her honor. She has since had the satisfaction of seeing her grandchildren pass through the school to which she made such crucial contributions.
12. For an informed discussion of "American" universities in the Gulf and Middle East, see Shafeeq Ghabra, "American-style universities prove popular in Arab world," *Kuwait Times* website, July 29, 2007 <<http://www.kuwaittimes.net/read_news.php?newsid=NTIOMjk3OTk0>>.
13. Claudia al-Rashoud, "American Business Council of Kuwait," March 2012.

14 Ibid.
15 The league was begun in 1980 and was formally chartered by Little League International, Williamsport, Pennsylvania, in 1987. The succession of seasons was broken only in 1991 due to the disruptions of the Iraqi occupation.
16 Iddris Seidu, "KLL kicks off new season at Salem Field," *Arab Times*, January 13, 2011.
17 Claudia al-Rashoud, "Kuwait Little League," February 2012. KLL added T-Ball teams in the late 1980s while I was serving there. Today, it has a Challenger Division with two teams of players who have been diagnosed with Autism Spectrum Disorder or Down Syndrome. It is the only Challenger Division in the Middle East.
18 Anecdotal evidence suggest that a notable proportion of these residents, and their children, elect to return to Kuwait on further assignments or in other capacities. See, for example, the case of John Peaveler later in this chapter.
19 Except as otherwise indicated, the material for these profiles is drawn from Claudia al-Rashoud, "Contributing to Kuwait," March 2012.
20 Latham, *Occupation Diary*, p. 49.
21 During my service in Kuwait, I had a number of fascinating conversations with a young man who was a very conservative Muslim. A major focus of his charitable work in Somalia at that time was the collection of used prescription eyeglasses that could be matched to the needs of Somalis.
22 Ibid.
23 Since Islam forbids the consumption of pork, bacon and sausage are made of seasoned turkey or beef. I was pleasantly surprised by how close these "substitutes" are in taste to the "real thing."
24 Farkas, *Kuwait Before and After the Storm*, p. 202.
25 The hospital buildings along the coastal road had been unoccupied and deteriorating since the American Mission was dissolved in the 1960s. Their restoration and use had been discussed for decades, including conversations between Shaikha Hussah and me during my time as ambassador in the 1980s.

Appendix E Select Excerpts from Diaries ...

1 Roberta and John Hogan *Trapped in Kuwait: Countdown to Armageddon*, with Linda D. Meyer (Lynnwood, Washington: Chas. Franklin Press, 1991), p. 4.
2 Hogan, ibid., p. 32.

688   Notes

3   Ibid., p. 34. These exchanges relate to an operation to move citizens who felt vulnerable to safer quarters.
4   Ibid., p. 35.
5   Ibid., p. 41.
6   Ibid., p. 42.
7   Ibid., p. 44.
8   Ibid., p. 48.
9   Ibid., p. 52.
10 Ibid., p. 54.
11 Ibid., p. 58. The report of a shooting at the Embassy was erroneous.
12 Ibid., p. 59.
13 Don Latham, *Occupation Diary: The Diary of an American In Kuwait, August 2, 1990 until December 10, 1990* (Kuwait: Noureya Al Saddani, 1992), p. 13. The announcement was days earlier.
14 Hogan, *Trapped in Kuwait*, p. 90. There were, in fact, four women on the compound.
15 Ibid., p. 96.
16 Ibid., p. 98.
17 Ibid., p. 100.
18 Latham, *Occupation Diary*, pp. 37–38.
19 Ibid., p. 45.
20 Hogan, *Trapped in Kuwait*, p. 107.
21 Latham, *Occupation Diary*, p. 49.
22 Ibid.
23 Hogan, *Trapped in Kuwait*, pp. 112–13.
24 Ibid., p. 116.
25 Latham, *Occupation Diary*, pp. 59–60.
26 Ibid., p. 62.
27 Ibid., p. 67.
28 Hogan, *Trapped in Kuwait*, p. 124.
29 Latham, *Occupation Diary*, p. 70.
30 Hogan, *Trapped in Kuwait* p. 129.
31 Michael Kano, "Hiding from Saddam: An American in Occupied Kuwait," manuscript, 1998, p. 55.
32 Hogan, *Trapped in Kuwait*, p. 132.
33 Ibid., p. 149.
34 Latham, *Occupation Diary*, p. 109–10.
35 Hogan, *Trapped in Kuwait*, p. 153.
36 Ibid., p. 155.
37 Ibid., p. 156.
38 Latham, *Occupation Diary*, p. 119.

Index

Page numbers in *italics* refer to images.

A-4 fighter planes 214, 236, 311, 626n74
Ababeel missiles 448
abaya protests 176–77
Abd al-Hadi Ghazali, Walid 429
Abdallah Ali Reza 195
Abdallah __ al-Sabah. *See* Abdallah II
Abdallah al-Sabah al-Sabah. *See* Abdallah I
Abdallah al-Salem al-Sabah. *See* Abdallah III
Abdallah al-Uthman 146
Abdallah I (Abdallah al-Sabah al-Sabah) 9–10, 11, 528n25
Abdallah II (Abdallah __ al-Sabah) 2, 15–16, 524n4
Abdallah III (Abdallah al-Salem al-Sabah) *131*; Ahmad's death and 121, 133; assessment of 199–200; British administration and 148, 167; British recognition of 134, 560n3, 560n7; on business reform 151–52; death of 201; donations by 146; on governmental reform 76, 139–40, 166–67; hospitality of 205, 582n17; transition at independence and 179–80
Abdallah Jabir 141, 143, 176, 195
Abdallah Mubarak 121, 162, 166, 189

Abu Alwan (Salim Garabet) 136
Abu Dhabi, United Arab Emirates: 1981 GCC conference in 278; schools in 583n25, 584n30; U.S. Embassy in 213, 241, 534n36, 556n13, 564n44, 575n21, 582n17, 594n44; U.S. oil embargo and 592n25. *See also* United Arab Emirates (UAE)
Abu Hnaich (John Bagot Glubb) 67, 545n44
'Abu-Jasim, Muhammad 95–96
Abu Nidal (Sabri Khalil al-Banna) 312, 626n77, 629n97
Adair, Red 165
Ado, Sergio *352, 353,* 360, 402, 663nn22–23
Al-Adsani, Ibrahim 468
Agnew, Spiro 239, 250, 589n72, 598n82
agriculture 4, 675n77
Ahmad Abdallah al-Sabah 454
Ahmad al-Hamoud al-Sabah 683n61
Ahmad I (Ahmad al-Jabir al-Sabah): on 1929 desert boundary settlements 67–68, 545n46; 1929 'Uqair Conference and 60–61, 67, 541nn5–6; 1946 oil ceremony 110; Advisory Council and 59, 72–73, 75–76, 547n61, 548n77; automobiles and 79, 549n89; on British loyalties 67–70, 546nn46–47; British oil com-

Ahmad I *(continued)*
panies and 58; children of 121, 559n55; Dasman Palace and 79, 541n106; death of 120–21, 559n54, 559n55; first telephone call by 94; health of 90–91, 120; Ibn Saud and 63, 547n59; Mylrea and 90–91, 553n34; reputation of 121, 559n56; on slavery 78
Ahmadi, Kuwait: 1950s description of 181; community of 113, 164, 207, 557n33; establishment of 109–12; military cargo at 552n26; oil explosions in 164–65. *See also* Kuwait
Ahmad Said 170
Al-Ahram (newspaper) 234
air-conditioning 93, 144, 357, 359, 553n43, 558n40. *See also* climate
aircraft: A-4 fighter planes 214, 236, 311, 626n74; F-4 fighter planes 236, 592n24; F-18 fighter planes 311, 626n75; first use in oil exploration 554n64. *See also* weapons systems
airline activity: 1990 American evacuations 373–75, 652n52, 653nn53–56; 2003 restrictions 444–45, 680n24; first Kuwait routes 70, 546n54. *See also* plane hijackings; *specific airline companies*
Ajman tribe 14, 47–49, 538nn72–73
Akins, James E. 196, 579n71
Akio Shirota 632n8
The Alamo (movie) 361, 648n17
Alani, Mustafa 192–93
Alayon, Felipe 395, 661n2

Albert, Carl 250, 599n84
alcohol: arrests related to 454; PTSD and 439–40; regulations on 534n24, 613n30, 618n16
Aldakheel, Maureen 327, 373–74, 404–5
Alexander Gibb and Partners 173
Alexander the Great 526n5
Ali al-Mo'men 459
Ali Khalifa al-Sabah 172, 280, 281, 293, 294, 349, 611n19
Ali Sabah al-Salem al-Sabah 376
Allahu Akbar (expression) 377, 654n66, 655n67
Allison, Mary 64–65, 162, 557n34
Amal militia 626n78
Amarat tribe 5
Al-Ameer, Fatima 441–42
American Baccalaureate School 474
American Business Council of Kuwait (ABCK) 474–75
American community in Kuwait: 1940s–50s life 108–13; 1956 protests and 162, 570n25; 1961 evacuation 191–92; 1970s–80s withdrawal of 247–48; 1980s Iranian violence and 255–56; 1980s life in 296–98, 307; 1990–91 occupation residents 396, 402; 1990 escape tactics by 327–28, 636nn27–28, 656n78; 1990 Iraqi request for 331–32, 638n38; 1993 visit of 425–26; 2003 evacuation advisory 444, 680n22; on 2005 safety 452–53; August 2, 1990 migration to Embassy 323, 632n8; bus transport for 1990 evacuation 373, 632n6; casualties

Index 691

American community in Kuwait *(continued)*
during Iraq occupation 401, 661n3; charitable organizations 476–79 (*See also* American Women's League (AWL)); communication of 319, 556n14, 556n16; dancing and 405, 464, 686n9; globalization and 464–67, 686n3; hiding *vs.* embassy refuge 399, 662n12; initial arrival of 533n15; local acceptance of 37–39, 42–43, 53–54, 463–64, 575n15; musical performances and 116, 299, 619n24; oil communities *vs.* Town residents 113–14, 142, 143, 182, 563n42; population statistics 66, 174, 206, 635n25; reception of women from 205, 582n17, 582n20; recreation of *228, 230,* 250, 298, 619nn19–21; reputation of, in British community 116–17; return residents 557n32, 687n18; as target of terrorism 265, 306, 452, 606n67; taxes and home leave of 297, 619n17; theatrical performances of 283, 299, 613n32; waterski performance 619n23. *See also* oil industry of Kuwait; schools; siege of U.S. Embassy (Kuwait, 1990); United States
American Community School (Abu Dhabi, UAE) 584n30
American Foreign Service Association 599n88
Americani Cultural Centre (Kuwait) *355*
American Independent Oil Company (AMINOIL): chairman of 135; consular services for 118, 144; establishment of 112, 557n29; first strike of 113; nationalization of 217, 247–48, 597n70, 612n28
American International School (AIS) 446, 681n30
American Life Insurance Company 306
American Mission and hospital (Kuwait) 26–27; 1910 agreement 486; 1920 city walls and 50; 1920s support of 63, 543n20; 1930s–40s accommodations of 91–95, 544n29, 544n32, 552n20; 1934 procedure load 64–65; 1940s nurses training 95–96; 1950s conditions 145–47; 1951 diagram of *125;* in 1960s 181, 207; Battle of Jahra and 53–54, 56; chapel 70–71, 547n55; closure of 208, 247, 575n19; *colporteur* (term) 532n4; construction of 39–42, 70, 114, 146–48, 535n40, 535n42, 544n34; doctor's residence 39, 55, 535nn39–40; early acceptance of xiv, 31–33, 183–84, 532n6, 532n8, 532n10; establishment of ix, 31–34, 531n1, 533n15, 533n17; failed religious conversion 36, 43, 208, 463, 566n61; gifted property to 57, 535n50; Ibn Saud and 47; looting during 1990 siege 376; meetings of 566n59; oil industry and 113–14; original role of 36, 534n28, 574n13; outpost facilities of 95, 145–46;

American Mission and hospital (*continued*)
vaccinations 65, 182, 544n33, 575n16; World Missions Board 183, 575n19. *See also* Calverly School; *specific persons*
American School of Kuwait (ASK) 419, 473–74, 671n28, 671n30, 686n11. *See also* International School of Kuwait (ISK)
American University (Beirut) 176, 580n82
American University of Kuwait (AUK) 474
American University of the Middle East (AUM) 474
American Women's League (AWL) 226–27; 1993 Bush visit and 426; charity bazaar 298, 405, 471–72, 686n7; on EOD 421; post-2006 life and 472–74; role of 466, 468–71
Amir Abdallah 181
Anaza tribe 5
Ancona (ship) 18
Ang, Melvin 362–63
anger in post-traumatic recovery. *See* post-traumatic stress disorder (PTSD)
Anglo-Iranian Oil Company (AIOC) 58, 99–100, 110, 122, 560n62, 566n70. *See also* Kuwait Oil Company (KOC)
Anglo-Ottoman Convention (1913) 18–20, 46, 171, 530n43, 534n36, 537n59
animals: birds 675n77; charitable organizations for 478–79; Islam on 687n23; pets 326, 336, 641n57
anthropology reports. *See* Lienhardt, Peter

Al-Anzi, Fareed 426, 672n46
Arab Cooperation Council (ACC) 628n95. *See also* Gulf Cooperation Council (GCC)
Arabian Mission of the Reformed Church in America. *See* American Mission and hospital (Kuwait)
Arabic language schools 42, 543n25
Arab-Isreali War (1967) 211–12, 585n45, 586nn49–50
Arab League: Kuwait's application to 188, 200, 576n30; Mutual Defense Pact 193, 578n60
Arab Legion of Transjordan 545n44
The Arab of the Desert (Dickson) 34, 133
Arab Times 422
'Arafat, Yasir 543n26
ARAMCO 248, 555n10, 565n56
archaeology 181, 526n5
ardha (sword dance) 423, 569n6
arfaj (camel thorn) 4, 27, 92
'Arif, Abd al-Salam 234
Armitage, Richard 349
Ashland 557n29
ash-Sha'ab (weekly newspaper) 170
Ashura 258
Aspin, Les 616n65
Al-Assad, Hafiz 271
assassinations: of Abu Nidal 626n77; attempt on Bush 428–30, 673n66, 674n68; attempt on Habib 271; attempt on Jabir III 262, 604n44, 618n14; of Iraqi diplomat and son (1985) 609n2; of U.S. ambassadors 241, 245
'ataba (term) 6, 527n7

Atack, Norrie 371–72, 652n47
Al-Atiqi, Abdul Rahman *131*, 180, 237, 256, 601n11
Atlantic Monthly 610n4
automobiles: Ford Motor Company 59, 92, 219, 590n81; GM dealership in Kuwait 218–19, 563n41; introduction in Kuwait 38, 58, 59; of Kuwaiti military 579n75; special tires for 541n105; of U.S. Consulates 142, 565n55
Avis 306
Al-Awadi, Abd al-Rahman 417
AWARE (Advocates for Western-Arab Relations) 467–68
Awazim tribe 34, 67, 69, 546n46, 607n83

Baath Party of Iraq 234, 590n5, 600n3. *See also* Iraq; Saddam Hussein
Al-Bader, Abdul Fatah 293, 294
Bader al-Baijan 418, 671n25
Bader Saud al-Abdul Razzaq 562n32
Badria, Shaikha 564n51
Baghdad, Iraq: -Kuwait railroad lines 18, 35, 45; U.S. Consulate in 116–17, 196–97. *See also* Iraq; U.S. Embassy (Baghdad, Iraq)
Baghdad Pact (proposed) 172, 572n59, 573n63
Baharna (term) 540n99
Bahra, Kuwait 101. *See also* Kuwait
Bahrain: 1920s oil interests in 98, 554n53; 1970s U.S. relations 212–15, 236–37, 587n58; Al-Khalifa and 10, 528n20; missionaries in 31, 33; parliamentary experiment of 243; pearl traders and 20; U.S. Consulate in 103, 213, 617n4; U.S. Embassy in 213, 241; U.S. Naval base in 115, 212, 586n54; WWII and 551n10. *See also* Manama, Bahrain
Bahrain Petroleum Company (BAPCO) 99
Bahr al-Uloom, Ayatollah Mohammad 680n21
Bahr al-Uloom, Mohammad Hussein 459, 685n89
Al-Baijan, Nabil 441
Baker, James 393
Al-Bakr, Ahmad Hassan 209–10, 254, 590n5
Al-Banna, Sabri Khalil 312, 626n77
Al-Baqsami, Thuraya 654n67
Barber, Brian 678n2
barge construction. *See* shipbuilding industry
Al-Barges, Barges 296
Barney, Ester 557n34
Barrak 6
baseball leagues *228*, 250, 298, 475, 687n15, 687n17
Basra, Iraq: 1988 description of 609n1; British control in 46–47; diplomatic relations in pre-20th century 10–11, 528n25; migration of Sabah family to 530n42; missionaries in 31, 32; trading history of 1, 4, 5–7; U.S. Consulate in 118, 121, 140, 558n47. *See also* Iraq
Battle of Jahra (Kuwait, 1920) 49–56, 539n77, 539nn84–85, 540nn94–95, 574n13
Battle of Riqa'i (Kuwait, 1928) 66, 545n41

Bayne, Marmaduke G. 586n54
Bayt-ar-Rabban 33
BBC (British Broadcasting Corporation) 332, 370, 448, 651n42
Bechtel Corporation: facilities of 109; personnel of 204, 205, 556n17; U.S. Army and 206, 437
bedouin tribes: al-Sabah relations with 684n78; camel caravans and 57–58; citizenship of 458–59; missionaries and 37, 532n6; settlements of 5, 63, 133–34, 541n6; urbanization and politics of 457–58, 684n79, 685n82. See also *specific tribes*
Beecher, "Skip" 116
Begin, Menachem 271
Behbehani, Jaafar 440
Behbehani Compound 64, 66, 107
Beirut, Lebanon: 1982 invasion 271–72, 608n90; Kuwait Embassy bombing 629n97; military in 257; reputation of 143, 398; schools in 176, 576n27, 580n82; U.S. Embassy in 398, 575n21, 601n13, 638n35. See also Lebanon
Beirut College for Women (renamed Beirut University College) 64, 576n27
Belgium Embassy (Kuwait) 656n75
Bell, Gawain 152, 164
Bender, Michael 321
Beni Ka'b tribe 10, 528n23
Beni Khalid regime 5–6, 9
Beni 'Utba 6, 527n7
Bennett, Arthur 32, 33, 533n15, 533n17
Bibby, Geoffrey 526n5

Big Five company controversy 149–51
Bilkert, Henry 69, 546n50
birds 675n77
Bishara, Abdullah 278
Bishara, Ahmed 409
Bishop, Robin 270
bitumen deposits 101
Black September 245
Bneid al-Gar, Kuwait 158
BOAC (British Overseas Airways Corporation) 70, 546n54
Bodine, Barbara: on citizen help 329, 637n31; communication by 330, 389, 632n5, 637n34; embassy evacuation and 334, 337, 363, 390, 397; on Iraq invasion 318, 663n22; siege operations by 339, 345, 404, 634n18, 640n47, 659n105
Boeing 609n98
Boghardt, Lori Plotkin 624n63, 639n41, 668n59
Bogosian, Richard 242, 249, 252, 588n69, 595n47
Bombay Marine 12
Bonn conference (1990, Germany) 316
boom (Arabic cargo vessel): as symbol 81, 86, 87, 107; as term 524n5; water cargo on 106, 172. See also maritime commerce; pearl diving industry
Boots, Paul 101
border disputes (Iraq-Kuwait): in 1928–29 60–62, 67–68, 541nn5–6, 545n46; in 1973 235–36, 591n18; 1990 initial invasion 321–25, 631n1; 1993 427–28; in 1998–99 432–33; demarcation politics 171–72, 308–9, 572n57, 625n66, 668n62

Index   695

border disputes (Iraq-Saudi Arabia)   577n50
Boucher, Richard   662n10
Bourahmah, Debbie   469
Bovenkerk, Henry   146
Bowden, William   654n62
Al-Braikan, Hazem   669n3
Braun Construction Company   280
Brewer, William D.: on 1953 water pipeline project   172, 573n63; appointment of   144; on early Kuwait   532n14; on Mubarak   58; report by   115–16; at St. Paul's Church consecration   164
Bridgeton (tanker)   290–91
Briscoe, Kevin   321
British Airways   70, 546n54
British community in Kuwait: 1956 protests and   162; 1990 evacuation of   325, 639n41; celebrations of   299–300; death during siege   371; education system of   206, 583n25, 583n28, 598n77, 619n18; population statistics   174; reputation of   150–51, 568n84. See also British political agency in Kuwait
British Council Centre (Basra, Iraq)   176
British East India Company   9, 10, 12, 528n25, 543n19
British Embassy (Kuwait)   180, 635n24
British Fusilier (oil tanker)   110
British-India Steam Navigation Company   14, 38, 529n34
British Ladies Society (BLS)   450, 477
British military in Kuwait: in 1927–29   66–69, 546n47; 1961 intervention   189–94, 576n44, 577n50, 577n57; after Battle of Jahra   54–56, 540nn94–95; cargo at Ahmadi   552n26; withdrawal of   210, 585nn40–41
British military in Saudi Arabia   67
British oil concessions in Gulf region   58, 97–99, 175
British Petroleum   217
British political agency in Kuwait: 1899 protectorate agreement   18, 33, 35, 179, 187, 576n33; 1913 Anglo-Ottoman Convention   18–20, 46, 171, 530n43, 534n36, 537n59; 1929 'Uqair Conference and   60–61, 541nn5–6; 1950s conditions   115, 135–39, 148–49, 160–66, 567n73; on 1953 pipeline project   173; 1960s conditions   579n69; 1961 independence agreement   179–80; Embassy   180, 635n24; first American missionaries and   33, 38; first oil concessions of   97–99, 554n51; recognition of Abdallah III   134, 560n3, 560n7, 568n89; residence of   28; sentiments of Gulf political agents on   62; U.S. relations with   97–103, 114, 118–19, 137, 594n42. See also British community in Kuwait; British military in Kuwait
Brooks, Dennis   290
Brown, Paul   352, 354, 359, 657n92
Brown and Root   303
Bubiyan Island, Kuwait   187, 245, 308, 672n50
Buckley, John and Joan   113–14
Buraimi oasis, Saudi Arabia   574n5, 595n46

Burgan, Kuwait 79, 101, 550n92
Burrows, Bernard 118–19
Bush, George H. W.: 1993 Kuwait visit of 422–24; at 1996 building dedication 437, 678n109; assassination attempt on 428–30, 673n66, 674n68; children named after 551n16; Sa'd Abdallah and 311, 626n71
businesses 151–52, 564n51. See also *specific types*
Butler, Richard 433
Bwambale, Hassan 468

cable communications 38, 58, 72, 209
Calverly, Edwin 29, 31, 534n38, 574n13. See also American Mission and hospital (Kuwait)
Calverly, Eleanor 26; children of 534n38; descriptions of Kuwait by 35–36; work of 31, 42, 557n34. See also American Mission and hospital (Kuwait)
Calverly School: closure of 64, 70, 207, 543n26; establishment of 42, 44; reputation of 64, 543n23, 543n25; students of 29, 29, 44, 57, 64, 536n54; teachers of 536n53. See also American Mission and hospital (Kuwait)
Calvert system of homeschooling 206
camels and camel caravans 27, 57
camel thorn 4, 27, 92
Camp David Agreement 269
Canadian Embassy (Kuwait) 654n62, 656n75

Capps, Michael 338
Carlucci, Frank 349
Carradine, Charlie 358, 388
Carroll, Jim 364
Carter, Jimmy 269
Carter Doctrine 269
Ceauşescu, Nicolae 313, 315
Cecil, Charles 211, 585n46
Chancery and residence, U.S. Embassy 224, *351*; 1983 bombing on 257–58; construction of 195, 240–41, 583n21, 593nn38–39, 594nn40–41; school in 206–7; security of facilities at 255, 323, 359, 612n27. See also siege of U.S. Embassy (Kuwait, 1990); U.S. Embassy (Kuwait)
charitable organizations 476–79, 687n21. See also American Women's League (AWL)
Charles, Sandra 321
chemical warfare: by Iraq 327, 384, 629n98; pollution from 308, 339; preparation for 444, 445–46. See also weapons systems
Cheney, Dick 431
Chesapeake City (tanker) 633n9
Chesapeake Shipping, Inc. 290
Cheslick, Virginia 582n20
childbirth practices 42
child custody case 270, 608n85
children: 1990 deaths and violence against 397, 406, 441, 663n17, 679n10; animals and 478; citizenship and 250, 259, 270, 608n85, 687n18; community groups for 468–70; education of (*See under* education); embassy siege and evacuation of 337, 362–65, 369, 372, 373,

Index 697

children *(continued)*
418, 662n10; entertainment for 619n20, 634n18; EOD and 421; health effects of war 407, 419, 445–47, 666n40, 666n45; medical care for 65, 96, 450; plane hijackings and 263; separation due to war 636n27, 638n36, 641n56, 653n56; sports for (*See* Little League baseball). See also *specific communities in Kuwait*
Chippendale, Nancy 582n20
cholera epidemics 12
Christmas holidays 93, 260, 603n32, 617n6, 686n8
Christopher, Warren 607n79
Chun, Gladys 601n12
churches: National Evangelical Church in Kuwait 70–71, 207, 531n1, 547n55; St. Paul's Church in Ahmadi 164, 207. *See also* American Mission and hospital (Kuwait); religion
Churchill, Winston 149
circumcision 65, 544n31
citizenship: Battle of Jahra and 57, 540n100; of bedouin tribes 458–59; children and 250, 259, 270, 608n85, 687n18; of Lewis Scudder, Jr. 208, 603n31; of Palestinians 197, 603n31; U.S. students and 186
Clarke, Ramsey 363, 434
class system 158, 164. *See also* merchant (middle) class
climate conditions: during 1990 embassy siege 359, 647n12; during 2003 invasion 449, 682n42; housing and 3–4, 525n14. *See also* air-conditioning
Clinton administration 429–30
clothing: constitutional mandate on 458; foreign influence on 157, 184, 525n10; as symbol of national identity 157, 185, 423, 641n52; veil-wearing protest 176–77
clubs and organization: 1950s protests of 160–66, 570n28, 571n36; of 1960s 580n6; Ahmadi women's 113, 557n33; surveillance of 245, 596n55
Cluverius, Wat 213
CNN 397, 448, 466, 641n52
Coca-Cola Company 250
colporteur (term) 532n4
Colwell, Luz Marina 365, 649n26
Commander Middle East Force (COMMIDEASTFOR): 1970s retention of 213; communication with Manama 616n1; establishment of 115, 558n39; seaplane tenders of 558n40
Committee of the Clubs protest (1956) 160–64
Committee on Foreign Investment in the United States 280
communication: during 1990 embassy siege 360–61, 366–67, 370, 403, 647n13, 650n35; of consulate officers 561n9; diplomatic relationships and subtleties in 216, 588n69, 588nn67–68; during social unrest 259, 265–66, 602n21, 602n27. *See also* language
communication systems: cable 38, 58, 209; for embassy wardens 259, 602n27; initial consular methods 142–43, 564n45;

communication systems *(continued)*
  telephone 94, 143; telex 584n36
communist party: exclusion from Kuwait 596n56; in Iraq 209, 234; in Lebanon 580n82; U.S. on 159
Connor, Marsha 426–27
Connor, William 426
constitution (1962, Kuwait) 198, 247, 597n67
Convention on International Trade in Endangered Species of Wild Fauna and Flora (CITES) 479
Cottam, Howard Rex 211, 237–38, 585n48, 589n72
Cox, Percy 47, 60–61
Crane, Charles R. 69, 546n50
Crichton, G.C.L. 148, 150
Crist, George 624n63
Crocker, Ryan 437, 647n14
Crouse, Ruth 557n34
Crowe, William J., Jr. 213, 214
Crystal, Jill 122
Cuban Missile Crisis (1962) 197
Culbertson, Lloyd 366, 650n31
Cunningham, Pat 562n32
currency 152, 167, 209, 380, 417, 571n43
Czech Embassy (Kuwait) 619n21

Dabbagh, Colonel 193–94
Daily News (Kuwaiti English-language newspaper) 239
dancing: in American community 405, 464, 686n9; in Kuwaiti community 76, 423, 569n6, 585n46
Dar al-Athar al-Islamiyyah (DAI) 355, 402, 413, 480–81, 671n25
Dartmouth College 474

Dasman Palace 50, 322, 323, 541n106
dates and date trade industry: in 1930s 82; on embassy grounds 299, 383, 620n25, 657n92; groves as gifts 13, 16, 530n39; of Jabir III 618n12
Davies, Ralph 112
Davies, Roger 241
Al-Dawish, Faisal 50, 51, 54, 56, 66
De Gaury, Gerald 71, 549n79
DeJong, Gerrit 70, 96, 133, 164
deportations: in 1960s 203; in 1980s 261, 264, 305, 605n56; of persons with TB 477
depressions, economic 29, 38, 44, 63, 78, 83–85, 95
desert agriculture 4, 675n77
desert border. *See* border disputes (Iraq-Kuwait)
"Desert Peace" 425–27
development. *See* urban development; *specific industries*
Dhahran, Saudi Arabia 104, 142, 242, 551n10, 554n64, 558n47, 594n42
dhows (term) 524n5. See also *boom* (Arabic cargo vessel); maritime commerce
diabetes 32, 439
Dickman, François M.: on Haig's instruction 271–72, 608n88; on Kuwait foreign investments 278, 590n7; on Kuwait nonalignment policy 268; security of 606n69; on successor Grove 273; on Suq al-Manakh 276; as U.S. Ambassador 255–56, 258
Dickson, Harold: on 1929 'Uqair Conference 60–61; Ahmad and 68, 70; *The Arab of the*

Index   699

Dickson, Harold *(continued)*
  Desert 34, 133, 607n83; as British political agent 39; on first oil concessions 99–100, 554n56
Dickson, Violet 28, 375–76
Dilmun civilization ruins 526n5
Dimna, Kuwait 156, 569n3
diseases. See *specific diseases*
dishdashas 157, 185, 420, 423, 525n10, 641n52
distillation plants, seawater: establishment of 106, 110, 149; output of 573n62; protection of 295; second plant 152, 168, 568n87. *See also* water
diwanniya system: modern political discourse and xiv, 160, 300, 309, 313–14, 627n83; term 536n53; tradition of 64, 143, 468, 596n15, 613n31; war recovery and 679n6
DNA testing 412, 441, 451
Doha, Qatar 242, 594n45
donkeys 26, 51, 106
Dorfman, Dan 279
drugs and PTSD 439–40
dual-national families 185, 250, 259, 270, 418, 470, 608n85
Dubai, United Arab Emirates: gold trade and 550n7; U.S. businesses and 589n79; U.S. oil embargo 236–37. *See also* United Arab Emirates (UAE)
Dulles, John Foster 573n63
Duncan, Bruce 325, 656n82
Duncan, Enoch 126, 135, 136, 140, 561n9
DuPont 541n105
Al-Duri, 'Izzat Ibrahim 245
Dutch East India Company 8, 9
Dutch Embassy (Kuwait) 656n75

Eagleburger, Lawrence S. 393–94, 661n124
The Early Bird (restaurant) 479–80
Eastern and General Syndicate (EGS) 98–99
Eastern Gulf Oil Corporation 98–99, 108
Eastman Kodak 555n64
economic activities of Kuwait: pre-20th century 1–3, 7–8, 10–11, 13, 524n1, 525n7; 1980s crisis 276, 610n4; currency 152, 167, 209, 380, 417, 571n43; depression eras 29, 44, 63, 78, 85, 95; foreign investments 218, 278–79, 665n34; Mubarak and 19–20; treasury 149–50, 218. See also *specific trades*
The Economist 678n2
education system in Kuwait: in 1980s 207; affected by 1956 protests 162–64, 570n21, 570n27; collegiate system of 249–50, 297–98; culturally diverse instruction 175–76, 570n21, 573n72; for girls 43, 79, 175; homeschooling 206. *See also* Kuwaiti Department of Education; schools
education system outside of Kuwait: collegiate system for 249–50, 297–98; first students of 186; for girls 576n27; in Gulf region 64, 584n30; societal changes due to 136–37, 175–76; statistics on 249; U.S. programs 185–86, 249, 575n24, 598n80; U.S. *vs.* British systems 598n77. See also *specific schools*
Edwards, Lovey 240
Egypt: 1956 Suez Crisis 160–68,

Egypt *(continued)*
  186, 570n28, 571n36; on 1961 British intervention 577n54; -Israeli peace treaty 269, 285. *See also* Nasser, Gamal Abdel

Egyptian community in Kuwait: agitation from 12, 134, 159, 161–63, 203, 581n12; educators from 175–76, 573n72

Eids. *See* holidays

electricity: in 1940s 106; in 1980s 553n42; in American Mission and hospital 94; early power stations 89, 106, 110, 149; during embassy siege 357, 361–62, 365, 382, 646n2, 647n13, 664nn27–28; of U.S. Consulate 141

Embassy Beach, Kuwait 196, 579n70

emotional effects of war. *See* post-traumatic stress disorder (PTSD)

English, Clifton 121, 133, 135, 560n8

English language schools. *See* schools

entertainment: in 1930s–40s 93, 107; during embassy siege *350, 353,* 361, 362, 388–89, 647n7, 648n17; musical performances 116, 299, 619n24; theatrical performances 283, 299, 613n32. *See also* holidays

Entertainment City 421

environmental pollution from war 407, 420, 671n31, 671n33

explosive ordnance disposal (EOD) 420–22. *See also under* mine warfare

eye diseases 32, 65, 531n2

F-4 fighter planes 236, 592n24

F-18 fighter planes 311, 626n75

Fahad Ahmad al-Sabah 633n10

Fahad Salem, Shaikh of Kuwait *126;* American relations with 136, 138–39, 166; British relations with 136, 561n16; children of 138, 561n14, 564n51; description of 139, 561n16, 562n25; reception of U.S. consulate by 136, 143, 564n51; schooling of 57, 64, 561n13

Failaka Island, Kuwait 295, 526n5, 617n5

Faisal ibn Turki 15

Fakhri Qadduri 235, 591n16

Fao Peninsula, Iraq 285, 294–95

Farrington, Edna 267

Fatah (Palestinian organization) 626n77

Fawzi Dalloul 237

FBI (Federal Bureau of Investigation) 429, 673n66

Federal Highway Works Administration (FHWA) 282

Fell, Egbert 182–83

Filipino community in Kuwait 337, 341, 342, 548n70, 634n21, 644n77, 681n35

fire services 106, 165

Firestone Tire and Rubber Company 541n105

fireworks 110, 447

fishing settlements, historical 5–6, 526n5

flags, national: 1990 embassy siege and xii, 392, 658n94, 660n120; 1993 Bush visit and 422; confiscation of 302, 574n5, 655n71; Howell children and 594n45; of Kuwait 81, 180, 381, 655n71; Little

Index 701

flags, national *(continued)*
 League and 475; on Mylrea Memorial Men's Hospital *128*, 147; protests burning 272; tanker protection and 288–91, 310, 633n9; on U.S. official vehicles 330, 337–38, 624n59
food: breakfast restaurants 479–80; fast food restaurants *231*, 297, 298, 472, 618n15; supermarkets 297, 556n13
footwear 634n21
Ford, Gerald 280, 611n18
Ford Motor Company 219, 250, 590n81
Foreign Service Nationals (FSNs) 237, 257–58, 355
Forties, David L. 328
fortification, pre-20th century 6, 8–9, 526n1, 528n17, 528n24, 529n26. *See also* walls, city
France 586n53, 592n22, 655n74
Freeth, Zahra 71–72, 106, 112, 540n99, 575n16
French Embassy (Kuwait) 655n74
Fulbright, William 589n72, 599n86
Fund for Future Generations 218, 279, 665n34
Funk, Thomas G. 338
Al-Fuzai, Muna 474–75

Gallman, Waldemar J. 573n63
G. and J. Weirs 152, 568n87
gangrene 53
Gatch, John 585n48
gates, city 23, 93, 553n38. *See also* fortification, pre-20th century; walls, city
Geerhart, Wilton and Mrs. 111, 556n17
gender customs. *See* women

General Electric 186
General Motors (GM) 218–19, 563n41
generator, power 58, 59, 553n42
geology of oil exploration 101
George V, King 58
Germany 18–19, 46, 75, 316, 537n59, 675n79
Getty Oil Company 144, 169, 206, 563n42, 565n56
Ghabra, Shafeeq 198, 381, 409, 456–58, 466, 628n86
Ghadanfari, Habib 624n58
Al-Ghanim 563n41
Ghazi, King of Iraq 75
Al-Ghunaym, Khalid 64
girls, education of 43, 79, 175, 576n27. *See also* women
Glaspie, April 318–19, 585n48, 630n104
Glen Eagle Company 310
Globe Oil and Refining Co. 557n29
Glubb, John Bagot "Glubb Pasha" 67, 545n44
Gnehm, Edward "Skip" 404, 418, 647n14
gold 550n7
Graham, Laurie 354
Graham, Maurice *354*, 388
Grane (term) 5, 526n1
Great Britain. *See under* British
Griffin, Philip J. 274
Grobba, Fitz 75
grocery stores 297, 556n13
Grove, Brandon 273
Gulf Cooperation Council (GCC) 272–73, 278, 286–87, 628n95
Gulf Exploration Company 100–101
Gulf islands: 1970s Iraq-Kuwait relations on 245, 591n18;

702 Index

Gulf islands *(continued)*
    Bubiyan 187, 245, 308,
    672n50; Kubbar Island 113;
    Kuwaiti declaration on 246;
    Qaru Island 113; Umm al
    Maradim Island 113; Warba
    Island 245
Gulf Kit (attire) 93
Gulf Oil Company 118, 139, 217,
    247–48
Gulf Protection Regime. *See* Operation Earnest Will
Gulf University of Science and
    Technology (GUST) 474
Gulzaman Khan 237, 564n43,
    592n28

Habib, Phillip 271, 608n89
Haidar al-Khalifa 96
Haidar Mohammed al-Khalifa
    567n78
Haig, Alexander Meigs, Jr. 271,
    272, 608n87
Haji Ahmed bin Salmon 88
Hamburg-Amerika Line (ship) 38
Hamdan, Ghazi 323
Hammadi, Sa'dun 246
Al-Hammadi, Abdallah 439
Al-Hamoud, Mudi 458
Hanken, Bethen 400
harbor. *See* Port city of Kuwait
Harb tribe 67
Harrison, Ann 533n18, 546n50
Harrison, Paul 27; book of recollections and 533n18; child
    of 64; duties of 31, 33, 37;
    Ibn Saud and 538n67; on
    local acceptance 37; on pearl
    diver's health 536n51
Hart, Jr., Fred L. 328
Hart, Parker T. 131, 180, 204, 205,
    581n15

Hassouna, Abdul Khalek 193
Hassounah, Jane 446, 447
Hasted, Major General (Indian
    Army) 148, 150–51
Hatfield, Mark 250
Hawaiian Dredging Co. 168
Hawk missiles 214, 236, 273, 284,
    295, 330, 367
Haynes, Philip 39, 41
health effects of war: environmental pollution and 420, 449,
    671n31, 671n33; on Foreign
    Service personnel xii–xiii;
    Howell on 665n36; physical
    injuries 450; on vulnerable
    populations 407, 666n40,
    666n45. *See also* post-traumatic stress disorder (PTSD)
Heath, Edward 179, 656n82
Hebrew language schools 543n24
Hejaz conquest 66–67, 545n42
Herzberg, Mark 358, 386, 390
Heusinkveld, Eleanor 96
Higgins, Odessa 338, 363, 642n62
Higgins Industries, Inc. 90,
    552n30
hijab (head covering) 458
hijackings. *See* plane hijackings
Hilton Hotel, Kuwait 196, 255,
    293, 585n47, 682n48
Hinchcliff, Peter 300
HMS *Bulwark* 191
HMS *Wren* 133
Hoffman, Miles 401
Hoffman, William 267
Holden, David 194
holidays: Christmas 93, *231*, 260,
    603n32, 617n6, 686n8; facilities
    for 299; Independence Day
    celebrations 127, 206, 229,
    298–99, 619n22; military 299,
    672n44; shaikhs-American

holidays *(continued)*
call tradition 93, 143–44, 527n15, 565n53; sword dance 423, 569n6; Thanksgiving 353, 388, 648n18. *See also* entertainment
homeschooling 206
Hooper, James 293
Hospital of Psychological Medicine 407
hospitals: effects of Iraq occupation on 329, 397, 636n29; first construction 39–41; Mylrea Memorial Men's Hospital 41, 127, 128, 146–47, 355, 687n25; Olcott Memorial Hospital for Women 71, 94, 136, 355; postwar 114, 557n37. *See also* American Mission and hospital (Kuwait)
housing: 1950s redevelopment plans 130, 155–57; climate considerations of 3–4, 525n14; inflation and 567n78
Howell, Margie Saunders 227, 231, 355; award for 648n16; as AWL chair 227, 298; communication during siege 360–61, 365, 366; DAI and 481; Dorothy Scudder and 597n69; Glaspie and 630n104; on women's suffrage 599n88
Howell, W. Nathaniel 349, 350, 352, 353, 355; 1967 June War and 586n50; 1980 Zubair bombing and 606n72; 1982 Israeli conflict and 608n86; on 1983 Iraq policy 613n38; 1985 plane hijackings and 606n67; 1990 Iraq invasion buildup 319; 1990 Iraq invasion communication 321, 325–27, 631n1; 1990 meeting with Iraqi Embassy 330, 637n34; at 1996 building dedication 678n109; 2003 Iraq visit 680n21; appointment to Embassy Kuwait 291; on authority over citizens 331; baseball and 619n19; on British acceptance of American presence 534n36; British celebrations and 300; DAI lecture by 481; decorations of xi; description of 327, 588n67; *diwanniyas* visits of 300; in Doha 594n45; Dorothy Scudder and 597n69; at Embassy Abu Dhabi 534n36, 556n13, 564n44, 575n21, 582n17, 588n68; at Embassy Beirut 575n21; on eyewitnesses 633n14; on Fahad Ahmad 633n10; family of 594n45, 596n57, 641n57 (*See also* Howell, Margie Saunders); on flags 624n59; on Gulf regional conference 316, 629n96; initial consultations as ambassador 294; Jackson and 323–63, 648n20; on Kuwaiti's nonalignment 588n67; language prowess of 599n86; musical skills of 619n24; personal effects and evacuation x–xi; role as evacuee of 333, 640n45; on Shi'a politics in Lebanon 626n78; siege momento 392, 660nn117–18; as US Central Command 303, 615n52. *See also* siege of U.S. Embassy (Kuwait, 1990); U.S. Embassy (Kuwait)

Index

Hudson, Daniel K. 321, 338
Hug, Rita M. 652n52
Al-Humaidhi, Ayeshah 478–79
hunger 69, 84
Hungry Bunny (fast food restaurant) *231*, 298
Hunt, John 295, 618n7
Hunter (U.S. tugboat) 302
Husayn, 'Ala' 434, 676n91
Hussah Sabah al-Salem al-Sabah *355*, 481
Hussain, Fatima 177
Hussein, King of Jordan 211, 372

Iacocca, Lee 250
Ibn Saud: 1929 'Uqair Conference and 60–61, 541nn5–6; Ahmad and 63, 547n59; Ajman tribe and 47, 48, 538n72; American Mission and 47; on authority over Kuwait 541n7; on authority over Qatar 61; embargo on Kuwait by 49, 63, 70, 542n16; Harrison and 538n67; Hejaz conquest and 66–67, 545n42; Mubarak and 45; Mylrea and 45, 538n74; Rush on 49, 538n73; Scudder on 45; Wahhabi *Ikhwan* and 60, 66, 545n42, 546n53. *See also* Saudi Arabia
Al-Ibrahim, Yusuf 16, 17, 19
IIS (Iraqi Intelligence Service) 428–30, 674n68
Ikhwan. *See* Wahhabi *Ikhwan*
Ikhwan al-Muslimeen (Muslim Brothers) 143
Imperial Airways 70, 546n54
Independence Day (U.S.) celebrations *127*, 206, 229, 298–99, 619n22

India: foreign retirement in 90, 91; gold and 550n7; Kuwaiti currency of 152; maritime trade with Kuwait 2, 7–10, 12, 81–83, 528n25, 529n34; missionary work in 92; schooling in 177; U.S. opposition by 103
Indian community in Kuwait 108, 122, 174, 182, 342, 441
inflation 84, 150, 567n78
influenza epidemic (globally, 1918) 47, 537n62
International School of Kuwait (ISK) 207, 474, 686n11. *See also* American School of Kuwait (ASK)
Iran: 1972 foreign policy 607n81; 1980s air attacks on Kuwait 614n44; 1980s Kuwaiti relations with 285, 529n38, 613n36, 623n51; 1986 tanker attacks by 287–88; 1987 missile attacks 294–95; 1988 U.S. action on 303–4, 621nn32–33; embassy seizure in 255–57, 601n12, 613n36; mine warfare by 301–2, 620n32; oil industry in 280, 281, 566n70; Shatt al-Arab 105–6, 172–73, 235, 308, 526n3, 573n63, 606n71; Shiite community in 253–54; U.S. asset freeze of 256, 269, 601n11; WWII and 87. *See also* Iraq-Iran War (1980–88)
Iran Ajr (ship) 301–2, 620n28, 620n32
Iranian community in Kuwait: in 1940s 95; 1970s–80s political agenda of 253–54, 261–62, 264, 603n41; in diplomatic offices 260; population

Index 705

Iranian community in Kuwait
(continued)
statistics 174; terrorism by 256, 259, 262–63, 305, 605n61, 605n62, 623n47; in trade industries 87, 88, 261
Iranian Navy 301, 620n27
Iraq: 1930s Kuwait relations 73–78, 548n70, 548n75; 1950s Kuwait relations 172–74; 1960s propaganda 577n54; on 1960s U.S.-Kuwait relations 196–97; 1961–62 claim to Kuwait 187–88, 233–34; 1961 military resistance against 189–94, 576n44, 577n50, 577n57; 1963 Kuwait visit 234, 584n39; 1963 recognition of Kuwait 194; 1973 border disputes 235–36, 591n18; 1980s Kuwaiti relations 308, 529n38, 625nn63–66; 1990 initial border invasion 321–25, 631n1 (*See also* Iraqi occupation of Kuwait (1990)); 1992 Shi'a Muslim homeland destruction 432, 675n77; 1993 border disputes 427–28; 1994 Republican Guard attack 432, 675n79; 2003 invasion of Kuwait 439, 443–47, 447–49, 449–50, 681nn34–35; 2010–11 Kuwait relations 459–61; Baath Party in 234, 590n5, 600n3; Baghdad-Kuwait railroad lines 18, 35, 45; education system on Kuwait 675n81; export control on 629n98; IIS 428–30, 674n68; Khazima province 333; -Kuwait frontier demarcations 171–72, 308–9, 572n57, 625n66, 668n62; Kuwaiti loans to 234, 308, 316–17, 584n39, 625n65; oil industry in 97–98, 281; puppet government of Kuwait by 333, 639n41, 676n91; Shatt al-Arab and 105–6, 172–73, 235, 308, 526n3, 573n63, 606n71; Soviet Union military assistance to 448, 614n39; tribal incursions in 60, 66. *See also* Al-Qassem, Abdul Kareem; Saddam Hussein; *specific regions*
Iraq Embassy (Kuwait) 330, 630n100, 637n34, 638n36
Iraqi Airways 372, 493
Iraqi community in Kuwait 159, 174, 262, 263
Iraqi occupation of Kuwait (1990–91): babies and 397, 661n5; border invasion, initial 321–25, 631n1; buildup to 316–19, 630n103, 630n105; captives and targeted nationalities 399, 401–2, 662n9; capture of Iraqi soldiers 323–24; conclusion of 415, 418, 665n35, 670n12; destruction of monuments 402; evacuation statistics 662n10; exposure of collaborators 407, 415–16, 427–28, 433–34, 667n46, 670n9, 676n87; eyewitness accounts and 324–25, 633n14; footwear 634n21; Kuwaiti resistance movement 376–79, 654n67, 655nn68–69; military assistance by students 669n3; national unity and 409–10, 414, 667n53; Operation Desert Storm 426–27, 431, 672n44; resistance training in 401;

Iraqi occupation of Kuwait *(continued)*
    statistics on 412, 668nn63–64; UN resolutions on 395, 408; U.S. flanking maneuver 395–96; U.S. oil companies and 598n74; U.S. troop statistics 661n1. *See also* Kuwait; Kuwaiti community; siege of U.S. Embassy (Kuwait, 1990)

Iraq-Iran War (1980–88): conclusion of 285, 304, 622n42; initial incidents in 266; Iraqi missile attacks on U.S. in 622n41; Kuwait-Iran relations due to 275, 285; Kuwait-Iraq relations due to 246, 285; Kuwaiti response to 254–55, 268–69, 607n77, 607n79; logistics of disarray 268, 607n75; tanker war 301–3; total loss of 304; U.S. response to 266, 268, 269–70, 285, 607n79

Iraqi Southern Desert Camel Corps 67

Iraq Petroleum Company (IPC) 98

Irwin, Lee 616n2

Islam: animals and 478–79, 687n23; description of worship 43; in early Kuwait 561n18; studies abroad and 250

Islamabad, Pakistan 602n20

Islamic extremism: in 1970s Iran 254; incidents at Mecca, Saudi Arabia 602n20, 623n50; political agendas of 458; terrorism as jihad 262, 601n19, 609n2; war as punishment 667n50

Ismael, Jerry 469

Israel: 1967 Arab-Israeli War 211–12, 585n45, 586nn49–50; 1982 invasion of Lebanon 269, 271; -Egypt peace treaty 269, 285; Palestinians migration to Kuwait from 549n90, 562n31. *See also* Palestinian community in Kuwait

Isra'il, Mu'allim 64

Ives, Dr. 7

Jaafar, Ezzat M. 560n3, 562n23, 562n26

Jabar Abdallah Umayri 416

Jaber al-Khaled al-Sabah 454

Jaber al-Mubarak al-Hamad al-Sabah 456

Jabir al-Ahmad al-Sabah. *See* Jabir III

Jabir al-'Ali 143, 246, 565n52, 684n78

Jabir al-Mubarak al-Sabah. *See* Jabir II

Jabir __ al-Sabah. *See* Jabir I

Jabir I (Jabir __ al-Sabah) 12–14, 47, 529n28

Jabir III (Jabir al-Ahmad al-Sabah): 1985 public appearance 297; Ahmad's death and 120–21; appointment of 201, 253; assassination attempt 262, 604n44, 618n14; on Bush 424; death of 442; description of 559n55, 618n12, 679n12; on National Assembly divisions 203; Rockefeller and 589n79; U.S. visit of 562n23

Jackson, Jesse 362–63, 648n18, 648n20

Jahra, Kuwait 95. *See also* Battle of Jahra

Japan: Embassy Kuwait 619n19, 632n8; military assistance by

Japan *(continued)*
  620n28, 621n35; mine countermeasures and 302, 621n35; oil exports to 113; pearl industry of 63; WWII and 84
Jewish community in Kuwait: call for deportation of 265; in education 543n24; migration to Israel 175; population statistics of 64, 66
J. H. Pomeroy 168
Johnson, Lyndon 586n53
Joint Task Force Middle East (JTFME) 290
Jones, G. Lewis 118–19, 558n48
Jordan 193, 211, 578n60, 590n2. *See also* Transjordan
Jordan, L. T. 110, 142
Jordanian community in Kuwait 174
Joubaydi, Saadoun 362, 648n19
Joyce, Miriam 116–17, 120, 187–88
JP-5 (aviation fuel) 611n20
J. S. Abercrombie 557n29
judicial system: postwar 116–17, 558n48; prewar 116; State Security Courts 244, 596n53, 601n19, 605n59, 609n2; transition at independence 180
Jugar, Jeff 390, 664n27
Al Jumhuriya 675n79
June War (1967) 211–12, 585n45, 586nn49–50

Kaifan resistance cell 377, 654n65
Kamp Kuwait group xiii
Kano, Michael 371–72, 380–82, 656n78
Kay and Associates 329
Al-Kazima (magazine) 543n27
Kelly, John H. 316, 365

Kennedy, John F. *131*, 181
Al-Khalifa family 10, 528n20
Al-Khatib, Ahmad 170, 199, 307, 572n53, 580n82
Khaz'al, Shaikh of Muhammera (Khoramshar, Iran) 20, 32, 47, 538n65
Khazima 33
Khomeini, Rouhollah 254, 604n46
Khrushchev, Nikita 202, 581n7
Khuzistan Province, Iran 4
Kiawah Island (South Carolina) 278
Kreuzeman, Tom 663n19
Kubbar Island 113
Kuwait: pre-20th century trade economy 1–3, 7–8, 524n1, 524n5, 525n7; pre-20th century descriptions 6, 8–9, 13–14, 526n15, 527n13; 1899 British protectorate agreement 18, 33, 35, 179, 187, 576n33; 1900s–20s descriptions 34–35, 531n2; 1913 Anglo-Ottoman Agreement 18–20, 46, 171, 530n43, 534n36, 537n59; 1920 Battle of Jahra 49–56, 539n77, 539nn84–85, 540nn94–95, 574n13; 1928 Battle of Riqa'i 66, 545n41; 1929 'Uqair Conference and 60–61, 541nn5–6; 1930s–40s modernizations 58, 59, 93, 94, 106–7, 541n105; 1930s descriptions 65, 66, 81; 1958 regional Arab relations 172–74, 573n66; 1960s–1980s general conditions 243–45; 1961 independence agreement 179–80; 1967 June War and 211, 585n45; 1970s–80s Iranian politics in 253–54,

708   Index

Kuwait (continued)
261–62, 603n41, 623n51; 1970s foreign policy 250–52, 268, 597n65; 1980s visa suspension and deportations 261, 264, 272, 286, 605n56; 1990–91 Iraq puppet government in 333, 639n41, 676n91; 1990–91 resistance movements 376–81, 654n67, 655nn68–69; 1993 border conflict 427–28; airplane routes, first 70, 546n54; anniversaries, national ix, 133, 195, 560n3; arrival cards 566n59; climate 525n14; constitution 198, 247, 597n67; currency 152, 167, 209, 380, 417, 571n43; environmental pollution from war 420, 671n31, 671n33; establishment of 5–6, 526n5; foreign investments by 218, 278–79, 590n7, 665n34; government-in-exile 408, 667n47; historic maps of 24–25; infrastructure damage from war 402, 406; -Iraq frontier demarcations 171–72, 308–9, 572n57, 625n66, 668n62; Iraq-Iran War and 268, 270, 275–76, 607n77, 607n79; list of rulers 485; martial law 415, 416, 433, 668n59; nationalist movements 151, 160–66, 198–99, 570n28, 571n36; National Kuwaiti People's Congress 410, 414, 417; night curfew 415, 670n10; nonalignment policies of 215–16, 268, 278, 587n63, 588n67; parliamentary system and (See National Assembly, Kuwait); post-occupation violence 416–17, 668nn59–60; post office administration 72, 547n60; punishment for crimes in 263, 312, 627n82, 628n92; railroad lines 18, 35, 45; as refuge for Ajman tribe 49, 538n73; Saudi embargo on 49, 63, 70, 542n16; Soviet Union military assistance to 287, 311; spy arrests 685n93; State Security Courts 244, 596n53, 601n19, 605n59, 609n2; terms for 5, 6, 526n1, 527n7; treasury of 149–50, 218; U.S. export embargo and 212, 217, 236–37, 282, 592n25; on U.S.-Soviet Union relations 276, 610n8; war crimes trials 433–34, 676n89. See also Iraqi occupation of Kuwait (1990–91); Kuwaiti community; other nations; specific industries; specific leaders; specific regions

Al-Kuwait (magazine) 64, 543n27
Kuwait Action for the Care of Children in Hospital (KACCH) 450
Kuwait Air Force (KAF) 324, 613n34, 626n75
Kuwait Airways 246, 263, 609n98
Kuwait Democratic League 160
Kuwait Drilling Company 248, 317
Kuwait Fire Service 165
Kuwait Fund for Arab Economic Development 234, 590n7
Kuwait Handicapped Society 228, 298, 471, 659n108
Kuwaiti Army: 1967 June War and 211; development of 174, 188–89; French acquisitions by 592n22; U.S. acquisitions

Index   709

Kuwaiti Army *(continued)* by 197, 214, 217, 236; vehicles of 579n75

Kuwaiti community: 1932 smallpox epidemic 65, 544n33; 1940s American relations with 108–9; 1950s cultural/ideological change in 157–59, 174–75; 1988 July incident on 304, 622n40; 1990–91 abuse and violence on 380–81, 396, 656nn81–82, 663n17, 666n45; 1990–91 hostages/missing/deaths 396, 403, 412, 441; acceptance of missionaries by 37–39, 42–43, 53–54, 575n15; citizenship and 57, 540n100; cultural diversity of 11, 57, 66, 525n11; dancing and 76, 423, 569n6, 585n46; description of xiii, 252, 547n63; dual-national families 185, 250, 259, 270, 418, 470, 608n85; education and internal employment 175; globalization and 464–67; leading family structure 8, 11, 17, 75, 527n15; merchant (middle) class 73, 547n63; national unity in war 409–10, 414, 667n53; network during Iraq occupation 399–400; popular dissent (*See* protests); population statistics 35, 65, 105, 174, 184; post-traumatic recovery (*See* post-traumatic stress disorder (PTSD)); postwar identity 410–12, 667n52; return of exile population 417, 419, 422, 670n15; weapons and 407, 415, 416, 666n43. See also *specific elements*; *specific industries*; *specific nationalities in Kuwait*

Kuwaiti Department of Education: 1956 protests and 162–64, 570n27; culturally diverse instruction 176, 573n72; U.S. study programs and 185–86. *See also* education system in Kuwait

Kuwait Industrial League (softball) 230

Kuwait Institute of Scientific Research (KISR) 621n39

Kuwait International Hotel 325, 332, *351*, 391

Kuwait Investment Company 278

Kuwait Little League (KLL) *228*, 250, 298, 475, 687n15

Kuwait National Day 133, 195, 560n3

Kuwait National Guard 612n27

Kuwait National Petroleum Company (KNPC) 611n16

Kuwait Oil Company (KOC): in 1942 88; 1952 workers of *126*; 1961 intervention and 191; Brewer and 144; charitable organization support by 474, 479; concessions of 100–101, 217; Dickson and 102; effects of war on 106, 402, 664n31, 666n40; facilities of 107, 110–11, 168, 552n20; fireworks 110; on Gulf Protection Regime 625n69; London office attacks 260; management of 217, 582n19; personnel statistics 111, 556n25, 561n19. *See also* Anglo-Iranian Oil Company (AIOC); oil industry of Kuwait

Kuwait Oil Tanker Company (KOTC) 289, 293, 303, 617n7. *See also* Operation Earnest Will
Kuwait Petroleum Company (KPC): bombings at 617n3; European outlets of 279, 611nn16–17; formation of 279–80. *See also* oil industry of Kuwait
Kuwait Police Department 211, 668n63, 670n8
Kuwait Regency Palace Hotel 228
Kuwait Society for the Protection of Animals and their Habitat (K'S PATH) 478–79
Kuwait University 249, 306, 435, 629n98

"laissez passer" 267
language: American accents 108, 556n14; American-Gulf Arab slang 109, 556n16. *See also* communication; schools
Latham, Donald 401
Latifa Fahad al-Sabah 470, 471
League of Nations 97–98. *See also* United Nations (UN)
Lebanese community in Kuwait 159, 174, 262, 263
Lebanese Phalange 608n90
Lebanon: on 1961 Kuwaiti defense 578n60; 1982 Israeli invasion 269, 271; terrorism from 312, 608n90. *See also* Beirut, Lebanon
Lee, James E. 582n19
Levins, John: on 1990 military action 396, 632n5; on embassies roles in siege 638n38, 651n44; on Howell's departure 391–92; on international media 397; on medical evacuees 648n24; network of help and 331, 399; on siege communication 403–4, 664n28
Libya 280, 578n60, 626n78
Lienhardt, Peter 181–82, 183, 575n20
Life (magazine) 186–87
liquor regulations 534n24, 613n30, 618n16
Little League baseball 228, 250, 298, 475, 687n15
Locher, A. 1, 3–4, 524n5, 526n15
Lockheed Corporation 248
Logsdon, Mimi 353, 354, 370, 390, 647n7
Logsdon, Wayne 354, 358, 385–86, 390, 647n7
Loken, Keith 267
Luce, William 179
Lumsden, George Quincey 238, 248, 596n55, 598n82

MacDoughal, Eoin 399
MacNeil, Donald 543n26
MacPherson, James 135, 142
Madrid murders (1982) 261, 603n37
Maestrone, Frank E. 255
magazines 64, 543n27
Magwa, Kuwait: oil explosions at 164–65; oil personnel camp in 102, 108, 556n12
Al-Mahri, Kuwait 617n3
Mairza, Hussein 476
Mairza, Sheryll 475–76
majlis system 158, 590n83
Mak, Dayton 131; on 1960s British position 579n69; on Egyptian community in Kuwait 581n12; on facilities 582n21;

Mak, Dayton *(continued)*
  as first chargé d'affaires 180, 204; on Kuwaiti officials 205–6; on U.S. military assistance 197
malaria 20, 35, 45, 531n2
malnutrition 84
Manama, Bahrain: British foreign office in 152–53; U.S. Embassy in 213, 241. *See also* Bahrain
Marble Arch 107
maritime commerce: of 19th century 1–2, 7–8, 524n1, 524n5, 525n7; in 1930s 63, 81–83; Baharna (term) 540n99; dhow (term) 524n5; piracy and 6, 9, 10, 12, 528n23; WWII and 83–84. See also *boom* (Arabic cargo vessel); pearl diving industry; shipbuilding industry
marriage 185, 561n14
Martyrs Bureau 441–42, 679n10
Marzook, Yusuf 77
Masters, Clyde Lee 186
Mavericks missiles 311, 626n72, 626n74
McClelland, Walter 236
McDonald's (fast food restaurant) 297, 618n15
McGhee, George C. 139
McHenry, Donald 610n9
McWilliams Dredging Co. 168
Mecca, Saudi Arabia: camel caravans to 57–58; seizure by Islamic extremists 602n20, 623n50
media reports: on 1956 protests 165, 570n25; on 1977 terrorist hijacking 246; on 1980s military assistance 287, 311; on 1980 Zubair bombing 267–68; on 1990–91 Iraq occupation 397–98, 416; on 1993 Bush visit 422–23; on 2003 buildup 446–47, 681n30; on Ceauşescu overthrow 313; on Chancery construction 240; on embassy populations 635n25; in Iraq 235, 577n54, 591n18; misinformation or carelessness by 397–98, 413, 669n4; on Suq al-Manakh 620n4; on tanker protection regime 616n2
medical equipment and facilities: in 1920s–30s 59, 70, 544n29; of 1940s oil companies 556n12; shortage of medicine 551n11. *See also* American Mission and hospital (Kuwait); hospitals
medical procedures: in 1930s 42, 64–65; local acceptance of Western 65, 71–72, 544n33; payment of 85; vaccinations 65, 182, 544n33, 575n16
Medina, Saudi Arabia 67
mental health. *See* post-traumatic stress disorder (PTSD)
Menting, Peter 452–53
merchant (middle) class: in 1950s 121–22, 164, 560n61; description of 547n63; politics and 13, 73–74, 457; real estate and 548n66; revolt of 1910 19–20, 536n55; revolt of 1938 76–77. *See also* Kuwaiti community; wealth distribution; *specific industries*
Meridian Hotel 332, 634n21
Mickey Mouse 326, 634n18
Middle East Economic Survey 256
MIDEASTFOR 213, 290

Index

Midhat Pasha 15–16
migration: after assassinations 530n42; due to Israel 549n90, 562n31; history of 5, 155, 525n11; of Al-Khalifa 10, 528n20
Miller, Ardith 593n31
Miller, Reagan 362
Miller, William 256
El-Miloudi, Hamid 354, 384, 401–2, 651n40, 658nn94–95, 663n22
Mina al-Abdallah, Kuwait 113, 114
Mina al-Ahmadi, Kuwait: 1986 attacks on 609n2; attacks on 305, 623n47; capacity of 110, 556n23; establishment of 110; oil explosions at 164–65; personnel of 113–15
Mina Saud, Neutral Zone (Kuwait-Saudi Arabia) 557n31
mine warfare: explosive ordnance disposal (EOD) 420–22; in Iraq-Iran War 301–2, 620n32–33; Japan countermeasures on 302, 621n35; minesweeping 302, 304, 406, 620n33, 665n38; "pollution" research and 621n39. *See also* Operation Earnest Will; weapons systems
Ministry of Higher Education 297–98
Mirage (aircraft) 236, 592n22
Mireles, Tony 358, 386, 388, 657n86
missiles. *See* weapons systems
missionaries. *See* American Mission and hospital (Kuwait)
Mitchell, Benny 367, 650n35
Moberly, Robert E. 140

Mobil Oil 98
Mohamad Reza 253–54
Mohammad al-Salem al-Sabah 456
Mohammad Khaled al-Sabah 435
Molotov-Ribbentrop Pact (1939) 615n57
Mooneyham, John 336, 631n1
More, J. C. 51, 574n13
Morris, Joe Alex 662n7
Mosher, Dennis and Mary Ann 399
Mothers of Young Children 468, 469
Al-Mubarak, Massouma 454
Mubarak al-Kabir (Mubarak the Great) Medal of Honor 424
Mubarak I (Mubarak al-Sabah al-Sabah): 1913 convention and 20; acceptance of missionaries by xiv, 31–33, 36, 42, 532n10; on city walls 50; death of 44, 45–46; on female beauty 58; on first hospital construction 39–41; Ibn Saud and 45, 538n74; merchants revolt of 16–20, 536n55; oil concessions and 58, 97
Al-Mubarakiyah (school) 42, 253, 543n25
Mughawi, Buthayana A. 407
Muhammad I (Muhammad al-Sabah al-Sabah) 16–17, 530nn41–42
Al-Mukawa oil field attacks 609n2
Munais, Ahmad bin 76–77
munitions dumps 421, 428, 672n37, 673n55
Murphy, Caryle 397–98
Murphy, Richard 288
Murphy, Sean 447
Al-Musaed, Abd al-Aziz 676n92

Musayd, 'Abd al-'Aziz 245
Muscat, Oman 241
museum, national. *See* Dar al-Athar al-Islamiyyah (DAI)
musical performances 116, 299, 619n24
Muslim Brothers *(Ikhwan al-Muslimeen)* 143
Muslim communities. *See under* Islam; Islamic; Shiite Muslim community; Sunni Muslim community in Kuwait
Mutair tribes: incursions in Iraq by 60; incursions in Kuwait by 62, 67, 542n14, 546n46
Mutawa, Sulaiman 416
Al-Mutawa, Faisal 64, 186
Mu'ti Haroun, Abdul 237, 565n55, 592n27
Mylrea, Bessie 43, 566n58
Mylrea, Stanley: Ahmad and 90–91, 553n34; assistants of 96; on Battle of Jahra 51–52, 55, 539n77, 539n84, 574n13; death and burial of 145, 565n57; description of xi, 39, 43, 54, 93–94, 534n31; Ibn Saud and 45; on Ibn Saud's priorities 538n74; on local acceptance 37–38; on Mubarak and first hospital 40–41; residence of 39, 55, 535nn39–40; transportation of 536n52; work of 33, 43, 53, 71
Mylrea Memorial Men's Hospital 41, *127, 128,* 146–47, *355,* 687n25

Naif Avenue, Kuwait Town 156
Najd desert region 63, 542n16
Najem, Muhammed 579n78
Najib Sayyid Hashim Rifa'i 261
Al-Najjar, Ghanim 443
Al-Naqib, Rajab 32
Nasir Mohammad al-Ahmad al-Sabah 443, 454, 456
Nasser, Gamal Abdel: 1950s Arab nationalism and 143, 151, 160, 176; 1967 June War and 211; platforms of 161, 169–70. *See also* Egypt; Suez Crisis (1956)
National Assembly, Kuwait: 1960s opposition in 203, 209, 234, 581n8, 584n38; 1970s opposition in 217; 1973–75 security measures by 246–47; 1981 redemption of 270; 1989 reinstatement controversy of 313–15, 627n84, 628n86; 2003–07 opposition in 453–54, 683n59; 2011–12 opposition in 453–57, 683n64, 683n66; bills proposed in 435–37, 677n107; Bush on 425; dissolution of xiv, 203, 247, 260, 265, 435–36, 581n8; dissolution *vs.* abandonment 628n87, 628n90; elections of 140, 198, 202, 204, 434–35, 624n61; on foreign investments 280; formation of xiv, 202–3; fraud and 455, 684n70; Howell on 595n51; Kuwaitis in Saudi Arabia and 685n87; post-occupation and 410; Shi'a *vs.* Sunni representation on 260, 602n28, 684n77; Twinam on 243–44. *See also* Kuwait
national banking system 152, 567n82
National Evangelical Church in Kuwait: 1990–91 Iraq

714 Index

National Evangelical Church in Kuwait *(continued)*
  occupation and 212, 325, 376, 654n63; facilities of 70–71, 247; success of 207, 531n1, 547n55
nationalist movements: in 19th century 17; in 1950s 136–37, 140, 151; 1956 protests of 160–66, 570n28, 571n36; independence and 179–80, 198–99. See also *specific nations*
National Kuwaiti People's Congress (October 1990) 410, 414, 417
National Organization of Women (NOW) 413–14, 669n4
naval mining. *See* mine warfare
Nawwaf al-Ahmad al-Sabah 264, 443
Neutral Zone (Kuwait-Saudi Arabia): division agreement of 283, 598n72; first concessions in 112–13; port access in 557n31; security in 1960s 179
New Street 157
New Yorker magazine 87, 674n68
New York Times 246, 256, 416, 630n105
Al-Nidaa 433
Niebuhr, Carsten 8, 526n1, 527n13
Noel, Cleo 241
Norwegian Embassy (Kuwait) 632n8
Noyes, James 589n72
nuclear warfare 629n98
Nuri al-Said 172, 573n63
Nykerk, Gerald 114, 182, 565n57

oil industry of Bahrain 98, 554n53. *See also* Bahrain).

oil industry of Iran 280, 281, 566n70. *See also* Iran
oil industry of Iraq 97–98, 281. *See also* Iraq
oil industry of Kuwait: 1920s–30s concessions 97–101, 553n34; 1940s–50s production statistics 109–10, 113, 566n70; 1940s production process 108; 1980s operation-sharing 279–80; 1990 production rates 317; Ahmad and 79, 550n92, 553n34; damage from 2003 conflict 402, 407, 417, 449, 664n31, 666n40, 669n66; descriptions of American personnel 108–9, 556; European retail outlets 279, 611nn16–17; free market ideals and 281–82; Mubarak and 58, 97; nationalization of 217–18, 247–48, 283, 597n70; in Neutral Zone 112–13, 557n31; oil refinery stations 110, 279; post-occupation recovery of 417; production costs of 555n11, 612n23; profit-sharing agreements 574n80; suspension during WWII 85, 97, 102, 555n10; urban planning and development in 109–14, 168–69, 572n49; U.S. export embargoes 212, 217, 236–37, 282; U.S. military supplies from 611n20. *See also* Kuwait; *specific companies*
oil industry of Saudi Arabia 248, 281, 555n10, 565n56
Olcott Memorial Hospital for Women 71, 94, 136, 355
Olympic Games 633n10

Index   715

Oman: independence 594n43; Iraq-Iran War and 269–70; U.S. Embassy in 241
Operation Bellringer 191, 577n49
Operation Desert Fox 431, 674n76, 675n80, 676nn83–84
Operation Desert Storm 426–27, 431, 672n44. *See also* Iraqi occupation of Kuwait (1990)
Operation Earnest Will 349; con-
Operation Earnest Will *(continued)* clusion of reflagging tankers 310, 625n69; initiation and activity of 288–91, 293, 615n53; mine warfare and 301–2, 620n32–33; mobile sea base 303–4; personnel of 615n52
Operation HOPE Kuwait (OH) 476–77
Operation Iraqi Freedom 443–44, 452
Operation Vantage 191–94
Organization of Petroleum Exporting Countries (OPEC): 1990s production and 317–18, 629n99; fluctuations and 217, 280–81; Kuwait's enrollment in 167
Ottoman Empire: 19th century Kuwaiti relations with 10, 13–17, 537n59; 1913 Anglo-Ottoman Convention 18–20, 46, 171, 530n43, 534n36, 537n59; expulsion from Eastern Arabia 5–6, 17

Pacific Dredging Co. 571n47
Pacific Western Oil Corporation 112, 113
Pakistani community in Kuwait 108, 122, 174, 262, 548n70
Palestine Liberation Organization (PLO) 271–72, 277, 611n10

Palestinian community in Kuwait: 1990–91 occupation and 644n77; citizenship of 197; conflict refugees from 211, 549n90, 562n31; deportation of 263; education system and 79, 549n90, 579n78; in foreign office positions 582n18, 596n55; local acceptance of 197, 575n15; oil jobs and 143, 169, 549n90; population statistics 174, 244–45; protests of 607n82; temporary refuge for 605n54
Pan American Airlines 306
parliamentary system 73, 243–44, 595n51
Parrish, Connie 390, 664n27
Patrick, Tom 107, 110
Paul, Ron 434
Pauley Petroleum Inc. 557n29
pearl diving industry 2, 8; in 1920s–30s 38, 63, 81–83; films on 550n4; health of divers 536n51; Japan and 63; migration of traders 20. *See also* maritime commerce
Peaveler, John 478–79
penicillin 539n77, 551n11
Penniman, Mike 367, 404
Pennings, Alfred 182
Pennings, Gerrit 33, 37
Peppers, Ray 267–68, 283
Percy, Charles 250
Persian Gulf Command (Sayre) 87
Persian-Ottoman conflict 10
petroleum market: 1980s conditions of 612n22; 1990s conditions 317, 629n99; barrel price index 280–81; base strategy of 282, 612n25. *See also under* oil industry

716   Index

pets 326, 336, 641n57
Philby, J. B. 62, 542n12
Philippine Embassy (Kuwait) 632n8
Phillips Petroleum 557n29
photography 467, 555n64
piracy 6, 9, 10, 12, 528n23
plane hijackings: in 1977 246, 604nn47–48; in 1980 260–61; in 1984–85 265, 604n43, 606n67; in 1988 263, 312, 604n43, 627nn80–81. See also airline activity
PLO. See Palestine Liberation Organization (PLO)
pollution from war 407, 420, 671n31, 671n33
polygamy 561n14
Popular Front for the Liberation of Palestine (PFLP) 246, 604n47
Port city of Kuwait 28, 30; descriptions of 5, 31, 34, 81; development of 135, 168, 571n47; Iraq's use during Iraq-Iran War 268, 607n77; as strategic location 538n74; during WWII 86. See also Kuwait; maritime commerce
Porter, Jadranka 367, 633n12, 650n36, 651n44
ports. See *specific port names*
post offices 72, 547n60
post-traumatic stress disorder (PTSD): 1991 liberation and 407–9, 426; 2003 resolution and 405; 2012 statistics 439; anger and 406, 407, 665n36; children and 407, 445–47, 666n45; *diwannyas* on 679n6; factors of severity 678n2; false alarms and 445, 688n25; first imperative of 430; Iraqis with 674n70; population statistics and 441, 678n4; reoccurring 406, 448, 681n37; social and societal effects of xii–xiii, 439–42; social stigmas and 414, 440, 666n42, 669n5; Twinam on 406. See also health effects of war
Powell, Colin 311
power, electrical. See electricity
printing press 543n27
profit-sharing agreements in oil industry 574n80
prohibition of urban vices 534n24
prostitution 534n24
protests: 1950s nationalist 160–66, 570n28, 571n36; 1982 of anti-American sentiments 272; 2011–12 demonstrations 453–55, 683n62, 683n64, 683n66, 684n67; on National Assembly 314, 628n89, 628n92; of Palestinian community 607n82
psychological effects of war. See post-traumatic stress disorder (PTSD)
Psychological Medicine Hospital 678n3
PTSD. See post-traumatic stress disorder (PTSD)
Pyron, Walter B. 108

Q8 611n17
Al-Qabas 455
Qaddafi, Muammar 626n78
Qaru Island 113
Al-Qassem, Abdul Kareem 173,
Al-Qassem, Abdul Kareem *(continued)* 187–89, 209, 233, 576n33. See also Iraq

Al-Qatami, Jasim   170
Qatar: Ibn Saud on   61; U.S. Embassy in   242, 594n45; U.S. oil embargo   236–37
Qatif   6
Qibla Quarter   8, 66, 527n15
Al-Qitami, Muhammad   77
Quainton, Anthony C. E.   276, 281, 284, 286
Al-Qudeeri, Muhammad   654n67
Raad al-Assadi   429
Radha, Abbas   96
radio stations: in Egypt   170; in Kuwait   159, 560n6; tactics in crisis incidents   267–68, 606n73
Radisson SAS Hotel   332, 446
raft races   *230*, 299
Al-Rageeb, Latifa   407
railroad lines, Baghdad-Kuwait   18, 35, 45
Rajab, Jehan   400, 663n15
Ramadan al-Khalifa   96
Ransom, David   647n14
Ras al-Khaimah   594n43
Rasha al-Sabah   677n107
Rashadat platform, Iran   295
Rasheed, Abdul Aziz   64
Al-Rashids   19, 45
Al-Rashoud, Claudia Farkas   669n1; 1991 description by   420; 2003 Iraq invasion and   446, 448–49, 451, 452; on Kuwaiti society   465
Al-Rashoud, Salah   451
rationing, WWII   83–86
rats   567n74
Ray, Nancy   426
Al-Ray al-Amm   260
Raymond Concete Pile   571n47
Raytheon Corporation   248, 330
Razzak, Ghazi al-Abdul   324

Reagan, Ronald   *223*, 271, 272, 311
recreation   *228*, *230*, 250, 298, 619nn19–21. *See also* baseball leagues
Red Fort, Jahra, Kuwait   539n85
Reed, Karla   267
Al-Refai, Maxine   419–20, 468, 473–74, 671n28
refineries. *See under* oil industry
religion: failed Christian conversion   36, 43, 208, 463, 566n61; Islam   43, 250, 561n18. *See also* churches; *specific communities*
restaurants   *231*, 297, 298, 472, 479–80, 618n15
reunions of foreign service personnel   xii–xiii, *354*, 393–94
Reynolds Aluminum Company   111
Richmond, J. C.   180, 193
Al-Riggaee Center   440, 678n3
Rinehart, Jack   *352, 354*; description of Howell   363; on embassy evacuation   390–91, 650n37; on initial hotel evacuation   332–33, 638n40; plumbing and   358; on power during siege   357; on siege communication   371
Riyad, Mahmoud   235
Riyadh, Saudi Arabia   45, 47, 278, 537n62. *See also* Saudi Arabia
roads   144, 155–57, 565n55
Robertson, Iva   536n53
Robertson, Raymond   388
Rockefeller, David   589n79
Rodriguez, Paul G.   321, 323
Rogers, Gale   322, 372, 390, 653n55
Rogers, William P.   250, 589n72, 599n83
Romania   313

Rosenthal, Benjamin 279, 280
roundworm disease 65
Royal Air Force 67, 68
Al-Rumaihi, Mohammad 273
Rush, Alan: on Abdallah III 199–200; on al-Sabah family 7; on early maritime commerce 9, 10, 11; on Ibn Saud 49, 538n73; on National Assembly 203
Rusk, Dean 190
Russia. *See* Soviet Union
Ryan, Mary 647n14

Al-Sabah, Duaji 529n28
Al-Sabah, Jarrah 16, 17, 530n42
Al-Sabah, Mubarak. *See* Mubarak I
Sabah al-Ahmad 120, 278, 287, 559n55, 562n23, 614n45
Sabah al-Ahmed al-Sabah. *See* Sabah IV
Sabah al-Jabir al-Sabah. *See* Sabah II
Sabah bin Jabir [Muhammad]. *See* Sabah I
Al-Sabah family: in 1960s–80s 243; 2006 transition of power and 442–43, 679n17; on Ahmad's council 548n77; Arab nationals on 170, 572n53; debt of 547n64; early influence of 7, 8, 11, 17, 75; practice of succession 201, 580n3. *See also* 'Utub federation; *specific persons*
Sabah I (Sabah bin Jabir [Muhammad]) 7, 9
Sabah II (Sabah al-Jabir al-Sabah) 14
Sabah III (Sabah Sabah al-Salem al-Sabah): 1960s Iraq visits by 235, 584n39, 591n15; 1967 June War and 210–11; 1968 U.S. visit by 212, 216, 586n53; accession of 201, 580n1; death of 252; Mak on 205
Sabah IV (Sabah al-Ahmad al-Sabah) 443, 580n3
Sabah Sabah al-Salem al-Sabah. *See* Sabah III
Sa'd al-Abdallah: 1988 U.S. visit of 223, 311, *350*; 1989 Iraq visit by 308; 1993 U.S. visitors and 425–26; accession of 253, 580n3; appointments of 434, 435; health of 442–43, 679n14; marriage of 561n14; on National Assembly divisions 203, 265; professional life of 253; on Soviet embassy 215; on war crimes trials 433–34
Al-Sadar, Musa 626n78
Saddam Hussein: in 1980 on Shatt al-Arab 606n71; 1990 invasion motive 333; 1990 on U.S. involvement in Gulf 315, 628n95; 1993 Bush assassination plot and 430, 674n68; 1994 Republican Guard attack 432, 675n79; awards by 309; body doubles of 448, 681n38; demonstrations on 448, 682n39; on Egypt-Israel peace 286, 315; final conclusion of 439, 448; on Kuwait territory 631n106; occupation survivors on 667n48; on petroleum market 317, 612n25, 630nn101–2; rise to power of 254; September 1990 policy change 372, 652n49. *See also* Iraq; siege of U.S. Embassy (Kuwait, 1990)

Index   719

Mrs. Saddam Hussein   254, 600n4
Saddoun, Ahmed   655n68
Sadiq Qutabzadeh   260
Sa'dun bin Mohammed bin Ghurair al-Hamid   6
Safat Square   35, *130*
Safat Square, Kuwait   9, 527n17, 533n14
Safeway   297, 373, 493, 494, 652n52
Safir International Hotel   671
Safwan, Kuwait   171–72, 187, 572n57
Saif Abbas Abdallah   424
Salem al-'Ali al-Sabah   683
Salem al-Sabah   273, 406
Salem I (Salem al-Mubarak al-Sabah): Ajman independence campaign and   47, 48, 538n72; Battle of Jahra and   49–52, 54, 56, 539n77; death of   56, 59; Jabir and   47; religious policies of   48, 534n24; support of American Mission by   56–57
Salim Garabet (Abu Alwan)   136
Salmiya, Kuwait   569n3
Saloom, B. George   *354*, 360, 402, 663nn22–23
Al-Samoud missiles   448
Sanhouri, Abdul   171
Sanna, Mark   256, 266–67
Santa Fe International   280
Al-Saqr, Jasim   235
Al-Saud, Abd-al-Aziz. *See* Ibn Saud
Al-Saud, Abdallah ibn Faisal   14
Al-Saud family   13, 14, 19
Saudi Arabia: 1940s Kuwait relations   102–3, 574n5; 1961 Iraq border   577n50; Buraimi dispute   574n5; embargo on Kuwait   49, 63, 67, 70, 73, 100, 542n16; Hejaz conquest   66–67, 545n42; historical droughts in   5; Kuwaiti citizens and politics of   685n87; oil industry in   248, 281, 555n10, 565n56; U.S. oil concessions in   554n51. *See also* Ibn Saud; Neutral Zone (Kuwait-Saudi Arabia); *specific regions*
Saudi ARAMCO magazine   585n46
Saud Nasir al-Sabah   435, 452, 672n44, 677n98
Al-Sayer, Hilal   450
Al-Sayer, Margaret   450
Sayf bin Ghobash   597n57
Sayre, Joel   87
Al-Sayyad   591n18
schools   474; 2003 preparations and   446–47, 681n29; Ahmad and   79; American International School (AIS)   446, 474, 681n30; American School of Kuwait (ASK)   419, 473–74, 671n28, 671n30, 686n11; Anglo-American school in Ahmadi   112, 557n26; Arabic language schools   42, 543n25; British schools   206, 583n25, 583n28, 619n18; commencement exercises   *228*; for girls   43, 79, 175, 576n27; Hebrew language schools   543n24; homeschooling   206; International School of Kuwait (ISK)   207, 474, 686n11; for missionaries, in India   583n27; Al-Mubarakiyah school   42, 543n25; in other Gulf states   580n82, 582n17, 584n30; postwar recovery and   419–20, 666n45, 671n30; Universal American School   474; in U.S. Embassy   207. *See also*

720 Index

schools *(continued)*
    Calverly School; education system; *specific schools*
Sciolino, Elaine 630n105
Scott, L. D. 110
Scudder, Dorothy: 1964 schoolbooks and 207; Ahmad and 120–21; on AWL 469–70; on Christmas 93; death of 229; dedicated entry for 229,
Scudder, Dorothy *(continued)*
    299; on Haidar 96; historical evidence of 212; Howells and 597n69; initial arrival of 92–94, 559n55; on telephones 94; work of 91, 92, 557n34
Scudder, Ethel "Beth" Talcott 92
Scudder, John 92
Scudder, Lewis, III 531n2, 535n39
Scudder, Lewis, Jr. *127, 128, 129;* 1939 descriptions by 91–92, 569n2; Ahmad and 90, 120–21; appointment of 91; death and burial of 565n57, 584n33; description of 93–94; health of 182–83; on Ibn Saud 45; tires for Oman mission 85
SCUD missiles 448, 681n35
scurvy 531n2, 536n51
Sea Isle City (tanker) 295
security: in 1970s 245–47; 1980s of Kuwaiti officials 261–62, 604n44; bedouin tribal raids 57–58; of embassy facilities 225, 257, 282, 294, 601n13, 602n22, 612n27; of embassy personnel 240–41, 597n57, 606n69; history in Kuwait regime 6; independence and 179; in Neutral Zone 179; strategy during embassy siege 365–66, 385–86, 397–98, 649n29, 657n91. *See also* terrorism; *specific conflicts*
Seelye, Talcott W. 168, 171
Seif Palace 34
seismology of oil exploration 101
Al-Shaheen, Sulaiman 294
Al-Shaheen, Sulaiman Majed 325–26
Shakespear, William 39, 533n15, 538n72
Shamia secondary school 306
Shammas, Alie Yaqoub 96
Shammas, Farida Yaqoub 96
Shammas, Suleiman Sim'an 96
Al-Sharekh, Mohamed 211
Sharon, Ariel 271, 608n87
Sharq Quarter 8, 473, 527n15
Shatt al-Arab 105–6, 172–73, 235, 308, 526n3, 573n63, 606n71
Shatti, Ali 96
Shaw, Charles 39, 41
Al-Shayji, Abdallah 442, 460–61, 685n90
Sheraton Hotel 324
Shiite Muslim community in Iran 253–54
Shiite Muslim community in Kuwait: 1980s conflicts and 261, 264, 305, 603n39, 605n61; 1992 homeland destruction 432, 675n77; Ahmad's council and 76, 549n77; Amal militia 626n78; holidays of 258; on National Assembly 602n28; population statistics 174; post-WWII 174–75; terrorism by 256, 259, 262–63, 305, 605n61, 605n62, 623n47
Shiite Muslim community in Lebanon 626n78
Al-Shimaari, Mankhi 433
Shinn, Sandy 418

shipbuilding industry: of 18th century 10–11, 13; during Iraq-Iran War 295–96; during WWII 83, 86–90, 114–15, 552n26. *See also* maritime commerce
ships. See *boom* (Arabic cargo vessel); *specific names*
Shuaiba port, Kuwait 417
Shultz, George 272
Shuwaikh, Kuwait, barge assembly in WWII 88–89, 552n26
Sibel, Charlie 336
Sidewinder missiles 311, 592n23
siege of U.S. Embassy (Kuwait, 1990): air-conditioning 357, 359; ambassador and officers' roles 659n105; beginning of 325–33; books on 357, 367–68; bunker 385–86, 658n99, 659n104, 659nn101–2; celebrations and entertainment 350, 353, 361, 362, 388–89, 647n7, 648n17; citizen help in 329, 637n31; citizen recollections 369, 381, 492–99, 660n113; civilian evacuation flights 373–75, 652n52, 653nn53–56; climate conditions 359, 647n12; communications 360–61, 366–67, 370, 403, 647n13, 650n35; construction during 657n86; description of compound 358–59, 647n9; destruction of classified files 322, 326, 632n5, 632n7; final departures 389–92, 660n119, 661n121; food 360, 362, 383, 389, 632n8, 657n90; garbage disposal 359; garden 359–60, 384, 658n95, 658n97; generators and power 357, 361–62, 365, 382, 646n2, 647n13, 664nn27–28; hygiene and health 353, 362, 364; inaccurate histories on 367, 633n12, 634n15, 650n36, 651n44; initial embassy evacuation mandate 333–35, 641n51; initial evacuation, remaining personnel 334–35, 640nn45–50; media attention on 364, 365, 366, 649n26; medical evacuations 363, 648nn20–21; nickname for 647n10; returning evacuees 369; reunion of survivors 354, 393–94; security strategy 365–66, 385–86, 397–98, 649n29, 657n91; September policy change 372, 652n49; sound system 387, 659n106; vegetation on grounds 658n93; warden system communication 366–67; water 352, 358, 383–84, 646n6, 650n31, 657n92. *See also* Iraqi occupation of Kuwait (1990–91); U.S. Embassy (Kuwait)
Signal Oil and Gas 557n29
Silkworm missiles 275, 294–96, 617nn5–6, 681n35
Simon, John 100
Simon, William 589n72
Simonian, Bianca 479–80
Skodon, Emil M. 335–36, 641n53
Slade, Ernest 97
slavery 78
smallpox 65, 182, 544n33, 552n28, 575n16
Smith, Jimmy 321
smoking 534n24
smuggling trade 46, 48, 84
Social Development Office 440, 679n6

722   Index

Socony Vacuum   98
softball   *230*, 298
Solarz, Steve   250
Souq Sharq   447–48
Southwell, C. A. P.   *126*
Soviet Union: 1960s Kuwait relations   188, 587n65; on 1961 British intervention   577n54; 1979 invasion of Afghanistan by   268–69, 607n80; early Kuwait interests of   18; in Gulf waters   585n43, 614n48, 615nn55–56; on Kuwaiti rulers   202, 581n7; military assistance by   287, 311, 448, 614n45; Molotov-Ribbentrop Pact (1939)   615n57; relations with GCC   272
Sri Lankan community in Kuwait   644n77
Al-Srour, Salem   324, 633n13
Standard Oil   98, 112
Stark missiles   622n41
starvation   69, 84
Steffen, Linda   453
Stinger missiles   287, 614n43
Stoltzfus, William A., Jr.: on 1973 Iraq-Kuwait relations   235–36; appointments of   143, 239, 243, 563n37, 578n65, 591n19; Chancery and residence of   224, 240–41, 593n38, 594nn39–41; on communication and relationships   216; facilities standards of   240–41, 257, 595n48; on local reception of initial consulate   143; sheep of   240; on U.S. defense of Kuwait   194–95
St. Paul's Church, Ahmadi, Kuwait   164, 207
Striker (U.S. tugboat)   302

Subahyah, Kuwait   55, 56
Al-Subayh, Nuriya   458
Sudan   193, 578n60
Suez Crisis (1956)   160–68, 186, 570n28, 571n36
suffrage of women   260, 436, 453, 599n88, 603n30, 628n93, 677n108
suicide bombers. *See* terrorism
suicides   407, 669n3
Suleiman Pasha   528n25
sulphur (for medicinal use)   94, 551n11
Sungari (tanker)   295
Sunni Muslim community in Kuwait   76, 260, 549n77
Sunni Muslim extremists   602n20, 623n50
Sunray Mid-Continental Oil Company   557n29
supermarkets   297, 556n13
Suq al-Manakh trading market   276, 610n4
Sutherland, Peter   255
sword dance   423, 569n6
Symmes, Harrison M.   141, 142, 563n35, 568n93
syphilis   531n2
Syria   271

Tafla, Fatima   433, 676n87
Tahir, Mohsin Shawkhat   434
Tanker Protection Regime. *See* Operation Earnest Will
T-Ball league   687n17
TCOM   437, 678n111
Tehran, Iran   255–57, 601n12, 613n36. *See also* Iran
telegraph. *See* cable communications
telephones   94, 143
terrorism: 1980 on Kuwaiti popu-

Index   723

terrorism *(continued)*
lation 260; 1980 on Zubair, Iraq 266–67; 1981 bombings in Kuwait 629n97; 1983–87 incidents 275, 294–95, 605n49, 609n2; 1983 on Embassy Kuwait 257–58, 262, 274, 601n17, 601n19; 1985 assassination attempt 262, 604n44; 1987–88 bombings 295, 306, 617n3, 624n57; 1990 hotel bombing 378–79; Americans as targets of 265, 306, 452, 606n67; Kuwaiti sleeper cells 452–53, 682n56; at schools 306. *See also* plane hijackings; security
Texas Oil Company (Texaco) 99, 283
Thanksgiving 353, 388, 648n18
Thatcher, Margaret 372
theatrical performances 283, 299, 613n32
Thoms, Sharon 32
Thoms, William Wells 92
Al-Tikriti, Hardan 235, 245
tires, automobile 541n105
Tomahawk missiles 430
Transjordan Arab Legion 545n44. *See also* Jordan
transportation: camels and camel caravans 27, 57; donkeys 26, 51, 106; innovations in 58; railroad lines from Baghdad-Kuwait 18, 35, 45. *See also* airline activity; automobiles
tribes. *See* bedouin tribes; *specific tribe names*
Triumph of the Righteousness (ship) 81
Trucial State administration 210, 241, 558n47, 559n51

truck bombings (1983) 257–58, 262, 274, 601n17, 601n19
Truman, Harry S. 104
tuberculosis (TB) 477, 531n2, 536n51
Tueller, Matthew 475
Tunisia 193, 578n60
Turkey-Kuwait diplomacy. *See* Ottoman Empire
TWA (Trans World Airlines) 604n43, 606n67, 609n98
Twinam, Joseph: as ambassador to Bahrain 213, 214; epitaph of Scudder by 208–9; on hospitals 182; on political systems 243–44; on recovery 406; on reregistration of tankers 289; on U.S.-Gulf relationships 109, 219–20, 251, 590n83; work of 584n34

ululation 377, 654n66
Umm al Maradim Island 113
Umm Qasr port, Iraq 187, 308–9, 585n43, 591n18
UNESCO 167
UNICEF 450
United Arab Emirates (UAE): formation of 594n43; gold trade and 550n7. *See also* Abu Dhabi, United Arab Emirates; Dubai, United Arab Emirates
United Arab Republic (UAR) 170, 174, 193, 578n60. *See also* Nasser, Gamal Abdel
United Nations (UN): on 1990–91 Iraq occupation of Kuwait 395, 408; on 1994 Iraq attack 432; Iraq-Iran War and 285, 624n60; on Iraq-Kuwait border demarcation 428; Kuwait's application to 188, 200, 215, 588n65

724 Index

United Nations Iraq-Kuwait Observation Mission (UNIKOM) 432–33, 673n52

United States: 19th century commercial trade of 1, 38, 524n1; 1950s involvement in local unrest 159; 1960s priorities of 210, 585n43; 1961 Kuwait-British intervention and 189–90, 576n44; 1970s relations with Bahrain 212–15, 587n58; 1982 protests against 272; 1991 Kuwait defense pact 431, 674n73; barrel price index 280; citizenship and students 186; early aerial Gulf exploration 554n64; establishment of 5; export control of Iraq 629n98; first oil concessions in Gulf region 97–101, 103, 554n51; foreign study program 185–86, 575n24, 576n27; Gulf Protection Regime 288–89, 614n49, 615nn52–53; immigration process of 662n13; initial awareness of Kuwait in 185–87; intelligence cooperation of 428–30, 429, 673n61, 674n68; Iranian asset freeze 256, 269, 601n11; on Kuwait oil nationalization 217–18; as model for recovery 667n52; oil embargoes and 212, 217, 236–37, 282, 592n25; oil personnel from (*See* oil industry of Kuwait); post-occupation visits by 422–27; relations with British political agency 97–103, 114, 118–19, 137, 594n42; response to Iraq-Iran War 266, 268, 269–70, 285, 607n79. *See also under* American; U.S.

Universal American School 474

'Uqair Conference (1929) 60–61, 541nn5–6

urban development: in 1950s *130*, 155–56; for barge construction 86–90, 134; city buildings and 34, 135; city walls and 8–9, 23, *129*, 528n26; fortification and 6, 8–9, 526n1, 528n17, 528n24; for oil industry 109–14, 168–69, 572n49; of waterfront 135. See also *specific regions*

U.S. Army 87–89, 552n26

U.S. Army Corps of Engineers 437

U.S. Bureau of Near Eastern Affairs (NEA) 241, 316

USCENTCOM 288, 310, 323, 615n52, 616n61, 661n1

USCINCCENT 303

U.S. Coast Guard 290, 614n49, 625n69

U.S. Consulate (Baghdad, Iraq) 116–17, 196–97

U.S. Consulate (Basra, Iraq) 118, 121, 140, 558n47

U.S. Consulate (Bneid al-Gar, Kuwait) 158

U.S. Consulate (Dhahran, Saudi Arabia) 142, 242, 551n10, 558n47, 594n42

U.S. Consulate (Kuwait): 1960s facilities 195–96, 579n70; 1961 British intervention and 191–92, 577n50; communications of 142–43, 564n45; costs of 120, 559n51; establishment of 116–20, *126*, 135–36, 558n47, 559n50; initial facilities of 141, 563n35; initial

Index 725

U.S. Consulate (Kuwait) *(continued)* Kuwaiti partners 563n33; list of personnel 487–89; local reception of 143; State support of 142–43, 564n44; transition at independence and 180

U.S. Consulate (Manama, Bahrain) 103, 213, 617n4

U.S. Department of Defense. *See* U.S. military in Kuwait; *specific branches*

U.S. Department of State: on 1961 Qaseem declaration 189–90; first oil concessions and 97–103; on Saddam in 1970s 254. See also *specific agencies*

U.S. Embassy (Abu Dhabi, UAE) 213, 241, 534n36, 556n13, 564n44, 594n44

U.S. Embassy (Baghdad, Iraq): 1980 status of 266; 1990 occupation and 318, 321, 362, 394; Embassy Kuwait evacuation and 336, 372, 402, 661n123, 663n24. *See also* U.S. Consulate (Baghdad, Iraq)

U.S. Embassy (Beirut, Lebanon) 398, 575n21, 601n13, 638n35

U.S. Embassy (Cairo, Egypt) 662n7

U.S. Embassy (Doha, Qatar) 242, 594n45

U.S. Embassy (Islamabad, Pakistan) 602n20

U.S. Embassy (Kuwait) 225; 1960s activities 206, 210–12, 585n49; 1960s facilities 195–96, 206, 224, 579n70, 579nn72–73, 582n21; 1970s–80s personnel 255; 1970s official visits to 239, 250, 589n72, 598n82; 1973 inspection and morale in 238–39, 593n34; 1979 incidents and evacuation of 256, 258, 259, 600n8, 602n25; 1980s official visits 277, 610n9, 611n18; 1983 ambassador transition 273–74, 276–77; 1983 terrorist attack on 257–58, 601n17, 601n19; 1990 invasion, initial communications 321–25, 631n1, 631n3; 1990 missile attack on 631n3; 1990 siege of (*See* siege of U.S. Embassy (Kuwait, 1990)); 1996, new building and transition 437, 466–67; baseball game of 619n19; communication with other embassies 333, 635n24; destruction of classified files 322, 326, 632n5, 632n7; establishment of 131, 180, 195; evacuation convoy of 336–38, 641nn54–57, 642nn58–60; Foreign Service Nationals and 237, 355; as governing representative 243, 595n46, 595n49; on Kuwait-Soviet relations 277, 610n8; nonimmigrant visas and 584n35; personnel 237, 293, 487–89, 593n31; post-siege conditions 404, 418, 664n32; provisions for 328–29, 333, 632n8; satellite networks of 641n52; school in 207; security of facilities 225, 257, 282, 294, 601n13, 602n22, 612n27; security of personnel 240–41, 597n57, 606n69; State honor awards for 211, 257, 268, 606n72, 607n74; supply shortages of 242, 284, 595n47; on Suq al-Manakh 610n4;

726   Index

U.S. Embassy (Kuwait) *(continued)* surveillance of   300–301, 327, 620n26, 635n23; USLOK   214–15, 255, 287; warden system of communication   259, 366–67, 602n27; water source of   338–39. *See also* Chancery and residence, U.S. Embassy; *specific incidents*; *specific personnel*

U.S. Embassy (Manama, Bahrain)   213, 241

U.S. Embassy (Muscat, Oman)   241

U.S. Embassy (Tehran, Iran)   255–57, 601n12, 613n36

U.S. Foreign Buildings Office (FBO)   141

U.S. Information Service (USIS)   299

U.S. Liaison Office Kuwait (USLOK)   214–15, 255, 287

U.S. Marines: annual ball   299, 665n33; assignment to Kuwait   255, 600n6; residence of   284, 293, 593n39

U.S. military in Kuwait: 1960s activities   189–94, 197; 1991 defense pact   431–32, 674n73; 1998–99 border action   432–33; aircraft sales of (*See* aircraft); equipment and weapons sales (*See* weapons systems); interactions of   451; prepo arrangement   431, 674n76, 675n80, 676n83–84; support in Iraq-Iran War   621n36. See also *specific branches*

U.S. Navy: 1950s officers gathering   126; 1987 SEAL operation   301; in Bahrain   115, 212, 586n54, 587n58; communication with Bahrain   616n1; Gulf protection by   288–91, 615nn52–53, 616n65; list of ship visits   490–91; at Mina al-Ahmadi   115; on Mission residence as landmark   535n40; reflectors on decoy barges   295–96

U.S. Office of Military Cooperation (OMC-K)   680n19

U.S. Persian Gulf Command   87

USS *Bridgton*   620n33

USS *Duxbury Bay*   126

USS *Greenwich Bay*   558n40, 578n68

USS *La Salle*   213

USS *Maury*   133, 560n4

U.S.S.R. *See* Soviet Union

USS *Robert G. Bradley*   633n9

USS *Samuel B. Roberts*   621nn32–33

USS *Ticonderoga*   524n1

USS *Valcour*   195, 212, 213, 558

USS *Vincennes*   304, 622n40

'Utub federation   6–7, 9, 527n7, 528n18. *See also* Al-Sabah family

vaccinations   65, 182, 544n33, 575n16

Van Ess, John   33, 38, 144, 532n14

Van Pelt, Mary (Khatem Miriam)   63, 92, 557n34

Van Rye, Bill   650n36

veil-burning   176

Veldman, Jeannette   96

Vellekoop, Laurens C. "Dutch"   329

vices   534n24

Villiers, Alan   81–82, 184

visas: for non-immigrants   584n35; suspensions and deportations   261, 264, 272, 286, 605n56

Index 727

Voice of America (radio station) 159, 332, 370, 651n42
Voice of the Arabs (radio station) 170
volleyball 298, 619n21
voting rights of women 260, 436, 453, 599n88, 603n30, 628n93, 677n108

Wahhabi *Ikhwan*: Battle of Jahra and 49–56, 539n77, 539n84, 540n94; British desert troops and 67, 545n44; buildup to 1928 tribal rebellion 63, 66, 542n16; fortification against 528n24, 529n26; Ibn Saud and 49, 60, 66, 545n42, 546n53; tribal rebellion in Iraq 66; on urban vices 533n24
Walker, Harold "Hooky" 376, 653n59
walls, city: 1920s built 50, 65; 1940s description of 544n35, 569n2; destruction of 129, 569n7; history of 8–9, 528n26. *See also* fortification, pre-20th century; gates, city
Walsh, John Patrick 238–39, 593n31
Walters, Vernon 661n122
Warba Island, Kuwait 245
war crimes trials 433–34, 676n89
Wasat (center) quarter 8
Washington Post 430, 616n65
water: as a scarce resource 94–95; Shatt al-Arab 105–6, 172–73, 235, 526n3, 573n63; of U.S. Embassy 338–39, 352. *See also* distillation plants, seawater
waterfront. *See* Port city of Kuwait
waterski performance 619n23
Al-Wazzan, Jassim Mohamad 186

wealth distribution: in 1950s 149–51, 568n83; dissension in 202; in historic Kuwait 7–8, 19–20. *See also* merchant (middle) class
weapons of mass destruction (WMDs) 316, 433, 629n98, 681n36
weapons systems: 1970s companies for 248; of 1980s 287; Ababeel missiles 448; explosive ordnance disposal 420–22; Hawk missiles 214, 236, 273, 284, 295, 330, 367; Maverick missiles 311, 626n72, 626n74; Patriot missiles 448, 681n35; Al-Samoud missiles 448; SCUD missiles 448, 681n35; Sidewinder missiles 311, 592n23; Silkworm missiles 275, 294–96, 617nn5–6, 681n35; Stingers missiles 287, 614n43; Tomahawk missiles 430. *See also* aircraft; chemical warfare; mine warfare
Webster, Ron 352, 357–59, 378, 386–87, 646n3, 647n9
Weinberger, Caspar 616n65
Westinghouse 152, 168, 568n87, 631n1
Wilk, Bill 421, 672n37
Wilson, Arnold 55
Wilson, Joseph 321
Wolle, William D. 238, 239, 593n33
women: 1950s protests by 176–77, 571n36; 1980s rights of 283; Ahmadi women's group 113, 557n33; American Women's League 226–27, 298; Baharna beliefs and 540n99; clothing

women *(continued)* 176, 283, 458; entrances for 536n53; Fahad Salem on rights of 561n14; of influence, American Mission 557n34; Islamists on rights of 458; in Kuwaiti businesses 564n51; misrepresentation of rights of 413–14, 669n4; reception of American 205, 582n17, 582n20; study abroad programs for 576n27; suffrage of 260, 436, 453, 599n88, 603n30, 628n93, 677n108. *See also* girls; *specific persons*
World Missions Board 183, 575n19
World War II: combat operations in Kuwait 551nn9–10; end of 104, 105; maritime commerce in Kuwait 83–84; oil industry suspension during 85, 97, 102, 555n10; rationing 83–86; report of effects in Kuwait 84, 551n13; shipbuilding in Kuwait 83, 86–90, 114–15, 552n26. *See also* depressions, economic
Wrampelmeier, Brooks 266–67, 283
Wyss, Patricia 469

x-ray technology 94, 544n29, 553n40

Al-Yacoub, Jassim 408
Yard, Molly 414
Yasin, Yusuf 102–3
Yemen 205, 269, 578n60, 581n15
Young, Andrew 277
Al-Yousifi, Kim 472

Al-Zayyat, Muhammad 235
Zoetmulder & Van Winkel 571n47
Zubair, Iraq 267–68, 606nn71–72
Zwemer, Samuel 31, 32, 532n8

www.ingramcontent.com/pod-product-compliance
Lightning Source LLC
Chambersburg PA
CBHW031956220426
43664CB00005B/41